Y0-ARF-476

SIR WALTER SCOTT

From an engraving by William Walker
after a painting by Sir Henry Raeburn

EDWARD WAGENKNECHT

Cavalcade of the English Novel

WITH SUPPLEMENTARY BIBLIOGRAPHY

In short, every secret of a writer's soul, every experience of his life, every quality of his mind is written large in his works, yet we require critics to explain the one and biographers to expound the other. That time hangs heavy on people's hands is the only explanation of the monstrous growth.

Virginia Woolf: *Orlando*

HOLT, RINEHART AND WINSTON
NEW YORK—CHICAGO—SAN FRANCISCO
TORONTO—LONDON

June, 1965

29166-0314

PRINTED IN THE
UNITED STATES OF AMERICA

TO

WALTER DE LA MARE

And there was a Horse in the
King's Stables; and the name
of the horse was, Genius.

By Edward Wagenknecht

PSYCHOGRAPHY: THE MAN CHARLES DICKENS (1929); JENNY LIND (1931); MARK TWAIN, THE MAN AND HIS WORK (1935); HENRY WADSWORTH LONGFELLOW, AMERICAN HUMANIST (in preparation)

CRITICISM: VALUES IN LITERATURE (1928); UTOPIA AMERICANA (1929); A GUIDE TO BERNARD SHAW (1929); CAVALCADE OF THE ENGLISH NOVEL (1943); CAVALCADE OF THE AMERICAN NOVEL (1952)

ABOUT THE THEATER: LILLIAN GISH, AN INTERPRETATION (1927); GERALDINE FARRAR, AN AUTHORIZED RECORD OF HER CAREER (1929)

ANTHOLOGIES: THE COLLEGE SURVEY OF ENGLISH LITERATURE (with others) (1942); SIX NOVELS OF THE SUPERNATURAL (1944); THE FIRESIDE BOOK OF CHRISTMAS STORIES (1945); THE STORY OF JESUS IN THE WORLD'S LITERATURE (1946); WHEN I WAS A CHILD (1946); THE FIRESIDE BOOK OF GHOST STORIES (1947); ABRAHAM LINCOLN, HIS LIFE, WORK, AND CHARACTER (1947); THE FIRESIDE BOOK OF ROMANCE (1948); JOAN OF ARC, AN ANTHOLOGY OF HISTORY AND LITERATURE (1948); A FIRESIDE BOOK OF YULETIDE TALES (1948); MURDER BY GASLIGHT (1949); THE COLLECTED TALES OF WALTER DE LA MARE (1950); AN INTRODUCTION TO DICKENS (1952)

INTRODUCTIONS by E. W.: THE CHIMES, BY CHARLES DICKENS (LIMITED EDITIONS CLUB) (1931); LIFE ON THE MISSISSIPPI, BY MARK TWAIN (LIMITED EDITIONS CLUB) (1944); A TALE OF TWO CITIES, BY CHARLES DICKENS (MODERN LIBRARY) (1950)

PREFACE

In one of his prefaces, John Galsworthy describes the drama as "simply a string of almost unrelated achievements, appearing like the outstanding figures of history, who knows when and why—as the dramas of Shakespeare appeared among the dullness of that crew of second-raters, the other Elizabethans."

It would be an exaggeration to say that I have approached the English novel in this book as Galsworthy approached the drama, but I am quite in sympathy with his fundamental thesis, as I understand it. Literary history is not an organism.

Personally I am more interested in literature, which is an art, than I can ever be interested in the factors by which it is conditioned. I have, I hope, kept the importance of backgrounds in mind, but, as a famous critic once expressed it, I have been careful not to permit the frame to take the place of the picture. In other words, my primary concern is with value-judgments.

I might add that for me reading a book is an act of communion between myself and the man who wrote it. "To know a work of literature," says Middleton Murry, "is to know the soul of the man who created it, and who created it in order that his soul should be known." During the six years this book has occupied me, I have found it necessary to commune with many souls. Naturally I have not found them all equally congenial, though there have been surprisingly few that I could honestly describe as antipathetic. And in every case my first object has been, as Barrett Wendell once put it, to "set forth the man . . . as that man saw himself, and to explain him on his own terms." When Miss Willa Cather said of the writer that "he fades away into the land and people of his heart, he dies of love only to be born again," she was not thinking of the critic. But there is a sense, I hope, in which the words may apply even to him.

In such a book as this, it is naturally impossible to be entirely "original." Hundreds of observations have been made which, to the best of my knowledge, have not been made before. But my primary object has not been to display my "originality"; I have tried to give the work of each of the writers I have considered as comprehensive a treatment as might be within my limitations of space.

Specific indebtedness is indicated in many footnotes; in addition, I must avow a general indebtedness to my bibliography as a whole, and to what the world has been thinking and saying about many of the writers I have discussed over a long stretch of years. In general, footnotes give bibliographical information only for those books which are not described in the general bibliography for the chapter in question; many of these books are not "sources"; they are merely cited for illustrative purposes. In some cases, however, I have described a "source" in a footnote; an example is Albert Morton Turner's *The Making of "The Cloister and the Hearth,"* which it seemed to me might more usefully be considered on page 249 than in the back of the book. I have no general "rule" which covers all these cases, but every case has been carefully considered on its own merits.

The absence of a chapter on Henry James may perhaps call for a word of explanation. James is often mentioned in the course of this book, but his work is nowhere discussed as such. Since the writer has in preparation a companion study of the American novel, it seemed logical to hold James over for consideration in that place; had no such book been contemplated, I should certainly have considered him here.

The following persons have read and evaluated for my guidance the sections of my book indicated in parentheses following their names. I am grateful to all of them for the trouble they took, the suggestions they made, and the generous encouragement they gave me. It must be understood, however, that none of them are, in any sense, responsible for what I have written:

Professor Joseph Warren Beach, of the University of Minnesota (Meredith and Hardy); Professor Frederic T. Blanchard, of the University of California at Los Angeles (Fielding); Dr. R. W. Chapman, of Oxford University (Jane Austen); Mr. Barrett H. Clark (George Moore); Professor L. P. Curtis, of Yale University

(Sterne); Mr. Walter Dexter, of *The Dickensian,* and Mr. J. W. T. Ley (Dickens); Dr. John Dozier Gordan, of The New York Public Library (Conrad); Professor Charles Brockway Hale, of the University of Maryland (Thackeray); Professor Will T. Hale, of Indiana University (Fanny Burney); Mr. Clayton Hamilton (Stevenson); Professor Joseph B. Harrison, of the University of Washington (the "stream-of-consciousness" chapter); Mr. A. Arthur Hemenway, formerly of the University of Washington (Surtees); Professor Annette B. Hopkins, of Goucher College (Mrs. Gaskell); Professor Clyde K. Hyder, of the University of Kansas (Wilkie Collins); Mr. H. V. Marrot (Galsworthy); Professor Alan D. McKillop, of the Rice Institute (Samuel Richardson); Professor Robert G. Mood, of the Municipal University of Wichita (Maria Edgeworth); Dean Edward S. Noyes, of Yale University (Smollett); the late Dean F. M. Padelford, of the University of Washington (the Elizabethan novelists); Professor William Lyon Phelps, of Yale University (Kipling and Barrie); Miss Fannie E. Ratchford, of the University of Texas (the Brontës); Mr. Michael Sadleir (Trollope); Professor A. W. Secord, of the University of Illinois (Defoe and his contemporaries); Professor Robert Shafer, of the University of Cincinnati (Gissing); Professor Morris E. Speare, of St. John's University (Disraeli); Dr. David Harrison Stevens, of the Rockefeller Foundation (the Seventeenth Century); Professor A. Lionel Stevenson, of the University of Southern California (Lever, Marryat, and Carleton); Mrs. Clara G. Stillman (Samuel Butler); The Reverend Montague Summers (the Gothic Novel); Professor Emerson Grant Sutcliffe, of Purdue University (Charles Reade); Professor Bruce Sutherland, of Pennsylvania State College (Maurice Hewlett); Mrs. Margaret Farrand Thorp (Kingsley); Professor W. Y. Tindall, of Columbia University (D. H. Lawrence); Miss J. M. S. Tompkins, of the University of London (the chapter called "Sentimentalists and Revolutionaries"); the late Lord Tweedsmuir, known to all lovers of good books as John Buchan (Sir Walter Scott); Mr. Carl Van Doren (Peacock); Professor Harold H. Watts, of Purdue University (Bulwer); Mr. Geoffrey West (Bennett and Wells); Professor Blanche Colton Williams, formerly of Hunter College (George Eliot).

When I was in Los Angeles in the summer of 1938, my friends Professor and Mrs. John R. Adams, of San Diego, found it enter taining to spend several warm summer evenings listening to me read as much of the manuscript as had then been completed and making useful suggestions concerning it. But I am even more heavily indebted to two of my colleagues at the University of Washington—Professor Ottis B. Sperlin and Professor Lawrence J. Zillman—both of whom have read the entire manuscript at my request.

Gratitude for many favors is due also to the University of Washington Library, and especially to Miss Bernice Shorrock, whose eager and efficient co-operation in arranging innumerable interlibrary loans made her almost a collaborator.

E. W.

Autumn of 1942

PREFACE TO THE 1954 EDITION

By the time these words appear in print, *Cavalcade of the English Novel* will have rounded out more than a decade of service in American colleges and universities. This 1954 edition is not a revision; errors of fact have been corrected throughout but the text is otherwise unchanged. A great deal of valuable material has, however, appeared in print since the publication of the first edition of this book, and in some cases—that of Thackeray, for instance—this has been of very great importance. The addition of the "Supplementary Bibliography" to that printed in 1943 gives *Cavalcade of the English Novel* much the fullest working bibliography of scholarship concerning the English novel that the student will find anywhere available. It is hoped that this will further increase the usefulness of the book.

E. W.

Boston University
September 12, 1953

CONTENTS

INTRODUCTION

"And what are you reading, Miss —— ——?" "Oh! it is only a novel!" replies the young lady; while she lays down her book with affected indifference, or momentary shame. "It is only 'Cecilia,' or 'Camilla,' or 'Belinda' "; or, in short, only some work in which the greatest powers of the mind are displayed, in which the most thorough knowledge of human nature, the happiest delineation of its varieties, the liveliest effusions of wit and humour, are conveyed to the world in the best chosen language.

JANE AUSTEN: *Northanger Abbey*

The novel probably comes closer to the lives of modern men than any other type of literature. What the epic was to men of the olden time, what the drama was to the Elizabethans, the far more "inward," more analytical novel is to us.

Yet nobody knows just what a novel is, and nobody knows just where the novel begins. For convenience' sake, we generally begin the history of European fiction with the unknown authors of the Milesian tales, that of English fiction with the Elizabethans. But neither of these groups invented fiction.

Haughtily self-assured as the novel is today, it may be well for us to remind ourselves that, not much over a hundred years ago, Sir Walter Scott published *Waverley* anonymously because the profession of novelist was still considered unbecoming to a man of his dignity. Julia Ward Howe's "Cousin Nancy" Greene wished very much to read *The Annals of the Schönberg-Cotta Family*. But learning that it was a work of fiction she decided not to break her rule.

We should remember too that it is convenience, not logic, which impels the modern bookseller to classify a new novel by Aldous Huxley as "Fiction," while a play by Sean O'Casey or a narrative poem by John Masefield must go into the "Non-Fiction" class. A story is a story whether it be told in prose or verse, whether it divide itself into scenes or chapters. Chaucer's "Pardoner's Tale" is more than a short story; it is a "short-story," even in the highly specialized sense in which Brander Matthews defined that term after studying the practice of Maupassant and Poe; [1] the *Troilus and Criseyde,* on the other hand, can hardly be more exactly described than as a long narrative poem. But had Chaucer lived in Shakespeare's time there can be no question *Troilus and Criseyde* would have been a play. And were he living today it would certainly be a psychological novel.

There is fiction in the Old Testament—in such narratives as Jonah, Esther, and Ruth—and certainly in the Apocrypha, where we read of Tobit, of Susanna, of Bel and the Dragon. Some of the best short stories in the world are among the parables of Jesus:

> A certain man went down from Jerusalem to Jericho and fell among thieves, which stripped him of his raiment, and wounded him, and departed, leaving him half dead.

Plot, character, setting—the essential ingredients of fiction; all are here in a single sentence. The action does not take place *in* Jerusalem nor yet *in* Jericho, but on the road which joins them. The "man" is not individualized; his name is not given; his character and appearance are left undescribed. But for the narrator's purpose in this instance, such details could only detract from the universality of the theme. "A certain man" is enough. He is any man. He is you or I, or the man next door. And so the tale is brought into vital contact with every member of the little company to which it was first addressed.

But there was fiction long before the Bible was written. For that matter, there was fiction long before anything was written. The very term "literature" is a misnomer; it stands as a symbol of our bondage to the printed page. The ultimate sources of all literature are oral, and we recognize this fact frankly enough when we are discussing the epic or the ballad. There is an apostolic succession in art as well as in religion; behind Joseph Conrad and Arnold Bennett, Storm Jameson and Sheila Kaye-Smith stretches an unbroken line of narrators back to some ancient Arab campfire where an old

[1] *The Short-Story: Specimens Illustrating its Development,* edited by Brander Matthews (American Book Co., 1908).

man sits rehearsing tribal memories to the little company gathered about him in the desert night. When the first mother whispered the first bedtime story to the first tired little girl, then fiction was born. When the first teacher devised the first myth to satisfy the curiosity of the first scholar concerning the origins of things, then fiction was born. When the first fisherman returned home excusing the contemptible littleness of the fish he brought with him and dilating on the wonders of the magnificent creature that got away, when the first hunter held his trembling wife close in his arms while he spoke of the dreadful monsters of the forest from which he had so narrowly escaped, then fiction was born.

"Fiction" is, of course, a much wider term than "novel," and, as I have already suggested, "novel" has never been satisfactorily defined. Sir Harry Johnston once complained with some bitterness that we have in English no really adequate term "to express that study of people's lives and emotions which has become in many ways the most fascinating form of literature to the majority of people able to read." Etymologically, he reminds us, "novel" indicates something new, while "fiction" implies falseness. Yet the best novels have always owed their vogue, their power over the imagination, to their inherent truth, the success with which they turn their mirror on human nature.[2] The eighteenth century got around this particular difficulty by calling its expansive narratives "histories," but to speak of Virginia Woolf's novels as histories certainly would not help our present confusion very much. There are even those who insist that they are not novels!

The distinction between a novel and a short story is not merely a matter of length; some short stories are longer than some novels. The distinction is rather one of problem. A short story deals with a single situation, a novel with a chain of circumstances. But it is not well to be too dogmatic in these matters. Bias appears even in Sir Harry Johnston's incidental definition of a novel, which I have quoted above, for Sir Harry is opposing romanticism.

Must a novel be realistic? As far back as 1785, Clara Reeve, herself a novelist, attempted to distinguish between novel and romance.

[2] "On the Writing of Novels," *Yale Review,* XI (1921), 58-67.

"The novel," she said, "is a picture of real life and manners, and of the times in which it was written. The romance, in lofty and elevated language, describes what never happened nor is likely to happen." Yet for all the battles that have been fought in this field, a complete separation between realism and romance is impossible. Every great writer is both realist and romancer. Surely George Saintsbury was right when he said, "A crowd of fantastic imaginings or additions, to supply the main substance, and a certain common-sense grasp of actual conditions and circumstances to set them upon, and contrast them with—these are the great requirements of Fiction in life and characters." Take realism away altogether and you get something as abstruse as the novels of E. R. Eddison. Take romance away altogether and you get—I know not what, for not even Theodore Dreiser has been able to achieve it. The personality of Émile Zola, high-priest of modern naturalism, was as important an element in the books he wrote as the personality of James Branch Cabell is in his.

The test of truth does not apply to the fairy tale in quite the same way as it applies to a realistic novel, but if the tale have quality it will still apply. No lover of Grimm need be reminded that the *Märchen* owe much of their charm to the rich German homeliness, the warm, earthy quality that is never quite lost even in the most imaginative passages. The French fairy tales of Charles Perrault and Madame la Comtesse d'Aulnoy lack this, but they have instead a *joie de vivre,* a bright social quality which is characteristically Gallic. And it has often been remarked that *The Tempest* holds our interest as it does because, though its subject-matter involves the unbelievable, the moral nature of the characters concerned is still presented as true to the life that we know.

The only quite accurate definition of the novel is the history of the novel. To this we now turn.

CHAPTER I

FICTION IN SHAKESPEARE'S TIME

But what was the sun like, before it came up?

WALTER DE LA MARE

1. *The Elizabethan Inheritance*[1]

Though it is not quite accurate to say that prose fiction begins in England during the reign of Queen Elizabeth (1558-1603), that period still affords the best point of departure for our survey. Some works worth mentioning had, to be sure, appeared earlier. A version of the Apollonius of Tyre story, derived from a late Greek original, had come into being as far back as Anglo-Saxon times. In 1485, with Sir Thomas Malory's *Morte d'Arthur,* the greatest of the medieval romance traditions reached an advanced stage of development; and 1516 brought the *Utopia* of Sir Thomas More, the first of a long series of studies of the ideal commonwealth, whose tradition reaches backward to Plato's *Republic* and the Hebrew prophets' visions of the New Jerusalem and forward to Edward Bellamy, Samuel Butler, and H. G. Wells.

Primarily, the *Utopia* is social and political criticism. Part I describes intolerable conditions in Henry VIII's England; Part II presents directly, by way of contrast, the ideal civilization of Utopia. But as the narrative of the sailor, Raphael Hythloday, whom the author purports to have met through "one Peter Giles, a citizen of Antwerp," the book still claims classification as a work of fiction. The introductory letter to Giles, the mention of real people like Amerigo Vespucci and Cardinal Morton, More's own remark that Hythloday had also described other lands ("peradventure in another

[1] Cf. Ernest A. Baker, *The History of the English Novel,* Vol. I, for a detailed account of English fiction before the Elizabethans.

place I will speak of it")—here is essentially the same effort toward verisimilitude that Swift and Defoe were to make, and while much of the *Utopia* is straight expository writing, the exposition is enlivened from time to time by interesting anecdotes, most notably perhaps in the account of the humiliation of the Anemolian ambassadors.

Moderns generally think of the Elizabethan period as a very romantic time. So it was in its loftiest reaches, but Elizabethans did not live perpetually in the mood of *The Faerie Queene*. It was Mary Stuart, not Elizabeth, who embodied the romantic ideal, and the age led Mary Stuart to the block. The Wars of the Roses were over, and England was a more comfortable country to live in than it had ever been before. The minstrel had disappeared or was disappearing; the clouds of illiteracy were lifting a little; the middle class had quite definitely thrust its head through the ruins of feudalism. All these tendencies encouraged literary experimentation.

Yet Elizabethan fiction produced no masterpiece. Fundamentally, the untutored "romantic" conception of the age is correct; the dominant literary temper remains idealistic. It was an age of great poetry, and when the poet wished to draw closer to the level of daily life than either the lyric or the epic would take him, it was the drama, not the novel, to which he turned. Here a form and a public were both found waiting for him, and here he need not deny himself the harmonious exaltations of verse. A good prose narrative style is still waiting to be developed, and when the fashionable writers do turn to the new medium, they do not, at the outset, understand it very well.

Still, Elizabethan writers had at their disposal a rich heritage of materials for fiction. First of all, there were the Greek and Roman "novels" of such writers as Heliodorus and Xenophon, Longus and Tatius, Lucian, Petronius, and Apuleius. *Daphnis and Chloë* (Longus) and *The Golden Ass* (Apuleius) are now the most widely read works of these writers. They concern themselves, for the most part, with love and adventure. Hero and heroine wander over the earth with fine disregard of all time- and place-relations, and they are almost as sure to survive the dire machinations of their enemies as the dramatic personae of a modern slapstick farce. The heroine may indeed perish at the hands of pirates, but when she does we can always be fairly sure that she will soon come to life again. The probabilities, then, are handled much more freely in these romances than in either *Captain Blood* or *To Have and To Hold,* but the enduring popularity of this kind of story today is an impressive testimonial to the continuity of human interests.

More important than these works were, for the Elizabethans, the medieval romances. These came into English literature during the Norman period. The life and deeds of King Arthur were first elaborately recorded in Geoffrey of Monmouth's *Chronicle* (c. 1147), and the legend developed steadily in detail and glamor until Malory achieved a comprehensive history in his *Morte d'Arthur* of 1485. Malory omitted some of the best narratives, as that of the Green Knight, and in some cases employed inferior versions, but for many generations the Arthur of the English people was his Arthur. This writer is repetitious and lacking in unity, but he realizes his characters vividly in points of detail, if not always as complete units, and he knows how to create atmosphere. On one occasion at least, he thrusts himself into the narrative as commentator (Book XVIII, Ch. 25), thus providing precedent for the "asides" of Thackeray, George Eliot, and many other writers.

But not all medieval romance material was Arthurian. French, classical, and Oriental sources entered the picture, and there were a number of English (as distinct from British) heroes, of whom much the most important was Robin Hood. A number of comparatively brief medieval tales—*Aucassin and Nicolette* among them—were destined for long life, as were also some of the French fabliaux, and, at a later date, some Spanish rogue tales like *Lazarillo de Tormes*. By Elizabeth's time, too, the romances themselves had been acted upon by pastoral influences; from Italy came Boccaccio's *Ameto* (1343) and Sannazaro's *Arcadia* (1502), from Spain Montemayor's *Diana* (1559?).

Collections of brief tales from abroad served dramatist and novelist alike as source-books. The *Gesta Romanorum,* compiled originally in Latin, about 1300, had been translated into English prose during the reign of Henry VI. Boccaccio's *Decameron* was not completely Englished until 1620, but there was considerable Boccaccio, as well as some Bandello, in Painter's *Palace of Pleasure* (1566-1567); and Bandello appeared again in Fenton's *Tragical Discourses* (1567). In *The Petite Palace of Pettie his Pleasure* (1576) the originals are sometimes modified. There is probably one new story in Whetstone's *Rock of Regard* (1576), and five out of eight stories are new in Riche's *Farewell to the Military Profession* (1581).

Without printing, none of these works could ever have become so influential as they did; for this reason, William Caxton, Wynkyn de Worde, William Copland, and their successors had an important influence on English fiction. Caxton set up his press at Westminster in 1477. Conservative in his literary tastes, he gave the romances the permanence and the wide distribution of printing, not only placing a great treasure-house of material at the disposal of Elizabethan writers but importantly affecting the taste of the rising generation.

2. *Two Predecessors of Lyly*

Though most histories of the English novel still begin with *Euphues,* it was as early as 1913 that Percy W. Long first called attention to the antecedent work of Gascoigne and Grange. *A Pleasant Discourse of the Adventures of Master F.J.,* by George Gascoigne, first appeared anonymously in *A Hundreth Sundrie Flowers Bound Up in One Small Poesie* (1573). The plot seems to have been drawn from a contemporary intrigue in which Gascoigne himself may have been involved. When he acknowledged the work in a second edition (1575), the change of title,[2] the transfer of scene to a foreign country, and the disclaimers and apologies included in the Preface addressed "to the reverend Divines" all indicated a desire to obscure the real life basis of the tale. *Master F.J.* has excellent characterization for its period and a well-developed plot. The letters introduced from time to time advance the action, the numerous poems are at least connected with it, and the two questions posed reveal the personalities of their propounders with some skill. At one point at least, Gascoigne's discussion of his alleged authenticating sources is very interesting. There is a controversy, he says, as to whether one of the poems included was actually written to Elinor, the un-

[2] *The Pleasant Fable of Ferdinando Jeronimi and Leonora da Valasco, translated out of the Italian Riding Tales of Bartello.*

worthy heroine of the story; it may have been addressed to another flame of F.J.'s, one Helen.

Leicester Bradner, who has studied *Master F.J.* with sympathy and enthusiasm, declares that "For a realistic picture of social life in the English nobility we must wait nearly two hundred years for anything equal in fulness and charm to Gascoigne's story." There can be no question concerning the realism at least; some may feel that Gascoigne pursues it in disregard of the canons of satisfactory story-telling. Stubbornly disdaining the fine, womanly daughter of the household, whom he was intended to woo, the hero centers his attention instead on the daughter-in-law, who is as faithless as she is charming. In the original version we are left hoping that things may finally come out "right," but the revision tells us specifically that the disillusioned F.J. has turned to an abandoned course of life, while the daughter, "the worthy Lady Frauncischina . . . did shortly bring herself into a miserable consumption, whereof (after three years' languishing) she died."

In 1577, John Grange, a law student, published *The Golden Aphroditis*. This time the scene is ancient Greece and the heroine, A.O., a daughter of Diana. But, despite some supernatural machinery, the psychology is Elizabethan, and Elizabethan customs furnish the background. I.I., an old flame, tries to break up the affair between A.O. and her lover, N.O., but he is overcome in a duel with staves. There is much feasting, visiting, dancing, and listening to music. Gods and goddesses attend the wedding at the close, and much nectar and ambrosia are consumed. *The Golden Aphroditis* resembles *Euphues* stylistically much more than does the Gascoigne tale. There is much learning in it, and Grange borrows freely without acknowledgment from other writers.

3. *The Prescience of* Euphues

In 1578, John Lyly (1554?-1606), Elizabethan poet and dramatist, published his "novel," *Euphues: The Anatomy of Wit*. The plot is slight. The hero, a young gentleman of Athens (Oxford), finds his way to Naples (London), "a place of more pleasure than profit and yet of more profit than piety." Rejecting the wise counsels of old Eubulus, he chooses as his bosom companion one Philautus, the affianced lover of Lucilla. Himself attracted to Lucilla, Euphues betrays his friend, only to be discarded in his turn for another lover. Hereupon he permanently outgrows frivolity. "I will to Athens there to toss my books, no more in Naples to live with fair looks." Lucilla, like Robert Henryson's Cressida, dies at last, a harlot, in the streets.

Two years later, Lyly published a sequel, *Euphues and his England*. Here the Italian mask is cast aside. Euphues and Philautus come to England, where the latter devotes himself to a long, vain, earnest attempt to win the love of the lady Camilla.

Since virtually every important speech made in the course of these narratives runs several pages, the progress of the action is slow. Even so, the "novel" takes up less than two-thirds of Lyly's total space. The rest is devoted to letters and treatises written by Euphues after his conversion: a discussion of child-rearing, a refutation of atheism, and the passionate glorification of England and England's Elizabeth that we know as "Euphues' Glass for Europe."

Lyly draws freely on the Elizabethan inheritance. His title is from his contemporary, Ascham; Plutarch, Pliny, Ovid, Erasmus, the Spanish Guevara, Castiglione and his *Courtier* all come to mind as one turns his pages. Philautus and Eubulus are both from William de Volder's scholastic drama, *Acolastus* (1529), and Lucilla plays refinements on Volder's courtesan, Lais. The betrayal of Philautus by Euphues develops the false friend situation, as in Boccaccio's story of Tito and Gisippo.[3]

There is some growth of character in Euphues himself, though the distinctly religious turn at the close of the first work is not developed in the sequel. Philautus is never more than a lay-figure. If we believe in Lucilla's tortured self-upbraidings when she forsakes Philautus, we can hardly accept her cruelty of spirit later on. *Euphues and his England* flounders badly in getting started: there are three stories instead of one, and they are sadly lacking in variety. Yet when we come at last to the Philautus-Camilla comedy, we find a treatment of the sex duel which, despite its formality, is nearly poignant.

[3] *Decameron,* X, 8.

To the reader of English fiction, Lyly's work seems curiously prophetic. Its theme is love. It has three stock types—the coquette, the fickle lover, the malcontent. It uses letters to advance the action. It employs the introduced story or special narration. The author occasionally acts as chorus and attempts some psychological analysis of thought and feeling. Above all, Lyly is profoundly ethical. In printing Malory, Caxton had hoped his readers might "take the good and honest acts in their remembrance and . . . follow the same." Lyly thinks of fiction in Caxton's manner. His attack on Oxonian immoralities and his expressed loathing of drunkenness and sexuality may have been pious genuflections, but the effect remains. He struck a dominant note in English fiction, and it has gone on ringing down the centuries.

Much less important, for our purpose, is Lyly's famous "euphuistic" style. He did not create it out of hand, but he probably brought it to its highest point of development, and he certainly contributed notably to its vogue. Weymouth defines its fundamental principle as "transverse alliteration in conjunction with parisonic antithesis." Rhetorical questions abound, and an amazing wealth of illustrative material is introduced—from classical sources, from proverbial lore, above all from the "unnatural natural history" of Pliny and the medieval bestiaries. Lyly was one of the most allusive writers who ever lived, and when none of his authorities would serve him, he manufactured his allusions out of hand. But artificial as euphuism is, it was no mere affectation. Foreign influences aside, it was bound to come, for it developed tendencies toward alliteration and balance which run clear back to Anglo-Saxon times. And here Lyly was decidedly not prophetic, for in general English novelists have not been greatly preoccupied with style. Not before *Tristram Shandy* shall we encounter another novel that is so emphatically "written."

4. *Sidney's* Arcadia: *Fiction and Heroic Poesy*

But if *Euphues* takes us on to the novel of manners, then *The Countess of Pembroke's Arcadia* (1590) draws us back into the world of the medieval romances. Or one might say that the novel, that most prehensile of all literary types is already reaching out to absorb the materials of the romances.

Sir Philip Sidney (1554-1586) was the ideal gentleman of Elizabeth's England, the apotheosis of a romantic ideal. When he was killed in battle in Holland, the fashionable nation virtually went into mourning for him, and no light or gaudy apparel was worn by gentlemen for months. So keen an observer as William of Orange judged Sidney "one of the ripest and greatest counsellors of estate . . . that at this day lived in Europe," which he certainly was not. Personally, however, he was of dauntless courage, and his proud spirit did not hesitate to cross Elizabeth's own when a real issue was at stake. It was indeed during a period of banishment from court that he wrote the *Arcadia* on his sister's estate at Wilton.

"Now it is done only for you, only to you," he wrote her. "Your dear self can best witness the manner, being done in loose sheets sent unto you, as fast as they were done." His self-disparagement must not be taken too seriously. There was a large conventional element in it; he is speaking moreover only of the "old" *Arcadia,* the original form of his work. Had he regarded the book literally as a trifle, he would hardly have undertaken the elaborate rewriting to which he gave himself. *Amadis of Gaul,* Sannazaro's *Arcadia,* Montemayor's *Diana,* and Malory's *Morte d'Arthur* all served as sources. There were influences too from the *Aethiopica* of Heliodorus, and there are many echoes from the classics and the Greek romances. Professor Myrick has shown that the revision carefully observes Minturno's rules for the heroic poem, and that when Sidney departs from Minturno, he departs consistently, in obedience to his own critical tenets, as laid down in *The Defence of Poesy.*

"Poesy" was what he himself considered the *Arcadia*—heroic poesy, not fiction, which was an inferior thing. To his way of thinking, a poem need not necessarily be written in verse. His revision stressed the heroic aspect and played down the pastoral. We wrong him, as Spenser has often been wronged, if we think of his masterpiece as belonging to the literature of escape. For him it was a serious interpretation of life—didactic, idealistic. His contemporaries approached it as such, and could find no praise too high for it. "Here are amorous courting (he was young in years)," wrote Gabriel Harvey, "sage counselling (he was ripe in judgment), valorous fighting (his sovereign profession was arms), and delightful pastime by way of pastoral exercises." Later critics have been less enthusiastic; Hazlitt judged the book "one of the greatest monuments of the abuse of intellectual power upon record." The main story, the history of Basilius and his family, though highly involved, is coherent enough in the original draft. But in the revised version it is so elaborately intermingled with other material—the adventures of Pyrocles and Musidorus before they enter the main plot, the touching history of Argalus and Parthenia, the story of the king of Paphlagonica (from which Shakespeare derived the Gloucester plot in *King Lear*), the machinations of the wicked queen Cecropia—that the reader needs the patience and the ingenuity of an expert in jigsaw puzzles to figure out the intricate relationships.

The pattern is there; no question can arise as to that. The *Arcadia* is no ragbag structure; it is a carefully integrated work of art. It has indeed, though in what seems to our modern impatience a hopeless confusion, just about everything one could ask for in a work of fiction, with the single exception of what moderns value most highly of all—that is, the realistic portrayal of living characters. Even this is approached at times in the person of Gynecia, the love-tortured woman. The rest of the eighty-eight name characters are, for the most part, types, but their variety is astonishing. Almost every kind of love appears from the virginal purity of Pamela to the senile doting of Basilius. There is humor too, though moderns sometimes fail to perceive it, and there is much serious criticism of life, as in Pamela's ardent refutation of the Lucretian atheism of the wicked Cecropia.

Stylistically, "Arcadianism" stands opposed to euphuism. "Now for similitudes in certain printed discourses," wrote Sidney in *The Defence of Poesy,* "I think all herberists, all stories of beasts, fowls, and fishes, are rifled up, that they may come in multitudes to wait upon any of our conceits, which certainly is as absurd a surfeit to the ears as is possible." But his own style is quite as artificial as Lyly's, and on the score of structural formlessness it is decidedly inferior. Repetition and rambling parentheses are the main structural devices employed; what Ruskin called the pathetic fallacy is used intensively and often most tastelessly. In fairness it must be added that there are noble passages like Pamela's famous prayer (which so comforted King Charles I in his imprisonment), in which all these affectations are cast aside.

5. *"Real Life" and History in Thomas Nashe*

With Thomas Nashe (1567-1601) and Thomas Deloney (1543?-1607?) we come closer to what the modern reader expects a story to be. Marlowe's friend, Nashe, university wit and writer of parts, brushed the skirts of fiction in several of his didactic, satirical, and informational pamphlets, but his real contribution was *The Unfortunate Traveler, or, The Life of Jack Wilton* (1594).

This work shows the influence of the Spanish picaresque novels, though the hero is much more sympathetic than Lazarillo de Tormes or Guzman de Alfarache. We meet him first in 1513 before Tournay, a page in the army of King Henry VIII, living largely on his wits. His first victim is a Falstaff-like victualer, whom he tricks into distributing free cider to the army. After the English victory he returns home to witness a terrible plague (which he describes in the manner of a young Defoe); back on the continent, he sees the battle of Marignano and the bloody suppression of the Anabaptists at Münster. Later he enters the service of the Earl of Surrey. They meet Erasmus and Sir Thomas More, and hear a public disputation between Luther and Carolostadius. Having exchanged roles in order that Surrey may enjoy "more liberty of behavior," both master and man are imperiled by a wicked Venetian courtesan, but Nashe's literary idol, Aretino, comes to their rescue. At Florence, Surrey enters the lists to defend the beauty and virtue of his lady, the Fair Geraldine.

The last part of the book is better unified, and Nashe's gift for gory melodrama finds full expression. Unjustly accused of murder, Jack is delivered by an English earl, who reads him a lecture on the sins of Italy. A wicked Jew sells him to a physician for anatomical purposes; he is saved by that monster of iniquity, Juliana, mistress of the Pope. In the end Jack gives over his sinful life, marries his mistress Dianeme, whom he had picked up in prison, and rejoins the English army on the Field of the Cloth of Gold.

A mere series of episodes structurally, *The Unfortunate Traveler* finds such unity as it commands in the simple fact that the same character is concerned in most of them. Jack is a human being, not a mere peg on which to hang speeches; the masterly description of Dianeme is suggestive of Chaucer's portrait of Alison in "The Miller's Tale"; Jusserand thought the victualer a possible source for Falstaff. There are a number of episodes which stamp themselves on the memory—the tragic death of the virtuous matron, Heraclide, for one; for another, Cutwolfe's murder of Esdras the desperado, whom he tricked into disclaiming his salvation in the hope of preserving his life, then "shot him full in the throat with my pistol: so did I shoot him that he might never speak after or repent him. His body being dead looked as black as a toad: the devil presently branded it for his own."

In his youth, Nashe had felt Lyly's influence: "*Euphues* I read when I was a little ape in Cambridge, and I then thought it was *ipse illo:* it may be excellent still for aught I know, but I looked not on it this ten year, but to imitate it I abhor." He had no need to imitate it. He has a rich vocabulary of his own, a strong, essentially metaphorical style, which, though sometimes too decorated for modern taste, still redeems its Elizabethan exuberance by a certain concrete vividness of expression. His book has been called the first historical novel and the first international novel, but he uses his history very freely, disturbing or even reversing chronology whenever it seems convenient to do so. His business is to tell a story, and he understands his business well.

Though Nashe is by no means the unqualified realist that some critics would make him, the bent of his mind was definitely in that direction. We know that he disliked the romances. He shies away from extravagant idealisms also, though his attitude toward life is fundamentally serious. The nobleman who saves Jack from hanging shares Ascham's views on Italian immorality; Heraclide speculates at length on the subject of predestination; and when it comes to heresy Nashe sacrifices consistent character-drawing to put his own sentiments into his hero's mouth. "Hear what it is to be Anabaptists, to be puritans, to be villains. You may be counted illuminate botchers for a while, but your end will be: 'Good people, pray for us.' "

6. *Deloney, An Elizabethan Dickens*

Yet with all his gifts, Nashe had no particular charm. Thomas Deloney had charm and to spare, and it makes him today, after long neglect, the most beloved of Elizabethan fictionists. He was no university wit. Probably of French origin ultimately, a silk-weaver and a ballad-peddler, he knew how it felt to be pilloried as a vagrant. Deloney wrote for the common people, and his popularity with them survived into the eighteenth century. He is at once more realistic than Nashe and less. He uses traditional materials freely, when they happen to suit his purpose, but at his best he draws directly upon his own first-hand knowledge of tradesmen and craftsmen. Yet no more than Dickens is he interested in the accurate delineation of manners for its own sake. An idealized, romanticized conception of common life is what he gives us, and M. Chevalley's London *Times* reviewer was not far wrong in comparing him with "those anonymous and often excellent novelists of the *Family Herald Supplement,* who told of servant-girls marrying peers."[4]

His fame rests on three works: "*Jack of Newberry* (1597) and *Thomas of Reading* (1600)—both devoted to the clothiers—and the two parts of *The Gentle Craft* (1597, 1598), which glorifies the shoemakers. They are all, in a sense, propaganda novels: Deloney wished to impress the powers-that-were with the importance of basic industries for the state and the vital necessity of permitting them to continue unhampered by governmental interference.

Jack of Newberry is developed, first, biographically, then, episodically. Jack lays the foundation of his fortunes by marrying, at her request, a wealthy widow, and gains the goodwill of King Henry VIII by furnishing 250 men, at his own expense, for Flodden Field. He obtains a reversal of Wolsey's economic policy; he finds himself at last established in benevolent affluence. In the last half, Jack's household is still the center of operations, but he himself is no longer the leading figure. An Italian who had sought to seduce an Englishwoman is put to bed in the dark with a sow; Mistress Frank, the gossip, who had persuaded Jack's wife to stint her servants' rations, is carried drunk through the town in a basket; Sir George Rigley,

[4] *London Times Literary Supplement,* March 24, 1927, p. 210.

having seduced a servingmaid, is tricked into marrying her in the guise of a rich widow.

The Gentle Craft has even less unity. The first nine chapters of Part I are devoted to history and legend. Deloney handles it charmingly, but it is not his own material. In one scene, where the prince-apprentice, Crispin, secretly married to the king's daughter, Ursula, comes to tell his mistress he has gotten a maid with child, the narrative comes suddenly alive, and in the woman's excitement we hear the authentic accent of common speech. From Chapter X on, the first part of *The Gentle Craft* is pure Deloney—the history of Simon Eyre (which Dekker dramatized in *The Shoemaker's Holiday*): how, through his wife's counsel and a lucky speculation, he rose from a cobbler's apprentice to be Lord Mayor of London. Part II comprises three distinct narratives. In the first, a brilliant apprentice, Richard Casteler, the Cock of Westminster (who had been mentioned by Holinshed), is vainly loved by two girls, one of them Long Meg of Westminster, already a personage in the chapbooks.

The scene of the third novel, *Thomas of Reading,* is set back during Henry I's reign, probably to avoid censorship difficulties. The book contains an even wider variety of material than its predecessors, though the structure is perhaps a bit tighter. The wooing by Robert, Duke of Normandy, of the daughter of the banished Earl of Shrewsbury, who has disguised herself as a maid in the service of one of the great clothiers, is a conventional piece of old-fashioned romance. There are sidelights on genuine English customs, on the other hand, as in the picture of the fair and the account of the establishment of the standard yard measure, and there may be a touch of social criticism in the incident of the rogue condemned to death who escapes his just punishment because nobody is willing to act as hangman. Deloney's familiar set of domestic high jinks appears notably in the yarn of the man who is made to believe that his nose is enlarged and can only be cured through a mock operation. Finally there is a powerful piece of bourgeois tragedy.

Deloney's style is simple, inelegant, and unpretentious, but except where, in conventional romantic passages, he imitates Lyly and others, it is generally pleasing. He uses dialect, not too convincingly, and his conversation is far and away the best of its time. His characterization, lacking psychological subtleties, is apt and vivid, mostly along the good old English line of external idiosyncrasy. His humor is broad, earthy; his speech, frank, honest, and inoffensive. The murder of Old Cole by the innkeeper and his wife, in *Thomas of Reading,* has been praised *ad nauseam* but never too highly; the suggestion that Shakespeare may have taken a hint from it for Macbeth's murder of Duncan is by no means absurd. Here, and here alone, Elizabethan fiction stands for a moment alongside the Elizabethan drama.

7. *Lodge, Greene, and the Disciples*

Gascoigne, Lyly, Sidney, Nashe, Deloney—these five blazed the trail. The others must be disposed of very briefly.

Of the followers of Lyly and Sidney, the most important are Robert Greene (1558-1592) and Thomas Lodge (1557-8?-1625). Greene, one of the most prolific of the Elizabethans, wrote not for fame but for bread, and was always prepared "to yark up a pamphlet" in a night and a day. He was a Master of Arts from both universities, but unwise habits brought him to an early grave, and he died calling down maledictions upon a prudent young man from Stratford who, many years later, using Greene's *Pandosto* (1588) as the source of a play called *The Winter's Tale,* was to give him a much firmer hold upon the attention of posterity than he could otherwise have commanded.

Making due allowance for the fact that Shakespeare had genius and Greene had not, readers of *The Winter's Tale* will know what to expect of the novelist. Strongly influenced by the Greek romancers, he shared their contempt for the probabilities. Though his women have a certain charm, he attempted little characterization; his forte was narrative. Despite his abandoned life, the tone of his work is idealistic, and he is much given to puritanical moralizing. *Pandosto* and *Menaphon* (1589) are today his best-known works.

Lodge, whose father was a grocer, began his career as a law-student, took his fling on two buccaneering expeditions, and died a rich physician of London. Like Greene's *Pandosto,* his *Rosalynde*

(1590) owes much of its popularity to Shakespeare, who, as all the world knows, changed the title of his dramatic version to *As You Like It.* But *Rosalynde* would be quite interesting enough without Shakespeare; indeed it is probably the happiest production of the whole euphuistic school. Lodge's other works include *Forbonius and Prisceria,* which is dedicated to Sidney, and *A Margarite of America,* an historical romance with a tragic ending.

Other writers who imitated one phase or another of the work of Sidney and Lyly (and later of Greene) include Anthony Munday, Brian Melbancke, William Warner, John Dickenson, and Emanuel Forde. Homage to Lyly sometimes appears even in their titles. Munday's *Zelauto* (1580), was "Given for a friendly entertainment to Euphues, at his late arrival into England"; Dickenson's *Arisbas* (1594) was subtitled "Euphues amidst his slumbers." Forde's *Parismus* (1598), a prosaic *Romeo and Juliet,* enjoyed a long popularity.

When we turn to the historians of low-life, Greene enters again, now drawing directly from his own experiences. *The Cony-Catching Pamphlets* (1591 ff.) professed a reforming purpose: the author wished to put honest citizens on their guard against the rogues who lay in wait for them. But many must have read them for the thrills they contained, and it is impossible to believe that Greene was unaware of this appetite or that he did not cater to it. *A Quip for an Upstart Courtier* glorifies the tradesman at the expense of the courtier, and *The Black Book's Messenger* is a story of crime. *Greene's Groatsworth of Wit, Bought with a Million of Repentance* and *The Repentance of Robert Greene* are frankly autobiographical, though the former does contain some fiction. Henry Chettle, Samuel Rowlands, and Nicholas Breton follow Greene along this line, to say nothing of a really important dramatist, Thomas Dekker, who, however, connects more directly with Nashe and Deloney. Breton's *The Miseries of Mavillia,* "the most unfortunate lady that ever lived," was a work of some fame but no quality. Dekker did not write fiction, strictly speaking, but he is like the Elizabethan realists in many tracts and pamphlets, notably *The Bachelor's Banquet* (1603) and *The Gull's Horn-Book* (1609).

CHAPTER II

THE SEVENTEENTH CENTURY

. . . one can live so intensely with one's characters and the experiences one creates or records, it is a life in itself, far better than the vulgar thing people *call* life. . . .

D. H. LAWRENCE

1. *Elegant Wasteland*

Few modern readers find it easy to become deeply interested in seventeenth-century fiction. The Elizabethans, tentative though their efforts were, had at least experimented interestingly with several prophetic types. Now, for a hundred years, if we except Bunyan, Mrs. Behn, and, in their own specialized and restricted field, the character-writers, we have practically nothing. Mrs. Behn's name, moreover, was long unmentionable in polite society, and Bunyan almost stands outside literary history altogether.

Charlotte Morgan distinguishes sharply between literary and popular types in seventeenth-century fiction:

From 1625 or earlier, to about 1700, the literary fiction consisted almost exclusively of translations and imitations of the continental narratives which were in vogue at the Stuart courts. The popular fiction . . . consisted to a very large extent of redactions of the Elizabethan romances and of journalistic narratives imbued with the political and religious temper of the time.

Though the fashionable narratives were by no means all of the French heroic type—Miss Morgan herself distinguishes no less than seven varieties—the heroic romances still enjoyed a tremendous vogue. That vogue continued well into the eighteenth century, for as late as 1752 Charlotte Lennox produced an intelligible burlesque in *The Female Quixote*.

Foreshadowed in the *Astrée* (1610-1627) of Honoré d'Urfé, and in John Barclay's curious *Argenis* (1621), the French heroic romance came into its own with Gomberville, La Calprenède, Madeleine de Scudéry, and the salon of the Hotel de Rambouillet. Englishmen read these authors both in the original and in translation; and such *précieuses* as Mrs. Katherine Philips, "the matchless Orinda," and Margaret, Duchess of Newcastle, formed their own salons, and tried to bring the tone and temper of favorite books into their own lives and those of their friends. In 1654, Roger Boyle, Earl of Orrery, a member of Mrs. Philips's circle, began to publish his *Parthenissa,* the earliest important English imitation of the French romances. He was followed, among others, by Sir George Mackenzie (*Aretina,* 1660) and by John Crowne (*Pandion and Amphigenia,* 1665).

Readers who are able to recall the so-called "heroic drama" of Dryden and his school will have a very fair idea of the general tone and temper of these romances. Love and honor is the theme, and the characters possess both a superhuman valor and a Marie Bashkirtseff-like tendency to torturing self-analysis. The background is martial, the scene wide-ranging, confused, with real and imaginary countries lying side by side. Pseudo-history, rather than history, provides the background; La Calprenède wins considerable leeway when he makes Cleopatra's daughter, not Cleopatra herself, the heroine of the romance which bears that famous name.

What the drama cannot suggest is the vast length and unbelievable complication of these romances. As in the *Arcadia,* the central action may be coherent enough, but elaborately interwoven episodes do their best to obscure it. Each new character has his own tale to tell, and in these tales we may well meet other persons who must be heard in their turn.

> Thus [says Sir Walter Raleigh, wittily], the introduction of a new character is a thing the reader learns to fear; it will probably delay the main action for a book or two. And when he finds himself plunged deep into the adventures of one who has no existence even among the characters of the main story, but leads a parasitic life, the shadow of a shade, in the narration of one of these, his patience is apt to fail. The stories are arranged one within another, as if they had swallowed one another in succession, and it is not until they are successively disgorged that the reader can get back to the enveloping story, which after all may disappoint him by proving itself to be the merest covering, with no particular structure or object of its own.

The marriage of Clélie and Aronce impends at the beginning of Madeleine de Scudéry's *Clélie,* but it does not take place until the end of the tenth volume, which was published more than six years later. And Roger Boyle is even worse than Madeleine. His Parthenissa strikes despair to the heart of her lover when he sees her enter a grove with an affectionate escort, and to this day she has never emerged to relieve his anguish.

The heroic romances are more sophisticated, more sentimental, than their predecessors of the Middle Ages had been. They are salon products—thin-spun, fine, and bloodless. Love, the all-consuming passion, is sicklied o'er with the pale cast of a febrile and decadent Platonism, whose silly idealism produces the very evils it pretends to deplore. It may seem absurd to use the word realism in connection with such works, yet the passion for analyzing motives, the detailed descriptions of dress and manners, the use of dialogue to present models for conversation, the allegorical presentation of contemporary persons and contemporary problems—all these are realistic notes. As the eighteenth century advances, we shall become very familiar with the sensitive, languishing heroine of the romances and with the hero who is at once a lover and a man of action. Such considerations may cause us to wonder whether the romances did not exercise more influence on the main stream of English fiction than they are generally given credit for.

Correctives, too, were soon ready to hand. In France, Charles Sorel, Scarron, Furetière, Molière, and Cyrano de Bergerac all attacked the sentimental excesses of the Rambouillet *précieuses.* In England, rogue stories, like the Mary Carleton narratives, and like that hodge-podge of picaresque adventure compiled by Richard Head and Francis Kirkman and known as *The English Rogue* (1665-1671), led, less self-consciously, less intelligently, in the same direction. Character-writings, diaries, letters, biographies and autobiographies—some real, some feigned—all link up with the introspective temper of the century, and come to appeal to it more directly, as time goes on, than the romances had ever appealed. The same might be said of the scandal-histories about Elizabeth and Essex and others, a type later developed elaborately by Mrs. Manley. In 1678 came a translation of the famous *Letters of a Portuguese Nun*

(Paris, 1669), which set the tone for a much franker, less decorous, if no less hysterical, analysis of emotion than had appeared in the romances.

The tendency toward realism in the ordinary sense of the term appears in a number of other works also. To the author of *Parthenissa,* another, very different narrative is ascribed in *English Adventures* (1676), which concerns the same characters as that famous American novel of the 1890's, Charles Major's *When Knighthood Was in Flower,* and which also gives us, for good measure, in an introduced story, the plot of Otway's great tragedy, *The Orphan.* Henry Nevile's *The Isle of Pines* (1668) is a direct, simple narrative, with considerable regard for verisimilitude, which is interesting as one of the precursors of *Robinson Crusoe.* Only, instead of being shipwrecked alone, George Pine has four women with him! The frank animalism of the book is redeemed by the fact that, unlike the contemporary Restoration comedy, it never leers. It is interesting to note in passing that the famous dramatist, William Congreve, contributed to fiction in 1692 his youthful *Incognita,* a play in novel form, with easily anticipated results in the way of directness and simplification.

2. *Mrs. Behn, the First Woman Novelist*

Another Restoration dramatist, much more important for fiction, is Aphra Behn (1640-1689). Her maiden name was Amis, and she was born at Wye in Kent. While she was still very young, her father (or possibly foster-father) was appointed governor of Surinam, the country on the north coast of South America now known as Dutch Guiana. He died at sea. His family, however, seems to have spent some time in Surinam, and here the future novelist is supposed to have met her most famous character, the Negro prince, Oroonoko.

Her Dutch husband must have played a very brief part in Mrs. Behn's life; by the summer of 1666 she was doing secret service work for the British government in Antwerp. In this capacity, she warned the authorities of the contemplated Dutch raid on the Thames, but the warning was disregarded. The raid materialized in June, 1667. The next year, having painfully made her way back to England, Mrs. Behn was cast into debtor's prison. It is possible that Killigrew may have delivered her from this impasse; in any event, a contemporary biographer assures us that "the rest of her life was entirely dedicated to pleasure and poetry." Her career as a dramatist began in 1670. She was the first Englishwoman who ever earned a living with her pen, and she has a long list of poems, plays, novels, and miscellaneous writings to her credit.[1]

Much the most elaborate—and most forward-looking—of Mrs. Behn's novels was *Oroonoko, or The Royal Slave* (1688).

> I do not pretend . . . to entertain my reader with the adventures of a feigned hero. . . . I was myself an eye-witness of what you will find here set down; and what I could not be witness of, I received from the mouth of the chief actor in this history, the hero himself, who gave us the whole transactions of his youth. . . .

Whatever may be the truth concerning Mrs. Behn's own experiences in Surinam, that portion of the story she claims to have witnessed—the slave insurrection and the tragic death of the noble black and his beloved wife—has a reality and poignancy that we do not find in the account of Oroonoko's youth in his own kingdom and his being carried into slavery.

On the other hand, nothing could be more misleading than the oft-encountered statement that in *Oroonoko* Mrs. Behn produced a seventeenth-century *Uncle Tom's Cabin*. Her own warm, ardent, enthusiastic sympathy has misled the critics at this point. That sympathy proceeds from temperament, not from conviction; Mrs. Behn has nothing to say against slavery as an institution. Life brought her her material by chance, and she used it as it came to hand, with no inclination or necessity to illuminate the general social problem involved.

If we must have a didactic Mrs. Behn, a much better case can be made for her having anticipated the primitivism of Rousseau, Cha-

[1] Mrs. Behn's whole biography is a tissue of problems; cf. V. Sackville-West, *Aphra Behn, The Incomparable Astrea* (Viking Press, 1928). Ernest Bernbaum's argument that she never went to Surinam—see *Kittredge Anniversary Papers* (Ginn, 1913) and *PMLA,* XXVIII (1913), 432-453—convinced few special students of the subject; H. G. Platt, Jr. would now seem to have closed the matter with his "Astrea and Celadon: An Untouched Portrait of Aphra Behn," *PMLA,* XLIX (1934), 544-559. Cf. also Edward Wagenknecht, "In Praise of Mrs. Behn," *Colophon,* Part XVIII (1934).

teaubriand, and Bernardin de Saint-Pierre.[2] The whole effect of *Oroonoko* is to contrast the corruptions of civilization with the innocencies of barbarism. "And 'tis most evident and plain, that simple nature is the most harmless, inoffensive, and virtuous mistress. 'Tis she alone, if she were permitted, that better instructs the world than all the inventions of men." Men and women live naked together in Surinam, yet one never sees "an indecent action or glance, and being continually used to see one another unadorned . . . it seems as if they had no wishes, there being nothing to heighten curiosity; but all you can see you see at once and every moment see; and where there is no novelty there can be no curiosity." Polygamy is practiced, of course, but never is a woman turned off, abandoned to want, shame, or misery. "Such ill morals are only practiced in Christian countries," writes Mrs. Behn scathingly, "where they prefer the bare name of religion, and without virtue or morality think that sufficient." Oroonoko himself could never be brought to take the doctrine of the Trinity seriously, and indeed he had little reason to be attracted to Christianity, its professors living as they lived before his eyes.

Among Mrs. Behn's other stories at least four titles should be mentioned. *Agnes de Castro* (1688), an idealized account of a famous incident in Portuguese history, presents one of the most tragic situations in the world, a good man married to one good woman and in love with another one, all three persons high-mindedly resolved to do only right, and breaking their hearts in the process. There has always been some difference of opinion as to whether *The History of the Nun, or The Fair Vow-Breaker* (1689) is a true tragedy or merely a tragic melodrama; one reader at least owns himself considerably shaken by it. If there is no such detailed presentation of character in *The Fair Jilt* (1688), at least Miranda embodies, unsentimentally and with fine honesty, one type of the eternal wanton for whom men perish, while she herself lives on to a comfortable and respected old age. *The Dumb Virgin, or The Force of Imagination* is a powerful incest-tale in the manner of Bandello.

[2] Cf. Edward D. Seeber, "*Oroonoko* in France in the XVIII Century," *PMLA*, LI (1936), 953-959.

Mrs. Behn used every means of attestation known to the fictionist of her day. The case of *Oroonoko* has already been cited. The story of *The Unfortunate Happy Lady* was related to her "by one who lived in the family," and as for *The Fair Jilt,* "to the great part of the main I myself was an eyewitness." She heard the story of *The Wandering Beauty,* in which she presents the servant-girl who marries above her station long before *Pamela,* from a lady of her acquaintance when she was not more than twelve years old. And she "lodged within three doors" of the tragic family of *The Dumb Virgin,* arriving on the scene in time to witness the bloody dénouement of their drama.

How freely are we to discount these protestations? Very freely, say Mrs. Behn's enemies. But the larger discount we take, the more must we attribute to her imagination, and the greater writer does she become! She is most convincing when she attests indirectly, as she does in numerous passages, some of them almost worthy of Defoe. "The officer received for answer that the money should be called in and paid at such a time, setting a certain time, which I have not been so curious as to retain or put in my journal-observations." And the casual addendum to *The Fair Jilt* is masterly: "Since I began this relation, I heard that Prince Tarquin died about three quarters of a year ago." Like Thackeray, Mrs. Behn understood that a comment made by the writer *in propria persona* may create illusion as well as destroy it. She herself is the most real character in *Oroonoko,* and we tend to accept the others because we believe in her.

Why, then, is her genius not more widely recognized? The answer must be that, unlike Defoe, she uses none of her talents very consistently, nor, indeed, very intelligently. In one of her dedicatory letters she complains that "poetry (my talent) has so greatly the ascendant over me, that all I write must pass for fiction. . . ." Her facts were right; her explanation was wrong. It was not poetry that betrayed her, but sentimental claptrap. She had no artistic principles. She was the coarse-natured spokesman of aristocratic tradition in a transitional age, and she used the materials of life and of fiction with equal relish. Intrigued by a romantic situation, she cannot treat it on the high imaginative level; she "authenticates" it, as it were, makes "history" of it, in the light of the novelistic theory and practice of her day; and so she sprawls ungracefully between two stools. Take *The Adventure of the Black Lady,* for instance. The local color is perfect: "About the beginning of last June (as near as I can remember) Bellamora came to town from Hampshire, and was obliged to lodge the first night at the same inn where the stage-coach set up. The next day she took coach for Covent Garden," etc. The girl's plight is real, and truly observed. She has given herself to her lover, and carries his child in her body, but she does not wish to marry him: "ever since I have abhorred the sight of him"—a singularly psychological touch for the seventeenth century. But the kind landlady stretches out the long arm of coincidence to find him again; the reunion is managed in good old story-book fashion, and we hear no more of Bellamora's scruples. In much finer stories we encounter similar disappointments. In *Agnes de Castro* the analysis of emotion is fine and moving, while the trick by which Constantia is made to believe Agnes unfaithful is the most transparent artifice in the world. All in all, Mrs. Behn takes her place in our literature as a writer who just missed the highest achievement of which she was capable because she failed to understand and correctly to define her genius. But her failure was not remarkable. The only wonder is that, working under the conditions in which her lot was cast, she should have been able to accomplish so much.

3. *John Bunyan, an Artist in Spite of Himself*

Very different was the experience of her contemporary, the "mechanick preacher," John Bunyan (1628-1688). When he wrote *The Pilgrim's Progress* (1678) in Bedford County Jail, he created a masterpiece which today exists in more than one hundred languages and dialects. This remarkable book, an allegory of the Christian way, has a threefold significance for students of fiction: it is at once a fairy-tale, a picaresque adventure-story, and a realistic novel.

For a hundred years *The Pilgrim's Progress* was read only as a pious book, mostly by those who considered fiction in general a snare of the devil. Its devotees never realized the complicated nature of the charm to which they were surrendering themselves, and the usual view is that Bunyan himself did not realize it either. This view needs some qualification.

The characters of his great allegory came to Bunyan in exactly the same way in which the personages of one of the most popular religious fictions of our own day, *Magnificent Obsession,* came to the author of their being, Dr. Lloyd C. Douglas, forcing their way in upon a consciousness engaged in producing a non-fiction work.

> Nay, then, thought I, if that you breed so fast,
> I'll put you by yourselves, lest you at last
> Should prove *ad infinitum* and eat out
> The Book that I already am about.

Once Bunyan had brought forth, his offspring rather appalled him. Should he publish, or no? Would such a book redound to God's glory? He sought advices, and it is very significant that though his counselors were unable to agree—

> Some said, It might do good; others said, No—

print it he did. It would have taken wild horses to stop him.

> At last I thought, Since you are thus divided,
> I print it will; and so the case decided.

Having got the book out into the world, he was sure he had done all for the glory of God, but that was later. If you had talked to him of the literary significance of his work, he would have stared. Nevertheless he wrote his story, as every other important piece of fiction has been written, because he could not help himself, because this was the work that he had come into the world to do.

There is a large conventional element in all Bunyan's books. He belonged to a group, and he took care that his experience should conform to the pattern approved by the group. This is true even of the famous autobiography, *Grace Abounding to the Chief of Sinners* (1666). Generations have been taken in by Bunyan's lurid account of his sinful youth, yet, profanity aside, what real wickedness did he commit?

Conversion may have utterly rooted out the Old Adam in John Bunyan the man; that is a secret between him and his God. What we may be sure of is that, as a writer, the saint made the best possible use of the materials that the sinner had accumulated. For it is now clear that *The Pilgrim's Progress* is by no means exclusively based upon the Bible, plus *The Plain Man's Pathway to Heaven,* by Arthur Dent, plus Deguileville's *Pilgrimage of the Life of Man,* plus *The Practice of Piety,* by Lewis Bayly, plus Foxe's *Book of Martyrs,* Luther's commentary on Galatians, and the few more respectable books to which attention was long ago directed, but that it owes quite as much to the author's remembrance of the "beastly romances, and books full of ribaldry, even such as immediately tended to set all fleshly lusts on fire" that he read in his unregenerate youth.[3]

The Pilgrim's Progress is not a perfect piece of art. Sometimes, as Coleridge remarked in the case of Passion's treasure, the details are too vague to carry conviction; sometimes the allegory is absurd. Sometimes, too, Bunyan's eagerness to expound doctrine betrays him. William Vaughn Moody complains of "the deliberate and rather hair-splitting conversation between Christian and Apollyon." He is right, but this too is determined by the allegory. Bunyan has a point to make, and he must make it, even though the unintended effect is to make the hideous monster seem unexpectedly reasonable and patient!

But all such faults are insignificant beside the positive merits of the book. Bunyan's rugged, epigrammatic, Anglo-Saxon style is unsurpassed in kind. The Valley of the Shadow, the Delectable Mountains, the Hill called Difficulty, By-Path Meadow—merely to speak the words is to be thankful that one has learned the English language. Style glorifies even Bunyan's ignorance and his partisanships, and we see Giant Pope "grown so crazy and stiff in his joints that he can now do little more than sit in his Cave's mouth, grinning at pilgrims as they go by, and biting his nails because he cannot come at them."

[3] *The Seven Champions of Christendom* and *Bevis of Hampton* are particularly noteworthy. Richard Bernard's *Isle of Man* and other allegorical writings may have exercised some influence. The Giant Despair episode may be indebted to the story of "Jack and the Beanstalk." The influence of *The Faerie Queene* is at best doubtful.

Professor Lowes had much to say of Bunyan's style some years ago, commenting in his own inimitable fashion on a brief passage at the very beginning of *The Pilgrim's Progress:*

> The man therefore read it, and looking upon Evangelist very carefully, said, "Whither must I fly?" Then said Evangelist, pointing with his finger over a very wide field, "Do you see yonder wicket-gate?" The man said, "No." Then said the other, "Do you see yonder shining light?" He said, "I think I do."

Says Mr. Lowes:

> That is not description; it is the thing itself. A man intently reading a roll; the lifting of his eyes to scrutinize another man; the pointing finger; the wicket-gate; the shining light; the anxious travelling of the eye across the field and back again to the pointing finger, and once more peeringly across the field and back again—was there ever, I wonder, another passage into which, within such brief compass, so many visual impressions have been packed? It is easy to say what a thing is *like,* and thousands have the trick. Direct vision, with the power of evoking it in us, is the gift of few, and among them are the greatest. Bunyan has it, and it is with his unswerving intensity of vision that we see: "Behold I saw"; "I looked and saw"; "I saw also"; "as I perceived"; "I looked then, and saw"; "So I saw in my Dream." It is no wonder that the pictures live and breathe. And one reason why the book itself has lived is a reason which it shares with *The Divine Comedy* and the *Iliad* and the *Odyssey* and a hundred passages in Shakespeare (to name no more)—the power of striking out, in a few naked, simple words, a picture which is ineffaceable.[4]

Characterization is quite as masterly. The personages bear the names of abstractions, but blood flows through their veins; they are Bunyan's compatriots, moving through the English towns and countryside he knew so well. As he uses it, "Christian" is not a generic term but a proper name, and we are in no danger of confusing the man who bears it with Faithful and Hopeful, who tread the road to heaven along with him. Bunyan has, too, Shakespeare's great gift of inventing a distinctive, individual turn of speech for his characters. "I perceive then that our talk must be about the

[4] John Livingston Lowes, *Essays in Appreciation* (Houghton Mifflin, 1936), pp. 53-54. Quoted by permission of the publishers.

power of things," says Talkative. "Well, 'tis a very good question, and I shall be willing to answer you. And take my answer in brief thus. . . ." It is as perfect as Juliet's immortal Nurse.

Yet these things alone do not explain the survival of the book. It lives because, fundamentally, after all allowances for Bunyan's unenlightened Calvinism have been made, it is true; it bores down to the rock-bottom of our lives. Every man, whatever his creed, must, in one form or another, answer the age-old question, "Wilt thou join with the dragons? wilt thou join with the gods?" Every man has wallowed in the Slough of Despond, and battled with Giant Apollyon in the Valley of Humiliation; every man has starved and thirsted in the dungeons of Despair. And every man knows, however he may try to forget it, that he must go through the River at last.

All things considered, the Vanity Fair episode is perhaps the greatest in the book. Nowhere else did Bunyan come so close to a realistic picture of contemporary English life, and nowhere is he more universalistic in his implications. In the trial of Christian and Faithful, the whole question of the relationship between the social order and the individual conscience is involved; write the name of any despised minority group of today in the place of the pilgrims' names, and the picture will still be accurate.

> But the men being patient, and not rendering railing for railing, but contrariwise blessing, and giving good words for bad, and kindness for injuries done, some men in the Fair that were more observing and less prejudiced than the rest, began to check and blame the base sort for their continual abuse done by them to the men; they therefore in angry manner let fly at them again, counting them as bad as the men in the cage, and telling them that they seemed confederates and should be made partakers of their misfortunes.

It might all be quoted from tomorrow morning's newspaper.

The second part of *The Pilgrim's Progress* (1684), which is the story of Christian's wife and children on their way to Paradise, is much inferior to Part I. At the outset, it was Bunyan's idea to have Mr. Sagacity tell the story to the Dreamer; then, apparently, he realized the clumsiness of this plan, and Sagacity was summarily dropped. Bunyan seems now to be writing for women and children. But a picaresque narrative needs a hero, not a heroine.

At the outset, Bunyan substituted an assault on Christina's chastity for the physical combats in which her husband had participated. But he was unable to do much with it, and in any event such a device could not very well have been repeated. When combats do occur, it is not Christina but her guide, Greatheart, who is involved in them. There is less adventure and more exposition in Part II than in Part I, and much of it is dismal. Even the death of Giant Despair, which ought to have been a climax to the thrilling adventures of Part I, is comparatively tame.

Yet there are touches as fine as anything in Bunyan. Greatheart himself, Mr. Valiant-for-Truth, Mr. Honest, and Madame Bubble are all memorable characters. Abstractions come to life as of old in those weak Christians, Mr. Fearing and Mr. Feeblemind—how wise, how tender, and how deeply Christian Bunyan is in his treatment of them! When Ready-to-Halt dances with Despondency's daughter, Much-Afraid, there is a welcome touch of humor. When Mercy falls in love with Christian's son, Matthew, and marries him, and bears him a child, we are coming close to the novel of domestic life. Finally (and this *is* in the heroic mood of Part I), we have the great picture of the crossing of the River. Despondency's daughter went over singing, "but none could understand what she said." With Mr. Valiant-for-Truth the situation was different: "all the Trumpets sounded for him on the other side."

Bunyan himself presents *The Life and Death of Mr. Badman* (1680) as a pendant to *The Pilgrim's Progress.* "It came again into my mind to write, as then, of him that was going to Heaven, so now of the life and death of the ungodly, and of their travel from this world to hell."

The description is misleading. *Mr. Badman* is not an allegory; it is a realistic story of contemporary English life. It has more morality than its great predecessor and less religion; as Bonamy Dobrée points out, the virtues praised and the vices castigated are, in general, those that help and hinder, respectively, the progress of trade. Bunyan weakens his narrative somewhat by having Mr. Badman dead before the book opens; his history is narrated in retrospect, with much prosy moralizing, by tiresome old Mr. Wiseman to his friend, Mr. Attentive. The villain-hero's downward progress occasions many other brief narratives, some of them childishly naïve, some of considerable power. Bunyan achieves a subtle variation of the customary judgment-tale when he gives Mr. Badman a quiet, peaceful death; for the unrepentant sinner (such is the implication) such a death is the most hopeless of all.

Bunyan's last work of fiction, *The Holy War, Made by Shaddai upon Diabolus, for the Regaining of the Metropolis of the World, or, the Losing and Taking Again of the Town of Mansoul* (1682), has little significance for the novel. Military symbolism here replaces the old figure of the pilgrimage. *The Holy War* is remarkably clear, for so elaborate an allegory, though there are shades of meaning, especially in Bunyan's references to the ecclesiastical and political life of his day, that a modern reader may easily miss. In the Biblical story, which is localized in a garden, the forbidden fruit is a finely effective symbol of sin. It seems sadly out of place, however, in a story of warfare. The narrative skill displayed in *The Holy War* runs far ahead of anything in *The Pilgrim's Progress,* but there are no such powerful characterizations and there is no such splendor of style.

Bunyan's contribution to the development of fiction has been most variously estimated. His personal achievement is unquestioned, but because a novel is one thing and a religious allegory another, it is sometimes maintained that he had nothing to do with the novel. A fairer judgment will perceive, first, that in many passages of the second *Pilgrim's Progress,* and in almost all of *Mr. Badman,* Bunyan is himself just on the edge of the realistic novel of manners; second, and far more importantly, that the methods he employed were by no means limited in their usefulness to the particular kind of fiction in which he was interested. He turned away from the meaningless heroism of the romances; he gazed on men and women in their habit, as they lived. But he did not view them cynically, as the picaresque writers had done, but earnestly and sympathetically, and he described their adventures in simple, moving style. Let the increasingly matter-of-fact years go on accumulating materials for fiction in this realm, let a middle-class reading-public begin to develop, then let a great writer appear who has the wit to recognize this need and the skill to cater to it, and the pre-novel will be over, the novel here. During the first quarter of the eighteenth century these conditions were to be fulfilled.

CHAPTER III

DEFOE AND HIS CONTEMPORARIES

To be an artist is a great thing, but to be an artist and not know it is the most glorious plight in the world.

Sentimental Tommy

1. *The Strange Case of Mrs. Veal*

In 1706 there appeared in London a brief work known as *A True Relation of the Apparition of One Mrs. Veal.* Though long regarded as fiction, we know now that it was a masterly piece of reporting of an incident well known in Kent, the kind of thing that might appear today in the *Proceedings* of the Society for Psychical Research.[1]

On the eighth of September, 1705, in her house at Canterbury, Mrs. Bargrave was surprised by a visit from her old friend, Mrs. Veal, "who was in a riding habit: at that moment of time the clock struck twelve at noon." Mrs. Veal was just starting on a journey; she had given her brother the slip, but she must see Mrs. Bargrave before going away. When Mrs. Bargrave offered to kiss her, she complied "till their lips almost touched, and then Mrs. Veal drew her hand cross her own eyes, and said, 'I am not very well,' and so waived it." She had indeed been subject to fits, and when she began to talk, as it seemed to Mrs. Bargrave, very strangely, asking her to write to the aforementioned brother to give directions concerning the disposition of some of Mrs. Veal's trinkets, Mrs. Bargrave feared that a seizure must be coming on. "And to divert Mrs. Veal as she thought she took hold of her gown sleeve several times and commended it. Mrs. Veal told her it was a scoured silk and newly made up."

[1] Cf. George C. Aitken, *XIX Century,* XXXVII (1895), 95-100; Sir Charles Firth, *Review of English Studies,* VII (1931), 1-6; Dorothy Gardiner, same, pp. 188-197.

The two ladies discussed various trivial themes, comforted each other in their tribulations, and exchanged much pious counsel. At last Mrs. Veal sent Mrs. Bargrave out to a neighbor's to fetch her daughter, but when Mrs. Bargrave returned she found her visitor already at the door. "She said she must be going, though perhaps she might not go on her journey till Monday." Mrs. Bargrave watched her down the street "till a turning interrupted the sight of her, which was three quarters after one in the afternoon."

The next paragraph begins: "Mrs. Veal died the seventh of September at twelve o'clock at noon, of her fits." She died, in other words, twenty-four hours before she called on Mrs. Bargrave.

Testimony skilfully adduced, verisimilitude, corroborative and irrelevant detail, minute particularity—almost every device that a narrator can employ to disarm skepticism and win credence is employed in *Mrs. Veal.* Thus, it is not enough that Mrs. Bargrave should be a lady of unquestioned respectability. We must be made to see that even if she were a liar she could gain nothing by lying in this particular instance. Furthermore, the skeptical reader's doubts are personified in Mrs. Veal's brother, whose attack upon Mrs. Bargrave we are made to resent. It is the very absence of what we commonly think of as a weird or ghostly atmosphere that is impressive in this narrative: surely if a man were "making up" a ghost-story, he could do better than this! And Mrs. Bargrave's chance mention of the scoured silk dress is a touch of genius. "Then Mrs. Watson cried out, 'You have seen her indeed, for none knew but Mrs. Veal and myself that the gown was scoured.'"

Mrs. Veal offers in miniature virtually all Defoe's salient qualities, thus affording an excellent introduction to the study of his technique. That the piece itself should be fact, not fiction, happens, as we shall see, to illustrate a valuable point.

2. *A Novelist's Way*

Defoe was nearly sixty when he published *Robinson Crusoe* in April, 1719, and forthwith launched the career which was to cause him to be labeled "father of the English novel." Born in London in 1660, the son of a pious, dissenting butcher, Defoe was intended by his parents for the ministry. He chose instead a much more exciting career in which journalism, secret service, and highly varied business activities all played their part. He went bankrupt; he stood his term in the pillory (incidentally winning a hostile crowd over, so that he became in effect the hero of his own disgrace); he lent his literary gifts to Whigs and Tories alike. By the time he died in 1731, he had an enormous amount of work to his credit; he was possibly the most prolific writer who ever lived.[2]

As early as 1705 Defoe tried his hand at a clumsy fantastic romance called *The Consolidator.* In *The Family Instructor* (1715) both narrative and dialogue played a considerable role. In this discussion our attention must be largely confined to the eight major novels on which his fame most securely rests, but it should be remembered that no absolute line can mark them off from the rest of his work. They were all published as fact, and in a sense they are fact; often they merely perform variations upon historic record. It is not what is true that convinces in art but what seems true, and Defoe knew it well: "neither is it of the least moment to inquire whether the Colonel hath told his own story true or not; if he has made a history or a parable, it will be equally useful. . . ."

The success of *Robinson Crusoe* was immediate. In four months Defoe had a sequel ready, the much inferior *Farther Adventures* through Russia and the Far East. (*The Serious Reflections of Robinson Crusoe,* 1720, which was not a novel but a book of essays, failed as ignominiously as it deserved to fail.) *Memoirs of a Cavalier* (1720) details the history of an English soldier, first under Gustavus Adolphus on the continent, then in the English Civil Wars, and provides Defoe for once with a gentleman hero. Two weeks later appeared *Captain Singleton,* which W. P. Trent describes as "at once a treasure-trove story, a sea and pirate story, a travel story, a hunting story, a trading story"! With *Moll Flanders* (1722) Defoe gave us the first of his two books about women, at the same time making his first considerable excursion as novelist into the demimonde. His next book, *A Journal of the Plague Year* (1722), was much soberer in tone. It was occasioned by the plague at Marseilles

[2] Defoe published anonymously, and much of his work is still unidentified. The list of separate titles attributed to him in *The Cambridge Bibliography of English Literature* runs to fourteen double-column pages.

in 1720, but it purports to describe the London plague of 1665. The *Journal* has no plot of any kind, and misinformed librarians have sometimes classified it as history. *Colonel Jacque* also belongs to 1722. It opens brilliantly, rather in the manner of *Oliver Twist,* with a sympathetic account of a small boy in London who is taught to steal before he knows that thieving is not a legitimate trade. Unfortunately the military and trading portions of the book are dull, though Jacque's matrimonial adventures bid fair to rival Moll Flanders's own. The last great novel, *Roxana, or The Fortunate Mistress* (1724), which technically at least is the most interesting of them all, gives us the counterpart of Moll Flanders in a higher social sphere.

3. *Defoe's Narrative Method*

Defoe spares no pains to convince us that he is telling the truth. The *Cavalier* manuscript was found accidentally "among other valuable papers in the closet of an eminent public minister, of no less figure than one of King William's secretaries of state." Moll Flanders's history has been rewritten so as to cause her "to tell her own tale in modester words than she told it at first." An "N.B." in the *Journal of the Plague Year* explains that the narrator was himself buried in one of the cemeteries of which he speaks.

With a show of disarming honesty, Defoe presents evidence con as well as pro; like Mrs. Behn, he knows the value of a profession of ignorance. Things must not fit together too perfectly; if they do the illusion of life will be destroyed. Captain Singleton is not sure about the dates in his early life, "for you may be sure I kept no journal." Nor is it known whether or not Wilmot's men still inhabit the colony they settled. A preacher walks through the streets of plague-stricken London crying, "Yet forty days, and London shall be destroyed." But, "I will not be positive," adds Defoe, "whether he said yet forty days or yet a few days."

No writer has ever surpassed Defoe's skill in choosing the vivifying detail. It is not enough that Crusoe should give us the bare fact that he made a sieve or a kiln or a boat; he must describe the process of its making every step of the way. Singleton tells us how the ornaments were made that he traded off to natives in the heart of Africa for substantial benefits, and when a pirate's arm is injured he describes just how it was injured and why the man never regained control over that member. By the time he is through, that injury is real to the reader, and if the injury is real then the man who sustained it must be real also. Let us look for a moment at the supper Colonel Jacque shared at the inn with his prospective third wife.

I provided what the house afforded, which was a couple of partridges and a very good dish of stewed oysters. They brought us up afterward a neat's tongue and a ham that was almost cut down, but we eat none of it, for the other was fully enough for us both, and the maid made her supper of the oysters we had left, which were enough.

"They brought us up afterward." "But we eat none of it." "And the maid made her supper of the oysters." How insignificant these touches are! And how they make the picture live!

All Defoe's novels are autobiographical narratives in the first person; an elaborate, deliberately "artistic" arrangement of materials was, therefore, out of the question. *Crusoe* is very imperfect structurally. Apparently it was planned, if it was planned at all, with the island sojourn as one episode among several, but Defoe gets so deeply interested in the island, and develops Crusoe's experiences there with such unrivaled authenticity, that the reader finds himself hurrying through what he thinks of as the preliminaries, and when at last the island drops below the horizon, the book is dead. In *Moll Flanders, Captain Singleton,* and *Colonel Jacque,* we have a series of elaborately developed episodes, connected by curt and meager summaries of what happened between them. "It concerns the story in hand very little," writes Moll, "to enter into the farther particulars of the family, or of myself, for the five years that I lived with this husband, only to observe that I had two children by him, and that at the end of the five years he died."

One cannot say that Defoe never uses suspense—Crusoe's agony between the discovery of the footprint in the sand and the arrival of the cannibals comes immediately to mind—but he does not use it often. His favorite method is to proceed step by step, without preparation or foresight, to touch lightly and pass on. The death of Gustavus Adolphus, which marks a climax in the Cavalier's life, is reported so casually that the careless reader often misses it altogether.

Defoe will make elaborate plans for something which altogether fails to come off and then continue his story quite calmly along another line [3]—a method quite as vivid in his hands as when Chaucer has the logical order of his tales upset by the quarrel between the Miller and the Reve, so that the Monk never does follow the Knight as narrator, even though decorum and Harry Bailly had both decreed that he should! Defoe's method here bars him from many achievements, yet it is difficult to speak of it as a defect, for it was part of a simplicity which had its own special virtues. As narrator pure and simple this man is the best that English fiction has to show.

4. *What Defoe Lacked*

Yet for all his microscopic circumstantiality, Defoe is far from being a realist in the higher sense of the term. His errors are not very important in this connection, nor the numerous conflicts and inconsistencies in his work, nor yet his confused historical relationships. Ignorance and realism may well go along together, and haste and careless workmanship can explain much. His difficulties with dialogue and especially with dialect are not worth worrying about either, for it was too early in the day to expect perfection along these lines. The real difficulty is more fundamental. It is true that when we compare Crusoe with its sources,[4] we observe that Defoe has omitted many picturesque details. But he has omitted other things as well. Dickens objected justly that *Crusoe* "exhibits a man who was thirty years on that desert island with no visible effect

[3] Crusoe sends Friday's father and the Spaniard off to the mainland to arrange for the deliverance of their party, but before his emissaries return he sights the stranger vessel which is destined to save him by other means. Amy makes a special trip to the continent in search of Roxana's Dutch husband, spends four or five months tracing him from country to country, hears at last that he is living in London, with much difficulty secures his address; meanwhile her mistress has met him again by pure chance! In *Captain Singleton* there is an impressive account of the siege of a hollow tree in which some savages have taken refuge. The besiegers make a ladder to scale the tree, then decide it would be impracticable to try to use it, yet finally they do use it! An interesting variation of this technique occurs in *Colonel Jacque,* where the hero discovers Moggy's pre-marital waywardness quite by chance after her death, when it is too late for the discovery to affect their relations in any way.

[4] Cf. E. G. Gudde, *Philological Quarterly,* IV (1925), 110-120.

made on his character by that experience." The real-life Crusoe, Alexander Selkirk, lived alone less than four and a half years, yet he had already become more than half savage by the time he was rescued. Now Defoe knew that he was open to criticism along this line. He forestalled it as much as possible by making his Crusoe an extremely practical, matter-of-fact sort of person; if any man could go through such experiences and live, it must be this man. And this is very characteristic of his manner of working. Having disarmed initial incredulity, he feels no obligation to be true to nature, but he is always ready with some clever trick to obscure the issue and prevent inconvenient questions from being raised.

Defoe's comparative failure as a creator of individual character connects directly here. We know Crusoe in the sense that we understand him thoroughly, but he is less an individual than he is Anglo-Saxon manhood face to face with the primal forces of nature. And most of the others are Crusoe's brothers and sisters; even when they are wayward brothers and sisters the family resemblance is clear. William Watson, the Quaker pirate of *Captain Singleton,* is more complex, and so are several personages of the last great novel. One of them, oddly, is again a Quaker, the unnamed Quaker with whom Roxana lodges, "a cunning as well as an honest woman." Another is that strange combination of unselfish devotion and ruthless violence, the maid Amy. Finally there is Roxana herself, concerning whom a whole chapter might well be written. Yet Defoe's art is not quite equal to his conception of Roxana's character. He has true and penetrating touches, as in the wicked woman's refusal to pollute the confessional for selfish purposes—a keen-sighted realization of the bewildering complexity of human character—but there are times too when he fails. In view of the extenuating circumstances involved, Roxana's sense of guilt while living with her first protector seems almost worthy of a Victorian gentlewoman; it is poor preparation for the inexpressibly shocking scene in which, not long afterwards, she forces her maid into her paramour's arms. Even here, I think, Defoe has intellectually got the thing right. A woman as complicated as Roxana might do just that, and her remorse might be the very thing that would impel her, deliberately, as if in desperation, to fling the last shreds of decency to the winds. But as we read the scene we are not convinced. We need painfully to reason the matter out; the author has failed, not in conception but in communication.

Defoe also lacks what we generally call atmosphere. It was his habit to concentrate absolutely upon the task in hand, and for all the vividness with which his world is realized, it is still a narrow world, the world of the immediate question at issue, with no sense of wider impingements. From the point of view of atmosphere, indeed, the greatest of the desert island romances is the poorest of them all. Both Dickens and Walter de la Mare fall foul of what they consider Defoe's emotional shallowness. Dickens calls *Crusoe* "the only instance of a universally popular book that could make no one laugh and could make no one cry," while de la Mare indicts the hero's transformation in Part II to a mere buccaneering globe-trotter, "with a sigh of petulance and surfeit dismissing even his island itself from all remembrance." He adds: "This wanton attempt of an author to ruin his finest piece of handiwork is, so far as I know, unparalleled in English literature." Both writers are shocked by the Friday episode. "I will venture to say," remarks Dickens, "that there is not in literature a more surprising instance of an utter want of tenderness and sentiment than the death of Friday." And de la Mare complains of Crusoe's thought of "returning to his island in search of a facsimile" which very likely he might have called "Monday Morning."

5. *Defoe's Attitude Toward Life and Fiction*

For all his unemotionalism, Defoe never approached the naturalistic ideal of presenting his material without comment. Good and bad alike, his characters moralize incessantly. "It is impossible to express the horror of my soul while I did this," says the thief Moll Flanders. Defoe's moralizing has often been called insincere, and there can be no doubt that he was cannily aware of the appeal such passages would exert. But fundamentally he was himself a part of the pious dissenting audience for which he wrote. John F. Ross rightly calls *Crusoe* "a success story, a handbook on how to succeed on a desert island." The utilitarian point of view apparent in Defoe was typical of the Puritanism-gone-to-seed that he knew as religion, and disinterested idealism was as uncharacteristic of his milieu as it was of himself. "Religion joined in with the prudential," remarks Robinson Crusoe in one connection. It generally does with Defoe.[5] Of course he knows the difference between true and false repentance. Moll Flanders feels a sentimental reaction against thievery, but she cannot bring herself to make restitution, and she has too much sense to suppose that tears can avail without it. The Quaker pirate, however, is a more complicated matter. That he is a hypocrite is clear enough, but this does not quite cover the case. Defoe's attitude toward him wavers a little; the rascal has something of the dissenter's stubborn determination to make the best of both worlds. This tendency always crops up in Defoe when money is in question. Crusoe, finding the gold in the wreck, apostrophizes most edifyingly: "O drug, what art thou good for?" and much more to the same effect. But the next sentence reads: "However, upon second thoughts, I took it away."

But Defoe can go deeper than this. His occultism is in large part, no doubt, the superstition of his class. But it is not all superstition. Colonel Jacque and the Cavalier's mother have remarkable dreams. Roxana experiences premonitions, and there is a famous example of telepathy in *Moll Flanders*. Crusoe, of course, is an avowed spiritualist and on one occasion at least he is clairvoyant. It is this side of Defoe which explains why, for all the minute particularism of his bourgeois soul, he yet brings us into a larger world than the modern naturalist can inhabit.

More interesting still is Defoe's by no means negligible social criticism. Roxana believes in free love; she will not submit herself and her property to the discretion of a husband's whim. For himself Defoe is careful to disclaim the implication of sexual looseness involved, but he understood her point of view, for he had shown his sympathy toward the unfair discriminations under which women suffer as far back as his *Essay on Projects*. Moll Flanders rightly sees herself as more sinned against than sinning, the inevitable product of a social system which makes starvation the only alternative to prostitution for an unprotected girl and then smugly casts

[5] The best discussion of this problem is Hans H. Andersen's "The Paradox of Trade and Morality in Defoe," *Modern Philology,* XXXIX (1941), 23-46.

stones at her because she chooses to live. Most significant of all in this connection is *Colonel Jacque;* the outcast children sleeping in the warm ashes at the glass house are a modern equivalent of Dante's unbaptized infants.

Defoe's share in the development of English fiction was a very important one. It is true that Professor Bernbaum has now discovered that his type of narrative had been somewhat anticipated in the Mary Carleton stories and in *The Complete Mendicant* (1699).[6] Yet Defoe's glory suffers no serious diminution as a consequence. Great writers are seldom highly original thinkers, nor does it often fall to the lot of him who invents a new literary genre to do very distinguished work in it. Fact and fiction were much confounded in Defoe's day, as indeed in some ways they are still. He produced, on a larger scale than had been the custom hitherto, stories of believable human beings in circumstances for which his art was generally adequate to secure credence and sympathy; whether his books were "novels" or not, in the modern sense of the term, is largely an academic question. Quite clearly, he pointed out the road along which many writers, some of them greater than himself, were to travel.

6. *Mrs. Manley and Some Others*

Defoe dominated the fiction of the early eighteenth century, but he was by no means the only one who contributed to it. In a rapid survey his work alone can be considered in any detail, but he must not be thought of as the only writer of his time.

Mention must be made, first, of a number of women writers. The earliest was Mrs. Behn's admirer, Mary de la Rivière Manley (1663-1724), whose own life was as colorful and scandalous as those of her heroines. *The Adventures of Rivella* (1714) is said to be autobiographical. Mrs. Manley's books have no great merit, but the several parts of the at once sentimental and sensual work known as *The New Atlantis* (1709-1710) have considerable historic interest in connection with the scandal chronicles or "secret histories" in which

[6] Cf. Ernest Bernbaum, *The Mary Carleton Narratives, 1663-1673, A Missing Chapter in the History of the English Novel* (Harvard Universitv Press, 1914).

much tiresome allegorizing and considerable epic machinery overlies a veiled exposé of the sins of famous personages of the time. Mrs. Manley draws closer to "real life" than did Mrs. Behn; it was her own opinion that in scenes of passion she achieved "such a representation of nature as to warm the coldest reader." She believed too, or pretended to believe, that her exposures served the cause of truth and decency, thus paying lip service at least to the dominant idea of the time, that fiction must have an ethical purpose.

Mrs. Eliza Haywood (1693?-1756) had a long and varied career. She imitated Mrs. Behn; she imitated Mrs. Manley; her last books and her best—*Betsy Thoughtless* (1751) and *Jemmy and Jenny Jessamy* (1753)—are both imitations of Richardson. If not fine art, they are at least remarkable examples of an aging writer's ability to adapt herself to a new style.

Mrs. Elizabeth Rowe (1674-1737), much admired of Pope, Watts, and Dr. Johnson, was as proper as her predecessors were prurient: Charlotte Morgan thinks her heroines suggest Elsie Dinsmore. Proper too was Mrs. Jane Barker (*fl.* 1688-1718), though possibly there was more prudence than idealism in her propriety. Turning to fiction after an unhappy love-affair, Mrs. Barker not only made literary capital out of her own emotions but had the realistic courage to present a hero with "nothing extraordinary" about him. Mrs. Penelope Aubin (*fl.* 1721), a learned lady and a Catholic, deliberately set out to improve fiction, illustrating "purity of style and manners." She imitated Defoe's chronicles of adventure, but never neglected to reward the pious for their fidelity. Heidler points out that the title of the first collected edition of her works "summed up the claims of the novelists of the period." It reads: *A Collection of Entertaining Histories and Novels, Designed to Promote the Cause of Virtue and Honor. Principally Founded on Facts, and Interspersed with a Variety of Beautiful and Instructive Incidents.* Other women writers of the time were Mary Davys, Arabella Plantin, and Elizabeth Boyd.

Incidental and intermittent use of the methods of fiction influenced many types of utilitarian and informational writing in the seventeenth and eighteenth centuries. We may speak here of only one type—the character-sketch.

Character-writing is as old as Theophrastus; there is a good deal of it in medieval literature and the Elizabethan "humors" comedy; all students of English literature are familiar with some of its most distinguished examples in the Prologue to *The Canterbury Tales.* The increasingly introspective temper of the seventeenth century favored the genre; a sketch of its development during the period would have to include Overbury, Earle, and Hall, Nicholas Breton, Samuel Butler and his *Hudibras,* and, in its own way, Clarendon's distinguished portrait-painting in his *History of the Rebellion.*

By the time we come to Addison and Steele and the Sir Roger de Coverley papers of the *Spectator* series (1711-1712), we are much closer to fiction as we ordinarily understand it. Add a thread of continuity to the adventures of Sir Roger, and you are not very far from *The Pickwick Papers.* Sir Roger is indeed a "character," much in the *Pickwick* manner. The reader does not think of him, Andrew Freeport, Captain Sentry, and Will Honeycomb as the Country Gentleman, the Merchant, the Soldier, and the Gallant (which is what the seventeenth century would have made of them); he thinks of them as individuals. Fortunately they are well enough known so that this point need not be labored here.

7. *Swift as Fictionist*

Gulliver's Travels (1726), the masterpiece of Jonathan Swift (1667-1745) has shared *Crusoe's* fate: it lives largely, in an expurgated state, as a nursery classic. ("It is like turning down the glare of a volcano," says Kipling, "to light a child to bed.") There was no love lost between Swift and Defoe; the Dean of Saint Patrick's was in the old aristocratic tradition while the hard-working journalist was supplying reading-matter for the new middle class. *Gulliver* was not Swift's first flirtation with fiction. There is fiction in *A Tale of a Tub* and *The Battle of the Books* (both 1704), and there is keen-sighted portrayal of character in *Genteel Conversation* and *Directions to Servants.* What has been written of Defoe's verisimilitude can be repeated of Swift's, yet it would be difficult to prove indebtedness. As John F. Ross has remarked, Defoe deals with "acknowledged possibilities," Swift with "sheer figments, impossible fantasies." Whatever may be thought of Defoe, the extravagant nature of Swift's material precludes, in his case, the suggestion that he wished to deceive. He wrote in the tradition of the imaginary voyage,[7] and the most important of his many sources were Cyrano, Lucian, and Rabelais. Yet the difference between Gulliver's kind of voyage and Crusoe's is probably much clearer to us than it was to Swift's contemporaries, and we know that an Irish bishop denounced *Gulliver's Travels* for its inaccuracies. It is startling to the modern reader when California is mentioned, and in Book III Gulliver actually visits Japan, along with such make-believe countries as Laputa, Glubbdubrib, and Luggnagg.

Chapters I, II, and VI of the First Book—the Voyage to Lilliput—make use of material originally designed in 1714 for the *Memoirs of Martin Scriblerus*. In these chapters Lilliput is Utopia, the nursery-tale atmosphere secures a willing suspension of disbelief, and the author's attitude toward his characters is, on the whole, sympathetic. Between 1714 and 1721, when he took the story up again, Swift re-charactered his material; Lilliput has now ceased to be Utopia and become England. And now the Dean introduces many references to English politics; it is clear he means to suggest that his country-men are morally dwarfish. In Book II he extends his field: now Gulliver in Brobdingnag is an insignificant Englishman traveling among admirable people built on an heroic scale.

Books III and IV have generally been considered much inferior. It is true that Book III makes a scattered impression, though its relativity, its spiritualism, and its eugenics are all of much interest, and the individual hits are as brilliant as ever. Brilliant would be a mild word for the last book, the voyage to the land of the Houhynhmns, where affairs of administration have been turned over to the horses, while the Yahoos, who are humans, live under them in unspeakable filth and degradation. It is this portion of Swift's masterpiece—"the ripe, mature, and all but rotting fruit of his scorched brain," Shane

[7] Philip Babcock Gove has now laid the foundation for the scholarly investigation of this type of literature in *The Imaginary Voyage in Prose Fiction. A History of its Criticism and a Guide for its Study, with an Annotated Check List of 215 Imaginary Voyages from 1700 to 1800* (Columbia Universitv Press, 1941). Gove gives considerable attention to *Robinson Crusoe*

Leslie called it—that is largely responsible for the popular conception of him as cynic and misanthrope.

Scott unfortunately helped to establish this view in 1814, in the "life" included in his edition of the Dean's works; and so did Thackeray in those lectures on *The English Humorists of the Eighteenth Century* in which the great Victorian managed to spit on the graves of a considerable number of his distinguished predecessors.[8]

At present this view has little critical standing. Charles Whibley led the attack in the Leslie Stephen Lecture of 1917; Ernest Bernbaum made an important contribution in his 1920 edition of *Gulliver;* in 1936 Ricardo Quintana brought out the definitive modern study of Swift. Whibley saw Swift's master-passion as "anger against injustice and oppression." The Dean was slandered "for the very reason that he was not a cynic. He did not write for his own pleasure, or to put money in his pocket." Bernbaum emphasized Swift's adherence to the Great Tradition of classical-Christian civilization. Neither the materialism of Mandeville nor the sentimentalism of Shaftesbury ever seduced him. He never denied man's capacity for mental and spiritual advancement. But in actual experience it hurt him to find men so seldom concerned to exercise this capacity.

There is some danger perhaps of carrying this defense too far. Swift was an heroic figure at times—an Anglican churchman who hated Ireland yet risked his personal safety and, in some measure, did destroy his professional future, to fight the battle of a Catholic people against English and Anglican injustice—but it would be a mistake to try to picture him as a genial figure. He died mad. He agreed with Sophocles and Thomas Hardy that not to have been born is best. The fascinated horror with which he regarded the physical life of man suggests a deep-seated sexual maladjustment. It is true that the noble Houhynhmns have "human" qualities as well as the degraded Yahoos, but the fact that in Swift's fable only the latter wear the semblance of humanity cannot be wholly without significance. It would be a mistake to make too much of the fact that the horse is hardly a quite satisfactory symbol of perfection.

[8] Cf. Merrel D. Clubb's important article, "The Criticism of Gulliver's 'Voyage to the Houhynhmns,' 1726-1914," *Stanford Studies in Language and Literature* (Stanford University, 1941).

Symbols of perfection are hard to come by; even Dante found this to be true when he turned from the horrors of hell to the glories of heaven. But Professor Quintana himself accuses Swift of sensationalism in "developing the theme of bestiality," and complains that he draws attention away from "the concurrent statement of the life of reason." And W. B. C. Watkins finds that as he goes on he tends more and more to identify man with the Yahoos alone. But when all reservations are made, the new view of Swift stands—in its broad, general outlines, if not always in its details. There is no excuse today for failing to realize that the man was a great idealist, one of those uncomfortable idealists who ask more of mankind than mankind can ever give.

With all this, however, the main line of the English novel had very little to do. Fiction is neither myth nor prophecy; it is a thing grounded on patient observation of human nature; it accepts the fundamental conditions of our life on this earth; the blazing fury and the mountain-peak idealism of the Yahoos and the Houhynhmns are at once below it and above it. In so far as the English novel developed along the lines suggested by Jonathan Swift, it gave itself to interests he shared with the vulgar journalist whom he despised.

CHAPTER IV

PSYCHOLOGICAL REALISM BEGINS: SAMUEL RICHARDSON

The characters no longer did anything, and then went and did something else: you were told instead how they did it.

Tommy and Grizel

1. *Richardson's Life and Works*

Samuel Richardson passed his fiftieth birthday without having written anything of literary significance; he died one of the famous novelists of the world. He was born in Derbyshire in 1689, the son of a cabinet-maker. As a child his schoolmates called him "Serious and Gravity," and his parents saw him as marked for the church. But financial difficulties intervened, and he was apprenticed to a printer. He married into his master's family in the good old story-book fashion. His business prospered; he printed the Journals of the House of Commons; in 1754 he became Master of the Stationers' Company. He died in 1761.

Like Walter Scott, young Samuel told his schoolmates stories; like Thomas Hardy, he was employed by the illiterate girls of the neighborhood as an amanuensis. One day in 1739, the London booksellers, Rivington and Osborn, called to ask him to write them a volume of model letters. Many of these turned out quite conventional in character—letters of congratulation and condolence, letters employing servants or paying debts. Others, more ambitiously, developed a situation. Letters XV to XXI constitute a love-story. Letters CXLIX to CLIX give us a critical description of London life. Most suggestive of all is Letter CXXXVIII—"A Father to a Daughter in Service on Hearing of her Master's Attempting her Virtue." While Richardson was working on it, he recollected an interesting real-life story he had heard along this line. The result was the publication, in November, 1740, of *Pamela, or Virtue Rewarded.*

The story is simple. After the death of her mistress, Pamela Andrews, a comely servant girl, is solicited dishonorably by the young squire, Mr. B. When she resists him he treats her harshly and violently, once even attempts rape. Pretending to send her home, he transfers her instead to a lonely estate in Lincolnshire, where she is guarded by a bawdy old she-dragon, Mrs. Jewkes. Here Pamela suffers many indignities; once she is nearly driven to suicide. Ultimately her noble constancy awakens her master's better nature; he offers honorable marriage, and is accepted.

Pamela's popularity was enormous. Defoe had broken with the romances, but Defoe's material was still adventure and crime. Addison and Steele had found their inspiration in the citizen's own daily experiences, but they wrote only brief sketches. This new book glorified the precise virtues of industry, chastity, solemnity, and sobriety that Puritan morality held most dear;[1] its intense introspective quality also struck a responsive chord. Clergymen praised it from the pulpit; a dramatic adaptation enlisted the talents of David Garrick; it even appeared as a waxworks show. John Newberry, publisher of *Goody Twoshoes,* brought it out in a special edition for children, and it inspired no less than sixteen imitations and burlesques. Even beyond England—and Puritanism—its influence extended: Goldoni made a play of it in Italy, Voltaire in France.

Not that the burlesques came from admirers. In the cleverest (and one of the bawdiest), *An Apology for the Life of Mrs. Shamela Andrews,* which was probably written by Fielding, Pamela's behavior is motivated not by chastity but by business acumen. She has a commodity to sell, and she will not let it go except at the highest market price. A purported sequel, *Pamela in High Life,* prompted

[1] In 1740, Puritanism had already formed its alliance with the commercial spirit of modern England. It is noteworthy that, suspicious as he is of art, Richardson does not condemn rank and fashion. The model Clarissa even plays cards occasionally for small stakes, though under protest, for sociability's sake, while Harriet Byron "loves to go to the public places, and often goes, and makes a brilliant figure there." Nor is Richardson dazzled by the clergy. Dr. Lewen, of *Clarissa,* is a noble soul, and Parson Williams, of *Pamela,* is well-meaning though ineffectual. But his neighbor, Mr. Peters, is as contemptible a cleric as any in Jane Austen, and the filthy suspicions of Elias Brand add much to Clarissa's trials.

Richardson to add two dull volumes to his own work, in which he described Pamela's model life as wife and mother. There is some good comedy in her contacts with the snobbish Sir Jacob Swynford and the free-spoken Sir Simon Darnford, whom she very neatly puts in his place, but only in the single incident of Mr. B.'s threatened return to his old libertinism does the reader catch a glimpse of Richardson's true power.

Fielding's scorn for *Pamela* has often been echoed. Sidney Lanier thought the book ought to have been called "Vice Rewarded"; Mr. B., he said, is the one who gets the reward. But possibly Lanier did not allow sufficiently for the gap between servant-girl and squire in early eighteenth-century thinking. A cipher of a characterization to begin with, Mr. B. is not rewarded until he has put his vices behind him, and unconvincing as his change of heart seems to us, it is simply the familiar phenomenon of instant conversion, so frequently encountered in the Elizabethan drama as an inheritance from unpsychological old tales. We accept Griselda's final reconciliation with her husband; we assume that Helena and Bertram will be happy after the final curtain falls on *All's Well That Ends Well;* why should we ask embarrassing questions here?

Moreover, Pamela loves Mr. B. It is true that Richardson was not, at this stage in his career, qualified to show us anything in that poor creature that could reasonably be expected to rouse a chaste girl's passion. But passion is not always reasonable, and once we get over this hurdle, we cannot deny that the author has traced developments with considerable skill. None of this means, however, that Pamela would ever have yielded to her passion at the cost of what she considers her honor, and it is a little hard to understand why those admirers of modern naturalism who excuse any indecency in contemporary fiction on the plea that the writer must at all costs face the facts, should so unanimously fall foul of Richardson for taking as his heroine an actual woman of her class rather than a plaster saint.[2]

[2] Richardson fought the moralists of his own day on this issue, as McKillop has shown. "In my scheme I have generally taken human nature as it is; for it is to no purpose to suppose it angelic, or to endeavor to make it so." If he were to be of service to those in whom the passions predominated, he

But virtue does not always triumph in this world: the Book of Job would be greater without its epilogue. In Richardson's second novel, *Clarissa, or The History of a Young Lady,* the epilogue is conspicuously absent. The longest novel in the English language—2,065 pages in the Heinemann edition—it was published, in seven volumes, in 1747-1748.

Clarissa Harlowe, favorite younger daughter of a wealthy family, has two suitors—Robert Lovelace, a glittering, personable rake, and Roger Solmes, an odious, elderly churl. Clarissa's family opposes the immoral Lovelace as a possible suitor for the girl, and soon finds itself in the position of attempting to foist Solmes upon her. Suffering intensely under petty domestic tyranny, Clarissa finally permits herself to be spirited away by Lovelace, with a view to seeking asylum with the respectable ladies of his family. He conducts her instead to a private brothel in London, and there, after a long and stubborn contest of wills, drugs and violates her. Her personality outraged, and the taste of life turned bitter in her mouth, Clarissa dies, at long last, of a broken heart. Lovelace perishes miserably in a duel at the hands of her kinsman, Colonel Morden.

The story of Clarissa's martyrdom is a story of sainthood achieved, a rare theme in English fiction. Miss Sheila Kaye-Smith may indeed observe in her "a mingling of obstinacy and irresolution which is essentially human and essentially feminine," may even find that she "comes sometimes dangerously near a fool." Clarissa lacks the sound common sense of her sprightly friend, Miss Howe, but perhaps it is not common sense for which one goes first of all to the saints. Clarissa might have lived on, had she chosen to do so; so, for that matter, might Jesus Christ. She is conceived in the tradition of the heroic tragedy, being less realistic than the other characters and exalted above them. Scott says finely that "it was reserved to Richardson to show that there is a chastity of the soul which can beam out spotless and unsullied even after that of the person has been violated." Clarissa knows that. But she knows too, as did Adam Bede,

insisted, he could not write so as to interest only the grandmothers. When we find Richardson prudish, we might do worse than to glance at his imitators and successors, the later sentimentalists, who, incidentally, have much to say concerning the indelicacy of *Pamela.*

that "There's a sort o' damage . . . that can't be made up for." Even the desire to see her friends forsakes the heroic girl as the end draws near. "God will have no rivals in the hearts of those He sanctifies." One may "agree" with her or not; one cannot deny her a touch of grandeur. She stands, among the imperishable things of fiction, against the frozen heights.

Lovelace may have been influenced by Philip Duke of Wharton, Colley Cibber, or le Comte de Grammont; his literary forebears include Noval, in *The Fatal Dowry,* by Massinger and Field, and Lothario, in Nicholas Rowe's *Fair Penitent.* The character has been most variously judged—as Lucifer, as the energy of life, as an eighteenth-century Byron, as a caddish schoolboy soaked in lust. Lovelace has refinement, culture, power, and will. He is no infidel. He is capable of generosity. Fastidious in his loves and not particularly a sensualist, he is more interested in the lure of the chase than in mere possession. He loves Clarissa, as he is capable of loving; he might have won her if only he had gone about it rightly. Why, then, did he choose to tread the path of outrage and shame?

Students have found so many answers to this question that the villainy of Lovelace may be called almost as variously motivated as that of Iago:

1. He wants revenge on the Harlowe family for having scorned his suit.
2. He has the rake's disinclination to wed.
3. His family is superior to that of the Harlowes.
4. He wishes to revenge himself upon all womankind for a wrong he suffered in his youth.
5. He doubts that he and Clarissa are suited to each other.
6. Resenting Clarissa's superiority to himself, he wishes to drag her down to his level.
7. He feels that he must test Clarissa before accepting her as his wife.
8. He enjoys playing the man-woman game for its own sake.[3]

[3] I throw out such passages as those which describe his unthinkable plot to abduct Miss Howe, her mother, and her suitor Hickman, to take them on shipboard, there to seduce Miss Howe and throw Hickman overboard, and the cold-blooded enumeration of the mistresses who died in childbirth. These things are out of the picture. Richardson's hand falters; he is "working up" his villain. Charlotte Smith (*Desmond,* 1792) is by no means the earliest writer who finds Lovelace old-fashioned. There are no Lovelaces today, she

Toward so complex a character almost any view can be justified. The portrait is not all of a piece. It is realistic and romantic, psychological and conventional, a failure and a success. But the best touches more than justify Balzac's praise. Lovelace has never a doubt that once he has violated Clarissa she must have him. It is his tragedy in life that the one woman he desires supremely should be the very woman that, even when she is on the verge of loving him, rakish tactics cannot win. Yet his passion touches no depths in him, for there are no depths. Cursed by a fatal levity, he is no more capable of repentance than of love. Poseur to the end, he dies in character, crying, "Let this expiate!"

Clarissa was, in a sense, a reaction against *Pamela;* Richardson's last novel, *Sir Charles Grandison* (1753-1754), the portrait of a good man, was designed as a pendant to *Clarissa.* It is the best-balanced, the most varied in tone and incident of his three books. Ruskin placed it with *Don Quixote* at the head of European fiction, and it was warmly admired by Jane Austen and George Eliot. As a drawing-room novel and a transcript of manners, it probably comes closer to what the novel of the future was to be like than anything else Richardson ever did. Yet there must be few people alive today who would read it through except for money. Richardson's understanding of men ran far behind his understanding of women, he was ignorant of aristocratic ways, and he knew nothing of the Italy in which for a time his scene is laid. Sir Charles goes about doing good, but he wins his triumphs far too easily. He encounters plenty of wicked people, it is true, but they are all so constituted that they must needs love the highest when they see it, at least when they see it in him.

Grandison suffers too in comparison with Richardson's other novels in that there seems to the reader no such vital issue at stake. Shall Sir Charles marry Harriet Byron, whom he has rescued from abduction by the wicked Sir Hargrave Pollexfen, or shall he unite himself to the high-born Italian lady, Clementina della Poretta, whose life and reason are perhaps menaced by her love for him but

says; "there is no modern man of fashion who would take a hundredth part of the trouble that Richardson makes Lovelace take to obtain Helen herself. . . ."

who fears for the loss of her immortal soul should she wed a heretic? Sir Charles would prefer to marry Harriet, but not for a moment would he evade his duty toward Clementina, and we hardly feel that he is likely to suffer a broken heart whatever happens. Until Clementina finally withdraws from the picture—the Amazonian Lady Olivia and Sir Charles's gentle ward, Emily Jervois, do not really count—Miss Byron's happiness is indeed in some danger, but Miss Byron is no favorite with modern readers. Her role is an undignified one, and she seems shamefully lacking in sexual pride. Designed to stand midway between Pamela and Clarissa, she has neither the pussy-cat charm of the one nor the magnificence of the other.

Sir Charles himself is generally dismissed as an impossible prig. Actually, the trouble is less with Sir Charles than with Richardson's method of presenting him. Himself a leading narrator, he is obliged to expound his own virtues, and the effect is not pleasant. We choke, too, in the fumes of the incense burned perpetually before him by his female adorers, though he himself seems to breathe them with ease. These things give an hysterical Miss Nancy quality to the book. The Clementina tragedy might have been poignant, but for that it must have needed a nobler simplicity than Richardson was able to find for it.

2. *The Epistolary Method*

Richardson was not the first writer to attempt to tell a story in the form of letters, but he carried the method to its highest point of development, and he remains in English its great exemplar.[4] In the original *Pamela* the method is still primitive. There are thirty-two letters in all; twenty-eight of these Pamela writes to her parents, and the other four are replies. Then communication is cut off, and Pamela continues the story in her journal. There is one brief narrative section by "the Editor."

[4] The letter emerges as a formal literary type in the sixteenth century. Singer (*The Epistolary Novel*) finds it used before Richardson to present "a story of travel, a scandal, a history, a pseudo-history, politics, manners, and, above all else, a story of lovers." Black (*Harvard Studies and Notes in Philology and Literature,* XV [1933], 291-312) enumerates no less than twelve distinct varieties of epistolary fiction.

Clarissa and *Grandison* are much more complicated. *Clarissa* comprises 547 letters. Most of these pass between Clarissa and Miss Howe, or between Lovelace and John Belford, but nearly all the numerous characters take pen in hand at some time. Footnotes furnish corrections and cross-references; occasionally they summarize and offer supplementary information.

Unlike the convention of the omniscient author (which Fielding was soon to establish for English fiction), the epistolary method aids verisimilitude by forcing the author to account for all his information; unlike Defoe's autobiographical narrative, it makes for intimacy and immediacy of impression. Sometimes, especially in *Grandison,* where letters are enclosed within letters, and our attention is consequently carried back into the past, Richardson foregoes this advantage, and begins to justify Hazlitt's criticism that he made his characters act upon reflection, not, as people do in life, on the impulse of the moment. But he has his distinguished successes too. Professor McKillop praises "the elaborate counterpoint" of Clarissa's correspondence with Miss Howe, as when, for example, the latter is made to comment on Clarissa's affection for Lovelace before Clarissa has discovered it herself. The method suits Richardson's prolixity, his determination to analyze his characters as well as to create them. Finally, it is intensely dramatic. When Richardson is at his best, each letter is as illuminating an utterance as a soliloquy in a great play.

But there are striking artificialities also. Not all life-experience naturally finds its way into letters, nor do we ever find a social group every member of which is afflicted with *cacoëthes scribendi.* It is difficult to believe that Pamela could have found time to write six long letters on her wedding-day. To write a successful epistolary novel, an author must be master of many styles; to enjoy it, a reader must be willing to piece many fragments together. In *Grandison,* both Lucy and Dr. Bartlett are the colorless recipients of letter after letter to which they never reply. Harriet writes fifteen successive letters retailing the past history of the Grandison family, and when she comes to the courtship of Lady Clementina, she encloses letters from Dr. Bartlett which in turn enclose letters from Sir Charles and the della Porettas!

On the whole, his method suited Richardson well. He attempted no direct transcript of experience; he did not know the world well enough for that. His devices to prolong the action (as in the case of Pamela's repeatedly delayed departure from Mr. B.'s house) are often pretty transparent; in *Clarissa* the central situation itself seems impossible. Yet once we accept the element of "given," an astonishing impression of reality results. The slow pace of the narrative is too closely attuned to the rhythm of life itself to make full use of the emotionalized heightening which is the special prerogative of art, yet there is plenty of suspense. The late entry of Lovelace, and more particularly of Grandison, is as finely managed as that of Tartuffe in Molière, and no sophisticated novelist of today knows any device that Richardson fails to employ in his complicated account of the abduction of Harriet or of Clarissa's rape. He creates suspense also in lesser matters. Will Clarissa be remitted to her uncle's custody or not? What will her brother say to her latest plea? What attitude will Colonel Morden take when he shall arrive in England? We await the answers to these questions nearly as breathlessly as she.

Richardson was a moralist: like Bernard Shaw, he would not have faced the labor of writing a single sentence for art's sake alone. It would have hurt him could he have lived to hear Southey's opinion that he was a man of most impure imagination. But he was conscientious not only as a man but also as an artist, and when art and morality came into conflict, it was by no means a foregone conclusion that art must be sacrificed. His minor characters are delightfully natural, and he had a special fondness for sprightly, rather hoydenish girls.

Often, of course, Richardson's moral inspiration and his artistic inspiration coincide. We need have no sympathy with the pernickety notion that it would have been unfitting for Clarissa to be permitted to achieve final happiness because in that event the sad results of parental disobedience could not have been illustrated in her case. It remains a fact, however, that the tragic ending to which that notion led was the right ending, and Richardson stood like a wall of granite against all the voluble sentimentalists who cried for treacle and honey. It is to his feeling that sin must be punished that we owe also the impressive Hogarthian realism of the death of Mrs. Sinclair, the brothel-keeper, to say nothing of the tragedy of Lovelace's own destruction.

3. *Ancestors and Descendants*

Richardson's relationship to the fiction which preceded him is a difficult subject. H. D. Traill long ago pointed out that "the sufferings of Clarissa are those of an imprisoned princess in a fairy-tale: [while] the cruelty and power of Lovelace is that of the giant ogre of the same order of fable." There are suggestions of allegory also, but no direct indebtedness can be proved. Richardson's absorption in problems of conduct has English precedent clear back to Elizabethan fiction (whence, of course, Pamela's name, from the *Arcadia*), and the heroic romances of the seventeenth century were much preoccupied with the analysis of motives. McKillop has suggested that periodical apologues like *Spectator* #375 may have contributed to *Pamela* also, to say nothing of current "scandalous narratives of seduction and rape"—not quite suitable reading for the pious printer. In French fiction, *Pamela* has an obvious affinity with the *Vie de Marianne* (1731-1741) of Marivaux.[5] Richardson knew Madame de LaFayette's masterpiece, *La Princesse de Clèves* (1678), but he seems not to have approved of it.

What is indisputable is the influence of the drama. *Clarissa,* a "Dramatic Narrative," divides naturally into five acts, and the postscript is an elaborate discussion of dramatic theory and practice. Richardson defends Clarissa's death by reference to Addison and Rapin, opposing the strict application of the doctrine of poetic justice in tragedy. Here and elsewhere he gives us lists of *dramatis personae*—in *Grandison* the personages are grouped under three headings: Men, Women, and Italians—while dialogue appears on the page, *à la* Defoe, in the manner of a printed play. Many specific incidents clearly echo contemporary and Restoration dramatists. There is some affinity of spirit with Steele's *Conscious Lovers.*

[5] Direct influence, often asserted, has never been proved. Cf. G. C. Macaulay, *Modern Language Review,* VIII (1913), 464-467; H. S. Hughes, *Modern Philology,* XV (1917), 491-512; R. S. Crane, *Modern Philology,* XVI (1919), 495-499, as well as McKillop's discussion in his *Samuel Richardson.*

Pamela witnesses another play of Steele's, *The Tender Husband,* and criticizes it in detail, as she does also *The Distressed Mother,* by Ambrose Philips.

But descendants are more important than ancestors. Wilbur Cross finds Hardy, Meredith, and James "in direct descent" from Richardson, and suggests interesting comparisons between Clarissa and Tess, between Grandison and Sir Willoughby Patterne. He also finds Richardson prophetic of the "stream-of-consciousness" method:

> In the letters his characters write under the impulse of the moment, they display their thoughts, intentions, and emotions as they arise, perhaps more naturally than in the novels of Virginia Woolf, whose art is more restrained.[6]

Richardson's immediate influence, however, was on such writers as Sarah Fielding, Frances Sheridan, Susannah and Margaret Minifie, and Susannah's daughter Elizabeth, and the playwright, Hugh Kelly, whose *Louisa Mildmay* (1767) is cited by Dr. Ernest A. Baker as "the masculine rejoinder to *Clarissa.*" Miss Fielding's *David Simple* (1744-1753) and Mrs. Sheridan's *Memoirs of Miss Sidney Bidulph* (1761) are the most distinguished novels of this group. What happens to Richardson's special theme in the hands of sensationalists may be seen by reference to such books as the anonymous *Jessy, or The Bridal Day,* by a Lady (1771) and John Cleland's *Fanny Hill* (1748-1749), which has led a vigorous life in the literary underworld clear down to our own time. Irrespective of special theme, Richardson's prestige naturally contributed notably to the vogue of the epistolary novel, of which Black finds 506 examples between 1740 and 1799.

With the later developments of some of the sentimental tendencies notable in his own work, Richardson could have had little sympathy, either as they appeared in Sterne and his followers or, on the continent, in the romantic morbidness of *La Nouvelle Héloïse* (1760), by Jean Jacques Rousseau, and the great Goethe's *Die Leiden des jungen Werthers* (1774). Richardson opposed the later developments of sentimentalism under Shaftesbury's influence. His own was always pious, moral, austerely disdainful of enthusiasm,

[6] *Yale Review,* XIX (1929), 181-183.

steadily mindful of what in our own time the late Irving Babbitt, arch-enemy of Rousseauism, called "the inner check." Rousseau admired Richardson, however, and so did other Frenchmen—Alfred de Musset, George Sand, even the Marquis de Sade. In Germany, Richardson was honored by Gellert, Hermes, Sophie La Roche, Wieland, and Klopstock. That he could have produced such offspring seems inconceivable, but Lord Ernle reminds us that when he began luxuriating in sentiment he was playing with fire. "Experience shows that sentiments cannot always be 'curbed by virtue,' or regulated by moral maxims, when the sanctions of both restrictions are doubted or denied."

In England it never quite came to that. Richardson had given characterization new scope and meaning in English fiction—that was the important thing. Though only the first of his three novels dealt importantly with "common" people, he still drew the novel down into the world of every-day experiences and emotions as the middle-class understood them. And "common" people have never objected to reading about their "betters." That he himself, despite his extreme propriety, relied largely on the seduction motif is not especially important, nor is it so surprising as, on first consideration, it seems. He was largely a woman's novelist, and he lived in an age when woman had but one function: as wife and mother she must fulfill her destiny, or being "ruined" she must fail to do so. Not before Meredith was there another English male writer who understood women quite so well. Richardson's special theme was not widely imitated; toward sex, his successors, until nearly the dawn of the twentieth century, were evasive or superficial. With the revival of interest in such matters which came later, Richardson had very little to do.

CHAPTER V

FIELDING AND THE PROSE EPIC

A novel is an epic with its wings clipped. . . .

GILBERT CANNAN

1. *The Novelist Unashamed*

Richardson vs. Fielding! Dickens vs. Thackeray! Here are the two great historic rivalries in the history of the English novel. At present Fielding and Dickens are so far ahead that their opponents seem at times to have given up the running, and Fielding's *Tom Jones* would probably get more votes as "the greatest English novel" than any other book. Yet Robert Louis Stevenson could still speak of it as "dirty, dull, and false," and as late as 1907, Sir Arthur Conan Doyle, presiding at the bicentennial dinner, was able to find nothing better to say of its author than that he was not the father of the English novel but "more like the wicked uncle who stole the baby"! Thackeray imitated Fielding but that did not prevent his slandering him; Dickens, though launching his own ship under Smollett's banner, was far more just. Yet when he came, in *David Copperfield,* to write of his childish fondness for *Tom Jones* and other eighteenth-century novels, even Dickens passed a sop to Cerberus when he added, for David and for himself, that they "did me no harm; for, whatever harm was in some of them, was not there for me; *I* knew nothing of it." "I have been Tom Jones (a child's Tom Jones, a harmless creature) for a week together."

Henry Fielding was born, April 22, 1707, in Somersetshire, of a distinguished family. He was educated at Eton and the University of Leyden. His early literary career was in the drama, where his criticism of Walpole's government was increasingly outspoken until the Licensing Act of 1737 put him out of business. He turned next to the law. Halfway through his thirties, he suffered a breakdown in health. He finished himself in unremitting service for the commonweal, then sailed away to die at Lisbon, October 8, 1754, at the early age of forty-seven.

Richardson, who hated his rival, was quite willing to take the responsibility for having made a novelist of him.

> The *Pamela,* which he abused in his *Shamela,* taught him how to write to please, though his manners are so different. Before *Joseph Andrews* (hints and names taken from that story, with a lewd and ungenerous engraftment) the poor man wrote without being read.

To be sure, it is easy to exaggerate the differences between the two writers.[1] Partly the contrast was that between crabbed age and youth, for Fielding was dead and in his grave before reaching the age at which Richardson began to write. Fielding was quite as much the moralist as Richardson, but his morality was less negative, less passive. He knew that prudential virtue was quite likely to find its reward in this world, but such virtue did not interest him very much. His blood was warmer than his rival's, and it moved less sluggishly in his veins; he spent himself eagerly—in his work, in his life and love. Hate he had no time for, save as he hated crime and murder and drunkenness and vice, against all which, sick as he was, he fought such a fight as magistrate, toward the heroic close of his life, as no Englishman had ever fought before him.[2]

Fielding was the first unashamed novelist in England. He does not pretend to be writing autobiography like Defoe; he does not rifle the postbag with Richardson. He himself assumes control of the narrative, interpreting and commenting in his own person whenever he chooses to do so, and establishing the convention of the omniscient author who enters into the minds and thoughts of

[1] Heinz Ronte, *Richardson und Fielding: Geschichte ihres Ruhms* (Leipzig: Tauchnitz, 1935), sees Richardson as essentially Christian while Fielding derives rather from classical culture. Graham Greene has something of this in mind in his fine essay on Fielding and Sterne in Bonamy Dobrée's *From Anne to Victoria:* "his [Fielding's] books do represent a moral struggle, but they completely lack the sense of supernatural evil or supernatural good." Cf. A. D. McKillop, "The Personal Relations between Fielding and Richardson," *Modern Philology*, XXVIII (1931), 423-433.

[2] The best book on this aspect of Fielding's work is B. M. Jones, *Henry Fielding, Novelist and Magistrate* (Allen & Unwin, 1933).

all his characters—(the assumption "that God is the writer, or that the writer is a god") [3]—which has remained dominant in the English novel clear down to the present day. "He had the boldness to present fiction as fiction . . ." says John Buchan finely. "Verisimilitude is to be attained by the inherent logic of the characters and their doings; the illusion he seeks is not that of history but of art." It is true, to be sure, that Fielding described his books as "histories," thus occasioning much learned speculation. Most of this speculation, however, is quite unnecessary, for though Fielding's use of the term "history" was not quite Aristotelian, all he really meant was that he was not writing a romance but trying to project a true picture of human life.

Fielding knew that his was a new type of fiction; he hoped "that when the little parlor in which I sit at this instant shall be reduced to a worse furnished box, I shall be read by those who never knew nor saw me, and whom I shall neither know nor see." As he thought of it, a novel was a comic epic in prose, though differing from the comedy of the theater "in that it has more extended action, more incidents, greater variety of character." The sense of comedy arises [illegible] affectation, in turn, proceeds either from vanity or from hypocrisy. Fielding was willing to admit caricature in diction but not in characterization. And the purpose of comedy, as he saw it, was ethical: "to laugh mankind out of their favorite follies and vices."

When Fielding's theory does not agree perfectly with his practice, the reason is generally that the latter is wider and more generous. His greatest comic character is Parson Adams. Now that inspired lunatic illustrates humor as affectation perfectly when we learn that the thing of which he is most proud is his sermon against vanity, or when, immediately after having rebuked Joseph Andrews for giving too free a rein to his affections, he receives the (erroneous) information that his favorite child has been drowned, "and soon began to stamp about the room and deplore his loss with the bitterest agony." Yet Parson Adams as a whole cannot be compressed into a formula. Even in the last example cited, we sympathize with him far more than we laugh at him.

[3] Sidney Lanier.

Fielding was never in too much danger of being bound to a theory. Few persons would deny that *Tom Jones* is a modern prose epic. But why? Because it contains invocations and mock-invocations, elaborate comic battles, Homeric similes, interpolated tales, and other epic paraphernalia? Much more, surely, because Fielding looks at his own age with an epic eye, achieving what M. Digeon describes as "a complete expression of a moment of collective life, a fragment of the legend of the centuries." Had he not been able to do that, all his learning must have proved only a hindrance to him, and his masterpiece must have smelled badly of the lamp. As it is, he illustrates how a great writer uses tradition. Inspired, not fettered, by it, he approaches his own age with as clear an eye as the ancients turned on theirs. In this sense, truly, as Pope declared, to copy nature is to copy them.

Such a writer is, obviously, a realist. In the famous bill-of-fare chapter which opens *Tom Jones,* the only dish Fielding offers is human nature. This dish is less common than people think, and generally it is not too well served. Developing the novel-epic analogy, Fielding could not well ignore the question of the supernatural. The gods, it goes without saying, are dead. Elves and fairies are "mummery." Ghosts are sometimes admissible, but they should be employed sparingly. For the modern writer, indeed, surprise may be thought of as taking the place of the old supernatural, and surprise may be used freely, if only it is used with skill.

The same principles are applied to characterization. Fielding found few perfectly good and few completely bad people in his journey through life, and we meet few such in his books. Even Mr. Allworthy, often criticized as too perfect, he makes credulous to a fault, and often, by way of consequence, very unjust to Tom. Sophia, the beloved heroine, would have been beautiful if her forehead had been higher. Conversely, Square and Thwackum, the deist and the bigot (both of whom Fielding greatly disliked), "could not be supposed to have holden none but wrong principles, and to have uttered nothing but absurdities." Fielding develops his personages by degrees, permitting them to reveal themselves naturally in dialogue and in action, and he has the great gift of choosing the significant idiosyncrasy. When Lady Booby, of *Joseph Andrews,* boasts that she has admitted no visitors since her husband's death, "though it is almost six weeks (it wants but a day) ago," we know at once that such careful computation of time is incompatible with the grief she proclaims.

2. *The Books*

As novelist, Fielding rests essentially on three works: *Joseph Andrews, Tom Jones,* and *Amelia.* There are two short pieces also, both somewhat uncertain as to date of composition, and both first published in the *Miscellanies* of 1743: *A Journey from This World to the Next* and *Jonathan Wild.*

The *Journey,* a Lucianic apologue, opens with the narrator's death, and relates a journey to the other world by stagecoach. Having visited the City of Diseases and the Palace of Death, the company arrives at last at the Gate of Elysium. In the subsequent examinations, presided over by Minos, Fielding finds much scope for his satire, his humor, and his humanity, but the reader's interest wanes when he runs off into a long account of the various incarnations of Julian the Apostate.

The History of the Life of the Late Mr. Jonathan Wild the Great is one of the most impressive pieces of sustained irony in English. The historic Jonathan, hanged at Tyburn in 1725, was a thief and racketeer whose biography had already been written by Defoe and others. Fielding's work is fiction, composed in a style of mock-admiration for the "Great Man," the fundamental premise being that greatness as this world conceives it is incompatible with goodness. The satire is directed against two types of scoundrel—the military conqueror and the corrupt politician, and especially against Fielding's old enemy, Sir Robert Walpole.[4] Newgate factions represent English political parties, and distinctive headgear indicates party differences. White is black and black is white in such a book. All decent human emotions are "low"; when the hero, at rare intervals, shows some rudimentary sense of pity, his biographer must apologize for his "weakness." *Jonathan Wild* has never been popular and never can be; it is, in Bernard Shaw's sense of the term, an "un-

[4] Walpole fell in 1742, and much of the specific satire was removed in the revised (1754) edition, the basis of most modern reprints.

pleasant" book. But the intelligent reader will perceive that Fielding is fighting with rather uncongenial weapons the same fight for human decency that he carries on in his major works.

Fielding's comic manner is seen at its best in *The History of the Adventures of Joseph Andrews, and his Friend Mr. Abraham Adams* (1742). "Written in Imitation of the Manner of Cervantes," the book begins as a burlesque of *Pamela* with a picture of her brother Joseph's virtuous resistance to the seductions of a female relative of Mr. B.'s clan. Fielding has enlarged the family considerably; he has also discovered the surname, which is Booby! Joseph is as chaste as his Biblical namesake. When his lady is shocked that he should dare prate to her of his virtue, he reminds her that he is "the brother of Pamela, and would be ashamed that the chastity of the family, which is preserved in her, should be stained in him." Twice he writes his sister letters in the best *Pamela* style, but he does not correspond with his sweetheart Fanny—(Fielding has seen to that!)—for Fanny can neither read nor write. Cast out upon the road, he is joined, on one pretext or another, by Parson Adams, by Fanny herself, and by Mrs. Slipslop, Lady Booby's hideous and lascivious maid. Against the homely background of the English countryside, the most delightful series of adventures any English novelist had yet described is now set forth.

Adams is the great character. In creating him Fielding has not really imitated Cervantes. Using the materials of his own experience, he has wrought against a native background in a similar, though less exalted, mood. Like the Don, Adams lives in an ideal world, and when he comes in contact with reality the impact is terrific. It is not the reading of romances that has turned his head, however. His mind has been nourished on classical literature, his soul on the ideals of primitive Christianity. He assumes that all men are as honest and as unselfish as he is. Evil rouses surprise and indignation in him; he grasps his crabstick and rushes to the fray. But he is never permanently disillusioned. When he is pleased, he snaps his fingers violently, then takes "two or three turns about the room in an ecstasy." Fielding submits Adams to dreadful indignities in the course of the narrative, yet he is never degraded. In all essential duties of his calling, he is faithful unto death, and when the vicious Lady Booby (who holds his living in her hands), seeks to persuade him to withhold his protection from Joseph and Fanny, he draws himself up suddenly to prophetic stature and addresses her in words that might have fallen from the lips of John Knox.

Though *Joseph Andrews* is more loosely constructed than *Tom Jones,* it is by no means innocent of structure. As Ethel Thornbury has pointed out, it surpasses *Don Quixote* in this respect, the pursuit of Joseph by Lady Booby and Mrs. Slipslop providing what Cervantes never provided, a "single thwarting force." M. Aurelien Digeon finds in the book the pattern of the French classical comedies. It is easy to cite the absurdity of straightening out a complicated series of relationships at the close of the book by reference to a strawberry mark on the hero's breast, but there was high precedent for this in what Aristotle described as the Greek drama of revolution and discovery, nor was Fielding ever taken in by the time-honored device. He used it; he laughed at it as he used it. It did double duty for him; the very fact that it was unconvincing added to the fun.

The History of Tom Jones, A Foundling (1749) is the book to which the epic-analogy really applies. This time the structure is well-nigh perfect. Even if one does not go all the way with Coleridge, who declared that the *Oedipus Tyrannus, The Alchemist,* and *Tom Jones* are the three most perfect plots ever planned, it is still difficult not to agree with Scott, who wrote of the novel as "a story regularly built and consistent in all its parts, in which nothing occurs, and scarce a personage is introduced, that has not some share in tending to advance the catastrophe."[5] Yet Fielding masters his structure as he had mastered his learning, and it is a tribute to the surpassing, careless ease of the book that one popular manual should actually

[5] "Compare the careful architecture of *Tom Jones:* the introductory essays which enable the author to put his point of view and to leave the characters to go their way untainted by the uncharacteristic moralizing of Defoe's; the introduction of parody in the same way and for the same purpose as Joyce's in *Ulysses;* the innumerable sub-plots which give the book the proportions of life, the personal story of Jones taking its place in the general orchestration; the movement back and forth in time as the characters meet each other and recount the past in much the same way as Conrad's, a craftsman's bluff by which we seem to get a glimpse of that 'dark backward and abysm' that challenges the ingenuity of every novelist." Graham Greene, *op. cit.*

speak of its build as "loose"! Probably very few readers ever suspect Bridget Allworthy to be Tom's mother before Fielding chooses to reveal the secret, yet as Wilbur Cross remarks, when one looks back over the story, one perceives that she has consistently behaved "just as a woman of her character would in the circumstances."

Uncertainty of birth—that time-honored motif—furnished then the mainspring of the plot. The method, as in *Joseph Andrews,* was again to turn the principal characters loose upon the road. But the canvas is now much wider, and there is more variety in the adventures which ensue. An epic must end happily, but it can and should be serious. The historical background of *Tom Jones* is slight but unmistakable, involving the five weeks in November and December, 1745, while the Duke of Cumberland was marshaling his forces against the Young Chevalier. Squire Western and Partridge are Jacobites, while Tom and Mrs. Western are Hanoverians. Once on her travels Sophia is mistaken for the Pretender's mistress, Jenny Cameron. The antecedent action (Books I-IV) covers some twenty years; the main action falls well within a twelvemonth, thus agreeing with the precepts of Renaissance critics of the epic. No less epical is Fielding's use of scene. What the poet Gray observed of *Joseph Andrews* applies quite as well here: the author was "well read in stage coaches, country squires, inns, and inns of Court," and the progress of his characters can be traced on a map.

The finest characterization in the book is that of the heroine's father, the hard-drinking, foul-mouthed country squire, Western. In some of his aspects he is as repellent as Adams is lovable, yet he awakens sympathy as people we know intimately always do, no matter what their faults, and Fielding's achievement in animating him is no less wonderful because he had been a stock figure in the drama for many years. As for his daughter, she is made to live on the printed page with such surpassing ease, such total absence of Richardson's prolix, deliberate analysis, that Schiller ranked her with Juliet. Like Clarissa, she will agree not to wed without her father's consent but refuses to carry filial obedience to the length of accepting a suitor her heart abhors. She is as pure as Clarissa in her heart, but she has a practical efficiency, an ability to make terms with the world that Clarissa never acquires. Yet Fielding's achievement is not so great as Richardson's. Fielding was always tempted to idealize his women, and the fact that in this instance he was drawing from his dead wife did not lessen his chivalry.

In the heroine of *Amelia* (1752), the beloved Charlotte lives again. This book was too far ahead of its time to be other than "damned." It came out of Fielding's work as magistrate; it is a propaganda novel, a serious arraignment of conditions breeding vice and crime in the fashionable gambling section of London. It begins with marriage (instead of ending with it, as so many novels do), and its intimate picture of family life, its searching study of economic distress were new notes in English fiction. The comic spirit is dead, and save for the presentation of antecedent material through interpolated narrative, the epic machinery is largely abandoned also. Professor Sherburn acutely compares Booth's recital to Miss Matthews with the tale Aeneas tells to Dido. "A touch worthy of James Joyce is the using of Newgate Prison to parallel the palace of the Carthaginian queen and the cave where was consummated the fateful *furtivum amorem*."

Perhaps *Amelia* is not an unqualified success; read immediately after *Tom Jones,* it may even seem dull. But no book of Fielding's will yield its full meaning on one reading, and in any event *Amelia* must not be judged by the standard of its predecessor. It is no more like *Tom Jones* than *Samson Agonistes* is like *Paradise Lost.* In *Amelia,* Fielding broke new ground whose cultivation was to be left largely for remote successors.

3. *The Moral of It*

The moral nihilists of the twentieth century will no doubt find it both inappropriate and offensive that a discussion of Fielding's contribution to the novel should end with the consideration of his morality. Unfortunately the subject cannot possibly be omitted. Not only have all the historic battles of Fielding criticism been fought in this arena but the subject was one of vital importance in Henry Fielding's own thinking.

Fielding wrote as a moralist, and it is impossible to understand his work without attempting to meet him on his own ground. But perhaps understanding is not the special forte of moral nihilists.

Some of the questions that have been raised about Fielding's personal morality are indeed wholly irrelevant. He was a faithful husband and father; even the widespread impression that he was "wild" in his youth rests on general probabilities rather than specific evidence.

But there still remains the sexual looseness of Tom Jones. Arnold Bennett complains of Fielding to his journal: "He seems to think that so long as Tom goes in for a little miscellaneous fornication he will be saved from priggishness."

Yet Fielding nowhere commends or justifies Tom's looseness. Certainly he never apologizes for the most revolting episode in Tom's career—his becoming, even though temporarily and unwillingly, the gigolo of Lady Bellaston. Thackeray was wrong when he traced this incident back to Fielding's own feelings having been blunted by an irregular life, and he is answered conclusively by Wilbur Cross. Tom "had only one weakness approaching a vice, and for that weakness Fielding resolved to degrade him and make him suffer to the utmost."

There are still those who feel that he did not suffer enough; that Sophia was soiled by her too ready acceptance of him afterwards; that, in the later novel, Amelia was degraded by her "easy" forgiveness of a husband who has carried Tom's ways into middle life. The great magistrate hated to condemn his fellowmen. Very few transgressors go to the bottomless pit in his *Journey* to the Other World, though many are sent back to earth to try over again. Where, as in Tom's case, sexual looseness has involved no settled inhumanity, then, though he holds the balance even, Fielding is likely to be lenient in his judgment. He would have agreed with Dante that fornication is the least among mortal sins, but no one who recalls his Paolo and Francesca need be reminded that it was not Dante's impression that fornicators must therefore be excused!

The matter happens to be of considerable historical significance because of the way it connects Fielding with the sentimental movement. In his attack on Richardson, he thought of himself as opposing sentimentalism. In so far as sentimentalism is tearfulness and effeminacy, this is true. But, as we have seen, there are limits to Richardson's sentimentalism; he has nothing to say to Shaftesbury's notion that virtue is a matter of "good" instincts. Despite Parson Adams's clear condemnation of "enthusiasm," Fielding is less successful here. Reacting against Richardsonian formalism, he falls in grave danger of Rousseauism. His emphasis on feeling was quite disproportionate; because the "heart" is right, both Tom and Booth are permitted a latitude which is at best unseemly. So Sir John Hawkins declared that Fielding was "the inventor of that cant phrase, goodness of heart, which is everyday used as a substitute for probity," and added that "he has done more towards corrupting the rising generation than any writer we know of." This condemnation is intemperate and extreme, but it was unfortunate that Fielding should have left himself open to such an attack.

He himself came to see the danger before the end. *Amelia* seems on first consideration the most sentimental of his books, for his old laughter has now been replaced by free-flowing tears. Actually the book is much less sentimental than *Tom Jones*. For Booth's problem is essentially the problem of conversion. For the first time, Fielding insists on Christian dogma and Christian ethics.[6]

It was significant that such a book should have resulted from Fielding's life as a magistrate; in the gin-soaked London slums good intentions play the part proverbially assigned to them in hell. Fielding grew to the end—as an artist and as a man. He brought the developing novel a theory and a background, but his books have more than an architectonic or philosophical significance. They have the greatness that can only get into a book out of the soul of a great man.

[6] Cf. George Sherburn, "Fielding's Amelia: An Interpretation," *ELH,* III (1936), 1-14. This is much the best study of *Amelia.*

CHAPTER VI

SMOLLETT AND THE NOVEL OF HUMORS

It is the business of the novelist to create characters, not to write fine prose.

ALPHONSE DAUDET

1. *Smollett's Attitude Toward Fiction*

With Richardson and Fielding the eighteenth-century novel is firmly established. Smollett and Sterne are often accused of having broken it down structurally just after their predecessors had built it up. In Smollett's case, at least, there is some justification for this charge.

Born in March, 1721, of an excellent Scottish family, Tobias Smollett received only a good education to face the battle of life. Neither in London nor in Bath does he seem to have been notably successful as a physician; during the expedition against Carthagena in 1741 he served as surgeon's mate on a warship, and returned to England with a Creole wife and material for the most vivid chapters of *Roderick Random*. He first wooed fame with a bad tragedy called *The Regicide;* he wrote some poetry; he contributed to the literature of medicine. In later life he operated a kind of literary mail-order house which turned out, among other things, an elaborate history of England designed to compete with Hume's. He also edited *The Critical Review*. Smollett died in Italy, September 17, 1771.

Smollett's novels[1] are five in number: *Roderick Random* (1748);

[1] I exclude *The History and Adventures of an Atom* (1769), an allegory of political affairs from 1754 to 1765, which, though fiction, is not a novel. It has an obvious affinity with the "secret" histories" of Mrs. Manley, and her school. A number of works during this period make an inanimate object, not a personality, the focusing-point of a narrative. The most important is Charles Johnstone's *Chrysal, or The Adventures of a Guinea* (1760), which hits governmental corruption, avarice, gambling, ecclesiastical abuses, and legal discriminations between rich and poor.

Peregrine Pickle (1751); *Ferdinand Count Fathom* (1753); *Sir Lancelot Greaves* (1760-1761); *The Expedition of Humphry Clinker* (1771). *Random* uses the autobiographical method of Defoe. *Clinker* is an epistolary novel. The other three books are written from the point of view of the omniscient author.

"A large diffused picture, comprehending the characters of life, disposed in different groups, and exhibited in various attitudes"—here is Smollett's conception of the novel. The principle of cohesion he found in the central character, who is needed to "attract the attention, unite the incidents, unwind the clue to the labyrinth, and at last close the scene, by virtue of his own importance." It was probably the influence of the masterly critical chapters with which Fielding opened every book of *Tom Jones* that caused Smollett to begin both *Random* and *Pickle* with a discussion of his art. But the discussion is not impressive, nor was he ever notably successful in regulating his practice by his theory.

Smollett praises Cervantes for bringing fiction into vital contact with life, but his direct model was the *Gil Blas* (1735) of the famous French novelist, Alain René Le Sage (1668-1747). This great picaresque novel Smollett finds defective only in that some of the "uncommon" or "extravagant" situations contained in it tend to "excite mirth rather than compassion," the hero's shifting from bad fortune to good being so sudden "that neither the reader has time to pity him, nor himself to be acquainted with affliction." With such a model before him Smollett could hardly be expected to achieve an organized plot. As Scott says,

> the heroes pass from one situation in life, and from one stage of society, to another totally unconnected, except that, as in ordinary life, the adventures recorded, though not bearing upon each other, or on the catastrophe, befall the same personage.

This does not mean that characters once dropped never turn up again. On the contrary, they are forever turning up, but their reappearance is governed by mere chance. Smollett ends his books with marriage or a happy windfall. When Roderick Random has had adventures enough, he finds a long lost wealthy father in South America, and the hitherto unattainable Narcissa drops into his lap like a ripe plum. A hundred odd chapters in *Peregrine Pickle* means roughly that same number of adventures, and Smollett develops narrative in the summary style of the old novelle, crowding as much story into a paragraph as even Boccaccio could have managed, the motivation of his characters being simply declared by their creator, and never, properly speaking, depicted at all.

If Cervantes and Le Sage influenced Smollett's narrative art, then Ben Jonson, though Smollett himself never actually says so, seems to have been the dominant influence in characterization.[2] Like Jonson, he sets his personages forth in terms of one dominating trait or "humor." His characterization is thus necessarily, one might say, external. It is not that his people are not vivid. The trouble is rather that they are too vivid. They are more vivid than life itself. It is of course true that "art is the right kind of exaggeration," but there is a difference between the exaggeration of a portrait-painter and that of even a superlatively fine cartoonist. Smollett loved idiosyncrasy, as he loved incident, for its own sake.

This art of characterization in terms of "humors," which Smollett derived from Jonson, he passed on to Dickens. Thus he became an important link between the Elizabethan drama and the Victorian novel.

2. *From* Roderick Random *to* Humphry Clinker

Smollett's first two novels are straightforward, unadulterated adventure stories. Roderick Random, a surgeon's apprentice, starts out from his native Scotland to make his fortune in London, and the first third of the book which bears his name is full of the lore of inns and highways, packed with broad farce and bloody adventure. Kidnaped by a press-gang, the hero next embarks upon the Carthagena expedition, and Smollett draws directly upon his own experience[3] for vivid descriptions of carnage, filth, brutality, and sharply etched portraits of a variety of seagoing men. After Rod-

[2] Cf. L. M. Ellison, "The Elizabethan Drama and the Works of Smollett," *PMLA,* XLIV (1929), 842-862.

[3] Cf. L. M. Knapp, "The Naval Scenes in 'Roderick Random,'" *PMLA,* XLIX (1934), 593-598; L. L. Martz, "Smollett and the Expedition to Carthagena," *PMLA,* LVI (1941), 428-446.

erick's return to England, the love element appears briefly, the conventionally lovely Narcissa being presented in the spirit of an idyll, while her aunt—a grotesque, middle-aged, half-mad poetess—is the broadest of caricatures. Here would seem to be sufficient variety for one book, but Smollett is only half through. Military service on the continent, the life of a fashionable gambler in London, a trading voyage to South America—all this and more we must savor before Rory's adventures can come to an end. In *Peregrine Pickle* we keep to the European side of the Atlantic, and the sea dogs gambol not on shipboard but on land. One of the brightest parts of the book concerns Cadwallader Crabtree, an elderly misanthrope, who, feigning deafness, learns everybody's secret sins, with astonishing results when he disguises himself and sets up as a fortune-teller.

The third novel, *Ferdinand Count Fathom,* is different. Inferior in quality, it was yet an effort of imagination for its author in a sense in which his first two books never were. But the villain-hero is never easy to manage. He was not easy even for the Elizabethans; it is no accident that among all their experiments in this genre, *Macbeth* alone should have emerged one of the great plays of the world. Smollett does not attempt the sustained irony of Fielding's *Jonathan Wild.* The reader's mind is divided between reprobation for Ferdinand's villainy and admiration for his "smartness." Nor does it help that the villain himself should sometimes be the victim.

Towards the end of the book, Smollett imposes upon the picaresque structure of Fathom's own adventures an elaborate plot in which a number of that scoundrel's victims are involved, but in order to develop this, he finds it necessary to keep the reader away from Fathom himself for so long that he is almost forgotten. The development involves pseudo-supernaturalism of the kind afterwards cultivated by Mrs. Radcliffe. Monimia is not dead (though we have seen her waste away, like Clarissa, before our eyes), nor is it, as he believes, her apparition that manifests itself before her repentant lover in the old church at midnight, it is her living presence. More impressive in a similar vein is the scene in the hut of the forest robbers, "a tale of natural terror," says Scott, "which rises into the sublime; and, though often imitated, has never yet been surpassed." To us who have Blackwood and de la Mare—to say nothing of

Scott himself—it may seem less magnificent than it did more than a hundred years ago. As an anticipation of what the Gothic novel afterward achieved, it is still, however, sufficiently remarkable.

Sir Lancelot Greaves is a direct imitation of *Don Quixote,* and the story is vitiated at the outset by the fundamental absurdity of its design: an armored knight-errant against the background of eighteenth-century England simply will not do. As a matter of fact, Smollett was never very happy when he drew his inspiration from books. Yet *Sir Lancelot* starts excellently. The opening scene at the inn is the best "interior" in English fiction so far, and the dialogue is not only lifelike but is used skilfully to advance the story. This book had a strong influence on *Pickwick:* the Eatanswill election, Mr. Pickwick's adventure in the pound, Bob Sawyer's landlady, and Mr. Jingle's peculiar style of conversation were all derived from it.

But if *Sir Lancelot* is Smollett's poorest book, its successor, *Humphry Clinker,* is clearly his best. *Humphry Clinker* concerns the pilgrimage of the kindly, irascible Matthew Bramble, with his ménage, to Bath and other English health resorts, and finally up into Scotland. It has been suggested that Smollett's epistolary method differs importantly from Richardson's, in that Richardson uses letters to tell the story while Smollett employs them rather to present contrasting points of view, and the influence of Sterne's *Sentimental Journey* and of Anstey's *New Bath Guide* (1766) has been cited at this point.[4] Such contrasts do appear. Matthew's impressions of Bath and of Vauxhall differ notably, for example, from those of his sentimental niece, Lydia Melford. But the contrasts are strongest where there is least to be told, and as story-interest increases we tend more and more to forget the narrators.

Humphry, the pious footman who gives the book its name, seems to have been an afterthought. The scene of his introduction, where his almost naked poverty shocks Miss Tabitha's modesty without in the least touching her heart, is almost worthy to stand beside what may have been its prototype in *Joseph Andrews.* Two slight lines of

[4] For a careful discussion of several possible influences upon the epistolary form of *Clinker,* cf. L. L. Martz, *The Later Career of Tobias Smollett,* 131 ff.

narrative interest are added, somewhat unnecessarily, to the plotless history of the pilgrimage itself: Lydia has a mild love-affair, and the unknown Humphry turns out to be Mr. Bramble's natural son.

In only one aspect has the book been overpraised: it has been said that it registers an advance in the use of scene. The scene is unassimilated. When *Humphry Clinker* devotes itself to scene it stops being a novel and becomes a book of travel. In still other passages, it turns into a physician's discourse on medicine or sanitation, or an essay on economics, sociology, and the glories of Scotland.[5]

3. *The Sea Dogs and Other Eccentrics*

Smollett's most distinctive group of characters consists of his sea dogs in *Random* and *Pickle*. Trunnion, Hatchway, Pipes, Bowling, Ratlin—we get nothing like these again till we come to Marryat. Perry's friend, Trunnion, who (like Wemmick of *Great Expectations*) lives in a garrison behind moat and drawbridge, and, until his marriage to Perry's Aunt Grizzle, succeeds in reproducing shipboard discipline on dry land, is probably the greatest of the lot. But Morgan, the Welsh surgeon of *Roderick Random,* who derives directly from Shakespeare's Fluellen, though with distinctive features of his own, is a character of whom no novelist would need to be ashamed; and the brutal Captain Oakum, who chains Roderick to the poop of the vessel during a battle, and who reduces the sick list by the simple expedient of ordering all hands on deck, makes Bligh of *Mutiny on the Bounty* look like a sentimentalist. Smollett was the first novelist to use a professional jargon, and the scene in which Trunnion orders his tombstone is often compared to the death of Falstaff:

> As for the motto . . . I do desire that it may not be engraved in the Greek and Latin lingoes . . . but in plain English, that when the angel comes to pipe *all hands* at the great day, he may know that I am a British man, and speak to me in my mother tongue.

[5] Martz, *The Later Career of Tobias Smollett,* points out that half of *Clinker* "deals with historical matter, topographical, social, and political." Martz would attribute all the important differences, stylistic and otherwise, between *Clinker* and the earlier books to Smollett's intervening work in the production of historical and geographical compilations.

In *Humphry Clinker,* there are no sea dogs, yet Smollett's hand never falters. If ever a character was permitted to talk herself alive, it is Tabitha Bramble:

You say the gander has broke the eggs [she writes home to the housekeeper] which is a phinumenon I don't understand; for when the fox carried off the old goose last year, he took her place, and hatched the eggs, and protected the goslings like a tender parent.—Then you tell me the thunder has soured two barrels of bear in the seller. But how the thunder should get in there, when the seller was double locked, I can't comprehend. Howsomever, I won't have the bear thrown out, till I see it with mine own eyes. Perhaps it will recover—at least it will serve for vinegar to the sarvants.

As Gamaliel Bradford would say, "A human being does not often have a chance to damn himself more completely than that." Tabitha's maid, Winifred Jenkins, who was always pious save when piety conflicted with the keener excitements of love-making, reaches no such depths as her mistress, but she is quite bad enough:

Present my compliments to Mrs. Gwillim, and I hope she and I will live upon dissent terms of civility. Being, by God's blessing, removed to a higher spear, you'll excuse my being familiar with the lower sarvants of the family; but, as I trust you'll behave respectful, and keep a proper distance, you may always depend upon the good-will and protection of yours, W. Loyd.

Bramble, a completer characterization and much less of a grotesque, must have been harder to do, but the Scotch lieutenant, Lismahago, who is the wildest grotesque in the whole gallery, is the greatest achievement of all, for without bating a jot of his grotesquerie, Smollett digs deeper and deeper into the man until at last, beneath all his idiosyncrasies, a sterling character is revealed.[6]

4. *The Spirit of Smollett*

Such achievements go far to atone for the brutality and obscenity of much of Smollett's work. He did not, as the saying goes, love the gentle race of men, but as he aged he mellowed. Signs of mellowing appear first in *Fathom,* and the last two books are predomi-

[6] Martz, *The Later Career of Tobias Smollett,* Ch. 7, is the fullest study of the sources and purpose of Lismahago.

nantly humane. Fathom himself is, of course, the worst scoundrel Smollett ever created, but Smollett knows it. The astonishing thing about Roderick Random is that Smollett seems to like him.

I have attempted to represent modest merit struggling with every difficulty to which a friendless orphan is exposed, from his own want of experience, as well as from the selfishness, envy, malice, and base indifference of mankind.

As attached to Roderick, "modest merit" seems one of the supremely inappropriate labels of all time.

But even if we pass Roderick, we shall surely balk at that unconscionable cad, Peregrine Pickle. It may be that the worst episode in his history, his brutal attempt to seduce the girl he professes to love, must be discounted somewhat on the ground that Smollett was more interested in burlesquing *Clarissa* than he was in maintaining consistency of characterization. But even aside from this matter Perry's promiscuous and disgusting sensuality is unbearable, while the senseless cruelty of his practical jokes marks him blood-brother to the Katzenjammer Kids.

Smollett has taken pains to prevent our identifying him completely with his heroes.

The only similitude between the circumstances of my own fortune, and those I have attributed to Roderick Random consists of my being of a reputable family in Scotland, in my being bred a surgeon, and having served as a surgeon's mate on board of a man of war, during the expedition to Carthagena. The low situations in which I have exhibited Roderick, I never experienced in my own person.

From other evidence we know that Smollett lived a good life, that, in spite of a ferocious temper, he was basically a kind and a generous man. Why, then, as an author, this enormous appetite for dirt?

There are numerous explanations, though perhaps no complete or wholly satisfying explanation. Smollett lacked great natural delicacy of taste, and what he had was very likely not fostered by his medical training. He probably felt that bawdry was a necessary element in comedy, for he was a classical scholar, and he could cite classical precedents for everything he did. Lewis Melville adds charitably that Smollett wished to reveal the ugliness of vice by showing it as it is; Ernest A. Baker that, being himself an abnormally sensitive man, he was more impressed than other men are by the filth and horror of the world. I cannot agree with either. There is a tremendous gusto in Smollett's obscenity but never a trace of the *saeva indignatio* of a Swift.

Smollett, then, introduced considerable new material into English fiction; there are few novelists of the sea who have not felt his influence. He was interested also in national traits and qualities, and he stamped a typical character upon many of them which long endured. His influence upon Sterne and Dickens, each in his own way quite antipathetic to his spirit, testifies clearly to his vitality.

Compared to Richardson and Fielding, he is weakest in form. In the Fielding sense of the term, he is hardly a novelist at all, and Howard S. Buck does not slander him when he remarks that though he is rich in the stuff of great art, "it is only rarely that we see it actually transmuted." Perhaps Sir Walter Scott was misled by patriotism when he championed his countryman against Fielding.

One point, however, Scott made which still stands; he paid due tribute of regard to Smollett's magnificent ease.

> He never shows the least desire to make the most either of a character, or a situation, or an adventure, but throws them together with a carelessness which argues unlimited confidence in his own powers.

Artistic lawlessness in fiction has a charm and even a value of its own. If it was not until the twentieth century that the novel became an intellectual discipline and a crossword puzzle book, the fortunate circumstance is due largely to the fact that England has never long been left without novelists like Tobias Smollett.

CHAPTER VII

THE TRIUMPH OF SENSIBILITY: LAURENCE STERNE

It is a great convenience to a man in haste, that there are three distinct roads between Calais and Paris, in behalf of which there is so much to be said by the several deputies from the towns which lie along them, that half a day is easily lost in settling which you'll take.

First, the road by Lisle and Arras, which is the most about—but most interesting, and instructing.

The second, that by Amiens, which you may go, if you would see Chantilly—

And that by Beauvais, which you may go, if you will.

For this reason a great many choose to go by Beauvais.

Tristram Shandy

1. *The Road to Sterne*

The reader of Laurence Sterne is likely to be impressed—and bewildered—first of all by his idiosyncrasies: asterisks and diagrams, blank, black, and marbled pages, and a good many other things one hardly expects to encounter in a novel. Sterne omits one section of *Tristram Shandy* altogether because what it contained was so good that all the rest must have been spoiled in comparison; he omits Chapters 18 and 19 of his last volume only to supply them after we have read Chapter 25; he breaks off conversations in the middle and takes them up again fifty pages later or not at all. Corporal Trim tries again and again to tell the story of the King of Bohemia and his Seven Castles, but he hardly ever gets beyond the opening sentence, and the story is still waiting to be told.

If we wish to be annoyed by all this, nobody can take that right away from us, but we must not assume that Sterne was trying to write like Richardson and Fielding and not succeeding. He was not interested in the conventional kind of novel at all. His novel was different, developed moreover with meticulous care, and in obedience to the exactions of its own informing principle. The title—*The Life and Opinions of Tristram Shandy, Gentleman*—is only part of the fun. Tristram is not born before the third volume and he does not wear breeches until the sixth. Ostensibly he is the narrator, but he could not possibly have known most of the things he narrates. The foreground is occupied by his father, Walter Shandy, and his mother, his Uncle Toby and Corporal Trim, Dr. Slop the man-midwife, Susannah the bungling maid, and others. "If anyone insists upon knowing who Tristram was," says A. Edward Newton, "I shall reply that he was the nephew of Uncle Toby—and that is honor enough."

It was not Sterne's tricks that made him a great writer, and not all of them originated with him. Rabelais, Swift, John Arbuthnot (*Memoirs of Martin Scriblerus,* 1741), Robert Paltock (*Life and Adventures of Peter Wilkins,* 1751), and the anonymous *Life and Memoirs of Mr. Ephraim Tristram Bates* (1756) [1] all preceded him in nonsense fiction. There were mad books like Thomas Amory's *Life and Opinions of John Buncle, Esq.* (1756-1766), which Sterne may not have read, and the writings of Tom D'Urfey and John Dunton, which he certainly did. Sterne read widely. He read standard authors—Horace, Erasmus, Montaigne, Bacon, Burton, and Hall. He read scholarly books on the learned professions. He read curious, out-of-the-way treatises on subjects as unrelated to each other as obstetrics and military engineering. He did not read any of them as a scholar; he went to them, as Katherine Mansfield would say, for "the life in the life of them." When he wrote he drew on them freely. Yet he is one of the most original writers who ever lived, presenting everything from the peculiar slant that marks Laurence Sterne and nobody else on earth.

Sterne was born in Ireland, November 24, 1713. His father, an army ensign, came of Yorkshire stock. After an unsettled childhood, he took both the bachelor's and the master's degree at Cambridge, and settled down, an Anglican priest, at Sutton-in-the-Forest, about eight miles north of York. He was married in 1741, not too fortunately, to Elizabeth Lumley. Having discovered his literary gift acci-

[1] Cf. Helen Sard Hughes, "A Precursor of Tristram Shandy," *Journal of English and Germanic Philology,* XVII (1918), 227-251.

dentally, through a local skit, he published the first two volumes of *Tristram Shandy* at the end of 1759, and came up to London to find himself the lion of the season. Elated, he announced his intention to bring out two more volumes every year for the rest of his life, and he nearly kept his word. The ninth volume came out alone in 1767; on March 18, 1768, tuberculosis finished Sterne and his book together. Meanwhile he had been feted in Paris, and had published in 1768 *A Sentimental Journey Through France and Italy* (so the book is called though Sterne died before he could write the Italian part of it) a few weeks before the end.

2. *Style, Method, and Point of View*

Of *Tristram* Sterne declared that "If 'tis wrote against anything, —'tis wrote . . . against the spleen!" With the *Sentimental Journey* he hoped "to teach us to love the world and our fellow creatures better than we do." Seriously or not, he had glanced obliquely at the two outstanding aspects of his work. But he does not give us humor in one book and tenderness in the other; on the contrary he has an artful blending of elements that no man can disentangle.

He believed sincerely in both humor and tenderness. Like another great consumptive, Robert Louis Stevenson, he felt that there was no duty men so much underestimate as the duty of being happy. He deliberately sought "to fence against the infirmities of ill health, and other evils of life, by mirth; being firmly persuaded that every time a man smiles,—but much more so, when he laughs, it adds something to this Fragment of Life." And for him at least such happiness could best be fostered by deliberately cultivating his sensibilities, by making himself hypersensitive to all the tender emotions. Happiness does not degrade man—it uplifts him. The traveler of *A Sentimental Journey* observes "an elevation of spirit" manifesting itself among the rural merrymakers. "In a word, I thought I beheld Religion mixing in the dance. . . ."

Sterne himself cited three sources of his inspiration: "the study of Locke," "the daily reading of the Old and New Testaments," and "an organization in which predominated the sacred principle which forms the soul, that immortal flame which nourishes life and yet devours it, which suddenly exalts and modifies all sensations, and which we call *imagination* or *sensibility,* according as it is used to depict scenes or to portray passions." Sterne was a "character," a "fantastick," an "original," as the humorist is likely to be. His frail body shrank from the brutalities of the age, as Pope's did; unlike Pope's, his mind could not nourish itself on the cut-and-dried sterilities of the "Age of Reason." (It was not for nothing that the original meaning of "humor" was "moisture.") But though the third source was the most important, the other two cannot be ignored. When Sterne read Locke he made vital contact with a philosopher who stressed sensation as the primary source of knowledge. He read his Bible not only as a priest but as an artist, and the art of the Bible, as Walter Sichel has pointed out specifically in this connection, is essentially impressionistic.[2]

Sterne might have cited a fourth influence—his love of music—for music is the most impressionistic of the arts. His books move to music. "Attitudes are nothing, madam—'tis the transition from one attitude to another—like the preparation and resolution of the discord into harmony. . . ." None could manage these transitions better than he. In *A Sentimental Journey* picture forever dissolves into picture, and the result is a flowing, melodious harmony unsurpassed in English prose. And in *Tristram Shandy* "the speech and movement of his characters . . . are all deftly attuned to musical harmony."[3]

Sterne's characters were his primary interest, and he came close to enlisting all the resources of all the arts to cause them to live on the printed page. It has often been pointed out that, compared to the characters in a modern novel, the Shandys live in a vacuum. Walter and Uncle Toby are related to no complex social or economic background,[4] for both are presented to us after their active lives are over. Toby has spent his life as a soldier, and even now his ruling passion is to be forever fighting Marlborough's campaigns in minia-

[2] *Sterne, A Study* (London: Williams and Norgate, 1910), 173-175. See also Kenneth MacLean, *John Locke and English Literature of the Eighteenth Century* (Yale University Press, 1936).

[3] Wilbur Cross.

[4] The historical background, however, is of some importance. Cf. Theodore Baird, "The Time-Scheme of *Tristram Shandy* and a Source," *PMLA,* LI (1936), 803-820.

ture upon the bowling-green. Yet Toby is so preternaturally humane that it is impossible for him to kill so much as a fly that has been annoying him. In a sense, these people, like Smollett's, are in the "humors" tradition, though in Sterne's case Jonson's influence is much less important than Pope's doctrine of the ruling passion, which he accepted as the psychological basis of his work. And if he does not do much in the way of presenting his personages against a background, he does make them live intensely in relationship to each other. Walter Shandy is all head—an hypothesis-ridden fool who is firmly convinced, among other things, that a man's character is importantly influenced by the size of his nose and the name bestowed upon him in baptism. Over against him stand his wife—who has never grasped one single idea in all her life—and his brother Toby. As Ernest Baker and others have remarked, Toby, who is all heart, is Walter's Sancho Panza, but Trim is Toby's Sancho Panza. The brothers spend their lives together and are devoted to each other, yet neither ever gets the faintest glimmer of an understanding of the other's nature.

Had Smollett presented such characters, they must have been developed strongly and obviously. Sterne's development is anything but obvious, for if his psychology is crude his art is consummate. He adds, as it were, another dimension to his characters, partly through his own intense sympathy—that capacity which only the greatest artists have of getting inside a character's skin and setting him forth on his own terms—and partly through the extraordinary richness and variety of the technical devices he employs. Look at his description of Trim reading Sterne's own sermon on conscience.[5] Consider his use of properties in the scene where Robert's death is announced to the servants' hall.[6] Sterne had not studied painting for nothing; neither had his theater-going time been squandered in idleness.

Sterne's facetious remark that his way of writing a novel was the most religious of all because he simply wrote the first sentence and trusted in God for the second has been taken much too literally. He was firmly convinced that a work of art cannot be measured by

[5] *Tristram Shandy,* Book II, Chapter 17.
[6] *Tristram Shandy,* Book V, Chapter 7.

rule of thumb, that rules were made for the artist, not the artist for rules, and he is quite serious when he insists that if he is to tell his story at all he must tell it in his own way. But though there is much whimsy in his method, and more than a little that is "smarty" and cocksure, it is a method; not even Fielding was surer what he wanted to do or went about it more unerringly. He refuses to play the preceptor; his function is to quicken our sense of life. When Susannah the maid hears of Robert Shandy's death, the first thing that pops into her head is "a green satin night-gown of my mother's, which had been twice scoured," and that dress is followed through her brain by the whole rainbow procession of her mistress' wardrobe, all quite useless now to a lady in mourning. "—My father thrust back his chair—rose up—put on his hat—took four long strides to the door—jerked it open—took no notice of the bad hinge—" so it goes on. And it is pretty close to life.

Of Sterne's style perhaps enough has been implied already. His ideal was one of colloquial ease, and he would break any rule if necessary to achieve it. "Writing, when properly managed . . . is but a different name for conversation." The famous set pieces may grow a bit stale—their studied negligence is sometimes too obvious—but nothing can spoil the lovely cadence of "God tempers the wind to the shorn lamb" (which we quote every day or so, generally under the impression that we are quoting the Bible), and there are quite uncelebrated passages also in which one exclaims suddenly as one comes across the perfect phrase. Mrs. Wadman does Uncle Toby's business for him by persuading him to look into her eye on the pretense that there is a foreign body in it, and the first time he comes to call thereafter, she is found looking out her chamber window "with an eye ready to be deflowered again." With Sterne it is literally true that the style is the man, quite as much the man as his employment of what a hundred and fifty years afterwards has come to be called the "stream-of-consciousness" method. His style reflects the fluidity of his spirit; it is the element that the people of his world must breathe. As Lytton Strachey said of Pope, his style *is* his criticism of life; he tells his story, he paints his picture by the mere fact of writing as he writes. That is why, as we read his books, we feel that we are forever in the presence of the man himself, yet he is never an intruder in his own world as so many novelists often are.

3. *Yorick Vindicated*

No great writer has been more misunderstood than Sterne. As a man, we now know that he was more freakish than wicked. As an artist, he still needs not apologists but expositors. There are greater books than *Tristram Shandy* but there is no other book quite like it; try to inject what it lacks into it and you will only spoil it. It has been urged that it never touches the idealistic heights of *Don Quixote*. It does not, but it would be less humorous if it did. It has been urged that if we regard even the beloved Toby seriously, we shall be forced to conclude that he is a fool. So we shall, but is it necessary to regard him seriously? This is a mad world that Sterne has created, but it fits together perfectly; Goethe knew whereof he spoke when he called its creator the freest spirit of his century. Admit common sense into such a book and everything is over, or, as Coleridge declared, the very essence of humor consists in "a certain reference to the general and the universal, by which the finite great is brought into identity with the little, or the little with the finite great, so as to make both nothing in comparison with the infinite."

There is the Victorian objection against Sterne's prurience. Fortunately much of his bawdry has become so obscure through the passing of time that, unless she has a carefully annotated edition, what the Victorians liked to call "the purest maiden" may now read him without danger of either understanding or contamination! As a clergyman, he knew that there were passages in *Tristram Shandy* which must cause the moralists to fall foul of him, knew and deliberately decided to run the risk. He could not be a humorist and a preacher at the same time, he said, and he was right. But his prurience is intellectual, not emotional; there is no passion, no seduction in it. He himself defended Rabelais, Scarron, and Cervantes in this connection: they all wrote books which excite laughter, not lust, for "there is no passion so serious as lust." The spirit of humor is naturally irreverent; in so far as we agree to exempt certain subjects from ridicule, in so far the humorous view of the world fails. All bodily processes are decent, but some bodily processes are exquisitely humiliating, and so long as incongruity is regarded as one of the great sources of humor, it is futile to ask that they shall never be exploited.

There is, again, the objection to his sentimentality. He skates over pretty thin ice here, but he rarely breaks through. His sensibilities were less perverted than has often been assumed; he was by nature unusually sensitive, and he was sincere when he ascribed sensibility to a divine origin. Cruelty in any form is obnoxious to him; he handles even his grotesques in the full consciousness that they are God's children, and Hazlitt calls Uncle Toby "one of the finest compliments ever paid to human nature." We may pass over the dead ass and the Recording Angel's tear if we will. It is still difficult not to be touched by the mendicant monk's true Christian forgiveness in *A Sentimental Journey,* and one responds in spite of oneself when Uncle Toby's great cry breaks in on Walter Shandy's dry-as-dust harangue on hidden resources:

> 'Tis by the assistance of Almighty God, cried my Uncle Toby, looking up, and pressing the palms of his hands close together—'tis not from our own strength, brother Shandy. . . .

Sterne's sensibility has an intellectual background also; in the famous case of Uncle Toby's fly, it is no mere humanitarianism that moves us (as Edwin Muir has shown in his brilliant essay), but rather a novel and hitherto unsuspected relationship between two living things. When Sterne feeds a macaroon to an ass, he is not incited by pure benevolence; he wants to see how an ass will eat a macaroon. But he says so frankly; he never pretends to be better than he is. Tristram sits down beside the mad Maria, "feeling the full force of an honest heartache," and describes how she looked alternately at the goat and at himself. For a moment the reader is afraid that Sterne will go too far. With superb nonchalance he breaks the spell: "Well, Maria, said I softly—What resemblance do you find?"

Virginia Woolf says rightly of *A Sentimental Journey* that in it Sterne centers our attention not on what he sees but on his own reaction to it. "A girl may be more interesting than a cathedral; a dead donkey more instructive than a living philosopher." But it does not necessarily follow, as she goes on to say, that Sterne is hinting that there is no universal scale of values.[7] "I think I can see the precise and distinguishing marks of national characters more in these nonsensical *minutiae,*" he says (and Virginia Woolf herself quotes him), "than in the most important matters of state; where great men of all nations talk and stalk so much alike, that I would not give nine-pence to choose among them." The logical outcome of Sterne's sensationalism might very well be a world without values, a mere welter of impressions, but if many of us followed the natural bent of our temperament to the end with absolute consistency, we should probably have been removed to the madhouse long ago. Sterne did not so follow his. He was a Christian, in so far as he understood Christianity, and though dogma never interested him greatly, his religion, such as it was, seems to have been perfectly sincere. The famous sermon on conscience, as Herbert Read has observed, sees moral sensibility "operating within a fixed world," and goes far toward justifying Read's conclusion that fundamentally Sterne is classical, not romantic, in his point of view.

There is finally the objection referred to in the beginning, the objection to Sterne's method. Like the cross-eyed man, he seems to be aiming at nothing in particular, and as a matter of fact that is what his imitators—Thomas Bridges, Courtney Melmoth, George Keate, John Williams, Isaac Brandon, and others—did often aim at. But Sterne himself always has his delicate instrument in perfect control. Consider, for example, his digressions. It would hardly be an exaggeration to say that *Tristram Shandy* is all digression. But—Sterne might retort—what else is life? He is right when he claims that his work is digressive and progressive at the same time—"I constantly take care to order affairs so that my main business does not stand still in my absence." Everything is arranged according to Locke's doctrine of the association of ideas which may originally have made up to each other by mere chance but which now

> always keep in company, and the one no sooner at any time comes into the understanding, but its associate appears with it; and if they are more

[7] "The 'Sentimental Journey,'" in *The Second Common Reader* (Harcourt, Brace, 1932).

than two which are thus united, the whole gang, always inseparable, show themselves together.[8]

Nothing is finished, and nothing ever really begins. Out of chaos a cosmos emerges, a universe in which everything is intimately connected with everything else. The road of excess leads to the palace of wisdom, and so far is Sterne from destroying the order of the universe that in the last analysis he is doing just the opposite. In his own elfish way, he is saying what Tennyson said in his address to the flower in the crannied wall. The unity at which he aims is deeper, profounder, more philosophical than that which can be set up as a rhetorician's goal.

[8] John Locke, *An Essay Concerning Human Understanding* (1690).

CHAPTER VIII

SENTIMENTALISTS AND REVOLUTIONARIES

Go on, cried the countess; go on—I insist upon it! I love to weep—I joy to grieve—it is my happiness, my delight, to have perfect sympathy in your sorrows.

The Fool of Quality

1. *Backgrounds of Sentimentalism*

The Golden Age of eighteenth-century fiction extends from the publication of *Pamela* in 1740 to that of *Humphry Clinker* in 1771. This period is dominated by the four great writers whose work we have just surveyed. The remaining twenty-nine years are more difficult to summarize. Thanks to what Elizabeth Griffith, herself a novelist, called "those slopshops of literature," the circulating libraries, quantity increased enormously but quality declined. Most of the novels of this period were frankly ephemera, and many titles do not exist today in so much as a single known copy.

Every conceivable kind of novel appears, but it would not be correct to speak of "the sentimental novel" as a type. Sentimentalism invades all types. Mrs. Radcliffe is generally considered queen of the terror-romances, but Mrs. Radcliffe's novels ooze sentimentalism. Indeed the terror tale itself is one phase of the sensibility cult; its exponents simply employed a stronger form of stimulus than some of their contemporaries.

Our study of Sterne has already shown us that sensibility was something more than lachrymosity. The philosophy of life which informed it is usually traced to France, to Jean Jacques Rousseau (1712-1778). But Rousseau did not invent Rousseauism. England merely reaped what she had sown, for the original impulse had come from her. English anti-monarchists even as far back as Buchanan and Algernon Sidney rejected the divine origin of the state and in one form or another accepted the social contract theory. Lord Herbert of Cherbury attempted the establishment of religion on a non-supernatural basis. Shaftesbury and Hutcheson thought of man as a social animal with naturally benevolent instincts and an intuitive moral sense. Butler, Hume, and Adam Smith all, in one form or another, connect with this general movement, and Tom Paine was its press agent among the people.[1] What Rousseau did was to take familiar ideas and infuse them with the kind of power that appears when either a truth or a dynamic heresy for which an age has been waiting is restated by a man of genius.

Paul Elmer More has pointed out [2] that, like the Christian, Rousseau was conscious of a deep, distressing dualism within himself. But he rejected the traditional view that this disquiet is caused by a conflict between the desires of the natural man and the will of God; instead he tended to shift the responsibility upon external forces. Man is good. He catches his corruption, like an infectious disease, from the social order. Primitive men follow healthy animal instincts. They claim their own but they are kept from injuring others by that feeling of sympathy and pity which is, after self-preservation, the second law of nature.[3] It is only when private property enters the picture that sympathy is destroyed by envy.

Here is something new under the sun; here is a philosophy of life which breaks with both the great traditions from which our civilization derives—the Graeco-Roman and the Hebrew-Christian. It is true, as Walter Francis Wright has recently reminded us, that the primitivism of the great prophets of sensibility has often been overstressed. Shaftesbury recognized the existence in untutored humanity of forces which make for chaos. He begged the question by calling them "unnatural affections," but he did recognize them, and he saw humanity as called to the task of destroying base passions and nourishing unselfish impulses. And Rousseau knew that the sav-

[1] Cf. R. S. Crane, "Suggestions Toward a Genealogy of the 'Man of Feeling,'" *ELH,* I (1934), 205-230, and the references therein contained.

[2] In *Shelburne Essays,* Sixth Series (Houghton Mifflin, c. 1909).

[3] Cf. C. B. Tinker, *Nature's Simple Plan* (Princeton University Press, 1922); H. N. Fairchild, *The Noble Savage* (Columbia University Press, 1928).

age sometimes did wrong, despite the intuitive moral sense he attributed to him; what he wanted was not that civilized men should become savages but that they should so remold the social order in which they lived as to get rid of the artificial desires which breed conflict. But these nice distinctions could not always be maintained consistently either by the founders of the movement themselves or by their much less discriminating followers.

It does not take much imagination to figure out what some of the consequences will be. Some sentimentalists will content themselves with private benevolence, or even with shedding tears over poor, misvalued humanity. Others will perceive that this is not enough. If society is corrupting mankind, then we must change society. We can do this through education—a peculiar kind of education which is almost the negation of what men have ordinarily understood education to be—or, if we are impatient for immediate action, we can do what Rousseau's French followers did—we can rush to the barricades. All these types of mind appear among late eighteenth-century novelists.

2. *Sentimentalism and Benevolence: Goldsmith and Mackenzie*

The book generally accepted today as the masterpiece of the sentimental school may be said to belong to it only in a general way. Like another Irishman, Oscar Wilde, Oliver Goldsmith (1730?-1774) was remarkable for his ability to handle a wide variety of literary types. *The Vicar of Wakefield* (1766) is his only novel, and excepting *Robinson Crusoe* it is probably the most widely read piece of eighteenth-century fiction today. It is like *Crusoe* in that its vogue has cut through national boundaries and exercised a considerable influence on continental literature.

Goethe coupled Goldsmith with Sterne as having saved him from despair. But Goldsmith hated Sterne. As a man he shied from his ribaldries; as an artist he was offended by his idiosyncrasies. Goldsmith was readily moved by pain and sorrow; the contemplation of purity and unselfishness always thrilled him. But the primitivistic tendencies of the sentimental movement never touched him. His opposition to luxury, as in "The Deserted Village," is based on sound economic grounds; it proceeds from no delusions as to the Noble Savage.[4]

This determined march down the middle of the road, though a torture of spirit to pigeon-holing critics, is the very thing that has kept *The Vicar of Wakefield* alive. The fable is trite enough, the old eighteenth-century seduction theme. In Olivia and Sophia we have the stock contrast between the showy daughter and the demure one; the villain never comes alive; Mr. Burchell's role is frankly equivocal. Yet the book stands in English literature a perfect prose idyll—"Fragonard in English prose"[5]—with the Vicar himself taking his rightful place beside Parson Adams and the beloved Priest of Chaucer's Prologue. He is not, like Chaucer's Parson, a perfect character. He is vain and opinionated, a fanatical Whistonian, and even with the lesson of his son Moses having traded the horse for a gross of green spectacles spread out before him, he must walk, as it were, eyes open, into the tender clutches of Ephraim Jenkinson. The artificiality of the epilogue has often been objected to. It would be quite as reasonable to object to the piling up of calamity on calamity in the fable itself. Like Job, the Vicar goes through a series of "tests," and his story is less convincing than Job's, for life does not often deal her cards so designedly as Satan. But though the situation may be artificial the man never is, and the arbitrary ending was largely a matter of literary convention. What Goldsmith is

[4] Cf. W. F. Gallaway, Jr., "The Sentimentalism of Goldsmith," *PMLA,* XLVIII (1933), 1167-1181; E. A. Baker, *The History of the English Novel,* V, 79-85. Baker overstates Goldsmith's anti-sentimentalism, however, and he takes the shifting of his machinery much too seriously, especially as it moves about to bring in a happy ending. Gallaway, too, is on uncertain ground momentarily when he suggests that "Goldsmith set out to describe the disasters of the gullible sentimentalists . . . but was prevented by a growing love for his own creation from leading him beyond the brink of what in any existing society would have been inevitable ruin." A scientific, Zola-esque approach to the problems of fiction could never have appealed to Goldsmith under any circumstances, and I do not understand why his somewhat cavalier handling of his *deus ex machina* ending should disturb anyone who remembers that he was also a dramatist and is familiar with the theatrical tradition that he inherited. For another discussion of Goldsmith's sentimentality, see Walter Francis Wright's *Sensibility in English Prose Fiction, 1760-1814.*

[5] Oswald Doughty.

really saying is not that goodness always triumphs in this world (which would be sentimental in the bad sense because it is untrue), but rather that the heart which rests in the Eternal is forever unconquerable because in spite of all that the world can do, it will be upheld to endurance and spiritual victory in the end.

Yet this interpretation fails to do justice to the book, if only because it conveys little suggestion of its humor. Moses at the fair, the absurd family picture which was painted in the kitchen and must stay there forever because it turned out to be too big to get through the door, the fatuous Mrs. Primrose with her vanities and her silly proprieties, all melting away at the mere suggestion of a chance to find a man for one of her girls—men will delight in these things as long as English fiction is read. In the discussion of prison conditions at the time of Primrose's incarceration, the book strikes a more serious note and touches the novel of purpose.

There is much less moderation in Henry Mackenzie (1745-1831). "The Scottish Addison" was a great man in Edinburgh—a poet, a playwright, a periodical essayist, and an editor. Liberal, forward-looking in his sympathies, he was a member of both the Royal Society and the Highland Society. It was his lecture on German drama that kindled the enthusiasm of the youthful Scott; students of Shakespeare owe him a grudge as one of the first proponents of the now exploded theory of a weak, procrastinating Hamlet. Mackenzie was a lawyer by profession, though, like his own Man of Feeling, he was disgusted by the law's more heartless aspects and finally gave it up.

Like Goldsmith, he disclaims the influence of Sterne, but when one opens *The Man of Feeling* (1771) it is difficult to accept his disclaimer. His first chapter is numbered XI, and it is a digression. He is following an old manuscript which a sporting clergyman had used for gun wadding, and omissions and discontinuities are explained on this basis. The truth of the matter is that while Mackenzie imitated Sterne's method, he remained impervious to his spirit. His own serious, idealistic temper allied him rather with Richardson and with Marmontel.

Like Yorick, the hero of *The Man of Feeling* is something of an epicure in sorrow; unlike him, he really does succeed in relieving distress. He goes about doing good, and for all his sensitiveness he is no prig. Once he restores a prostitute to her father, who, having been himself a freethinker, must share the blame for her fall. Only when it comes to regarding his own interests is he impractical. In love his shyness is unconquerable, and it costs him his life. Even had he not, incorrectly, suspected a rival and literally broken his heart over it, he might very well never have mustered courage to speak until it was too late.

Henry Morley indexed the tears that fall in *The Man of Feeling;* his list has forty-seven entries. The introduced story of old Edwards, whose misfortunes are climaxed when he offers himself to a press-gang as a substitute for his son, illustrates Mackenzie at his best and at his worst. When the soldiers arrive in the midst of the happy family's Christmas festivities, a strong contrast is created, but the contrast itself is pushed to an extreme when, in the face of the father's sublime sacrifice, the ruffians themselves burst into tears. As for Harley's feeling for the mad girl at Bedlam, it utterly passes the bounds of all rational compassion and steers straight toward the inanities of Wordsworth's tribute to the idiot boy.

The Man of the World, "In Two Parts" (1773), manifests Mackenzie's ability to cope with the exigencies of a coherent narrative, but it has much less of his peculiar "tap" than *The Man of Feeling.* Beginning with the romance of the Reverend Richard Annesly and Harriet Wilkins, it passes on to an account of the mildly Rousseauistic education they give their children, but soon thereafter transforms itself into a tale of rakish villainy. Sir Thomas Sindall first corrupts the son and succeeds in getting him transported; then he turns his attention to the daughter. Like Clarissa, she is drugged and violated. Unlike Clarissa, she returns home, to her kind father, to bear a daughter, and to die.

In Part II the incest theme appears. The vicious Sir Thomas is now seen weaving his toils about another girl. After having been wounded by her high-minded lover, he learns that she is his own daughter, and dies repentant. The reader has no difficulty in agreeing with the pious Mrs. Wistanly that "of those who have led his life . . . few have closed it like him!"

Mackenzie's last brief, epistolary novel, *Julia de Roubigné* (1777), which has a French setting, is a Rousseauized *Othello*. His aim was to produce a tragedy in which the catastrophe should arise

> not out of schemes of premeditated villainy, but from the excess and over-indulgence of passions and feelings, in themselves blameless, nay, praiseworthy, but which, encouraged to a morbid excess, and coming into fatal though fortuitous concourse with each other, lead to the most disastrous consequences.[6]

Believing the man she loves married to another, Julia marries the gallant but elderly Count de Montauban out of gratitude for his kindness to her father. When Savillon returns unwed she consents to a meeting that she may bid him farewell. Montauban, believing her an adultress, kills her with poison, then, learning the truth, commits suicide. This story might have been a masterpiece. It is not, though the narrative is well sustained, and there are moments of some power. Savillon's account of his adventures in far-off places introduces one more noble savage, Yambu, into eighteenth-century fiction—Mackenzie had already managed to drag a record of Cherokee life and torture into *The Man of the World*—and includes a discussion of the slavery question from the liberal point of view.

3. *Sentimentalism and Education: Brooke; Day; Mrs. Inchbald*

"Let us lay it down as an incontrovertible rule that the first impulses of nature are always right; there is no original sin in the human heart, the how and the why of the entrance of every vice can be traced." From this follows naturally Rousseau's theory of education. "It consists, not in teaching virtue or truth, but in preserving the heart from vice and the spirit from error." So Emile is separated from family and comrades and placed in the country under the care of a guardian who can be trusted to carry out this program. Throughout his earlier years books are taboo; information comes through play and through observation. Self-expression, not discipline, is the ideal, and the question whether what is expressed is worth expressing is never very clearly raised.

The English educational novels do not get quite so far as that. *The Fool of Quality* (1764-1770), by Henry Brooke (1703?-1783),

[6] Scott, *Lives of the Eminent Novelists and Dramatists*.

won the enthusiastic endorsement of at least two famous English men: John Wesley edited it, and Charles Kingsley reintroduced it to the Victorians. And even today so fine a critic as Miss J. M. S. Tompkins can write of it that

> nothing can obscure the nobility of this devout fairy-tale. It sprang from a mind which, in old age, was like an overgrown garden, a fragrant wilderness, still visited at rare and burning moments by the angels of God.

The tribute is richly deserved, for *The Fool of Quality,* though one of the strangest, is also one of the most charming books in the language. The main theme is clear enough: the training of a boy from his earliest years to his marriage. But no fewer than eleven other stories are woven into it, to say nothing of numerous fables and anecdotes (including those of Damon and Pythias, Diogenes and Alexander, and the Burghers of Calais) and lengthy essay passages on many weighty themes. Critics in general have greatly exaggerated the difficulty of holding the thread, however; except at the very end, where the attempt to reflect actual life is apparently given over altogether, the book is consistently easy and delightful reading.

Brooke's sentimentalism troubles most readers less than Mackenzie's. He calculates his emotional effects very neatly; he builds to scale. We get further away from the real world than Mackenzie takes us; consequently the standards of the real world do not so often intrude. There is more action, more melodrama, even an occasional surprising touch of worldliness, as in the discussion of duelling, or of brutality, as in the young hero's practical jokes. For all its tearfulness, there is nothing in *The Fool of Quality* to please a prig.

As an educator, Brooke does not rely on experimentation alone. Fables and instructional tales are employed freely. Physical activities are heavily stressed, however, and the boy is not rebuked when he does outrageous things so long as his intentions are right. He must learn Latin and Greek, but his young mind need not concern itself with the mysteries of deep divinity; the law precedes the gospel. Fear of the supernatural is acquired, not innate, and must never, therefore, be encouraged. All this is worked out in the contrast which appears between the proper education which the neglected child, Henry, receives at the hands of the philosopher, Mr. Fenton, and the fashionable education bestowed upon his brother. Mr. Fenton's aim is to rear a Fool, in the lofty sense in which Saint Paul used that term. A fool by the standards of conventional society, Henry has all the deeper wisdom of the soul.

Brooke's political teachings are somewhat contradictory. Theoretically he throws class distinctions over altogether. Every emperor has a beggar somewhere among his ancestors, every beggar has an emperor among his. After this his long, fervent eulogy of the British constitution seems something of a non sequitur. Practically he looked to the farmer, the manufacturer, and the merchant as the real pillars of society.

Religiously, Brooke has been strongly influenced by the German mystic, Jacob Böhme (1575-1624), and his English disciple, William Law. That is to say, he thinks of God as "an infinite and eternal Good Will," manifesting Himself both in the physical world and, on a higher level, in the moral nature of man. This divine beauty draws us to itself through all creation, for God alone is lovely and nothing else can be loved. Our spiritual bodies are already forming within us from the divine seed of the second Adam, and death will deliver us from the corruption of mortality. Christ is the principle of redemption in the bosom of all living things, even of those who have never heard his name, and each living thing can find its place in life only as it is able to break through the shell of self. "There are millions of worthy people and affectionate saints upon earth; but they are as a kingdom within a kingdom, a grain within a husk—it requires a kindred heart and a curious eye to discover them." Brooke wrote a second novel, *Juliet Grenville* (1774), but it added nothing to his fame.

The famous *Sandford and Merton* (1783-1789) of Brooke's admirer, Thomas Day (1748-1789), is more completely a pedagogic novel. Unlike Brooke, Day addressed the children directly, having discovered a "total want of proper books to be put into their hands, while they are taught the elements of reading." [7] But having written *Sandford and Merton,* he hesitated long before he could bring him-

[7] Cf. F. J. Harvey Darton's charming book, *Children's Books in England* (Cambridge University Press, 1932).

self to publish, and then he put it out anonymously, this the only one of his writings that has been spared by the oblivion of Time! Day was an admirable, though hilariously eccentric, man, a friend of Maria Edgeworth's father, Richard Lovell Edgeworth, and of Dr. Erasmus Darwin, the Sewards, James Watt, and others of the liberal group in Lichfield.

Sandford and Merton concerns two boys—Tommy Merton, the son of a rich Jamaica planter, who is ignorant and spoiled, and Harry Sandford, a poor farmer's son, who, under the stern, kindly tutelage of Mr. Barlow, develops rapidly into a paragon of strength and courtesy. The type-pair had already appeared in *The Fool of Quality* (whence Day may have derived them), but Brooke, concentrating on one boy, failed to develop the contrast which is Day's whole theme. When Harry saves the fearful Tommy from a snake that has coiled itself round his leg as he walks in the garden with his nurse, Mr. Barlow is persuaded to take the rich boy in hand also, and the association of Sandford and Merton is begun.

Day accepts Rousseau's comfortable theories concerning human nature, thus choosing the easiest way. Harry, spoiled though he is, is a boy of excellent capacity, with no real vice in him. What he needs is a chance to recover from the false training he has already received. Mr. Barlow's scheme of education is admirably comprehensive, and he relies fruitfully upon the method of learning by doing. You do not learn the principle of the lever, for example, until you find it necessary to move a huge snowball, and a knowledge of astronomy turns out to have considerable practical value to a boy who finds himself wandering benighted with nobody to lead him home. In the moral life the method is the same. Tommy does not have to work, since he thinks work beneath the dignity of a gentleman, but if he does not, then of course he cannot expect to receive the reward of work; consequently he must go hungry (which is uncomfortable) or subsist upon Harry's charity (which is humiliating).

Yet Day recognizes the importance of accumulated race-experience. Individual trial and error is necessary, but we are silly if we fail to compare notes with those who have traveled the road before us. So *Sandford and Merton* becomes a tissue of inserted stories some short and pithy like the story of Androcles and the Lion (which is used to teach kindness to animals), one—the Oriental tale of Sophron and Tigranes—so elaborate that a large part of the third volume must be given over to it.

Sandford and Merton remained a classic until almost the beginning of the twentieth century. Even today, despite its quaintness, formality, and occasional priggishness, one finds much in it that the world cannot afford to relinquish. It is narrowly moralistic in its attitude toward the arts, however, and it encourages the class-conflict by picturing all fashionable people as cold-hearted, bad-mannered snobs. As a guide to the conduct of life, its most serious fault, however, is that it pictures the world as a place where vice is always punished and virtue rewarded. This vicious pseudo-morality is at its worst in the stories of the Good Natured Little Boy and the Bad Natured Little Boy, which, as they passed down to him through hundreds of Sunday School books, Mark Twain ridiculed so mercilessly in *Sketches New and Old*. Day continued the exposition of his ideas through *The History of Little Jack* (1788), which has a hero who was suckled by a nanny goat and reared by an old soldier, and in which he shows an advance structurally over *Sandford and Merton*.

As a Roman Catholic, Elizabeth Inchbald (1753-1821) may seem somewhat out of place among the radicals. But Catholics were a group much discriminated against in eighteenth-century England; as such, they were naturally very conscious of the faults of government. Mrs. Inchbald has two priests among her characters in *A Simple Story,* and priests are rare in the literature of the time. On the whole, however, both religion and purpose appear less prominently in her work than is sometimes supposed.

Mrs. Inchbald herself was as interesting as any of her books. A farmer's daughter of Norfolk, she ran away from home and became an actress. She married an actor, probably not for love, and was early widowed. Red-haired, pretty, lisping, and vain, she had men about her all her life, some as high-minded as John Kemble, others no better than they should have been, yet her name was never touched by scandal. She deprived herself of almost the necessities of life to ensure the success of her private charities, yet her treatment of Mary Wollstonecraft, whose marriage to Godwin she seems to have resented, showed her capable of the meanest feminine spitefulness.

Besides her many plays, Mrs. Inchbald wrote two novels—*A Simple Story* (1791) and *Nature and Art* (1796). Both are generally classified as educational novels, though Dr. William McKee argues that the closing statement of *A Simple Story,* where we are informed that all Miss Milner's woes might have been avoided if only her father had given her a proper education, was merely an afterthought. Very likely he is right. We have seen nothing of Miss Milner's education in the course of the book. The problems she faces are personal problems, and her faults all seem faults of temperament.

In *Nature and Art,* on the other hand, the *Sandford and Merton* contrast appears again. This time the child of nature, Henry, has been reared on an island off the coast of Africa; his cousin William has a selfish worldly cleric for a father while his mother is a fool. Nothing in eighteenth-century fiction is more delightful than the scene in which the sophisticates try vainly to convince the young philosopher that war and murder are not synonymous terms.

The boys grow up; the contrast between them is well sustained through their respective love affairs. But at this point the book breaks. Mrs. Inchbald becomes so deeply interested in the pathetic story of the girl William has seduced that she drops everything else to follow her through poverty, prostitution, and crime, to her final condemnation, unrecognized, at the bench of the judge who is simply the boy that ruined her life, grown older.[8]

With this matter out of the way, Mrs. Inchbald tries to return to the central theme of the book, but her effort is not successful. Yet she manages her dénouement well. Barring one or two convenient accidents, like the infidelity of William's wife, character is fate, as it should be. The good do not escape the ills of life, but because they

[8] A similarly ironic situation has been used in many later works, including Fanny Burney's *Cecilia,* Bulwer-Lytton's *Paul Clifford,* and the popular French play, *Madame X,* by Alexandre Bisson. Mrs. Inchbald has one wonderful touch at the close of the girl's letter to her betrayer: "Hope you will excuse all faults, as I never learned but one month."

are what they are they find a happiness even as outcasts that the unrighteous rich can never know.

Mrs. Inchbald was not a good novelist, but she did know how to develop a "strong" situation, and she carried over from her dramatic training considerable skill in dialogue. She could not narrate. At her worst she merely scribbled stage-directions; at her best she visualized clearly in terms of the theater. Halfway through *A Simple Story,* she jumps over seventeen years in a chapter, kills off Lady Elmwood, and starts over again with the widower and his daughter. This book contains the materials for a superb study along the *Manon Lescaut* line, but their possibilities are never realized.

4. *Sentimentalism and Revolution: Holcroft and Godwin*

Thomas Holcroft (1745-1809) was the perfect radical. As Ford K. Brown puts it, he was "the first to exhibit in the English novel a complete sociological, philosophic creed, just as Disraeli and Kingsley in a later period evolved social Toryism and Christian socialism in the novel." This does not mean that Holcroft ever advocates violence. To avoid violence is, on the contrary, the alpha and the omega of all his striving. He wished to warn the upper classes that this could only be done through voluntary relinquishment on their part of the special privileges they held. But in practice Holcroft was always distinctly meliorist. The poor must be educated first; they can be elevated afterwards. Holcroft indeed was enamored of reason. He carried his faith in the power of the mind even to the length of maintaining that pain, disease, and death had no existence save in relationship to it, and could all be effectively controlled by it.

The son of a shoemaker and peddler, Holcroft spent his childhood tramping the roads of England. He became stable-boy in a racing establishment, later himself a shoemaker's apprentice. He was an actor and a playwright (*The Road to Ruin* long held the stage), a hackwriter, a reviewer, and a voluminous translator, also in a small way a poet and a musician. In 1794 he was accused, with gross unfairness, of high treason. The case was hastily dismissed without his having been given a chance to clear his name; it irked him that he must live thereafter as "an unconvicted felon." In private life, despite his notorious irritability, Holcroft was high-minded, unselfish, and incorruptible, much the same kind of man he has portrayed in the philosopher Turl, of *Hugh Trevor.*

Holcroft wrote four novels—*Alwyn, or The Gentleman Comedian* (1780), *Anna St. Ives* (1792), *Hugh Trevor* (1794), and *Memoirs of Bryan Perdue* (1805). The second and third are much the most important.

Anna St. Ives is the *Sir Charles Grandison* of the radical movement. It is unfortunate that only the villain, Coke Clifton, should be permitted to talk like a human being, or that when he discusses the problem of marriage with Anna and her all-right, all-competent lover, Frank Henley, he alone should talk sense. Once indeed Anna goes so far as to tell Frank that "if anything could make you dearer to me than you are, it must be weakness." But we feel the sentiment quite out of character in a girl who freely acknowledges her love for a good man yet prepares instead to marry a bad one so that she may fulfill her obligation to society by reclaiming him.

Anna is the daughter of a baronet; Frank is the son of her father's estate agent. But this social difference creates no barrier between them. Anna states her creed and Holcroft's in the series of tests she propounds to Clifton:

> Dare you think the servant that cleans your shoes is your equal, unless not so wise or good a man; and your superior, if wiser and better? Dare you suppose mind has no sex, and that woman is not by nature the inferior of man? Dare you think that riches, rank, and power are usurpations; and that wisdom and virtue only can claim distinction? Dare you make it the business of your whole life to overturn these prejudices, and to promote among mankind that spirit of universal benevolence which shall render them all equals, all brothers, all stripped of their artificial and false wants, all participating in the labor requisite to produce the necessaries of life, and all combining in one universal effort of mind, for the progress of knowledge, the destruction of error, and the spreading of eternal truth?

She adds that "all the false wants of luxury . . . are the necessary offspring of individual property," and that what Clifton possesses is not his own but rather "the property of him who wants it most."

Naturally Clifton does not enjoy being reformed, nor does he relish the moral superiority he cannot help feeling in Anna. She takes no pains to conceal from him the fact that she is conscious of it also. "Mind can do all things with mind," she says, and "those who, mature in reason, are superior to prejudice" cannot suffer. Even if she were violated, Anna could take no shame to herself. "For you perhaps I might weep, but for myself I would not shed a tear! Not a tear! You cannot injure me—I am above you!" She is nearly put to the test, for Clifton finally has her abducted, confining Henley meanwhile in a private madhouse. But virtue triumphs in the end, and Anna comes to an admirably common-sense conclusion: "Let us never cease our endeavors to reform the licentious and the depraved but let us not marry them."

But it does not seem as silly as all that in the actual reading, and *Hugh Trevor,* despite its conventionally romantic ending, is much closer to being an actual portrayal of life. This account of the making of Thomas Holcroft—for that is what it amounts to—involves plenty of denunciation. The church, the state, and the school are all equally corrupt. A soldier is "a hireling cut-throat." The students at Oxford are a gang of lazy sots and evil livers. As for the bishop, Holcroft is not content to have him steal Hugh's discussion of the Thirty-Nine Articles and publish it as his own, but he must involve him in an ugly seduction episode besides.

Hugh works his way toward sanity through the wise counsel of his friend Turl, who is Holcroft as he finally came to think of himself, even as Hugh is Holcroft in the making. Turl urges Hugh not to seek personal revenge upon those who have injured him. He has larger fish to fry; he must serve the commonweal.

> Speak, but speak to the world at large, not to insignificant individuals. Speak in the tone of a benevolent and disinterested heart, and not of an inflamed and revengeful imagination! otherwise you endanger yourself, and injure society.

Turl believes, furthermore, that

> Man becomes what the mistaken institutions of society inevitably make him: his tendency is to promote his own well being, and the well being of the creatures around him; these can only be promoted by virtue; consequently, when he is vicious it is from mistake, and his original sin is ignorance.

Holcroft's friend, William Godwin (1756-1836) had a precocious, pious, studious, and physically delicate youth; he began his career, not too successfully, as a dissenting clergyman. By his brief marriage to Mary Wollstonecraft, he became the father of the poet Shelley's second wife. In 1793, by way of rejoinder to Burke's *Reflections* on the French Revolution, he wrote his *Enquiry Concerning Political Justice,* and it made him, if only for a short time, a great man. His first two novels—*Caleb Williams* (1794) and *St. Leon* (1799) inspired encomiums which seem very extravagant today. Byron, Shelley, and Keats were all fascinated, and *Caleb,* dramatized by Colman as *The Iron Chest,* won great stage triumphs in England, France, and America.

As a thinker, Godwin stands between Hobbes, Helvetius, and Holbach (who see man as governed wholly by selfish impulses) and Rousseau. To his way of thinking, we come into the world without predisposition, good or bad; in other words heredity is nothing and environment everything. If you would achieve reforms you must first convince men's minds; this accomplished, the necessary changes may be brought about by constitutional means.

Godwin's most famous novel, *Caleb Williams,* has lived, indeed, less as a *Tendenz-roman* than as a pioneer detective story and a study in morbid psychology. And the question at once arises: Does *Caleb Williams* express Godwin's philosophy?

He himself described the novel both as "the offspring of that temper of mind in which the composition of my *Political Justice* left me" and as "a paraphrase on the story of Bluebeard." He was right on both occasions, and one of his critics pays him an unintended compliment when she points out that Falkland's persecution of Williams is not typical of social oppression in general. Godwin's point is that even in the extreme situation that he has conceived, even when the poor man has discovered that the rich man is a murderer, still poverty has no chance against riches in the courts of the land. The mere fact that the situation is not typical must clear Godwin of the charge that he was simply a propagandist with no interest in fiction as such.

In *Caleb Williams* the criminal is the pursuer, not the pursued.

Godwin conceived his book backwards. Volume III was to contain "a series of adventures of flight and pursuit; the fugitive in perpetual apprehension of being overwhelmed with the worst calamities, and the pursuer, by his ingenuity and resources, keeping his victim in a state of the most fearful alarm." For Volume II, Godwin planned "a dramatic and impressive situation adequate to account for the impulse that the pursuer should feel, incessantly to alarm and harass his victim." Finally, in Volume I, he developed the pursuer's past life up to the time when his victim came into it.

As we read, our sympathies, unfortunately, are somewhat divided. In the first part of the story, Falkland is made so attractive that when the author suddenly bids us change our attitude toward him we find it difficult to obey. We can forgive him his murder of the loathsome Tyrrel, for his provocation was great, but his having permitted the Hawkinses to die for the crime is another matter. And the Caleb who ferrets out his secret, as Saintsbury complains, "is actuated by the very lowest of human motives, sheer inquisitiveness."

Godwin thought so well of the central situation in *Caleb Williams* that for some time he feared he could never find another to equal it. Finally it occurred to him that if he could mix "human feelings and passions with incredible situations," he might do so. The result was *St. Leon, A Tale of the Sixteenth Century,* which is quite contemporary, unfortunately, in its psychology. The incredible situation involves the philosopher's stone and the gift of immortal life.

Once St. Leon has accepted these boons, he is cut off gradually from human fellowship. His son runs away from home and his wife dies of a broken heart. His apparently boundless wealth wakens the suspicions of the authorities; even when he tries to use it unselfishly, as in the attempted rehabilitation of ravaged Hungary, he encounters only disaster. The revolutionary note in the book is probably to be connected with its unmasking of the hollowness of wealth and power.

St. Leon has almost epic sweep and range and sometimes, at least, considerable power. Bethlem Gabor, the monstrous misanthrope who wrecks the Hungarian adventure, is nearly a masterpiece of his kind.[9] Sprague Allen points out that Goethe, Schiller, or Byron might have been unsocial enough to make a hero out of him.

The remaining novels are less important, though *Fleetwood* (1805) complements *St. Leon* in an interesting way. Fleetwood finds the solution to life's problem, which had eluded his predecessor, but his history never leaves the common level of daily life. The humanitarian interest of the book is very strong, and there is a really moving and powerful description of child-labor conditions in the silk mills at Lyons. The last part of the novel is a good study of marriage between a young girl and a middle-aged man, complicated by an Iago-like intrigue set in the frame of a typical eighteenth-century inheritance story. *Mandeville* (1817), the picture of an inverted, brooding misanthrope, is indebted to Brockden Brown's *Wieland,* which Godwin himself had inspired. In the two novels of his old age, *Cloudesley* (1830) and *Deloraine* (1833), Godwin borrows heavily from *Caleb Williams* and from books by other hands; *Cloudesley* involves ambitious Russian and Italian backgrounds.

Godwin began *Caleb Williams* in the third person, but he soon adopted instead the form of autobiographical narrative as "infinitely the best adapted, at least, to my vein of delineation, where the thing in which my imagination reveled most freely, was the analysis of the private and internal operations of the mind. . . ." His analysis was too formal to be completely successful, but it was a new note in English fiction, and during the early nineteenth century only Maturin succeeded in improving upon it. Through Godwin's influence on the American, Brockden Brown, his interest in psychology passed on, with Hawthorne and Henry James, to assume a tremendous importance in modern fiction.

5. *Bage and Other Propagandists*

Holcroft and Godwin had many imitators, including Mary Robinson (Garrick's "Perdita"), whose romantic liaison with the Prince of Wales was one of the great scandals of the time; Mary Hays

[9] One of his descendants is a character in George Preedy's powerful novel, *General Crack* (1928).

(*Memoirs of Emma Courtney,* 1796),[10] and Charles Sedley (*Asmodeus, or The Devil in London,* 1818). It is tempting to linger over Godwin's wife, Mary Wollstonecraft, who, though she owes her fame to her *Vindication of the Rights of Women* still contributed two novels well worth reading: *Mary, A Fiction* (1788) and *The Wrongs of Women* (1798). But in the few paragraphs available here it will be more profitable to glance at the more diluted radicalism of Bage and some others.

Robert Bage (1728-1801) was a Warwickshire paper manufacturer who turned novelist at fifty-three to take his mind off business reverses. His strongest tendency-novel is *Hermsprong, or Man As He Is Not* (1796). Hermsprong was reared among the North American Indians, from whom he learned the value of simplicity and the importance always of telling the truth, even (or especially) when it hurts. Hermsprong is a great walker, a bather, and a water-drinker, and his path through life is marked by many benevolences. It is interesting to compare him with the hero of Dr. John Shebbeare's *Lydia, or Filial Piety* (1755), who, being himself an Indian prince, achieves even completer detachment in his comments on European civilization.

In the course of his adventures, Hermsprong is called upon to face an English mob.

> My friends [he tells them], we cannot all be rich; there is no possible *equality* of *property* which can last a *day*. If you were capable of desiring it, which I hope you are not, you must wade through such scenes of guilt and horror to obtain it as you would tremble to think of.

Bage might sympathize with revolution in France, but he wanted none of it in England.

He never took the novel too seriously as an art-form, and he did not object to providing entertainment for his readers. *Mount Henneth* (1782), *Barham Downs* (1784), *The Fair Syrian* (1787), and *James Wallace* (1788) all have plenty of adventure. There are plenty of ideas also, but the plot and the ideas do not always get together. *Mount Henneth* attacks war, with specific reference to the American

[10] Cf. M. Ray Adams, "Mary Hays, Disciple of William Godwin." *PMLA,* LV (1940), 472-483.

Revolution and England's adventures in India, and combats the dominant idea that a woman who has been indiscreet must thereafter be regarded as "ruined."

Bage's sexual morality shocked Sir Walter, who included some of his books in Ballantyne's Library but solemnly warned his readers against this aspect of them. And this is not the only difficulty one encounters in seeking to evaluate him fairly. Miss J. M. S. Tompkins credits him with having brought the novel "a great increase of intellectual content." Saintsbury finds that he "never entirely 'comes off.'" Both judgments are correct. There are passages in *Hermsprong* that recall Fielding and passages that recall Sterne, but none are sustained.

Charlotte Smith (1749-1806) was a gifted and versatile writer who has only recently been studied with the care she deserves.[11] *Desmond* (1792) is her best book to consider along the line of this chapter's interests.

By the simple expedient of sending her hero off to France, where he comes into contact with those who oppose the Revolution as well as those who support it, and by permitting him to discuss his own ideas not only with them but also with his friends in England, the author is able to reflect almost every shade of contemporary opinion. She is careful, however, to give a friendly picture of revolutionary France, and all her discussions are so conducted as to leave no doubt in the reader's mind concerning the fundamental justice of the people's cause.

The plot remains personal: Desmond is in love with another man's wife. Charlotte Smith does not involve her hero and heroine in the Revolution, as almost any modern novelist would have done. And I do not know how better to contrast eighteenth-century morality with that of our own day than to glance at her treatment of the marriage problem. Though Varney's brutality and debauchery are unspeakable, it never occurs either to Geraldine or to Desmond that his wife might be justified in leaving him for another man. Yet for no better reason than to evolve a clumsy mystery and create suspense, the author does not hesitate to involve the "faithful" lover

[11] Cf. Florence M. A. Hilbish, *Charlotte Smith, Poet and Novelist (1749-1806)* (University of Pennsylvania Press, 1941).

in a casual intrigue with a Frenchwoman, and Geraldine herself seems to take the vulgar affair (and the child that comes of it) quite as a matter of course.

By the time she wrote *The Banished Man* (1794), Charlotte Smith had already begun to entertain some doubts about the Revolution, and *Marchmont* (1796) repudiates French republicanism altogether. In *The Young Philosopher* (1798) we have a disillusioned disciple of Rousseau who seeks the better life in America.

It must not be supposed that it was only the radicals who used fiction as a means of propagating their ideas; the conservatives and the reactionaries were eager to do the same. Among the most rabid of these were George Walker and Charles Lucas. Walker's *Vagabond* (1799), which is subtitled *Whatever is Just is Equal, but Equality Not Always Just* attempted a comprehensive criticism of the reformers.[12] Agreeably to its title, *The Infernal Quixote* (1801) by Charles Lucas, opens with a Prologue in which Satan is seen marshaling his forces for a new attack on England. Walker and Lucas may have been sincere in their view that the reformers were ambitious self-seekers, deliberately corrupting society under the cloak of a professed idealism, but if so they had not much brains or sympathy mixed up with their sincerity.

Charles Lloyd, Elizabeth Hamilton, and Isaac D'Israeli were more fair-minded. Lloyd (*Edmund Oliver,* 1798) had begun as a liberal. Disgusted by the violent course of the Revolution, he abandoned his faith in reform through legislation but he did not abandon his humanitarianism. In Mrs. Hamilton's *Memoirs of Modern Philosophers* (1800), Godwin and Holcroft appear as Mr. Myope and Mr. Glib respectively; in D'Israeli's *Vaurien* (1797) their names are Mr. Subtile and Mr. Reverberator.

Thomas Skinner Scurr's *The Magic of Wealth* (c. 1815) is the earliest thoroughgoing discussion of economic problems in English fiction. Opposed to the revolutionaries Scurr is yet oppressed by the condition of the poor. He sees and deplores the woes that are coming to England in the wake of the Industrial Revolution and his proposed remedy is a modified feudalism.

[12] Cf. H. H. McMullan, "The Satire of Walker's *Vagabond* on Rousseau and Godwin," *PMLA*, LII (1937), 215-229.

In times of transition we should not be surprised to find liberal and conservative ideas in the same writer. Amelia Opie, beautiful wife of the painter, moved freely in radical circles, and her father, Dr. James Alderson, held his revolutionary faith unshaken through all the dark days of the Terror. Yet *Adeline Mowbray* (1804), the story of a girl who tried to carry out Godwin's ideas on marriage, is distinctly conservative.[13] The somewhat fatuous Hannah More was thoroughly conservative, and her sincerity at least cannot be impugned, for she put forth her propaganda stories as tracts, at her own expense. Dr. John Moore's *Zeluco* (1786), *Edward* (1796), and *Mordaunt* (1800) are hardly either radical or conservative; they are merely novels of ideas, and the interest lies in the discusion itself.

The late eighteenth century may have produced few masterpieces in the realm of the English novel, but it certainly did much to illustrate the potential range of the most protean of all literary forms.

[13] Cf. Jacobine Menzies-Wilson and Helen Lloyd, *Amelia, The Tale of a Plain Friend* (Oxford University Press, 1937).

CHAPTER IX

THE RENASCENCE OF WONDER

Take

An old castle, half of it ruinous.
A long gallery with a great many doors, some secret ones.
Three murdered bodies, quite fresh.
As many skeletons, in chests and presses.
Assassins and desperadoes, *quant. suff.*
Noises, whispers, and groans, threescore at least.

Mix them together, in the form of three volumes, to be taken at any of th water-places before going to bed.

The Spirit of the Public Journals for 1797

1. *The Gothic Revival*

One type of late eighteenth-century fiction must have a chapter to itself. This is the so-called Gothic Novel.

The Gothic Novel had long roots. Miss Edith Birkhead wisely reminds us that the Tale of Terror as such did not make its first appearance in literature at this time. "The universal myth of a great flood is perhaps the earliest tale of terror." And the *Babylonica* of Iamblichus "is laid in tombs, caverns, and robbers' dens, a setting remarkably like that of Gothic story."

The eighteenth-century terror tale was but one phase of the pre-romantic movement in literature and in life. Sooner or later the reaction against neo-classicism was bound to come, for fundamentally the English people have always been incurably romantic.[1] *The Arabian Nights' Entertainments* found a warm welcome when they came in from France at the beginning of the century; so did the fairy tales of Perrault and Madame la Comtesse d'Aulnoy; *The Spectator* recognized the continued popularity of the old heroic ro-

[1] Cf. Raymond D. Havens, "Romantic Aspects of the Age of Pope," *PMLA*, XXVII (1912), 297-324.

mances by denouncing them; oral tradition must have satisfied many appetites to which standard authors refused to cater.

Gothic tastes appeared in gardening, in architecture, and in painting. If you could not go in for antiquities on the Walpole or Beckford scale, at least you could have a ruin set up in your garden—and spend considerable money to keep it in repair! In poetry, as everyone knows, we have Gray and Collins, Ossian and the wonder-boy Chatterton, and Bishop Percy's rediscovery of balladry in 1765. The critics, too, were affected. Thomas Warton's *Observations on the Faerie Queene* (1754) is only a straw in the wind; twenty years later came the *History of English Poetry* in which the same writer set out to trace the origins of romantic fiction in Europe. Burke's essay on the Sublime and Beautiful (1757) enunciated principles the romantics were to find no difficulty in accepting, but the writer who went farthest of all was Bishop Hurd, in his *Letters on Chivalry and Romance* (1762). Hurd was not satisfied to maintain that Gothic art had wonders and beauties of its own, by reference to which, and not by classical standards, it must be judged. He declared Gothic "manners" and Gothic "superstitions" superior to the classical per se. Homer himself would have used them had he had the chance.

Once accept this point of view, and there cannot possibly be any difficulty about finding Gothic "sources." There are Shakespeare and Spenser, to begin with. ("The elder Hamlet . . . was the godfather of the Gothic romance," says Miss Tompkins, "and the weird sisters rocked the cradle of the towardly child. . . .") There is the French Abbé Prévost (1697-1763), author of *Manon Lescaut* and (more importantly in this connection) *Cleveland* and *Le Doyen de Killerine,* who being, unlike Shakespeare, himself an historical novelist, furnished models in kind.[2] Later, when these things have begun to grow tame, "frantic novels" and "sickly and stupid tragedies" from Germany can be added to give the proper spice.

The term Gothic itself has had an interesting history in England. It changed "from a race-term to a sneering-word, from a sneering-word to a cool adjective, from a cool adjective to a cliché in criti-

[2] Cf. Benjamin M. Woodbridge, "Romantic Tendencies in the Novels of the Abbé Prévost," *PMLA,* XXVI (1911), 324-332; James R. Foster, "The Abbé Prévost and the English Novel," *PMLA,* XLII (1927), 443-464.

cism." Its original reference was, of course, to the Gothic races, which were considered barbarous. Bishop Hurd used it as a synonym for medieval, and so Walpole and Clara Reeve seem to have understood it. But since their self-styled Gothic tales also included elements of supernaturalism and terror, the word came at last to indicate grotesque, ghastly, violent, and superhuman. This usage belongs to the very late century, however, and is not sanctioned by the Gothic romancers themselves.[3]

2. *Horace Walpole and* The Castle of Otranto

The Castle of Otranto (1765) is generally called the first Gothic novel. This is not quite accurate. There are two elements in Gothicism: the historical (or pseudo-historical) and the wonderful. Leaving Nashe and Defoe out of it, and saying nothing of the Calprenède romances and the secret histories which have already been noted in these pages, we shall still have Walpole anticipated by three years, on the historical side, by the Reverend Thomas Leland's *Longsword, Earl of Salisbury,*[4] and by a much longer period, on the wonder side, by Smollett's *Ferdinand Count Fathom.*

Horace Walpole (1717-1797) was the dilettante son of Sir Robert Walpole, the great prime minister of Fielding's detestation. An exquisite to his finger-tips, he shrank from both Fielding's robust realism and the bourgeois tendencies of Samuel Richardson. Architecturally, he carried out his dreams in the ornate magnificence of Strawberry Hill, which is often spoken of as a castle but which was in fact a cross between a chapel and a country-house, decorated with

[3] Cf. Alfred E. Longueil, "The Word 'Gothic' in Eighteenth Century Criticism," *Modern Language Notes,* XXXVIII (1923), 453-460; Clara McIntyre, "Were the Gothic Novels Gothic?" *PMLA,* XXXVI (1921), 644-667.

[4] *Longsword,* in a sense our first historical novel, deserves more attention than it generally gets. It purports to deal with the adventures of a natural son of Henry II by Fair Rosamond, and it involves elaborate intrigue and adventure in both England and France, arranged in a pattern that will not be too unfamiliar to readers of Scott. Leland's preface disclaims depth, historical accuracy, and the desire to force a moral upon the reader. He achieves no particular characterization, and he is given to long speeches rather than to anything that could properly be described as dialogue. Cf. Edward Wagenknecht, "Precursor to Ivanhoe," *Coronet,* I, December, 1937, 15-17.

every species of ornamentation known to the Gothic designers. *The Castle of Otranto* is the literary equivalent of Strawberry Hill.

Walpole put it out timidly as having been "translated by William Marshall, from the original Italian of Onuphrio Muralto, canon of the Church of St. Nicholas at Otranto." The fact that he made no less a person than the poet Gray afraid to go to bed may perhaps have encouraged him; by the time the second edition was called for he was ready to avow authorship and state his aims. He had made, he said,

an attempt to blend the two kinds of Romance, the ancient and the modern. In the former, all was imagination and improbability; in the latter, nature is always intended to be, and sometimes has been, copied with success. Invention has not been wanting; but the great resources of fancy have been dammed up, by a strict adherence to common life.

In other words, Walpole realized that his contemporaries had far surpassed the old romancers in characterization. But he also believed that it was possible to apply the new methods to a much less pedestrian kind of subject-matter than any his contemporaries seemed disposed to employ. In the drama something like this had been done long ago. "That great master of nature, Shakespeare, was the model I copied."

The modern reader can hardly feel that he copied very closely. A gigantic helmet with enormous black plumes crashes into Manfred's courtyard at the beginning of the tale, killing the son of the house upon his wedding day, and there it stays, its plumes waving afresh from time to time to indicate the approach of some new calamity. A statue bleeds at the nose; a portrait sighs, heaves its breast, quits its panel, and descends to the floor "with a grave and melancholy air." At the end, the giant who had previously appeared, as one might say, seriatim, is brought upon the scene all in one piece. "The walls of the castle behind Manfred were thrown down with a mighty force, and the form of Alfonso, dilated to an immense magnitude, appeared in the center of the ruins," thus fulfilling the old prophecy (never made too clear), that Manfred's usurping line must be expelled from Otranto when the rightful owner should have grown too large to inhabit the castle.

Most of this machinery is, in Hazlitt's phrase, "matter of-fact impossibility"; it has "no purchase upon the imagination." But *The Castle of Otranto* was a pioneering work. That Walpole himself should afterward virtually have repudiated it is not surprising; that such a man as he was should have succeeded in writing it at all is surely one of the minor miracles of English literature. It is interesting to see how many of the elements of the complete Gothic novel, as it finally developed, are already present in Walpole's brief novel. There is the setting, the castle itself. Mrs. Radcliffe was to describe it more elaborately, and Lewis would enlarge its dungeons, but the primary essential properties are already here. Walpole's hero and heroine are colorless, but they remain colorless in his successors. He has the Byronic villain [5] and (inherited from Shakespeare) the talkative servant, both of whom became stock types; he has churchmen also, though they are not yet depraved. In Manfred's plan to take his son's destined bride to himself, there is even a hint of the afterwards popular incest theme. Above all else, he was fundamentally right in his preference for a real, as opposed to a sham, supernaturalism, as his successors, Clara Reeve and Mrs. Radcliffe, were fundamentally wrong.

3. *Clara Reeve, Sophia Lee, and Charlotte Smith*

Of Walpole's imitators and successors, Clara Reeve (1729-1807) was the earliest of any importance. Her contribution to the renascence of wonder came in 1777 with a story called *The Champion of Virtue*. A year later it was reissued under its better-known title, *The Old English Baron*.

Clara Reeve was a born theorist; *The Progress of Romance* (1785) was one of the earliest attempts made in England to develop a standard for criticism of fiction. She had decided ideas as to what a romance should and should not contain; she wanted "a sufficient degree of the marvelous to excite the attention; enough of the manners of real life to give an air of probability to the work; and enough of the pathetic to engage the heart in its behalf." In *The Old Eng-*

[5] I am not saying that he invented the type; neither did Mrs. Radcliffe, though she has often been given credit for it. Cf. Clara McIntyre, "The Later Career of the Elizabethan Villain-Hero," *PMLA*, XL (1925), 874-880

lish Baron she attempted to show how *Otranto* ought to have been written. The trouble with Walpole is that his

> machinery is so violent that it destroys the effect it is intended to excite. Had the story been kept within the utmost *verge* of probability, the effect had been preserved, without losing the least circumstance that excites or detains the attention.

That Clara Reeve perceived the fumbling quality in Walpole's supernaturalism is to her credit as a critic, but she was mistaken when she assumed that the difficulty could be taken care of by "toning down." There is nothing much worse in the Gothic novel than the scene in which, his light blown out in the haunted chamber, Edmund works himself up to a height of nervous terror under the influence of mysterious knocks and noises apparently of supernatural origin, only to find at last that all have emanated from the faithful Joseph who is just coming in to build the fire! But this is *The Old English Baron* at its worst, and must not be taken as altogether typical.

The theme (frankly repeated from Walpole) is the re-establishment of the rightful heir, and Clara Reeve handles it with a direct simplicity by no means without its charm. She has no suspense, however, for Edmund's dream (which, by the way, is not explained naturally) gives away the solution at the beginning. Nor is there much medieval coloring. The scene of the action is less like a medieval castle than a great country house of Clara Reeve's own time, but in adding a disused, half-ruined, reputedly haunted wing to it she contributed a tremendously important "property" to the Gothic horde. Clara Reeve also attempted straight historical fiction in *The Exiles* (1788) and *Memoirs of Sir Roger de Clarendon* (1793). *The Two Mentors* (1783) and *The School for Widows* (1791) are moral, sentimental tales in a contemporary setting.

A more important historical novel than anything of Clara Reeve's is *The Recess* (1783-1785), by Sophia Lee (1750-1824). The recess itself is a vast underground cavern, equipped with sliding panels, trapdoors, and other exciting paraphernalia, where the two heroines, twin-daughters of Mary Queen of Scots by an imagined marriage to the Duke of Norfolk, are concealed. The elaborate plot defies summary. One girl makes a trip to Jamaica, the other flees to Ireland disguised as a man, to be captured by the rebel Tyrone and finally to lose her mind. History is treated very freely in *The Recess.* Leicester loves one girl, Essex the other; the Armada precedes the execution of the Queen of Scots. The characterization is conventional, but the story proceeds at a breathless pace and is still immensely entertaining. The significance of Miss Lee's work in our present connection may be stated in the words of Professor James R. Foster: "From the crucible into which she threw [Prévost's] *Cleveland* we see emerging traits long thought to be exclusively Radcliffian." [6]

Professor Foster has also called attention [7] to the importance in this connection of a writer we have already had occasion to consider as a radical. Charlotte Smith notably anticipated Mrs. Radcliffe in her use of scene. Her landscapes cover a wide range: England, France, Italy, America; mountains, forests, and fields. Abundant evidence exists in *Emmeline* (1788), *Ethelinde* (1789), and *Celestina* (1791), but the modern reader is most likely to encounter it in *The Old Manor House* (1793), which, excepting the work of the acknowledged masters, is surely one of the best romances in the whole realm of English fiction.

The Old Manor House, to be sure, contains much besides the Gothic element. There are political and social criticism, one really distinguished piece of character-drawing in old Mrs. Rayland, and

[6] For other works by Sophia Lee and her sister Harriet, and for an account of the development of the historical novel before Scott, see E. A. Baker, *History of the English Novel,* Vol. V; J. M. S. Tompkins, *The Popular Novel in England, 1770-1800,* ch. 6; Montague Summers, *The Gothic Quest,* p. 164 ff. James White (cf. J. M. S. Tompkins, in *Review of English Studies,* III [1927], 146-156, and an entirely different study in her book, *The Polite Marriage,* Cambridge University Press, 1938) burlesques both the historical novel and contemporary vagaries, trying to prove "that our forefathers were as foolish as we are ourselves." When the demand for accuracy arrives, it brings mere antiquarianism with it, as in Joseph Strutt's *Queenhoo-Hall* (1808). Jane Porter's *Thaddeus of Warsaw* (1803) and *The Scottish Chiefs* (1810) are closer to our idea of what an historical romance should be, as their considerable popularity still attests.

[7] "Charlotte Smith: Pre-Romantic Novelist," *PMLA,* XLIII (1928), 463-475.

an exotic adventure-sequence in which the hero, fighting in the American Revolution, is captured by the Iroquois and befriended by a young warrior who manifests "the secret sympathy between generous minds."[8] The Gothic elements are plentiful, nevertheless: the old crumbling house, the roaring of wind and the flashing of lightning, the secret passage through which the hero travels on his chaste visits to his sweetheart's room, the supposedly haunted chapel which turns out at last to be only the refuge of smugglers. Corresponding sources of excitement appear in the plot—the lost will, the scoundrels who ingeniously set to work to deprive Orlando of his inheritance, the imprisonment of an indispensable witness as a lunatic (a touch suggestive of Wilkie Collins or Charles Reade), the mysterious disappearance of Monimia. When Orlando returns to the deserted house after his absence in America, the scenery takes on the somber colors of the approaching situation and constitutes a fine piece of atmospheric preparation for the events lying just ahead.

4. *Mrs. Radcliffe, Queen of Terror*

To such an extent has Mrs. Radcliffe's fame now faded that we are in danger of supposing that Michael Sadleir exaggerates when he speaks of her as "the most influential woman novelist there has ever been." In her own day she was "the Great Enchantress," "the Shakespeare of Romance." She was admired, translated, and imitated in many countries, and when Sir Walter Scott appeared on the scene his admirers could think of no higher tribute to his genius than to acclaim him her successor.

She was born, Ann Ward, in London, July 9, 1764. Her conventional education was supplemented by wide reading in romantic literature. She traveled widely in England and made one jaunt to Holland and Germany, but she never saw the Italy where she loved

[8] Many eighteenth-century novelists depict the American scene. Cf. Charlotte Lennox, in *The Life of Harriot Stuart* (1751) and *Euphemia* (1790); Frances Brooke, in *The History of Emily Montague* (1769); Courtney Melmoth, in *Emma Corbett* (1780); Gilbert Imlay, in *The Emigrants* (1793); George Walker, in *Cinthelia* (1797). For Mrs. Lennox, cf. Miriam R. Small, *Charlotte Ramsay Lennox* (Yale University Press, 1935) and G. H. Maynadier, *The First American Novelist?* (Harvard University Press, 1940). For the general field, cf. R. B. Heilman, *America in English Fiction, 1760-1800* (Louisiana State University Press, 1937) and the literature therein cited.

to lay her scenes; her Italy is a dreamland. At twenty-three she married William Radcliffe, lawyer and editor, and it is said that she began writing to pass long winter evenings when his business kept him away from her. She was a small pretty woman, unusually shy, "a little formal, reserved in manner, and too proud to enter any circle where her full equality was not acknowledged." It seems strange that all her books appeared within eight years. Her long silence following the publication of *The Italian* in 1797 has never been quite explained, but there is no foundation for the picturesque contemporary legend that the terrors conjured up by her own imagination had driven her mad. She died February 7, 1823.

Her first book, *The Castles of Athlin and Dunbayne* (1789), is brief and unimportant. In *A Sicilian Romance* (1790), she begins to find herself, but the book is over-plotted and crowded with hair-breadth escapes. *The Romance of the Forest* (1791) is much better. As the title implies, it belongs to one of the loveliest traditions in English literature—the Robin Hood–*As You Like It* tradition. The deserted abbey in which the ruined, half-criminal La Motte and his family take refuge together with Adeline, the girl so strangely entrusted to their care, provides a splendid background, and while the love-story is conventional enough, the tortured La Motte himself is an interesting character.

Such was the success of *The Romance of the Forest* that Mrs. Radcliffe's next book was awaited with breathless interest. When *The Mysteries of Udolpho* appeared in 1794, it can hardly have disappointed many readers. The plot is loosely knit, but the atmospheric background against which the exciting story unwinds is wide and impressive, and the development of the terror-theme while Emily is virtually held prisoner in the Apennines is masterly.

Yet *The Mysteries of Udolpho* is not Mrs. Radcliffe's masterpiece. That honor was reserved for *The Italian* (1797). Like her other books, it deals with young lovers persecuted by entrenched wrong and terrified by nameless fears, but the malign monk, Schedoni, who pursues them relentlessly only to find his fate involved in theirs, is such a character as she had never achieved before. The posthumous *Gaston de Blondeville* (1826) was distinctly an anticlimax.

Mrs. Radcliffe's historical coloring is of no importance. That is why her first novel, with its medieval setting, failed. She locates her castle on the "northeast coast of Scotland, in the most romantic part of the Highlands," she gives her characters a few Scottish names, and then she imagines she is through. Actually, no matter what her period, she never gets out of the eighteenth century. The past fired her imagination but she never took the trouble to acquire any information concerning it. She is much less the scholar even than Charlotte Smith, who was so proud of her knowledge that she paraded it in footnotes.

But when it comes to developing suspense and terror against marvelously picturesque backgrounds, then Mrs. Radcliffe need apologize to nobody. It is true that we can no longer believe, as we once believed, that no novelist ever had this feeling for background before her, nor yet that she evolved her pictures wholly from within,[9] but that is not important. The point is rather that what she did was done with marvelous skill. And it is greatly to her credit as an artist that passionately as she loved scenery, she never described it for its own sake; we get it always as it inspires and as it intensifies the moods of her characters.

She had a psychological interest in terror, which she distinguished sharply from horror. The first, not the second, is the source of the sublime: it "expands the soul, and awakens the faculties to a high degree of life." We have had a hundred and fifty years of experimentation along this line since Mrs. Radcliffe laid down her pen; no doubt the modern reader will feel that she sometimes lacks subtlety. Long before Emily visits Udolpho, she sees her father, one day, weeping over a woman's picture. Before he dies, he asks her to burn certain papers without reading them. She obeys him, but her eye inadvertently falls on two lines (withheld from the reader) that she knows she can never forget. Later the servant Ludovico disappears from a supposedly haunted room, and Emily herself sees a human face beneath the rising pall on the bed of the late marchioness.

The classical instance is, of course, the story of the Black Veil. In

[9] Cf. Clara McIntyre, *Ann Radcliffe,* ch. 2; J. M. S. Tompkins, "Ramond de Carbonnières, Grosley, and Mrs. Radcliffe," *Review of English Studies,* V (1929), 294-301.

an unused chamber at Udolpho Emily comes across a mysterious picture covered with a black veil. All she knows is that some terrible secret is supposed to be connected with it. After the reader's curiosity is as tortured as her own, she musters enough courage to go back and look at it. She

> passed on with faltering steps; and having paused a moment at the door . . . she then hastily entered the chamber. . . . She paused again, and then with a timid hand lifted the veil; but instantly let it fall—perceiving that what it had concealed was no picture, and before she could leave the chamber she dropped senseless to the floor.

And that is all we are told until the end of the book.

One reason for Mrs. Radcliffe's immense popularity was that she gratified the current taste for terror without ever violating the gentility, the sensibility which the times prized. It is not what happens in her books that terrifies us but only the fear of what may be about to happen. All her heroines are variants of the same noble type; her favorite word to indicate conduct of which she disapproves is "coarse." When Emily is imprisoned at Udolpho her maid gets hungry, but Emily herself is much too refined to think of eating. Prudery actually inspires grandeur in Mrs. Radcliffe's heroines; they achieve an impressive severity whenever they find it necessary to oppose their superior delicacy to the comparative commonness of the pursuing male. And they have the habit of coyly pushing the indelicate suggestion of early marriage far away from them on the basis of wholly fantastic scruples, even when in so doing they let themselves in for much additional misery (and the reader for many more thrills). When in *The Romance of the Forest* Adeline thanks Theodore for his generosity, he replies frankly, "Ah! call it not generosity, it was love!" And the tone of the scene is so delicate that the reader is almost shocked.

Mrs. Radcliffe's extreme sensibility does not help her with the modern reader, but this is not her most serious defect. Her real trouble is that except for Schedoni she created no character who is good enough for her plots. Her dialogue is unnatural, "refined." Miss McIntyre acutely links this shortcoming with the indifference to people which appears in Mrs. Radcliffe's journals and the general impression we get of her life. She was a recluse by temperament.

"The fairies gave her many gifts, but they held back the one which a novelist most needs."

As has already been indicated, her attitude toward the supernatural is unsatisfactory also. It is like her attitude toward the Roman Catholic Church, which fascinated her as an artist and repelled her as a woman. She must have supernaturalism; she cannot get her best effects without it. But since she is a cultured lady of the Enlightenment, she must attempt the impossible task of saving her cake and eating it too. In *A Sicilian Romance,* Madame de Menon does indeed discuss the whole psychic question in a scientific, open-minded way, but the same can hardly be said for Mrs. Radcliffe's own comments in *Udolpho.* Except for *Guy de Blondeville,* where she does have a bona fide ghost, her aim seems to have been to follow the bad example of Smollett and Clara Reeve (not Walpole's good one), and to offer at the close of her book neat naturalistic explanations for all the wonders the reader has met. It was with this in mind that *The Quarterly Review* put its finger on her failure to learn the lesson that Shakespeare might have taught her:

We can believe in Macbeth's witches, and tremble at their spells; but had we been informed at the conclusion of the piece, that they were only three of his wife's chambermaids disguised for the purpose of imposing on the Thane's credulity, it would have added little to the credibility of the story, and entirely deprived it of its interest.[10]

Even where no question of the supernatural is involved, Mrs. Radcliffe sometimes "manipulates" her materials too obviously. When Schedoni is about to murder Ellena, his eye falls on a miniature which causes him to believe that she is his daughter. Terrified, he asks her name:

"Have pity, holy father!" exclaimed Ellena in agony.

"Why do you not say whose portrait that is?" demanded he, forgetting that he had not asked the question before.

"Whose portrait?" repeated the confessor in a loud voice.

[10] In later life at least, her theory concerning the use of the supernatural seems to have been sounder than her practice. Cf. A. D. McKillop, "Mrs. Radcliffe on the Supernatural in Poetry," *Journal of English and Germanic Philology,* XXXI (1932), 352-359.

"Whose portrait!" said Ellena with extreme surprise.

"Ay, how came you by it? Be quick—whose resemblance is it?"

"Why should you wish to know?" said Ellena.

"Answer my question," repeated Schedoni, with increasing sternness.

"I cannot part with it, holy father," replied Ellena, pressing it to her bosom; "you do not wish me to part with it?"

"Is it impossible to make you answer my question?" said he, in extreme perturbation. . . .

Evidently it is, and his "perturbation" communicates itself to the reader.

In *Northanger Abbey,* Jane Austen burlesqued the famous passage in *A Romance of the Forest* where Adeline's candle is blown out just as she is on the point of a startling discovery in the mysterious manuscript she found in her room. Though the most obvious devices are employed here to postpone further reading, Mrs. Radcliffe is still well within her rights as an author. It is at least a question whether she does not usurp special privileges, however, when (as in the case of the Black Veil or the two dreadful lines in the St. Aubert manuscript) she withholds from the reader vital information which the characters are allowed to possess. At the end of the book we are told what it was that the Black Veil really concealed. It was a realistic wax effigy of a human body in a hideous state of decomposition. Emily's single glance left her with the impression that this was the actual corpse of a former inhabitant of the castle whom she suspected Montoni of having murdered. As a matter of fact, however, it was created for another person altogether to aid him in his penance! Thus the most famous incident in *The Mysteries of Udolpho* turns out a gratuitous thrill, entirely unconnected with the action of the book.

5. *"Monk" Lewis and Charlotte Dacre*

No Radcliffian skepticism troubled Matthew Gregory Lewis. Lewis was born July 9, 1775. He was a tiny man, with queer, bulging eyes, like an insect's; a fantastic creature, sexually abnormal. He had a wealthy father and an artistic mother; his youth was precocious and delicately indulged. Lewis knew Paris and Weimar; he was at one time a member of the British diplomatic staff at the

Hague and was elected to Parliament. The fame with which the meaning of life for him was bound up, he sought in poetry, fiction, and drama. Opposed to slavery on principle, Lewis inherited a Jamaica plantation, where the blacks adored him. Returning from Jamaica, May 14, 1818, he died of yellow fever, and was buried in the Atlantic.

Lewis's most famous novel, *The Monk* (1796) [11] was an amazing production for a boy of twenty. Lewis passionately admired Mrs. Radcliffe, whose *Italian* he probably influenced. But though he considered *The Mysteries of Udolpho* "one of the most interesting books that has ever been published," he could not create under its influence alone. He needed the headier draught of continental romances—Schiller's *Räuber,* Kotzebue and Tieck, and the French anti-clerical playwright, Boutet de Monvel. These influences manifested themselves, first, in such descriptions of sexual ecstasy as English fiction had never yet known (so that the law required alterations in a later edition, and the proprietress of a Dublin lending library could defend herself against an irate parent only by pointing out that she had carefully underscored all the improper passages in the book, thus warning young lady readers against them!), and, second, in a sensationalism which balked neither at the physically nauseating nor at the introduction of the Archfiend *in propria persona.* "I wants to make your flesh creep," says the Fat Boy in *Pickwick*. So does Lewis. And few can doubt that he succeeds.

The book is well put together, cleverly at least if not vitally. The use of the fortune-teller to forecast the action was a less hackneyed device then than it is now, and the erring nun's curse on the seemingly impregnable Ambrosio looks forward to his later woes. Lewis has three groups of characters which he develops separately, but all come together in the end. His style is simple and direct, without literary pretensions.

The principal action revolves about this Ambrosio, the idol of Madrid.[12] His sanctity mere pride at bottom, he readily falls into

[11] Not 1795, as generally stated. Cf. F. Coykendale, "A Note on 'The Monk,'" *Colophon,* New Series, Vol. I (1935), 87-96.

[12] He is called a monk and an abbot; actually he is a Franciscan friar and the guardian of a Capuchin house. (Cf. Summers, *The Gothic Quest,* p. 221.) The Gothic novelists are sometimes described as anti-Catholic. They were less

carnal sin through the temptations of Matilda de Villenegas. Lewis's conception of Matilda changes radically in the course of the book: at first she is merely a woman versed in cabbalistic lore; later we are told that she herself is a fiend; and the two conceptions are never reconciled. His passions awakened through her, Ambrosio gives his sensual race the run, and soon turns to the fresher charms of the innocent Antonia, who, though he knows it not, is his own sister. He violates Antonia, having first, in the course of the intrigue, murdered his mother; in the end, both he and Matilda fall into the hands of the Inquisition. To escape the stake, they sell their souls to Satan (who surely had them already!), but Ambrosio has failed to scrutinize carefully the terms of the demonic contract. The Fiend carries his prey to the mountains, and

> darting his talons into the monk's shaven crown, he sprang with him from the rock. The caves and mountain rang with Ambrosio's shrieks. The demon continued to soar aloft till reaching a dreadful height he released the sufferer. Headlong fell the monk through the airy waste; the sharp point of a rock received him; and he rolled from precipice to precipice till, bruised and mangled, he rested on the river's bank.

The subordinate plot concerns young Lorenzo's love for Antonia and his friend Don Raymond's devotion to Lorenzo's sister Agnes, who is forced into the cloister and, though released by ecclesiastical order, detained by an evil abbess to live through almost unreadable horrors in the convent dungeons. Much of the Raymond-Agnes story takes place in Germany, which circumstance gives Lewis a chance to bring in the Legend of the Bleeding Nun. With this fearful being Raymond actually elopes, believing her to be his sweetheart, and it is only through the occult skill of the Wandering Jew, who makes a brief but impressive appearance at this point, that he is delivered from her.

Lewis's brand of sensationalism appears again notably in Charlotte Dacre ("Rose Matilda"), who was influenced by him. She was born, possibly of Hebrew parentage, in 1782, and she died some time before 1842. Charlotte Dacre wrote four romances. One of

anti-Catholic than colossally ignorant of all Catholic matters. Lewis brings the strictly cloistered Poor Clares out into the street in procession; Mrs. Radcliffe has monks and nuns inhabiting the same cloister.

these—*Zofloya, or The Moor,* 1806—has been made available to modern readers through the Montague Summers reprint.[13] It may therefore be examined as typical of her work.

Victoria de Loredani is a cruel young Italian of the type made abundantly familiar to us in the later Elizabethan drama. Zofloya, the seemingly all-powerful Moorish servant through whom she works out her plots and poisonings, turns out at last to be the Devil himself. The last scene of the book is an unabashed imitation of the finale of *The Monk*.

Unrestrained violence does not begin so early in *Zofloya* as in Lewis's work; the first part of the book runs along on a fairly even keel. But the last part more than atones. "Now she clasped her hands, and twisted her fingers in each other," we are told of the disconsolate Lilla, "and now tore, by handfuls, the hair from her head, strewing it in agony over the lifeless body of Henriquez."

Charlotte Dacre is much given to explaining the motives of her characters; if they do not hold together, at least she has fully considered their disparate elements. Yet in spite of its obviousness, *Zofloya* is an absorbing narrative—one of those books that it is easy to sneer at and impossible to put down.

6. *Maturin and the Gothic Masterpiece*

To complete this brief survey of the Gothic Novel, it is necessary to cross the century line (which indeed I have already done for Charlotte Dacre). No less a writer than Shelley completed two romances of terror—*Zastrozzi* (1810) and *St. Irvyne, or The Rosicrucian* (1811). Both were written under the influence of Charlotte Dacre and the poet's father-in-law, William Godwin. But neither is anything like so important as Mrs. Shelley's *Frankenstein* (1818).

Mary Shelley was among the first of the long line of writers who have exploited science and pseudo-science for horrific purposes. Her frame, which may have been due to Shelley's insistence that the book be lengthened, is more than a little clumsy, but the story itself

[13] Published by The Fortune Press, 1928. For further comment on Charlotte Dacre, cf. Summers's essay, "Byron's 'Lovely Rosa,'" in his *Essays in Petto* (Fortune Press, 1928), which includes detailed plot-summaries of all her novels.

still conveys a genuine thrill. Gothic terror and humanitarianism blend in its pages, for society casts out Frankenstein's scientifically man-made monster, hungry for fellowship though he is, and its scorn turns him into a menace. In other words, *Frankenstein* is a "thriller" with an idea behind it.[14]

But it was the wild genius of that eccentric Irish clergyman, Charles Robert Maturin (born, 1780;[15] died, October 30, 1824) that produced the greatest of the Gothic Novels. "If I possess any talent," said Maturin, "it is that of darkening the gloomy, and deepening the sad; of painting life in extremes, and representing the struggles of passion when the soul trembles on the verge of the unlawful and the unhallowed."

Not all Maturin's work conforms to the Gothic pattern. *The Albigenses* (1824) is a historical novel; *The Milesian Chief* (1812) reflects his interest in Irish nationalism; *The Wild Irish Boy* (1808) and *Women, or Pour et Contre* (1818) are studies of character and society. But sensational material is employed in all of them. *The Wild Irish Boy* has a plot which makes Hardy's in *The Woodlanders* seem very tame, and in *The Milesian Chief* we meet a girl who believes herself to be a boy because her mother has told her so, and who goes through all the tortures of believing herself perverted when she finds herself falling in love with a man!

[14] *Frankenstein* grew out of a contest suggested as a pastime in 1816 at Lake Geneva, Shelley, Byron, and Dr. J. W. Polidori being members of the party. Byron's story never came to anything, but Polidori's *The Vampire* (1819) is interesting, especially as the vampire has been strangely neglected in Gothic romances in general. Montague Summers has reprinted it in his anthology, *The Grimoire and Other Supernatural Stories* (Fortune Press, 1936). Mrs. Shelley wrote five novels after *Frankenstein*. *Valperga* (1823) and *Perkin Warbeck* (1830) are historical novels; *Lodore* (1835) is largely autobiographical, and both Shelley and Harriet Westbrook appear in it; *Falkner* (1837) is a complicated mystery story; *The Last Man* (1826), the most remarkable of the group, takes us to England in 2073. Cf. R. Glynn Grylls, *Mary Shelley* (Oxford University Press, 1938); W. E. Peck, "The Biographical Element in the Novels of Mary Wollstonecraft Shelley," *PMLA*, XXXVIII (1923), 196-219; Sylvia Norman, "Mary Shelley: Novelist and Dramatist," in *On Shelley* (Oxford University Press, 1938).

[15] The date is usually given as 1782, but cf. Niilo Idman, *Charles Robert Maturin*, p. 312.

Women is a much more important book. A mother—a great actress and singer—wins a lover away from her long-lost daughter, for whom she has been searching diligently, and causes the girl's death. The saintly Eva was studied from Maturin's niece, Susan Lea, who died at eighteen. *Women* includes an interesting study of evangelical society in Dublin, and its relentless analysis of motives—to say nothing of its unequaled portrayal of human suffering—mark it as an outstanding achievement of its period. But for the real Gothic thrill we must go to *The Fatal Revenge* (1807) and the acknowledged masterpiece, *Melmoth the Wanderer* (1820).

Modern neglect of *Melmoth* is a strange phenomenon. Despite its complicated narrative structure, the book is not difficult reading, nor should its undisciplined character quite carry the day against it in a country in which form has always been so little regarded in literature (and especially in fiction) as it has in England. Melmoth is the Faust and Mephisto of Goethe rolled into one with strong suggestions of the Flying Dutchman and the Wandering Jew. Having bartered his soul to Satan, he has been roaming the world since the middle of the seventeenth century in a vain search for someone who will exchange destinies with him. Like the genius of suicide, he manifests only to those in the last extremity of man's needs, a sinister figure with eyes "such as one feels they had never seen, and feels they can never forget," and when "the unutterable condition" is communicated the sufferer always recoils in horror.

The contemporary John Melmoth first hears of his frightful ancestor when summoned from Trinity College, Dublin, to attend the deathbed of his miserly old uncle in County Wicklow. After the old man's death, John destroys Melmoth's portrait and reads the manuscript history of an Englishman, Stanton, who encountered the Wanderer first in Spain in 1676, later in an English madhouse. Melmoth himself appears briefly to his descendant, but John does not learn much more about him until a Spaniard, Moncada, who is wrecked on the Irish coast in a terrible storm, tells the story of his life.

Moncada's tale (like *The Monk, The Italian,* and *St. Leon*) is set against a grisly background of monastic life and the Inquisition, and it leads to the fantastic history of Immalee, which Moncada has copied out, in an underground cavern, at the command of a learned Jew with whom he found refuge after escaping from the Inquisition just before an *auto-da-fé*. *The Edinburgh Review* described Immalee as "a species of insular goddess, a virgin Calypso of the Indian Ocean, who, amid flowers and foliage, lives upon figs and tamarinds, associates with peacocks and monkeys, is worshipped by the occasional visitants of her island. . . ." The most important visitor, of course, is Melmoth, and Maturin is at his best in his description of how the unspoiled child of nature grows into tortured womanhood through her love for him.

We see her next in Spain, where she has been reunited, most unhappily, with the parents from whom she had been separated in infancy. In one of the greatest scenes in all Gothic fiction, she marries Melmoth secretly, at an old monastery in the mountains, her hand being placed in her husband's by the icy touch of a hermit who, as she learns afterwards, had himself died the day before. Melmoth reveals himself to her family at a ball, and having killed the brother of Isidora (as she is now called), leaves her with her new-born child to be thrown into prison. The resemblance to *Faust* is very close at this point. The baby dies, and the mother is unjustly accused of having killed it. Her own death cheats the executioner and it cheats Melmoth, who, true to form, has appeared before her at the end to offer deliverance on the old "unutterable condition." [16]

"The Tale of the Indians," as it is called, has twice been interrupted. Aliaga, the father of Isidora, hears "The Tale of Guzman's Family" from a fellow-traveler. In this narrative Melmoth makes the usual offer to a German musician, Walberg, whose family is starving to death before his eyes in Spain. Walberg's wife is to Maturin what Amelia is to Fielding. The other story, "The Lover's

[16] There is one wonderful touch at this point. The priest is trying to comfort the dying Isidora:

"My daughter, you are passing to bliss—the conflict was fierce and short, but the victory is sure—harps are touched to a new song, even a song of welcome, and wreaths of palm are weaving for you in paradise!"

"Paradise!" uttered Isidora, with her last breath—*Will he be there?*"

Tale," a tragic narrative involving the downfall of a great family in Restoration England, is told to Aliaga by Melmoth himself.

With Isidora dead, we return at last to Moncada and young Melmoth, to whom the Wanderer now appears, announcing that the term of his prolonged existence has at last come to an end. He shuts himself up in a room, where, during the night, a terrific struggle takes place. In the morning the room is empty, and there are footprints leading out to a rock which overlooks the sea.

This is eccentric story-telling with a vengeance. (I have told the story at some length because the book, of which a reprint is urgently needed, is very difficult to come by.) The younger John Melmoth lives his own story, he reads Stanton's out of a manuscript, and Moncada's is told to him. Moncada has read (and presumably renarrates) the story of Immalee, to which Walberg's tale and the story of the lovers is merely tacked on. Yet the work as a whole is a performance which no other English novelist can match in kind. It opens with a quite unsentimental picture of rustic Ireland. It has two brilliant terror-tales, each quite unlike the other in tone; with these the idyll of the island contrasts sharply but effectively. The suffocating world of economic and domestic want closes in on us in the Walberg story, and the closing tale brings us into the atmosphere of large affairs.

"There are no quiet scenes or motionless figures in *Melmoth,*" Miss Edith Birkhead has remarked. "Everything is intensified, exaggerated, distorted. The very clouds fly rapidly across the sky, and the moon bursts forth with the 'sudden and appalling effulgence of lightning.'" The timidities of Mrs. Radcliffe never came near Maturin, nor did he need Lewis's coarse stimuli.

The critics have never been fond of Maturin—did he not break all the rules? Both Scott and Byron thought well of him, however, and his *Melmoth* thrilled Rossetti, Victor Hugo, Baudelaire, Poe, Balzac (who wrote a satirical sequel), Thackeray, and Stevenson (whose "Bottle Imp" may have been indebted to it). Like Shakespeare, he himself was an inspired plagiarist; he took what he wanted wherever he found it, but he never fails to make it his own. No doubt Maturin's interest in morbid psychology indicates an abnormal streak in him, but this is not the whole story, and his idealistic attitude toward women is greatly to his credit. In *Melmoth* Gothicism justified itself in a masterpiece.

7. Vathek *and the Oriental Tale*

The Gothic Novel was not the only type which opposed the classical strain in eighteenth-century culture. Another was the Oriental Tale. The Oriental craze—which owed much at the outset to the inspiration of *The Arabian Nights*—affected both England and France. Martha Pike Conant, the only scholar who has studied the Oriental Tale in England in any detail, classifies under four headings the works which appeared: The Imaginative Group; The Moralistic Group; The Philosophic Group; and The Satiric Group. In all except the first the periodical essayists played an important part. Addison's "The Vision of Mirza" (*Spectator* #159) is the acknowledged masterpiece in this field.

The line between Miss Conant's second group and her third wavers somewhat. Dr. Johnson's *Rasselas* (1759) she calls philosophical; the *Almoran and Hamet* (1761) of his follower, John Hawkesworth, she classifies as moralistic. *Rasselas* is a monument of Christian pessimism. The Prince of Abyssinia and his sister escape from the Happy Valley where they have lived the thralls of ennui and undertake a systematic survey of various ways and conditions of life. But nothing can ensure happiness, for "human life is everywhere a state in which much is to be endured and little to be enjoyed." Work, duty, common sense, and the hope of a better world beyond this one—these things alone can bring us through. The narrative interest is not strong in *Rasselas*—even the kidnaping of the heroine's maid by the Arabs fails to excite us—and the Oriental coloring is thin. The book is good reading not because it is "Oriental" but because it is full of Johnson's warm humanity and sturdy good sense.

Almoran and Hamet has much the same earnestness. The contrast between the good king and the bad one is well developed, and while magic is employed freely the really determinative influence is character. John Langhorne's *Solyman and Almena* (1762) never quite makes up its mind whether it is a love story or the history of a pilgrimage in search of knowledge. Mrs. Frances Sheridan's *History of Nourjahad* (1767) is an interesting story detailing the miseries and ultimate enlightenment of one who asked of fate inexhaustible riches and "prolongation of his life to eternity to enjoy them," but when we come to the end to find that all the wonderful events described were part of a gigantic hoax, we do not feel that Nourjahad alone has been tricked. In the essays known as *The Citizen of the World* (1762) Oliver Goldsmith criticized contemporary society from the point of view of an hypothetical Chinese observer who is very nearly the man from Mars.

The two masterpieces of the imaginative group did not come along until the eighties. Clara Reeve's *Charoba* (which was included in *The Progress of Romance,* 1785), is only a short story, but it catches the true spirit of Oriental fantasy. William Beckford's *Vathek* (1787) is almost as fantastic as the life of the immensely wealthy dilettante who wrote it or the "Fonthill Abbey" in which he lived. The Abbey crashed but the book has lived for a long time now, and there are many who admire it greatly. Vathek catches both the horror and the uproarious horseplay of *The Arabian Nights.* There are pastoral interludes also, and it has often been remarked that the last few pages rise to a height of tragic power which Dante alone has surpassed. It is too bad that this impressive close has not been prepared for; the book as a whole is something of a hodgepodge. The caliph Vathek has a palace with five wings (each devoted to the pleasures of one of the five senses), an eye so terrible in its anger that "the wretch upon whom it was fixed instantly fell backward, and some times expired," and a mother, the sorceress Carathis, whose horrible wickedness shames the worst devices of the evil old women of Grimm. Yet with all its absurdities, *Vathek* remains a work of genius, one of the minor classics of English literature.

The Oriental tale in England never succeeded in assimilating native materials or connecting itself in any way with vital English interests; hence it remained a mere recreative novelty. When in the eighties a serious, scientific study of Orientalism got well under way, its day was done. Horace Walpole tried conducting a very gay funeral service in his *Hieroglyphic Tales* (1785).

8. *The Life and Death of The Gothic Novel*

Many ladies and gentlemen who contributed prolifically to late eighteenth-century romanticism do not survive today by so much as a name. The novels of this period are among the rarest of all English books; they were bought for the circulating libraries and literally read to pieces. The survival of seven titles that must otherwise surely have perished we owe to Jane Austen's glorious fun in *Northanger Abbey,* yet for many years, until Michael Sadleir and Montague Summers resurrected them, it was generally assumed that Jane Austen had made up a list of fantastic titles out of her head.[17] The Minerva Press catered to those who would read these Gothic tales in high-priced editions; at the other end of the scale were the cheap "bluebooks" which inherited the old chapbook tradition, and provided condensed versions of even the most famous novels at sixpence and a shilling.[18] "Shockers," old and new, continued to circulate among the common people long after the critics had forgotten that they ever existed.

That must have been an ignominious end, had it been the end. Actually the Gothic influences lived on importantly through the nineteenth century, making important contributions (to take no

[17] The titles in question are *Clermont* (1798), by Regina Maria Roche; *The Castle of Wolfenbach* (1793) and *The Mysterious Warning* (1796), both by Eliza Parsons; *The Orphan of the Rhine* (1798), by Eleanor Sleath; *The Midnight Bell* (1798), by Francis Lathom; *The Necromancer* (1794), a translation by Peter Teuthold from the German of Lawrence Flammenberg, pseudonym of Karl Friedrich Kahlert; and *The Horrid Mysteries* (1796), translated by P. Will from the German of Karl, self-styled Marquis of Grosse. *The Necromancer* and *The Horrid Mysteries* were reissued in London in 1927 by Robert Holden, with valuable introductions by Montague Summers, who also contributed an introduction to a private reprint of *The Mysterious Warning* a year later. This book is now excessively rare. For discussion of these six titles, cf. Michael Sadleir, *The Northanger Novels,* English Association Pamphlets, No. 68, 1927. Jane Austen was not alone in burlesquing such things. See Eaton S. Barrett's novel, *The Heroine* (1813) and cf. Winfield H. Rogers, "The Reaction Against Melodramatic Sentimentality in the English Novel, 1796-1830," *PMLA,* XLIX (1934), 98-122.

[18] On this subject, William W. Watt's delightful essay, *Shilling Shockers of the Gothic School* (Harvard University Press, 1932) is not to be missed. Cf. also Robert D. Mayo, "The Gothic Short Story in the Magazines," *Modern Language Review,* XXXVII (1942), 448-454.

more examples) to the work of the Brontës and the whole Dickens school, and we who are contemporaries of Miss Daphne du Maurier certainly ought not to need reminding that Gothicism can still be made extremely popular and profitable.

With all its extravagances, the Gothic revival was immensely worth while. Miss Tompkins has remarked of Mrs. Radcliffe that "none of her Gothic edifices are ever fully known, even to their inhabitants, whose steps are always liable to stray, as in a dream, into unfamiliar apartments and down crumbling stairways." But is it not very much the same with all of us in this House of Life? And may this not be one reason why the Gothic Novel interests us as it does? Fielding was a very great writer. Yet he says, "I must confess I should have honored and loved Homer more had he written a true history of his own times in humble prose than those noble poems that have so justly collected the praise of all ages." It would have been a very bad thing for the development of the novel had all novelists agreed with Fielding.

The Gothic novelists contributed to the plot-development of the English novel, though they failed unfortunately to connect plot with character. They contributed to psychology in narrative through their interest in feelings of fear and terror. But their most important contribution was the demonstration they offered that "reason" alone could never control English fiction. They set the novel in the presence of the Unseen, fronting squarely that great, impenetrable Mystery which enfolds our little life.

CHAPTER X

THE ROMANCE OF THE TEA-TABLE

> Jane lies in Winchester—blessed be her shade!
> Praise the Lord for making her, and her for all she made!
> And while the stones of Winchester, or Milsom Street remain,
> Glory, love, and honour unto England's Jane!
>
> RUDYARD KIPLING

1. *Fanny Burney, The First "Lady Novelist"*

In a sense, the "lady novelist" existed in England as far back as the novel itself. No doubt it would be possible to argue that Mrs. Behn was not quite a lady. As a writer, indeed, Mrs. Behn was hardly a lady at all.

The feminine point of view in fiction is evidently a highly relative matter. John Cowper Powys is prepared to maintain that no novelist ever wrote from the woman's point of view before Dorothy Richardson.[1] Most readers will feel, however, that the three novelists who are to be considered in this chapter—Fanny Burney, Maria Edgeworth, and Jane Austen—came much closer to expressing the feminine point of view than many of their predecessors. They contrast sharply not only with Mrs. Behn, who tried to look at the world from a man's point of view, but even with Mrs. Radcliffe, who steadfastly refused to look upon it at all.

Maria Edgeworth's was the widest scope among these three writers; Jane Austen was incomparably the finest artist. But Fanny Burney (1752-1840) was the pioneer. She often gets less than her due in the history of fiction, for her fame rests on but two novels[2]—

[1] See *infra*, p. 507, 510-511.

[2] Her two later books—*Camilla* (1796) and *The Wanderer* (1814)—were clothed in "the worst style that has ever been known among men"; they added nothing to her fame nor to the history of fiction.

Evelina (1778) and *Cecilia* (1782)—and neither of these calls for much analysis. Yet she discovered the novel of manners. She established the kind of fiction in which women have since peculiarly excelled.

This does not mean that she wrote for women merely. It means simply that she wrote with integrity. The most intelligent men of her time—and it was not an age noted for effeminate men—sat up all night to read her books.

We today do not sit up nights for *Evelina,* but it still holds our interest. It is precisely the kind of book one would expect to see "date" quickly, for its whole *raison d'être* is to mirror the idiosyncrasies, the peculiar temporalities of London life. But these things are real to us because they are vividly realized in the mind of the girl who comes in contact with them. Miss Burney admired her great predecessors in English fiction, but she wisely refused to imitate them. Her aim was not "to show the world what it actually *is,* but what it *appears* to a young girl of seventeen. . . ."

Daughter of a well-known musician whose house was visited by a wide variety of celebrities, Miss Burney had unusual facilities for the study of character-types. Though she was a backward child in her studies, she began writing for her own amusement almost as soon as she could read; but because her stepmother did not consider fiction a genteel avocation for a young lady, the young author felt constrained to burn *The History of Carolyn Evelyn* in which we might otherwise have read the story of Evelina's mother. She published *Evelina* when she was twenty-six, and immediately became a pet of the Johnson circle. In 1786 she was appointed a keeper of the robes in the Queen's household. The experience contributed some incomparable passages to the Diary which many readers prefer to even the best of her fiction, but it broke both her health and her spirits. In 1793 she married a penniless French refugee, General d'Arblay; she wrote her third novel, after the birth of their only child, in an attempt to help keep the wolf from the door. Ten years she spent in France; in 1812 she was back in England. Nearly a generation afterwards, having outlived her husband, her son, and most of her contemporaries, she died in the third year of Queen Victoria.

Unlike Jane Austen, Miss Burney never precisely defined her gift. When she aimed at magnificence, as in her last two novels, she failed disastrously. Even *Cecilia* suffers from a Johnsonian prolixity.

She had specifically declared her disinclination to transport her readers "to the fantastic regions of romance, where fiction is colored by all the gay tints of luxurious imagination, where reason is an outcast, and where the sublimity of the marvelous rejects all aid from sober probability." But she never really meant that. Even *Evelina* has a silly mystery which must be cleared up before the heroine can establish her identity in her father's eyes. And *Cecilia* has much more of what I presume Miss Burney must have considered imagination.

There may be some difference of opinion concerning the sequence of events which culminate in the spectacular suicide at Vauxhall of the heroine's gamester-guardian, Mr. Harrel. But surely nobody now admires the scene by which Miss Burney was willing to have *Cecilia* stand or fall—the description of the long contest of wills between Mrs. Delville and her son, which ends as the mother cries, "My brain is on fire," and forthwith bursts a blood-vessel! Nor would anyone defend the lingering Richardsonian ending in which the heroine is temporarily driven mad by an ingeniously-contrived arrangement of very unnecessary sorrows. Miss Burney may not have cared for the romances, but she never realized that the kind of thing she could do supremely well was capable of carrying the burden of a novel without adventitious aids.

Evelina and *Cecilia* are similar in plan; the first deals with "A Young Lady's Entrance into the World" and the second presents "Memoirs of an Heiress." *Cecilia* is twice as long as its predecessor and at least twice as complicated. The heroine is older and a bit more sophisticated than Evelina, and the central problem of her history is more serious. In craftsmanship, *Cecilia* is much the better book, but it lacks the spontaneity of its predecessor, and its character-types are more deliberately "arranged." The hero, however, comes much closer to reality. If we are to accept Evelina's Orville at all, we must accept him as a seventeen-year-old girl's dream of the perfect lover, never as an objective portrait.

But in neither book is the plot the important thing; what counts is the way the author puts her heroines through the paces of fashionable London life. There is probably no place where Londoners can go which they do not visit, and there are not many types of human being, male or female, that they do not meet. Of course Miss Burney is not uniformly successful in presenting these. Evelina's coarse grandmother, Madame Duval, she makes only a monstrosity, and when she comes to the sea dog, Captain Mirvan, she simply throws up the sponge. It would be very unseemly for a young lady to attempt a realistic portrayal of a coarse man whose every other word was an oath.

Yet Fanny Burney was not afraid of vulgarity—the Branghtons fairly set one's teeth on edge—and she was not afraid of reality. Gamaliel Bradford complains of her Diary that "she was always flying out of life to preserve it—in syrup." In her novels, she uses syrup sometimes in her high-toned love-scenes but never when she is concerned with character-types. For her time, she was a very unsentimental writer. She is so determined that the hero and heroine of *Cecilia* shall neither "be plunged in the depths of misery, nor exalted to *unhuman* happiness," that she makes the end of the book almost cynical. There are practical jokes also that shock us in their unabashed reflection of eighteenth-century brutality, and Professor Will T. Hale has pointed out the total absence on Fanny's part of that tenderness toward eccentrics that so charms us in Dickens.

Dickens is quite apropos here, for Miss Burney's is the method which Smollett learned from Ben Jonson and which Dickens was to lift above itself by pouring into it all the manifold resources of one of the richest creative gifts the world has ever known. ("She constructed her personages," says M. E. Christie, "not from within [as is the modern fashion] but by means of a thousand minute touches showing their conversation and behavior in an infinite variety of such small circumstances as make up the daily round of existence.") And she lacked more than Dickens's sympathy; she lacked his range. The first time Mr. Meadows is bored we are amused, but the performance is less impressive the fifth or sixth time he goes through it. This, indeed, is what is meant by the common criticism that *Cecilia* is too long. By the time she finished it, Miss Burney had nothing more to give the novel; she had almost completed her contribution, indeed, with *Evelina.*

2. *The Work and Influence of Maria Edgeworth*

Like Wilkie Collins in the mid-nineteenth century, Maria Edgeworth (1767-1849) exerted an important influence on a number of writers who were much greater than she was herself. Before her time the peasant's main function in literature had been to furnish comic relief. She pointed the way to a more penetrating treatment. From her conscientious, sympathetic study of provincial life and manners both Scott and Turgenev derived the inspiration for the same characteristic element in their own work. Her contribution to the "local color" movement was, therefore, very great, but this is not her only claim. She contributed outstandingly to the international novel and the family-history chronicle (she is, indeed, often said to have created them), and at least one authority would credit her besides with having given "new shape and importance to the short story." Finally, in *Castle Rackrent,* she anticipated Henry James's favorite device of establishing the comparatively detached "point of view" of a minor character and viewing her material consistently from this angle.

Originally an English family, the Edgeworths had crossed the Irish Sea as far back as 1583, but Maria was born in Oxfordshire, and did not come to "Edgeworthstown" to live until she was sixteen. Mistaken critics sometimes rejoice in the "detachment" this circumstance lent her work. One cannot be detached from something one has never possessed. Maria Edgeworth wrote of her neighbors as intelligently and sympathetically as an outsider can.

Her father, Richard Lovell Edgeworth, has already entered this chronicle in connection with his no less eccentric friend, Thomas Day. Edgeworth was much given to ingenious contraptions; at least one visitor to Edgeworthstown was afraid to close the lock he had placed on her bedroom door lest she should never be able to get it open again! He and his daughter lived and worked in perfect harmony: Maria began her career by helping him with his treatise on *Practical Education,* and he was almost a collaborator on her novels. His influence is generally thought to have been bad, but it is by no means certain that he contributed only didacticism, and it may be of some significance that the one long novel Maria Edgeworth published after his death, *Helen,* is not among her best books.

In a sense, Maria Edgeworth belongs with the educational novelists who have been discussed in Chapter VIII. It was only the humanitarian side of the Revolution that touched her, however; she was quite indifferent to politics, and she was always less preoccupied with the "rights" of man than with his duties. "All the world, according to Maria Edgeworth," says Miss F. V. Barry, "was a School, the men and women merely pupils." But she adds: "What made this tolerable was the fact that she thought of School as an Adventure."

It is good to know that in her early days Maria had loved the Gothic romances she afterwards scorned, and that one character in an unpublished story owned "a mask made from the dried skin taken from a dead man's face, which he put on when he wished to be disguised, and which he at other times kept buried at the foot of a tree"! There is not much romance in her mature work, however, and her religion is largely morality, as free of mysticism as it is innocent of dogma. Jeremy Bentham's utilitarianism had indeed got a strong hold on her, and she just missed being dry and arid by her kindness of heart, her sweet, unselfish nature, and a personal charm that made everyone forget that this tiny woman who reminded Scott of "Whippity Stourie, the fairy so much renowned in Scottish nurseries," had, even in her youth, been quite free of personal beauty.

Of all her books, *Castle Rackrent* (1800) is the one which most flatters our preconceptions of what a work of fiction ought to be. It is unique in its time, this quiet, objective, undidactic—almost amoral—picture of a family of Irish gentry steadily destroying itself under four successive masters. We do not forget the litigious Sir Murtagh ("Out of forty-nine suits which he had, he never lost but seventeen . . ."), nor yet Sir Kit, the gambler, who locks up his Jewish wife for fourteen years when she refuses to surrender her jewels. "And it was a shame for her, being his wife, not to show more duty," says Thady, the old steward-narrator, and a superb example of indirect characterization, "not to have given it up when he condescended to ask so often for such a bit of a trifle in his distresses, especially when he all along made it no secret he married for money." Maria Edgeworth was not the historian of the tea-table in *Castle Rackrent,* but she *was* a poet in the sense in which Rupert Brooke defined the term: "It consists in just looking at people and things in themselves—neither as useful nor moral nor ugly nor anything else; but just as being."

Ennui (1809), *The Absentee* (1812), and *Ormond* (1817) are generally spoken of as Irish novels. Actually, each has an international setting, but good native materials appear in all of them. Nothing in *Castle Rackrent* is more impressive than the squalor and suffering of the peasants, under rapacious agents, on the neglected estates of luxurious absentee landlords, in the two first books named, nor does the strong propaganda element involved interfere at all with the realism of the picture. In *Ormond,* Cornelius O'Shane, self-styled King of the Black Isles, is an eccentric worthy of Smollett.

But in all these books Maria Edgeworth does what she refused to do in *Castle Rackrent:* she uses conventional novel-motifs freely. Unlike the Rackrent people, for example, the Clonbronys of *The Absentee* do not meet the ruin they deserve. The last part of *Ormond* takes the hero off to Louis XV's Paris, and we get a topical picture of French society life, indistinguishable in tone from Miss Edgeworth's studies of social life in England.

The English novels are largely in the Burney manner. The picture of contemporary life and morals presented in them is not unimpressive; many passages recall the study of the breakdown of established standards which the post-war novelists of the nineteen-twenties presented. *Leonora* (1806) excoriates fashionable sensibility. The author develops naturally the interesting situation of the French coquette who started out with nothing more in mind than having a flirtation with Leonora's husband, only to be caught in her own trap, but the dénouement is artificial. *Vivian* (1812), though it uses some of the time-honored devices of melodrama, still remains a rather strong, grim study of a man who had a wishbone where a backbone ought to be. *Patronage* (1814) is a contrasted study of two families; one looks to patronage for advancement while the other relies on the exertions of its members. *Harrington* (1817) was written to apologize to Jews for the harsh portrait of the money-lender, Mordecai, in *The Absentee*. (Incidentally, the hero's Jewish sweetheart turns out to be a Christian, after all!) The opening scenes of *Harrington,* which show how an ignorant nurse and other prejudiced persons create fear and hatred toward an alien race in the mind of a little boy looks forward to Dickens's studies of childhood in *Oliver Twist* and elsewhere; and the book connects with another Dickens novel, *Barnaby Rudge,* when it comes to describe the "No Popery" riots of 1780.

Belinda (1801) and *Helen* (1834) probably deserve more extended comment. *Belinda* was the first of the English novels, and it has always been the most famous. It has the same theme as *Evelina,* a girl's introduction to fashionable life in London. But it suffers from a divided unity. Because Lady Delacour, the society woman to whom Belinda is entrusted, is surrounded with mystery, we are more interested in her than we are in the heroine. The mystery is soon dispelled. Lady Delacour, angered by her husband's neglect, has abandoned herself to reckless living, and a man she sincerely esteemed has been killed in a duel as the result of her folly. In addition to all this, she believes herself to be dying of an incurable disease. After this delusion is cleared away, both she and her husband reform. Not only is this change unconvincing in itself, but it necessitates the development of a new interest in the second half of the book. Belinda loves Clarence Hervey, a somewhat trifling Grandison, but Hervey fancies he has an obligation to a "child of nature" whom, like Thomas Day, he had adopted in a fit of Rousseauistic idealism. The scandalmongers view the situation as anything but an ideal one, and not until the end of the book are the misunderstandings cleared away.

The first part of *Helen* is mostly talk; the book seems to have no skeleton. The last part is much better. Helen herself is much too perfect to seem convincing, but there is reality in her friend, Lady Cecilia Clarendon. Lady Cecilia is married to a man (the author evidently regards him as quite perfect) who insisted that his bride must be completely virginal, not only in body but in mind. She never found the courage to tell him that she herself had been briefly, though innocently, infatuated with a roué. Now the roué is dead, and his memoirs, with some of Cecilia's letters in them, are about to be published. To save herself, Cecilia permits Helen to take the blame for her indiscretion, even though the girl's own romance with another male paragon must thus be endangered. The theme of social scandal is very striking in this novel, but Miss Edgeworth loads all the dice against Cecilia. One false step leads inevitably to all the others. I am afraid life is neither so logical nor so decent as Miss Edgeworth would have it.

Maria Edgeworth's short stories hardly fall within our province here, nor yet the tales for children. Saintsbury dismisses those who do not like the latter as "idle paradoxers, ill-conditioned snarlers at things clean and sweet, or fools pure and simple"! And indeed one does not envy the child who has never encountered "Simple Susan," "Rosamond and the Purple Jar," and "Waste Not, Want Not; or, Two Strings To Your Bow." In the best sense of the term, Maria Edgeworth was always a child-like person. She loved children dearly and knew them well—her father's four prolific wives took care of that!—and she wrote for them as "experimentally," as "scientifically" as Lucy Sprague Mitchell and her associates at the Bureau of Educational Experiments today. It was a neat little sideline for the woman who may be said to have created Irish fiction.

3. *The World and Jane Austen*

The tea-table novel would still have justified itself abundantly had it done nothing more than prepare for Jane Austen. Responsible critics have compared "England's Jane" to Chaucer, Shakespeare, and Molière, to Mozart, to Vermeer, and to sunshine. She has, it is true, her enemies—Charlotte Brontë, Madame de Staël, Mark Twain, Alice Meynell, Owen Wister's *Virginian,* and H. G. Wells in *The Brothers*—but, formidable as they are, the weight of critical opinion is overwhelmingly against them.

She is perhaps the star example to refute the thesis that it is impossible to be a great novelist without having had a wide experience of life. She was born, a clergyman's daughter, at Steventon, in Hampshire, December 16, 1775. She moved, with her family, to Bath, Southampton, and Chawton, finally to Winchester, where,

July 18, 1817, she died. In an age when class distinctions were sharper than they are today, and when, in rural England at any rate, life seemed less threatened by change, her days ran along quietly in the contented world of the country gentry and the upper middle class.

To this world, as a writer, she confined herself absolutely. Her brother narrowly missed Trafalgar; her cousin's husband actually died in Paris on the guillotine. Though her indifference to such matters has often been exaggerated,[3] they are not important for her fiction. Her creative range was limited to humanity in its social—more particularly, in its family—relationships.

The literary world of her time never knew Jane Austen; except at the end, when the Prince Regent took her up, she had virtually no encouragement outside her own family. She never needed it. She worked in the family sitting-room, scribbling on small pieces of paper which could be hastily shoved under a blotter if need arose. Nobody ever suggested a subject to her except the librarian at Carlton House, and he wanted her to write "an historical romance illustrative of the august House of Cobourg"!

> I could no more write a romance than an epic poem [she replied]. I could not sit down seriously to write a serious romance under any other motive than to save my life; and if it were indispensable for me to keep it up and never relax into laughing at myself or at any other, I am sure I should be hung before I had finished the first chapter.

But she was as fastidious as she was modest. A painter of two-inch ivory miniatures she calls herself. Her major novels are only six in number and some of them were extensively rewritten.[4] In time- and place-relationships her exactitude stands comparison with

[3] Cf. Laura M. Ragg, "Jane Austen and the War of Her Time," *Contemporary Review*, CLVIII (1940), 544-549.

[4] Jane Austen's major novels were published in the following order: *Sense and Sensibility* (1811); *Pride and Prejudice* (1813); *Mansfield Park* (1814); *Emma* (1816); *Northanger Abbey* and *Persuasion* (together, posthumously, 1818). But these dates are misleading. *Sense and Sensibility* was written, as *Elinor and Marianne,* in the form of letters, about 1795. Recast in 1797-1798, it was further revised in 1809-1810. *Pride and Prejudice,* originally *First Impressions,* seems to date from 1796-1797, and to have been revised in 1812. *Northanger Abbey* was first called *Susan,* 1797-1798. Revised, it was accepted by a publisher in 1803, but not printed.

Fielding's or with Emily Brontë's. More than one critic has observed—and the figure suits her admirably—that she never drops a stitch.

Like Fielding, too, and again like Thackeray, Jane Austen began with burlesque. The juvenilia first printed not so many years ago in *Volume the First* and *Love and Freindship* [sic!] contain some of the most delightful nonsense in English literature. Nor are they unrelated to her maturer work.[5] *Sense and Sensibility* excoriates the sentimental novel; *Northanger Abbey* attacks the Gothic school. But here we must pull up sharply. For nothing could be more absurd than to assume that because Jane Austen burlesqued Mrs. Radcliffe and her contemporaries she must have disliked their books. Critics have made the same mistake here that has sometimes been made concerning her personality. And the latter point had better be cleared up first.

In her first three novels particularly, and even more in her letters, Jane Austen has enough sharp, "smart" judgments to outfit a new Dorothy Parker. So she has been called a cynic and a Heine in petticoats. Specifically, she has been reproached as irreligious and cold-hearted toward children. Yet we have irrefutable evidence that she was charming to live with and that children adored her. Surely Emma's dancing with the disappointed boy in *The Watsons,* after Miss Osborne has rudely snubbed him, is one of the most gracious incidents in fiction!

Jane Austen saw life from the satirist's angle. She did not agree with Mrs. Johnson, of *Lady Susan,* that "facts are such horrid things!" and she could perceive neither honor nor charity in calling black white. Her sense of honor, indeed, is one of her most striking characteristics; it is one of the few masculine qualities she has. Yet her tolerance extends to many personages whom the reader finds it hard to embrace—("I am going to take a heroine," she wrote of Emma Woodhouse, "whom no one but myself will much like"); and Elizabeth Bennet speaks for her creator as well as herself when she says, "I hope I never ridicule what is wise or good." Disillu-

[5] Cf. Annette B. Hopkins, "Jane Austen's 'Love and Freindship': A Study in Literary Relations," *South Atlantic Quarterly,* XXIV (1925), 34-49, and "Jane Austen the Critic," *PMLA,* XL (1925), 398-425.

sioned skeptics who rally round Miss Austen's banner display, indeed, in this connection, all the customary obtuseness of skepticism. She was as moral, she was as reverent fundamentally as Maria Edgeworth herself, though, to be sure, she was much less in earnest.[6] The fundamental moral and religious postulates she took absolutely for granted; unlike her descendants, she did not, therefore, find it necessary to start from scratch on a fresh examination of them every time she put pen to paper. She was free in a sense in which the emancipates never know freedom; her creative energies were released for other tasks.

To come back, now, to her attitude toward fiction. She tells us specifically that she and her family were "great novel-readers and not ashamed of being so." I think she was no more ashamed to enjoy Mrs. Radcliffe than many a cultivated person is today to gulp down a detective story or a hair-raising ghost story or a rollicking blood-and-thunder romance. When it came to creating on her own there was a different tale to tell, though even here it is possible to trace the influence of the fiction she is supposed to have abhorred.

She has a great time in *Northanger Abbey* with Catherine Morland, herself the antithesis of Mrs. Radcliffe's fine ladies, whose head has been so turned by reading novels that when she comes to the Abbey on a stormy, romantic night, she must needs go through all the drawers in the old cabinet until in the very last she finds a mysterious document. Precisely as in *A Romance of the Forest,* her candle blows out as she is about to read it; the next morning she

[6] Some passages might throw doubt even upon this reservation. Her preference for Richardson over Fielding on grounds of delicacy and her criticism of the *Spectator's* coarseness are hard morsels to swallow. Apparently she saw nothing wrong in playing cards for money, but "Sunday travelling" is a serious item in the indictment Anne Elliott draws up against Henry. The reader of today is likely to find the moral tempest awakened by the private theatricals in *Mansfield Park* more than a little silly, but in order to judge this situation fairly it is necessary to understand what *Lovers' Vows* (Mrs. Inchbald's adaptation of Kotzebue's *Das Kind der Liebe*) meant to Jane Austen's contemporaries and what object she had in mind in introducing it here. The play itself may be read in Chapman's edition of *Mansfield Park;* cf. also M. A. Pink, *XIX Century and After,* CII (1927), 125-134; William Reitzel, *Review of English Studies,* IX (1933), 451-456; E. M. Butler, *Modern Language Review,* XXVIII (1933), 326-337, and H. W. Husbands' reply, *Modern Language Review,* XXIX (1934), 176-179.

finds it to be a laundry-list! Even more outrageous are her suspicions that her host, General Tilney, has murdered his wife, or, at the very least, that he keeps her in solitary confinement in some out-of-the-way corner of the Abbey. Yet *Northanger Abbey* as a whole is aimed much less at Mrs. Radcliffe than at her credulous, undiscriminating readers; and the model young Henry Tilney carefully repudiates the idea that serious men of good taste do not read fiction, and praises the author of *The Mysteries of Udolpho* specifically and intelligently. What is even more to the point is the fact that *Northanger Abbey* develops a neat little mystery of its own before we have done with it, and the same thing is true of several others among Jane Austen's books.

Furthermore, it cannot honestly be claimed that Jane Austen is always superior to Mrs. Radcliffe in the way she manages the resolution of her plots. She misleads us in *Emma* concerning Frank Churchill's secret engagement to Jane Fairfax. I know she is preparing a surprise; I know, too, that the situation is viewed largely through Emma's eyes; yet I find it very hard to swallow what Frank has to say about the hair and the complexion of the girl he loves! Towards the close of *Sense and Sensibility* Elinor believes herself to have lost Edward Ferrars. He loves her, but he has felt honor-bound to be true to his engagement with the odious Lucy Steele. Elinor is told, first, that Lucy is now Mrs. Ferrars, then that she is not Mrs. *Edward* Ferrars, but Mrs. *Robert* Ferrars, for at the last minute the minx decided that Edward's worthless brother had more than himself to offer her. Elinor finds this easy solution, so accommodatingly arranged for her convenience, "unaccountable," and the reader agrees with her. The clumsy business of Mrs. Smith, in *Persuasion,* is even more unpardonable. Many a Gothicist cleared up far more vital matters with less to-do.

4. *Jane Austen's Characterization*

Humpty Dumpty is the patron saint of those who feel that Jane Austen's character-range is narrow:

> "I shouldn't know you again if we *did* meet," Humpty Dumpty replied, in a discontented tone, giving her one of his fingers to shake; "you're so exactly like other people."

"The face is what one goes by, generally," Alice remarked, in a thoughtful tone.

"That's just what I complain of," said Humpty Dumpty. "Your face is the same as everybody has—the two eyes, so—" (marking their places in the air with his thumb) "nose in the middle, mouth under. It's always the same. Now if you had the two eyes on the same side of the nose, for instance—or the mouth at the top—that would be *some* help."

Jane Austen has many eccentrics in her supporting casts, but with her principals she never chooses the easiest way. It is true that such energetic, capable girls as Elinor Dashwood, Elizabeth Bennet, and Emma Woodhouse have much in common. So have the more passive, gentle girls, like Fanny Price and Anne Elliot. But no reader is ever in danger of confusing Elinor with Elizabeth or Anne with Fanny. Mr. Collins and Mr. Elton are both clergymen, and both are contemptible, but neither owes anything to the other. We hate Lady Catherine de Bourgh, and we hate Lady Denham, of *Sanditon*. But we keep for each the particular hatred that is all her own.

Jane Austen's heroines were very real to her; she used to look for their portraits when she went to exhibits. "I must confess," she writes of Elizabeth, "that I think her as delightful a creature as ever appeared in print, and how I shall be able to tolerate those who do not like *her,* at least, I do not know." But she keeps her feet on the ground—and theirs. In general, "pictures of perfection" made her "sick and wicked." Elizabeth's singing is "pleasing, though by no means capital." She has a physical energy very uncommon in the novels of the period. She goes out walking in very unladylike fashion; she is not a bit afraid of getting wet or dirty. And Catherine Morland commits *faux pas* upon *faux pas,* but without forfeiting our sympathy.

As for the men, it would be unfair to suggest that Jane Austen was not successful with them. They are, however, less complete than her women. She presents men in a woman's world, sees them as they appear in a woman's eyes; and there is something in every man that no woman ever sees. So scrupulous is she about keeping within the range of her own knowledge that she never writes a scene in which men alone appear. There is always a woman present, and the scene is described from the woman's point of view.

Of course it would be absurd to say that Jane Austen never fails in characterization. Margaret, the youngest sister in *Sense and Sensibility,* never comes to life at all; Mary Bennet is a caricature. Jane Fairfax fails for a different reason; she is kept in the background too long; we never come to realize her. In *Mansfield Park,* Henry Crawford's seduction of Maria is not too convincing. Probably Jane Austen designed him as a conventional villain. But she made the mistake of vitalizing him; she even gave him a certain charm; and when she forced him back into the role she had originally designed for her puppet, he was unable to turn in a good performance. In *Northanger Abbey* one finds it difficult to believe that the pedantic Henry Tilney would choose a girl like Catherine Morland as a confidante and, later, as a sweetheart. Jane Austen herself seems to have sensed a false note here; she stops to remind us that men always marry brainless girls. Perhaps they do, but she has not made it seem quite inevitable that this one should.[7]

Jane Austen has almost no formal description of her characters; what there is along this line is conventional and unimpressive. Analysis she leaves to the reader; she is satisfied to create.

This creation she achieves largely through dialogue. The influence of the theater probably enters at this point, and especially the influence of those private theatricals at Steventon with which Jane Austen herself was concerned. Meredith observes that "Emma and Mr. Elton might walk straight into comedy, were the plot arranged for them." With some of the minor people, this method leads occasionally to a summary, externalized kind of characterization.

Another notable feature of Jane Austen's art is her ability to set her people forth on their own terms without ever actually identifying herself with them. She is *like* Elizabeth Bennet, but she is not Elizabeth Bennet. She maintains a cool, critical detachment. We are always conscious of the fact that the most interesting character of all will never step on the stage. "Lord, what fools these mortals be!"

[7] Other instances of characters who fail to come off are alleged by A. R. Turpin, "Jane Austen: Limitations or Defects?" *English Review,* LXIV (1937), 53-68.

5. *Her Limitations and Her Greatness*

Janeites have never been able to decide which is the best of Jane Austen's novels. Probably nobody would vote for either *Northanger Abbey* or *Sense and Sensibility,* but each of the others would find its special advocates.

Northanger Abbey is probably the most entertaining book Jane Austen ever wrote, but the fun is coarser in quality from that presented elsewhere. The author's attitude toward her heroine wavers somewhat; she views her satirically and affectionately at the same time. In *Sense and Sensibility* the contrast between the two girls is pretty formal, as is also that between the solid worth of Colonel Brandon, Marianne's true lover, and the flashy, uncertain Willoughby, by whom, for a time, her girlish imagination is enthralled. In her attitude toward morality and emotion, Jane Austen is a true classicist. She is not cynical about love, and she scorns the marriage of convenience, but she believes that decency is more important than happiness, and she knows that though marriages may be made in heaven, they must be lived on earth.

Emma is the book which best exemplifies Jane Austen's irony. Emma is a girl who has a passion for arranging other people's lives, together with a complete inability to understand her own. She breaks up an eminently suitable match between her stupid little protegée, Harriet Smith, and a young farmer, because she believes the Reverend Mr. Elton to be in love with the girl; actually, he is in love with Emma herself. With Frank Churchill she makes just the opposite mistake. Frank is secretly engaged to Jane Fairfax, but Emma thinks he loves her; for a time she is even in danger of loving him in return. She soon transfers him mentally to Harriet, however, and not until the girl confesses her love for Mr. Knightley who had loved Emma in secret for some time, does that wise young lady wake up to the realization that she herself loves Knightley, and that nobody else is going to have him! The development of Emma's character is well-handled. Darcy, of *Pride and Prejudice,* changes, but Emma grows.

Nevertheless it is the story of Darcy's romance with the sprightly Elizabeth Bennet, who hated him for his pride, while he looked down on her for her family connections, which is unquestionably Jane Austen's most brilliant book, and which will probably always be the general favorite. Disraeli was not alone in having read it seventeen times; probably no classical novel is more alive today. *Pride and Prejudice* is an excellent book, too, in which to study Jane Austen's plot-development, for it comprises four romances—Elizabeth and Darcy, Jane and Bingley, Lydia and Wickham (if that can be called a romance!), Charlotte Lucas and the Reverend Mr. Collins—and the book is so arranged that Elizabeth's romance becomes the determining factor in every other affair.

No doubt it is easy to overpraise Jane Austen. Poetry and passion were not within her range, and the lyrical note in her books is thin. "Let other pens dwell on guilt and misery. I quit such odious subjects as soon as I can. . . ." David Rhydderch has counted the kisses exchanged in her canonical works. He finds sixteen in all, with never a lover's kiss among them. Yet no one can doubt that Anne Elliot has deeply loved, or even, in her own wild young way, Marianne Dashwood. Between Anne's deep still feelings and the larger attention given to scene in this last novel, *Persuasion,* it seems as if Miss Austen might have been on the verge of new developments when she died. There is very little tartness in her last three books, and the grotesques themselves—notably Mr. Woodhouse and Miss Bates—are lovingly handled.

When sexual irregularity does skirt the fringes of Miss Austen's world, there is no squeamishness in her treatment of it. Furthermore, her heroines are always honest in their attitude toward love; there is no trace of the libidinous mock-modesty so popular at the time. Very likely her avoidance of passion and her avoidance of scenic background may have been determined in part by her reaction against the popular novels in which these elements were so sadly overworked. A dramatic "scene" she could create with the best of them when she chose. No reader ever forgets the Box Hill party in *Emma* or the private theatricals of *Mansfield Park,* and there is a fine, restrained intensity in Elizabeth's clashes with Darcy and in the picture of the final mutual surrender of Anne Elliot and Captain Wentworth.

Once, in the picture of the Price family in *Mansfield Park*, degradation and squalor came within Jane Austen's province, and she faced it without flinching. The fragment, *Lady Susan,* deals with a thoroughly bad woman; *Lady Susan* is Jane Austen's *Jonathan Wild.*

She never violates the integrity of personality, but she gives herself to no petty apportionment of reward and punishment. She never made the vulgar error of supposing that realism inheres in detailed descriptions of furnishings—nor yet in the detailed description of bodily functions which lie south of the solar plexus. She did not have the impression that unassimilated disquisitions on social, political, and economic theory can somehow enlarge the scope and dignity of fiction. She did know that it is possible for a lady to be a great artist, that in the parlor, as in the prisons and on the battlefield, men are called on for decisions in which every essential quality of character must be tested. Perhaps the profoundest observation ever made concerning her is Robert Morss Lovett's remark that, though she never heard of the Will to Live in its biological sense, her work is still almost exclusively concerned "with a condition fundamental to the future of families and the race, viz., the right mating of individuals." In an age when all our enlightened emancipation has at last brought us to the place where our death-rate begins to equal our birth-rate, perhaps nothing else could testify more cogently to Jane Austen's fundamental understanding of life.

CHAPTER XI

THE HEIGHTS

The Prince, the King, the Emperor, the God Almighty of novelists.

WILKIE COLLINS

1. *The Making of Sir Walter Scott*

Jane Austen's achievement made it clear, though as a matter of fact there were few to realize it at the time, that the strange decline into which the novel had fallen after the death of Sterne was not to be a permanent thing. Her contemporary and warm admirer, Sir Walter Scott, was to bring this comforting truth home forcefully to every man who was able to read.

For a hundred years Scott was almost universally regarded as the greatest of all British novelists, and though this view has now been vigorously challenged, it is difficult to see any very cogent reason why it should not still stand. Scott's careless construction and careless writing may be admitted freely, likewise his frank disinclination to handle some of the intellectual and emotional problems with which contemporary criticism would have the novelist concern himself first of all. But with all his limitations he still reaches heights of tragic grandeur to which few British novelists have even dreamed of aspiring; he is still the only British novelist whose work can, without absurdity, be compared to Shakespeare's.

Like most great men, Scott chose the right place for his birth and breeding.[1] He was born to an old Border family, August 15,

[1] Mr. Edwin Muir, indeed, does not think so. In *Scott and Scotland* (Robert Speller, 1938), he argues that Scott's genius was conditioned unhappily by his northland residence and inheritance. Since Scotland had no homogeneous literary language, no real union of feeling and intellect could be achieved. The "nation which should have formed both his theme and his living environment is irremediably melting away around him"; thus he is inevitably thrown back into the past. It is impossible to do justice in a footnote to the

1771, in romantic, historic Edinburgh. His father, an earnest Calvinist, was a lawyer; his mother was a walking encyclopaedia of old Border lore. In his infancy he was fortunately lamed by infantile paralysis; the active career he always thought he would have preferred to that of the writer was thus closed to him. He became a learned man; he had Latin, French, German, Spanish, and Italian; his knowledge of history and romantic literature was immense. Even his work as a lawyer was of value to him; it disciplined his imagination, and it brought him into contact with a wide variety of character-types. Only his early, unhappy love for Williamina Belsches would seem to have refused to fit into the picture. He soon married Charlotte Carpenter, and the marriage was successful; only, as he himself remarks, those who have been nearly drowned in bathing do not venture out a second time beyond their depth. So far as love is concerned, Scott did not venture much further in his novels than he did in life.

Scott's earliest writings were produced under the influence of "Monk" Lewis and exuberant German romanticism; his first important publication was the great ballad collection, *Minstrelsy of the Scottish Border* (1802-1803). This achievement opened up the world he was to possess in the long narrative poems with which he came definitely into his kingdom: *The Lay of the Last Minstrel* (1805); *Marmion* (1808); *The Lady of the Lake* (1810). But by the time *Rokeby* came along in 1813, Scott found himself writing against the competition of Byron, whose subtle depravity he could not have matched if he would, and would not if he could. So he dug out the first seven chapters of a piece of prose fiction which he had begun and abandoned about 1805, and completed it. It was *Waverley, or 'Tis Sixty Years Since,* a story of the Jacobite uprising of 1745.[2]

closely reasoned argument. I do not accept it. Had Scott not been a Scotsman he would not have been Scott; and I have no more intention of evaluating the novels that have never been written than I have of determining what song the sirens sang.

[2] *Waverley* gave its name to the entire series, which is known collectively as The Waverley Novels. Authorship was not formally acknowledged until 1827. Scott had various motives for secrecy. At the outset he was doubtful of success; he doubted too the propriety of a Clerk of Session turning novelist. Of late some writers have sought to disturb the chronology of the

2. *The Waverley Novels, A Survey*

Waverley (1814) is not the best of Scott's novels, but it does contain most of the essential elements. Very effective contrasts are created by bringing a young Englishman first to the Lowlands and then to the Highlands. There is no end of thrilling adventure, and Fergus McIvor's death for the cause of legitimacy is very moving.

Its successor, *Guy Mannering* (1815), differs in that while the scene is still set midway in the eighteenth century, the interests represented are those of private life. *Guy Mannering* is not important for its plot, which is a conventional story of the missing heir, but such characters as Dominie Sampson, Dandie Dinmont the farmer, Paulus Pleydell the lawyer, and Dirk Hatteraick the smuggler are all among Scott's most memorable creations; above all, there is the gypsy, Meg Merrilies, who was drawn with one eye on the actress Mrs. Siddons.

The Antiquary (1816) moves down to nearly the end of the eighteenth century, and despite the presence of a number of conventional elements, comes considerably closer to realism than either of its predecessors. The missing-heir motif carries over from *Guy Mannering*. Nobody is greatly interested in the love-story, nor indeed in the heir as such, but his thread in the plot links up with another of Scott's great ghastly figures, Elspeth of the Craigburnfoot, who years ago had her share in a great wrong, and who now, in her dotage, clears her conscience and opens up the way for the union of the lovers. Chapter 31—the scene in the fisherman's hut—is surely one of the greatest in all fiction; there is also a marvelous storm scene. The finest character in the book is the old Scottish beggar, Edie Ochiltree, who has more than a little of the spirit of the prophets, and in whom the ancient nobility of his people shines forth.

With *The Black Dwarf* (1816), Scott met his first failure. He designed it originally as a full-length novel, but recognizing that

Waverley Novels; I find their arguments quite inconclusive. Cf., with references therein contained, M. C. Boatright, "Scott's Theory and Practice Concerning the Use of the Supernatural in Prose Fiction in Relation to the Chronology of the Waverley Novels," *PMLA*, L (1935), 235-261.

deformed misanthropes were not his forte, he brought it to an early end. (When it was published, anonymously, as all save Scott's last novels were, Mrs. Leigh attributed its authorship to her brother, Lord Byron). But *Old Mortality* (1816), which with it constitutes the first series of "Tales of My Landlord," more than atones for the shortcomings of *The Black Dwarf*. *Old Mortality* deals with the Covenanters insurrection of Charles II's reign. Here, for the first time, Scott found it necessary to rely on written records—so far oral tradition had sufficed him—but his imagination proved equal to the emergency; only a perfectly sane man could have created the balanced and dispassionate picture of fanaticism which Scott paints here. Graham of Claverhouse is one of the great historical portraits, and the speech on death (Chapter 34) is a justly celebrated piece of eloquence.

Rob Roy and *The Heart of Midlothian* make up the second series of "Tales of My Landlord" (1818). *Rob Roy* was Stevenson's favorite among all Scott's novels. It repeats the *Waverley* formula, involving a young Englishman—somewhat unconvincingly, one must admit—in the Jacobite uprising of 1715. *Rob Roy* has clumsy plot-machinery, elephantine preliminaries, obscure and artificial villainy, but none of this can spoil the charm of Andrew Fairservice, Nicol Jarvie, Rob Roy himself, nor Diana Vernon—Scott's best romantic heroine, "one of the deathless daughters of dreams." But the happy ending of the love-story has not been prepared for; it may have been an afterthought, like Pip's union with Estella in Dickens's *Great Expectations*.

The Heart of Midlothian is often considered Scott's greatest novel. Structurally, to be sure, it is one of his worst. It is very slow getting started, and it "makes up" for this, as the saying is, by going on for a whole volume after the story is over. The Porteous riots, too, while vividly described, do not make an ideal introduction to a domestic drama centering about alleged child-murder. But Jeanie Deans, as Agnes Muir Mackenzie has remarked, "is the type of peasant that helps one to understand St. Joan." She will not lie in court, even to save her innocent sister from the gallows,[3] but she will go alone to

[3] "In the great trial scene Jeanie Deans makes a tragic choice as certainly as Antigone when she scattered dust upon her brother's body; and that . . .

London on foot, to win a pardon from the Queen. Jeanie is an ideal character, but she is not idealized—"the puritan in whom there is neither sourness nor fanaticism," says John Buchan,[4] "whose sane, rational instincts are wholly impregnable, whose severity is for herself alone and not for others." It takes Scott forty pages to tell the story of her journey to London and her interviews with Argyll and the Queen. In that brief space, as Sir Hugh Walpole once pointed out, he has managed to present almost "every sort of human life."

In his third series of "Tales" (1819)—*The Bride of Lammermoor* and *A Legend of Montrose*—Scott is still concerned with his native Scotland (and in the former with the eighteenth century), but his mood grows increasingly romantic. The production of these books coincided with the first serious break in his health; *The Bride* was dictated from a bed of such grueling agony that when the printed copy was first placed in his hands Scott read it as the unfamiliar work of another man.

Brooded over by supernatural portents, *The Bride of Lammermoor* stands, in its tortured intensity, somewhat apart from all the rest of Scott's work save, perhaps, *The Fair Maid of Perth;* and there has always been some difference of opinion as to whether it really is the Scottish *Romeo and Juliet* or merely a masterpiece of Gothic romance. Lockhart, Tennyson, and Gladstone all considered it Scott's finest novel; Emerson compared it to Aeschylus. Scott himself seems to stand, as he so often does, on the side of the enemy —"I felt it monstrous gross and grotesque, but still the worst of it made me laugh, and I trusted the good-natured public would not be less indulgent"—and so does John Buchan, who finds that "it wounds without healing, and perturbs without consoling. Its tragedy is a ballad tragedy, cruel and inexplicable, for the ballads have no

whether with the author we feel she did the right thing, or think with Mr. Bernard Shaw that she should have lied. . . . In the first case the tragedy is . . . a fatal conflict between two great principles, . . . between the love of her sister and the fear of God. If the other be the right view, if she was in bondage to a too scrupulous, superstitious conscience, then the tragedy is that which Aristotle defines." Sir H. J. C. Grierson, "Scott and Carlyle," *Essays and Studies by Members of the English Association,* XIII (The Clarendon Press, 1928).

[4] This quotation and all others from the same author in this chapter are cited from John Buchan, *Sir Walter Scott* (Coward McCann, 1932).

philosophy." It is true that the narrative is hurried and summary at times, and that Lady Ashton is a figure of melodramatic villainy. But I will not admit the strictures often directed against Caleb Balderstone; it is no slight achievement to create a figure in terms of comedy, and raise him at the end, if only for a moment, to the level of tragic dignity and courage.

A Legend of Montrose, which involves the conflict in the Scottish Highlands during the English Civil War, is much less important. The method of treatment is essentially pictorial; the book is a capital romance, presenting an unbroken succession of vivid, thrilling scenes; there are no dull moments in it. But the great Montrose is only incidentally presented, nor are the wild, savage, half-human Children of the Mist the principal focus of interest. Scott confessed that Dugald Dalgetty, mercenary and military pedant, literary offspring of Smollett's Lismahago, led the tale whither he would.

Accumulating romanticism reached a brilliant climax in *Ivanhoe* (1820), where, for the first time, Scott jumped the Border-line and for the first time invaded the Middle Ages. *Ivanhoe* is Exhibit A in the museum of historical romance; it established patterns which are still employed. With it, too, Scott's European vogue began.[5] John Galt and Sir James Barrie are probably alone in placing this book at the top of Scott's bent, though Coleridge is ridiculous when he lumps it with the "Bride of *Ravensmuir,* or whatever its name may be,"—"two wretched abortions." The truth of the matter is that *Ivanhoe* is a tour de force, and that only one character, the Jewess Rebecca, calls forth Scott's deeper resources.

In *The Monastery* and *The Abbot* (both 1820), he returned to Scotland, but this time he did not come beyond Reformation times. *The Monastery* is an indubitable failure. Scott was quite beyond his depth in a novel concerned with Reformation controversies, and the White Lady of Avenel is surely the clumsiest piece of bungling in the use of the supernatural that any writer of quality ever permitted himself. But *The Abbot,* which is a kind of half-sequel, is another story altogether. Scott had refused to write a biography of Mary Queen of Scots "because his opinion was contrary to his feel-

[5] Cf. G. H. Maynadier, "Ivanhoe and its Literary Consequences," *Essays in Memory of Barrett Wendell* (Harvard University Press, 1926).

ing." Centering his fiction about her during her captivity at Lochleven, he was able to yield to her spell without actually committing himself on any of the controversial questions. Most novelists who write about brilliant women are obliged to content themselves by telling us every now and then that the lady is brilliant. Scott does not need to tell us that Mary is brilliant; he shows us. He is indeed prodigal of women in this book; as a young romantic heroine, Catherine Seyton knows no superior save the inimitable Die.

Kenilworth (1821), a pendant to the two preceding books, resulted from the booksellers' plea that Scott do for Elizabeth's reign what he had already done for her lovely rival's. History is treated very freely in *Kenilworth,* and the introduction of famous personages like Shakespeare and Raleigh is not accomplished in a very subtle manner. Elizabeth herself, however, is a fine piece of craftsmanship, a genuine study in temperament. "No historian's Queen Elizabeth," said Thomas Hardy, "was ever so perfectly a woman as the fictitious Elizabeth of *Kenilworth.*" Scott is chivalrous; he gives us "no scandal about Queen Elizabeth," though there is plenty about Leicester, for the Amy Robsart story furnishes the plot. There is much melodrama in the book, but there is some real tragedy also, the finest touch of all being Tony Foster's outcry as he peers down into the vault upon the murdered Amy: "I see only a heap of white clothes, like a snowdrift. O God, she moves her arm!"

The next three books stand each alone. The first, *The Pirate* (1822), goes back to the beginning of the eighteenth century in the Shetland and Orkney Islands. Scott had visited this region in 1814. He gets the feeling of the wild northern life very well—indeed, he had never been more successful in his treatment of landscape—but the story itself is not very satisfying, and the novel has never been a favorite.

The Fortunes of Nigel (1822), on the other hand, even aside from its wonderful portrait of King James I—a fool, yet royal—is one of the best adventure stories ever written. Essentially it belongs with Scott's romances, though it has aspects which reveal the realistic side of his genius. It deals with the Scots in London, and there is a serious study of social corruption during James's reign. Margaret, though a conventional heroine, is individualized, not merely by her willfulness, which is common with Scott's heroines, but also by a touch of bad temper, which is not. The miser Trapbois and his daughter are vivid characters, and the scenes leading up to the old man's murder are wonderfully eerie.

The scenes of *Peveril of the Peak* (1822) are laid in London, Derbyshire, and the Isle of Man, and the action revolves about the Popish Plot of Restoration times. It is the longest of all Scott's novels, and he himself feared it would "smell of the apoplexy." One of its characters, King Charles II (an acceptable, though not a brilliant, portrait) sums up the book's shortcomings when he says, "Here is a plot without a drop of blood; and all the elements of a romance without its conclusion. Here we have a wandering island princess . . . a dwarf, a Moorish sorceress, an impenitent rogue, and a repentant man of rank, and yet all ends without either hanging or marriage."

The next two books were both experiments, the first a gloriously successful experiment. In *Quentin Durward* (1823) Scott first dared to lay his scene abroad, but he took a Scottish hero along with him! His conception of Louis XI, who fascinated him as an artist and repelled him as a man, lacks the complete reality of his James I, but it is wonderfully vivid, and it has remained the dominant conception to this day. Nothing in *Quentin Durward* has any particular reality, nor is it meant to have; John Buchan says all when he calls the book a fairy tale. Quentin himself is "the eternal younger son who goes out to seek his fortune." Louis is "the treacherous stepmother." There are also "ogres and giants," "good companions," "malicious elves," "a warlock," and a "conventional fairy-tale princess." The book is Scott's supreme achievement in an artificial genre.

St. Ronan's Well (1824) has had its distinguished admirers; Balzac, who was strongly influenced by it, put it in the front rank of Scott's achievement. Alone among Scott's novels, it aimed "to give an imitation of the shifting manners of our own time." The book cannot be judged fairly in its present state, for the puritanical publishers refused to accept Clara Mowbray's tragedy as Scott originally wrote it, and he recast the situation disgustedly, warning them that the effect would be "to perplex and weaken the course of his narrative, and the dark effect of the catastrophe.[6] He was right. As the situation now stands it is inexplicable and unbelievable. There are some dark moments of splendor, but the characters seem hysterical and sentimental because we do not understand the nature of the forces which cause them to behave as they do. The vivid, slightly malicious sketches of the "menagerie" at the Wells are much better, however, than Sir Walter thought them, and Meg Dods the innkeeper is one of his unforgettable characters.

St. Ronan's Well was followed by the last great Scotch novel, *Redgauntlet* (1824), which takes Scott back to the Jacobites in the eighteenth century, and of which Lockhart says that "it contains perhaps more of the author's personal experiences than any other . . . [novel], or even than all the rest put together." The tale wavers as to method: part of it is direct narrative; part is written in the form af a journal; part comprises an interchange of letters. *Redgauntlet* skirts the incest theme when Darsie falls in love with his unrecognized sister, Green Mantle; their relationship discovered, she is transferred to his friend, Alan Fairford, with a nonchalance which even *The Two Gentlemen of Verona* can hardly surpass. Nanty Ewart's tragedy, sketched parenthetically in Chapter 14 and later consummated before our eyes, has the stuff of a whole great novel in it. "Wandering Willie's Tale" is one of the greatest pieces of *diablerie* in English or any other language, and if the great scene on Solway Firth, where the sacred cause finally collapses, is not the greatest in Scott, it comes pretty close to it.

Of the "Tales of the Crusaders" (1825), *The Betrothed* is universally condemned—Scott himself nearly destroyed it unpublished—while *The Talisman* has always been a great favorite. Yet the first three-fourths of *The Betrothed* gives promise of leading up to a tragic situation as fine as anything in *The Bride of Lammermoor;* even Damian's illness and Eveline's skill as a healer reinforce the emotional overtones of the situation by suggesting the *Tristram and Iseult* motif. But Scott lacked the courage to develop it logically—probably because this might have involved staining the purity of the Lady Eveline—and the book ends with some romantic hocus-

[6] Cf. J. M. Collyer, *Athenaeum,* Feb. 4, 1893, and E. A. Baker, *History of the English Novel,* VI, 193-198.

pocus by no means in his best vein. Yet Eveline's passionate nature is well-portrayed, Wilkin Flammock, the faithful Fleming, is an excellent portrait, and Rose, Wilkin's pert but courageous and high-souled daughter, is the kind of girl with whom Scott never fails. *The Betrothed* does not deal with the Crusades at first hand; rather, it traces their effect on those who stayed at home. The scene is the borderland of Wales during Henry II's reign, and Prince Richard—not yet king—makes a brief appearance toward the close. Coeur-de-Lion had already played his part in *Ivanhoe;* he reappears full-length in Syria, with his noble opponent, Saladin, in *The Talisman,* which, for all the praise it has received, is merely first-rate swash-buckling.

Scott's next book—*Woodstock, or The Cavalier* (1826)—was written, as we shall soon see, under very difficult circumstances. It is a book of great technical skill and mastery, but remembering that the author was Scott, we cannot but feel that it lacks charm. Scott did not admire Cromwell; as that great man appears in *Woodstock,* he is not always in command of his faculties. But Scott's fundamental decency nowhere shows more attractively than in his partisanships, and John Buchan, who admired Cromwell almost as much as he admired Scott himself, accepted the fundamental accuracy of the portrait. The Prince of Wales, later King Charles II, appears in *Woodstock,* disguised as a page to conceal him from his enemies; Scott's analysis of the faults of his character is in harmony with the findings of modern biographers.

It was while Scott was engaged with *Woodstock* that financial disaster descended upon him. He had for years been publisher as well as author, his great estate at Abbotsford ate up money faster than even he could earn it, and his business affairs had tangled themselves into confusion worse confounded. Too honorable to take advantage of the bankruptcy laws, Scott assumed a debt of more than £100,000, and, as all the world knows, literally wrote himself to death to pay it off.

Naturally the work he did during this final period cannot all rank with his very best, but it is clear that many of the people who condemn it most heartily have never read any of it. Not much can be claimed for *The Surgeon's Daughter,* the longest item in the first series of "Chronicles of the Canongate" (1827). The first part, in Scotland, is pleasant enough eighteenth-century domestic melodrama; the last part, which takes place in India, is nearly unreadable. But both *The Highland Widow* and the short story, "The Two Drovers," achieve powerful drama. Certainly Scott never did anything greater than "The Two Drovers."

The Fair Maid of Perth, or Saint Valentine's Day, the principal item of the second series (1828), is the wildest and darkest of all Scott's books. It begins with the cutting off of a man's hand; in the course of the action a criminal is hanged on the gallows, later to be cut down and revived; Dwining, a really horrible villain, commits suicide; so, probably, does the pitiable Conachar; even the fool, Oliver Proudfute, is murdered in the streets. The hero, Henry Smith, is less civilized than Scott's heroes generally are, a fighting fool whose life is stained with sin, and whose heroic qualities are not always under control. The almost saintly heroine, Catherine Glover, stands out very effectively against this dark background. Scott himself declared that he was impelled to write *The Fair Maid* by the consideration that "no attempt had hitherto been made to sketch [the] manners" of the Scottish Gael. The book is certainly not one of his healthiest productions but it is an experience not to be missed. Of the remaining "Chronicles," "The Tapestried Chamber" is one of the best of all stories of haunted rooms, but "My Aunt Margaret's Mirror" is only fair Gothicism, and "Death of the Laird's Jock" is too far beyond the range of modern experience to move us as it was intended to do.

The Wizard had three novels left to write. *Anne of Geierstein* (1829) goes back to fifteenth-century Switzerland and neighboring countries, and introduces, among other historical personages, Margaret of Anjou, René king of Provence, and Charles the Bold, who had already appeared in *Quentin Durward*. *Anne* goes as far into Gothic mystification as Scott ever ventured, but it is a mistake to regard the book as the work of his dotage; his hand never leaves the throttle.

His career closed with the fourth series of "Tales of My Landlord" (1832). I can find nothing good to say of the pasteboard

Count Robert of Paris; the Byzantine Empire at the time of the First Crusade was no subject for Scott; indeed *Count Robert* suggests Italian motion picture spectacles at their worst. In *Castle Dangerous* he gets his foot on his native heath again, and though the book is no masterpiece, it is much better than *Count Robert of Paris.*

They had taken Sir Walter to the Mediterranean in search of health—a Whig government generously placed a frigate at the disposal of the great Tory—but nothing was gained. Even if he had been well, Scott could not have lived away from the sight of the heather. He died at Abbotsford, September 21, 1832.

3. *Scott and the Historical Novel*

There is, or there has been, a curious impression among critics that the historical novel is somehow an inferior branch of fiction. But Professor Ernest Bernbaum has shown effectively that the modern attack on historical novels has proceeded from "that school of thought which philosophers call Empiricism or Naturalism," and that the assumption on which it rests—"that faith and imagination are not rational uses of the mind"—is really "hostile to all imaginative literature." [7] In a sense it is true that the historical novel encourages shoddy workmanship—it is more difficult to detect an error in a novel of Richard I's time than in one of George VI's—but to say that a form of art is difficult is not to say that it is illegitimate. Moreover, no novel can stand or fall essentially on the accuracy of its backgrounds. To write a really good historical novel, a writer must have the same insight into character that he would need if he were writing about his contemporaries; in addition to this, he must

[7] "The Views of the Great Critics on the Historical Novel," *PMLA,* XLI (1926), 424-441. On the historical novel, cf. also Brander Matthews, *The Historical Novel and Other Essays* (Scribners, 1901); George Saintsbury, in *Collected Essays and Papers, 1875-1920,* III (Dent, 1923); H. Butterfield, *The Historical Novel* (Cambridge University Press, 1924); A. T. Sheppard, *The Art and Practice of Historical Fiction* (Toulmin, 1930); Hugh Walpole, "The Historical Novel in England Since Sir Walter Scott," in Grierson's *Sir Walter Scott Today;* Elizabeth C. Bentley's Ph.D. thesis, *The English Historical Novel Since Scott* (Cornell, 1931); and two cogent papers in Dale Warren's *What is a Book?* (Houghton Mifflin, 1935): "Historical Fiction," by Rafael Sabatini, and "Why the Past?" by Esther Forbes.

have sufficient knowledge and imagination to be able to think and feel his way back into an alien mode of life.

Something has already been said in these pages concerning historical fiction before Scott. The line traces, through Nashe, the French heroic romances, Defoe, Mrs. Manley, the Gothic novelists, and such anti-romantics as de Sandras and Anthony Hamilton, down to Leland's *Longsword* and the later experiments of the Lee sisters, James White, Godwin, and others. With *Longsword* the pattern which Scott himself was to employ would seem to have been fairly well developed.

But the suggestions thrown out by Leland were not taken up by other writers with anything like the avidity one might have expected. Even Scott credits Ariosto rather than Leland with having furnished a model for the technique he used so brilliantly in his description of the siege of Front-de-Boeuf's castle and elsewhere, developing several groups of characters simultaneously, carrying each group up to a crisis, then taking the reader off with him to follow the fortunes of another until that group also is brought up to the moment of crisis.

Scott did not use the past as a springboard from which to leap into a world of fantasy, as James Branch Cabell does; such a writer escapes many obligations. Nor did he go the whole way with Balzac, who in *Droll Stories* actually tried, as R. K. Gordon had said, "to write and feel and think as if he were a Frenchman of the sixteenth century." Scott "is always aware that he is writing about the past, that he is looking at it from another period, making allowances for it, interpreting its strangeness to us."

He had an example of the antiquarian method before him in Joseph Strutt's *Queenhoo-Hall,* which had been left unfinished by that writer's death, but though he tinkered with it and published it, he did not altogether approve of it. The gist of his criticism was that Strutt had overlooked "that extensive neutral ground, the large proportion . . . of manners and sentiments which are common to us and to our ancestors"—in other words, that he had neglected to keep in mind that continuity of racial experience without which neither historian nor novelist can ever succeed in vitalizing the past. Scott himself attempted to exclude the definitely "modern" from his own books, but he felt free to confuse "the manners of two or three centuries" when, as in *Ivanhoe,* it seemed necessary to do so in order to secure a desired effect.

Here, of course, Scott is open to criticism. For while accuracy as such has no value for creative writing, so long as it is the business of the novelist to interpret human life, a picture which is true to the spirit of no time, and which presents a set of characters incited by the motives of no particular period, must always labor under a heavy handicap. When Scott writes of Scotland he never falls under this condemnation, and when he is writing of a period he knows through oral tradition the temptation never comes near him. A modern novelist often gives the impression of having worked up his background a chapter at a time. He is not writing about Mary Queen of Scots, for example, because he is interested in her. He never was interested in her until it occurred to him that she might be a good subject for a novel. With Scott the emphasis is reversed. He had the historic sense as strongly as any man who has ever lived. He saw men as products of the forces that impinge upon them out of the past. He could not possibly have confined himself as novelist to the little hour in which he wrote, for that hour failed to confine his life. Scott lived through his material imaginatively long before he ever dreamed of writing about it; he reached back to tap springs of racial memory. Save when he touches the supernatural, his method is always the good old solid foursquare method of the eighteenth century.[8] But he immensely widened the scope of fiction by adding, as it were, a fourth dimension to it, and that fourth dimension was the vista of time past. Brunetière says justly, ". . . if the sense of history consists in the perception of differences which distinguish epochs, in the thorough knowledge of characteristic details, and especially in the knowledge of the bearing of 'manners' upon customs and usages and laws, it may be truly said that this is what novelists before Walter Scott did not possess."

Scott's kind of historical novel was, it will already have appeared, very different from Hewlett's and from the kind that such writers as Heinrich Mann and Margaret Irwin are producing today. "None

[8] See, in this connection, a heart-warming article by J. R. Moore, "Scott and Defoe," *PMLA,* LVI (1941), 710-735.

of the characters in this book is imaginary," says a note prefixed to Miss Irwin's *Royal Flush* (1932). Scott used historical characters for atmosphere, color, and background; the plot-action was entrusted to imaginary personages whom he might manipulate as he would. As I have already suggested, interesting attempts have recently been made to break away from this method. The results have often been of great interest, but there is always grave danger that the new type of historical novelist may fall between two stools. For what do we use art if not to satisfy the needs which life still leaves unsatisfied? Does not the writer who chooses to make historical fiction mere novelized history relinquish most of the advantages which the novelist enjoys over the biographer? Scott at least ran no danger of that. His method, as C. A. Young observed, "wedded the probability of history to the probability of romance." [9]

And, of course, Scott is not all romancer. It is no romancer who finds his best heroine in Jeanie Deans, and who writes of *Waverley* that "It may really boast to be a tolerably faithful portrait of Scottish manners." All Scott's best interpreters agree upon this point. "He was a realist working in a romantic world," says Sir Hugh Walpole, "a poet transforming a realistic world." "Scott's love of romance is like that of Dumas," says R. H. Hutton, "his love of common life like that of Cervantes." "He combines the substance of the realist with the fantasy of the romantic," is the way Lord David Cecil sums it up: "he had a foot in two worlds and made the best of both of them." And John Buchan generalizes impressively on the basis of General Campbell's words in *Redgauntlet:*

> They are far more effective than any desperate stand or heroic dying words, for they suddenly make the romance a tremendously real thing by linking it to our ordinary life. This seems to me perhaps Scott's greatest gift—the power of taking us to the summits and yet keeping us always cognizant of our homes and workshops in the valley below. . . .

4. *Merits and Demerits*

Walter de la Mare says that a poem is a deed. And Joseph Conrad declares that "An artist is a man of action, whether he creates a

[9] For a reasoned defense of what is, in essence, the Scott method, cf. Preface to Wilkie Collins, *Antonina*.

personality, invents an expedient, or finds the issue of a complicated situation." Had Scott been able to agree with them he might have rated his own work more highly than he did. As it was, he was never able to bring himself to believe that a man who merely described great deeds could ever stand on a level with the man who performed them. It was for this reason and not, as some writers suppose, because his attitude toward fiction was essentially a contemptuous attitude, that he was inclined to place a modest evaluation on his work. It is true that he says, "I was . . . far from thinking that the novelist or romance-writer stands high in the ranks of literature." But he also says that if it is well done the historical novel deserves to rank with the epic.

Professor Hillhouse points out that Scott's own comments "show how consistently the germ or nuclear idea and inspiration of the novels was . . . historical and social. . . ." Scott himself calls the plot "a string by which to draw up a succession of scenes"; and he says, "I must not let the background eclipse the principal figures. . . ." This does not mean that Scott despises plot. He recognizes its importance, and he recognizes his own deficiencies in handling it. But he has found through experience that he writes best when he writes rapidly, that it is impossible for him to adhere to a preconceived plan. Fielding's *Tom Jones*—and "perhaps" *Amelia*—he saw as the perfect novel, but in himself he recognized more kinship to Smollett and Le Sage. "These great masters have been satisfied if they amused the reader upon the road; though the conclusion only arrived because the tale must have an end. . . ."

Modern readers criticize Scott for what they call his "padding" and for his slow approach. The latter is surely censurable when it throws the book out of proportion, or when, as in *Guy Mannering,* he prepares for a situation deliberately, and then decides not to develop it. Yet in the main his instinct was sound; we go slowly while we are winning our way into a story; once we hold the material firmly in our grasp, astonishing speed and vividness can be achieved. In other words, the aria seems all the more brilliant because the tenor spared himself in recitative passages.

Scott felt that dialogue rather than narrative was his forte. The reader of a novel is not satisfied to be told what is taking place (which is all that he would know in life), "but he is desirous, while reading for amusement, of knowing the interior movement occasioning the course of events." That you can only set forth as you permit your characters to talk themselves alive.

What, then, of these characters?

His heroes—and his heroines—are generally condemned. Of the former, nobody has spoken more contemptuously than Scott himself. "I am a bad hand at depicting a hero . . . and have an unfortunate propensity for the dubious characters of Borderers, buccaneers, Highland robbers, and all others of a Robin Hood description." Lord David Cecil explains the shortcomings of the heroes on the basis that they generally connect not with Scott's own particular interests but rather with those of the plot, which he was always inclined to treat more or less perfunctorily. And Agnes Muir Mackenzie points out that when Scott wrote his novels he was a mature man, and his day for becoming greatly excited about romantic love had long gone by.

One might ask the critics, what more do they want in the young hero than Scott gives them? How much more does Shakespeare give? Is not the romantic hero in general, as Hazlitt declares, a kind of blank which the author leaves for the reader to fill in as he pleases?

To any general condemnation of Scott's heroines several exceptions have already been entered in these pages; it is interesting in passing to note the opinion of the authors of *Pamela's Daughters,* who know all there is to be known concerning the heroines of English fiction, and who certainly cannot be accused of any prejudice in favor of the absurdly proper and the sentimental:

> One or two of Scott's heroines are pale and passive; Mary Avenel is one, but such figures are not typical of him. For the most part he gives us vigorous human girls with solid figures, active minds and active bodies.

In character-parts his skill has never been denied. His range is not universal: he has no Hamlet, no Cleopatra, no Iago; no Emma Bovary, no Raskolnikoff, no Alyosha. The dark struggles of the soul divided against itself do interest him increasingly after *St. Ronan's Well.* Had he chosen, he might have won distinguished success here; he was a master of the twilight world, but he preferred the sunshine. Yet he has created literally hundreds of memorable characters, and it would be ridiculous to assume that simply because he believed the novel to be a work of art, not a stamping-ground for Freudian quackery, he did not understand the characters he created.

The case against Scott as a stylist has been stated with great force by the admiring Robert Louis Stevenson,[10] and every charge he makes can be sustained. But I think it might hurt him could he read Virginia Woolf's essay on *The Antiquary:*

> These slips and slovenlinesses are pauses, changes of attitude to uncramp the muscles which give the reader breathing space and air the book. Moreover, it is only perfunctorily that one either notices or condemns them; read currently, in their places, as Scott uses them, they fulfil their purpose and merge perfectly with their surroundings.

Of the great storm scene in this novel, Mrs. Woolf felt specifically that, despite all its clichés, it was far ahead of the more carefully-described storm in *Kidnapped,* which "never so much as wet the sole of a lady's slipper."[11]

But whatever we may say of Scott's narrative style, it is in the great dramatic moments that he is supreme and unassailable. Evan Dhu's offer to die for Fergus, Meg Merrilies denouncing the laird of Ellangowan, Edie Ochiltree facing death calmly on the tide-swept cliff, Nicol Jarvie's refusal to buy his life from Helen Campbell at the cost of perjury, Jeanie Deans's plea to Queen Caroline—these things can die only with the language in which they were written.

5. *The Soul of Sir Walter*

John Buchan has a fine phrase for Scott: "He stood at the heart of life." Yet his character was not simple. He was an astonishing combination of the practical man and the dreamer, of sensibility and stoicism, of sickness and health. He did not manage his business life wisely, and he immolated himself to atone. But he was not a greedy man. Business was an outlet for his energy and a means of giving employment to many needy people. Abbotsford was a poem

[10] Cf. "A Gossip on Romance," in *Memories and Portraits.*

[11] *New Republic,* XLI (1924), 42-43.

in stone. He had never felt that art could take the place of life; he had to live the life of the medieval Scotch laird as well as write about it.

Scott has suffered, as George Washington has suffered, from the admiration of hysterical and sentimental adorers. All the life runs out of such a man as soon as one seeks to canonize him; this never happens with the true saints. Scott understood sainthood; Henry Warden's rash testimony before Julian Avenel in *The Monastery* and the contrast in *The Fair Maid of Perth* between Father Clement's absolute loyalty to the spiritual ideal and the worldly caution of the worthy Samuel Glover are alone enough to show that. But he did not desire sainthood for himself; he was a Border laird; his ideal was that of an honorable man of this world.

His Christian faith was absolute and unwavering; he had no more doubt of God or Christ or immortality than he had doubt that the sun would rise tomorrow morning. It is not strange that Cardinal Newman should have loved Scott, and thought he had prepared the way for the Oxford Movement by turning men's minds in the direction of the Middle Ages. George Borrow makes similar assertions from his own violently anti-Catholic point of view in *The Romany Rye*. Scott himself was anti-Catholic so far as his conscious opinions were concerned, but this was, as it were, a mistake. If ever a human being had the Catholic temperament, Scott was that man; he would have been a happier man and a better Christian in the Church of Rome than either the Anglicans or the Presbyterians were ever able to make of him.[12]

[12] Cf. articles on "The Religion of Sir Walter Scott," by W. S. Crockett and W. Forbes Grey, *Hibbert Journal*, XXVII (1928-1929), 483-497, and XXXI (1932-1933), 47-60. On the allied matter of his attitude toward the supernatural, cf. M. C. Boatright, "Witchcraft in the Novels of Sir Walter Scott" and "Demonology in the Novels of Sir Walter Scott," *University of Texas Bulletin, Studies in English*, Number 13 (1933), 95-112, and Number 14 (1934), 75-88. Scott uses supernaturalism freely, "not to excite fear of supernatural things in my reader, but to show the effects of such fear upon the agents in the story." He is not absolutely consistent; he himself saw a ghost on at least one occasion, yet he could speak contemptuously of ghost-seers. His great gift was, of course, his ability to create characters like Meg Merrilies which hover on the verge of the supernatural and become the mouthpiece of impersonal forces without actually going over.

Scott's political views were those of an extreme Tory; he saw the Reform Bill as the prelude to a French Revolution in England and he fought it bitterly. No doubt the enormous popularity of his novels was determined partly upon this basis in an age when England was growing increasingly conservative.[13]

Yet despite his politics Scott was a great democrat, and his democracy was closely connected with his religion. "He was, with all his errors," says G. K. Chesterton, "profoundly possessed with the old religious conception, the only possible democratic basis, the idea that man himself is a king in disguise." In a sense, class distinctions were drawn very closely in old Scotland; the lord was a lord and the beggar was a beggar. But before being either a lord or a beggar, each was a man, and men respect each other and meet on a basis of mutual understanding which few of the eager young geniuses who talk about the necessity for the artist to line himself up in the class conflict today have even begun to understand. In *Old Mortality,* Claverhouse would distinguish between the life of the developed man and the life of the clod, but Morton will have none of it: "Your distinction is too nice for my comprehension. God gives every spark of life, that of the peasant as well as of the prince; and those who destroy his work recklessly or causelessly must answer in either case." Dickens feels love and pity for the poor; it is not too much to say that Scott finds grandeur in them.

Even if Scott had not one word to speak to the men and women of today he would still be the most important of all British novelists historically. To name all whom he influenced would be virtually to call the roll of nineteenth-century British novelists. Nor was his influence confined to Britain; Balzac, Vigny, Mérimée, Victor Hugo, and Dumas owned his influence in France; Ebers,

[13] Mark Twain (*Life on the Mississippi*) made the fantastic charge that Scott foisted an idealized feudal system upon the South, and thus became responsible for the Civil War! Cf. H. J. Eckenrode, "Sir Walter Scott and the South," *North American Review,* CCVI (1917), 595-603; Grace Warren Landrum, "Sir Walter Scott and his Literary Rivals in the Old South," *American Literature,* II (1930-1931), 256-276; G. Harrison Orians, "Walter Scott, Mark Twain, and the Civil War." *South Atlantic Quarterly,* XL (1941), 343-359.

Galdos, Jokai, Sienkiewicz, Dostoevsky, Strindberg, and many more, in other countries.[14]

Naturally such a man influences life even more than he influences literature. And Sir Herbert Grierson pays Scott an impressive tribute as "the great reconciler":

> He reconciled Highlands and Lowlands, Celt and Angle. . . . But he reconciled also Scotland and England. . . . He even helped to reconcile Britain to the continent and the continent to Britain after the long years of exile and isolation. Goethe hailed in him the first exponent of the worth of German literature. A passionate supporter of the long war with Napoleon, he never wrote of the French with the contempt which was common in his day, and earlier. . . . He reconciled Presbyterian and Episcopalian, for . . . his treatment of the Covenanters has left no bitterness in Scottish hearts. He reconciled rich and poor. . . .[15]

But Scott's importance is much more than merely historical, for he represents an attitude toward life which has as much validity today as it had a hundred years ago. He even flatters some of the dominant interests of the moment; he is a regionalist; he is, on one side of him, a determinist. "The privilege of free action belongs to no mortal," says Redgauntlet: "we are tied down by the fetters of duty, our moral path is limited by the regulations of honor, our most indifferent actions are but meshes of the web of destiny by which we are all surrounded." John Buchan pays tribute to Scott's "very clear philosophy, of which the basis is the eternity and the wisdom of the divine order of things." But "If he makes the world more solemn he also makes it more sunlit." He has "the insight of the healer and the reconciler." He "loves mankind without reservation, is incapable of hate, and finds nothing created altogether common or unclean. This Border laird, so happy in his worldly avocations that some would discard him as superficial, stands at the end securely among the prophets, for he gathers all things, however lowly and crooked and broken, within the love of God."

[14] Cf. Louis Maigron, *Le Roman Historique à l'epoque romantique; essai sur l'influence de Walter Scott* (Paris, Champion, 1912).

[15] From "Scott and Carlyle" in *Essays and Studies by Members of the English Association*, XIII, 104-105 (The Clarendon Press, 1928).

CHAPTER XII

FROM SCOTT TO DICKENS

> There are nine and sixty ways of constructing tribal lays,
> And every single one of them is right.
>
> RUDYARD KIPLING

Chronologically the pause between Scott and Dickens was inconsiderable. Scott died in 1832; Dickens's first novel appeared in 1836. There were, however, a number of writers who may be regarded as younger contemporaries of Scott and older contemporaries of Dickens. In a history of the novel these fall to be considered at the point where we have now arrived.

1. *Bulwer the Virtuoso*

Sir Edward Bulwer-Lytton [1] was possibly the most important—certainly he was the most spectacular—of this group. Bulwer was the most remarkable virtuoso in the history of English fiction. As a novelist he manifested the same kind of ability that Sarah Bernhardt displayed in the theater. He could take up a line of fiction, exploit it for all it was worth, and then, just when he seemed to have written himself out, he could turn to an entirely different kind of fiction and repeat the performance. Bulwer was very shrewd in guessing which way the cat would jump; he both anticipated public taste and created it.

That he never became a supreme master in any of the numerous fields he invaded may have been due in part to the fact that he tried to do too much and in part to his somewhat professional atti-

[1] Edward George Earle Lytton Bulwer was made a baronet in 1838, became Bulwer-Lytton in 1843, when, upon inheriting Knebworth from his mother, he added her maiden-name to his own, and was elevated to the peerage in 1866 as Baron Lytton of Knebworth.

tude toward literature. But the fundamental difficulty was in his own temperament and character. Bulwer had brains, great talent, much wisdom and idealism. But his taste was subject to sudden, strange lapses, and he had very little sense. Shameless charlatanry and prophetic insight stand cheek by jowl in his fictions, pedantry defaces his vast knowledge, the sublime and the ridiculous are grotesquely commingled, and the coxcomb too frequently replaces the serious artist. It is not true, as some writers have managed to suggest, that Bulwer's vogue—which, like Scott's, was a European phenomenon—had only a popular significance. As a matter of fact, many serious critics have paid their tribute to him. But it is true that the pretentious absurdities from which his pages were never free for long made it very easy for those who were so disposed to overlook his solid merits.

To know Bulwer's life-experience, however, is to know why he wrote as he did. He was born in London, May 25, 1803. His father was a general, his mother a great heiress; his youth was petted and spoiled. He felt the influence of Byron, as most sensitive young men did in those days; he went through a perfect story-book love affair; he was victimized by Byron's inamorata, the mad Lady Caroline Lamb. For a time he even wandered about with the gypsies. Bulwer was educated at Trinity College, Cambridge, and published his first important novel, *Pelham,* when he was twenty-five.

And he married, married as unfortunately as Byron himself, married after a violent courtship, in defiance of his doting mother's wishes, and was disowned by her in consequence. With plenty of faults on both sides, the marriage was so desperately unhappy that even after the lapse of a hundred years it is painful to read about it. Separation came in 1836, but that was only the beginning, for Rosina, who was probably not a sane woman, devoted the rest of her life to torturing her husband. Once when he was electioneering, she appeared before him (as mysteriously as the supernatural portents in his novels), and denounced him to his constituency. Bulwer lived in the shadow of this fantastic scandal for many years, and it says much for him that he should have been able to accomplish what he did in the face of a situation so ideally calculated to cause a man to appear ridiculous. He was dramatist [2] and poet as well as novelist; and, like Disraeli, he was also a politician. His political career impresses us today less than Disraeli's, though he once held the office of Secretary of State for the Colonies. That no touch of color might be wanting in his life, he was also offered the throne of Greece! He died January 18, 1873.

When he comes to formulate his theory of fiction Bulwer is much preoccupied with effects of tragic grandeur. In discussing these, he inclines to take his illustrations from the Greek drama, for the simple reason that he does not find them readily to hand in English fiction. He thought of English novelists for the most part as having concerned themselves with manners and humors; even Scott had no "grandeur of conception," for he lacked the "strong desire to render palpable and immortal some definite and abstract truth." Such desire is indispensable for the finest fiction, for while Bulwer agreed that characters are more important than either plot or background, he felt that they ought always to be developed with reference to some central idea behind the book. This did not mean that the novelist must forever be teaching "lessons"; the moral usefulness of a work of art is not "confined to the peculiar idiosyncrasies of character it selects"; otherwise *Macbeth* could have value only for those who are plotting murder in order to seize a throne. But the general tendency must be sound.

Bulwer's fundamentally ethical, fundamentally idealistic attitude toward the novel is thus beyond question. "There is as much truth in the poetry of life as in its prose," he declares. And "of all the signs of a corrupt heart and a feeble hand, the tendency of incredulity is the surest."

This idealism impels Bulwer powerfully in the direction of allegory, not only in metaphysical stories like *Zanoni,* not only in *Ernest Maltravers* and *Alice,* which, though nearly forgotten today, have more that was important to him in them than his better-

[2] *Richelieu* and *The Lady of Lyons* were the most distinguished plays in an undistinguished period of British drama; the former has been acted in our own times by Robert Mantell, Walter Hampden, and George Arliss. Both were written for the greatest English actor of the mid-nineteenth century, William Charles Macready.

known works, but even in *The Disowned,* where Algernon typifies "the Heroism of Christian Philosophy," even in *Godolphin,* a study of "the frustration or abuse of power in a superior intellect originally inclined to good," and even in crime stories like *Lucretia:*

> In Dalibard, the intention was to portray the wary, calculating, and laborious intellect, which, rightly directed, leads to science; in Varney, the versatile, lively, impressionable fancy, which, purified and guided, may conduct to art; in Lucretia, the energy and active will, which, nobly sustained and trained, may lead to eminence and success in the outward concerns of life.

The allegorical intention determines the fate of the leading characters in this book. Varney, who had indulged and pampered his senses, suffers the coarsest of hardships; Lucretia, who had made a god of the intellect, "is cursed in the intellect."

Bulwer had his own classification of his fictions, extending his first period from *Pelham* to *Paul Clifford* to cover four novels in which he "rather observes than imagines." Between *Paul Clifford* and *Eugene Aram* he passed "the boundary of invention" and turned from the errors of society to those hidden in the human heart; here too, for the first time, he seized "those more ideal images" with which he was to concern himself increasingly in later books.

The critics generally make their divisions on a somewhat more mechanical basis. There are, we are told, Fashionable Novels, like *Pelham* (1828) and *Godolphin* (1833); Stories of Crime, like *Paul Clifford* (1830), *Eugene Aram* (1832), *Night and Morning* (1841), and *Lucretia* (1846); Historical Novels, like *Devereux* (1829), *The Last Days of Pompeii* (1834), *Rienzi* (1835), *The Last of the Barons* (1843), and *Harold, or The Last of the Saxon Kings* (1848); Stories of the Supernatural, like *Zanoni* (1842), *A Strange Story* (1862), and the famous short story, "The Haunters and the Haunted, or The House and the Brain" (1857); Family Chronicles, or Stories of Character, like *The Caxtons* (1849), *My Novel* (1853), and *What Will He Do with It?* (1859); to say nothing of his utopia, *The Coming Race* (1871), and other experiments.

It may be that Bulwer's own classification is better, for he understood the fundamental unity of his work in his own heart and brain. Probably few readers have perceived an organic connection between the Stories of Crime and the Stories of the Supernatural. But for Bulwer there was a connection, for he believed that crime and the supernatural were the only two sources of tragic pity and terror available for the modern novelist.

Pelham, too, has elements that cannot be accounted for as "Fashionable." Its picture of society derived (to say nothing of the author's own experience) from Disraeli's *Vivian Grey,* but there were other elements from Godwin and Mrs. Radcliffe; and there is a residue which can only be described, if the term be not too pretentious, as "philosophical." There is philosophy too, for that matter, in both the stories of crime and the historical novels. Godwin himself had been a philosophical as well as a sensational novelist. Bulwer had already taken Falkland's name (out of *Caleb Williams*) as the title of a novel, but he saved the murder-mystery for *Pelham,* and to make the connection inescapable he called the victim Tyrrel. In other words, we have not accounted for *Pelham* when we note that the name became a contemporary epithet for a young bounder, nor even that the book established the vogue for black evening clothes which has endured to this day. For the hero is at once "a fop and a philosopher, a voluptuary and a moralist"; he is "somewhat better than the voluptuary, and somewhat wiser than the coxcomb." He is intensely annoying at times, as Bulwer himself was, but he is in no greater danger than Bulwer was of making shipwreck of his life. *Pelham* still has some of the Byronism or Wertherism of the author's earlier scribblings, but in more important aspects it marks his emancipation from these aberrations. The post-war hardheadedness is about it; it helped "to put an end to the Satanic mania,—to turn the thoughts and ambition of young gentlemen without neckcloths, and young clerks who were sallow, from playing the Corsair, and boasting that they were villains." *Ernest Maltravers* (1837), *Alice* (1838), and *Kenelm Chillingly* (1873) are maturer books in a somewhat similar vein.

The crime stories all professed the most serious moral purpose. *Paul Clifford,* the highwayman's history, shows how society forces boys to grow up in conditions which must inevitably make criminals of them, and then tries to make things right by hanging the criminal. Paul is sentenced by that whited sepulcher, his illegitimate father. "Your laws are but of two classes," he tells the old villain and the England behind him; "the one makes criminals, the other punishes them. I have suffered by the one—I am about to perish by the other." But the tendency toward sensationalism that always betrayed Bulwer's high resolves appears in this book also; Paul's defiance of society is magniloquent, and some passages describe the ways of criminals almost in a spirit of epic glorification. As for *Eugene Aram,* its subject is a famous English crime which had recently been revived by Thomas Hood. Bulwer has a perfectly legitimate interest here: what could cause a high-minded scholar of gentle ways and spotless reputation to commit a murder? [3] Yet many agree with R. Ellis Roberts, who classified the book with the "bad thrillers," because the author, "uneasily aware that his criminal was a sordid rogue, deliberately sentimentalized him."

Bulwer's public references to his contemporaries are likely to be fulsome, but he generally manages to convey the idea that he has decidedly advanced beyond them. The references he makes to Scott in the course of his discussion of the historical novel are a case in point. Scott's method was "picturesque"; his own is "intellectual"! And it is true that *The Last Days of Pompeii,* which was largely written in Italy, attempts a reconstruction of ancient society which is probably more thorough (certainly it is far more ponderous) than anything in Scott. But it is also true that both here and in *Rienzi,* where he attempted the rehabilitation of a fourteenth-century Italian dictator, Bulwer indulged in an extravagant sensationalism that Scott's finer taste must surely have disdained.

Indeed, though *The Last Days of Pompeii* is now by far Bulwer's most popular book, both *Harold* and *The Last of the Barons* are far superior to it. Unlike Scott, Bulwer does not shy from making bona fide historical characters the leading actors in his novels. The Earl of Warwick is the central figure in *The Last of the Barons;* the novelist does not pervert facts but elucidates them; when history is silent as to the motives of his characters, his imagination can provide them.

[3] In later editions, Aram is not actually a murderer.

Supernaturalism appears, not too convincingly, in *The Last Days of Pompeii.* Occult powers are attributed to Arbaces, but Bulwer cannot resist proving that he himself is an intellectual by learnedly explaining most of them away. *Zanoni,* which is a novel of the theater, a novel of the French Revolution, and a novel drenched in Rosicrucian or Theosophical wisdom, takes its occultism much more seriously. Bulwer regarded *Zanoni* as his masterpiece; if the truth be known, he regarded it as unique in English fiction.

> As man has two lives—that of action and that of thought—so I conceive that work to be the truest representation of Humanity which faithfully delineates both, and opens some elevating glimpse into the sublimest mysteries of our being, by establishing the inevitable union that exists between the plain things of the day, in which our earthly bodies perform their allotted part, and the latent, often uncultivated, often invisible, affinities of the soul with all the powers that eternally breathe and move throughout the Universe of Spirit.

That the perfect novel will have to do all this, I do not doubt. That Bulwer himself did it in *Zanoni,* I am not convinced.

Sensationalism does go utterly by the board, however, in *The Caxtons,* one of the best derivative novels in all fiction. Were not the reader continually being reminded of *Tristram Shandy,* he would surely call it a first-rate novel. But then, if there had been no *Tristram Shandy,* the story of *The Caxtons* would never have been written! It is a beautiful book, nevertheless, and something of its spirit carries over into *My Novel* and *What Will He Do with It?* though here complicated plots are used again, and the latter, at least, is less Sterne than Dickens.

It is interesting that though Bulwer illustrates the novel in more varied aspects than any other famous writer, its ultimate destiny would probably have been very much the same if he had never written at all. It is true that he tried to smash Scott's pattern in the historical novel, but he was not influential here; when Hewlett and others finally did break that mold they were not tracing his footsteps. An exception should perhaps be made in the case of the novel of crime, in which connection he had many imitators and influenced the careers of both Dickens and Thackeray. Of course none of this means that Bulwer wrought in vain. Novelists do not write for the purpose of influencing other novelists, nor yet for the sake of "The Novel." They write to give pleasure and refreshment to their readers. Bulwer gave both to uncounted thousands.

2. *Disraeli and the Political Novel*

"These two," wrote Sir Edmund Gosse, "the author of *Pelham* and the author of *Vivian Grey,* raced neck and neck at the head of the vast horde of 'fashionable' novel-writers, now all but them forgotten." Primarily, however, Benjamin Disraeli, later Lord Beaconsfield (1804-1881), was a political novelist, and of course literature was only an incident in his spectacular career. "It was not originally the intention of the writer to adopt the form of fiction as the instrument to scatter his suggestions," so he declares in one of his prefaces, "but, after reflection, he resolved to avail himself of a method which, in the temper of the times, offered the best chance of influencing opinion."

Yet Disraeli's fiction and his statesmanship come very close together. He declared his ideals in his novels; as prime minister he himself was privileged to exemplify them. There is a puzzling mixture of cynicism and high-mindedness both in his writings and in his life; the same Oriental imagination that conjured up the cinema-like splendors which in *Tancred* and *Lothair* turned the Holy Land itself into an *Arabian Nights* fairyland, crowned Victoria Empress of India.

Disraeli's novels arrange themselves in three groups: (1) those from *Vivian Grey* (1826-1827) to *Venetia* (1837), in which a young man, not yet able to secure a foothold in politics, made his first bid for fame; (2) the trilogy—*Coningsby* (1844); *Sybil* (1845); *Tancred* (1847)—in which the leader of the Young England Party (still far from the premiership) achieved a comprehensive statement of his principles; (3) the two books of Disraeli's old age—*Lothair* (1870) and *Endymion* (1880).

No more exuberantly irresponsible first novel was ever written than *Vivian Grey*. The young hero sets out to make a name for himself in politics, but since Disraeli's own principles are still undefined, he can have no political faith; he is only "precociously convinced of the necessity of managing mankind, by studying their tempers and humoring their weaknesses." He establishes his omniscience by quoting authorities which never existed; and when a young lady expresses a desire to own an autograph of Washington Irving, he accommodatingly offers to write one, adding (should it please her) those of Scott, Southey, Milman, Byron—and Disraeli! When the political bubble bursts at last, Vivian leaves for Germany and embarks upon a series of adventures which reflect both Peacock and the Gothic novelists and anticipate Meredith's *Adventures of Harry Richmond.*

Vivian Grey has no continuity and no harmony of tone. Vivian's humanitarianism toward John Conyers is much in the tone of *Sybil,* yet the Conyers episode comes in the midst of the most frivolous part of the book. Mrs. Lorraine's insufficiently motivated attempt to poison Vivian is sheer melodrama, and her death, from a broken blood-vessel, is unintentionally amusing. So, in a different manner, is the death of the consumptive Violet Fane, in the hero's arms, from the shock of his proposal to her! There are many essay-passages—criticisms of contemporary fiction, music, and philosophy—and the book ends with a tremendous storm-scene.

This was the note on which Disraeli began his career, and though he wrote better books afterwards, he never quite got away from it. Thackeray takes off his Oriental magnificence very happily in *Codlingsby:*

> The carpet was of white velvet—(laid over several webs of Aubusson, Ispahan, and Axminster, so that your foot gave no more sound as it trod upon the yielding plain than the shadow did which followed you)—of white velvet, painted with flowers, arabesques, and classic figures, by Sir William Ross, J. M. W. Turner, R.A., Mrs. Mee, and Paul Delaroche. The edges were wrought with seed-pearls, and fringed with Valenciennes lace and bullion. The walls were hung with cloth of silver, embroidered with gold figures, in ruby, amethyst, and smaragd. The drops of dew which the artificer had sprinkled on the flowers were diamonds. The hangings were overhung by pictures yet more costly. Giorgione the gorgeous, Titian the golden, Rubens the ruddy and pulpy (the Pan of Painting), some of Murillo's beautiful shepherdesses, who smile on you out of darkness like a star, a few score first-class Leonardos, and fifty of the masterpieces of the patron of Julius and Leo, the imperial genius of Urbino, covered the walls of the little chamber. Divans of carved

amber covered with ermine went round the room, and in the midst was a fountain, pattering and babbling with jets of double-distilled otto of roses.[4]

Disraeli took his revenge with a cruel caricature of Thackeray himself in *Endymion,* but he wreaked it upon a dead novelist.

It is not necessary to consider the other novels of the first group in any detail.[5] For Disraeli's fame as a novelist must rest at last on the trilogy of his middle period. In all these books the pattern is the same: the hero is a young aristocrat, and the plot describes the devious ways in which he is groomed to serve his country. In *Coningsby,* which opens with the Reform Bill of 1832 and closes with the Tory victory of 1847, the emphasis is on politics; in *Sybil* the call for social amelioration is sounded, and industrial conditions are described in a manner prescient of Mrs. Gaskell and Charles Reade; *Tancred* develops the religious implications of Disraeli's creed.

That creed it is important to understand if one would understand Disraeli's novels. He was willing to admit that the divine right of kings could no longer be practically maintained in England, but he still insisted that "the divine right of government is the keystone of human progress." In modern England, as he saw it, liberalism had undermined "all the institutions which were the bulwarks of the multitude," and gone far toward destroying the idea of the community. Representative government was no solution; Tancred refused to enter Parliament because he could not discover the principle on which the state was founded. In fact, Disraeli could not see the true representation of the people in Parliament; for that, he

[4] The reader who thinks this burlesque unfair to Disraeli should read the description of the Rose of Sharon in her garden, in *Tancred,* Book III, ch. 4.

[5] *Popanilla* (1828) is an attack on the Utilitarians in the form of a Lucianic apologue. *The Young Duke* (1831) is in the manner of *Vivian Grey.* In *Contarini Fleming* (1832), the hero is the son of a Scandinavian minister of Italian origin who wishes to be a poet, but being unable to write, he becomes a robber chieftain instead! *Alroy* (1833) depicts a twelfth-century Jewish struggle against the Mohammedans. *Henrietta Temple, A Love Story* (1836) is remarkable for Disraeli in that it has nothing to do with politics. The characters of *Venetia* (1837) suggest the experiences of both Byron and Shelley.

added somewhat lamely, they must turn to the press! The natural guardians of the rights of the people were the young aristocrats, not the bloated materialists who had been created by modern commerce and firmly entrenched in power by the iniquitous Reform Bill, and it was to an alliance between the aristocracy and the masses that Disraeli pinned his hopes.

It will be clear, then, that faith and imagination play a large role in Disraeli's conception of the state; like Carlyle, he believed that man was "made to adore and to obey." Hence the importance of the Church, by which Disraeli means the Church of England—"if the Church were to be destroyed, Europe would be divided between the Atheist and the Communist." An atheistic society is inevitably anarchic; whatever militates against the spiritual view of life must, therefore, be destroyed, whether it take the form of an "assault on the divinity of the Semitic literature by the Germans" or "recent discoveries of science, which are hastily supposed to be inconsistent with our long-received convictions as to the relations between the Creator and the created."[6] Disraeli's religious attitude was thus nicely calculated to satisfy both his Jewish birth and his Anglican baptism. He thought of his own people as having been peculiarly endowed with mystic sensitiveness and of their country as primarily the land of revelation. But the "Asian principles" committed to them, "although local in their birth, are of divine origin, and of universal and eternal application." As Philip Guedalla expresses it, for Disraeli a Jew was a "proto-Christian," a Christian a "completed Jew."

In *Coningsby,* the Jewish prophet-financier, Sidonia, sets forth these ideas with much sententious epigram. Though Sidonia has been widely praised as a character-creation, he is never convincing; his cynical worldliness simply will not blend with his idealism. "In

[6] Disraeli did not accept the evolutionary hypothesis; he originated a famous phrase when he remarked that if he had to choose between apes and angels he was "on the side of the angels." One of the most delightful passages in fiction is that in *Tancred* (Book II, Ch. 9) in which Lady Constance tries to interest the hero in *The Revelations of Chaos,* which is Disraeli's burlesque title for Robert Chambers's *Vestiges of the Natural History of Creation* (1844), a rather superficial, but widely-read, book on pre-Darwinian evolution.

his organization there was a peculiarity, perhaps a great deficiency. He was a man without affections." Such men may exist, but that is beside the point; Disraeli does not make this one seem real. The Duke of Monmouth, who may have been studied from the same original as Thackeray's Lord Steyne, is an interesting character; and so is the Manchester manufacturer, Millbank, who wants a real aristocracy in England, not a sham one, based on "the spoliation of the Church; the open and flagrant sale of its honours by the elder Stuarts; and the borough-mongering of our own times," and whose daughter the hero marries. There are many "originals" in *Coningsby;* the hero himself was studied from George Smythe, later Viscount Strangford.

Sybil is set against the Chartist background of 1837-1844; the hero is an aristocrat, the saintly heroine a Chartist's daughter whose pedigree finally emerges as nobler than his own! Sybil opposes the use of physical force in labor disputes, as does her incredible admirer, Stephen, and when Stephen at last betrays this principle, it costs him his life. Disraeli perceived the power of the general strike; he knew that though labor's cause is hopeless when violence is employed, a courageous, unyielding commitment to non-violent non-co-operation must have a good chance for victory. Yet Sybil's class-consciousness is as unyielding as that of Karl Marx, and the book which bears her name arrays class against class as uncompromisingly as Marx himself was to do it:

"Well, society may be in its infancy," said Egremont, slightly smiling; "but say what you like, our Queen reigns over the greatest nation that ever existed."

"Which nation?" asked the younger stranger, "for she reigns over two."

The stranger paused; Egremont was silent, but looked inquiringly.

"Yes," resumed the younger stranger after a moment's interval. "Two nations; between whom there is no intercourse and no sympathy; who are as ignorant of each other's habits, thoughts, and feelings, as if they were dwellers in different zones, or inhabitants of different planets: who are formed by a different breeding, are fed by a different food, are ordered by different manners, and are not governed by the same laws."

"You speak of—" said Egremont, hesitatingly.

"The Rich and the Poor."

It is not all as doctrinaire as that, for the study of suffering among miners and weavers (and of the immorality and degradation to which it leads) was based on first-hand knowledge, and their woes are strikingly, if somewhat artificially, contrasted with the purposeless lives of the young aristocrats. Disraeli uses Scott's technique of weaving backwards and forwards, but he is more indirect than Scott; like the modern novelist, he leaves more to inference; a letter may arrive in one chapter, for example, and not be written until the next. Dickens might have conceived Baptist Hatton, the antiquary who looks up pedigrees, and who can make a peer though not a baronet; and the fiery death of Master Joseph, the young ogre of the tommy-shop, would find itself quite at home in *Barnaby Rudge*.

James Russell Lowell called *Tancred* "an epigram in three volumes post octavo" with "no principle of cohesion except the covers." A principle of cohesion is precisely what the very earnest young hero cannot find in England (Disraeli's young heroes grew increasingly earnest and increasingly less independent with the passing of time), and this is why he goes to the Holy Land to explore "the Asian mystery." Amazing Oriental adventures ensue—some of them much in the manner of Rider Haggard's *She*—involving the highly intellectual and horribly argumentative and completely annoying Rose of Sharon, who smokes "a confection of roses and rare nuts" through "a flexible silver tube, tipped with amber," and whose final amorous collapse, "cold, insensible," upon the hero's shoulder, gives the book all the termination it gets. Fakredeen's proposition to move the seat of the British Empire to the Orient is interesting in view of Disraeli's own imperialism:

> Let the Queen of the English collect a great fleet, let her stow away all her treasure, bullion, gold plate, and precious arms; be accompanied by all her court and chief people, and transfer the seat of her empire from London to Delhi. There she will find an immense empire ready made, a first-rate army, and a large revenue.

Disraeli left it to the statesman of Bernard Shaw's *Back to Methuselah* really to accomplish something like that, but he certainly made the Orient an important part of English concerns.

Religious matters play a large role also in *Lothair,* which is much the more important of the Prime Minister's two novels. *Endymion,* which covers the period from the death of Canning to the Crimean War, is interesting for its many portraits of contemporary figures, and as a striking example of Disraeli's woman-worship, but it is insignificant beside the study of the Catholic question, which had been suggested to Disraeli by the recent conversion of the Marquis of Bute. Disraeli was fascinated by the Catholic Church; the Catholic case against "progress" is stated with great force in this novel; there are many passages which might have come straight from a Catholic writer. Yet in the end Disraeli always manages to load the dice against the Roman Church. The Lady Corisande's juvenile prejudices against Catholicism are treated very reverentially; and when the Italian patriot, Theodora, is on her deathbed, she makes Lothair promise he will never submit to conversion. The author seems quite unaware of the monstrous unfairness of such conduct, on the part of a mature woman, toward a boy who adores her; in fact, when Lothair is later in danger of wavering, Theodora's ghost comes back to him in the Colosseum by moonlight to remind him of his pledge! This is presumably the true miracle of the book, opposed to the false, Catholic miracle, which would transform the peasant woman who saved Lothair on an Italian battlefield into the Virgin, miraculously interposing in his behalf, and which is supported by Cardinal Grandison (Cardinal Manning) with reasoning so "Jesuitical" that Lothair himself is almost persuaded at last that he fell fighting for the Pope instead of against him! *Lothair* gives an excellent idea of the work of the revolutionary secret societies of the 'sixties—the Fenians in Ireland, the Mary Anne in France, and the Madre Natura in Italy. Mr. Phoebus's "Aryan principles" afford coarser entertainment, but they interest the modern reader greatly in the light of recent world-developments. The Italian campaign in *Lothair* suggests Meredith's *Vittoria.* The principal fault of the book is that after the Italian campaign, and especially after Lothair's return from Jerusalem, its structure collapses.

Disraeli's imperfect cohesion weighs heavily against him with modern critics. He leaves both plots and ideas hanging in the air; he devotes a whole book to the "Asian mystery," for example, yet the book ends before either hero or readers find out what it is. He was too topical, also, for lasting popularity; few contemporary readers have the detailed knowledge of Victorian politics one must have to peruse his pages with easy enjoyment. And the epigrams, brilliant as they are, often bring in the suggestion of insincerity which has always militated against Disraeli, and which was further reinforced by his lack of emotional depth. In *Coningsby,* Lucretia faints:

> "The brain cannot be affected, with that pulse," said the surgeon; "there is no fracture."
>
> "How pale she is!" said Lord Monmouth, as if he were examining a picture.

That is the way Disraeli "examines" the human heart.

3. *Charles Lever and the Anglicized Irish*

Among Irish novelists, Maria Edgeworth and C. R. Maturin have already been considered in this book. A considerable number of the sons of Erin turned to fiction during the period with which we are now concerned; unfortunately several of them must be relegated to the Appendix. Charles Lever and William Carleton, however, fall for consideration here: Lever, if for no other reason, because his contacts with the literary life of London and his English and American popularity made him, and make him still, the best-known of the entire group; Carleton, because he stands, by common consent, at the head of Irish fiction.

Dr. Baker speaks of Lever's most famous book, *Harry Lorrequer,* as "very Irish in the stagey sense, very unreal." A fairer judgment of his work as a whole is that of the Jesuit writer, Stephen J. Brown, who calls Lever "by far the greatest of that group of writers who, by education and sympathies, are identified with the English element in Ireland. He was untouched by the Gaelic spirit, was a Tory in politics, and a Protestant." Father Brown continues: "His books give a wonderful series of pictures of Irish life from the days of Grattan's Parliament to the Famine of 1846. Many of these pictures, though true to certain aspects of Irish life, create a false impression by directing the eye almost exclusively to what is grotesque and whimsical." But he gives warm praise to Lever's "portrait gallery," "one of the finest in fiction": here are "the dashing young soldiers of the earlier books; the comic characters, an endless series; diplomatists, doctors, lawyers, politicians, usurers, valetudinarians, aristocrats, typical Irish squires, adventurers, braggarts, spendthrifts."

Lever was born of a good family with its just share of eccentrics, in Dublin, August 31, 1806; his father was a building contractor. He was of high spirits from childhood, with always a strong inclination toward pranks and practical jokes. After his graduation from Trinity College, Dublin, in 1827, he came to America, and amused himself by living with the Indians, who bestowed tribal privileges upon him, and from whom he is said to have escaped with difficulty. He studied medicine at Göttingen, and served his apprenticeship under difficult, almost heroic, conditions in rural Ireland, where he saw a cholera epidemic at first hand; later he was a kind of unofficial doctor to the embassy at Brussels. From 1842 to 1845 he edited the *Dublin University Magazine,* but left his native city when his unwillingness to take the thoroughgoing partisan's attitude toward the political disputes of the day lost him the favor of more than one group. The rest of his life he lived at various fashionable continental resorts, and was finally employed in the diplomatic service in Italy and Austria. He died at Trieste, June 1, 1872.

Lever's literary career opened with *The Confessions of Harry Lorrequer* (serially 1837-1840, in book form, 1839), which started as a disjointed series of sketches of military life, and grew gradually into a novel (if, indeed, it can be said ever to have become one), more because of the interest of readers and editors than on account of the author's own. "Such was our life in Cork,—dining, drinking, dancing, steeplechasing, pigeon-shooting, and tandem-driving, filling up any little interval that was found to exist between a late breakfast and the time to dress for dinner. . . ."

And such is the book. Early in the narrative, Harry falls in love with the daughter of the Earl of Callonby, whom at the end he wins in spite of much misunderstanding and cross-purposing. In between the two events is a series of practical jokes and amusing experiences as loosely related to each other as if Smollett had written it; Harry is mistaken for a physician, for a distinguished composer at the opera, for a well-known diplomat at a royal reception, and enjoys himself hugely or suffers hugely in every contingency. And, as in the earlier case of Tom Jones, we are intended to remember that, in spite of his propensity for getting into difficulties, he has a very good heart!

There was no depth to any of it, but it was bright, vivid, and good-humored, and it revealed an admirable story-telling gift. On it, and on the same kind of thing in *Charles O'Malley, The Irish Dragoon* (1841), *Jack Hinton, The Guardsman* (1843), and *Arthur O'Leary* (1844), Lever's contemporary popularity largely rested, and it is on such books that what there is left of it still rests today. *Charles O'Malley* is a truer military novel than *Lorrequer,* for it takes in the Peninsular Campaign, and we see the soldier in action as well as in the mess and on the parade-ground.

Tom Burke of "Ours" (1844) was a more ambitious undertaking. The plot is still unorganized, but the aim was "to portray, with as little aid from fiction as might be, some lights and shadows of the most wonderful and eventful period of modern history,—the empire of Napoleon." The Irish hero goes to France while the Corsican is still first consul, and the narrative follows through to a romantic and theatrically touching picture of the fall of the Empire. All the elements of good romance-making are here, even Minette, the Ouida-like vivandière—"a regular vivandière of the melodrame—virtuous, high-minded, and intrepid"—who worships the hero in vain, is killed gloriously in action, and dies in his arms! Here, as elsewhere in his work, Lever's attitude toward war is merely juvenile, and the reader who thinks nothing better could have been expected in his day need only compare the anti-militarism of Peacock or of Surtees. *Tom Burke* gives a vivid picture of the terror under the Consulate, a less common theme in fiction than Robespierre's terror. Everything in it, indeed, is vivid, but it is the vividness of a good film, not the vividness of *The Dynasts.* Lionel Stevenson calls the hero

> a well-sustained though depressing study of the melancholy, touchy temperament of a young man driven to be a soldier of fortune through complete alienation from family and country. Lever [he continues] caught something of the profound world-weariness of the Celtic nature, and his

picture of a soldier who is brave through indifference is strangely convincing, and the very antithesis of his previous gay blades.

No doubt it is this element which impels some critics to find in *Tom Burke* the first signs of the disillusionment that undoubtedly does exist in Lever's later books.

With *The O'Donoghue* and *St. Patrick's Eve* (both 1845), in any event, the old high spirits are gone forever. *The O'Donoghue,* whose action takes place in Glenflesk and Killarney around 1796, when rebellious Irishmen flirted with the idea of a French invasion to help them throw off the English yoke, gives us the picture of a decaying gentry, trying to live on in feudal splendor without having enough to eat. *St. Patrick's Eve,* which was suggested by Dickens's bitterest book, *The Chimes,* concerns the economic problems of peasants and small farmers.

Political events are relatively more and economic conditions relatively less important in *The Knight of Gwynne, A Tale of the Time of the Union* (1847), which Lionel Stevenson calls the first of Lever's novels to have a soundly-constructed plot, and in whose titular hero he finds suggestions of Colonel Newcome. *The Martins of Cro' Martin* (1847) is something like *The Knight of Gwynne,* but the scene is laid on a great estate in Connaught a generation later. This ambitious and complicated novel is sometimes rated very high. To me its heroine is rather too good to be true. On one side of her, Mary Martin inherits the saint's legend tradition; since she also possesses a definite physical prowess, she was evidently intended to make a somewhat comprehensive appeal. There is a secondary heroine, Catty Henderson, who is revealed as a revolutionary (with much melodramatic fanfare) in the Paris of 1830. The book has considerable discussion of ideas concerning the state of Ireland, as well as the general European problem, but the discussion is never permitted to halt the story. Similarly, though the bias is distinctly what we should now call proletarian, there is little overt propaganda.

More than twenty novels followed *The Knight of Gwynne,* and it is not necessary to speak of all of them here. "I wrote as I felt—sometimes in good spirits—sometimes in bad—always carelessly—for, God help me, I can do no better." So Lever said of his first book, and so he might have said of the last. Like Dickens, he was never far ahead of the printer; unlike Dickens, he often missed his dates. He never kept a copy of what he wrote, and having written an installment he immediately forgot it, so that when a manuscript was lost in transit, as sometimes happened, he was always obliged to set to work and concoct something entirely different! He wrote for bread, for bread and to pay his gambling debts; for while Lever did not live a dishonorable life, he was distinctly on the rackety side. Had he been willing to use the sense he was born with, and adjust his scale of living within reasonable bounds, he might perhaps have added a more illustrious chapter to the history of fiction.

Professor Stevenson is well within his rights when he points out that it is not fair to label Lever either "military" or "Irish" novelist and let it go at that: "both his life and his novels covered more of the continent of Europe than did those of any other British author." Indeed, he did not always confine himself to Europe, not even in the books in which Irish themes and characters predominate.[7] The hero of *Confessions of Con Cregan* (1849) is shipwrecked on an American island and finally marries a lady from Mexico. All the opening scenes of *Roland Cashel* (1850) are laid in Colombia, and several chapters of *One of Them* (1861) suggest *Martin Chuzzlewit* in their picture of life on the mid-western American frontier.

Lever experimented interestingly in several of his later books. *Davenport Dunn* (1859) is a study of social and political corruption, and *Gerald Fitzgerald, "The Chevalier"* (serially 1858-1859) is Lever's only conventional historical romance; the hero is the son of the Young Pretender by a secret marriage with an Irish lady. Most unusual of all, however, was *A Day's Ride, A Life's Romance* (1863), which, when it was serialized in *All the Year Round*, so greatly reduced the circulation of the magazine that its editor, Charles Dickens, was driven to advertising the date on which the story would end; but which Mr. Bernard Shaw, in the preface to *Major Barbara*, assures us had had a larger influence on his own

[7] This group includes (in addition to titles already cited) *Roland Cashel* (1850); *Sir Jasper Carewe* (1855); *The Fortunes of Glencore* (1857); *Barrington* (1863); *The Bramleighs of Bishop's Folly* (1868); and *Lord Kilgobbin* (1872).

work than any of the distinguished continental progenitors with whom he is popularly accredited. What held Mr. Shaw in *A Day's Ride* was, of course, the book's anti-romanticism, the somewhat acrid contrast it presents between the real world and the world of dreams, between what the commonplace son of a Dublin apothecary actually is and what he believes himself to be.

Of Lever's general characteristics and his place in the history of the novel possibly enough has been said already. He himself believed that "any skill I possess lies in the delineation of character and the unravelment of that tangled skein that makes up human motives." It is one of the worst self-judgments on record. What he really could do was just the opposite: he could achieve vivid surface pictures of whole cross-sections of human society, whole areas of human life. Lewis Melville may seem to start unfairly when he says, "He was at his best when describing the men who drank deep, rowed hard, gamed heavily, fought bravely, and led a devil-may-care life"; but when he goes on to add: "but also he depicted with graphic pen the wretched state of the peasantry, and drew with no unskilful hand the pitiful lot of the decayed Irish gentleman," he achieves a just appraisal. The Gaelic spirit in its profounder aspects passed Lever by, as, for that matter, everything that was profound passed him by. But he had a vast fund of "Irishness," and his contemporaries found it enough.

4. *Dark Rosaleen: William Carleton*

William Carleton's (1794-1869) was a very different story. He did not shy from the stage Irishman: the traditional association of Paddy and his pig owes much to one of his sketches. He even resembles Lever in his lack of mysticism. But he was a much greater writer, and his attitude toward his work was very different.

It was Carleton's own opinion that

> there never was a man of letters who had an opportunity of knowing and describing the manners of the Irish people so thoroughly as I had. I was one of themselves, and mingled in all those sports and pastimes in which their characters are most clearly developed. Talking simply of the peasantry, there is scarcely a phase of their life with which I was not intimate. That, however, is not so much in itself, because many have

had the same advantages, but not only a cultivated intellect, but strong imagination, and extraordinary powers of what I may term *unconscious* observation, existed in my case. . . . My memory, too, although generally good, was then in its greatest power; it was always a memory of association. . . . With the natural habits of my life, arising as they did from my position, accompanied as they were by the gifts which God had bestowed upon me, is it surprising that I have painted the Irish people with such truthfulness?

This accurate self-assessment suggests Carleton's limitations as well as his powers. His creative range was limited to his own peasant-class. In the "hedge-schools" to which Catholic masters were reduced in his day, he managed to pick up a good deal of scholarship, but his great powers remained undisciplined. The same inability to put his economic house in order that kept him, as a famous novelist, never more than two steps ahead of the poorhouse manifests itself also in the imperfect "development" of his longer stories. Nor does he always succeed in making the jump from the particular to the universal. "We remember him well," he writes of a clergyman in *The Tithe-Proctor,* "as who of his survivors that ever knew him does not?"

Probably no other novelist of Carleton's rank ever achieved quite his straightforward simplicity. At its best this is a great virtue in his work. But has the convention of the omniscient author anywhere else been quite so frankly "given away" as in this passage from *The Emigrants of Ahadarra?* A character has just locked up a letter in his desk. "As we, however," says Carleton, "possess the power of unlocking his desk, and reading the letter to boot, we now take the liberty of laying it in all its graphic beauty and elegance before our readers."

Carleton was a very serious writer. His biographer reminds us that "his intention was not to amuse, but to inform and to reform. He took up the problem of Irish life and Irish character with the desire of solving it. . . ."

Such a program cannot be followed through without much treading on sensitive corns, and Carleton changed sides often enough so that before he was through he had managed to tread on all of them. A born Catholic, he early left the fold, and his first tales were contributed to a virulently Protestant paper; his later books, on the other hand, are generally pro-Catholic in their sympathies.

He wrote some Nationalistic stories for bread, but his heart was not in them. He was a moderate by temperament, and he satisfied the partisans as little as Bryan McMahon in *The Emigrants of Ahadarra,* who, having voted for a Protestant, is denounced from the altar, and nearly mobbed.

In such books as *Parra Sastha, or The History of Paddy-Go-Easy and his Wife Nancy* (1845), in which he castigated Irish sloth and filth, and *Art Maguire, or The Broken Pledge* (1847), which linked up with Father Mathew's temperance movement, Carleton's didacticism is obvious. Above all, he hated the secret societies—the Ribbon lodges, the Orangemen, the Whiteboys. All appear in his pages as using terrorism and murder under the cover of high ideals, and victimizing the peasants to enrich their leaders. Naturally the sensational interest afforded by the machinations of such groups did not make them any less attractive as material to a novelist so lacking in invention as Carleton was and so prone to repeat his effects. But his fundamental sincerity is not to be impugned.

His cogent defense against the charge of his critics that he was betraying his country by revealing her faults to the world applies to more than one realist:

If they [the faults] had not existed, I could not have painted them. . . . I endeavor to paint Ireland, sometimes as she was, but always *as she is,* in order that she may see many of those debasing circumstances which prevent her from being what she *ought to be.*

Carleton's natural genius found its appropriate form of expression in the short stories included in that extensive collection of *Traits and Stories of the Irish Peasantry* (1830-1833) which contains some of his best work and is still perhaps his greatest monument.[8] He wrote his first long fiction, *Fardorougha the Miser* (1839), because his

[8] Carleton was working here in a field also cultivated by such writers as Thomas Crofton Croker, Gerald Griffin, W. H. Maxwell, Samuel Lover, Miss Mitford, and Mrs. S. C. Hall. Croker's *Fairy Legends and Traditions of the South of Ireland* (1825), however, goes into a mystic realm which Carleton could not enter.

sensitive pride smarted under the imputation that he lacked "strength of wing for a long-sustained flight."

He was not wholly successful in disproving the charge, for *Fardorougha* is a *mélange* of disparate elements, and the development of the plot involves melodrama which is far from convincing; yet the best of the book touches greatness. Essentially, *Fardorougha* is a study in pathology. Avarice grows on the miser through the years until he has actually convinced himself that unless he saves every penny he can lay his hands on, a dog's death from starvation is in store for him. Passionately as he loves his only son, he cannot bring himself to make the settlement which will enable the boy to marry the girl he loves; instead he advises him to carry her off and then refuse to marry her until her father "comes through"! Shylock's ancient cry, "My daughter and my ducats!" sounds through this book in all its grotesque pathos, for the boy is unjustly accused of arson, which in those days was a capital offense. Fardorougha would die for Connor if he could; he refuses to testify against him, and himself faces prison unafraid. But when it comes time to hire a lawyer, he suffers the tortures of the damned.

We see Fardorougha from his own point of view, as we see Shylock. In a way he is "redeemed" in the end, but he is never sentimentalized, and the probabilities are not outraged. "Your heart was hard and godless, Fardorougha," says his wonderful wife, when things look blackest: "and surely, if Connor's death'll be the manes of savin' his father's sowl, wouldn't it be a blessin' instead of a misfortune? Think of it in that light, Fardorougha, and turn your heart to God." The old man says his prayers, and when he has finished he turns to his wife. "I'm afeard," he says, "that my heart wasn't properly in them, for I couldn't prevent my mind from wandherin' to our boy."

After *Fardorougha,* probably Carleton's best novels are *The Black Prophet* (1847) and *The Emigrants of Ahadarra* (1848). Written during a terrible famine and typhus-plague, the *Prophet* was audaciously dedicated to Lord John Russell, the prime minister, to remind him of his duty to do something about the conditions described. The background is as wonderful a "drop" for a tale of moral evil as Chaucer found in a similar situation in "The Pardoner's Tale." In *The Emigrants* the emphasis is on careless landlordism.

Other novels by Carleton certainly worth mentioning include *Valentine McClutchy* (1845), whose central figure is a rascally land-agent, and which makes great fun of the proselytizing efforts of the "New Reformers" whose zeal was stimulated by fear of Catholic emancipation; *Roddy the Rover* (1845), which is said to have been responsible for the disbanding of 600 Ribbon lodges; and *The Tithe-Proctor* (1849), which is built around the resentment of a Catholic people that they should be taxed to maintain a Protestant church in Ireland. *The Tithe-Proctor* does not quite get justice from Carleton's critics. It is true that its plot-development is not very satisfactory, for the Cannie Soogah (Jolly Pedlar) is a kind of deus ex machina who is obliged to act as leader of the Whiteboys and protect their victims at the same time, but it is also true that those who condemn the book pass over other similar faults elsewhere. In the last analysis, the feeling against *The Tithe-Proctor* must be explained on non-literary grounds; it pictures the Irish in a most unamiable light. Carleton's most popular book, *Willy Reilly and his Dear Colleen Bawn* (1855), was never taken seriously either by the author or his critics.

Carleton's character-range is extremely wide, but his idealized women and girls have always come in for special praise. Honor, in *Fardorougha,* is his portrait of his own mother. As to the reality of these women, perhaps only an Irishman can judge. To the present writer, the death of Mrs. McMahon in *The Emigrants* seems a very formal "set" piece, with a Catholic sermon added to the secular sentimentalities of English death-bed scenes in the same period. It may be, for all that, a straightforwardly honest piece of reporting, though the question would still remain whether Carleton might not have been a greater artist if he had exercised more restraint. He never knew restraint, in the expression of emotion at any rate, and for some readers the accumulated woe of the scene in which Connor parts from his mother and his sweetheart quite passes the bounds of art.

In any event, Una O'Brien (*Fardorougha*), Mave Sullivan (*The Black Prophet*), and Kathleen Cavanagh (*The Emigrants of*

Ahadarra) represent the Carleton heroine at her best. One thing is certain: there is no weakness about her. Her nature is passionate, her figure voluptuous. But the strength of her character matches the charms of her body. Mave's determination to risk her life in order to nurse her lover's outcast family through typhus strongly exemplifies the power of the Catholic ideal; we could hardly expect that of an English heroine, at least not before George Eliot. And a George Eliot heroine would be very self-conscious about it, while Mave simply takes it in her stride. The neglected Sarah McGowan in the same novel, whom Carleton audaciously introduces to us trying to stab her stepmother, is an interesting variation; through love and sorrow she draws back from the very brink of hell to manifest at last a really wonderful power of heroic devotion. Kate Hogan, the savage moonshiner's wife in the same novel, shows the influence of Scott's Meg Merrilies.

5. *Fiction, Fox-Hunting, and Surtees*

For many years, the novels of Robert Smith Surtees—expensively printed, with hand-colored illustrations, and handsomely bound in the sportsman's favorite red—have been an indispensable part of every hunting gentleman's library. This circumstance, placing as it were the stamp of a too narrow specialization upon him, has probably contributed adversely to Surtee's fame as a novelist. It is not his ability to describe the "run" that gives him his place in the history of the English novel; it is rather his ability to create characters like John Jorrocks. And Jorrocks may be enjoyed even by those (like the present writer) who are so far from relishing hunting that they take up toward it the attitude of such Englishmen as John Galsworthy and Thomas Hardy.

Surtees was born, the younger son of a country squire, in Northumberland, May 17, 1803. His family could trace back its history to the eleventh century. In 1822 he was articled to a solicitor; in 1831 he became co-founder of the *New Sporting Magazine*. By the death of an elder brother, he succeeded to the estate in 1838. During his later years he was an important man in his county, and did much magisterial and other public work. He died at Brighton, March 16, 1864.

John Jorrocks was created by Surtees in the third number of the *New Sporting Magazine.* He achieved the dignity of covers in 1838 in *The Jaunts and Jollities of that Renowned Sporting Citizen, Mr. John Jorrocks, of St. Botolph Lane and Great Coram Street,* a cum bersome Victorian title, which, by common consent, the world abbreviates to *Jorrocks' Jaunts and Jollities.* ("Not to know Jorrocks is indeed to argue oneself unknown.") In *Handley Cross,*[9] in which he appears as M. F. H. (Master of Fox-Hounds), the sporting grocer passes out of the sketch into the novel; in *Hillingdon Hall* (1845), he becomes a country squire and an agriculturist.

Though *Handley Cross* is now considered Surtees's masterpiece, it was not successful in its own time—the publisher Colburn actually wanted Jorrocks himself eliminated, or at least "toned down"!—and Surtees did not become popular until *Mr. Sponge's Sporting Tour* came out in 1853.[10] *Sponge* was followed by two lesser novels—*Ask Mamma* (1858), whose hero, Billy Pringle, hunts not because he enjoys it but because his mother tells him "it is the best of all possible sports, and there is none that admits of such elegant variety of costume," and *Plain or Ringlets?* (1860). Surtees's last novel, *Mr. Facey Romford's Hounds,* in which he revived several of the leading characters of *Sponge,* was posthumously published in 1865.

Surtees can hardly be said to have a "method"; indeed he makes something of a point of its absence:

> It may be a recommendation to the lover of light literature to be told that the following story does not involve the complication of a plot. It is a mere continuous narrative of an almost every day exaggeration, interspersed with sporting scenes and excellent illustrations by Leech.

Except for *Romford,* which does make some approach to an organized plot, one episode follows another in Surtees's books, and nobody cares particularly whether all the material is brought to bear

[9] *Handley Cross* began its serial career, which ran to twenty chapters, in 1838; it first came out in book form in 1843. But it did not reach its final state (eighty chapters) until 1854.

[10] Meanwhile Surtees had published *The Analysis of the Hunting-Field* (1846) and a minor novel, *Hawbuck Grange* (1847). *Young Tom Hall* (1851-1853), an uncompleted serial, did not see the dignity of covers until the Blackwood edition of 1926.

on a central theme or not. In *Ask Mamma,* Miss de Glancey is introduced as if she were to play an important role; then she is simply dropped. When the terrible Mrs. Jorrocks is not needed, she disappears from *Hillingdon Hall;* on her brief reappearance, the reader finds himself wondering how in the world Jorrocks was able to get away from her for so long, and how he was able to manage so many activities without her. When the Anti-Corn Law League needs a candidate, Mr. Bowker is reintroduced from a former novel, with no particular regard paid to the consistency of his characterization.

The trial scene in *Pickwick* would seem clearly to show the influence of Jorrocks's trial for the killing of Old Tom, the hare [11]—they get him for poaching when it is determined by foot-rule that the length of his great toe was across the line of Squire Cheatum's estate when he fired the fatal shot—and it must be admitted that even with Dickens's immortal bravura piece in mind, Surtees's dialogue is very amusing. There are those who believe that the general idea of *The Pickwick Papers* was suggested to its publishers, Chapman and Hall, by the success of *Jorrocks.* Both Dickens and Surtees go back to Smollett; one feels the influence more strongly in the older writer because his tone is predominantly farcical throughout his work, not merely in his first novel, as Dickens's is, and also because he comes closer to an eighteenth-century outlook. He lacks Smollett's brutality, to be sure, and Smollett's appetite for dirt, but he is as far from Dickens's intense Victorian earnestness as he is from his sentimentalism.

Jorrocks is a savage compared to Pickwick, yet there are many points of resemblance between them. Don Quixote had his Sancho Panza; Pickwick has his Sam Weller; Jorrocks has his huntsman, James Pigg. Jorrocks is not often so innocent as either of these other worthies (though once Pigg saves him from everlasting disgrace by yanking him out of a temperance procession into which he had strayed!), but what Frederick Watson calls "the contrast between the dry-tongued, uncouth, hard-riding northerner and the voluble,

[11] *Jorrocks' Jaunts and Jollities,* "Surrey-Shotting: Mr. Jorrocks in Trouble." The Jorrocks papers appeared serially, 1831-1834, but the book did not come out until 1838. Meanwhile *Pickwick* had taken England by storm, and poor Surtees was accused of plagiarism!

enthusiastic, but timorous cockney" is consistently maintained. Like Pickwick, the character changes notably; the buffoon of the *Jaunts and Jollities,* who loses his pants on the beach at Margate, is hardly the same man who gives those masterly "lectors" on hunting, and whom Surtees uses as the mouthpiece of his own ideas on agriculture and the Corn Laws. Mr. Pickwick in the pound is not a very pretty sight, but Pickwick is abstemious compared to Jorrocks, and his adventure with the lady in curl-papers is mild indeed compared to Jorrocks's Parisian sojourn with the Countess "Benwolio," or even his flirtations with Mrs. Markham and Mrs. Flather.

This does not mean that Jorrocks is necessarily the lesser achievement. He has the peculiar kind of vulgarity that is one of the glories of English literature, the vulgarity which first appeared notably in the Wife of Bath, and which reached its apotheosis in Falstaff. (Dickens himself achieved it not with Pickwick but with Mrs. Gamp.) With all his faults, Jorrocks has a refreshing freedom from meanness—his humanity as a magistrate is notable—yet I suppose many readers must be surprised to find themselves thinking of him so kindly as they do. No doubt his marvelous vitality has much to do with it, and so does his marvelous lingo.

"I'm a Post Hoffice Directory, not a Peerage, man," he cries. "Where I dine I sleep and where I sleep I breakfast." Mutton-broth reminds him of "a cold in the 'ead," and he calls French macaroni soup "water with worms in it." He refuses mince because he likes to chew his own meat, and he requires "a good fruity wine; a wine with a grip o' the gob, that leaves a mark on the side o' the glass." So enthusiastic is his love of hunting that he hunts in his sleep. "No man is fit to be called a sportsman," he declares in a public address, "wot doesn't kick his wife out of bed on a haverage once in three weeks!" His definition of hunting is famous—"the sport of kings, the image of war without its guilt, and only five-and-twenty per cent. of its danger." And his "COME HUP! I say, YOU HUGLY BEAST!" is still heard and understood among hunting Englishmen.

Surtees has many vivid characters besides Pigg and Jorrocks, but the best of them are surely those two "dead beats," Soapey Sponge and Facey Romford. By 1852 Surtees found it convenient to perform the conventional genuflexion before Mrs. Grundy; he created

Soapey, he tells us, "to put the rising generation on their guard against specious, promiscuous acquaintance, and [train] them on to the noble sport of hunting, to the exclusion of its mercenary, illegitimate off-shoots." There can be no question as to the sincerity of Surtees's opposition to the "low and demoralising pursuits" of "Prize-fighting, Bull-baiting, and Cock-fighting"—he would not so much as allow them to be treated in his magazines—but he did not create Soapey as a horrible example. He might even have agreed with Mr. Watson's enthusiastic defense of that engaging rogue.[12] The brutal ending of *Mr. Sponge's Sporting Tour*—the death of Jack Spraggon in a steeplechase—disturbs many readers, and the Defoe-like unemotionalism of Surtees's description is generally attributed to his own coldness of temperament. No doubt this element enters in, but it should not be forgotten that he has a point to make against racing.

It is in the *Sponge* books too that we get Lucy Glitters, whom Sponge marries, then deserts, when the cigar and betting rooms they establish are not going too well, and who is probably Romford's mistress, as well as his partner in the business alliance they set up. In general, Surtees is very cruel to women: an especially flagrant example is the marriage of the heroine's mother in *Plain or Ringlets?* to "the Jug" who does Jovey Jessup's drinking for him. Except for Jorrocks's niece, Belinda, who is too much of a lay-figure to count—and even Belinda "pets" mildly!—almost all Surtees's women, young and old, are selfish, spiteful, or shrewish. We are told specifically when we first meet Lucy Glitters that the ex-actress is only moderately virtuous, yet we are made to like her, and we feel that Surtees liked her also.

Though Surtees pays little attention to what may be called the intellectual life of his day, it must not be supposed that he was interested only in sport; he reflects his age, indeed, in so many aspects that a whole book has been devoted to the subject. He was deeply concerned over the agricultural problem, and *Hillingdon Hall* is one of the few books in which the modern reader may still find a statement of the case in favor of the Corn Laws. Surtees never

[12] *Robert Smith Surtees, A Critical Study*—Chapter 13, "A Word for Mr. Sponge."

rebelled against his age as Dickens did, but he was too intelligent to be entirely conventional; it has been argued that one reason why his hunting books were less immediately popular than Whyte-Melville's was that Jorrocks was not the early Victorian notion of what an M.F.H. ought to be. Huntsmen were not too comfortable under Surtees's chaffing; he did not quite hew to the "party line."

Surtees is one of the few English novelists who have never been "boomed." Lockhart, Thackeray, William Morris, Kipling, Theodore Roosevelt—these are among the few famous men who have expressed enthusiasm for him; yet he has safely come through his first hundred years. Both Kipling and Wingfield-Stratford have been horrified by the coarseness of the world he pictures; [13] unfortunately we have plenty of testimony that the picture was only too true. Surtees himself was one of the most fastidious of men, and apparently a very reserved man. He wrote because writing had become a habit, and published anonymously; it is said that his daughters never read his books, "because papa said there was nothing worse for young people than reading bad literature"! But because of his historic importance and his own creative powers, he now seems due for a revival, and there are some signs that he may get it. That it will reach the extent of the Trollope revival is doubtful, however, nor can one believe that such ill-considered judgments as André Maurois's statement that Jorrocks is the *chef d'oeuvre* of the English novel will contribute to it notably. Nevertheless it is high time Surtees was rescued from the stables.

6. *Captain Marryat, "The Enslaver of Youth"*

Like Surtees, Frederick Marryat had a specialty. He is the novelist of the old navy and of the sea. The critics never liked Marryat, and when, in his later years, he turned to juvenile fiction, they seized the opportunity to proclaim that he had never been a novelist at all but only a "story-teller." Yet when *Japhet in Search of a Father* was running its serial course, an American vessel ran up a signal to a British merchantman in mid-Atlantic to inquire, "Has Japhet found his father yet?" Today Marryat's name is rarely mentioned

[13] Rudyard Kipling, *A Diversity of Creatures,* "My Son's Wife." Sir Esmé Wingfield-Stratford, *Those Earnest Victorians* (Morrow, 1930), cf. index.

in literary circles, but anyone who thinks he is no longer read may disabuse himself quickly by looking through the British and American catalogues of books in print.

The indifference of the critics is not difficult to understand, for while Marryat's sheer narrative power is so great as to have misled Ford Madox Ford into calling him "the greatest of English novelists," he is a writer concerning whom there is very little to say.

> One may go to him [says Michael Sadleir] for cynical good sense; for knowledge of the world; for gaiety and laughter; for swift, uproarious pantomime; for plots that ripple easily to their end or swirl over rocks or slide dangerously between steep banks; for vivid pictures of a vanished world; for agile, simple English.

Marryat wrote sixteen novels for adults, of which twelve have nautical subjects, and six stories for children. He is more like Smollett than he is like anybody else, and he is more like Smollett than any other writer is like him. And that comes perilously close to being all that needs to be said.

Marryat was born in London, July 10, 1792. His father, an M.P. and a wealthy man, was of Huguenot descent; his mother came of a German family which had settled in Boston. The boy made several attempts to run away from school and go to sea before, in 1806, he was finally allowed to join the crew of the *Impérieuse*. He served with gallantry and distinction, with reckless, foolhardy, and apparently unself-regarding courage in both the Napoleonic War and the Burmese War. But though he became a commander in 1815, he never received the reward which he expected and probably had a right to expect in the navy—his outspoken opposition to impressment may have had something to do with this—and in 1830 he left the sea and settled down on land to spend the rest of his life as a gentleman farmer, a man of fashion, a dissipated buck, a magazine editor, and a novelist. He died August 8, 1848.

We do not know much about Marryat's personality; his daughter's memoir was both very late and very discreet; the evidence that still exists is full of contradictions. He was imperious in his household, we are told, yet his children called him "Baby." What his wife called him we do not know, for he separated from her after she had borne him eleven children. His portrait shows the kind of man generally described as "a handsome devil"; the chin is deeply cleft, and one eyebrow is higher than the other.

It would be unfair to say that Marryat lacked sensibility; not only did he speak out on impressment, but he opposed flogging, and he entertained liberal views on labor conditions and on slavery. He was an impulsive, generous, uncalculating friend to individuals and causes. Yet, despite all disclaimers, it is difficult to believe that the callous caddishness of Frank Mildmay and other Marryat heroes owes all to Smollett and nothing to Marryat. And even when all allowances have been made for thin-skinned American sensibilities, it is difficult to believe that he behaved very well on his stormy American tour.[14]

Not that it is sexual irregularity that troubles us in Marryat's heroes. Contemporary attacks upon him in this connection were quite unfair; his morality as a novelist was very proper; it was even prudish. But it takes a strong stomach to relish his appetite for physical horrors, and the calculating selfishness and hardness of his young men is more repulsive than lust alone can be.

When Jacob Faithful's brother falls overboard, his father hears the splash. "What was that? I shouldn't wonder if it wasn't Joe." But he does not move or stop smoking. By the time the child is found, "the eels and chubs had eaten off his nose and a portion of his chubby face, so that, as my father said, 'he was of no use to nobody.'" In the same novel, the death of Jacob's gin-soaked mother from spontaneous combustion is another case in point.

In a way, the degradations to which Marryat's heroes are submitted in the course of his narratives seem to have little effect on their characters. We are so absorbed by "the poetry of circumstance," to borrow a distinction of Stevenson's, that "the poetry of conduct" quite passes us by. But we should feel more comfortable about Marryat himself if he could give some indication of knowing that not all is quite as it should be.

The first book is the most objectionable from this point of view. *The Naval Officer, or Scenes and Adventures in the Life of Frank*

[14] Cf. Arno Bader's fascinating account of this adventure in "The Gallant Captain and Brother Jonathan," *Colophon,* New Series, II (1936), 114-129.

Mildmay (1829) is sometimes judged as having fallen between the two schools of fiction and autobiographical memoir. But nobody capable of enjoying Marryat at all can fail to relish *Peter Simple, Jacob Faithful* (both 1834), and *Mr. Midshipman Easy* (1836). The last named would deserve immortality if only for the unmarried wet-nurse whom Dr. Middleton brings to Mrs. Easy. When the latter objects to receiving into her house an unmarried woman who has borne a child, the offender drops a curtsey and explains that "if you please, ma'am, it was a very little one."

In *Peter Simple* the theme is the growth to manhood, through naval service, of the fool of the family; in *Easy* we have the contrast between naval discipline and the theories of liberty and equality with which the hero's father has indoctrinated him. Jacob Faithful does not join the navy; he is a waterman on the Thames. It would be too much to say that all the incidents in these books are quite convincing. But they are nearly all vastly entertaining.

Of the non-nautical novels, the picaresque *Japhet in Search of a Father* (1836) is the only one universally regarded as one of Marryat's best. *Snarleyyow, or The Dog Fiend* (1837) has some seafaring men, but the scene is set back in William III's time, and much of the action takes place in Holland. Some critics place *Snarleyyow* high among tales of supernatural horror. Marryat dabbled in the supernatural again in *The Phantom Ship* (1839), which concerns the old legend of the Flying Dutchman.

Marryat's juveniles hardly come within the range of this history, though there are still those who call them the best books for children that have ever been written. *Masterman Ready* (1841-1842) was the first and is probably the most popular. But *The Children of the New Forest* (1847) might run it a close second, and Marryat "fans" are generally very enthusiastic about *The Settlers in Canada* (1844). Marryat is said to have entered this field because he was disgusted over the unreality of *The Swiss Family Robinson.*

Marryat attempts little in the way of elaborate plot-structure or detailed characterization; his own judgment of himself was that his mind was like a kaleidoscope except that there was no regularity in it. He could always make the particular incident sufficiently absorbing to prevent our worrying too much about its relationship to the general design, and the idiosyncrasies of his characters sufficiently vivid to take our minds off the moot matter of their general reality.

What he has in the way of philosophy is conventional and superimposed. He moralizes about Jacob Faithful's resentment against his benefactor, Mr. Drummond, who had discharged him for an alleged fault, and he believes that the adventures of that hero in general go to show that "There is no such thing in the world as independence, unless in a savage state. In society we are all mutually dependent upon each other." But nobody ever remembers any of that in connection with *Jacob Faithful,* and the book would be quite what it is if the idea had never crossed Marryat's mind.

His heroines are generally lay-figures, but in Mary Stapleton, of *Jacob Faithful,* he did go in for psychology. Mary has inherited frivolity and love of adventure from a recreant mother, and she does not learn how to control herself until she has nearly destroyed the man she sincerely loves. And *Japhet in Search of a Father* has an interesting character of a more grotesque variety in Aramathea Judd, a young woman disguised as an old one, to take the place of her aunt, a deceased cultist whose reappearance after death had been promised to her followers. Aramathea finds she can no longer exist without the adoration to which she has now grown accustomed, even though she has had to turn to alcohol to keep going under the strain her life of duplicity involves.

In general, however, if we are to maintain Marryat's claim to a place among the English novelists, it must rest, as Sadleir has rested it, first of all on his style, "his easy, rakish mastery of words," and then, as has already been suggested, on his ability to resurrect a vivid, buried world.

Next after Smollett, the novelist he most strikingly recalls is Sterne. Midshipman Easy's parents are much like Tristram Shandy's and the same note is sounded in the enchanting porter scene at the beginning of *Japhet. Japhet* also reflects Sterne's interest in noses; the hero's is aquiline, and since his ruling passion in life is to find his father, nobody with a similarly constructed protuberance can hope to avoid a careful examination.

7. *The Individualism of Peacock*

Thomas Love Peacock was older than any of the other writers considered in this chapter, but I have placed him last because of the special character of his work. With the Time-Spirit he had little or nothing to do. If he had contemporaries, they were Aristophanes, Rabelais, and Voltaire, not the Lake Poets with whom his lot was cast and whom he often caricatured.

Peacock was born in or near Weymouth, in Dorsetshire, October 18, 1785. His father was a merchant, his mother the daughter of a master in the Royal Navy. He grew up in rural surroundings at Chertsey, and his formal schooling ended when he was thirteen; as a classical scholar he was self-educated. When his friend Shelley deserted his first wife, Harriet, Peacock staunchly took her part and served her, till her death, in every way he was capable. In his youth Peacock worked as clerk and secretary; in 1819 he came into the employ of the East India Company, where he rendered distinguished service for many years, being partly responsible for the introduction, first, of steam-propelled vessels, and later of iron (as replacing wooden) ships. He died at Lower Halliford, on the Thames, January 23, 1866.

With Peacock's poems and plays we are not here concerned, nor yet with his literary and musical criticism. His fame rests finally on his fiction—five "novels of talk" in a contemporary setting and two historical, or, rather, legendary, romances. *Headlong Hall* (1816); *Melincourt* (1817); *Nightmare Abbey* (1818); *Crotchet Castle* (1831); and *Gryll Grange* (1861) make up the first group; the second comprises *Maid Marian* (1822) and *The Misfortunes of Elphin* (1829).

Between these two groups the line of demarcation is less absolute than it is sometimes made to appear. There are plenty of ideas even in the rollicking *Marian,* and Peacock's wonderful gift for the elaborate demonstration of propositions patently absurd was never better exemplified than in some of Prince Seithenyn's speeches in *Elphin.*

Nor is it quite accurate to say that the country-house novels have no plot. Even *Headlong Hall,* the earliest and the simplest, has at least the materials from which a plot could be built, and a conventionally romantic one at that. Only, Peacock chooses not to build it: the incidents are all hurried out of the way as cavalierly as even Meredith might do it, so that our attention may be centered upon the ideas expressed. Consider, in this connection, the wonderful celerity with which a whole group of marriages is arranged in Chapter 14. The only person who makes any trouble at all is the phrenologist, Mr. Cranium, who will not agree to give his daughter to Mr. Escot unless the latter will give him the skull of Cadwallader in exchange! To arrange this little transfer is, of course, but the work of a moment.

In *Nightmare Abbey* we have the theater-situation of the disobedient lovers, which is familiar to us all in *The Rivals* and many other plays; and *Melincourt* has a perfect "movie" climax, the heroine being rescued by Sir Oran Haut-ton, in the very nick of time, from the villain who had abducted and imprisoned her.

This misplacement of emphasis was deliberate on Peacock's part. Citing Petronius, Rabelais, Swift, and Voltaire as his predecessors in the use of this method, he avowedly built his books around opinions, not characters. The characters of his earlier books—"Mr. Foster, the perfectibilian; Mr. Escot, the deteriorationist; Mr. Jenkinson, the statu-quo-ite" (all in *Headlong Hall*); Mr. Toobad, the eschatologist, who goes about crying, "The devil is come among you having great wrath"; and Mr. Asterias, who spends his days in search of a mermaid (both in *Nightmare Abbey*)—are only embodied idiosyncrasies in the humors tradition; but he introduced more shading in later books.

Moreover, Peacock's people are definitely placed in their world. It is a thin and narrow world compared to those the great novelists have created, but it is a world, and the soul of its creator impregnates it. Carl Van Doren has pointed out that the action in Peacock's books is largely independent of the people who take part in it. There can be little question of the depth of the author's insight at this point; in his own eccentric way, he illuminates the everlasting dichotomy between faith and practice, the word and the deed. The avidity with which his characters embrace the pleasures of the table is a testimonial to his own worship of Bacchus, but it is much more than that; as in the *Rubáiyát,* the symbolic is here much the larger significance.

The list of writers who influenced Peacock could easily be enlarged. He read in five literatures—Greek, Latin, English, French, and Italian. Later he added Spanish, but his dislike of transcendentalism always caused him to avoid German. In general, the writers he loved best had cool, crisp, but never bitter, minds. J. B. Priestley has observed that Euripides, Lucretius, Dante, and Milton all passed him by. His younger contemporary, Dickens, he did not discover until the last year of his life, when he read him with avidity, finding his favorite novel in *Our Mutual Friend.*

Peacock was a poet as well as a satirist. In his youth he loved unhappily, which is probably good for poets. As long as he lived he wore the girl's hair in a locket, and before he died (at eighty-one), he told his granddaughter that his lost love had been visiting him in dreams. But it is only in the exquisite natural beauty of the settings in his novels that he allows his romanticism full sway; love itself he handles always with a certain abashment. Indeed, Peacock is not often passionate, even about ideas, nor is he often a special advocate. He prefers the dramatic method, and he was well pleased when told that he himself had taken no sides in the argument.[15]

Many of the things Peacock disliked are, of course, perfectly clear —the universities, the rotten boroughs, spiritualism, paper money, slavery, Malthusianism, and much besides. But the interest is always in the discussion, and every phase of opinion is reflected somewhere. Peacock's own meditations on the tyranny of the state [16] have still, unhappily, as much vital significance as they had in his time or in

[15] John W. Draper is the only critic who has had the nerve to try to determine Peacock's own beliefs from his novels; his conclusions are pretty nihilistic. Cf. "The Social Satire of Thomas Love Peacock," *Modern Language Notes,* XXXIII (1918), 456-463; XXXIV (1919), 23-28.

[16] *The Misfortunes of Elphin, Ch. 6:* "The powerful took all they could get from their subjects and neighbours; and called something or other sacred and glorious, when they wanted the people to fight for them. They repressed disaffection by force, when it showed itself in an overt act; but they encouraged freedom of speech, when it was, like Hamlet's reading, 'words, words, words.'" Peacock himself contributed indirectly to the growth of imperialism through his service in the East India Company.

Elphin's; Mr. Crotchet's vindication of the decency of nakedness [17] is just as sound as ever it was; Mr. Forester's reflections on the responsibility of the individual for social sins [18] are unfortunately somewhat marred by that character's general priggishness. In *Melincourt* there is a fine critical examination of Wordsworth's curious notion that morality is somehow an emanation of the landscape.[19] Mr. MacLaurel anticipates some of Mark Twain's reasoning in *What Is Man?*,[20] and Dr. Opimian's conviction that most accidents are crimes suggests Samuel Butler.[21] Dr. Opimian also fears that "it is the ultimate destiny of science to exterminate the human race," [22] a fear which has certainly not lessened since Peacock was happily laid to rest.

Peacock uses virtually the same "frame" in all the country-house novels: an amiable crotcheteer gathers a group of assorted crotcheteers about him in his country-house; they talk, dine, drink, and (some of them) fall in love. Mr. Priestley has divided Peacock's characters into three classes:

> the crotcheteers in general, each with his dominating interest or theory; the caricatures of actual persons; and the more rounded and normal characters . . . who range from mere faint sketches to complete individuals.

Such controversy as the caricatures awaken centers today about the Lake Poets, for naturally many of the non-literary folk are no longer recognizable without a gloss. Southey's portrait as Feathernest and Wordsworth's as Mr. Paperstamp (both in *Melincourt*) are grossly unfair—Shelley thoroughly enjoyed himself as Scythrop in *Nightmare Abbey*—but in general Peacock's satire is not vicious. He attempts no actual presentment of a man's personality. What he does is to take a set of opinions and build an independent embodiment of his own around them.

It is not too difficult to pick and choose among Peacock's novels. In the country-house group, *Headlong Hall* is prentice work, and

[17] *Crotchet Castle,* Ch. 7.

[18] In *Melincourt.* To discourage slavery in the West Indies, Forester drinks his tea without sugar, as Peacock himself did.

[19] Ch. 37.

[20] *Headlong Hall,* Ch. 5.

[21] *Gryll Grange,* Ch. 7.

[22] Ch. 19.

Melincourt is, on the whole, unsatisfactory. The brilliant idea of making an orangoutang the central character in a novel gave the author a fine opportunity to satirize human nature in general and some of the particular theories of the primitivists in particular, but he made less of the opportunity than might have been expected. *Nightmare Abbey* is more successful. A mock-Gothic, with the supernaturalism all neatly explained at the end, *à la* Mrs. Radcliffe, it was written "merely to bring to a sort of philosophical focus a few of the morbidities of modern literature, and to let in a little daylight on its atrabilious complexion." But, good as it is, it seems slight compared to *Crotchet Castle,* in which this phase of Peacock's art was brought to its fullest flowering. Thirty years later, he recaptured the old method, if not quite the old verve, in *Gryll Grange;* and Peacockians are still divided on whether the lovely mellowness of that book atones for its banked fires.

In *Maid Marian* the present writer can find very little to distinguish it from many other versions of the Robin Hood story from Scott [23] to Howard Pyle. It is not surprising that Planché and Bishop made an opera of it; indeed, Peacock himself had almost saved them the trouble.[24] The heroine herself is rather unpleasantly Amazonian, but the skull-thwacking Friar Tuck is the best expression we have of Peacock's slapstick; as a character he ranks with the two clergymen—Dr. Folliott, of *Crotchet Castle,* and Dr. Opimian, of *Gryll Grange,* in which, unspiritual as they are, a pagan novelist sought to make amends to the church for the sots and gluttons he had presented as her representatives in his earlier books. *The Mis-*

[23] For a study of the problems involved in the resemblances between *Maid Marian* and *Ivanhoe,* cf. Sir Henry Newbolt, *Studies Green and Gray* (Nelson, 1926) and Halliford Edition of Peacock, I, p. cx ff.

[24] The comic opera spirit in Peacock is not peculiar to *Marian,* though it is strongest there. Songs and ballads appear in the text of all his novels. Falconer, of *Gryll Grange,* who lives (chastely) in a tower with seven girls to serve him, is very Gilbertian. Out of a sense of obligation to the seven maidens, Falconer hesitates to wed the lady of his choice; simultaneously, one of the maidens, Dorothy, is hesitating to accept the love of Harry Hedgerow because she does not wish to desert Falconer. Harry finally produces six friends, each of them quite as devoted to one of the remaining six maidens as he is to Dorothy. See Freeman, *Thomas Love Peacock,* p. 330 ff. for an argument that Falconer is Shelley.

fortunes of Elphin, however, is a much more ambitious affair. Here Peacock is working in the old Welsh legends, combining the story of Seithenyn, the story of Taliesin, and the story of Guinevere's abduction by Melwas. Seithenyn himself is as close an approach as can be made to Falstaff on the level of pure irony;[25] and the book as a whole is Peacock's austerest achievement; by it he may well be content to stand or fall.

[25] Seithenyn's refusal to keep the Royal Embankment in repair, actually because he is too lazy and drunken to care about it, is justified to his critics on grounds of conservatism in words which echo the public utterances of Tory leaders of the period. (Cf. Priestley, *Thomas Love Peacock,* pp. 191-192.) Perhaps the point is too obvious to be noted, but I have nowhere found any comment on the fact that this delightful speech is built on the model of Falstaff's own utterances in *1 Henry IV:* "Everything that is old must decay. That the embankment is old, I am free to confess; that it is somewhat rotten in parts, I will not altogether deny; that it is any the worse for that, I do most sturdily gainsay. It does its business well: it works well: it keeps out the water from the land, and it lets in the wine upon the High Commission of Embankment. Cupbearer, fill. Our ancestors were wiser than we: they built it in their wisdom; and, if we should be so rash as to try to mend it, we should only mar it." When the flood comes, Seithenyn draws his sword and leaps into the raging sea, surely an echo of *Hamlet,* III, 1:59—"Or to take arms against a sea of troubles."

CHAPTER XIII

WHITE MAGIC

"Yes—doesn't Charley D. make our little men smaller than ever—and such *pencil sharpeners*—"

KATHERINE MANSFIELD

Dickens's place among novelists is that of the woman in the Gospels who was a sinner. Much is forgiven him because he loved much. He has enough faults to sink a whole flotilla of lesser writers, but he sails serenely on in spite of them, propelled by that marvelous endowment of creative energy in which, among all English writers, he is surpassed only by Shakespeare and matched only by Scott. He alone among the Victorians has never lost his contemporary popularity, and insofar as there has ever been any critical reaction against him, it has now spent its force utterly. Yet it is significant that one never thinks of him in terms of literature alone. He was so vital that literature could not hold all of him. He was a great moral force, an apostle of spiritual power; he incarnated the hope of an age.

1. *The Life and Works of Charles Dickens*

Charles Dickens was born at Landport, February 7, 1812, but soon came to London, where all the formative influences of his life were centered. He is said to have preserved some of his father's characteristics in Mr. Micawber, his mother's in Mrs. Nickleby. Dickens had no formal schooling after he was fifteen, and not too much before that. Having mastered on his own initiative an unbelievably complex system of shorthand, he gained his first foothold in the world as a parliamentary reporter. The real beginning of his career as an author came in 1836, when the publishers Chapman and Hall asked him to furnish the letter-press to accompany a series of sporting plates by Robert Seymour. Seymour's suicide, just before the publication of the second number, left Dickens in charge of the enterprise, free to develop *The Pickwick Papers* (1836-1837) according to his own ideas.

The result was hardly a novel, but there is no other work of Dickens's in which art plays so small a role comparatively and genius so large a one. "A whole picture of rural England rose up," writes M. André Maurois, "a very eighteenth century and rural England, alive with that sort of childlike delight which the English take in simple pleasures, the enjoyment of roaring fires on the hearth, sliding in snowy weather, a good dinner, and simple, rather absurd love-affairs." There are hundreds of characters in *Pickwick,* mostly comic characters, for the book is predominantly farcical in tone, beyond anything else Dickens ever did. Yet even in the glorious hilarities of the Bardell-Pickwick Trial, his sharp impatience with institutionalism has already manifested itself, and there is some serious social criticism in the story of Mr. Pickwick's incarceration in the Fleet. Pickwick and his servant Sam Weller, that incredible yet disarming combination of cockney smartness and disinterested faithfulness, fall into the time-honored relationship of Don Quixote and Sancho Panza, as has already been noted in these pages. Chesterton called Pickwick a fairy, but Sam calls him "a reg'lar thorough-bred angel," an angel in tights and gaiters. Dickens sins somewhat against the canons of art, but never against those of humanity, when he permits the figure he designed as a butt to change as the story advances until at crucial moments his magnanimity brings tears to our eyes.

Dickens's second novel, *Oliver Twist* (1837-1839), which traces the fortunes of a poor foundling in his life among thieves, is as grim as *Pickwick* is jolly. The plot is melodramatic and impossible; scenes and personages observed with tremendous faithfulness are set beside much that can live only in the light shed from a glaring lime. Sikes and Nancy belong, mainly at least, in the first class; Fagin, the terrible Jew who trains boys to steal, probably belongs in both. *Nicholas Nickleby* (1838-1839), which was written concurrently, may be said to contain all the elements, good and bad, of Dickens's novels. Mystery and horror are here, and farce and tenderness, and moral purpose—this time in the form of an attack on brutal schoolmasters—and, best of all, Vincent Crummles and Mantalini and Mrs. Nickleby and the mad suitor who says it with vegetables. You may test yourself as a Dickensian by your ability to relish *Nickleby.* In later years Dickens worked hard to overcome the faults revealed in it, and up to a point at least he succeeded, but it is a question whether he did not lose more than he gained; for many men have achieved a pervasive plot in this world, but none other among all the countless millions of mankind has ever been able to turn out a *Pickwick* or a *Nickleby.*

Dickens's next venture was a huge miscellany to be known as *Master Humphrey's Clock,* but the public was not much interested. Consequently, *The Old Curiosity Shop* (1840-1841), which had originally been designed as a short piece, was expanded to a full-length novel; it and *Barnaby Rudge* (1841) came therefore to make up the bulk of the modified *Clock.*

Barnaby Rudge, which, except for *A Tale of Two Cities,* is Dickens's only historical novel, is in some ways even less characteristic of him than that great tragic melodrama. It shows the influence of *The Heart of Midlothian,* as well as that of the Gothic novels, and it is interesting to compare Dickens's more sensational picture of the "No Popery" riots with Scott's portrayal of the Porteous mob. The heroine, Dolly Varden, is Dickens's first study of a pretty little minx; Thomas Wright would seem to have overlooked her in his contention that Dickens did not portray this type of girl until after he had become acquainted with Ellen Ternan. *Barnaby Rudge* is a rather well-built book, but what we may call the "private plot" is not too well connected with the historical background, and in Barnaby himself the author has disregarded the law which prohibits the use of idiots and madmen as central characters in a serious work of art.

For Dickens's contemporaries, *The Old Curiosity Shop* was the story of Little Nell and her Grandfather. The intensity of their love for that innocent child is astonishing; no less astonishing is the animus she has awakened in our own time! Careful re-reading of the book in which she figures would perhaps convince many of her enemies that she suffers through confusion in memory with later inferior treatments of the type of character she exemplifies. Dickens surrounded Nell with monstrosities like the dwarf Quilp, and lovable eccentrics like Dick Swiveller and the Marchioness.

Dickens was now riding the crest of a tremendous popularity. In 1842 he made his first visit to America, where he was riotously welcomed and cruelly disappointed. Instead of the utopia of his young radical dreams, he found a land where many of the abuses of the Old World had already taken root, and along with them he found much of the coarseness and crudeness inseparable from a new country. He went home in disgust to write his *American Notes* (1842), which he followed with the novel, *Martin Chuzzlewit* (1843-1844), which contains many cruel caricatures of extreme, obnoxious American types. *Chuzzlewit* attacks a private vice, selfishness, instead of a public wrong. It is as formless and heterogeneous as *Nickleby* itself, but it is maturer in its outlook and it reaches greater heights. In *Chuzzlewit,* too, we get Mrs. Gamp, who is generally considered Dickens's masterpiece in characterization. A more genial event of the same period was the appearance in 1843 of what A. Edward Newton called "the greatest little book in the world," *A Christmas Carol.*[1]

Between 1844 and 1847 Dickens and his family were much abroad —in Italy, in Switzerland, and in Paris. At Lausanne in 1846 he began work on the novel which marks the beginning of his later, more realistic manner, *Dombey and Son* (1846-1848). The book itself is not wholly convincing. The intrigue which centers around the second Mrs. Dombey is forced, and Dickens lacked the courage to carry it to the logical conclusion he had planned for it. When Edith goes off with Carker it was originally intended that she should go as his mistress. Lord Jeffrey objected, and Dickens changed his plan. The inevitable result is that the reader is left wondering vainly why in the world she should run off at all. The death of Paul repeats the

[1] Later *Christmas Books* were *The Chimes* (1844); *The Cricket on the Hearth* (1845); *The Battle of Life* (1846); *The Haunted Man* (1848). Though the *Cricket* has always been very popular, neither it nor any of the others ever reached the *Carol's* standard. *The Chimes,* however, is very significant for Dickens's sociological ideas. Cf. my *Man Charles Dickens,* and especially my Introduction to the edition of *The Chimes,* with pictures by Arthur Rackham, published in 1931 by the Limited Editions Club.

Little Nell motif of *The Old Curiosity Shop;* in itself it is handled masterfully, but it breaks the book in two. I confess I think Florence Dombey a somewhat better heroine than most critics do, but there is no denying that the best thing about *Dombey and Son* is that when gorgeous eccentrics like Cap'n Cuttle wander into it, Dickens is still more or less disposed to let them go their own gait, without worrying too much about whether their antics link up with the theme of the book or not. During the years leading up to 1850 Dickens began his famous amateur theatrical performances for charity, and with the establishment of his weekly magazine, *Household Words,* in March, 1850, he found the beginning of the successful journalistic venture he had sought for long.

Halfway through the century came the great autobiographical novel, *David Copperfield* (1849-1850), the most beloved piece of fiction in the English language. The Micawbers, Peggotty and her brother, Aunt Betsy Trotwood, and Mr. Dick are well enough known to all persons who can read English so that no description of the book in which they appear is necessary; and this is fortunate, for no description is possible.

There are touches of melodrama in *Copperfield,* but they are only touches; fundamentally the book is God's truth. Objectively regarded, probably the Murdstones were not monsters. But that is irrelevant. We never see the Murdstones objectively; we see them only through the eyes of a small boy whom they frightened nearly to death. As for the marriage of David and Dora, Ernest A. Baker's tribute is well deserved; it is "a prose-poem of love and wedlock," "an enchanting idyll, which Dickens was sane enough to treat with delicate humour, whilst he entered whole-heartedly into all its transports."

Copperfield was followed by *Bleak House* (1852-1853), an immensely ambitious novel involving an attack on "the law's delay," especially the Court of Chancery. Here for the first time Dickens achieves a perfect plot of its kind, and every one in his long list of characters—the high and the low, the serious and the comic—is brought into relationship with it and developed with reference to it. But sensationalism does not disappear. W. C. Phillips has remarked that what *Hamlet* and *The White Devil* are to the Elizabethan tragedy of blood, *Great Expectations* and *The Moonstone* are to popular Victorian sensation fiction. Perhaps *Bleak House* would be a better example than either of the two novels chosen. The one thing in the book which no critic can defend is the use of Esther Summerson as narrator of part of the story. Esther herself is a bore; the technical device employed is not sustained, and it would not be worth the effort if it were.

Hard Times (1854), an attack on political economy of the Manchester school, with side glances at the English divorce laws, shows Dickens's sympathy with the views of Carlyle, but interests students of his fiction primarily as illustrating what a great genius turns out when he gets completely away from his own material and method. It is Dickens's only arid book. Something of its mood carries over into *Little Dorrit* (1855-1857), for though this book is more in Dickens's own manner, it probably marks the height of his sociological interest. Writers like Bernard Shaw who are interested in literature primarily for its propaganda values naturally place *Little Dorrit*—"a more seditious book than *Das Kapital*"—at the height of Dickens's achievement. A more disinterested judgment will probably see it as the titanic effort of a very tired man.

In 1858 Dickens separated at last from his wife,[2] and the sense of relief which supervened upon this resolution of a long intolerable domestic situation expressed itself in a fresh burst of creative energy. Neither *A Tale of Two Cities* (1859) nor *Great Expectations* (1860-1861) gives us quite the old Dickens, but in both we get something splendid. The *Tale* is "a picturesque story," "a story of incident," a

[2] Of late years the scandal-mongers have been very busy with this matter; cf. Thomas Wright, *The Life of Charles Dickens* (Scribners, 1935); Hugh Kingsmill, *The Sentimental Journey, A Life of Charles Dickens* (Morrow 1935); Gladys Storey, *Dickens and Daughter* (London: Frederick Muller, Ltd., 1939). Be it said once and for all that nothing approaching evidence has ever been brought forward to substantiate the contention of these writers that Ellen Ternan was Dickens's mistress. Edmund Wilson, however, has naïvely accepted the theory and states it as fact in his essay on Dickens in *The Wound and the Bow* (Houghton Mifflin, 1941), a completely irresponsible piece of criticism. For further discussion, cf. J. W. T. Ley's review of Thomas Wright's book, *The Dickensian*, XXXII, December, 1935, pp. 15-21, and my review of *The Wound and the Bow*, *Modern Language Quarterly*, III (1942), 161-164.

story for its own sake, a dramatization of Carlyle's *French Revolution;* and if Dickens has a true tragic character, Sydney Carton is his name. *Great Expectations* is a more "arty" *David Copperfield.* In *Our Mutual Friend* (1864-1865) he again essayed a full-length variegated book,[3] but the weariness he had held off for two novels is now seen creeping back upon him.

Dickens was indeed much too tired to write and much too nervous to rest. For refuge he turned to extensive reading-tours in England and in America.

There was for him no "city of the mind" against outward ills [wrote the man who understood him best, his biographer, John Forster], for inner consolation and shelter. It was in and from the actual he still stretched forth to find the freedom and satisfactions of an ideal, and by his very attempts to escape the world, he was driven back into the thick of it. But what he would have sought there, it supplies to none; and to get the infinite out of anything so finite, has broken many a stout heart.

The tours were phenomenally successful, the most successful of their kind in history. But they finished Dickens. Apoplexy took him on June 8, 1870, half way through *The Mystery of Edwin Drood* (1870), in which for the first time he had staked everything upon a plot whose secret nobody has solved to this day.

2. *The Influences on Dickens*

The great influences upon Dickens's life and work were the character of the age in which he lived; his early poverty; the books he read in his formative years and his love of the theater; his work as a reporter; and an unhappy love-affair at eighteen.

His age was a period of industrial development, marked by the rise of the middle class. Of this middle class he made himself one. For it he wrote. Its aspirations were his aspirations, its limitations were his limitations; its human kindliness he found reflected in his own heart. He was twenty when the first Reform Bill went through, twenty-one when Shaftesbury began his campaign to protect children in industry. Of what his work might have been like had he

[3] Both *A Tale of Two Cities* and *Great Expectations* are (like *Oliver Twist* before them) just one-half Dickens's usual length—about 500 pages in modern editions. *Hard Times* is even shorter.

lived in another age, we catch lovely glimpses in the rural scenes of *The Old Curiosity Shop.* As it was, this could be no more than an interesting divagation. He is urban. His scene is London, a vast, dark, lowering London, a mighty fungus-growth. It is a terrifying city that saps the strength out of men's souls; yet he loves it. It is an immense magic-lantern show to him; he has difficulty when he tries to write away from the stimulus of its mighty contact. Yet he hates it, and because he loves the men it is destroying he never quite makes terms with it, with the age, or with himself. Like Ruskin's, like Carlyle's, but with more of impulse and less of consciously directed intelligence, his voice cries out in the wilderness, but it is no undivided voice. For he is his age, with its iconoclasm, its worship of energy, its easy faith in progress; and when these things fail him at last there is nothing left but to kill himself with work.

Take the effect of the changing times as reflected in the most obvious, the most material thing of all—Dickens's method of publication. For Scott the novel was an aristocratic diversion: with *Kenilworth* he got the price up to thirty-one shillings, sixpence, and there it stayed. Most of Dickens's novels were first published in monthly parts at a shilling each. One result was an extension of the reading public; another was an inevitable looseness of structure in the work itself. Each installment must now be interesting, and the novelist is encouraged to think in terms of serial units, rather than in terms of the book as a whole. Moreover, he must use repetition freely to aid the memories of simple readers. Dickens was never very far ahead of the printer, and he often started with no definite plan in mind. Even when he had a plan, he found it possible to introduce modifications in response to public demand. But it was not only through the sales-reports that his readers influenced him. They created an atmosphere for him. The modern novelist finishes his book and sends it out into the world. It may be read for a year or for a hundred years. But he is through with it, save to cash his royalty checks, if there are any. His creative energy is enlisted in other things. Dickens, on the other hand, set a whole people to laughing or weeping together, as he should choose to give the signal, and they wept or laughed as he wrote.

In *David Copperfield* Dickens has described his own early reading in the great novelists of the eighteenth century. As I have already had occasion to point out, Smollett was particularly dear to him and (excepting his savagery) a strong influence upon him. He knew the essayists also, and Gissing is no doubt right when he ascribes to Dickens's thorough familiarity with them his general freedom from vulgarism in style. He knew the Bible, *The Arabian Nights,* Shakespeare (superficially), Ben Jonson, Carlyle best of all among contemporaries. Few other writers had a really important influence upon him; he was never, in any sense, a "reading man." But for his immediate models he needed something "smarter," more "up to date" than Fielding and Smollett; so he turned to such popular makers of *facetiae* as Pierce Egan and Theodore Hook.

Their influence upon him is commonly deplored, as is also that of the popular theater. But the theater brought Dickens more than sensationalism and claptrap melodrama. He created his characters as an actor creates them, and to this he owes his unparalleled vividness. "I have just burnt into Newgate," he writes Forster, while working on *Barnaby Rudge,* "and am going in the next number to tear the prisoners out by the hair of their heads." As soon as the idea of *A Tale of Two Cities* came to him, he became eager to "embody" it in his "own person."

Katherine Mansfield sensed this experiencial note in Dickens and chose it as the distinguishing quality which marked him off from her own contemporaries:

> There are moments when Dickens is possessed by this power of writing: he is carried away. That is bliss. It certainly is not shared by writers today. The death of Merdle: dawn falling upon the edge of night. One realises exactly the mood of the writer and how he wrote, as it were, for himself, but it was not his will. He *was* the falling dawn, and he *was* the physician going to Bar.[4]

Dickens's journalistic work taught him a method and provided a means to discipline his energies. Through it he established himself in the world; through it he acquired his intimate familiarity with

[4] *Journal of Katherine Mansfield* (quoted like the epigraph from Katherine Mansfield's *Letters,* at the beginning of this chapter, by permission of the publisher, Alfred A. Knopf). See my article, "Dickens and Katherine Mansfield," *The Dickensian,* XXVI, Winter, 1929-1930, pp. 15-23.

roads and inns and his always intense dislike for law and lawyers.

On the unhappy experiences of Dickens's youth it is more difficult to dogmatize. His contact with Maria Beadnell probably warped his view of women, whom he tended to think of for many years as either monsters or angels, with a special subdivision under the second rubric for mischievous angels. Maria, too, threw him straight into the arms of Catherine Hogarth, who, through no fault of her own, was of all the women in England the one least fitted to be his wife. More far-reaching still in its influence upon him was the deep suffering he experienced when he was taken out of school and put to work in a blacking warehouse. This ordeal developed a tremendous capacity for self-pity in his nature; at the same time it taught him, at a cruelly early age, that if he were to stand in the world, he must rest his weight on his own backbone. In a sense it made him stubborn and self-centered; what is remarkable is that it did not make him selfish. One may be annoyed by his self-pity, but one admits that he made the best possible use of it. In the blacking warehouse he received his baptism into the sufferings of the world. There were not many men of his time who tried harder to alleviate those sufferings than he.

3. *Towards Evaluation*

As a maker of plots, Dickens never approached his disciple, Wilkie Collins. He had to have a plot, an increasingly complicated plot as time went on, a plot abounding in melodramatic action and theatrical surprises. But some of his very best characters have virtually nothing to do with the action of the book in which they find themselves. Pecksniff and Micawber are utterly delightful so long as they are only called upon to be themselves, but the Micawber who unmasks Uriah Heep is quite unbelievable, and the end of the Pecksniff story suggests nothing so much as breaking a butterfly upon the wheel.

Dickens would have sympathized perfectly with Turgenev's pronouncement that the writer of fiction should begin with his characters and not with his plot. Once he had invented his personages and got them going, he felt strongly that it was their business to tell the story and not his. If they got out of hand and proposed to go their own way, he was always more or less inclined to let them go.

But how did he get them going? First of all, as Shakespeare did, as Scott did, by the simple expedient of permitting them to talk themselves alive. Except in dialogue, he is not a stylist, as Thackeray is a stylist, but how marvelous his dialogue is! When he has completely realized a character, he invents for him a distinctive utterance that is that character and nobody else on earth. We should know what Mrs. Gamp is from the rhythm of her speech alone even if we could not understand a word she says. And though he has his failures, it is not his great personages alone of whom this must be said. Dozens of characters make but one brief appearance in Dickensland, yet, like Shakespeare's First Gravedigger in *Hamlet,* in that instant they talk themselves into immortality. This is Dickens's greatest gift for characterization, but it is not his only gift; nor, since he is novelist, not playwright, could it alone suffice.

He had a great knack for "tagging" his characters. The "tag" may be physical, like Mr. Carker's teeth, or Uncle Pumblechook's "mouth like a fish, dull staring eyes, and sandy hair standing upright on his head, so that he looked as if he had just been all but choked, and had that moment come to." It may be a speech-tag, like "I never will desert Mr. Micawber" or John Jarndyce's frequent references to the east wind. Or it may take the form of a characteristic action, as when Traddles draws skeletons all over his slate. Shakespeare, it will be recalled, speaks of Juliet's habit of blushing, and Hamlet has the trick of repeating words and phrases—"Very like, very like." Such things do not necessarily "mean" anything, but they do cause a character to come alive on the printed page.

Some of Dickens's greatest triumphs were won along this line. Mrs. Gamp running her nose along the top of the fender, Plornish picking a bit of lime out of his whisker, Mrs. Gargery cutting bread —the pictures imprint themselves upon the film of the imagination forever.

He is equally adept in his use of properties—and here he shows with special vividness the influence of the theater. When Miss Murdstone came to the Rookery, "she brought with her two uncompromising hard black boxes, with her initials on the lids in hard brass nails. When she paid the coachman she took her money out of a hard steel purse, and she kept the purse in a very jail of a bag which hung upon her arm by a heavy chain, and shut up like a bite."

The mention of Miss Murdstone serves conveniently to remind us of the obvious fact that Dickens uses names as an element in characterization. Murdstone itself was probably intended to suggest both "stone" and "murder." And his methods here are more various than the casual reader would be likely to suppose.[5]

But I would seem to have played straight into the hands of the enemy. Most of the unfortunate people who are unable to like Dickens would grant much of what I have so far written. But, they would add, all this shows that he was second-rate. His personages lack reality. They are caricatures; they are types. His grotesques alone can he make even remotely convincing. His heroes and heroines are sticks; he never drew the portrait of a gentleman. He is quite unable to indicate developments, and he does not understand the characters he himself has created.

If we are to judge Dickens by his worst work, all these charges can be sustained. But if we judge him by his best, as he has a right to ask, there will be a very different story to tell.

As to the objective reality of his personages, it is difficult at this distance of time to enter a dogmatic judgment. That they were real to him is beyond disputing. He quotes them in his letters; to finish a book and dismiss them was agony unspeakable to him. But Time has thrown the world of which he wrote into the pack on his back; many of its types have simply disappeared from the earth. George Gissing, who saw the tail-end of those days, always defended the reality of Dickens; Santayana declared that those who accused him of exaggeration had no eyes nor ears but accepted things "conventionally, at their diplomatic value." But this, of course, is a secondary question. Naturally Dickens's characters are not "real" as life is "real." If they were they would be bad art, for literature is not life. But that they have amazing vitality as art, it were vain to deny. "There is nothing like them in life," write Batho and Dobrée, "but

[5] Cf. Elizabeth Hope Gordon, "The Naming of Characters in the Works of Charles Dickens," *University of Nebraska Studies in Language, Literature, and Criticism,* Number 1, 1917.

life is the poorer for being without them. If Providence did not create Mrs. Gamp, Chadband and the rest of them, it ought, we feel, to have done so."[6]

In Dickens, as in Scott, the hero and heroine are often much less vivid than the lesser characters. We have already observed that Dickens creates as an actor, and every actor knows how easily the "character" roles may become more vivid than the "leads." But Dickens improved steadily along this line. Pip is much better than Nicholas Nickleby, and Bella Wilfer than Rose Maylie. The same thing may be said of his gentlemen. The young radical had too much prejudice against the upper classes ever to look at them dispassionately: Sir Mulberry Hawk and Lord Frederick Verisopht are therefore as unreal as two characters might well be. But the creator of Sir Leicester Dedlock (though not yet completely successful), had got far beyond such nonsense. John Jarndyce is a gentleman; Mr. Crisparkle is a gentleman; Andrew Lang insisted that the boy who cried, "Shame, J. Steerforth!" was a gentleman.

The charge that Dickens did not understand his characters is made by no less sensitive a critic than Lord David Cecil, who cites Micawber's transformation, at the close of *David Copperfield,* into a successful magistrate. "It is as though, in the last chapter of *Pride and Prejudice,* Jane Austen were to inform us that Mr. Collins became the secret paramour of Lady Catherine de Bourgh." And he is right, but his rightness is more or less beside the point.

Dickens was not an intellectual in any sense. He lived through one of the most harrowing periods in the religious history of mankind, without, so far as written evidence goes, ever having heard of Darwin or evolution, certainly without having thought about them. What he conceived scientific research to be we may infer from his reference in *Pickwick* to the learned gentleman who wrote a treatise on the mysterious lights in the garden; his idea of a scholar is suggested in Mr. Curdle, of *Nicholas Nickleby,* who "had written a pamphlet of sixty-four pages, post octavo, on the character of the Nurse's deceased husband in Romeo and Juliet. . . ." We must not expect too much in the way of analysis from such a man.

[6] Edith Batho and Bonamy Dobrée, *The Victorians and After, 1830-1914* (McBride, 1938), p. 83.

Lord David Cecil himself, who appreciates Dickens, realizes that we have gained, as well as lost, through this limitation in him, citing for one thing his wonderful success when viewing life from the point of view of a child. But I think he takes the Micawber matter much too seriously. I am sure Dickens knew as well as we do that Micawber could never have been a successful magistrate. He is closing up his novel in a hurry, he has to account for everybody, and all the good people must be made happy. This is a novel—not a history; why should not Micawber become a successful magistrate? And especially since we never see him in that capacity, but only hear of him, far off in Australia, which was almost as mythical a country to Dickens, and to most of his readers, as Lilliput or Brobdingnag? In precisely the same fashion did Shakespeare lightly save the souls of Oliver and Duke Frederick so that everything might end "as you like it." These things are not at all in accord with what modern realists regard as the demands of fine art, but neither Shakespeare nor Dickens accepted those demands; their withers are unwrung.

Finally, there is what Gissing calls his inability to "develop character through circumstance." He progressed toward this end also in his later novels, and in Pip he had at least one striking success. But in general he does fail here, and again he is like Shakespeare, for the great Elizabethan has not many Cleopatras, many Lady Macbeths among his dramatis personae; for the most part, his characters are at the end as they were at the beginning. Yet when I say that he fails I am merely meeting the heathen on their own ground, for a man cannot fail at what he has never set out to do. Dickens is, besides being much else, a great folklorist, and perhaps he is greatest of all in this aspect. As Chesterton might say, his characters often fail as human beings but they rarely fail as gods. Adopt the modern realistic ideal, develop your characters through circumstance, subject them to the vicissitudes of existence, and what is the result? If you succeed, you have created a semblance of life. But Dickens was creating more than life; he was creating immortality. The characters described in a realistic novel are dead when the book is over, but nobody is dead in Dickens who ever was alive. Pecksniff and Mrs. Nickleby illustrate the curious paradox that external life on this planet is the exclusive prerogative of those who have never lived in the flesh; they go on forever in a land beyond a land. And they could not do that if they were not in some sense, as Dickens's detractors point out, "static" characters.

This folklore quality appears in many aspects of Dickens's work. Again and again in his pages the inanimate pulsates with life. Properties come to life. Scene comes alive.

> The room in which he had shut himself up was on the ground-floor, at the back of the house. It was lighted by a dirty sky-light, and had a door in the wall, opening into a narrow, covered passage or blind-alley. . . . It was a blotched, stained, mouldering room, like a vault; and there were waterpipes running through it, which, at unexpected times in the night, when other things were quiet, clicked and gurgled suddenly, as if they were choking.

Here Dickens has gone far beyond the theater, surely. One might say he had passed through the stage-door into the world of animism known to primitive man.

And it is important for the understanding of more than Dickens's characterization that this folklore quality should be kept in mind. From the fact that Dickens more than once altered a story in obedience to the real or imagined mandate of his public, it is sometimes assumed that he wrote down to his public. No judgment could be more completely mistaken. Dickens never wrote down to his public. *He was a part of his public.* His books were not made; they were born. They were begotten by him of his public. He is like the primitive folk-bard in this. And he is the only modern novelist of whom these things are true.

4. *Dickens and the Modern Novel*

The question is often asked: Was Dickens a realist or a romancer? Romancer in the Scott sense he certainly was not. He neither understood medievalism nor respected it, and the very idea of aristocracy was anathema to him. His public shared these feelings. As has already been indicated, they were not Scott's public but a wider and comparatively uncultivated public. It was the "here and now" they wanted to read about; they were not sufficiently familiar with the past to be curious about it. And they did not want kings and queens as the dramatis personae of their novels; they wanted ordinary men and women like themselves.

Moreover, Dickens was a reporter. His reporter's style may be seen at its best in the *Sketches by Boz* (1836), which he wrote before he had developed the more individual "Dickensian" style of his novels.

A good deal of evidence can be marshaled in support of the thesis that Dickens was a realist. Many scenes, many personages in his books were taken direct from life. Such passages as the death of Nancy in *Oliver Twist* and the horrible picture of the mob in *Barnaby Rudge* might even be termed naturalistic. When Dickens is criticized, as for the unmotivated change in Mr. Pickwick's character which appears in the course of the story, his defense is quite likely to involve a false parallel between art and life. And George Gissing, who ought to know, credits him in so many words with having taken a step toward naturalism. "Who, if not Dickens, founded the later school of English fiction?"

There can be no doubt that toward the end of his life Dickens's interest in realism was growing. The fairy world where Pickwick lived was closing her gates against him, but he was exploring new areas of this mundane world to the end and making them increasingly his own. Compare, in the matter of sex alone, the treatment of lust in such figures as Bradley Headstone and John Jasper with the way he had handled the problem in Steerforth and Little Em'ly earlier in his career. Dickens's strong interest in using his books to inculcate personal morality had always kept him away from unsavory subjects. He was still a moralist, but now he was inclined to give the moralist a little more leeway as to subject-matter than had once been the case. And there are passages in his notebooks which indicate that, had he lived longer, he might have gone considerably beyond Headstone and Jasper.

But if we are to describe the spirit of Dickens's work as it was rather than as it might have been (or as it might have become, had he lived fifteen years longer), then surely the naturalistic bias in it cannot be said to have been very strong. "In *Bleak House* I have purposely dwelt upon the romantic side of familiar things." He might have said the same of almost any of his books. What he thought of realism in painting we know from his bitter opposition to the Pre-Raphaelite movement in its first phase.[7] He took the same attitude toward literature:

It does not seem to me to be enough to say of any description that it is the exact truth. The exact truth must be there; but the merit or art in the narrator is the manner of stating the truth. As to which in literature, it always seems to me that there is a world to be done. And in these times, when the tendency is to be frightfully literal and catalogue-like . . . I have an idea . . . that the very holding of popular literature through a kind of popular dark age, may depend on such fanciful treatment.

Furthermore, Dickens's humor was as important an element as his morality in steering him away from naturalism. Gissing cites the amazing anomaly of Guster:

Plainly described, this girl is an underpaid, underfed, and overworked slavey, without a friend in the world, . . . and subject to frequent epileptic fits. And we roar with laughter as often as she is named!

The same anomaly appears in Mrs. Micawber, to say nothing of her more magnificent husband.

I have known her [says David Copperfield] to be thrown into fainting-fits by the king's taxes at three o'clock, and to eat lamb chops breaded, and to drink warm ale (paid for with two teaspoons that had gone to the pawnbroker's) at four.

How can one feel the pity and terror of poverty in the face of such a figure? It is her very greatness that she rises superior to all the common ills of life.

For this very reason, no doubt, some persons feel that Dickens is open to the same criticism sometimes brought against one of the greatest cockneys of the twentieth century, Charlie Chaplin, who has so strikingly inherited the Dickens tradition.[8] It is true that both

[7] Cf. "Old Lamps for New Ones," in *Miscellaneous Papers*.

[8] Or else, loving Dickens too much to give him up, the economic radicals choose the other road and try to prove that Dickens was one of them! The most elaborate attempt to square the circle along this particular line is T. A. Jackson, *Charles Dickens, The Progress of a Literary Radical* (International Publishers, 1938), a saddening example of how completely the use of Marxian blinders can vitiate what might otherwise have been a warm and generous book.

Dickens and Chaplin must always disappoint those who feel that progress is to be served by waving a red flag. Dickens warned England specifically of the danger of revolution, both in *A Christmas Carol* and in *A Tale of Two Cities;* but he could have taken no part in it had it come. And it is true that Dickens was very impatient with the inefficiency of democracy. But he would have made a very bad Fascist, Communist, or New Dealer. An individualist to the core, with a well-founded distrust of all government and all governmental enterprises, he placed his trust, his hope of amelioration exclusively in the impulse of private benevolence, the untutored common sanity of ordinary people.

In Chaplin's day the sky is darker; the little clown has a wistfulness that is not essentially Dickensian. He expects the worst and usually gets it; the most he can hope for is to snatch a few stolen moments of happiness while his dehumanized, regimenting superiors chance to be looking the other way. Our "brave new world" was not yet close enough to turning the corner for Dickens to catch a glimpse of it. Mark Twain, who died just forty years later, envisaged it well, and savored all its horror.

Yet Dickens cannot be quite dissociated from the modern novel, for probably none of our "advanced" writers have done anything that he did not, in one way or another, do before them. *Great Expectations* is a very rich book to compare with the "stream of consciousness" writers. Take this reference to Mrs. Gargery's ungentle washing of her little brother's face: "I suppose myself to be better acquainted than any living authority with the ridgy effect of a wedding-ring, passing unsympathetically over the human countenance." When the convict on the marshes gave Pip "a most tremendous dip and roll," the result was that "the church jumped over its own weather-cock."

That first chapter of *Great Expectations* is one of the most wonderful in all fiction; it is wasted labor to try to frame a definition of genius while such writing remains in the world. For here *is* genius:

As I never saw my father or my mother, and never saw any likeness of either of them . . . my first fancies regarding what they were like, were unreasonably derived from their tombstones. The shape of the letters on my father's, gave me an odd idea that he was a square, stout, dark man, with curly black hair. From the character and turn of the inscription, *"Also Georgiana Wife of the Above,"* I drew a childish conclusion that my mother was freckled and sickly. To five little stone lozenges, each about a foot and a half long, which were arranged in a neat little row beside their grave, and were sacred to the memory of five little brothers of mine—who gave up trying to get a living exceedingly early in that universal struggle—I am indebted for a belief I religiously entertained that they had all been born on their backs with their hands in their trousers-pockets, and had never taken them out in this state of existence.

Equally remarkable, though written almost at the beginning of his career, is Dickens's use of the irrelevant in his description of Fagin's end, and there are many subtle touches all through his work which it is difficult to particularize in such a discussion as this. Consider the revealing postscript to the enamored Fanny Squeers's report concerning Nicholas Nickleby's attack on her father in defense of Smike: "I pity his ignorance and despise him." Consider David Copperfield's sudden chilling realization of what it means that Dora should be speaking of herself in the past tense. Above all, consider the late short story, "George Silverman's Explanation," which is naturalistic and stream-of-consciousness at the same time.

I am glad you see a certain unlikeness to anything in the American[9] story [so Dickens wrote his sub-editor, W. H. Wills]. Upon myself it has made the strongest impression of reality and originality!! And I feel as if I had read something (by somebody else), which I should never get out of my mind!!!

All in all, it should surprise nobody that Dickens exercised a strong influence on writers so apparently unlike him, and each other, as Bernard Shaw and Marcel Proust.

One of the marked characteristics of the "stream-of-consciousness" writers, especially as they derive from Henry James, is their insistence upon a "point of view" in narrative. In general, of course, Dickens accepts the Fielding convention of the omniscient author. Three times at least he attempted an autobiographical narrative: in *David Copperfield,* in *Great Expectations,* and in that part of *Bleak House* that is told by Esther Summerson. About Esther the less

[9] "American" because at this time it had been printed only in *The Atlantic Monthly.*

said the better. In *Copperfield* he is careless; David reports in detail on conversations that took place before he was born. In *Great Expectations,* however, he is much more careful and much more successful along this line.

Dickens defended Fielding's and Smollett's use of what he calls the "introduced story," or interpolated narrative, on the ground that the material contained in it could not have been presented otherwise "without supposing the reader to be possessed of almost as much romantic allowance as would put him on a level with the writer." And he adds that in Miss Wade, of *Little Dorrit,* he attempted to make "the introduced story so fit into surroundings impossible of separation from the main story, as to make the blood of the book circulate through both." More interesting still is Forster's description of the original idea for *Edwin Drood:* "The story . . . was to be that of the murder of a nephew by his uncle; the originality of which was to consist in the review of the murderer's career by himself at the close, when its temptations were to be dwelt upon as if, not he the culprit, but some other man, were the tempted." This is another bit of evidence to indicate that Dickens was still growing when he died.

5. *The Greatness of Dickens*

It would be foolish to deny the presence in Dickens's novels of either sensationalism or sentimentality. But both are more annoying than important. There was no affectation in Dickens's sentiment, and his love of sensation never prevented him from being fundamentally just in his appraisement of life.

He himself considered it his "infirmity" sometimes to discern fantastic resemblances which were not evident to others. But though he loves his grotesques, he loves them always because they belong to humanity, not because they are set apart from it.

He loved humanity. He believed in humanity. He was an optimist because he had faith. As the great American reformer, John Peter Altgeld, once expressed it of himself, he believed that "the gravitation of eternal justice is toward the Throne of God." This is very significant. Galsworthy could not help being impressed by it. Dickens, he pointed out, "regarded . . . values as absolute; had no ironic misgivings, nor any sense that existence is a tragi-comedy." [10] Nathaniel Wright Stephenson compared him with Browning—

> a great intruder, a reincarnation of some younger, more trustful age, or else the herald of a mightier age to come. We smile at his crudities; we may condemn his methods; but the heart of man responds steadily to his exuberant conviction that in the long run right will win. If we show him a case in which "robber wrong" prevails, he replies, "That is an exception," and pounds on fearlessly with his gospel, "Be not afraid." [11]

Kate Douglas Wiggin obscurely felt the same thing when, as a little girl, her hero-worship was so great as to overcome her timidity and enable her to thrust herself upon him in a railway carriage: "I remember feeling that I had never known anybody so well and so intimately." Looking back upon her experience after many years, in what is surely the loveliest paper ever written about him, she summed up his case:

> He had his literary weaknesses, Charles Dickens, but they were all dear, big attractive ones, virtues grown a bit wild and rank. Somehow when you put him—with his elemental humor, his inexhaustible vitality, his humanity, sympathy, and pity—beside the Impeccables, he always looms large! Just for a moment, when the heart overpowers the reason, he even makes the flawless ones look a little faded and colorless.[12]

That was the spirit in which Dickens wrought his mighty deeds, and that is the spirit in which he must be apprehended. He was essentially one of the Good Enchanters of Men. There were some heights that he could not reach. He could not breathe the air of Scott's mighty world of tragic conflict and epic endeavor. But, if I may paraphrase George Radford's tribute to Falstaff, no writer has ever done more to make this vale of tears a less terrible dwelling-place than it would otherwise be.

[10] John Galsworthy, *Candelabra* (Scribners, 1933), p. 133.
[11] Cf. his *The Spiritual Drama in the Life of Thackeray* (Doran, 1916).
[12] *A Child's Journey with Dickens* (Houghton Mifflin, 1912). Quoted by permission of the publishers.

CHAPTER XIV

THE DISCIPLES OF DICKENS

The great man, with his free force direct out of God's own hand, is the lightning.

THOMAS CARLYLE

1. *The Dickens-Reade-Collins "School"*

The mighty shadow of Dickens falls across the whole Victorian novel-terrain. His example impelled novelists in two directions—toward sensationalism and toward didacticism. They wrote "thrillers," and they wrote "novels of purpose."

The really close relationship was that between Dickens, Collins, and Reade. These men came as close to forming a "school" as any novelists have ever come in England. No fewer than six of Collins's novels were serialized in Dickens's magazines, *Household Words* and *All the Year Round*. Reade's serializing experience was not so happy. *Hard Cash* reduced the circulation of *All the Year Round* by 3,000 copies, but this fact was not permitted to disturb the friendly relations between editor and contributor. Collins was very intimate with Dickens personally, he had a hand in nearly all the special Christmas numbers, and he acted in the Dickens theatricals many times. He influenced the master's later novels also, exercised indeed as strong an influence as a younger and lesser writer ever exerted on an older and greater one. Had it not been for him, we might never have had the elaborate plot-structure of *Bleak House* and *The Mystery of Edwin Drood*.

In his *Dickens, Reade, and Collins, Sensation Novelists,* Walter C. Phillips has commented illuminatingly upon this group. He sees them as influenced by the terror tradition, which traces back through Bulwer, Ainsworth, and others to the Gothic School; by the contemporary theater; and by the exigencies of serial writing, which encouraged them to include a "punch" in every installment. They all used the dramatic method wherever possible—(Reade calls *Christie Johnstone* "this 'dramatic story'—'novel,' by courtesy")—keeping commentary down, and consequently attempting comparatively little in the way of psychological analysis and exposition. It is interesting to note that Reade did not like the term "sensation novelist." "This slang term is not quite accurate as applied to me. Without sensation there can be no interest; but my plan is to mix a little character and a little philosophy with the sensational element." Nevertheless he carried sensationalism farther than either of the other two; Phillips is just when he finds in him the *reductio ad absurdum* of the principles of the sensation school.

The three writers are alike in their preoccupation with the "here and now," and they are alike in their taste for "the romantic side of familiar things." "Not one man in ten thousand living in the midst of reality," cries Collins, "has discovered that he is also living in the midst of romance." And Reade declares: "When we write a story or sing a poem of the great nineteenth century, there is but one fear—not that our theme will be beneath us, but we miles below it; that we shall lack the comprehensive vision a man must have from heaven to catch the historical, the poetic, the last features of the Titan events that stride so swiftly past IN THIS GIGANTIC AGE."[1]

Finally they are alike in their intense earnestness. Dickens and his followers saw sensation fiction as a serious criticism of life. This should help us to understand why Victorian "thrillers" are so much better than our own. In those days it was still possible for a "thriller" to be a serious novel.

"Nothing in this world is hidden forever," declares Collins, in *No Name*. "The gold which has lain for centuries unsuspected in the ground, reveals itself one day on the surface. Sand turns traitor,

[1] "Proximity is, indeed, one great element of sensation. It is necessary to be near a mine to be blown up by its explosion; and a tale which aims at electrifying the nerves of the reader is never thoroughly effective unless the scene be laid in our own days and among the people we are in the habit of meeting." So declared one of the ablest contemporary surveys of "Sensation Novels" in the *Quarterly Review*, CXIII (1863), 481-514. The article goes on to distinguish between Bigamy Novels (which exalt the mistress at the expense of the wife), Newspaper Novels (which fictionize recent crimes), Theological Novels, etc.

and betrays the footstep that has passed over it; water gives back to the tell-tale surface the body that has been drowned. . . ." And there is no cant in Walter Hartright's reflections when he looks upon the dead face of Sir Percival Glyde: "So, for the first and last time, I saw him. So the Visitation of God ruled it that he and I should meet."

Philosophically speaking, this point of view may be unspeakably childish and naïve; it must almost certainly seem so to the twentieth century reader. But it is, or it was in those days, a perfectly possible point of view for art; and it is only on some such basis that the sensation novel can be sincerely (and therefore greatly) written. When faith dies, art dies with it. What is left is tawdry and unreal.

2. *Wilkie Collins*

(William) Wilkie Collins was born, January 8, 1824, the son of one distinguished painter, the godchild of another. He was privately educated, did a little painting of his own, worked for a while for a firm of tea-merchants, studied law and was admitted to the bar, though he never practiced. His first, prentice novel, *Antonina* (1850), was an historical romance of the Bulwer school. He began to find himself in *Basil* (1852), and he came definitely into his kingdom with *The Dead Secret* (1857). His three most important novels —*The Woman in White*,[2] *Armadale,* and *The Moonstone*—appeared in 1860, 1866, and 1868 respectively. Other significant titles include *No Name* (1862), *Man and Wife* (1870), *The New Magdalen* (1873), and *The Two Destinies* (1876). In 1873-1874 he followed the master's footsteps in a reading tour of the United States.[3] He died September 23, 1889.

Collins is generally thought of first of all as a maker of ingenious plots; in so far as the modern mystery novel derives from an English inspiration, *The Moonstone* is that source. Certainly it would

[2] Evidently *The Woman in White* was, in his own view, Collins's greatest novel. The inscription on his tombstone in Kensal Green Cemetery, London, which was written by himself reads: "In memory of Wilkie Collins, author of 'The Woman in White,' and other works of fiction."

[3] Cf. Clyde K. Hyder, "Wilkie Collins in America," *University of Kansas Humanistic Studies,* Vol. VI, No. 4 (1940), pp. 50-58.

be difficult to overpraise the ingenuity of this book; it has enough stuff in it for a dozen mystery stories as they go nowadays.

But Collins's wonderful gift for creating atmosphere is at least as important as his unusual plots. It is on atmosphere that he relies for the thrills and chills which Reade gets through violent action; there is comparatively little action in his books.

He delights in scenes of solitude [says Walter de la Mare], gloomy woods, stagnant waters; and the most characteristic of his chapters are haunted with the dark; not, as with Bunyan, a darkness feared and detested, or one that gives the moon and stars a deep serene wherein to shine, but a darkness for its own sake, resembling a drug of the imagination.

No reader of *The Moonstone* can ever forget the Shivering Sand, under which Rosanna Spearman fears she must find her grave, and where she does find it in the end. (This may possibly be echoed in Eustacia Vye's feeling about the Heath in *The Return of the Native,* for Collins influenced Hardy deeply.) More impressive still is the great scene on Hampstead Heath at the beginning of *The Woman in White,* where Anne Catherick steps out of the darkness and places her hand on Walter Hartright's shoulder.[4]

The Woman in White is indeed drenched in atmosphere. Walter feels a mysterious reluctance to accept the position at Limmeridge House; Miss Fairlie's little Italian greyhound shrinks and shivers when Sir Percival Glyde tries to touch her; the death of another dog, on Marian's first day at Blackwater Park, is regarded as a bad omen; the lake "looks just the place for a murder." Marian feels "the ominous future coming close"; and simple remarks, like Count Fosco's "There will be a change tomorrow," are charged with significance. As time goes on, Walter is increasingly conscious of the force of destiny:

Yes! the time had come. For thousands on thousands of miles away—through forest and wilderness, where companions stronger than I had fallen by my side, through peril of death thrice renewed and thrice

[4] For the autobiographical basis of this scene, cf. Clyde K. Hyder, "Wilkie Collins and *The Woman in White,*" *PMLA,* LIV (1939), 297-303. This is in some respects the most important study of Wilkie Collins. It records facts concerning his carefully guarded private life not elsewhere available.

escaped, the Hand that leads men on the dark road to the future had led me to meet that time.

Armadale is nearly as remarkable from this point of view. The scene on the deserted timber-ship, the interview in the library with the storm beating against the windows, where part of the dream comes true, and the death scene in the corridor at the close of the book—these things come as close to holding the reader breathless as literature can come.

Collins's sensitiveness to landscape was no doubt influenced by his association with painters; the special ominous quality in his descriptions of it may have owed something to his use of laudanum.[5] There is much pathology in his novels, and the mentally and physically deformed play an important part. The admiring Swinburne, always so much more normal in his criticism than in his creative writing, considered this a grave fault. Though the mere title of *The Woman in White* carries a thrill, the character whom it designates is mentally deficient and therefore uninteresting.

Probably Collins's fundamental belief about the art of fiction was that a novel ought, first of all, to tell an interesting story. Hardy said of him:

> He probably stands first, in England, as a constructor of novels of complicated action that depend for their interest on the incidents themselves and not on character. Yet while he was writing he was scandalously ridiculed by the same critical papers that twenty years afterwards praised second-rate imitations of his methods.[6]

But it should not be assumed that Collins had no interest in characterization. He never believed that a careful artificer of plots

[5] In nineteenth-century England laudanum was sold freely by all English chemists for the relief of pain. Collins suffered ungodly tortures from rheumatic gout in his eyes; since no one knew enough to put atropin into them, he turned instead to laudanum, of which he came, in the course of time, to consume enormous quantities. Collins was something of a sybarite, and he did not live within the bounds of conventional morality. But he was kindly and unselfish; and it is only fair that the harsh things sometimes said about him should be balanced by such tributes as Hall Caine's in *My Story* (Appleton, 1909), and that of the fastidious William Winter, in *Old Friends* (Moffat, Yard, 1909).

[6] Quoted by S. M. Ellis, *Wilkie Collins, La Fanu, and Others,* pp. 3-4.

must necessarily neglect the other elements in fiction. *The Woman in White* is a sensation novel, but Marian and Fosco are characters of whom few novelists would need to be ashamed, and there is a warm human feeling all through the book which is very attractive. The heroine of *The Moonstone,* Rachel Verinder, is a gallant girl.

Collins's special preoccupation was, of course, with mystery. Now the commonest way of handling mystery is to withhold the facts at the outset from the reader and the characters alike. This is what Collins does in both *The Moonstone* and *The Woman in White.* In *The Dead Secret* there are two mysteries. What was in the letter which the dying Mrs. Treverton dictated to Sarah Leeson? And what happened to Sarah herself to turn her hair white before its time and stamp her face with the marks of suffering? When Rosamond finds the letter both questions are answered, and the rest of the book holds little interest.

But not all Collins's novels conform to this pattern. *No Name* opens with a mystery, but the mystery is soon explained, and we go on to the development of other interests. Sometimes Collins reaches back into the past to explain the situation which exists in the present; and sometimes he uses a Prologue of dread events, while the story proper concerns the next generation. In *Armadale* the whole action is outlined in advance in a dream, and the reader has only to wait breathlessly to see how the fulfillment will come. In *The Two Destinies,* the reader knows, as soon as ever Mrs. Van Brandt comes into Germaine's life, that she is his lost childhood sweetheart, Mary Dermody, but she does not know, and he does not know; and their common ignorance is the cause of all their sufferings. And in *The New Magdalen* the reader knows from the beginning that Mercy Merrick is masquerading as Grace Roseberry; here we are interested partly in whether she will escape detection but more in whether her own sense of honor will permit her to go on; in other words, our fundamental interest is in character.

Both *The Moonstone* and *The Woman in White* are composed of a series of documents supposed to have been written by the various personages involved. As in epistolary fiction, many interesting points of view can thus be presented; and the reader is compelled to take a hand in building up the story. A problem may be posed in one narrative, for example, and solved in another; when the pious housekeeper, Mrs. Michelson, is completely taken in by Count Fosco, we learn something about both characters. But many of the artificialities which have already been noted in connection with epistolary fiction appear again; Betteredge, for example, has more sensitive perceptions than could reasonably have been attributed to one of his class, and Miss Clack, "the evangelical hag," is frankly burlesqued. In *Armadale,* too, Miss Gwilt's diary is both tiresome and unconvincing; she could have had no motive for making so elaborate a record of her villainy.

Collins is better with Dickensian eccentrics than is Reade. Among the most striking in his novels are (in *No Name*) the unscrupulous Captain Wragge and his gigantic, half-witted wife, whose head buzzes terribly whenever she gets more than one idea into it, and who is perpetually falling crooked and run down at heel, and Old Mazey, the sea dog, who sleeps outside the Admiral's door to guard him against somnambulism, and who has a weakness for fine-grown girls—("I liked the make of you [especially about the waist] when you first came into the house. . . .") In *The Moonstone* we have Sergeant Cuff, the detective who loves roses, and Gooseberry, the boy-detective, with the M. G. Lewis eyes. In *The Woman in White* the dilettante invalid, Mr. Fairlie, is very good. Sarah Leeson's German Uncle Joseph, with the Mozart music-box, lends charm to *The Dead Secret,* and the dyspeptic Mr. Phippen, though quite an extraneous element, furnishes one very delightful scene. Some of these persons have more shading than Dickens habitually employs. Indeed Betteredge is so elaborately developed that it is probably not fair to call him a type-sketch at all, but his habit of using *Robinson Crusoe* as some people use their Bibles, opening the book at random and interpreting the first passage he turns up as a "message," is surely a "humors" touch; nor was the villain Fosco's tenderness for pet birds and mice uninfluenced by the same tradition.

There is comparatively little propaganda in the novels of Collins's prime, but in later years, possibly under Reade's influence, he became more interested in the novel of purpose. Neither *The Black Robe* (1881), in which he attacked the Jesuits, nor his anti-vivisection book, *Heart and Science* (1883), added much to his fame; and Swinburne is at least partly justified when he writes:

> What brought good Wilkie's genius nigh perdition?
> Some demon whispered, "Wilkie! have a mission!"

Some "tendency" does appear in more characteristic works, however. The [illegible] confusion of the British marriage laws is an import[illegible] *Man and Wife;* the same book airs Collins's well-founded and carefully reasoned opposition to athletic sports. One incident in *The Woman in White*—the incarceration of a sane woman in a madhouse—brings Collins close to one of Reade's favorite themes. Implicationally at least, *The New Magdalen* attacks moral snobbery, and at the end of the book the girl from the refuge marries the saintly clergyman, Julian Grey. Something like this occurs again in *The Fallen Leaves* (1879), whose hero befriends and afterwards marries a girl of the streets. But Collins goes farther here than he went in *The New Magdalen,* and as if determined to tramp on as many toes as possible, he makes his chivalric paragon a Socialist!

The Reverend Julian Grey is to Collins what the Reverend Mr. Eden, of *Never Too Late to Mend,* is to Charles Reade; and both men are chorus characters. This utterance of Grey's is characteristic of the whole Dickens school, and it helps to show why, despite its utter indifference to theological considerations, that school has always been thought of as distinctively Christian:

> Humanity is sacred. Humanity has its immortal destiny. Who shall dare say to man or woman, "There is no hope in you?" Who shall dare to say the work is vile, when that work bears on it the stamp of the Creator's hand?

In his *Autobiography,* Anthony Trollope—no unprejudiced witness, to be sure, in this connection—indicates an important weakness in Collins's novels. Trollope acknowledges that Collins "excelled all his contemporaries in a certain most difficult branch of his art"—plot construction. Then he adds:

> But I can never lose the taste of the construction. The author seems always to be warning me to remember that something happened at

exactly half-past two o'clock on Tuesday morning; or that a woman disappeared from the road just fifteen yards beyond the fourth milestone.

In other words, Collins did everything that can be done with art except one thing: he never caused us to forget it. He wrote story-books. T. S. Eliot has found the perfect phrase for it. In all Collins's work, he says, there is an "air of spurious fatality."

This is a serious defect in a writer one of whose special themes is the supernatural. To attempt supernatural themes at all in the grossly materialistic days of good Queen Victoria took courage. It is an honor to Collins that he ventured as far as he did, and surely it was a great service to the novel. "There are mysteries in life and the conditions of it which human science has not fathomed," says the doctor who has restored a dead man in "Brother Morgan's Story of the Dead Hand"; [7] "and I candidly confess to you that, in bringing that man back to existence, I was, morally speaking, groping haphazard in the dark."

But Collins is not always so satisfactory as this in his study of what passes ordinary human experience. *The Moonstone* hardly reaches quasi-supernaturalism. There is a curse on the diamond, to be sure, but material means are made to account sufficiently for everything that happens. In the Appendix, Collins declares that he has purposely left his readers

> with reference to the Dream in this story, in the position which they would occupy in the case of a dream in real life: they are free to interpret it by the natural or the supernatural theory as the bent of their own minds may incline them.

This method is legitimate enough. Essentially, it is the method Scott uses in "Wandering Willie's Tale." The trouble with *Armadale* is that we never are sure what attitude the author wishes us to take toward his material, or in what relationship toward it we are intended to place ourselves. Are the two Armadales actually under the spell of destiny, or are we merely supposed to interest ourselves in a psychological study of the effect of fear upon the human mind?

Collins's difficulty seems to be that he wants the supernatural thrill, yet is not quite ready to pay the price for it, as does Le Fanu,

[7] In *The Queen of Hearts* (1859).

for example, among his contemporaries. Again and again he "manipulates" this thrill, tries to bring it in without adequate motivation. There is, for example, a keen psychic interest at the beginning of *The Two Destinies*. But as the story proceeds, this effect is weakened; Collins seems, as the saying is, to be "turning on the works," and one recalls, perhaps not quite fairly, Andrew Lang's impression that there is in all his work "a kind of professional hardness."

With the single exception of Maria Edgeworth, there is no other English novelist, himself not absolutely first-rate, who has had so great an influence as Wilkie Collins. A whole school of sensationalists was indebted to him: Miss Braddon, Bertha M. Clay, Mrs. Henry Wood; later, Marie Corelli and Hall Caine; to say nothing of writers of contemporary mystery and detective stories. On a higher level, he influenced Blackmore, Meredith, Hardy, Stevenson, Conrad, and Arnold Bennett. In conclusion some mention should probably be made of modern English writers whose special field is the supernatural, like Algernon Blackwood, Arthur Machen, and, above all, Walter de la Mare.

3. *Charles Reade*

Charles Reade may well go down to posterity with a single book in his hand—*The Cloister and the Hearth* (1861)—that magnificent historical novel which modern criticism values above all the rest of his work together. But this was not the contemporary view, and most emphatically it was not Reade's view. "If that's your opinion," he told one who ventured to call *The Cloister* his masterpiece, "you ought to be in a lunatic asylum." *It Is Never Too Late to Mend* (1856) and *Put Yourself in His Place* (1870) were the kind of thing on which he prided himself.

Reade breaks with the classical tradition altogether; his pages look like those of a sensational American newspaper. In *Griffith Gaunt* (1866), twenty-five successive paragraphs are but a sentence each in length. Capitals indicate shouting; whispers are printed in microscopic type. "The lies of a seducing villain in *A Woman Hater* are printed in regular type, his truths in italics—in a fashion which reminds one of Eugene O'Neill's soliloquies of the subconscious mind in *Strange Interlude.* When two conversations go on at the same time, double columns give the impression of simultaneousness."[8]

Sometimes language fails Reade altogether. Then he uses pictures set into the text, like the nuggets on the knife-blade, and the picture of the Southern Cross, both in *Never Too Late,* or the amazing map in *Love Me Little, Love Me Long* (1859), in which Uncle Fountain's emotional geography is portrayed; the county is larger than all the rest of Britain, and Britain is larger than the rest of the world.

Reade's eccentricities are not always stylistic. When a character is in danger, the author may cry out a warning as if he were a small boy in the gallery at a melodrama theater; he also apostrophizes himself. He does not address the reader so often as do Thackeray and Trollope, but he surely breaks the illusion when he does: "Now would you mind closing this book for a minute and making an effort to realize all this. It will save us so much repetition."

Yet Reade had a far more cultivated background than Dickens. He was born June 8, 1814, the son of an Oxfordshire squire; he himself became an Oxford man, and was destined for the church. He rebelled against his destiny and turned instead to medicine, but his nerves could not stand the horrors of the dissecting-room. Like Collins, he studied law and was admitted to the bar, but never practiced. He became a fellow (later vice-president) of Magdalen College; for financial reasons he held his college fellowship all his life, thus preventing himself from ever contracting a legal marriage.[9]

The hardest thing to remember about Reade is that as a writer he was primarily interested not in the novel but in the drama. He collaborated with Tom Taylor in many plays; their first success was

[8] E. G. Sutcliffe, "The Stage in Reade's Novels," *Studies in Philology,* XXVII (1930), 654-688.

[9] Despite sensationalism, Reade's learned background shows in his work. He makes much use of the learned languages, and he has a weakness for pedantic explanatory footnotes, linguistic and otherwise. Though he championed a Saxon vocabulary and was merciless in his condemnation of "fine writing," there are times when he falls under his own condemnation, and then he is even more distressing than in his extreme colloquialism. In *The Cloister and the Hearth,* he writes that "the soil was strewed with dramatis personae," and again, "they fled quadrivious, shrieking." In *Hard Cash,* the

Masks and Faces, which Reade afterward turned into the novel *Peg Woffington* (1853). Reade was stagestruck all his life; there is no other word for it; he spent the money he made on successful novels on unsuccessful plays. He adapted many works of Scribe, Legouvé, Molière, and others to the English theater; but not until the very end of his career, when he turned Zola's *L'Assommoir* into a play called *Drink,* did he find a genuine "smash-hit." He died, rather forlornly, April 11, 1884.

Peg Woffington, though always popular, is an extremely artificial book; the material of *Masks and Faces* has not even begun to be transmuted into the new medium. Its companion piece, *Christie Johnstone* (1853), is better, for while the theater-influence is still strong here, we do get out into the world of open-air adventure, where Reade was always at his best. But it was not until *It Is Never Too Late to Mend* came out in 1856 that Reade really began to show what was in him.

Not that *Never Too Late* lacks theatrical quality. It too was partly based on a play (*Gold*); and its beginning on the farm in Berkshire, whence George Fielding is sent off to Australia and Tom Robinson to his hell of a prison, is a series of "arranged" scenes which have obviously been "set" with some care to get the story going. Moreover the winding up of the action at the close of the novel is quite as artificial. But the long prison episode is another matter altogether. Though it breaks the back of the book, it has terrible, almost sadistic, power.

It was to this work that Reade first applied the elaborate system of documentation which reminds us that he was a contemporary of Zola's, but which found its immediate inspiration in Harriet Beecher Stowe's *Key* to *Uncle Tom's Cabin.* He had begun "to make notes

vermin which devour Alfred in the asylum are spoken of as "insects, without a name to ears polite, but highly odoriferous and profoundly carnivorous." He had, too, even in dialogue, the bad habit of quoting, without acknowledgment, from history and from standard literature. "Oh, Sandy Liston," cries Christie Johnstone, "hoow could ye think to put an enemy in your mouth to steal awa' your brains?" When Lady Bassett learns that her enemy is to become a father, she echoes Queen Elizabeth's words when the news came of Mary Stuart's confinement: "That villain has married a fruitful vine, and . . . I am a barren stock."

with a view to writing fiction" as early as 1835, but he "thought so highly of that great and difficult art, that for fourteen years" he published nothing. It was his rule that whatever could be investigated personally, he must investigate; when this was impossible, he depended on encyclopaedic reading in "a multitude of volumes, pamphlets, journals, reports, blue-books, manuscript narratives, letters. . . ." As the novelist Rolfe, of *A Terrible Temptation,* who is Reade's portrait of himself,[10] puts it, "I feign probabilities, I record improbabilities." When Reade's accuracy was impugned, as it was, again and again, in the course of the many public controversies in which he saw fit to engage, he was always ready to cite chapter and verse.

What shall be said of this "method" of Reade's? I reply at once that it was a very unfortunate one.

The novelist rests on experience of course. But he is not using his experience when he takes a fact out of a newspaper and copies it down into a novel. Before facts can have much significance for art, the artist must assimilate them, he must absorb them, they must take on the color of his own personality. No doubt this is one reason why so much of our best fiction concerns itself not with the contemporary period but with a period about thirty years back, a time still held rich and warm in living memory, but not so close to the cluttering ephemera of day-by-day experience that one finds it impossible to see the woods for the trees.

In Reade's own case there was the further difficulty that temperamentally he was not a realist. The truth he was looking for was the truth that is "stranger than fiction." It has been pointed out before that the flood scene at the close of *Put Yourself in His Place* sounds like a burlesque of Reade's method rather than simply, as it is, an

[10] All students of Reade must be familiar with Chaps. 22-23 of this novel, where Rolfe's (and Reade's) study is described. "There was 'Index rerum et journalium,' 'Index rerum et librorum,' 'Index rerum et hominum,' and a lot more; indeed, so many that, by way of climax, there was a fat folio ledger entitled 'Index ad Indices.' " Rolfe is engaged in "writing a novel based on facts. Facts, incidents, living dialogue, pictures, reflections, situations, were all on . . . cards to choose from, and arranged in headed columns; and some portions of the work he was writing on this basis of imagination and drudgery lay on the table in two forms, his own writing and his secretary's copy thereof, the latter corrected for the press."

example of it. No doubt he could have cited a document for the ludicrous touch of the torn stockings:

> He tore her out of the water by an effort almost superhuman. Such was the force exerted by the torrent on the one side, and the desperate lover on the other, that not her shoes only, but her stockings, though gartered, were torn off her in that fierce struggle.

The whole thing illustrates what a writer naturally romantic in his tastes and tendencies is likely to do when he fears to trust his imagination and feels that he must make terms with the dominant *Zeit-geist* of a scientific age.

Put Yourself in His Place has its realistic element, for it includes a description of the "rattening" (sabotage) practiced by "the dirty oligarchy" which Reade saw in the labor unions. Outside of that, however, it is better, because more consistent, undiluted melodrama than *Never Too Late*. Melodrama in itself is, of course, a perfectly legitimate form of art; it becomes ineffective only when it is mingled unskillfully with incongruous materials; a "lime" gives no light in the face of "God's candle," the sun. There is nothing so painful in *Put Yourself in His Place* as the prison scenes of *Never Too Late;* and it has more picturesque material, some of it of great charm. The Christmas celebrations at Squire Raby's; the picture turned face to the wall, with "Gone into Trade" written on the back of it; the Gabriel Hounds (one of Reade's few flirtations with the supernatural); the great snow scene; the abandoned old church in which Henry sets up his forge; Jael Dence—best of all Reade's Amazons—her generous, unrequited love for the hero, and her narrowly averted suicide; the trick marriage, and the infuriated heroine's sensational attempt to kill her betrayer—people who cannot be excited by these things may be much more intellectual than the writer of this book, but they get much less pleasure out of fiction!

Reade uses suspense, more elaborately, perhaps, than any other standard English novelist has ever used it. He is following Scott's method here, but he goes much further than Scott. He cuts in anywhere, moving from one group of characters to another; no matter if the arrangement is purely arbitrary. In *Hard Cash* there is a scene in which the supposedly dead Captain Dodd is about to be buried at sea; suddenly we shift our attention to England, and not until long afterwards do we learn that Captain Dodd showed faint signs of returning life just as his body was about to be shunted overboard, and was consequently revived. Reade had a theory to cover such cases, and his fundamentally artificial conception of the novel shows in it clearly: "I never knew an interesting story allowed to proceed without a whole system of interruption."

Yet Reade often fails to thrill us, for he moves so rapidly that we are never left in doubt long. His insane speed gave him a natural affinity with short books, and while it is true that his principal works are very long, he achieves this length by combining great masses of often disparate material. Even so, he always seems rushing to catch a train. He sums up as curtly as Boccaccio; in *The Cloister and the Hearth,* old Martin, an important character, sickens and dies in the course of a single sentence.

As a reformer, Reade was interested, among other things, in prison administration (*Never Too Late*), labor unions (*Put Yourself in His Place*), factory conditions (*Put Yourself in His Place*), and the regulation of private insane asylums (*Hard Cash* and *A Terrible Temptation*). Even *The Cloister and the Hearth* has a strong propaganda element in its attack on the celibacy of the clergy, "an invention truly fiendish." Like Dickens, Reade was proud of the fact that his books inspired reforms. What Father Angelo says of Rolfe, Reade would say of himself: "He is a writer, and opinions vary as to his merit. Some say he has talent; others say it is all eccentricity and affectation. One thing is certain; his books bring about the changes he demands."

To his contemporaries, Charles Reade seemed a very daring writer. He gives more attention to the physical perfections of women than the other Victorian novelists, and his biology is franker. In *A Terrible Temptation* not only did he dare to include a "kept" woman, Rhoda Somerset—a quite unbelievable creature—among his characters, but he introduced us to her in her boudoir! Sir Charles Bassett, who discards Rhoda on the eve of his marriage to Bella Bruce, is sympathetically presented in this novel; worse still, Bella's aunt, Mrs. Molineux, treats the whole situation as a matter of course. A contemporary critic described the book as "this mass of brothel garbage," and Reade himself as "a slimy, snaky, poisonous literary reptile." There was some trouble, too, over *Griffith Gaunt,* which even Dickens found too strong for his stomach. When Wilkie Collins tried to enlist him as witness in a prospective lawsuit, the master declared that he considered *Griffith Gaunt* "the work of a highly accomplished writer and a good man," but admitted that there were some scenes in the book which, as editor of a popular journal, he could not have passed. "I should say that what was pure to an artist might be impurely suggestive to inferior minds. . . ."

Why did Reade rise so far above his usual level in *The Cloister and the Hearth?* The answer is comparatively simple. He got hold here of a great tragic theme, and it was a theme on which he could feel deeply, for his own life had been cursed by enforced bachelorhood. Furthermore, since he was now writing of the past, he had a subject better adapted to his method of elaborate documentation than many contemporary subjects could be; and the material he worked with was vastly superior to the kind of thing he ordinarily clipped from the daily press and pasted into his scrap-books.[11] For

[11] The "musty chronicle written in tolerable Latin, and in it a chapter where every sentence holds a fact" in which Reade found the story of the parents of Erasmus was identified by Andrew Lang with *Compendium Vitae,* Leyden, 1607. In 1938, Albert Morton Turner published *The Making of "The Cloister and the Hearth"* (University of Chicago Press), the most elaborate source-study of any English novel. Mr. Turner's list of Reade's sources includes seventy-four titles. Six of these Reade must have consulted in Latin, between nine and thirteen in French. Mr. Turner divides Reade's sources under eleven headings: I. Erasmus and his Works; II. Literary Works; III. Books on Literature; IV. The Fine Arts; V. Ecclesiastical Works; VI. Political History; VII. Social History, Etc.; VIII. History or Biography in the Form of Fiction; IX. Travels and Geography; X. Letters and Discourses; XI. Collections and Indexes. "From some [works] he took only one small point; from others he helped himself again and again." "The two classes of works from which Reade drew most . . . are books on social history—especially modern works in French—and Renaissance books of travel." He did not borrow equally for all parts of his novel. "The portions about Holland have comparatively few borrowings; those concerning the other countries have many." Sometimes he takes over specific facts, sometimes whole groups of facts. Sometimes he borrows ideas for scenes. "The degree of closeness with which Reade adheres to his original varies greatly." Generally he condenses, leaving out "the useless repetitions or the weaker details that would injure his account." He "is quite capable of increasing the bulk of an incident, but this is by adding specific details, and especially dialogue, in order

once he did not confine himself to the dramatic method but filled in an elaborate background; for once he used atmosphere freely. And for once he did not stop with describing his characters from the outside but entered intimately into all their joys and sorrows, and set them forth on their own terms.

It is true that not even this book sustains a single mood: Gerard's adventures on the road are wonderful picaresque material; in the Roman chapters we get almost everything. But after we return to Holland, where the conflict between cloister and hearth is finally fought out, we move within a much narrower circle, and there is a deeper probing into human motives, if that term can be used with Reade at all. Certainly both Margaret and Gerard are convincing characters, and certainly their cruel plight enlists our deepest emotions.

It is a wonderful thing that so learned a book should be so wildly exciting. A really enormous amount of knowledge went into it: on painting, on inns, on national character, on the "Bohemians" (i.e., the professional beggars) and their tricks, on medieval medicine and jurisprudence, on the church, on murder as a fine art in Renaissance Italy. There are more learned novels than *The Cloister and the Hearth,* but few of them have assimilated their learning so well.

Griffith Gaunt has had many distinguished admirers, notably Swinburne, who objected, however, to the subtitle *Jealousy,* and who thought that the use of bigamy was not well prepared for. Reade tried to be psychological in this book, but many melodramatic elements carried over. It is true that the first part—the wooing of Catherine—gives us no idea what the rest of the book is to be about; after the wedding it takes a deep breath and starts all over again. But at least Griffith and Catherine have been so portrayed that their later behavior seems credible.

Other books of Reade's introduce no fresh elements of much importance. In *Hard Cash,* Captain Dodd's adventures on the high seas are easily as thrilling as Fielding's in Australia, and Alfred Hardie's experiences in the asylum come close to the prison scenes

to make it more vivid." Or he may borrow from more than one source and mingle the elements taken. (The quotations in this note are made by kind permission of The University of Chicago Press.)

in *Never Too Late.* Reade's technical knowledge of seamanship comes out also in *Foul Play* (1868), which he wrote in collaboration with the playwright, Dion Boucicault; for good measure he threw in a financial panic and an idyllic desert island episode. William Dean Howells thought the heroine of this work "almost fit to match with Margaret in 'The Cloister and the Hearth.'" *A Simpleton* (1873) deals once more with pioneering, this time in South Africa; *A Woman Hater* (1877) presents Reade's conception of the "new woman" in the physician, Rhoda Gale; *The Wandering Heir* (1875) offers an eighteenth century parallel to the contemporary Tichborne case.

4. *The Two Mrs. Gaskells*

Dickens was not Mrs. Gaskell's first editor; that place had been pre-empted by William Howitt, for whom, however, she did nothing of importance. Her first novel, *Mary Barton,* was accepted by Chapman and Hall on the recommendation of the master's closest friend, John Forster. When *Household Words* was brewing, Dickens himself sent Mrs. Gaskell a most flattering letter: "there is no living English writer whose aid I would desire to enlist in preference to the authoress of 'Mary Barton,' (a book that most profoundly affected and impressed me. . . ." "Lizzie Leigh" accordingly opened the first number of *Household Words;* for it and its successor, *All the Year Round,* Mrs. Gaskell wrote most of her short stories, and in it *North and South* was serialized.

Dickens's own tastes, and those of his subscribers, may have determined the special emphasis on ghosts, horror, and crime in the tales Mrs. Gaskell sent him. This is not certain, however, for while these matters are not adumbrated in her novels, we know that Mrs. Gaskell was herself not uninterested in psychic themes; she showed great skill in telling ghost stories to her friends, and once, we are told, she herself saw a ghost. Moreover, Dickens's own ecstatic appreciation of *Cranford,* which began as a short sketch, and for whose continuation we are indebted to his enthusiasm alone, shows that he did welcome also a quieter kind of work.

In her novels, Mrs. Gaskell manifests an affinity for the spirit of Dickens, but there is little or no specific indebtedness to be shown.

Though he was the great exponent of the novel of purpose, he had no monopoly of it, and his first application of it to the labor question postdated hers. Her *Mary Barton* appeared in 1848, six years before his *Hard Times, North and South* in 1855, one year after it. Meanwhile Charlotte Brontë's *Shirley* had been issued in 1849 and Kingsley's *Alton Locke* in 1850. Reade did not become a didactic novelist before *Never Too Late* (1856), and his special study of labor problems, in *Put Yourself in His Place,* is as late as 1870. Disraeli, of course, had concerned himself with these matters as far back as *Coningsby* and *Sybil* in 1844 and 1845; and Mrs. Trollope's *Michael Armstrong, The Factory Boy* (1840), which incidentally has a Manchester setting, is even earlier.

As a matter of fact, Mrs. Gaskell was not really, by temperament, a didactic writer. That is to say, the greater Mrs. Gaskell was not. The lesser Mrs. Gaskell did write three very important purpose-novels. The first two—*Mary Barton* and *North and South*—deal, as we have already seen, with labor problems; the third, *Ruth* (1853) has what the Victorians considered the far more daring subject of the "fallen" woman. But the other Mrs. Gaskell, the more objective artist, wrote *Cranford* (1853), *Sylvia's Lovers* (1863), *Wives and Daughters* (1866), and that lovely idyll, its author's finest short piece, "Cousin Phyllis" (1864). And there is no didacticism in that Mrs. Gaskell; she even, as Stanton Whitfield has remarked, "sympathized with misunderstood aims, uncommon temperaments, and wavering consciences."

The truth of the matter is that Mrs. Gaskell's proper range was as closely drawn and as domestic as Jane Austen's; only, unlike Jane Austen, she did not always stay inside it. To be sure, even her domestic experience was wider and intenser than Jane Austen's. The latter was a daughter; Mrs. Gaskell was so completely wife and mother that today only the specialist remembers that her name was once Elizabeth Cleghorn Stevenson. And herein she differs not only from Jane Austen but also from her contemporaries, George Eliot and the Brontës.

She differs from these contemporaries again in being, in the ordinary sense of the term, an attractive woman, interested in society and in all feminine frills and furbelows. She was one of the first signers of the Married Women's Property Bill, yet she "would not trust a mouse to a woman if a man's judgment were to be had." ". . . I like a smelling and singing world," she cries. "Yes, I do. I can't help it. I like Kings and Queens, and nightingales and mignonettes and roses."

She had all these things (except the kings and queens) in her native south country: at Chelsea, where she was born, September 29, 1810; at Knutsford (Cranford), where her aunt brought her up; at Stratford-upon-Avon, where she went to school. No more than Margaret Hale, of *North and South,* was she prepared for the misery she saw when, as the Reverend William Gaskell's bride, she transferred her residence in 1832 to hungry Manchester, in the midst of one of the most horrible depressions in English history. Machines were piling up new profits for the cotton manufacturers, and throwing workmen upon the streets, their ranks swollen by the hopeless influx of agriculturists who flocked to the cities following disastrous crop-failures. The high tariff kept prices up, and Adam Smith's *laissez-faire* economics deprecated and discouraged any governmental interference. Neither Reform Bill nor Poor Law could solve the problem.

For thirteen years Mrs. Gaskell watched the situation in silence—and did the pitifully little any one woman could do to help. Then, in 1845, she lost a child, and herself had a serious illness. Her husband suggested that perhaps she might help herself through this difficult time if she were to turn to the composition of an extended work of fiction.

> Living in Manchester, but with a deep relish and fond admiration for the country, my first thought was to find a framework for my story in some rural scene; and I had already made a little progress in a tale, the period of which was more than a century ago, and the place on the borders of Yorkshire, when I bethought me how deep might be the romance in the lives of some of those who elbowed me daily in the busy streets of the town in which I resided.

It is easy to see what she wanted to do; we should know even if she did not tell us. The bitterness and suffering of the poor oppressed her; she yearned "to give some utterance to the agony which, from time to time, convulses this dumb people; the agony of suffering without the sympathy of the happy, or of erroneously believing that such is the case."

Mary Barton did this; too well, its critics said; it was "one-sided." In the book itself Job Legh had anticipated this objection: "I never see the masters getting thin and haggard for want of food; I hardly ever see them making much change in their way of living, though I don' doubt they've got to do it in bad times. But it's in things for show they cut short; while for such as me, it's in things for life we've to stint." For Mrs. Gaskell herself the objection had been anticipated even earlier, one day when a poor man she was trying to comfort and reconcile to his lot, grasped her arm, and cried, "Ay, ma'am, but have ye ever seen a child clemmed [starved] to death?"

The book rendered an important pioneering service, and this is its special distinction. It is not a very good novel. Technique as such never interested Mrs. Gaskell greatly, and there are passages in *Mary Barton* in which she seems to have no technique.

> She did all this with the same compressed lips, and the same stony look that her face had assumed on the first examination of the paper. Then she sat down for an instant to think; and rising directly, went, with a step rendered firm by inward resolution of purpose, up the stairs;—passed her own door, two steps, into her father's room. What did she want there?
>
> I must tell you; I must put into words the dreadful secret which she believed that bit of paper had revealed to her.
>
> Her father was the murderer!

There is considerable melodrama in *Mary Barton;* at one point the heroine goes to Liverpool and pursues a departing vessel, to bring back the man who can prove an alibi for her lover, Jem Wilson, unjustly accused of Carson's murder. But the power of the book is not in its melodrama, but rather in the impression it conveys of the attendant evils of the Industrial Revolution seen from the worker's standpoint, in its detailed pictures of the life of the poor—their work, their homes, their unions and burial clubs—and in the characterization of Mary's father, John Barton, who becomes a criminal through want, opium, and his disappointment in the failure of the Chartist movement.

North and South is a better balanced book than *Mary Barton,* and its tone is calmer. The miseries of the poor are presented again—Bessy Higgins dies because she has been poisoned by fluff—"little bits as fly off fro' the cotton, when they're carding it, and fill the air till it looks all fine white dust"—but the manufacturer, John Thornton, means to do right, insensitive in some ways though he is, and before he comes to the end, and his union with Margaret Hale, he realizes that he has not quite disposed of those who urge co-operation between master and man by asking, "Do you give your servants reasons for your expenditure, or your economy in the use of your own money?"

To array class against class was the last thing Mrs. Gaskell really wanted to do in either of these books, for she did not think of man as exclusively, or even primarily, an economic creature. "The most depraved have also their Seed of Holiness that shall one day overcome their evil. Their one good quality, lurking hidden, but safe, among all the corrupt and bad." Unions do ride rough-shod over all the rights of man; she is as sure of that as ever Charles Reade was. In *North and South* their persecution drives Boucher to suicide; in *Mary Barton,* Job Legh says frankly that he would much rather work for low wages than strike for none at all, but if he tries that he knows the unions will "worry" him. "Now clemming is a quiet death, and worrying isn't, so I choose clemming, and come into the union." Mrs. Gaskell herself probably agreed with Higgins, of *North and South,* that "It's the only way working men can get their rights, by all joining together." But she wished it were not so; it is her prayer that other men's eyes may open as John Thornton's are opened, that others may not need to go through Barton's agony to learn, as he does at last, that there are broad human interests which men and master share. Mrs. Gaskell is very fond of the reconciliation theme. Barton and old Carson get together at last, even with Harry's corpse between them; Sylvia forgives the dying Philip a deep personal wrong. Like Dickens, Mrs. Gaskell appeals to the conscience of England; like him she stops short of advocating any system, economic or otherwise. Machinery can never solve the human problem; effective readjustment is completely dependent upon the religious impulse of self-sacrifice in the individual human heart.[12]

Between *Mary Barton* and *North and South,* Mrs. Gaskell published *Ruth,* a book which actually encouraged Josephine Butler in her life of service to outcast women. *Ruth* is much Mrs. Gaskell's poorest novel, but it would be a mistake to permit either its technical deficiencies or the exaggerated burden of woes it piles upon its "fallen" heroine—she "atones" at last when she gives her life to nurse her seducer through typhoid fever!—to blind us to its prophetic significance. It is true that Victorian proprieties make it impossible for Mrs. Gaskell to treat the seduction itself convincingly. And because passion must not be portrayed, the unintended effect is that Ruth is degraded, for she seems to have become Bellingham's mistress almost casually. Once the deed is done, however, Mrs. Gaskell faces the consequences courageously. "Oh, my God, I thank thee!" cries the deserted girl, when she learns she is to have a child. "Oh, I will be so good!" Faith Benson is disgusted to hear her speak thus of the "badge of her shame," but Faith's cleric-brother takes a very different attitude:

> "Faith, Faith! let me beg of you not to speak so of the little innocent babe, who may be God's messenger to lead her back to Him. Think again of her first words—the burst of nature from her heart! Did she not turn to God, and enter into a covenant with Him—'I will be so good?' Why, it draws her out of herself! If her life has hitherto been self-seeking and wickedly thoughtless, here is the very instrument to make her forget herself, and be thoughtful for another. Teach her (and God will teach her, if man does not come between) to reverence her child; and this reverence will shut out sin,—will be purification."
>
> . . . .
>
> "These are quite new ideas to me," said Miss Benson coldly. "I think you, Thurstan, are the first person I ever heard rejoicing over the birth of an illegitimate child. It appears to me, I must own, rather questionable morality."

When Bellingham returns, Ruth is obliged to struggle hard to avoid yielding to her old love for him, but she wins the battle; she

[12] Annette B. Hopkins has a fine exposition of this idea in "The Social Teachings of Mrs. Gaskell," *Social Service Review,* V (1931), 57-73. Cf. also Josephine Johnston, "The Sociological Significance of the Novels of Mrs. Gaskell," *Social Forces,* VI (1928-1929), 224-227.

will not have him now, even as her husband. The gentle Ruth is closer to Tess of the D'Urbervilles than she is to Pamela; she too is "a pure woman faithfully presented."

Sir Walter Raleigh once said of Christina Rossetti's poetry:

> The worst of it is that you cannot lecture on really pure poetry any more than you can talk about the ingredients of pure water—it is adulterated, methylated, sanded poetry that makes the best lectures. The only thing Christina makes me want to do, is cry, not lecture.

This is almost as true of "pure fiction" as it is of "pure poetry," and one feels it strongly in leaving these inferior books of Mrs. Gaskell's, whose interest has now become largely historical, for those others which remain a joy forever.

Mrs. Gaskell does not make us cry precisely, in Sir Walter Raleigh's sense—though, in her mid-Victorian fashion, heaven knows she tried hard enough. But when one approaches her better books there are few handles to grasp hold of; if once she had no technique, then now she seems to have passed beyond the need of it. I have no idea how she makes the willful Sylvia so real to us, nor the two contrasted heroines of her last, perfect, uncompleted book, *Wives and Daughters*. But that she does do so is beyond dispute.

I do not mean that her gift for characterization was a new thing. In *Ruth* itself, though Bellingham is tinsel and pasteboard, Benson, the dissenting clergyman, is a convincing character; and old Sally is a worthy feminine counterpart of the servitors of Scott. But in *Cranford* and in *Wives and Daughters* Mrs. Gaskell does not attempt any of the things she cannot do well.

Cranford itself is fortunately so well known that analysis is as superfluous as it would be impossible. Nobody analyzes *Cranford;* one simply quotes and remembers. There is the green tea; the cat that swallowed the lace; the cow who, having fallen into a limekiln, went to pasture thereafter in flannels; Mr. ffoulkes, who spelled his name with two little ff's, and who never considered matrimony until he met Miss ffaringdon who did the same; Mr. Holbrook, who decided that Tennyson was a great poet because he knew that ashbuds were black in March. Best of all there is the immortal Miss

Matty: "Two people that we know going to be married. It's coming very near!"

Sylvia's Lovers, which concerns press-gang days at Whitby toward the close of the eighteenth century, is something of an historical novel. Smuggling and whaling are involved also, there is much local color, and the pictures of rural life suggest George Eliot. It is not surprising that *Sylvia's Lovers* should have given Mrs. Gaskell more trouble than any other book. She had a feeling for the sea which derived, ultimately, from her Scandinavian forebears. But she had to work up her data—historical and otherwise—from local worthies and local literature; moreover, for the first time in her experience, she is working with a setting she did not know intimately at first hand. It will be clear, then, that not all the material in the book is well adapted to her gifts. Daniel Robson, the heroine's father, is hanged after having led a mob to destroy the inn which serves as headquarters for the press gang; her cousin, Philip Hepburn, wins her as his wife through refusing to reveal his knowledge that her worthless lover, Charley Kinraid, the harpooner, is not dead, as she supposes, but only impressed. The action involved in these episodes Mrs. Gaskell manages satisfactorily, though not superlatively; but when, after Kinraid's return, Sylvia breaks with Philip, and both men go off to war somewhere at the ends of the earth, where Philip atones by saving his rival in battle, she is as far out of her range as Scott was out of his when he wrote *Count Robert of Paris.* All this part of *Sylvia's Lovers* one may safely relinquish. On the other hand, Sylvia and Philip themselves are not to be missed; the girl's development out of a willful youth, through passionate, frustrated love, into devoted motherhood and tolerated wifehood, then, through bitterness, when she learns that her husband has lied to her—("I tell thee my flesh and blood wasn't made for forgiving and forgetting") —into complete spiritual maturity at the end, is consummately done.

Wives and Daughters is a very simple, though very long and perfectly constructed, story of a country doctor and his daughter, his second wife and her daughter, their neighbors, lovers, and friends. I do not believe the author's attitude toward Mrs. Gibson is so friendly as the critics would make it; certainly mine is not. When her husband tells her that Lady Cumnor is worse, she exclaims,

"You don't say so? Poor dear lady! What a shock it is to me! I'm so glad I've had some breakfast. I could not have eaten anything." But Cynthia, her daughter, is another matter; no mere moralist could have created her.

Cynthia is Beatrix Esmond in a minor key; she is as much like Beatrix as so decent a girl can be. "How kind he is!" she exclaims to Molly, when Gibson offers to finance her trip to London. "But I ought not to take it. I wish I had known you years ago; I should have been different to what I am." She does take it, for she is her mother's daughter. But she is daughter, too, to the late Kirkpatrick, who, as his widow never tires of recalling, walked five miles in the rain to get her a muffin when she was ill. "Just what one of your sensible, cold-hearted, commonplace people would never have thought of doing. With his cough and all." Cynthia must not be permitted to draw our attention away from Molly, the doctor's daughter; for Molly is nearly as delightful as Trollope's girls, and it is only here and there that she seems for a moment too good to be true. But she is not so complex as her step-sister, who has, among other things, Beatrix's passion for self-analysis: "Oh, Molly, you don't know how I was neglected just at a time when I wanted friends most. Mamma does not know it; it is not in her to know what I might have been if I had only fallen into wise, good hands." But the reader is not deceived.

> The fault, dear Brutus, is not in our stars,
> But in ourselves. . . .

The Cynthias of the world leave the Enchanted Wood quite as they entered it.

Mrs. Gaskell died in a moment, one Sunday afternoon (November 12) in 1865, when she had only a few more pages of *Wives and Daughters* left to write. She was not a great novelist. She had neither the great attitude of the Brontës, for whose fame she did so much, nor the perfect clarity of Jane Austen's vision, nor the deep philosophic insight of a George Eliot. Nevertheless her contributions to the English novel were considerable, greater, perhaps, than she was ever aware. Gerald DeWitt Sanders has summed them up well:

Her chief general contributions to literature were those she made in the social novel and in the delineation of village life and customs in Victorian England. Her chief particular contributions were her incomparable characterizations of spinsters and doctors and servants, her excellent use of dialect, and her sympathetic understanding of the views of English workingmen. In the first of these she has no near rival in English literature; in the second she did much to add to a realistic presentation of characters by giving a correct representation of their conversations; and in the last she set the mode for others, until in time men became recognized as human beings and not as worthless chattels. To have done any one of these things would have been to live; to have done all three, and to have done them well, will insure her a lasting place among the worthies of English literary history.

5. *The Novels of Charles Kingsley*

Charles Kingsley (June 12, 1819, to January 23, 1875), who once described himself as "a Church of England parson and a Chartist," but who lived to become chaplain in ordinary to Queen Victoria and tutor to the Prince of Wales, Regius Professor of Modern History of Cambridge, and canon, first, at Chester, then, at Westminster Abbey, can be said to belong to the Dickens school only in a somewhat Pickwickian sense. To speak of Kingsley as an intellectual would no doubt amuse those who recall the ineptitudes of his controversy with Newman, or his juvenile glorification of physical prowess. He was a man who lived largely in his enthusiasms and emotions, and his imagination was quite undisciplined. Nevertheless his enthusiasm went out to "ideas" as Dickens's never did. His theology was indebted importantly to Frederick Denison Maurice, his social philosophy to Carlyle.[13] And it is perilous to sneer at his scientific studies, for they won the respect of both Darwin and Huxley, and were cited in *The Descent of Man.*

Dickens shared Kingsley's admiration for Carlyle, and he must surely have agreed with him in most of the specific reforms he advo-

[13] "Kingsley, like Carlyle," writes Stanley E. Baldwin, "advocates legislative interference in labor, sanitary and educational legislation, an organized emigration service, some system of profit-sharing, and the organization of labor. Kingsley, like Carlyle, attacks the aristocracy and the clergy for their listless attitude toward the social conditions in the country, and like Carlyle, Kingsley pleads with them to recognize their responsibility as the real leaders of the people." F. D. Maurice was one of the greatest Victorian preachers.

cated. He must have sympathized with his theology also, at least in a general way, though Dickens was not greatly interested in theology as such. Both men used the novel as an instrument of reform. It was not merely because Dickens was an immeasurably greater novelist that he never permitted the weight of his ideas to break down the structure of his books as Kingsley did; it was also because he was never particularly interested in ideas for their own sake.

That Kingsley wrote novels at all is an impressive testimonial to the importance the Victorians had come to attach to this once despised branch of literature as a vehicle of discussion and reform. The novel was never more than a sideline with him: he wrote *Yeast* at night, when the work of the parish was done, *Alton Locke* between five in the morning and family prayers at seven; and his six volumes of adult fiction make up a comparatively small part of the bulk of his collected works.

Three of Kingsley's novels—*Yeast* (1848 in *Fraser's Magazine,* 1851 as a book), *Alton Locke* (1850), and *Two Years Ago* (1857)—deal with contemporary problems. In the other three—*Hypatia* (1853), *Westward Ho!* (1855), and *Hereward The Wake, "Last of the English"* (1866)—he escapes into the past but manages to carry all the problems of the present along with him.

Yeast was inspired both by the terrible condition of the agricultural laborer in England after the repeal of the Corn Laws in 1846, and by a desire to combat the drift of "the more thoughtful" among English young people "towards Rome, towards sheer materialism, or towards an unchristian and unphilosophic spiritualism."

The drift toward Rome was, of course, the result of the Oxford Movement, which Kingsley fought all his life with fanatical zeal. In the course of the book, the fox-hunting, heart-hungry hero, Lancelot Smith, has an interview with Newman, but when the priest commends him to the Blessed Virgin, he cries, "I am not a

His theology, which was definitely Christo-centric, showed German philosophical influence. He repudiated the substitutionary theory of the Atonement; to his way of thinking, Christ removed sin, not merely the penalty of sin. He believed that men can know God through Christ on the score of their—and his—humanity, and that through the Incarnation mankind might be redeemed from all its ills. Hence followed his—and Kingsley's—rejection of the doctrine of eternal punishment.

child, but a man; I want not a mother to pet, but a man to rule me." The crucified Redeemer will not do either. "I want a live Christ, not a dead one."[14] The "unchristian and unphilosophic spiritualism" was pantheism, or, as Kingsley called it, "Emersonianism."[15] The "sheer materialism" might have been expected to be Darwinism, but it is not, for Kingsley was a devoted Darwinian, and Lancelot is sure that "Man's scientific conquest of nature must be one phase of his Kingdom on Earth, whatever else is not," and that "If that Hebrew Bible is to be believed by me, it must agree with what I already know from science."

As a work of art, *Yeast* is very loosely constructed; as Stanley E. Baldwin puts it, "The author shoots at a variety of evils of his day with buckshot." Yet there is life in it because so much of Kingsley's self went into Lancelot. He too was a strong young man who could neither deny the imperious needs of his body nor find his heart's rest in them; he too had gone through a shattering spiritual conflict; he too had been saved by the love of a woman. Argemone is Mrs. Kingsley, but in the book there is no happy ending; Kingsley seems to have felt it would be more artistic somehow to have the heroine die during a typhus epidemic. Tregarva, the sensitive game-keeper, awakens Lancelot's social consciousness; the mysterious, unbelievable Barnakill points him finally to "Jesus Christ—THE MAN." Almost every force working for or against the Kingdom of God in England, as Kingsley understood it, appears somewhere in this book, but comparatively few of the characters involved have anything more than an ideational interest.

Alton Locke, Tailor and Poet, An Autobiography, which is based on the career of the shoemaker-poet, Thomas Cooper, author of *The Purgatory of Suicides,* whom Kingsley knew, and whom he won

[14] It would be impossible to bring Newmanism and Kingsley's Broad Church principles into much sharper contrast than by reading *Yeast* along with Newman's novel, *Loss and Gain* (1848). (Incidentally, Newman's *Callista* [1856] only less diametrically opposes *Hypatia.*) But Newman was no novelist; to judge him fairly one must add his impressive autobiography, *Apologia Pro Vita Sua* (1864), which was occasioned by Kingsley's unfortunate charge of untruthfulness.

[15] Cf. the very beginning of *Yeast* and, in *Alton Locke,* Chapter 22—"An Emersonian Sermon."

back to his abandoned theism,[16] is a much better book than *Yeast*, especially in the impressive account at the beginning of the poor tailor's boy who struggles for an education in spite of poverty and Calvinism. Alton gets his poems published through the respectable patronage of Dean Winnstay, who shares Kingsley's passion for science, and who, at the end, serves as the author's mouthpiece to convince Alton that there is no necessary conflict between religion and science. But because the Dean has no social vision, the poems appear in an emasculated state, an outrage to which Alton submits only because he has fallen in love with the soulless beauty of Winnstay's daughter, Lilian. Not until the end of the book does he realize how much more he has in common with her cousin, Eleanor Staunton, and then it is too late; never was the Victorian passion for untimely death more perfectly illustrated than in Eleanor's quite needless passing!

Alton Locke centers around the Chartist crisis of April 10, 1848. The concrete demands of the Chartists were reasonable, but the method of their agitation brought up the old question of whether or not violence has a necessary share in the social struggle, and both frightened and alienated a great many people. Kingsley had an important part in this struggle.

> My only quarrel with the Charter [he said], is that it does not go far enough in reform. I want to set you *free;* but I do not see how what you ask for, will give you what you want. I think you have fallen into just the same mistake as the rich of whom you complain—the very mistake of fancying that *legislative* reform is *social* reform, or that men's hearts can be changed by act of parliament.

It is to this position that Alton comes at last through all his sufferings.

Eleanor's heroic social service is intended to show up the injustice of class discriminations. Carlyle is often referred to in *Alton Locke* and the Scottish bookseller, Sandy Mackaye, embodies his personality as well as his ideas. Cousin George, who sympathizes with the Tractarians, is contemptible and dishonest; his death, on the eve of his wedding, from typhus contracted through a sweated garment

[16] Cf. Louis Cazamian, *Kingsley et Thomas Cooper, Etude sur une Source d'Alton Locke* (Paris, F. Rieder et Cie, 1903).

is as bold and sensational a piece of divine retribution as Victorian fiction knows.

The last of Kingsley's contemporary novels was *Two Years Ago.* The inept title recalled the Crimean War, which Kingsley, like Tennyson in *Maud,* absurdly thought of as having regenerated England! In the book itself the cholera epidemic is more important than the war. Kingsley himself had done good service during epidemics; as he grew older, his interest in politics declined, and his passion for sanitary reform grew ever stronger.

Tom Thurnall, a rolling stone who becomes a doctor, is the hero of this book. The Puseyites and the Dissenters are damned as usual, but Kingsley pours out the special vials of his wrath on Ellsley Vavasour, who sees a terrible shipwreck only as a good subject for a poem. Kingsley had grasped the important truth that if the artist is only an artist he is nothing, but the accumulation of woe he brings down on Vavasour's head seems absurdly overdone.

The schoolmistress, Grace Harvey—half mystic and saint, half unbalanced fanatic—is a strange kind of heroine; equally strange in her own way is Marie Cordifiamma, an afterthought due to Kingsley's newly-awakened interest in abolition, whose story is quite unconnected with the rest of the book. Marie is an American mulatto, a slave, but she only needs Tom to convey her to free territory in order to become an international stage celebrity, and finally the wife of a wealthy American!

No book of Kingsley's is free from absurdities, and there are probably more absurdities in *Two Years Ago* than in any other. Yet for all its infelicities the book has a strange charm, the same kind of charm as *The Fool of Quality,* which Kingsley adored, and by which, it is clear, he was influenced.

Of the three historical novels, *Hypatia, or New Foes with an Old Face,* a picture of the struggle between Christianity and paganism in fifth century Alexandria, is the one which gets farthest away from Kingsley's own time in its setting and stays closest to it in spirit. The author's own valedictory suggests the great weakness of the book: "I have shown you . . . your own likenesses in toga and tunic, instead of coat and bonnet." He does. He even shows us Charles Kingsley's likeness as Bishop Synesius, who glorifies sportsmanship and married love. But none of this helps to take us into fifth-century Alexandria.

Kingsley was right in his feeling that, unlike religion, philosophy is always essentially aristocratic in its appeal; when Hypatia confronts the hapless Pelagia, she has "no gospel . . . for the harlot! No word for the sinner, the degraded!" And this gives him a chance to bring forward the cardinal tenet of Maurice's theology—and of his own—that the Incarnation is the answer to the human problem.

Unfortunately Kingsley was prevented from setting forth this idea very effectively by the fact that in *Hypatia* he is also trying to excoriate everything he hates most in ecclesiasticism—"those habits of doing evil that good may come, of pious intrigue, and at last of open persecution. . . ." The unfortunate result is that while paganism or "Emersonianism"—which is what Kingsley was really fighting, and which, of course, is not really paganism at all—is seen at its best in the book in Hypatia herself, the Christian party—the Bishop of Alexandria and his followers—have only a degraded Christianity to pit against it.

Critics of the past praised *Hypatia* for its elevation of tone. It has this elevation undoubtedly, and it has plenty of action also, but neither its Jews nor its Christians, its Romans nor its Goths, have any particular reality; and Howells was not unfair when he described the heroine as "a sort of Alexandrian Margaret Fuller."

To a certain extent these faults appear in *Westward Ho!* The respectability of the book is eminently Victorian, and the famous tribute to Queen Elizabeth was written with one eye on Kingsley's own sovereign. The Rose of Torridge elopes with Don Guzman, and Frank and Amyas Leigh cross the seas in pursuit. When, through an overheard conversation, Frank learns that his love is not the Spaniard's mistress, as he had feared, a great load drops from his mind. " 'Husband!' whispered Frank faintly to Amyas. 'Thank God, thank God! I am content. Let us go.' " Despite such absurdities, Kingsley understood the Elizabethan period much better than he understood Alexandria in the fifth century, and he had a much truer feeling for it. *Westward Ho!* is a highly idealized picture of the Elizabethan sea-rovers, but of its kind it is as good a picture as we are likely to get.

Morally, however, the book is open to serious objection. Kingsley's bitterness toward the Roman Catholic Church is very unpleasant, and his specific exemption, from his blanket condemnation, of "those Roman Catholics whose noble blood has stained every Crimean battlefield" is merely comic. This brings us to the second objection. *Westward Ho!* was a recruiting poster for the Crimean War, for Kingsley, forward-looking as he was on many social questions, was blind to the underlying purposes of imperialist war. So Drake, Raleigh and the others appear in his pages, though not without some historical justification, one must admit, as prophets of the modern imperialist expansion.

Hereward the Wake takes its place with Bulwer's novel and Tennyson's play about Harold as an important contribution to the Anglo-Saxon revival. Kingsley had a genuine love for the fen-country from memories of his youth, and his very limitations helped him to enter sympathetically into the experiences of the Saxon warrior. He develops his story episodically, and he is rather successful in catching the spirit of *The Anglo-Saxon Chronicle:*

> And now is Hereward to the greenwood gone, to be a bold outlaw; and not only an outlaw himself, but the father of all outlaws, who held these forests for two hundred years, from the fens to the Scottish border.

Of course it must be a woman, Torfrida, who leads Hereward into the right way, and of course when he deserts her, it must be the beginning of the end:

> But the grace of God had gone away from Hereward, as it goes away from all men who are unfaithful to their wives.

Even for that interpretation, however, there is some justification in the chronicles.

I do not wish to suggest that I consider Kingsley's achievements as a novelist altogether negligible. He was a writer of many gifts, and he knew how to tell an exciting story. But his arrows often failed to hit the mark at which he aimed them. He was right in his feeling that a man must be a good pagan before he can be a good Christian; nevertheless, it was Christianity that he wanted to preach. He can hardly be said to achieve his purpose, however, when he gives us heroes like Amyas Leigh and Tom Thurnall, who travel heroically through the books they inhabit in their pagan aspects, only to experience a hurried, offstage conversion at the close. Moreover, Kingsley's continual harping on his favorite ideas becomes very tiresome even to those who share them. To the development of the novel as such Kingsley contributed little; he applied it to social and economic problems, to be sure, but others had, as we have seen, done that before him. It is even doubtful that his novels had any important influence on the breakdown of structure so often apparent in later "novels of ideas." But certainly they themselves prefigure it.

CHAPTER XV

COUNTER-BLAST: W. M. THACKERAY

The Art of Novels *is* to represent Nature; to convey as strongly as possible the sentiment of reality—in a tragedy or a poem or a lofty drama you aim at producing different emotions; the figures moving, and their words sounding, heroically: but in a drawingroom drama a coat is a coat and a poker a poker; and must be nothing else according to my ethics, not an embroidered tunic, nor a great red-hot instrument like the Pantomime weapon.

W. M. THACKERAY

1. *Thackeray and Dickens*

From the beginning it seems to have been recognized that Thackeray was Dickens's great antitype. When Mrs. Carlyle read *Vanity Fair* she declared roundly that it beat Dickens out of the field. But her husband, repelled by what he considered Thackeray's cynicism, turned back to his old favorite as a refuge.

Thackeray himself recognized Dickens's power. He even praised enthusiastically some elements in Dickens's art which modern criticism tends to reject. But he knew his own power also. He felt that his novels were a serious picture of life such as Dickens had never achieved, and it hurt him to see the other novelist selling five books to his one. Personal relations between the two men, though not unclouded, were in the main creditable to both. But it is clear that there was no very intimate sympathy between them.

It is not necessary for the critic to sacrifice one great writer to another. But it is important that he should understand the differences between them.

2. *Thackeray's Career*

William Makepeace Thackeray was prepared for life by failing in every desire of his heart. He lost his fortune almost as soon as he had come into it; his beloved wife went mad; his talents were long comparatively unrecognized. This unhappy prelude to his artistic achievement must always be kept in mind in contemplating what Professor Dodds calls his "congenital melancholy," a melancholy "which often just avoids shading off into a grim morbidity, but which is saved always by a tenderness and a humour which are just as native to him."

Thackeray was born in Calcutta, July 18, 1811. He went to school at the Charterhouse (he called it the Slaughterhouse), then at Cambridge, where he published rimes and parodies in college papers but took no degree. He read law, half-heartedly; he wandered about Weimar and Paris in pursuit of art. When it became clear that he was going to have to earn a living, it was to art that he turned first. But the attempt proved abortive, and in 1837 he became one of Dr. William Maginn's writing hacks on *Fraser's Magazine*. This picturesque journalist was now engaged in a war against Bulwer-Lytton, editor of the rival *New Monthly Magazine*. In this war Thackeray's gift for burlesque caused him to be enlisted.

He attacked the novel of fashionable life in *The Memoirs of Mr. C. J. Yellowplush* and *The Diary of C. Jeames de la Pluche,* and the crime story, much more importantly, in *Catherine* (1839-1840). But he did not stop with Bulwer. In the course of time, Disraeli, Lever, G. P. R. James, Fenimore Cooper, and Mrs. Gore all fell into his clutches. His ridicule influenced contemporary fiction: James cashiered the solitary horseman with which he had been in the habit of beginning his novels, while W. H. Ainsworth and Pierce Egan both steered away from the novel of crime. Sometimes malice was involved in Thackeray's attacks, sometimes moral purpose. Fortunately there is no trace of either in his finest burlesque, *Rebecca and Rowena,* a history of the unhappy married life of Sir Wilfrid of Ivanhoe!

Thackeray then is like Cervantes, Fielding, and Jane Austen, in that his initial writing impulse derived from literature, not directly from life; he was out to demolish false ideals. Indeed he never relinquished occasional writing—his major novels make up less than half the bulk of his collected works—nor did he ever relinquish burlesque; as late as the *Roundabout Papers* (1863) he has a take-off on Wilkie Collins. In 1842 he began contributing to *Punch,* in whose pages the immortal *Book of Snobs* first appeared.[1]

In his crime-story, *Catherine,* which is something more than a burlesque, Thackeray's sincerity is beyond question; he believed that the contemporary Newgate novels were both morally vicious and artistically worthless.

> Over this part of Mrs. Cat's history we shall be as brief as possible; for, to tell the truth, nothing immoral occurred during her whole stay at the good Doctor's house; and we are not going to insult the reader by offering him silly pictures of piety, cheerfulness, good sense, and simplicity; which are milk-and-water virtues after all, and have no relish with them like a good strong vice, highly peppered.

The real Catherine Hayes was executed at Tyburn in 1726, and Thackeray's nauseating climax cleaves closely to history. Yet the book is only a qualified success. The author himself had no stomach for it, and his cries of distress do not help the reader. "And here, though we are only in the third chapter of this history, we feel almost sick of the characters that appear in it, and the adventures which they are called upon to go through." Contemporaries were shocked; modern readers are more likely to be caught by the gusto of the tale than admonished by its moral.

A more important book is *Barry Lyndon* (1844), a picaresque tale describing the disreputable adventures in love and war of a rascally Irish adventurer of the eighteenth century. Barry tells his own story in the absolute faith that he has always been right, yet every word that falls from his lips condemns him. People who dislike Thackeray's habit of commenting freely upon his narrative sometimes rate the objective *Barry* higher as a work of art than the major novels.

Such a view cannot, however, be upheld. Considered by itself, *Barry Lyndon* is a brilliant thing. But compare it with its acknowledged model, Fielding's *Jonathan Wild,* and it loses luster. Thack-

[1] *The Book of Snobs* portrays the principal varieties of English snob—military, clerical, university, club, etc. Thackeray starts out with the idea of the snob as a social climber. Unsure of his position, he pretends to be something he is not; thus he finds it necessary to look down upon his own class. As the sketches proceed, however, Thackeray widens his scope until snobbery comes to include almost all human failings.

eray could never have been more than a second-rate Fielding; the master's hard, magnificent irony is beyond him. (In Chapter VII, for example, in the scoundrel's tender reflections on his mother, the mask drops; and the face we see is the face of Thackeray.) Like *Esmond,* the book refuses to glorify war, thus taking one step toward the realistic war novel of recent times.

Unfortunately, *Barry Lyndon* did not attract the public; neither did *The History of Samuel Titmarsh and the Great Hoggarty Diamond* (1841), charming and tender as it is. Real recognition, however, came to Thackeray in 1847-1848, with the dazzling achievement which is *Vanity Fair.*

Vanity Fair began as "Pen and Pencil Sketches of English Society." It is not a highly unified book, for the material of many earlier papers was taken up into it. The frame-conception of a great puppet show was an afterthought, nor was the professed moral purpose—"to make a set of people living without God in the world"—in Thackeray's mind from the beginning. The novel is somewhat uneven, too, in its realism. Yet it constitutes probably the most serious picture and the most important criticism of society offered in English fiction up to its time.

The crisis centers in the Battle of Waterloo, and the Waterloo chapters are so good that any novelist worth his salt would give his eyeteeth to have written them. Thackeray does not take us to the battlefield. He portrays the great crisis indirectly, through its effect on the lives of those who stayed at home.

There are many fine characters in *Vanity Fair,* but so far as the world is concerned the book is first and foremost the story of Becky Sharp. The great length of the novel permits Thackeray to employ for all his major personages a method of gradual revelation. When they are first introduced we may not wholly comprehend them, indeed we may even miscomprehend them; then, as the pages fly beneath our fingers, we gradually live our way into their lives.

The conventions governing Victorian fiction obliged Thackeray to pass lightly over some phases of Becky's later career, but the book is not seriously affected by this limitation. Nathaniel Wright Stephenson overstates the case when he speaks of Becky's "intuitive sense of proportion, her natural delicacy . . . her courage, her amiability, her lack of malice, her poise, her serenity, her charm. . . ." It is true that Becky wants a position in the eyes of the world—she feels sure she could be a good woman on £5,000 a year—but she has a rackety side to her which Stephenson does not even glance at. Yet this does not mean that D. H. Lawrence would have done a better job by her than Thackeray. She is no nymphomaniac; indeed she is too cold to be capable of real passion. She would commit a sexually immoral act at a moment's notice if it seemed necessary in order to get something she wanted, but she would probably not find too much pleasure in it. Not for many moments, at best, would it keep her mind off the main chance.

Becky has courage and poise unquestionably. She even has a measure of serenity and charm. She has as much amiability and lack of malice as a woman can have without either heart or conscience. She is always kind when it costs her nothing, when there is nothing to be gained by being unkind. That is not much to say, but in a world in which there are far too many people busily engaged in producing mischief because they enjoy it, it is something. Becky has no reason to love Dobbin surely, yet she makes it possible for him to get his Amelia when she reveals at last the truth about George Osborne. It is part of Thackeray's irony that, worthless as Becky is, Rawdon should, like the knights of old, be purified through his love for her. And it is at once a tribute to her and to the depth and complexity of Thackeray's characterization of her that, as Dodds has reminded us,

> her point of greatest admiration for her husband should come when, having discovered her alone with Lord Steyne, he is striking the Peer in the face. It meant the collapse of Becky's fortunes, but she had a detached power of viewing life judicially as it swept by her.[2]

[2] Thackeray himself wrongs Becky egregiously when he throws out the suggestion that she murdered Jos Sedley. This is one of the worst blunders of characterization in all English fiction, a far more serious matter than making Micawber a magistrate in Australia. It refuses to fit into the picture at all; indeed, I think it completely fails to "register" with most readers. Catherine Branch Ely has a sensible, if somewhat colloquial, discussion of "The Psychology of Becky Sharp," in *Modern Language Notes,* XXXV (1920), 31-33. For the suggestion that the character may have been based on Sydney Owenson, Lady Morgan, cf. Lionel Stevenson, in *PMLA,* XLVIII (1933), 547-551.

Though Thackeray's method is discursive, he can develop great "scenes" when he needs them. The most famous scene in *Vanity Fair* is the one just referred to—Rawdon's return from the spunging-house. Equally powerful in a very different manner is the famous last paragraph of Chapter 32:

> No more firing was heard at Brussels—the pursuit rolled miles away. Darkness came down on the field and city: and Amelia was praying for George, who was lying on his face, dead, with a bullet through his heart.

But Thackeray does not need to turn on all the heat to be effective. Nothing could be sharper than his remark concerning Becky that "it was only from her French being so good, that you could know she was not a born woman of fashion." And the picture of her hypocrisy, "hemming a shirt for her little boy," is consummate. "Whenever Mrs. Rawdon wished to be particularly humble and virtuous, this little shirt used to come out of her work-box. It had got to be too small for Rawdon long before it was finished, though."

Despite all its verve, *Vanity Fair* is a profoundly disillusioned book. It is "A Novel Without a Hero," and Thackeray deliberately goes out of his way to make Dobbin unheroic, to emphasize his ugliness and clumsiness. The contrast is effective enough, but let nobody rest under the delusion that Thackeray is doing what Rostand did in *Cyrano de Bergerac.*

What Rostand is saying is that a man can be a great hero in spite of a grotesque physical handicap. Thackeray, on the other hand, is saying that when, once in a blue moon, nature does turn out a decent human being, she gives him a presence and a temperament that must inevitably cause his pure soul to lose half the power it might otherwise command. In the end, Dobbin wins his Amelia but not until he has learned how cruel and unjust she can be: in the last analysis the game is not quite worth the candle.

Pendennis (1848-1850) is Thackeray's biographical novel. It was modeled deliberately upon *Tom Jones,* though with the clear realization that Fielding's eighteenth-century frankness was now quite out of fashion. Thackeray conceived it in terms of a modern morality: the design on the yellow wrapper of the monthly parts shows a young man torn between the forces of good and evil, which are personified respectively in a mother with her children and a siren and imps. More than three-quarters of the way through the book the author defines his purpose: "our endeavor is merely to follow out, in its progress, the development of the mind of a worldly and selfish, but not ungenerous or unkind or truth-avoiding man."

The book is arranged throughout in blocks of action, which are connected with each other only by the fact that Pen participates in all of them. In the first two hundred pages, which concern his infatuation for the virtuous and rather bovine actress, Miss Fotheringay, the treatment is masterly but the subject-matter seems trifling. On the other hand, Major Pendennis, the hero's uncle, is a wonderful characterization, the most famous snob in English fiction. Without abating a jot of his snobbery, Thackeray makes him completely a human being, nor does he find it necessary to deny him the possession of every good quality. His kindness toward Pen is admirable; his skill in extricating the boy from his many difficulties is unfailing. And at the end, when, in one of Thackeray's big "scenes," Major Pendennis triumphs over his rascally valet, Morgan, who had conspired against him, he is nearly heroic.

There is a touch of "sensation" here, and there is more than a touch of it in the mystery centering about the reappearance of Lady Clavering's first husband, the worthless Amory. Here Thackeray seems trying to meet Dickens on his own ground.

The women of the book repeat the antithesis between good and bad with which we have already become familiar in *Vanity Fair*. Blanche Amory is a contemptible cheat, quite lacking in Becky's verve and spunk. The good women are Pen's mother, Helen Pendennis, and Laura Bell, with whose hand he is rewarded after he has been purged of his worst faults. We are evidently intended to admire Helen tremendously, but she strains our sympathy by her cruelty to Fanny Bolton, the little servant girl who has nursed Pen through an illness.[3] Of Laura, her husband says later, when they

[3] It is apparently to be a shining star in Pen's crown that he refrains from seducing Fanny. If one wishes to see what has happened to class distinctions since Thackeray's time, it is only necessary to compare this girl with the Little Model in Galsworthy's *Fraternity,* or with the heroine of the same writer's most celebrated short story, "The Apple Tree."

reappear in *Philip,* that she is "too certain of her own virtue . . . too sure of the correctness of her own opinion." This is a very mild expression of what many readers have felt.

Henry Esmond (1852), alone among Thackeray's full-length novels, was never published in parts. It is a beautifully built book, and one can hardly imagine its being omitted from any list of the great English novels.

Esmond is an historical novel, covering the years from about 1678 to 1718. Thackeray loved the eighteenth century, and succeeds wonderfully well in conjuring up its atmosphere. A triple background is involved in the book: (1) military campaigns on the continent; (2) Jacobite plots in England in behalf of the Old Pretender; (3) the social and literary life of Queen Anne's London.

The aged Esmond tells his own life-story, in the third person mainly. The method, though dramatic, involves no conflict with Thackeray's essentially subjective approach to fiction, for Esmond is as much given to moralizing as Thackeray himself. The novelist resists the temptation to make his hero a mere chorus-character, however. Esmond's judgment is sometimes at fault—as in his extreme contempt for Marlborough—and Thackeray adds footnotes written by other members of the family, to guide the reader's judgment and assist in creating verisimilitude.

In Beatrix Esmond this novel has, too, Thackeray's most fascinating heroine. Beatrix is of the sisterhood of Becky Sharp, but she wears her rue with a difference. She is selfish and hard, but she knows her faults as well as we do, and she sees out and beyond her to a higher plane of being toward which she knows she can never aspire. Her mother, Lady Castlewood, is another of Thackeray's "good" women, but she has not been a wise or understanding mother to Beatrix; and when we compare what the girl says of the mother with what the mother says of her, we may not feel that the advantage lies wholly on Lady Castlewood's side.

Beatrix's weaknesses are accentuated by the circumstances of her life. She is engaged first to Lord Ashburnham, but the engagement falls through, then to the Duke of Hamilton. Just as she is preparing for her wedding, Hamilton and Lord Mohun fight a duel, the same sword that had destroyed Beatrix's father taking the life of her affianced husband also. When Esmond and his fellow-conspirators bring the Pretender to England during the last days of Queen Anne, their plan to have him named as heir to the throne seems in a fair way to succeed, but Beatrix cannot resist placing her own interests above what she and they alike think of as the welfare of England, and when the crucial moment arrives, the Prince is not to be found, for he has gone away with her. This marks the break between Beatrix and her old life, and it cures Esmond of the long disease of his love for her. Yet Esmond had come closer to touching her heart than any other man; had he been more masterful and less humble he might have won her. There is an element of real tragedy in her history; and to meet such a woman, even in fiction, is to enlarge one's understanding of life.

The Newcomes (1853-1855) returns to the discursive manner of *Pendennis,* Pen himself being reintroduced as the narrator. This is a family novel covering three generations. Various phases of snobbery, worldliness, selfishness, and self-seeking are studied in various members of the Newcome clan; and all are contrasted effectively with the self-effacing worldliness of Clive's father, old Colonel Newcome. Clive, who is an artist, is not unlike Pendennis himself. Ethel is Thackeray's most successful attempt to create an intelligent and attractive heroine. Thanks to the faults of her upbringing, she starts out with the worldly ideal—her aim in life is to capture a rich husband. But what happens in the course of the story opens her eyes, and she chooses the better way.

Thackeray castigates the marriage of convenience in the union of Sir Barnes Newcome and Lady Clara Pulleyn, which ends tragically, and he is almost equally hard on the marriage of consolation in Clive's mating with Rosey Mackenzie, whom Clive marries when he seems to have lost Ethel, a blunder which piles up misery upon misery for everybody connected with it.

There is some satire on religious pretensions in Sophia Hobson Newcome; and there is some almost unbearable writing in the description of the slow torture to which Mrs. Mackenzie subjects the Colonel when, having lost all his money and all Rosey's money in the failure of the Bundelcund Bank, he is forced to live under her domestic tyranny. Surprise is used again at the close when the belated discovery of Sophia's will rehabilitates Clive's fortunes, though Thackeray uses this reversal much less sensationally than Dickens would have done. Charles Honeyman, the fashionable clergyman, is worth comparing in detail with Dickens's clerical hypocrites. The Dickens figures are more amusing, but Thackeray's is the finer touch.

If *The Newcomes* ties up with *Pendennis,* then *The Virginians* (1857-1859) was an outgrowth of *Esmond,* for it concerns itself with the grandsons of Henry Esmond, George and Henry Warrington. The historical background involves both the French and Indian War and the American Revolution, in which the brothers are enlisted on opposing sides. But most of the action takes place in England, where the two young men visit their kinsmen and run the gamut of the fashionable life of the day. Sundry types of worldliness and selfishness are presented again; and the stock eighteenth-century contrast between the studious young man and the gay young blade appears in the two heroes themselves. Harry's passion for his cousin, Lady Maria, varies the Fotheringay motif out of *Pendennis.* The leading social climber is Lydia van den Bosch, a rich young Dutch-American. The Lambert family furnishes welcome relief from the prevailing selfishness of the Castlewood clan.

But the most interesting character is again Beatrix Esmond, now the aged Baroness Bernstein. When she lies at last on her delirious deathbed, we learn, in broken French, that she has not been as bad as we believed her to be. She fled with the Pretender not as his mistress but as his affianced bride, and he deserted her. But her life since that day has been far from blameless, and she has now attained a graceless old age. Yet she is never a caricature, never a horror. Though the process of transformation is not shown but inferred, the character is recognizable despite all the ravages of the years. This is the kind of old woman that Beatrix Esmond must have become.

The Virginians completes the list of Thackeray's major novels. *Lovel the Widower,* a short book, serialized in the *Cornhill Magazine,* of which Thackeray became the editor upon its establishment in 1860, is not important. And though *Philip* (1861-1862), Thackeray's last long novel, has some fine things in it, as a whole it does illustrate the truth of his own saying, "All I can do now is to bring out my old puppets and put new bits of riband upon them." On the other hand, the fragment, *Denis Duval* (1864) is magnificent in its way; if he had only lived to finish it, it would surely have been one of the best of English romances.

Thackeray's health had long been bad. His eating and drinking habits did not tend to improve it; nor, probably, did his lecture tours on both sides of the Atlantic. On the morning of December 24, 1863, he was found dead in bed, in the fifty-second year of his life. The "poor little wife" who had brought him such joy and such sorrow outlived him in her madness by a generation.

3. *Technique and Point of View*

Thackeray's point of view is always that of an upper classman. He sees man as a social being, and he never fails to make an ethical judgment, but the "private" not the "public" virtues are his concern. In the modern sense of the term he has no social consciousness. Factory wheels are turning in the background of the *Newcomes* drama, but we never see them turn. Thackeray believed with Anthony Trollope that "all authors can do is to depict men out of their businesses."

Like Dickens, Thackeray considered himself a radical in politics. But on questions of international policy he saw more clearly than Dickens ever did. He hated militarism and imperialism, and he did not hesitate to say so out loud. His attitude toward America was refreshingly sympathetic and intelligent. But politics did not touch his art.[4]

That the world whose special historian he became was a world that had been created by the Industrial Revolution, Thackeray probably never stopped to consider. Yet his special *bête noire,* the snob, could have flourished only at such a time as that in which his own lot was cast, that is, after the old aristocratic barriers had begun to crumble and before the ideal of a classless society had become widely acceptable.

His art-study and his literary life in London added Bohemia to

[4] Cf. Robert S. Forsythe, "Thackeray, Critic of His Times," *The Quarterly Journal of the University of North Dakota,* XXII (1932), 191-203.

Thackeray's Mayfair. Continental experiences widened the scope of his picture, if not of his mind. His basis of judgment is always insular. To him Frenchmen are always frog-eaters. Unlike Kipling at a later date, he left India too early to derive local color from it. For Thackeray, India is a country to bring characters from or send them to.

Passion is outside Thackeray's range; he cannot write a love-scene. "I blush so, though quite alone in my study, that you would fancy I was going off in an apoplexy." And love is not the only one of the intenser human experiences he approaches gingerly. Dickens disliked in him "a pretence of undervaluing his art, which was not good for the art that he held in trust." "Let us not be too prowd," says his own Mr. Yellowplush, "and fansy ourselves marters of the truth, marters or apostels. We are but tradesmen working for bread, and not for righteousness' sake. Let's try and work honestly; but don't let us be prayting pompisly about our 'sacred calling.'" Thackeray had much religious sentiment, but he has no metaphysic, and the lives of his characters are never oriented in relationship to the Absolute.

Professor Charles Brockway Hale points out that of all Thackeray's major novels only *Vanity Fair* and *Pendennis* are written in the third person throughout. *Barry Lyndon, Esmond,* and *Denis Duval* are autobiographical narratives. *The Newcomes* and *Philip* are told from the point of view of a minor character. *The Virginians* begins in the third person, but in the last part Thackeray is supposed to be editing George Warrington's manuscript. Sometimes he forgets this and permits Warrington to comment on the manuscript as if he were outside of it. He is guilty of many contradictions and inaccuracies of this kind, though few of them are very important.

He is fond of beginning his narrative *in medias res,* and then going back to relate antecedent adventures. Like Balzac,[5] Trollope, Zola, and Howells, he links his novels one to another. He has the upper classman's interest in genealogy; and he dislikes branching out on something absolutely new.

Thackeray rendered an important service to realism in fiction.

[5] Cf. W. C. D. Pacey, "Balzac and Thackeray," *Modern Language Review*, XXXVI (1941), 213-224.

And if a realist is a man who refuses to create characters that are larger than life, then surely he deserves that title. He believed "that men are weak; that truth must be told; that fault must be owned; that pardon must be prayed for; and that love reigns supreme over all." When he was preparing to put George Washington into *The Virginians* what he wanted to know about him was whether he was "a funny old gentleman in a wig? Did he take snuff and spill it down his shirt front?" If Amelia quarrels with her mother, if Rachael Esmond Warrington nearly wrecks the lives of both her sons, if Charlotte Firmin is meanly and spitefully jealous of the Little Sister, all these things must go in. But Thackeray can never get his head and his heart together; consequently there is often a great gulf fixed between the worshipful comments he makes on his "good" women and the spiteful manner in which he permits them to behave.

His realism was modified too by his narrow moral outlook. Theoretically he believed that the artist must concern himself with "that strange and awful struggle of good and wrong which takes place in our hearts and in the world." Practically he left many aspects of that struggle unexamined. He was shocked by Goethe and Victor Hugo. He was even shocked by Richardson. As editor he once returned a story to Trollope because in it a character planned to run off with a married woman. Thackeray's prudery, which increased with the years, is seen at its worst in the Barnes-Clara episode of *The Newcomes*.

Perhaps Thackeray's realism was also modified by the fact that he never really liked the kind of novel he wrote. What he really wanted to write was a book with "an incident in every other page, a villain, a battle, a mystery in every chapter"; and in *Denis Duval* he nearly achieved his ideal. *Denis* represents indeed his capitulation to romance.

This capitulation was not surprising, for Thackeray mellowed as he grew older, as he traveled farther from the crushing disappointments of his youth. The pall lies heaviest over *Vanity Fair:* "Ah, *Vanitas Vanitatum!* Which of us is happy in this world? Which of us has his desire? or, having it, is satisfied?—Come, children, let us shut up the box and the puppets, for our play is played out." In

Philip the tone is very different: "Who says the world is all cold? There is the sun and the shadows. And the heaven which ordains poverty and sickness sends pity, and love, and succour." [6]

Whatever may be said of Thackeray's realism, his reality comes out most clearly in his treatment of character. And here, though the particular types he deals with are often very different, he is closer to Dickens than he is to George Eliot, for he does not construct his personages, he evokes them. His insight was uncanny. His daughter, Lady Ritchie, tells us that "he sometimes spoke of this conscious feeling he had about people at times, as if uncomfortable facts in their past history were actually revealed to him," and she gives the example of his having spoken of someone in good repute at the time as if he knew that the man had committed a murder. "You know it, then!" exclaimed his companion. "Who could have told you?" Nobody had told him. But he knew.

Thackeray is sincere, therefore, when he declares that he does not know what his personages are going to say or do next. "I wonder what will happen to Pendennis and Fanny Bolton; writing it and sending it to you somehow it seems as if it were true." He professes ignorance as to how far Becky really descended, and when he was reproached for having made Esmond marry the mother of Beatrix after Beatrix herself had eluded him, he declared, "I didn't make him do it; they did it themselves."

Perhaps some effects are beyond the writer who declines improvisation and plans all his work out in advance. Literature is one thing and life is another, yet the greatest writers are always making us forget it. We shall never know the whole truth about Hamlet any more than about Mary Queen of Scots: hence the perennial fascination of his character. It might still be argued, however, that wonderful as such creations are, they lack the simplicity which it is one special function of art to bring us, and for which we turn to art, away from life. Mrs. Stirling, the actress, put her finger on this point in commenting upon Clive's marriage to Rosey: "Really, it is

[6] From *Vanity Fair* to *Philip* the pall lifts steadily. The process is traced in some detail in Nathaniel Wright Stephenson's stimulating book, *The Spiritual Drama in the Life of Thackeray* (Doran, 1913).

very provoking of Thackeray that he will make his heroes and heroines marry the wrong people just as they do in real life."

On no other aspect of Thackeray's narrative art is opinion so sharply divided as on the matter of his habit of commenting *in propria persona* upon his story.[7] He himself defines this practice in *Vanity Fair:*

> And, as we bring our characters forward, I will ask leave, as a man and a brother, not only to introduce them, but occasionally to step down from the platform, and talk about them: if they are good and kindly, to love them and shake them by the hand; if they are silly, to laugh at them confidentially in the reader's sleeve: if they are wicked and heartless, to abuse them in the strongest terms which politeness admits of.

William Dean Howells unsparingly condemns Thackeray's tenency "to stand about on his scene, talking it over with his hands in his pockets, interrupting the action, and spoiling the illusion in which alone the truth of art resides." Henry Dwight Sedgwick is even more caustic: "He is like a timid mother, who will not let her brood out of sight while any one is looking at them."

But G. K. Chesterton, Lord David Cecil, Emerson Grant Sutcliffe, John W. Dodds, and Herbert J. Muller are all in the other camp. "Thackeray could not rest easy until the reader was acquainted with everything," says Sutcliffe, "not only what had happened, but what Thackeray thought about it. Only this was for him the complete truth." Dodds, somewhat similarly, finds in his comments "an artistic extension to what we may speak of boldly as his idea." "He is the novelist of memory," adds Chesterton, "that is, of the emotion of experience." Cecil sees him welding diverse material into unity through imposing his own personality upon it. And Professor Muller, "modern" as he is, boldly takes the bull by the horns:

> Although Fielding and Thackeray constantly embroidered their narratives with personal comment, their work is in a deeper sense highly impersonal. They preserved a philosophical if not an artistic detachment, and could enter their stories so freely if only because they so definitely stood outside them and commanded the show. They had a far firmer

[7] Cf. Albert H. Tolman, "The Author's Comment in 'Vanity Fair,'" in *The Views About Hamlet and Other Essays* (Houghton Mifflin, 1904).

grasp of their material than most contemporaries who on esthetic grounds fastidiously eschew their intimacy with the reader.

Just how, one might ask the objectors, do Thackeray's comments destroy his illusion? Do we blot a character out of existence by the mere expedient of talking about him? Might the case not be argued at least as effectively the other way round? Thackeray's characters *must* be real—otherwise he could not possibly talk about them!

Yet it does not follow that this habit of Thackeray's is to be unreservedly commended. The trouble with many of his comments is not that they destroy the illusion but that they are themselves tiresome and trite. He was not a thinker as Fielding was a thinker. He has only a few stops in his quill, and we soon become familiar with all the music he can play upon them. Like others, this habit grew steadily upon Thackeray as time advanced, and by the time we get to *Philip* we are reading a commentary upon a novel rather than the novel itself.

About Thackeray's style, on the other hand, there has been very little difference of opinion. It is almost universally recognized as having combined fine elegance with colloquial ease. Howells, to be sure, finds him bookish, and Charles Whibley complains that he is facile and uncontrolled. But this is eccentric criticism, and, in Howells's case at least, not unprejudiced criticism. Most essays on style, so they say, are abominably written; no comment shall be made here beyond this tribute from another great stylist:

> He blew on his pipe [wrote Max Beerbohm], and words came tripping round him like children, like pretty little children who are perfectly drilled for the dance, or came, did he will it, treading on their precedence, like kings, gloomily.

4. *Some Shortcomings*

Anthony Trollope pointed out Thackeray's most important weakness when he said, "There is a touch of vagueness which indicates that his pen was not firm while he was using it." He is a sentimentalist and a cynic, a worldling and an innocent; his boyish high spirits alternate with fits of melancholia. He cannot make up his mind even about his own characters: you can prove from his recorded utterances both that he admired Esmond, Amelia Sedley, and Colonel Newcome, and that he despised them.

He was a year older than Dickens, yet his first major novel, *Vanity Fair,* came out along with Dickens's sixth, *Dombey and Son.* And *Vanity Fair* itself did not give him confidence; nothing on earth could do that. In 1849 he sought a government appointment. He hoped he might last six years more in literature; he knew he was writing badly, but probably he could ride along that far on his reputation! After that he would have to depend on other work.

One reason why *Denis Duval* is so fascinating—was, indeed, under the circumstances, a minor miracle—is that here, for once, Thackeray did actually break with his past and attempt something new; it was as if he were starting all over again.

Part of the difficulty seems to have been that Thackeray did not really care for first-rate art. His conviction that *King Lear* is a bad play, his amazing notion that Othello's Desdemona really had had improper relations with Cassio—surely we do not need to add to these things his monstrous slander of Fielding, Swift, and Sterne to understand what Thackeray was worth critically.[8]

"A big, fierce, weeping man," Carlyle called him; "not a strong one." He was a giant. He had a giant's weakness and a giant's easy power.

Comparing him again with Dickens, one would be obliged to point out that Dickens moved within certain very definite limitations of temperament. There were some barriers that he could not cross. That may have been his Creator's fault; certainly it was not his. Of what had been given him to work with, he made absolutely the best that any human being could have made. His life was not, in every aspect, a happy one; yet one feels that he fulfilled his destiny.

With Thackeray one cannot feel this. It is true that if he lacked Dickens's horse-sense, he also lacked, happily, the "go-getter" qualities of Dickens. The attractive melancholy gentleness of his spirit demands sympathetic study; it yields itself less readily than Dick-

[8] Cf. Philip Enzinger, "Thackeray, Critic of Literature," *The Quarterly Journal of the University of North Dakota,* XX (1930), 318-333; XXI (1930-1931), 52-65, 145-160.

ens's warm, expansive geniality. Yet when all is said and done one is inclined to agree reluctantly with Frank Swinnerton that "He did not . . . essay the heights opened to him by his talent." This is the feeling that makes Thackeray the most difficult of all English novelists to evaluate, and that even causes a bit of his own melancholy to take possession of his critics.

CHAPTER XVI

THE NOVELIST AS NOVELIST: ANTHONY TROLLOPE

Have you ever read the novels of Anthony Trollope? They precisely suit my taste; solid, substantial, written on strength of beef and through the inspiration of ale, and just as real as if some giant had hewn a great lump out of the earth and put it under a glass case, with all its inhabitants going about their daily business, and not suspecting that they were made a show of.

NATHANIEL HAWTHORNE

1. *Trollope's Place in Fiction*

Anthony Trollope was not, as he has sometimes been considered, a disciple of Thackeray's. He did not "follow" Thackeray as Reade and Collins followed Dickens. Like Thackeray he was a realist; like him he opposed the exuberant sensationalism of the Dickens school. But he was not a minor Thackeray; he was a major novelist in his own right.

If it be the purpose of fiction to show the very age and body of the time his form and pressure, then Trollope achieves the purpose of fiction better than Dickens, better than George Eliot, better than Thackeray himself. He is the Great Victorian Mirror. He is not quite the Perfect Victorian, for while he honored all the surface conventions governing Victorian fiction, he managed at the same time to make it clear to all discerning readers that there was not much about men and women that he did not know. Probably he is not so great as Thackeray or Dickens. He adds less of that "something more" which is the peculiar tap of the greatest writers; the light and color of his own personality is not so dazzling that it stands between us and his world. But he was a writer of remarkable gifts, and it is good to see him, after a period of neglect, coming back into his own again.

If he is not the Perfect Victorian, there is a sense in which he does deserve to be called the Perfect Novelist. That is to say, he is not the Novelist-Sociologist, nor the Novelist-Reformer, nor the Poet-Novelist; he is not the Novelist as Intellectual nor as Metaphysician. He is simply the Novelist. He tells stories. He is not ashamed of telling stories. He never forgets that they are stories; indeed he reminds us of it again and again. It was his aim to create life-like characters in believable situations, and to make their often commonplace fate a matter of absorbing interest to his readers. It did not seem to him that you make the Novel more important by turning it into something that is not a novel.

Trollope's books were very popular during his lifetime; after his death they soon fell into desuetude, in England especially. This was partly because the enormous, unsorted bulk of his output placed a heavy burden upon those who attempted to read him; it was partly because both his themes and his temper were uncongenial to the febrile, decadent estheticism of the Beardsley period; it was partly because in his *Autobiography,* published after his death in 1883, Trollope did himself a great injustice.

Trollope forgot that there are tricks in all trades, and that there are some secrets a tradesman had just as well not reveal. He told how, when starting work on a new novel, he would begin a diary divided into weeks, allotting to each week the number of pages it would be necessary to write in order to have the novel finished by the date set. He always contracted with his publishers in terms of words; he prided himself on having his work ready on time, and never falling short of the stipulated number. After retiring from the postal service, he rose every morning at five-thirty, and wrote continuously for three hours with his watch before him, turning out 250 words every fifteen minutes. Having completed one book he would promptly start another; he could write anywhere, under any conditions—at home, at his club, in a railway carriage, or on the ocean. Instead of admiring such artistic mastery as they ought to have done—they sadly needed the example—the esthetes threw up their pretty hands, and exclaimed that no work done in this mechanical fashion could possibly have any value.

2. *Biographical and Statistical*

Trollope was born in London, April 24, 1815. He had a strange and unhappy youth, a worthy but eccentric father, only desultory schooling, and not too much money. The awkwardness and confusion of his early years he described directly in his *Autobiography,* indirectly in such novels as *The Three Clerks,* and in his self-portrait as Johnny Eames in *The Small House at Allington* and *The Last Chronicle of Barset*—"a hobbledehoy,—a calf, as it were, who had carried his calfishness later into life than is common with calves; but who did not, perhaps, on that account give promise of making a worse ox than the rest of them."

His mother was Frances Milton Trollope, a woman who lived obscurely for the first fifty years of her life, and who then, in 1832, found herself suddenly famous—or notorious—as the result of her book on the *Domestic Manners of the Americans,* written after a visit to the United States. Mrs. Trollope's was a very sarcastic pen, and no book ever published about America has made its inhabitants more angry than that book did. Having discovered that she could write, Mrs. Trollope continued writing for many years, thus supporting her family after her husband had finally demonstrated his inability to do so.[1]

At nineteen, Trollope became a clerk in the Post Office. He remained in the service until 1867, and was an extremely able official: the pillar post-box was one of his inventions. In 1841 he was sent to Ireland, where he remained, except for a two years interval, until 1859. Because of this circumstance his first two novels deal with Irish themes.

Neither *The Macdermots of Ballycloran* nor *The Kellys and the O'Kellys* attracted the public, but some of Trollope's modern readers

[1] For Mrs. Trollope (1780-1863), cf. "Anthony's Mother," the first section of Sadleir's *Anthony Trollope, A Commentary.* From 1836 to 1856 she published at least a novel a year, some of them (though she was by no means a thinker) novels of ideas. Among her best-known titles are *Jonathan Jefferson Whitlaw* (1836), an anti-slavery novel; *Michael Armstrong* (1840), an attack on child labor; *Jessie Phillips* (1843), which opposed the Poor Law; and the three novels about the Widow Barnaby. Anthony's older brother, Thomas Adolphus Trollope (1810-1892) was likewise a novelist.

—Hugh Walpole and Arnold Bennett among them—can find no praise too high for them. *The Macdermots* takes its point of departure from the ruins of an abandoned country-house, and works out, through stark tragedy, the picture of a decaying social order. This was not the kind of Irish fiction people wanted to read in the 'forties; so Trollope turned next to an equally ill-fated venture, *La Vendée,* a novel of the French Revolution from the Royalist point of view.

After *La Vendée* had failed also, Trollope did not bring out another novel for five years. But when *The Warden* appeared in 1855 it was clear that he had found his métier. With this book he began the Barsetshire series, descriptive of life in and about a cathedral city, which still constitutes his principal claim to fame.

The range and extent of Trollope's fiction can best be grasped by glancing at Michael Sadleir's classification:[2]

I. THE CHRONICLES OF BARSETSHIRE. *†*The Warden* (1855); *†*Barchester Towers* (1857); *†*Doctor Thorne* (1858); *†*Framley Parsonage* (1861); *†*The Small House at Allington* (1864); *†*The Last Chronicle of Barset* (1867).

II. THE POLITICAL NOVELS. **Can You Forgive Her?* (1864); *†*Phineas Finn: The Irish Member* (1869); **The Eustace Diamonds* (1873); **Phineas Redux* (1874); **The Prime Minister* (1876); **The Duke's Children* (1880).

III. NOVELS OF MANNERS, CONVENTION, AND SOCIAL DILEMMA. **The Three Clerks* (1858); **Orley Farm* (1862); **The Belton Estate* (1866); **The Claverings* (1867); **The Vicar of Bullhampton* (1870); **Ralph the Heir* (1871); **Sir Harry Hotspur of Humblethwaite* (1871); **Lady Anna* (1873); **The American Senator* (1877); *Is He Popenjoy?* (1878); **Ayala's Angel* (1881); *Marion Fay* (1882).

IV. SOCIAL SATIRES. *The Bertrams* (1859); **Rachel Ray* (1863); **Miss Mackenzie* (1865); *The Struggles of Brown, Jones, and*

[2] *Anthony Trollope, A Commentary,* pp. 415-419. I have placed an asterisk before the titles available in "The World's Classics" series, published by the Oxford University Press, and a dagger before those republished in "Everyman's Library." *The Kellys and the O'Kellys* and *The American Senator* have also been reprinted by Random House for the Trollope Society. The unmarked titles are still (1942) out of print, but the Oxford Press seems to be proceeding toward a complete Trollope. The classification of novels is reprinted with the kind permission of Houghton Mifflin Co.

Robinson (1862); **The Way We Live Now* (1875); *Mr. Scarborough's Family* (1883).

V. Irish Novels. *The Macdermots of Ballycloran* (1847); **The Kellys and the O'Kellys* (1848); *Castle Richmond* (1860); *The Landleaguers* (1883).

VI. Australian Novels. *Harry Heathcote of Gangoil* (1874); *John Caldigate* (1879).

VII. Historical and Romantic Novels. *La Vendée* (1850); *Nina Balatka* (1867); *Linda Tressel* (1868); †*The Golden Lion of Grandpère* (1872).

VIII. Psychological Analyses and Stories of Single Incident. *He Knew He Was Right* (1869); *An Eye for an Eye* (1879); **Cousin Henry* (1879); **Dr. Wortle's School* (1881); *Kept in the Dark* (1882); **An Old Man's Love* (1883).

IX. Fantasia. *The Fixed Period* (1882).

X. Short Stories. **Tales of All Countries* (1861, 1863); *Lotta Schmidt and Other Stories* (1867); *An Editor's Tales* (1870); *Why Frau Frohmann Raised Her Prices, and Other Stories* (1882).

In 1857 Trollope's travels began in the interest of the postal service. After his retirement in 1867 he traveled for pleasure. In the course of time he visited Egypt, the West Indies, South Africa, New Zealand, and the United States. He died December 6, 1882.

3. *Theory and Practice*

Trollope's theory of fiction was very simple. For "the amusement of the young people of both sexes," he designed "a picture of common life enlivened by humor and sweetened by pathos." This "picture" must be presented in terms of a story, and stories do not tell themselves. "If the reader will allow me," he says, "I will go back a little and explain this."

He is quite capable of setting forth a situation objectively, but he does not often choose to do so. When he essays sophisticated experiments—writes *in medias res,* or attempts a chapter in the epistolary style—he is clowning. "Were I possessed of a quick spasmodic style of narrative [like Charles Reade's, he might have added], I should have been able to include it all . . . in five words and half a dozen dashes and inverted commas." He likes to drive with a light rein, breaking into his scenes whenever he chooses to do so, giving us all the ins and outs of the situation from his own omniscient knowledge.

He does this partly, no doubt, because he hates mystery. He had no respect for the literary art which destroys itself in the process of its development. "Let the personages of the drama undergo ever so complete a comedy of errors among themselves, but let the spectator never mistake the Syracusan for the Ephesian. Otherwise he is one of the dupes, and the part of a dupe is never dignified."

In applying this principle Trollope is nearly fanatical. When Nina Balatka resolves to break with her Jewish lover, the author at once tells us that she is going to change her mind. When Eleanor Bold, of *Barchester Towers,* is persecuted by two unworthy suitors, he bids us "be under no misapprehension whatever," for she will marry neither of them. When the Major calls on Lady Eustace to clear up the mystery of the Eustace diamonds, Trollope says, "It may be as well explained at once, at this moment: the Major knew, or thought that he knew, every circumstance of the two robberies, and that his surmises were, in every respect, right." And when Phineas Finn is suspected of the murder of Mr. Bonteen we are soon reassured: "The reader need hardly be told that . . . Phineas Finn was as white as snow. The maintenance of any doubt on that matter . . . would be altogether beyond the power of the present writer."

In his *Autobiography,* Trollope tells us that *Orley Farm* suffered through the premature unravelment of the plot in the revelation of Lady Mason's guilt. But he handled the problem more artistically here than he generally does. We are sure of Lady Mason's guilt at a comparatively early stage, but at no point does Trollope actually poke his head through the curtains to tell us that she is guilty. And even when the revelation is made, it comes indirectly: the reader simply overhears Lady Mason's confession to Sir Peregrine.[3]

Even without mystery, Trollope is capable of big "scenes." "A good novel," he says, "should be both realistic and sensational, and

[3] There is some mystery, however, in *The Vicar of Bullhampton* and *The Last Chronicle of Barset.* In *Studies in Philology,* XXXVI (1939), 651-663, H. J. W. Milley writes plausibly and entertainingly on the thesis that the disappearance of the jewels and its sequelae in *The Eustace Diamonds,* that mystery novel without a mystery, were designed to burlesque *The Moonstone*

both in the highest degree." His own novels are not sensational "in the highest degree," but he has his moments.

Barchester Towers comes first to mind. *Barchester Towers* is to Trollope, I think, what *Pride and Prejudice* is to Jane Austen; it is probably not his greatest book, but none other presents so many brilliant confrontations and clashes. In the Parliamentary novels there are thrilling moments also: when Robert Kennedy tries to kill Phineas Finn; when Mr. Wharton returns upon the Lopez dinner party; when Lopez himself enters, just as Emily is extricating herself from Arthur Fletcher's arms.

Generally the shock in these scenes is psychological: Trollope did not often deal with the clash of physical conflict in the open air. But he is an old hand at atmosphere, and it is not always the spirit of the drawing-room that he evokes. The rustic episodes in *The Way We Live Now* are prescient of Hardy, the lower and middle class comedy in *Orley Farm,* of H. G. Wells. And when he went to Prague, to Nuremberg, and to Lorraine—as he did in those three charming novels, *Nina Balatka, Linda Tressel,* and *The Golden Lion of Grandpère*—he was as "picturesque" as anybody could have been.

In *The Small House at Allington,* the cold, clever Lady Dumbello is just on the verge of a dangerous flirtation when she comes to her senses, and rights herself with her husband, in the flicker of an eyelash as it were, by the simple expedient of showing him her mother's letter. In such an incident we see how "subtle" Trollope might have been, had he chosen to devote himself to a more implicational style of writing. But Archdeacon Grantly's interview with Grace Crawley in *The Last Chronicle of Barset* is more direct and more characteristically Trollopian. It is true that that interview takes an unexpected line of development, but everything we know of Grantly's character is summed up in it.

Tears flow freely at Trollope's command—when Lady Lufton swallows her pride and asks Lucy Robarts to be her son's wife, when the wayward Carry Brattle returns to her family, when the inflexible but conscientious Duke of Omnium tries so hard to meet the minds of his sons. And in the somber novels he wrote at the close of his career—*The Way We Live Now* is the greatest of them—a dark cloud seems to be spreading itself over the lovely English landscape.

4. *People*

Trollope's characters were very real to him:

> There is a gallery of them, and of all I may say that I know the tone of the voice, and the color of the hair, every flame of the eye, and the very clothes they wear. Of each man I could assert whether he would have said these or the other words; of every woman, whether she would then have smiled or so have frowned.

Sometimes they actually took possession of him:

> I have wandered alone among the rocks and woods, dying at their grief, laughing at their absurdities, and thoroughly enjoying their joy. I have been impregnated with my own creations till it has been my only excitement to sit with the pen in my hand, and drive my team before me at as quick a pace as I could make them travel.

Like George Eliot, he does not care for "heroes" and "heroines." "The persons whom you cannot care for in a novel because they are so bad, are the very same that you so dearly love in your life because they are so good." Saint Paul might be a model clergyman for an epic, but he will not do for a novel. Raphael's madonnas may be more lovable than Rembrandt's matrons, but in the latter you can believe.

It is interesting, at this point, to compare him with such confirmed analysts of character as George Eliot and Henry James. In general, he does not probe into hidden motives but contents himself with an astonishingly vivid description of human behavior. Probably his most elaborate formal analysis is that of the Reverend Mr. Crawley, half-madman, half-saint, whose inability to remember where he got a small check informs the vast pervasive plot of *The Last Chronicle of Barset*.

For there are times when Trollope does come close to the analysts of motives. Of course the tendency toward intense introspection is as old as English fiction itself. Phineas Finn's scruples as to whether or not he is free to woo Violet Effingham, now that she has rejected his friend, Lord Chiltern, would be quite at home in the seventeenth-century romances; Lily Dale's motives for rejecting Johnny Eames are less simple than they seem. Adolphus Crosbie, who jilts Lily, is Trollope's Tito Melema; comparing him with George Eliot's famous character, one is reminded how Mark Twain praised Trollope's American counterpart, Howells, because he could make his characters vivid "without analyzing the guts out of them, the way Hawthorne and George Eliot do." In Isabel Boncassen, of *The Duke's Children,* Trollope has James's favorite type-character, the American girl abroad. And Sadleir and others have pointed out that he was increasingly preoccupied with psychological problems in such later novels as *He Knew He Was Right, An Eye for an Eye, Cousin Henry, Dr. Wortle's School, Kept in the Dark,* and *An Old Man's Love.*

But Trollope is more like Jane Austen than he is like either James or George Eliot. The scene in *Doctor Thorne* in which Lady Arabella tries to persuade Mary to give up Frank is much like Elizabeth Bennet's famous interview with Lady Catherine de Bourgh; and Trollope's is much the more delicate touch at this point.

As for Trollope's "method" in characterization, it is his method to permit his characters to talk and himself to talk about them. He often thrusts himself into the narrative, once at least, in *Barchester Towers,* unfairly perhaps, but with deadly effect: "I never could endure to shake hands with Mr. Slope." Probably he is merely being casual here, not striving for verisimilitude, *à la* Daniel Defoe. But verisimilitude is unquestionably the effect.

He is certainly casual in what modern criticism must surely regard as a *faux pas*—his suggestion that we glance at Millais's illustrations to *Orley Farm* if we wish to know what Lady Mason looked like! Let no one suppose that he lacked confidence in his own ability to describe her! But he admired Millais's illustrations immensely; why in the world should he not refer to them if he wanted to? What was a novel, anyway, except a long conversation between the author and his readers?

He has other infelicities. At the beginning of *The Duke's Children* we are very likely to get the idea that Frank Tregear is going to be a much less worthy young man than he turns out to be. Of Frank Greystock we are told that he is a dual character, one of those men on whom "Satan obtains an intermittent grasp, from which, when it is released, the rebound carries them high amid virtuous resolutions and a thorough love of things good and noble." But the process is not traced, and probably few readers of *The Eustace Diamonds* ever think of connecting such a struggle with this character.

Sadleir accuses Trollope of inconsistency in Archbishop Grantly's portrait when he shows him furtively enjoying his Rabelais. I agree. Grantly is surely sophisticated enough and sensible enough to read Rabelais openly if he wishes to do so. I think too that our introduction to Grantly is infelicitous; it seems at the outset as if he were to be a henpecked husband. There is even some wavering in Mr. Harding's portrait. When we first meet him he is a weak, not too intelligent, clergyman, saved by his freedom from rancor and his ability to see the enemy's point of view, but before we are done with him he is nearly a saint.

Trollope departs from realism in the descriptive Dickensian names he gives many of his minor characters. Henry James remarks that when we read that Mr. Quiverful is the father of fourteen children we can accept either the name or the fact but we cannot accept both.

There are times, too, when Trollope offends by assuming too complete a control over his characters. Had Eleanor Bold given way and sobbed during her interview with Mr. Arabin, everything would have been explained. "But then," he asks, "where would have been my story?" He killed his most famous character, Mrs. Proudie, after he overheard two men abusing her—and him—at a club. He introduced himself to them, and promised to go home and kill Mrs. Proudie before the week was over. One wonders whether any other woman of comparable vitality was ever so frivolously slaughtered for a whim.

Trollope's young heroines have all the purity Victorian readers demanded, but they have too a reality which Victorian readers did not always get. They are not necessarily beautiful, but they are simple, passionate, earnest, and "proud-hearted." Lady Stavely would not have Madeline emulate Florence Nightingale. She thought it a young woman's duty to marry. "For myself," adds Trollope, "I am inclined to agree with her."

He has girls like Julia Brabazon and Laura Standish, who sacrifice love for money—and live to regret it. After Lord Ongar's death, Julia comes back to fight for Harry Clavering, tries every means in her power to get him away from Florence Burton. But she is a good loser; there is no malice and bitterness about her at the end. Laura, on the other hand, never finds a happy landing; there is something distasteful about this love-tortured woman, avowing frankly to all and sundry her passion for a man who is unable to revive his early affection for her.

Lady Glencora (later the Duchess of Omnium) is more interesting than either of these women. In her youth she had an unfortunate love affair. She recovered. She made a success of her marriage with Planty Pal. But she still carries her scars. Lady Glencora is ambitious; when her husband becomes prime minister she wants to be mistress of the robes. He refuses her, and she embarks upon an elaborate social program, partly to help him, but partly also because she enjoys power. Her judgment of men is bad; she is capable of hot resentment and blazing anger. Like her husband, she is one of Trollope's most complex creations. And there can be no question that she is alive.

Of Trollope's unworthy women the most elaborately studied is Lizzie Eustace. She is his Becky Sharp; in fact, he himself calls her "that opulent and aristocratic Becky Sharp." He is no sentimentalist toward her: neither is he ever a sadist.

> She knew what were the aspirations, what the ambition of an honest woman; and she knew, too, how rich were the probable rewards of such honesty. True love, true friendship, true benevolence, true tenderness, were beautiful to her, qualities on which she could descant almost with eloquence; and therefore she was always shamming love and friendship and benevolence and tenderness.

A contemptible little schemer in a lower social class is Amelia Roper, who tries to win Johnny Eames in the hilarious boarding-house sequence of *The Last Chronicle of Barset.* But Amelia is a pathetic little thing in her way, and all her scheming does not get her much; Trollope gladly lets her have her moment of sincerity.

Marie Melmotte, of *The Way We Live Now,* stands midway between Amelia and Lady Eustace. Compared to girls like Mary Thorne or Lily Dale, she is vulgar; in her position, no one could wholly have escaped contamination. But her loyalty and courage redeem her, and when she goes out of the book one wishes her something much better than she is likely to find.

Both Mrs. Peacocke, of *Dr. Wortle's School,* and Mrs. Askerton, of *The Belton Estate,* have lived beyond the bounds of conventional morality; Trollope's treatment of them is both generous and courageous for his day. George Hotspur's mistress, Lucy Morton, is so much better than the man she lives with that all our sympathies are with her. Mrs. Hurtle, of *The Way We Live Now,* has had a lurid career; she is a woman of violent passions, but her fundamental humanity is never obscured. In Carry Brattle, of *The Vicar of Bullhampton,* Trollope dared make a "fallen" woman one of his leading characters and to treat her with tender Christian sympathy but quite without sentimentality.

Trollope's worst woman is the horrible Sophie Gourdeloup, the Russian spy of *The Claverings.* I am indebted to Michael Sadleir for the idea that she may have been suggested by the French governess in Le Fanu's *Uncle Silas.* In any event, she is a shameless virago, venomous to her fingertips. Sophie might easily have passed over into caricature, but she never does. Her unscrupulous energy actually frightens the reader.

I would not for a moment insult Madame Goesler (afterwards Mrs. Finn) by suggesting that she is a bad woman. She is a very good woman from any point of view. Yet without her conscience and her great magnanimity she must surely have become an adventuress. She has the spunk for it, and certainly she has the resourcefulness.

Trollope's eccentrics are generally, though not always, older women. His dowagers range all the way from the heartless and bad-mannered Lady Aylmer, of *The Belton Estate,* to the gracious Lady Lufton, of *Framley Parsonage.* I am less enthusiastic than many about the Signora Neroni and her playmates in *Barchester Towers,* though they are much better than Clara Van Siever and her associates, whose story is the only bad part of that great novel,

The Last Chronicle of Barset. Clara herself will perhaps pass. But both her history and Signora Neroni's seem to me bathed in an air of Ouida-like fantasy which is not quite at home in the Trollope world. On the other hand, such an eccentric as Miss Thorne, with her fête champêtre at which knightly customs are to be revived, is emphatically at home in that world; and Lady Julia De Guest is almost equally charming. Charming would be the last word one could apply to Trollope's most famous eccentric, the bishop's managing wife, Mrs. Proudie. But what reader of English fiction can fail to be grateful to her for the pleasure she has given?

5. *Fundamentals*

Trollope's attitude toward life has sometimes been condemned as smug. His temperament was, no doubt, conservative. In *The Warden,* Mary Bold begs her brother not to make war on the hospital. He refuses to yield, and succeeds in putting an end to the situation he abhors, but though Mr. Harding loses the income, the old almsmen in whose behalf the fight was undertaken are not benefited. Indeed there is a touch at the close strongly suggestive of Galsworthy—"from the moment of Mr. Harding's departure, the twopence a-day, his own peculiar gift, must of necessity be withdrawn."

The Bishop's optimism in *The Way We Live Now* seems very easy-going. And Trollope's own attitude toward material things was not quite that of Saint Francis of Assisi or of Jesus himself.

> All material progress has come from man's desire to do the best he can for himself and those about him, and civilization and Christianity itself have been made possible by such progress.

The matter is important in connection with Trollope's fiction partly because of the large role which the Church plays in the Barsetshire Novels. Paul Elmer More had no difficulty in demolishing the common view that there is no religion in Trollope's fiction. More cites the account of Arabin's struggle in *Barchester Towers,* and in *The Bertrams* the description of George's dedication of his life to holiness while sitting on the hill above Jerusalem, "in its kind a veritable masterpiece of art and of delicate suggestion. It could have been conceived only by a writer who was himself deeply religious." We know that Trollope had his own definite religious convictions; when the *Fortnightly* was founded he made his connection with it dependent upon its agreeing to print no article that should deny the Divinity of Christ.

In general, however, it is the social, rather than the religious, lives of his clergymen with which Trollope is concerned. When Dr. Proudie is installed as bishop, Trollope says, "I will not describe the ceremony, as I do not precisely understand it." If there is any disrespect here, it is disrespect for fiction, not for religion. "It would not be becoming were I to travestie a sermon, or even to repeat the language of it in the pages of a novel."

As a novelist, Trollope had the same attitude toward religion as toward morality. He did not moralize very much, but he could not have held up his head if he had not been sure that "no girl has risen from the reading of my pages less modest than she was before," and that "no youth has been taught that in falseness and flashiness is to be found the road to manliness."

He was a Christian Stoic; as strongly as any writer who ever lived, he held the conviction which goes back in English literature at least as far as *Beowulf,* and which remains prominent in Anglo-Saxon moralizing today: a man must stand up to life; whatever comes to him, he must never "howl." Lily Dale proves that this philosophy can be made to apply to women also. There is no cant in what she tells Crosbie when releasing him from their engagement: "Nothing on earth can I ever love as I have loved you. But I have a God and a Savior that will be enough for me."

In the Parliamentary novels, which were the solace of Grover Cleveland's declining years, Trollope's fundamental conception of the character of fiction remained unchanged. M. E. Speare objects that the reader "never gains the intellectual stimulus which a novel with a political thesis is likely to give because . . . [Trollope] never is interested in novelizing a 'point of view,' a platform, a philosophy of conduct." But, as James Branch Cabell would say, Speare is declining to participate in a game of billiards on the ground that he is fond of herring. It is true that no fundamental questions are involved in Trollope's political novels. "Who desires among us to put down the Queen, or to repudiate the national debt, or to destroy religious worship, or even to disturb the ranks of society?" Even so, Phineas Finn and the Duke of Omnium are well worth knowing. Omnium is over-conscientious, painfully honorable, self-contained, thin-skinned, and ungenial. "He is fretful and makes enemies." He is so painfully anxious not to do the wrong thing that there are times when, through his very eagerness, he does it. But he is a noble soul, and he awakens a respect that is close to love.

Trollope himself was no obscurantist in either politics or religion.

> She hated Radicals [he is speaking of Miss Aylmer, in *The Belton Estate*], and thought that *Essays and Reviews,* and Bishop Colenso, came direct from the Evil One. She taught the little children in the parish, being specially urgent to them always to curtsey when they saw any of the family:—and was as ignorant, meek, and stupid a poor woman as you shall find anywhere in Europe.

There is more real democracy in some of Omnium's meditations than in those of a good many "advanced thinkers" today. And there are flashes in Trollope's own pronouncements on social and political questions which it would be hard to match in any English novelist before Meredith. When during the Civil War, the United States took to conscription, Trollope wrote thus to his American friend, Kate Field:

> This conscription is very bad. Was it absolutely necessary? My feeling is that a man should die rather than be made a soldier against his will. One's country has no right to demand everything. There is much that is higher and better and greater than one's country. One is patriotic only because one is too small and too weak to be cosmopolitan. If a country cannot get along without a military conscription, it had better give up—and let its children seek other ties.

But Trollope's idealism and the fundamental nobility of his spirit comes out most clearly in his treatment of love. This does not mean that in his novels love is febrile and bloodless. Hugh Walpole complains that "His heroine in love with a rogue must appear again and again an addlepated fool, because the real physical fascination that love has for her must be almost completely unanalysed." Unanalyzed it may be, but it is there.

His characteristic note is the almost religious devotion his heroines bring to the object of their passion. Lily Dale is the classical example, but Emily Hotspur, Mary Flood Jones, Nina Balatka, and many others share her spirit.

Trollope seems to have felt that a woman's gift of her heart must in the first instance be entirely voluntary; none of his heroines are swept away by uncontrollable passion. Probably it seemed to him that such passion would stain a girl's purity. Sometimes his treatment of this matter seems formalized and artificial. Of Violet Effingham he says:

> She was so constituted that she had never allowed him or any other man to be master of her heart,—till she had with a full purpose given her heart away. The day before she had resolved to give it to one man, she might, I think, have resolved to give it to another.

But once the gift was made, it was irrevocable. "My love was a thing to give," says Emily Hotspur, "but when given I cannot take it back." Mary Thorne takes up the same position. She admits the force of some of Lady Arabella's arguments against her proposed union with Frank Gresham. "But she had no power of going back; her troth was plighted, and nothing that any human being could say should shake her from it." All in all, Trollope must have devoted thousands of pages to describing the sufferings of fine young women who loved unworthy men and were unable to separate themselves from their love.

Emily Hotspur's is the most tragic fate among all these girls of Trollope's, but compared to Lily Dale, Emily herself is a shadowy figure. Like the heroines of the saint's legends, she is described in terms of a single quality; she is faithful unto death, and that is all we have of her. Lily, whether we "agree" with her or not (Trollope himself called her a "French prig") is alive in many more aspects.[4]

[4] But I must not leave the impression that none of Trollope's heroines ever succeed in overcoming their native quixotism in love. Linda Tressel voluntarily relinquishes her lover after an abortive elopement has revealed his worthlessness; Clara Amedroz somewhat shamefacedly accepts Will Belton after Captain Aylmer has shown himself no fit mate for her; Emily Wharton comes to her true love, Arthur Fletcher, after far more harrowing experiences.

6. The Value of Trollope's Limitations

Trollope did not love his characters too well; that is impossible for a novelist. One feels, however, that his books might have gained in variety if he had loved plot a little more. After one has beaten down parental opposition with his young lovers some fifteen or twenty times, one is ready to change the subject. But about all one gets, by way of variety, is the picture of a young man who engages himself to one girl and forthwith proceeds to consume three volumes while he makes up his mind either that he does or that he does not love another one better.

The only thing that redeems this latter situation in Trollope is his fundamental honesty in treating it. "A man, you say, delicate reader, a true man can love but one woman,—but one at a time. So you say, and are so convinced, but no conviction was ever more false." He goes on, however. "But it is not to be thought that I excuse him altogether. A man, though he love many, should be devoted only to one." This is an excellent illustration of Trollope's entire decency, combined with his entire freedom from the kind of hypocrisy which, to flatter ourselves, we like to label Victorian.

Another shortcoming of Trollope's—contemporary taste in fiction being what it is—is his deliberate lack of subtlety. To be sure, Sir Leslie Stephen defends him ingeniously by urging that the most naïve way of telling a story is really, in the last analysis, the most sophisticated:

> . . . the attempt to produce . . . illusions is really unworthy of work intended for full-grown readers. The humorist in particular knows that you will not mistake his puppet-show for reality, nor does he wish you to do so. He is rather of opinion that the world itself is a greater puppet-show, not to be taken in too desperate earnest.

But this defense applies with greater force to Thackeray than to Trollope.

Often Trollope gives the impression either that he does not trust his own ability to make his characters clear to the reader through action and dialogue, or else that he does not give the reader credit for sufficient intelligence to understand what he reads. "It was a disagreeable, nasty letter from the first line to the last." "Mr. Furnival was very wrong to swear; doubly wrong to swear before his wife; trebly wrong to swear before a lady visitor; but it must be confessed that there was provocation." There are hundreds of such passages in Trollope. They make his novels a welcome relief from those of our own day which are designed along the lines of a Chinese puzzle, but it may well have been a superabundance of this kind of thing in the novels of the past that encouraged the growth of the Chinese puzzle school.

On the whole, however, for readers of today, Trollope's limitations would seem to be quite as valuable as his special powers. He was pedestrian; he was comfortably mid-Victorian. He was blind to some of our great social problems; others, through the accident of time, he was lucky enough never to encounter. But there are times when we are thankful to be able to turn to a writer who helps us to forget these problems, and who reminds us that the only ceaselessly interesting thing in the world is human nature.

No doubt this was what Paul Elmer More had in mind when he declared that with the possible exception of Boswell's *Life of Johnson,* Trollope's novels had been more often in his hands than any other English books.

> I have not gone to them, naturally, for that which the great poets and philosophers and divines can give. But they have been like an unfailing voice of encouragement in times of joy and prosperity; they have afforded solace in hours of sickness and despondency and adversity; they have lightened the tedium of idleness and supplied refreshment after the fatigue of labor.

A writer who can do these things has no mean claim on our gratitude.

CHAPTER XVII

FIRE OVER YORKSHIRE

But O, the thorns we stand upon!

The Winter's Tale

1. *How It All Began*

Analogically at least, the Brontës disprove the old saying that lightning never strikes more than once in the same place. It struck twice at Haworth Parsonage. Few would deny Charlotte the name of genius, while Emily is not only one of the two or three best women poets of England but her one novel stands alone in world literature. A third sister, Anne, though certainly no genius, still manifested a very respectable talent. Some critics have believed that even the brother, Branwell, might have accomplished something if he had not succeeded in drinking himself to death, but Miss Ratchford, whose study of the Brontë juvenilia has recently revolutionized criticism, can find no evidence for this.

Branwell's tragedy is not the only splash of lurid color on the Brontë palette. That lonely Yorkshire parsonage, with the graveyard on one side of it and the open splendor of the moors on the other, was a Wuthering Heights kind of place for children to grow up in. They were not English children: the Reverend Patrick Brontë had come from Ireland, his wife from Cornwall. This circumstance explains much as to the character of the Brontë imagination. The mother died of cancer at an early age. The father has been greatly over-dramatized. Mrs. Gaskell's truthfully intended stories of how he fired pistols and sawed the legs from chairs, burned shoes and cut up dresses can no longer be taken at face value. He was an eccentric, nevertheless, and he can never have been too comfortable a man to live with.

In 1824 all the girls except little Anne were sent to the Clergy

Daughters' School at Cowan Bridge. (Charlotte was eight years old, Emily six.)[1] Early in 1825 both Maria and Elizabeth were brought home to die. Charlotte blamed unsanitary conditions at the establishment for this unhappy outcome; in *Jane Eyre* she castigates the Clergy Daughters' School and its administrator, the Reverend Carus Wilson (Mr. Brocklehurst). Her experience was much happier at Roe Head, which she entered in 1831, and in which she became a teacher. Like Emily and Anne, she also spent some time as a governess, but she was much too sensitive a person to be happy in this capacity.

At an early date the Brontë children discovered in themselves a strong myth-making faculty. It found the starting-point of its expression in a box of wooden soldiers which Mr. Brontë brought home in 1826. Between 1829 and 1845 a saga of amazing complexity developed in a series of tiny, home-made books, filled with microscopic handwriting which can only be read under a glass. In time the kingdom of Angria was created in Africa, and until Charlotte's departure for Roe Head, Angria was the spiritual home of all the Brontë children. Then Emily, rebelling against Branwell's claim of leadership, withdrew, and, taking Anne with her, devoted herself to the history of Gondal, a large island in the North Pacific.

The Gondal materials no longer exist, though the history of Gondal has been reconstructed in part from Emily's poems, many of which were part of the same enterprise.[2] About a third of the Angrian saga has, on the other hand, now found its way into print.[3]

[1] Charlotte Brontë lived from April 21, 1816, to March 31, 1855. Emily Brontë lived from July 30, 1818, to December 19, 1848. Anne Brontë lived from January 17, 1820, to May 28, 1849.

[2] In addition to what is now the definitive account of these matters in *The Brontës' Web of Childhood,* by Fannie E. Ratchford, and in C. W. Hatfield's edition of *The Complete Poems of Emily Jane Brontë* (Columbia University Press, 1941), see Fannie E. Ratchford, *Two Poems by Emily Brontë, with the Gondal Background of Her Poems and Novel* (Austin, Texas: Von-Boeckmann-Jones Company, 1934) (reviewed in *Modern Philology,* XXXIII, 209-210) and three articles by Madeleine Hope Dodds, *Modern Language Review,* XVIII (1923), 9-21; XXI (1926), 373-379; XXII (1927), 197-198.

[3] See *The Twelve Adventurers and Other Stories,* ed. C. W. Hatfield and Clement K. Shorter (Hodder & Stoughton, 1925); *The Spell,* ed. G. E. Mac-

And in *The Brontës' Web of Childhood* Miss Ratchford has made an impressive study of it.

This study demonstrates the essential unity and continuity of the Brontë lives. It deals the popular view that literature is necessarily autobiography the heaviest blow it has sustained in many years. Almost all the principal themes the Brontës are supposed to have derived from personal experience are now shown to have been described by them in another form before the experiences in question took place!

In 1841 the Brontë sisters conceived the idea of opening a school of their own. Because they felt the need of Continental training, Charlotte and Emily went to Brussels in February, 1842, and were enrolled at the Pensionnat Héger. In November, the death of their aunt, Miss Branwell, who had lent them the money for this adventure, drew them back home; and here Emily stayed. But Charlotte returned to Brussels in January for another term as pupil-teacher.

The Brontë school never materialized. And to Emily the Brussels sojourn apparently contributed nothing. But Charlotte manifested an uncanny ability to choose the experiences she needed to reinforce what she had already imagined. Brussels gave her a realistic setting for her Angrian materials.

In 1845, Charlotte discovered that Emily had been writing poetry. So had she. So had Anne. Emily is said to have been furious at first over this violation of her privacy, but she was finally brought to consent to the publication, next year, of *Poems,* by Currer, Ellis, and Acton Bell. Two copies were sold.

From poetry the sisters turned to the novel. Charlotte (Currer) wrote *The Professor,* Emily (Ellis) *Wuthering Heights,* Anne (Acton) *Agnes Grey*. Emily and Anne found a publisher at the end of 1847. Charlotte had preceded them by two months, not with *The Professor,* which never did see print during her lifetime, but with *Jane Eyre*.

Lean (Oxford University Press, 1931); *Legends of Angria,* ed. F. E. Ratchford and W. C. De Vane (Yale University Press, 1933); and the two volumes of *Miscellaneous and Unpublished Writings* in the Shakespeare Head Brontë.

2. *Charlotte Brontë Relives Angria*

We turn in disgust from those contemporary critics who found in *Jane Eyre* a picture of "courtship after the manner of kangaroos" and "a murmuring against the comforts of the rich and against the privations of the poor, which, so far as each individual is concerned, is a murmuring against God's appointment." Yet the accusation of coarseness is justified in part by the passage in which Rochester tells Jane of his disgraceful life with his mistresses; artistically speaking, this communication is both indefensible and inconceivable. The Brontë children were apparently quite unsupervised in their reading; there is much brutality and sexual delinquency in the Angrian stories. These tales, incidentally, are sometimes far ahead of the later work in their pictures of "society." The "society" part of *Jane Eyre* is as inept as the same element in *Nicholas Nickleby*.

And, like all Charlotte's books, *Jane Eyre* has no structure. Jane is abused by her aunt, Mrs. Reed, and neglected at Lowood School; she becomes a governess at Thornfield; the Byronic Mr. Rochester falls in love with her; their marriage-ceremony is interrupted at the altar by the revelation that he has a wife living; refusing to become his mistress, Jane runs away and nearly starves; she is saved by strangers who turn out to be her cousins, and in time learns that she has inherited a fortune; feeling that she has lost Rochester forever, she very nearly goes to India as a missionary; telepathy draws her back to a burned Thornfield and a free, blind Rochester. The last chapter begins, "Reader, I married him." [4]

[4] For the telepathy, cf. "Albion and Marina," in *The Twelve Adventurers*. A famous incident in Defoe's *Moll Flanders* has often been suggested as a possible source here. Charlotte Brontë herself had some psychic sensitiveness; how far it went beyond the creative artist's conviction of the reality of his characters and passionate absorption in them, it is difficult to say. She is now known to have written one of the most mystical passages formerly attributed to Emily, the last two stanzas of the poem called "The Visionary." Charlotte believed in Jane's telepathic experience. "It is a true thing," she told Mrs. Gaskell; "it really happened." One of Le Fanu's stories, "A Chapter in the History of the Tyrone Family" (1839), which has been reprinted in *Victorian Ghost Stories*, ed. Montague Summers (Simpkin Marshall, 1936) has some points of resemblance to *Jane Eyre;* cf. *Cambridge History of English Literature,* XIII, 407, 414-416; also Edna Kenton, in *Bookman* [N.Y.] LXIX (1929), 528-534.

The extravagance of the book is another matter. Probably neither Mr. Theodore Dreiser nor Mr. Sinclair Lewis could convince us that it would be possible for Rochester to keep a mad wife concealed in deep, impenetrable secrecy at Thornfield, but since neither Mr. Dreiser nor Mr. Lewis wrote *Jane Eyre,* that is not important. The whole story is keyed so high that its improbabilities never disturb the absorbed reader. ("I am an exaggerated person," said Marie Bashkirtseff; "it is like a piano a half-tone higher, it is exact, but it is exaggerated.") If art is the right kind of exaggeration, if a book achieves greatness only when it ceases to matter that it is bad, then *Jane Eyre* has a clear title. It has poetry too, along with its tension, as in the strange scene in which Rochester first rides into Jane's life. And Charlotte Brontë's instinct was unerring when she cast it into the form of an autobiography. It is immaterial whether or not things *were* like this; this is the way Jane saw them.

In her first novel, *The Professor* (which was not published until 1857), possibly by way of reaction against the extravagant romanticism of the Angrian stories, which she may by now have come to think of as childish, Charlotte Brontë had held her native impulses in check. She had not been able to sell the result; it may also be, as May Sinclair has suggested, that reading *Wuthering Heights* had convinced her that the Brontës were never meant to be literalists. On this hypothesis, *Jane Eyre* represents her return to romanticism, her discovery of a new, adult romanticism, which was as satisfying to the woman as the Angrian legends had been to the child.

In *Jane Eyre* Charlotte Brontë used Angrian materials freely. Rochester is clearly a rationalization of Zamorna, the Byronic hero of Angrian history. When Jane is tempted to go to the continent with Rochester as his mistress, Charlotte is simply harking back to Sir William Percy's proposal to Elizabeth Hastings, the earliest heroine she identified with herself. The original of Rochester's mad wife (whose maiden name was Bertha Mason) is Lady Zenobia Ellrington, who first appears in a story written in 1830, when Charlotte was fourteen; but she is crossed with the hag, Bertha, in "The Green Dwarf" (1833), who is, in turn, Ulrica of Scott's *Ivanhoe*. Says Miss Ratchford:

Ulrica, howling her song of revenge from a tower of the blazing castle, was a picture that long remained in Charlotte's mind, to reappear in her own novel as Bertha Mason Rochester on the blazing roof of Thornfield.

Whatever the specific faults of *Jane Eyre* may be, its method was, for Charlotte Brontë, the right method. This is exactly what one does not feel about the more objective *Shirley* (1849), and when Franklin Gary argued a few years ago [5] that Charlotte Brontë wrote it because she was attempting to meet George Henry Lewes's criticism of the earlier book, his arguments seemed on the whole convincing. The conflict between operatives and mill-owners over the introduction of machinery in Yorkshire between 1807 and 1812 plays an important part in the book; and one chapter follows the Leeds *Mercury* account of the attack on William Cartwright's mill.

One may still feel that labor struggles were not Charlotte Brontë's forte. One must certainly feel, after considering her satirical portraits of the curates, that she ought to have envied Jane Austen instead of despising her. But whatever Lewes's influence may have been, one can no longer overlook the fact that the social and economic disturbances of *Shirley* have roots which run as deep into Angria as anything Charlotte ever did. Moreover she had used the curates themselves as far back as 1835.

Nor was Shirley herself originally conceived as Emily Brontë, as most commentators have assumed. She was Jane Moore, "the beautiful Angrian," "the Rose of Zamorna." Her lover, Louis Moore, seems, as the book now stands, to have been introduced rather hastily, as if to provide a fit mate for her after it becomes clear that not she but her friend, Caroline Helstone, is to have his brother Robert. But Louis is a Percy of Angria, who had already appeared in another aspect as one of the Crimsworths of *The Professor*. "Between the Percy brothers and Jane Moore of Angria there existed the same complicated relations as between the Moore brothers and Shirley" (Miss Ratchford).

It should be noted that it was while she was working on *Shirley* that Charlotte Brontë suffered the greatest sorrows of her life. Bran-

[5] Cf. his "Charlotte Brontë and George Henry Lewes," *PMLA*, LI (1936), 518-542.

well's slow, deliberate suicide was consummated in September, 1848. Emily followed him to the churchyard before the year had closed. And in the spring of 1849, Anne too passed on, as gently as she had lived.

Charlotte's contacts had now broadened considerably. She was one of the most famous writers of her time. She had even been to London, where she was lionized as much as her shy temperament and censorious outlook would permit. She made new friends, but there were none to take the place of those who had gone. As a matter of fact, she herself had but one more book left to write.

It was *Villette* (1853), and it is her masterpiece. Here she reworks in the plenitude of her powers the Brussels experience which she had fumbled somewhat in *The Professor*.

Villette is the story of an English girl who teaches in Brussels; and its proudest achievement is its portrait of that bad-tempered saint, the teacher, M. Paul Emanuel, one of the most successful male characters ever drawn by a woman. Ever since 1913, when the four pitiful letters which Charlotte wrote her French teacher and employer, M. Constantin Héger, after her return to Haworth, were published in a London newspaper, it has been generally assumed that Paul Emanuel is M. Héger, and that with M. Héger Charlotte herself was desperately and hopelessly in love.

Today all this seems very doubtful. For *Villette* is "the most Angrian" of Charlotte Brontë's books. Dr. John Bretton is only superficially her publisher, George Smith; fundamentally he is again Zamorna. Paulina is Zamorna's two wives, Marian Hume and Mary Percy, with Marian Fairburne as a link between them. And Paul Emanuel himself is now seen clearly as Warner Howard Warner, home secretary of Angria, plus "the odd blending of Sir William Percy with Charles Townsend in the last years of the Angrian cycle"; even the storm which hypothetically engulfs Paul Emanuel at the close of the novel "has a long background in Angrian literature" (Miss Ratchford).

Of course this does not prove that no personal experience went into *Villette*. I have already spoken of Charlotte's ability to find experiences which would reinforce her imaginative perceptions. We know that the wonderful church scene in which, bigoted Protestant though she is, Lucy seizes upon the wonderful office of the confessional to pour her troubles into a sympathetic ear, describes what Charlotte herself did in Brussels.[6] The impassioned picture of Vashti's acting has its obvious kinship with an account of an imaginary appearance of Mrs. Siddons in the Angrian capitol of Verdropolis, written by Charlotte Brontë during her fourteenth or fifteenth year. But it is also clear that her own reaction to a performance of Rachel's which she witnessed in Brussels has been superimposed upon the earlier account.

Theoretically there is no reason why something of this kind may not have happened with M. Héger and Paul Emanuel. Madame Beck is clearly Madame Héger; there is no question that the latter was jealous of Charlotte; the Héger family seems committed to that much. Yet even when they are read in the light of these facts, Charlotte's letters to M. Héger are less conclusive than they seem. In tone they are much like the letters Charlotte had long before sent her friend, Ellen Nussey, from Roe Head, where, as now at Haworth, she was cut off from creative activity; moreover, the letters themselves use Angrian materials![7]

No more than *Jane Eyre* is *Villette* a flawless book. The old structural formlessness appears again; the early scenes in the home of Mrs. Bretton have no real connection with Lucy's life in Brussels, though Charlotte stretches the long arm of coincidence until it cracks to bring Mrs. Bretton and Dr. John and Paulina back into Lucy's life again. Many critics consider Paulina a masterpiece. To

[6] The common view has been that she confessed her love for M. Héger. Miss Ratchford believes she confessed that she had made a god of the creatures of her imagination. We know from other evidence that she tortured herself over this. There is a strikingly similar incident in *The Marble Faun,* by Nathaniel Hawthorne.

[7] Cf. F. E. Ratchford, "Some New Notes on the Brontë-Héger Letters," Bookman [London], LXXXV (1933), 180-182. M. Héger himself was an interesting and able man. Charlotte's first impression of him was not pleasant; she compared him to "an insane tom-cat" and "a delirious hyena." But in spite of his fierce temper, Héger gave himself to his pupils as the saints give themselves to God. It says much for his penetration that he should have discerned the genius of Emily, who disliked him, at this early date. Cf. Frederika Macdonald, *The Secret of Charlotte Brontë. Followed by Some Reminiscences of the Real Monsieur and Madame Héger* (Jack, 1914).

me she is about half real, and her early promise is not quite fulfilled. The ghost of the nun is in the old Radcliffe tradition; and the scene in which Polly confesses her love to her father is cheap, sentimental Victorian fiction.

But none of this bulks very large against the positive virtues of the book. The plot of *Villette* may be forgotten, but no reader will ever forget Madame Beck, as she travels silently, graciously, and with terrible efficiency through the rooms of her establishment on her missions of espionage. *Villette* gives a terrible picture of spiritual malady; it is a far more daring book than *Jane Eyre;* even today there are passages one can hardly bear to read. Quite distinctly, Charlotte Brontë here takes a long step toward the freer study of abnormalities which later novelists have permitted themselves.

On June 29, 1854, Charlotte was married to her father's curate, the Reverend A. B. Nicholls. He was a good, rather dull man whom she seems to have esteemed more than she loved. But they had not long to be together. She died, March 31, 1855.

3. *The Greatness of* Wuthering Heights

Of Emily Brontë less is known personally than of any other English writer of comparable genius. Except that the circumstance inspires ill-balanced persons to spin elaborate theories and paint fantastic portraits, it need not be greatly regretted. Emily was a mystic; her life was all within. Biographical data can add little to the understanding of such a life.

Her genius was less lyrical than Charlotte's and more dramatic. Even as a child, Miss Dodds notes acutely, she did not take sides in the Gondal wars. Books have been written in an attempt to identify the lover she commemorates in "Remembrance"; we know now that the poem is simply the imagined Rosina's lament for King Julius. From the world's point of view Emily had nothing; from her own she had everything. She was the happiest of all the Brontës, and repression never came near her. C. E. Vaughan has remarked of her that she was "a rebel so convinced that it never enters her mind to argue about the matter." In *Wuthering Heights* marriage is cavalierly disregarded—Cathy declares her intention of marrying Linton to help Heathcliff—yet sexually the book is cold as ice. The world cannot give much to people like Emily, and there is not much that the world can take away. Poverty and illness are incidents. Even in the Valley of the Shadow they fear no evil.

Wuthering Heights made its way slowly. Contemporary critics thought it the work of a "man of uncommon talents, but dogged, brutal, and morose"; as late as 1877 Wemyss Reid, who recognized its power, judged it the product of a morbid or diseased mind! Swinburne, on the other hand, compared it to *King Lear, The Duchess of Malfi,* and *The Bride of Lammermoor;* Maeterlinck was enthralled by it. Today, with C. P. Sanger [8] and Lord David Cecil, full understanding would seem at last to have been achieved.

There has been much discussion of the sources of *Wuthering Heights.* A story by the German Hoffmann has been suggested, and a story in the Brontës' beloved *Blackwood's.* The "mad Methodist magazines" that Aunt Branwell brought to the parsonage, "full of miracles and apparitions, of preternatural warnings, ominous dreams, and frenzied fanaticism," may possibly have exercised an influence; [9] and perhaps something came from a real life situation in Yorkshire. But however all this may be, it is now clear that *Wuthering Heights* was no sudden flowering in Emily's development; it was intimately inwrought with the whole Gondal saga; its roots lay deep in her own spiritual life.[10]

In the past even admirers of *Wuthering Heights* have generally been constrained to regard is as a "wild" book. The unusual way in which the story is told; the extravagant character of some of the incidents—Heathcliff sees a ghost and becomes so much interested in it that he starves himself to death—and the strange motives by which some of the characters are actuated; the way in which the

[8] *The Structure of Wuthering Heights,* by C.P.S. (Hogarth Press, 1926).

[9] *Shirley,* Ch. 22. Cf. G. Elsie Harrison's interesting books, *The Methodist Good Companions* (Epworth Press, 1935) and *Haworth Parsonage, A Study of Wesley and the Brontës* (Epworth Press, 1937).

[10] The best study of sources is Leicester Bradner, "The Growth of Wuthering Heights," *PMLA,* XLVIII (1933), 129-146. Special apologists have sometimes maintained that Branwell had an important share in *Wuthering Heights,* but this is now ruled out of court by Miss Ratchford's demonstration that *Wuthering Heights* is a Gondal novel, and with Gondal Branwell had nothing to do. Charlotte, not Emily, was his ally, and Charlotte remained loyal to him after Emily had given him up as a bad job.

first generation is killed off in the middle, leaving Heathcliff free to torture the second—surely all this is far removed from the norm of English novel-writing.

The special service of C. P. Sanger has been to prove conclusively that *Wuthering Heights* is a completely integrated work of art. Only three dates are directly stated in the book, but so accurately are time-relations held in mind that Mr. Sanger has been able to determine when every event recorded took place and to make out a dated pedigree for every important character. Topography is equally precise, and there is an amazing display of legal knowledge. Mr. Sanger points out "that during the major part of the book Mr. Lockwood is telling us what Ellen Dean told him, but sometimes, also, what Ellen Dean told him that someone else—for instance, Isabella—had told her," but he is able abundantly to justify this apparent eccentricity. If she had not begun the story in the middle, Emily Brontë could not have presented her amazing material so effectively as she did.

Lord David Cecil[11] regards *Wuthering Heights* as the greatest of all Victorian novels. He points out that Emily Brontë "sees human beings, not . . . in relation to other human beings, or to human civilizations and societies and codes of conduct, but only in relation to the cosmic scheme of which they form a part." For her, two principles are operative in the world—the principle of storm and the principle of calm. Neither is "good" and neither is "bad." Only when, in their earthly incarnations, they "are diverted from following the course that their nature dictates" do they become negative forces of weakness and destruction. "The conflict is not between right and wrong, but between like and unlike." Ultimately "the single principle" behind them both "imposes an equilibrium." Catherine is drawn to Heathcliff not because she admires him, and certainly not because she feels any tenderness toward him, "but because he's more myself than I am." And Heathcliff's nature does not find fulfillment in destruction, for it is not primarily destructive; its ultimate aim is union with Catherine. The book does not end in venge-

[11] The quotations that follow are from his *Early Victorian Novelists,* and are reprinted with the permission of Bobbs-Merrill Co.

ance, and it does not end in death—for Emily's vision blots out the line between the living and the dead—it ends in peace.

Such a book is no wild flight of fancy. "On the plane on which it is composed its every incident is the inevitable outcome of the situation. Still less is it remote from the central issues of human life." It concerns itself with "the ultimate issues which are generally looked upon as the subject matter of tragedy or epic."

4. *Anne Brontë's Novels*

Of Anne Brontë there is little to say; had she not been the sister of Charlotte and Emily, her two novels would now be forgotten. But as if to prove that no statement can be made about any of the Brontës that will go wholly unchallenged, no less a personage than George Moore rises at this juncture to call *Agnes Grey* (1847) "the most perfect prose narrative in English literature," and to declare that "if Anne Brontë had lived ten years longer, she would have taken a place beside Jane Austen."

Agnes Grey is another governess story, a Jane Eyre with all the fire left out. It has the familiar Brontë scorn of insincerity, the Brontë excoriation of selfish, vain, self-centered women, the Brontë preoccupation with love. But this time the lover is no Rochester. He is a good, faithful clergyman, just the kind of man who might have appealed to the youngest and gentlest and prettiest of the Brontës.

Didacticism carries over into *The Tenant of Wildfell Hall* (1848), in which a woman walks out and slams the door long before Ibsen's Nora was ever dreamed of, but this time it is didacticism with a difference. *Wildfell Hall* is not a very good novel, but it is an amazing book for a girl like Anne Brontë to have written; there was no weakness in that gentle heart. In *Agnes Grey* the picture of the boy who tortures birds had certainly not spared our sensibilities; here we get the story of a man who drives on steadily to the devil, as Branwell did. But he is not Branwell temperamentally; Charlotte's note is misleading on that point. It took courage, too, in those days, to disbelieve in eternal damnation, and say so frankly.

It is interesting that Anne begins *Wildfell Hall* in the middle, just where Emily began *Wuthering Heights*. Charlotte thought it a very improper book for her little sister to have written.

5. *What the Brontës Mean*

What, then, did the Brontës contribute to English fiction?

First, romanticism. The Gothic novelists had rebelled against the "reasonable" limitations of the eighteenth century, but they got bogged on the terror-tale and generally failed to go deep enough to make their revolt completely effective. The Brontës had what the Gothic people lacked: they worked against the background of that vast spiritual awakening which we call the Romantic Movement.

Scott was a romantic on the antiquarian side of romanticism, but in his attitude toward the expression of personal emotion in literature, Scott was a true classicist. In the Brontës, the Romantic Movement captured the English novel. Deserting the drawing-room and the town, they drove back, as Wordsworth did, to elemental things. "You are right," Charlotte tells Mrs. Gaskell, "when you say that there is a large margin in human nature over which the logicians have no dominion; glad am I that it is so."

Second, introspection. Richardson had opened up this field for the novelist. In his perverse way, Sterne had mapped out considerable tracts of it. But neither had the terrible Brontë lust for truth, the ruthless determination to dig down to the roots of the inner life. And few among the contemporaries of the Brontës had these things at all.

They themselves were not particularly analytical about it. They do not do it systematically, as James Joyce and Virginia Woolf were to do it in our own time. Their introspection takes the form of a tremendous outpouring. But they are in complete possession of the greatest single discovery of the Romantic Movement, its affirmation of the essential meaning of Christianity, its unshaken conviction of the infinite value and significance of each individual soul.

Third, passion. Again and again, Charlotte has been compared to George Sand. She would have been horrified, surely! But probably she is as close to George Sand as a decent British woman can come; she is a strange, northern, virginal George Sand. This was Jane Eyre's great indelicacy in the eyes of her contemporaries—that she loved unbidden and dared avow her love. And there is one passage in *The Professor,* where Frances frankly expresses her passion for Crimsworth, which must surely have seemed to the Victorians, had they read it when it was new, to surpass anything in *Jane Eyre.*

In life Charlotte Brontë accepted many narrow mid-Victorian views; on one side of her, she was a censorious, pernickety "old maid." In Brussels both her nationalistic insularity and her religious bigotry were appalling; she actually has Dr. John tell Lucy that at first he mistook her for a "foreigner," which, of course, is exactly what she is!

It is significant that in the very same passage in *Villette* in which she pours scorn on the voluptuous Cleopatra picture, Charlotte Brontë must also reject all meaningless, insipid pictures of merely "good" girls. The wonderful description of Vashti's acting in the same novel has more significance than many readers realize. Charlotte Brontë's letters make it clear that seeing Rachel brought her a genuine spiritual experience, that the great French tragedienne thrilled her even while she repelled. She sensed power—debased, degraded power, as she believed—but still power, life-force. "Well, if so much of unholy force can arise from below, may not an equal efflux of sacred essence descend one day from above?" At least she is intelligent enough to realize that what Rachel has represents a more advanced development in life than insipid goodness, and that there is no hope for the world if nothing better than an insipid goodness can be pitted against it.

Emily Brontë is greater than Charlotte—the imaginative power of *Wuthering Heights* is a thing the elder sister never matched—and she surrendered herself to her daemon with complete self-abandonment, instead of pitting the conscientious scruples of a conventional religion against it, as Charlotte so often did. Yet Charlotte has had a larger influence on the novel. And as much as any outstanding novelist's, hers is the importance of her own personality. "Lewes was describing Currer Bell to me yesterday," wrote George Eliot, "as a little, plain, provincial, sickly-looking old maid, yet what passion, what fire in her!"

Charlotte Brontë's intensity is terrible; some of her images are actually suggestive of Donne:

This longing, and all of a similar kind, it was necessary to knock on the head; which I did figuratively, after the manner of Jael to Sisera, driving a nail through their temples. Unlike Sisera, they did not die: they were but transiently stunned, and at intervals would turn on the nail with a rebellious wrench; then did the temples bleed, and the brain thrill to the core.

Sometimes she misses the effect she aims at, and then she is ludicrous, but she is glorious when she succeeds. Her heroines may call their husbands "sir," but they are feminists nevertheless, and not only Shirley but even the mild Frances Henri, who actually maintains—and successfully maintains—the economic independence of the married woman!

St. John Rivers offers Jane Eyre God, but God is not enough; she must live in this world too. Caroline Helstone, of *Shirley,* losing her lover, gives herself religiously to good works, but they do not fill the void in her life; she pines away. Charlotte Brontë was naked under her clothes, as Heine reminded the prudish lady—those stiff Victorian clothes! Like Richardson, she would have been shocked by the subsequent development of tendencies to which she stood already half-committed.

CHAPTER XVIII

THE "NEW" NOVEL: GEORGE ELIOT

Who fished the murex up?

ROBERT BROWNING

1. *A Survey*

With George Eliot the English novel turns away from the art of Dickens and Thackeray to head in the direction of the novel of today. The change was due to the circumstances under which George Eliot worked, to her own temperament, and to her experience of life.

Marian Evans was born at Arbury Farm, in Warwickshire, November 22, 1819. Her father, Robert Evans, was a land agent, some of whose characteristics survive in Caleb Garth, of *Middlemarch,* and in Adam Bede. Standing between his knees as he drove about the countryside, his daughter "drunk in knowledge of the country and of country folk at all her pores." It was upon her unpremeditated, eager childhood experiences that she based her earlier and more spontaneous books. Her self-portrait as Maggie, in *The Mill on the Floss,* shows that her nature was both passionate and intensely earnest, and both in the highest degree.

In her native environment, it was inevitable that this temperament should express itself first of all in an almost fanatical devotion to the ideals of evangelical Christianity. But when, in 1841, she and her father went to live in Coventry, and Marian, already distinctly an intellectual, though her formal schooling had not been superior to that of other girls of her class, came in contact with the Hennells and the Brays, her views were quickly altered. What we know as the modern historical school of Bible study had begun in Germany, and its conclusions were just now beginning to be made known in England. As the translator of David Strauss's rationalistic *Life of*

Jesus, Marian Evans was thoroughly exposed to them. The result was a formal renunciation of intellectual assent to Christian dogma.[1]

After the death of her father in 1849, Marian went abroad for a time; later she joined the staff of the *Westminster Review.* This work brought her in close touch with an "advanced" group of London intellectuals—the editor, John Chapman; Herbert Spencer; Harriet Martineau; above all, George Henry Lewes.

The meeting with Lewes marked Miss Evans's second great break with the traditions of her youth. He was living apart from his wife under circumstances which precluded a divorce; when she fell in love with him, Marian Evans first satisfied herself that their union could infringe the rights of no other person, then joined her life to his in what is known as a common law marriage.[2] In 1854 they went to Germany to give the storm a chance to blow over.

[1] The break came with appalling suddenness, as her letters show. The most penetrating observation in Anne Fremantle's little book on *George Eliot* (Macmillan, 1933) is that she could hardly have acted as she did, had she had any understanding of mysticism. "Faith, in the theological meaning of the word, she had never had: Hennell's *Enquiry* merely removed her beliefs." George Eliot later traced back her first skeptical impulses to the reading of Bulwer's *Devereux* and some of Scott's novels. Here for the first time she found characters who lived nobly without the sanction of specific creeds.

[2] For Lewes, cf. A. T. Kitchel, *George Lewes and George Eliot, A Review of Records* (John Day Company, 1933). He was a man of wide learning, though not an independent thinker in the fullest sense of the term; his interests embraced literature, philosophy, science, and music. The fact that in 1854 England still required an act of Parliament for every divorce must have placed that luxury beyond a man in his circumstances under any conditions; his case was complicated, however, both because he had once condoned his wife's adultery (thus closing the door on any future redress), and because both he and Thornton Hunt, her paramour, had been known as advocates of free love. Flippancy seems to have been characteristic of the earlier Lewes; serious people generally disliked him intensely, declaring that he had no reverence in him; this was George Eliot's own first impression. But his love for her seems to have exercised a wonderfully transforming influence upon him; his devotion went the length of adoration; he lived in her as completely as it is possible for one human being to live in another. It should be added that the two Georges supported not only Lewes's sons but the spendthrift wife, who lived on until 1902, more than twenty years after both of them had gone to their graves. Charles Lewes's testimony is very impressive: "George Eliot found a ruined life and she made it into a beautiful life. She found us poor motherless boys, and what she did for us no one on earth will ever know."

Marian Evans's first, tentative, fumbling effort as a writer of fiction had been made at least as far back as 1846,[3] but nothing had come of it. Now under Lewes's encouragement, she wrote her first story, "The Sad Fortunes of the Reverend Amos Barton." Lewes sent it to Blackwood, who fortunately recognized its quality at once. "Barton," "Mr. Gilfil's Love-Story," and "Janet's Repentance" make up George Eliot's first book, *Scenes of Clerical Life* (1858). The success of the work was instantaneous, though Dickens alone among celebrities was sure that the writer was a woman.

"Mr. Gilfil" is partly melodrama, though there is a real, and therefore touching, quality in Caterina. In both the other stories, George Eliot is consistently faithful to her announced Wordsworthian purpose of writing so as to make her readers conscious of the heroism and poetry in quiet lives. "Janet's Repentance," which involves the redemption by a devoted clergyman of an unhappy wife who has taken to drink, shows a true understanding and appreciation of the author's own discarded evangelicalism.

Increasing acclamation hailed the first full-length novel, *Adam Bede* (1859), probably the most beautiful and completely satisfying of all George Eliot's books. Primarily, it is not Adam Bede's story. (Adam, as Henry James observed, lacks "spontaneity and sensibility" and "the capacity to be tempted.") It is the story of pretty, shallow Hetty Sorrel, who was betrayed by her well-meaning but careless lover and led on into child-murder. It is the story of the epigrammatic Mrs. Poyser, who was never one of those to see the cat in the dairy and wonder what it had come after. It is the story of Dinah Morris, the Methodist woman preacher, a figure suggested by George Eliot's aunt, Elizabeth Evans, though not a portrait of her.

Despite George Eliot's known admiration of Scott, *Adam Bede* cannot be proved to have been directly indebted to *The Heart of Midlothian*. It is interesting, nevertheless, to compare Hetty Sorrel with Scott's Effie Deans. In a sense, George Eliot understands Hetty better than any man could have understood her, and the girl's passion is alluringly and seductively and sympathetically described.

[3] Cf. *Early Essays of George Eliot,* with an Editor's Preface by R (Privately printed, 1919), an extraordinarily interesting and prescient collection.

But if the novelist escapes being seduced by a kittenish beauty there are other dangers which she does not escape. She gives us so many more examples than we need of the shallowness and heartlessness of the girl that unfriendly critics have often reproached her with feminine spitefulness and jealousy. Even if we reject this extreme view, Scott still seems more generous-minded.

Mrs. Poyser ranks with the inhabitants of the Rainbow Inn in *Silas Marner* as a prime expression of George Eliot's humor; this is the more remarkable as the novelist had so little humor in life. Encouraged by Lewes's feeling that Mrs. Poyser grew "better and better as the book goes on," George Eliot confessed having written her speeches "with heightening gusto." Mrs. Poyser is a character part in the Smollett-Dickens tradition; if she has a fault it must be that she is too good.

The marriage of Adam and Dinah at the close of the book troubles many readers,[4] but George Eliot wrote Blackwood that she would have her teeth drawn rather than change it. Elizabeth Haldane, remembering George Eliot's own dependence upon men, thinks she could not bear to leave Dinah alone in the world. Hardy, of course, would have done so; and Hardy would have hanged Hetty as he hanged Tess. George Eliot, on the other hand, permits the girl's sentence to be commuted to transportation at the very foot of the gallows; this is the scene in which *Adam Bede* comes closest to popular Victorian sensation fiction. But there were good novels before Hardy; and George Eliot herself was very sure that Adam's "love for Dinah was better and more precious to him" than his love for Hetty had ever been, "for it was the outgrowth of that fuller life which had come to him from his acquaintance with deep sorrow."

In *The Mill on the Floss* (1860), George Eliot dipped once more into the storehouse of memory. The book shows a wonderfully true insight into the child mind and behavior—possibly the most wonderful in English literature—and also into the mental processes of country people. Maggie Tulliver has a restless, rebellious spirit which is typical of her time, and a wonderful capacity for devotion.

[4] Cf. John S. Diekhoff, "The Happy Ending of *Adam Bede*," *ELH*, III (1936), 221-227.

No wonder George Eliot was angry with those who felt that she did not want her readers to sympathize with Maggie's brother, Tom. He was her own brother, Isaac, and she never lost her love for him, even when he refused all contact with her through the long years of her union with Lewes. Yet Maggie is right when she calls Tom an uncomprehending and unimaginative Pharisee, and H. H. Bonnell is right when he calls him a prig. In the end, when the flood comes, Maggie gives her life for Tom. This is not quite satisfactory, and George Eliot knew it well. "The *Epische Breite* into which I was beguiled by love of my subject in the two first volumes, caused a want of proportionate fullness in the treatment of the third, which I shall always regret."

George Eliot's readers are not, of course, obliged to be as generous to Tom as she was; and if they feel, as I do, that he was not worth his sister's sacrifice, their feeling of dissatisfaction in the ending will surely not be lessened. But this is subjective criticism. George Eliot, clearly, felt that in one way or another she must cut the Gordian knot. It was Maggie's tragedy that she could not satisfy her legitimate needs and desires without hurting somebody who was dear to her. Had she accepted Philip Wakem, she must have broken her father's heart; had she gone off with Stephen, she must cruelly have stabbed both Phil and Lucy. Her creator evidently saw Maggie's love for Philip as a herald or harbinger of her deeper, truer love to Stephen. Possibly she herself had experienced something like this in her feeling for John Chapman,[5] or Herbert Spencer, or the unnamed early suitor of Mathilde Blind's biography, before George Henry Lewes came into her life. It was a daring thing in those days to create a heroine who was capable of changing her mind in love, and who only through an heroic effort could barely save herself from stealing another woman's lover.

> If the ethics of art [cried George Eliot, indignantly] do not admit the truthful presentation of a character essentially noble, but liable to great error—error that is anguish to its own nobleness—then, it seems to me, the ethics of art are too narrow, and must be widened to correspond with a widening psychology.

[5] Cf. Gordon S. Haight, *George Eliot and John Chapman, With Chapman's Diaries* (Yale University Press, 1940).

Whatever we may think of Stephen Guest himself—and he is, at any rate, something much better than the utterly graceless churl some critics have presented under his name—the fact remains that *The Mill on the Floss* helped break the mold of an old, in the bad sense, idealistic fiction. George Eliot's final verdict was that the book had "more thought and a profounder veracity" than *Adam Bede* but that *Adam* was better balanced.

The Mill on the Floss was followed in 1861 by George Eliot's shortest novel, *Silas Marner,* the idea of which came as "a sudden inspiration" while she was working out the plot of *Romola* and demanded to be written down at once, even though she felt that, "since Wordsworth is dead," nobody would care for it very much. Silas gives his heart to God; when, because of hideous injustice on the part of his co-religionists, he loses his faith, he can for a time find no better object in life than the accumulation of money. But when the child Eppie is cast upon his care, his deep human tenderness is fully awakened. In *Silas Marner* George Eliot came closer than anywhere else to a study of religious doubt in her fiction, but she still shies off. Whether she intended it or not, the story harmonizes well with the general tenets of her loosely-held Comtian "religion of humanity." In his normal, natural devotion to a child, Silas finds a more satisfying fulfillment of himself than ever the old supernaturalism had been able to give him.

The basic conception of *Silas Marner,* as George Eliot herself was aware, is that of an idyll:

> I have felt all through as if the story would have lent itself best to metrical rather than to prose fiction, especially in all that relates to the psychology of Silas; except that, under that treatment, there could not be equal play of humour.

The idyllic quality disappears, however, in the Godfrey Cass story, which is given far too much space. The long Chapter XI—completely out of place in so short a tale—witnesses to the author's always seductive tendency to fill in an elaborate background. The unhappy result is that Eppie is introduced comparatively late, and the resultant change in the character of Silas seems almost instantaneous.

In *Silas Marner,* George Eliot is still using native material, though imagination is playing a larger role and recollection a slighter one than in her earlier books. But in *Romola* (1863), an elaborate historical novel of Florence in the days of Savonarola and Lorenzo de Medici, she goes completely afield.[6]

After an heroic course of reading in the Magliabecchian Library and elsewhere, George Eliot filled in her backgrounds with archaeological conscientiousness. She is just when she points out that the background is no more elaborately indicated here than in her English stories. But she perhaps forgot that the English background in which she herself had lived was vitalized to a degree she could not achieve in dealing with tumultuous, tempestuous Renaissance Florence. Any less tremendous theme than the one George Eliot had chosen must have been swamped by such treatment. As it is, the book remains, despite all the considerations that may justly be urged against it, one of the great reading experiences of English fiction.

> My predominant feeling [such was her own final judgment] is—not that I have achieved anything, but—that great, great facts have struggled to find a voice through me, and have only been able to speak brokenly.

George Eliot understood the temptations of the saint. Except for the unsatisfactory treatment of his mysticism, the character of Savonarola is powerfully set forth in *Romola,* though there is too much analysis and too little drama. When Romola flees from Florence and her faithless husband, it is Savonarola who turns her back. The enlightened paganism on which she had been reared now proves inadequate to solve her problems; not until Savonarola has appealed

[6] Most critics recognize a change in the spirit and method of George Eliot's work at this point. Generally it is attributed to her increasing age and intellectuality. In an article on "The Influence of Contemporary Criticism on George Eliot," *Studies in Philology,* XXX (1933), 103-122, Mathilde Parlett argues ingeniously that the bad press received by *The Mill on the Floss,* following the revelation of "George Eliot's" identity with Marian Evans, was fundamentally responsible. Conservative Englishmen had not yet forgiven Miss Evans for her union with Lewes. Miss Parlett thinks she turned to imaginative themes to rule out all suggestions that she was using autobiographical material, and that, at the same time, she made her teaching more specific.

to her capacity for self-sacrifice and awakened her deeper nature does she reach the full development of which she is capable. But she does not surrender into his keeping the conscience that he has given her; and when at the end he sins by identifying his party with God's Kingdom, she repudiates him indignantly and stands alone. Romola may be more British than Italian, but she has the deep moral impressiveness which George Eliot manifested in her own life. Her husband, Tito Melema, is the most famous study of deterioration of character in English fiction, though one must admit that, here and there, he is a problem in ethics rather than a character in a novel.

Felix Holt the Radical (1866) presents a detailed picture of England's political turmoil in the days of the Reform Bill. Though it is set against a background of provincial life, very little of it was drawn from recollection. *Felix Holt* has an elaborate inheritance plot and a double mystery of parentage which suggests the possibility of Dickens influence. In writing this book, George Eliot took pains to consult Frederic Harrison in order to get her law right. It is generally considered her least important novel, though the development of the love affair between Felix and Esther Lyon, who is won away from selfish frivolities through her love for him, has great charm. As a political novel, *Felix Holt* is not important; George Eliot was much less interested in politics than a writer with so much social consciousness might have been expected to be.

Middlemarch (1871-1872), George Eliot's longest novel—"the magnificent book," Virginia Woolf calls it, "which with all its imperfections is one of the few English novels written for grown-up people"—is a study in frustration. Whether or not it is George Eliot's masterpiece depends on whether or not one can accept the wider and maturer view of life which it comprehends as an adequate substitute for the now lost spontaneity of *Adam Bede* and *The Mill on the Floss*.

Both Lydgate and Dorothea Brooke start out with the highest ideals, and both fail through circumstance; for George Eliot believed that "there is no creature whose inward being is so strong that it is not greatly determined by what lies outside it." Lydgate's failure is absolute. He marries Rosamond Vincy, a beautiful, selfish, uncomprehending woman; the unyielding tenacity of the weaker nature wears away the stronger; and he who began with the most unselfish plans lives a fashionable physician to paying patients, and goes gladly, still in the prime of life, to an undistinguished grave. Rosamond is loathsome, as only a thoroughly "blameless" woman can be loathsome; and it is when she is utterly graceless herself that she manages to put everybody else completely in the wrong.

Dorothea, who is potentially a modern Saint Teresa, recovers from her mistake in a measure; indeed George Eliot intends us to believe that she is happy in her second marriage with Will Ladislaw. But Ladislaw is a cheap motion picture hero in whom the reader finds it very difficult to believe. The first husband, the arid Casaubon,[7] is real enough, though one wonders how so intelligent a girl as Dorothea could have been so completely deceived. Casaubon is engaged upon a monumental (and, as it proves, incompetent) study of comparative mythology; and Dorothea is supposed to believe that in devoting herself to this purpose, she will find the duty that can give meaning to her life. Her miscomprehension of motives at the beginning of the book is a little like that of Jane Austen's Emma, with the significant difference that Emma had no higher object in life than to get people married, while Dorothea would devote herself to ideal aims, even though she is not quite sure what they are. Her growing disillusionment in marriage is powerfully portrayed, until at last the reader shares her "dumb inward cry for help to bear this nightmare of a life in which every energy was arrested by dread."

But *Middlemarch* is more than the story of two marriages; it is "A Study of Provincial Life," a picture of the life of a community. There is a third love affair, that of Fred Vincy, Rosamond's brother, and the sensible Mary Garth; and there is the fall of the hypocritical philanthropist, Bulstrode. A hypocrite, at least, is what any other novelist would have called him; George Eliot, whose tolerance is like the tolerance of God, understands that "he was simply a man whose desires had been stronger than his theoretic beliefs."

[7] Cf. Mathilde Parlett, "George Eliot and Humanism," *Studies in Philology,* XXVII (1930), 25-46.

She had one more novel to write: *Daniel Deronda* (1876).[8] Like *Middlemarch* it is composed of two main stories. Sidney Lanier, who thought *Deronda* "the most significant, the most tender, the most pious and altogether the most uplifting of modern books," has named these stories: "The Repentance of Gwendolen Harleth" and "The Mission of Daniel Deronda."

Gwendolen, who is introduced to us at the gaming-table, in a scene presented, for the sake of emphasis, out of its natural order in the story, seems at the outset likely to develop into a repulsive feminine counterpart to Tito Melema. Her marriage to the monstrous Grandcourt is as hopeless as Dorothea's to Casaubon; unlike Dorothea's it has been undertaken for purely selfish reasons. Catherine Arrowpoint, who imprudently marries Herr Klesmer for love, in defiance of the wishes of her parents, is intended as a contrast to Gwendolen.

But thanks to Deronda's influence, Gwendolen is saved at last, "as by fire." She comes in time to love Deronda, but that nineteenth-century Sir Charles Grandison has meanwhile given his heart to Mirah Cohen, a beautiful young Jewess, whom he rescues from suicide in her destitution, and through whom he discovers that he himself is a Jew, and gives his all to the Zionists. The Jewish part of the book, which involves considerable mystery, is very romantic and not too convincing. George Eliot's interest in the Jewish problem testifies to an attractive largeness of spirit, but she was not able to transmute it into the stuff of fiction. About Gwendolen herself there can be no question; she is one of the most powerfully portrayed women in English fiction. But her reality only shows up the comparative unreality of the rest of the book.[9]

[8] Two short pieces should be mentioned to complete the record of her fiction. "The Lifted Veil" (1859), though it links up with Lewes's interest in scientific experimentation, proves that clairvoyance was never designed as a theme for George Eliot. "Brother Jacob" (1864) is even worse; it reads almost as if she had set out to burlesque herself. The long dramatic poem, *The Spanish Gypsy* (1868) is also, of course, a work of fiction, and there are some brief narratives among her collected poems. Her last book, *Impressions of Theophrastus Such* (1879), is a collection of essays with a very thin fictional veneer.

[9] "Daniel Deronda: A Conversation," by Henry James (*Partial Portraits*) well indicates the differences of opinion which the book called forth. After

In later years the two Georges established their famous Sunday afternoons at the Priory, and here the ageing novelist presided like a sibyl over her reverential adorers. She had now attained the height of her fame, and her contemporaries were comparing her with Shakespeare, Dante, and Goethe. When Herbert Spencer served on the library committee for the London Library, he thought it unnecessary that any novels should be purchased for that collection, "except, of course, those of George Eliot."

She was prostrated in 1878, when Lewes died; she would see nobody; she had no business left in the world but to bring out his unpublished works. But in 1880 she astonished everybody by marrying the banker, John Walter Cross, who was much younger than she, and who became her biographer. For the second time in her life, she had found a man who was capable of giving her the adoration without which she could not live. But he could not give it her for long. On December 17, 1880, she took cold at a concert. Five days later she was dead.

2. *George Eliot's Originality*

The first significant difference between George Eliot and most of her predecessors is that she did not begin to write fiction until she was a mature woman with a fully developed, carefully formulated philosophy of art and of life. Even more significant than this is the fact that she was an intellectual in a sense in which none of her fellow Victorians among the novelists could wear that label. Her novels, constructed around ideas, are not entertainment; they are a serious interpretation of life. In them, for the first time, the modern novel widens its horizon to the intellectual breadth of the modern world.

One need not necessarily claim that it was better for that. In George Eliot's case, it is even possible to maintain that her intelligence was her undoing, that she would have done even finer work if she had not been handicapped by her learning. Indeed everybody who prefers *Adam Bede* and *The Mill on the Floss* to *Middlemarch* and *Daniel Deronda* is by implication committed to this view.

Lanier, Gardner and Browning are the critics of George Eliot who make the best case for it.

Critics sometimes berate Lewes for having led George Eliot, in her later books, toward an arid intellectuality. It is probably true that the peculiar character of her bond with him did cut her off, especially during the earlier years of their union, from what might well have proved a fructifying contact with her peers. George Eliot never doubted the righteousness of her course, but she was always careful not to impose her society upon those who might not care for it. What Lewes's critics fail to take into consideration, however, is that without his encouragement, George Eliot might never have written fiction at all.

Criticism must indeed tread warily at this point. The revolutionary character of George Eliot's novels is lost altogether on the casual reader. There was nothing of the iconoclast in her, and she did not make a clean break with the past. "Her methods were old-fashioned," writes Elizabeth Haldane: "her style was direct as the Bible: there were none of the modern allusionary modes of hinting at things not told."

But if it is possible to miss the differences between George Eliot's novels and those of her predecessors, it is also possible to exaggerate the differences between her earlier and her later novels. She herself was unaware of any difference: "The principles which are at the root of my effort to paint Dinah Morris are equally at the root of my effort to paint Mordecai." And it is true that Blackwood's one criticism of "Amos Barton" summed up, at the very beginning of her career, the most serious indictment in the case that criticism has against her: "Perhaps the author falls into the error of trying too much to explain the characters of his actors by description instead of allowing them to evolve in the action of the story."

Nevertheless, I think Sir Edmund Gosse is just when he points out that as time went on, George Eliot tended more and more to trust "to her brain rather than to those tired servants, her senses." It is true that she does not always use the expository method even as late as *Middlemarch*. When Brooke calls on Mr. Cadwallader, he is "shown into the study, where all the fishing-tackle hung." But because she was a critic and an essayist, as well as a novelist, she does not often choose to leave her readers to inference and deduction.

Her constant preoccupation with ethical problems did not help her at this point either. Nearly all her more elaborate portraits involve some question of guilt; she tests her characters for sin as carefully as a chemist tests the purity of a drug. Certainly the modern novelist is far more like her in method than he is like Dickens. It is ironical, therefore, that this "modern" note in her should lie at the root of all the pedantic idiosyncrasies that annoy the contemporary reader most—her lumbering reflections, her excessive explanations, her direct or confidential address to the reader, her exhortations to us not to misinterpret the facts that she has given us, her maddening habit of asking questions which she proceeds to answer a moment later, her tendency to expatiate on her own feelings toward her characters.

She resembles our contemporaries too in her bias toward actuality. The Dutch painters are her favorites;[10] the epigraph which she prefixed to one chapter of *Middlemarch* might well stand before her work as a whole:

> Let the high Muse chant loves Olympian:
> We are but mortals, and must sing of man.

Again and again, from *Clerical Life* to *Deronda,* she apologizes for directing our attention to such commonplace personages and themes. Real heroes, as distinct from book heroes, have an element of human fallibility about them; she hopes this will not destroy their interest for us; after all, heroism too has its roots in the soil of common life; "for the growing good of the world is partly dependent on unhistoric acts; and that things are not so ill with you and me as they might have been is half owing to the number who lived faithfully a hidden life, and rest in unvisited tombs." But at heart she is not apologetic, any more than Wordsworth was; she would woo us away from lollipops and develop our appetite for strong Positivist meat.

[10] Cf. *Adam Bede,* Ch. 17, the most important single statement of her literary creed.

3. *God and the Novelist*

Thus the temper of George Eliot's work is even more distinctive than its technique. F. W. H. Myers strikes the note here in his oft-quoted pen-portrait of her in her prime:

I remember how, at Cambridge, I walked with her once in the Fellows' Garden of Trinity, on an evening of rainy May; and she, stirred somewhat beyond her wont, and taking as her text the three words which have been used so often as the inspiring trumpet-calls of men—the words, *God, Immortality, Duty*—pronounced, with terrible earnestness, how inconceivable was the *first,* how unbelievable the *second,* and yet how peremptory and absolute the *third.* Never, perhaps, have sterner accents affirmed the sovereignty of impersonal and unrecompensing law. I listened, and night fell; her grave, majestic countenance turned toward me like a Sybil's in the gloom; it was as though she withdrew from my grasp, one by one, the two scrolls of promise, and left me the third scroll, only, awful with inevitable fates. And when we stood at length and parted, amid that columnar circuit of the forest-trees, beneath the last twilight of starless skies, I seemed to be gazing, like Titus at Jerusalem, on vacant seats and empty halls—on a sanctuary with no Presence to hallow it, and heaven left lonely of a God.

George Eliot's revolt against her inherited faith was based on intellectual grounds alone; it was a problem in historical criticism that stumped her. At no time was there a moral revolt. It was inevitable, therefore, that, being what she was, she should have spent the rest of her life trying to preserve the Christian morality without supernatural sanctions.

Here is this problem of selfishness, for example. George Eliot's novels hardly deal with anything else. The hapless Hetty Sorrel and the far more deeply criminal Tito Melema destroy themselves in their egoism; Arthur Donnithorne and Rosamond Vincy destroy those who trusted in them. Esther Lyon is a charming girl when we first meet her, and a good girl, but her interests in life are trifling and highly personal. She would have made a perfect heroine for almost any other novelist; George Eliot perceived that one must live for something larger than that.

When an egoist is saved, it must be as Gwendolen is saved, "as by fire." Maggie Tulliver is the most lovable of all George Eliot's egoists because she refuses resolutely to identify herself with her egoism. "I couldn't live in peace if I put the shadow of a willful sin between myself and God. I have caused sorrow already—I know it—I feel it; but I have never deliberately consented to it: I have never said, 'They shall suffer, that I may have joy.' "

"Our deeds are like our children that are born to us; they live and act apart from our own will." The tragic thing is that the egoist cannot himself absorb the evil he creates; he brings sorrow and suffering upon others also. "Men's lives are as thoroughly blended with each other as the air they breathe: evil spreads as necessarily as disease." Through suffering it is possible to learn humility and tenderness, but even on this basis only a partial atonement is possible. As Adam Bede points out, "There's a sort o' damage . . . that can't be made up for."

But the really good man is interested in something better than securing exemption. "Surely it is not true blessedness to be free of sorrow, while there is sorrow and sin in the world: sorrow is then a part of love, and love does not seek to throw it off." Dinah Morris, Daniel Deronda, and Dorothea Brooke know the secret; Romola learns it; we feel that Gwendolen Harleth may learn it in the end. In the directly didactic close of *Romola* the philosophy is clearly expounded.

It was no accident that while George Eliot was the first major English novelist who did not profess the Christian religion, none other should ever have set forth the Christian ethic with such intellectual power. Her intellect robbed her of God, but she made no god of the intellect. Love was the most imperious need of her nature at all times, from her childhood as Maggie Tulliver, when she gave her young adoration to her brother, Isaac Evans, until the last year of her life, when she trusted her decline to J. W. Cross. Adam Bede speaks for her as well as himself when he says, "it isn't notions sets people doing the right thing—it's feeling"; and, again, that "feeling's a sort of knowledge." The same philosophy lies at the heart of *Daniel Deronda,* so different from *Adam Bede* in other ways.

George Eliot was no clamorous atheist. She soon outgrew the first zest of her emancipation, and refused to wear a label, even the "rationalist," Positivist label; she simply waited patiently for more light. She found it difficult to believe that men had brought forth sublimer thoughts than the universe itself; and her faith in free will always separated her from the thoroughgoing naturalists. Dorothea Brooke identifies herself with the divine power against evil; and George Eliot herself speaks of "the breath of God within us." She refused to reject human values and take molecular physics as her dominant guide.

Some men might have been happy on that basis; George Eliot could not. It has often been pointed out that she never made loss of faith the principal theme of a novel. This was partly, as we have seen, because she was no iconoclast; it was partly because as an artist she had her roots in the world of her believing youth; it was partly because she never reached the certitude of unbelief. Like Renan she might have said, "I feel that my life is governed by a faith I no longer possess." Henry James observes of her with marvelous rightness that she is not naturally a critic and a skeptic—

> her spontaneous part is to observe life and to feel it, to feel it with admirable depth. Contemplation, sympathy and faith—something like that, I should say, would have been her material scale. If she had fallen upon an age of enthusiastic assent to old articles of faith, it seems to me possible that she would have had a more perfect, a more consistent and graceful development, than she has actually had.

This problem of faith concerns more than Marian Evans the woman; we must understand it if we are to understand George Eliot the novelist. She was great only to the extent that memory and her natural goodness made it possible for her to rise above her unfaith. If you had asked her what she thought of mysticism, she would have replied that she feared and distrusted it. But probably nobody ever succeeded in being a great writer without having something of the mystic in him; so it is not surprising to learn that George Eliot told John Walter Cross that "in all that she considered her best writing, there was a 'not herself' which took possession of her, and that she felt her own personality to be merely the instrument through which this spirit, as it were, were acting." But her unfaith made it difficult for that spirit, and the spirit did not always get through. Her most ambitious novel is an epic of failure; her books stand as an incomparably beautiful record of one dark hour in the history of the human spirit.

Her life was one, not many; and I think her tragedy is reflected even in her style. We are told that she played the piano "correctly, conscientiously but not with the *entrain* and charm of far inferior musicians." Edmund Gosse says, "Her prose has fine qualities of force and wit, it is practical and persuasive, but it misses one prime but rather subtle merit, it never sings." The Christians sang on the way to the arena, but they believed that they were going, through sharp, brief agony, into the very presence of God.

Yet there was more God in George Eliot than she ever knew; as Ethel Colburn Mayne says of Byron, what draws and holds us to her is her "enthralling humanity." She wanted our love, this sad, "rather smoke-dried" woman, as she calls herself, her face "with lines in it that seem a map of sorrows." In case it makes any difference to her in Elysium, there are those who still find it impossible to resist her.

CHAPTER XIX

THE POETIC COMEDY OF GEORGE MEREDITH

"Though," said she, "what it all meant, and what was the drift of it, I couldn't tell to save my life. Is it every day the same with you here?"
"Very much."
"How you must enjoy a spell of dulness!"

The Egoist *

1. *Some Comparisons*

With Meredith the "new" novel is upon us with a vengeance—obliqueness, indirectness, elaborate psychological analysis, sustained intellectuality, and all the rest of it. It will be interesting to compare him at the outset both with George Eliot and with Thomas Hardy.

Meredith's first novel, *The Ordeal of Richard Feverel,* came out the same year as *Adam Bede,* 1859. Incidentally, George Eliot was one of the first people to recognize the younger writer's genius. She had reviewed his "Arabian Entertainment," *The Shaving of Shagpat,* most favorably, calling particular attention to "the exquisite delicacy of its love incidents and love scenes."

Both Meredith and George Eliot were tremendously interested in the problems of human conduct, and both found the root of our difficulties in the same fault—selfishness. Nothing written by another hand could sound much more like George Eliot than these words from *Rhoda Fleming:*

> He closed, as it were, a black volume, and opened a new and bright one. Young men easily fancy that they may do this, and that when the black volume is shut the tide is stopped. Saying, 'I was a fool,' they believe they have put an end to the foolishness. What father teaches them that a human act once set in motion flows on for ever to the great account? Our deathlessness is in what we do, not in what we are.

* This quotation and all other quotations from Meredith's writings in this chapter are given by permission of Charles Scribner's Sons.

The differences between the two writers, however, are even more striking than their resemblances. George Eliot worked through tragedy, Meredith through comedy. So completely was he committed to the comic standpoint that he saw even the woeful story of Ferdinand Lassalle and Helena von Dönniges as the history of a pair of "tragic comedians." George Eliot wrote verses but Meredith was a poet, and, profoundly ethical though he was, his approach to fiction, unlike hers, was less a moralist's than a poet's. He was, too, a far more original, though a far less systematic, thinker than she. George Eliot identified religion so completely with the dogmas she discarded that, having lost the dogmas, she never found religious certitude again. Meredith, on the other hand, worked out a philosophy of life which, whether he was right or wrong, completely satisfied his conscious needs. Finally, George Eliot, though she rearranged her material to suit her thesis, still attempted a realistic representation of life. Meredith's picture of life, on the other hand, can be called realistic only if God is a Meredithian.

Meredith and Hardy both accepted the teachings of modern science, but so far as human life was concerned they deduced diametrically opposed conclusions. In Hardy, nature is coldly indifferent to man when she is not actively malevolent. Egdon Heath is the real hero of *The Return of the Native;* the human characters can find peace only as they submit themselves to it; whoever resists is crushed. How different is Richard Feverel's experience when he goes out walking in the rain on the darkest night of his life! "Nature Speaks." Nature speaks, for one thing, through the tiny leveret he had picked up and put in his breast:

> He was next musing on a strange sensation he experienced. It ran up one arm with an indescribable thrill, but communicated nothing to his heart. It was purely physical, ceased for a time, and recommenced, till he had it all through his blood, wonderfully thrilling. He grew aware that the little thing he carried in his breast was licking his hand there. The small rough tongue going over and over the palm of his hand produced the strange sensation he felt. Now that he knew the cause, the marvel ended; but now that he knew the cause, his heart was touched and made more of it. The gentle scraping continued without intermission as on he walked. What did it say to him? Human tongue could not have said so much just then.

Meredith himself had much to say to men to strengthen their courage for life; Hardy's is often interpreted as a voice of despair. Yet because Hardy's novels are easy, delightful reading they are a living force in men's lives today, while, thanks to the difficulties of their style, Meredith's too often stand, a set of books, in quiet dignity upon the shelf.

2. *The Publishing Record*

George Meredith was born at Portsmouth, February 12, 1828, the son of a tailor. He had some Celtic blood in his veins, less than is generally assumed by those who make much of the imaginative in his work, less perhaps, than he liked to have people think. His education included two years at a Moravian school in Germany. He attempted to study law. For eight years, despite his liberalism, he was staff contributor on a conservative newspaper; in 1866 he served as war correspondent in Italy; later he did editorial work on the *Fortnightly* and the *Pall Mall Gazette*. For thirty-five years he was a reader for the firm of Chapman and Hall, in which capacity he rejected *East Lynne,* Ouida's *Villiers, Erewhon,* Bernard Shaw's novels, *The Heavenly Twins,* and the work of John Oliver Hobbes, but encouraged Hardy, William Black, Edwin Arnold, and George Gissing. He was married in 1849 to Thomas Love Peacock's daughter, who was six and one-half years his senior (not nine, as he once stated). The marriage, which was very unhappy, dragged on until 1858, when Mrs. Meredith put an end to it by going to Italy with another man. In 1864 Meredith married Marie Vulliamy, and they established their home at Flint Cottage, near Box Hill, in Surrey, which, in the later years of Meredith's fame, became a literary shrine. In 1885 the wife died and the husband's health began breaking; in later years he was crippled by paralysis. In 1892 he became president of the British Society of Authors, succeeding Tennyson; in 1905 he received the Order of Merit. He died, May 18, 1909.

Meredith approached his first novel—*The Ordeal of Richard Feverel*—through two fictional anterooms. *The Shaving of Shagpat* (1856) presents Celtic material, from the *Mabinogian* and other sources, in an Oriental setting; *Farina* (1857) is a sly German Gothic. Both *Feverel* and its successor, *Evan Harrington* (1861), use autobiographical materials. In *Feverel* the comedy and the tragedy are imperfectly blended; when, in later years, Meredith revised the book, cutting some of the rich comic background material, he acknowledged in effect that the pathetic love story of Richard and Lucy had run away with the interest of the narrative. *Evan Harrington* is an elaborate comic treatment of the question whether a tailor can be a gentleman.

Sandra Belloni (1864)—originally called *Emilia in England*—and *Vittoria* (1867) have the same heroine, an opera singer. The first concerns her love affair with the arch-sentimentalist, Wilfrid Pole; in the second we see her in Italy against the revolutionary background of 1848-1849. Between these two titles came *Rhoda Fleming* (1865), a story of seduction which has elements in common with both *Clarissa* and *Adam Bede.*

The Adventures of Harry Richmond (1871), Meredith's only novel written in the first person, attempts a combination of romantic, and slightly fantastic, adventure with the comic spirit. It shows Meredith's understanding of the heart of a child, and marks his closest approach to such novels as *David Copperfield* and *The Mill on the Floss. Harry Richmond* has had a considerable influence on later "psychological romances," a conspicuous example being *Prince Otto,* by Robert Louis Stevenson.

Both *Beauchamp's Career* (1876) and *The Egoist* (1879) are distinguished books. *Beauchamp's Career,* which concerns the idealist in politics, reflects Meredith's own liberalism, and is said to have been his favorite novel. But it is *The Egoist,* of which there will be more to say later, that is generally taken to represent the highest development of his complex and subtle art.

Both *The Tragic Comedians* (1880) and *Diana of the Crossways* (1885) take off from contemporary scandals—Meredith puts his imagination to work on the material much as Browning might have done—and so does the next book but one, *Lord Ormont and His Aminta* (1894). The brief account of the Lassalle-von Dönniges tragedy cleaves close to the facts of history, but in *Diana,* the most immediately successful of all his novels, Meredith allows himself much freer rein. It is built around the story of Sheridan's granddaughter, Mrs. Caroline Norton, who was accused, unjustly as it appeared, of selling a government secret to the London *Times.* Later editions carried a disclaimer: "The story of Diana of the Crossways is to be read as fiction."

Meredith's last four novels are all concerned with the "woman question." In *Diana of the Crossways* one is less interested in whether or not Diana sold the secret than in the sympathetic study Meredith has made of a brilliant Irishwoman whose marriage goes to pieces through no fault of her own, and who is thrown upon her own resources to sink or swim in a world of men. *One of Our Conquerors* (1891), Meredith's most difficult as well as most daring book, presents the Meredithian heroine as a "common law" wife. *Lord Ormont and His Aminta* is based on the career of Charles Mordaunt, Earl of Peterborough. Aminta weds the hero she has worshiped since her schooldays, but he nurses his grievance against society by keeping her in such seclusion that the world thinks of her as his mistress rather than his wife. What she seemed to be toward him she becomes in earnest to another man who is generous enough to allow her a course of self-development as a human being. In *The Amazing Marriage* (1895), Fleetwood casts away the pearl of great price in the love of a woman—and learns its value too late.

The Amazing Marriage was Meredith's last work of fiction, though he had fourteen more years of life. He left one unfinished novel, *Celt and Saxon,* published in 1910. In addition to his novels, he wrote several long short stories—one of which, "The Tale of Chloe," is generally considered a masterpiece—the famous *Essay on Comedy,* and several volumes of poems.

3. *Philosophy of Life*

Meredith's novels were the result both of his philosophy of life and of his philosophy of fiction. First, we must consider his philosophy of life.

Basically, he was a nature-worshiper, deriving ultimately from Wordsworth.[1] His later views were modified by his study of Dar-

[1] My discussion is indebted at this point, among other authorities, to James Vertner Fletcher's unpublished Ph.D. thesis, *The Background and Development of George Meredith's Ethics* (cf. *Abstracts of Theses,* Vol. II, University of Washington, 1937).

win, who seems to have helped him to retain his optimism by making it possible for him to think of struggle and death as simply part of a vast cosmic process whose ultimate development should be perfection.

This is Meredith's new romanticism, a romanticism based on science and therefore not open to the objections which have been justly urged against the old evasive romanticism of the past. Meredith opposed both "dirty drab" and "rose pink"; poetry alone, in his view, could "hallow" energy. "Otherwise, we are in the breeding yards, among the litters and the farrows. It is a question of looking down or looking up. . . . Better say, life is holy!"

Meredith is not quite consistent in his use of the term "God." He called himself "a practical Christian," whatever that may be; but he also wrote, a few days before his death, "Nature is my God, and I trust in her." In 1872 he urged his son not to "lose the habit of praying to the unseen Divinity. Prayer for worldly goods is worse than fruitless, *but prayer for strength of soul is that passion of the soul which catches the gift it seeks.*" He rejected immortality—

> Into the breast that gives the rose,
> Shall I with shuddering fall?

Dr. Fletcher thinks he finds God always in the natural process, never outside of it, "God who represents a future ideal of perfection to which man is slowly approximating."

Though Meredith was an evolutionist, he did not share the easy faith in automatic progress which comforted such men as Macaulay and Herbert Spencer. He goes far deeper than they do. It is true that the evolutionary process has operated unconsciously in the past. But it is also true that on that basis it has produced an "all but sensational world." Now that the process has achieved a directive intelligence in the minds of purposeful men, better things are in prospect. Only, to serve the needs of life, man must get rid of self. "Service is our destiny in life and death." "I think that all right use of life, is to pave ways for the firmer footing of those who succeed us; as to my works, I know them faulty, think them of worth only when they point and aid to that end."

From Meredith's attitude toward nature follows inevitably his attitude toward love. He rejects asceticism; he will not disown his mother; the tree can grow only when it is "planted in good gross earth." A man who hates women hates nature, and men who hate nature are insane. Even a heart as weak as Sir Purcell Barrett's "has a new vital force, new health" when it "is stirred to love a woman." Meredith perceived that even the male demand for "purity" in women is often merely a means of feeding the male ego. "The young man who can look on them we call fallen women with a noble eye, is to my mind he that is most nobly begotten of the race, and likeliest to be the sire of a noble line."

But though the tree is "planted in good gross earth," it does not blossom there. Meredith was not interested in sex; he was interested in love. This does not mean that he shies from sex. He defends sex wholeheartedly against the Puritan, but that is because the Puritan attitude toward sex, as he sees it, is an impure attitude. His real interest is in something far transcending any physical relationship. "Spirit must brand the flesh that it may live."

Hating sensuality, Meredith hates sentimentalism also, for sentimentalism is a kind of ingrown sensuality. Sentimental people "fiddle harmonics on the strings of sensualism." Indeed sentimentalism is more dangerous than sensuality, for the very reason that its true character is disguised.

Sandra Belloni is Meredith's most uncompromising study in sentimentalism. Purcell Barrett, who wonders if he is not "constitutionally different from others," kills himself because he cannot bear disappointment; Wilfrid Pole loses his love. "So it is when you play at Life!" cries Meredith. "When you will not go straight, you get into this twisting maze." Better a thousand times to know real passion as Emilia does.

"Passion . . . is *noble strength on fire.*" The sentimentalist knows not passion; he cannot come close enough to life for that. Instead he rides the Hippogriff. He "goes on accumulating images and living sensations, till such time as . . . they assume a form of vitality, and hurry him headlong. This is not passion, though it amazes men, and does the madder thing."

But there is something worse than sentimentalism. That is egoism. "The Egoist is our fountain-head, primeval man. . . ." Sir Willoughby Patterne, in *The Egoist,* is the most wonderful portrait of an ass in English fiction.[2] Like Chaucer's Sir Thopas he rides forth to seek the elf-queen, for no other woman is worthy to be his wife. For a time he thinks he has found her in Clara Middleton, who has engaged herself to him, only to discover, when she knows him better, that it would kill her to live with him. Sir Willoughby wants the perfect union; Clara must pledge her word that she is his forever; death itself could make no difference. So far as Sir Willoughby knows, all this is sheer idealism on his part.

When at last he must release the girl, he releases her on a condition. If she will not wed him, then she must wed his kinsman, Whitford Vernon, for Willoughby feels responsible for Clara even though she is not to be his wife. What he has completely failed to perceive is that Clara and Whitford Vernon have been in love with each other for some time.

For himself, Willoughby is compelled to fall back on a woman he had previously jilted, Laetitia Dale. But this time he gets a Laetitia whose eyes are opened and who sees him as he is.

As might be inferred from this discussion of *The Egoist,* comedy is Meredith's favorite weapon in his war against egoism, sentimentalism and all their brood. "Man is the laughing animal; and at the end of an infinite search, the philosopher finds himself clinging to laughter as the best of human fruit, purely human, and sane, and comforting."

Stuart Sherman found the right phrase when he said that for Meredith the Comic Spirit was "a fine celestial sunlight in the mind, answering to the theological Grace of God in the heart." Meredith himself has set forth his views importantly in the *Essay on Comedy,* in the Prelude to *The Egoist,* and in "An Ode to the Comic Spirit."

Ever since Aristotle men have believed that it was the function of tragedy to purge the mind through pity and terror. If that is true, then it is the function of comedy—that "sword of the common

[2] In "*The Egoist* and the Willow Pattern," *ELH,* IX (1942), 71-78, Robert D. Mayo shows that Sir Willoughby Patterne's name comes from the Willow Pattern, "the most popular single design ever to be employed on English earthenware," and that his plight was suggested by the legend connected with it.

sense"—to "touch and kindle the mind through laughter." To Meredith as to Molière comedy is a great social force, a means of purging man of unsocial vices, and making it possible for him to live with his fellow men. A sense of humor could have saved Sir Willoughby Patterne. A sense of humor could even have saved Sir Austin Feverel, who tried to imprison his son in a system and only succeeded in wrecking the boy's life. "A good wind of laughter had relieved him of much of the blight of self-deception, and oddness, and extravagance; had given him a healthier view of our atmosphere of life; but he had it not."

It should be made clear, however, that Meredith is a humorist, not a satirist. "The satirist is a moral agent, often a social scavenger, working on a storage of bile." "You may estimate your capacity for comic perception by being able to detect the ridicule of them you love without loving them less, and more by being able to see yourself somewhat ridiculous to dear eyes, and accepting the correction of their image of you." "To love Comedy you must know the real world, and know men and women well enough not to expect too much of them. . . ." "If you laugh all round your victim, deal him a smack, and drop a tear on him, own his likeness to you and yours to your neighbor, spare him as little as you shun, pity him as much as you expose, it is a spirit of Humour that is moving you." So we are asked to "consider" even Sir Willoughby "indulgently." And Stevenson tells of the young man who came to reproach Meredith with having put him in a book. "Willoughby is me!" "No, my dear fellow," said the novelist; "he is all of us."

Both Meredith's attitude toward nature and his interest in social comedy prepare us for the large part which women play in his books. "Where a veil is over women's faces, you cannot have society."

In life, Meredith was a "feminist"; he believed that

> women of the independent mind are needed for any sensible degree of progress. They will so educate their daughters, that these will not be instructed at the start to think themselves naturally inferior to men because less muscular, and need not have recourse to particular arts, feline chiefly, to make their way in the world.

Being less muscular, woman obviously cannot win her battle against man by brute force; she is thrown back, therefore, upon her humor and her common sense. Here her position is very strong, for she is temperamentally much less inclined to ride Hippogriff than is man. She is closer to earth than he, less theory-ridden, less "idealistic." In love particularly she is more likely both to forget self and to keep her feet firmly on the ground.

The "ordeal" gets into the title of only one of Meredith's books, but it gets into the action of nearly all of them. Through his ordeal man proves his worth or fails to prove it; only thus can he change from "the happy bubbling fool" to "the philosopher who has come to know himself and his relations towards the universe." Again and again this ordeal comes through a woman. One of Storm Jameson's books is called *Women Against Men.* Meredith might have made *Women Against Men* the title of his collected works.

Between his faithlessness and the shame that follows—one part repentance and three parts pride—Richard Feverel nearly kills Lucy; he finishes the job when he gives way to the quixotism of which a Meredithian hero is never free for long by fighting Lord Mountfalcon. Wilfrid Pole loses Emilia because while he finds no difficulty in pledging himself to eternity, he shrinks from eleven o'clock the following morning. Edward Blancove betrays Dahlia Fleming, and is spurned by her as Lovelace was by Clarissa once he has awakened to her true worth. Beauchamp frees himself from his romantic attachment to Renée and offers himself to his true mate, Cecilia, only after she has accepted another man. Alvan might have had Clotilde had he taken her in the proud moment of her passionate surrender, but he was too great a man to make a runaway match. Lord Ormont loses his Aminta because he used her to feed his grudge against society. Victor Radnor sacrificed Nataly on the altar of his own worldliness. Fleetwood waited too long to right the wrong he had done Carinthia Jane. All in all, it is a pretty dismal record for a man to read.

For the female of the species, Meredith may well be more exhilarating, especially when the distinction of many of his heroines is taken into account. His types are varied—nor is his success uniform—but his womanly ideal, which is as far removed from prurience as from febrile decadence, is certainly one of the finest tributes ever paid the sex in the frame of art.

There are fine young English girls like Lucy Feverel and Rose Jocelyn—"If before others his eyes brought the blood to her cheeks, she would perhaps drop her eye-lids an instant, and then glance quickly level again to reassure him." There are exotic creatures, with something of an idyllic dream-quality about them, like the French Renée or the fairy tale princess, Ottilia, in her enchanted German forest. There is Kiomi, the gypsy-girl, who stands alone. There are women like Emilia and Rhoda Fleming, who are built on a vaster scale than any of these. Both have their roots in the soil. Rhoda is content with the integrity of growing things—a girl of wind and sun and earth. Emilia branches out toward artistic development and unselfish devotion to an impersonal ideal. There is Clara Middleton, the "rogue in porcelain," through whom the arch-egoist meets his match. There is Nataly, who lives beyond the bounds of conventional morality yet keeps herself unsmirched. There is the brilliant Diana, contaminated by the world perhaps, yet holding the reader's sympathy even when she loses his credence.

4. *A Difficult Form*

All this might have been done within the conventional framework of the Victorian novel. It was not.

It is a mistake to suppose that Meredith knew no influence from his predecessors. Shakespeare's influence appears in more than the "Ferdinand and Miranda" chapter of *Feverel.* Meredith admired Fielding. His early books are full of Dickensian grotesques, generally badly handled. Both *Clarissa* and *The Mill on the Floss* are reflected in *Rhoda Fleming;* Dr. Able sees Thackeray's *Barry Lyndon* in such characters as Richmond Roy, Old Mel, and the Countess de Saldar. More important than any of these was Meredith's father-in-law, Thomas Love Peacock, who anticipated a number of his themes and specific convictions.[3]

Yet he was one of the most original of writers. What he did was done deliberately. "The forecast may be hazarded that, if we do

[3] Cf. A. H. Able, III, *George Meredith and Thomas Love Peacock, A Study in Literary Influence,* University of Pennsylvania, 1933.

not speedily embrace philosophy in fiction, the Art is doomed to extinction under the shining multitude of its professors." As early as *Feverel,* he condemns "an audience impatient for blood and glory." The Philosopher whom he whimsically describes as collaborating with him in *Sandra Belloni* "maintains that a story should not always flow, or, at least not to a given measure." He is as much interested in the thoughts of his characters as in their emotions, but he insists on presenting them in action rather than in repose. "My method," he wrote in 1887, "has been to prepare my readers for a crucial exhibition of the personae, and then to give the scene in the fullest of the blood and brain under stress of a fiery situation."

The difficulty is that sometimes he does not prepare. He longed for an audience which would "feel the winds of March when they do not blow," which is perhaps not quite a reasonable demand. As a narrator he stands, among English novelists, at the opposite end of the scale from Defoe. If it be a pardonable exaggeration to say that Defoe is all narrative, then one may also say of Meredith that he has no interest in narrative and no gift for it. This is what that often surprisingly just and acute critic, Oscar Wilde, had in mind when he remarked that Meredith could do everything except tell a story.

As a narrator he never seems to know what to "develop." He may labor an unimportant point through pages and pages, and then pass over a vital crisis with a phrase. The central situation in *Rhoda Fleming* is poignant but it fails to move us as it should because, for fatally long periods, the author keeps the principals out of sight, while the foreground is occupied with minor characters like Algernon Blancove and Mrs. Lovell. Elaborate preparations are made in this novel for the meeting between Rhoda and her sister Dahlia. When at last it occurs, it takes place between chapters!

We follow Emilia through two long novels to find out whether she will wed Merthyr Powys or not, but when the last page of *Vittoria* has been turned, we still do not know. Much of *Beauchamp's Career* is given over to the hero's attempt to force his uncle to apologize to Dr. Shrapnel for having beaten him—which is surely a minor incident either in Beauchamp's "career" or in his life—while his marriage and death, for no particular reason, by drowning, are both crowded into the last two chapters.

Perhaps the real difficulty in such instances is not that Meredith goes too far but that he does not go far enough. Possibly, having broken away from so many elements in the Victorian novel, he ought to have broken away from one more—the plot. His plots have the unbelievable complexity of a Congreve comedy; and they are no easier to follow because, unlike Congreve, he presents them indirectly. As J. B. Priestley points out, there is no "middle distance" in his fiction. "Either we see his people as little puppets illuminated by lightning flashes of wit, or we are almost inside their minds, swayed hither and thither by their lightest emotions." At times they really are puppets, for Meredith is not incapable of violating the integrity of a characterization to serve the needs of a "theme" or a plot. Few readers are convinced that Richard Feverel really would have stayed away from Lucy—it was on this ground that Brownell dismissed *The Ordeal* as "sophisticated melodrama"—and few are convinced that Diana would have sold the secret.

The difficulties of Meredith's narrative art are only reinforced by the difficulties of his style. "Our language," he says, "is not rich in subleties for prose. A writer who is not servile and has insight, must coin from his own mint." He was not servile; there can be no question that he coined.

"It was an evening of incessant talking," so we read in *Harry Richmond;* "no telling of events straightforwardly, but all by fits—all here and there." There are times when Meredith as a stylist seems to have taken the advice of the Countess de Saldar: "Yes, dear Van!" she told her brother, "that is how you should behave. Imply things." And there are times when his readers seem prefigured in Wilfrid Pole shaking his head over Adela's letter: "Why doesn't she write plain to the sense?" he asks, but, having pondered the postscript, he begins to see "meanings in the simple passages, and none at all in the intricate ones; and the double meanings were monsters that ate one another up till nothing remained of them."

Sometimes, to be sure, Meredith only makes us the dupes of our own stupidity, and then we have no right to complain. The following passage from *Beauchamp's Career* is often cited as an example of his implicational style; all the essential clues are there:

> Captain Baskelett requested the favor of five minutes of conversation with Miss Halkett before he followed Mr. Austin on his way to Steynham. She returned from the colloquy to her father and Mr. Tuckham. The colonel looked straight in her face, with an elevation of the brows. To these points of interrogation she answered with a placid fall of her eyelids. He sounded a note of approbation in his throat.

We are to understand that Captain Baskelett has proposed marriage, has been rejected, and that the colonel approves.

But Meredith is not always as clear as this. And there are passages which are ineffective not because they are obscure but because they are affected and absurd. His women never walk; they swim; Diana swims to the tea-tray. The Countess de Saldar "rambles concentrically." Dahlia "eyes" Edward a "faint sweetness." When Sir Willoughby would embrace Clara, "the gulf of a caress hove in view like an enormous billow hollowing under the curled ridge. She stooped to a buttercup, the monster swept by."

5. *What Remains*

It was a tragedy—for Meredith and for his readers. Here is one of the finest minds that ever devoted itself to English fiction. Here is a writer who, in his fashion, achieved a solution of half the problems which beset the modern mind before very many people knew that they existed. Here is a thinker who, whether one accepts all the implications of his philosophy or not, did have something to say to his age in terms which that age ought to have been able to understand; yet because he was unable or unwilling to make himself clear to his contemporaries, he has never reached—and he never will reach—more than a fraction of his potential audience.

Henley said of Meredith that he preferred his cleverness to his genius; Brownell declares, "He does not love the obscure, but hates the apparent." Meredith seems to have been a man who could not bear to say even obvious things in an obvious manner; a visitor at Box Hill has recorded being invited to "lave" his hands before lunch. Unfortunately one cannot write a novel without saying a good many obvious things. And when they are not said obviously they are said badly.

It is impossible to read Meredith without noticing these things, but it would be a mistake to blame him for them. With him, as with all great writers, the style is the man. Katherinc Mansfield was perfectly correct when she perceived that she must change her Self before she could change her work. But Meredith lacked Katherine Mansfield's divine humility.

This is not to deny that he lived impressively. That tragic first marriage seems so little calculated to have groomed him either for the success of the second or for the magnificent tribute to womanhood which is the body of his fiction that there are times when one feels it might not be too Freudian to see in the latter achievement an offering of atonement to the poor ghost of Mary Ellen Peacock. Meredith seems very successfully to have freed himself of sentimentality; it would be too much to say that he freed himself either of egoism or of intellectual snobbery. He was estranged, in turn, from his father, his wife, and his son; he was so ashamed of his origin that he refused even to give the census-taker the name of his birthplace.

Temperamentally, Meredith was an extraordinary combination of pride and charity; the Moravian brothers taught him the long view but they did not teach him to crucify himself. Intellectually he nearly always gets the thing right; he will not judge even those of whom he most emphatically disapproves. But one feels that he would have made no particular effort to get on with them.

There is an element of self-castigation in his fiction. Sir Austin Feverel fails with his wife and child in something the manner that Meredith himself failed; and at the very time he was concealing the facts of his origin he revealed them as fiction in *Evan Harrington,* and in such detail that he made all his relatives squirm. If Thackeray, historian of snobbery, was himself a snob, why could not Meredith, authority on egoism, be an egoist himself? Especially since he himself declared that Willoughby was all of us?

Take such a man, with a natural dislike of banality and a natural tendency toward indirection (whether fostered positively by his Celtic blood and German schooling, or negatively by his lack of a sound English university training is not very important); subject him for years to consistent neglect as a writer (and we have positive evidence that Meredith smarted under that neglect and actively resented it); then bring him, in his later years, into widespread fame; and it is inevitable that he should indulge himself somewhat. In his early years, his head bloody but unbowed, he refused to cringe to you. In his mastery, by the lord Harry, he will make you cringe to him!

It is too bad that he was not able to rise above all this, but we who are human will understand only too well why he did not. And however he may try our patience, we can neglect him only at our peril. He was no poseur. Even those who are most annoyed by his idiosyncrasies find his work persistently coming back to them, long after they had imagined they were done with him. He has vitality despite all his indirection; a profound sincerity underlies his innumerable flourishes. In some inexplicable way, his pages seem curiously flooded with light.

CHAPTER XX

HARDY AND THE COSMIC DRAMA *

> Oh Thou, who Man of Baser Earth didst make,
> And ev'n with Paradise devise the Snake,
> For all the Sin wherewith the Face of Man
> Is blackened—Man's forgiveness give—and take!
>
> *The Rubáiyát of Omar Khayyám*

1. *Inheritor of Old Renown*

When Tess Durbeyfield and her mother were together, Thomas Hardy tells us, "the Jacobean and the Victorian ages were juxtaposed." In his novels the juxtaposition reaches even farther.

There is no trace in Hardy of Meredith's implicational style. There is no avoidance of plot or of sensationalism. He had no truck with his continental peers; even *Jude the Obscure,* as he himself points out, owes more to Fielding than to Zola. Technically he is a very old-fashioned writer.

In Hardy's expression is a curious combination of clumsiness and power; even as a poet he had a rugged horror of technical "perfection." A master of irony, he rejected no effect as too obvious. When Angel Clare goes home just after having learned of Tess's past, the family Scripture reading must needs be the Proverbist's praise of the virtuous wife; when Sue finds her children murdered, the organ in the neighboring chapel must choose that moment to play "Truly God is loving unto Israel." Arabella Donn's method of attracting Jude's attention strikes the keynote of her character unerringly, but the "property" employed is so broad that it would be more at home in the comic strip than in a serious novel.

* The quotations in this chapter from Hardy's *The Return of the Native* are made with the permission of The Macmillan Company; those from *Tess of the D'Urbervilles* and *Jude the Obscure* with the permission of Harper and Brothers.

Towards the end of his long life Hardy was often called the last of the Victorians. With almost equal propriety he might have been named the last of the Elizabethans. Every reader notices the resemblance between Hardy's rustics and Shakespeare's—there is the same earthiness and the same touch of poetry—but this is by no means Hardy's only Elizabethan note.[1] His melodrama is Elizabethan, his occasional neglect of careful motivation, his free use of coincidence and of comic relief, his love of contrast and incongruity. When his plots are summarized they sound ridiculous, like those of many Elizabethan tragedies, or like that of *Wuthering Heights,* which alone, except for Hardy, achieves among Victorian novels a cosmic outlook, but which the author of *Jude the Obscure* would never read because he had heard it was depressing!

I do not mean, of course, that all the hackneyed plot-devices Hardy employs are specifically Elizabethan. I certainly do not mean that he must have taken them direct from the Elizabethans. Many of them are very definitely the kind of Victorianism we find in Wilkie Collins, whom Hardy read with avidity and who influenced not only his first published novel, *Desperate Remedies,* but his whole conception of fiction. He loved Ainsworth also and G. P. R. James. But the point is that all these things descended to the Victorians from the Elizabethans and remoter ancestors in an unbroken line. And it was from these very aspects of the native tradition that the "advanced," the "intellectual," the "psychological" novelists of Hardy's time were trying very hard to break away.

It must be made clear, however, that I am not reproaching Hardy for any of these things. I am simply concerned to establish a fact and a contrast. Jacques Barzun has recently pointed out that when we berate Hardy for the large role he gives chance in his books we simply prove that we have not grasped his conception of the nature of the world:

[1] For Hardy's familiarity with Shakespeare, cf. *Shakespeare Association Bulletin,* IX (1934), 91-97, 162-163; XIII (1938), 87-95. M. L. Anderson, "Hardy's Debt to Webster in *The Return of the Native,*" *Modern Language Notes,* LIV (1939), 497-501, shows that the quarrel between Clym and Eustacia goes back to an original in *The White Devil.*

The truth is, we blame Hardy for failing to show adequate cause when the lack of adequate cause is what Hardy is trying to show. From beginning to end, Hardy seeks to make it plain that whereas human beings are aware of their wills and designs, the nature of inanimate things is unconscious and undesigning. The motives of human beings are therefore intelligible, because we are human ourselves; but the falling out of events is not intelligible, because the world of matter is not consciously organized.

In another article in the same valuable symposium which takes in Barzun's discussion,[2] Donald Davidson shows in masterly fashion that Hardy's art rests finally on a traditional basis. He is full of the stuff of popular balladry because he grew up in an environment in which ballad materials were vitally alive, "where fiction was a tale told or sung." When he tried to be "literary"—as in *The Hand of Ethelberta* or *A Laodicean*—he failed. Tradition was far more important than iconoclasm in Hardy, and Professor Davidson has no difficulty in showing that what prudish Victorians thought of as his grossness, and even what misinformed intellectuals still call his pessimism both have their roots in the old world of folk art, folk morality, and folk belief.

Yet, of course, his novels mark important departures. It was always difficult for those meeting Thomas Hardy to connect this preternaturally kindly little man, conservative in his ways, deeply reverent in his spirit, with the "blasphemer" of *Jude* and many of the poems. And it is difficult for us to remember how much dynamite he packed into his story of the "ruined" girl when, looking over the Table of Contents in *Tess of the D'Urbervilles,* preliminary to our first reading, we find that the first division is entitled "The Maiden," the second "Maiden No More," and the fifth, actually, "The Woman Pays"! If ever a man poured new wine into old bottles it was Hardy. And, incidentally, so long as our young intellectuals sit up nights to read his books while they leave Meredith undisturbed upon the shelf, it will be difficult to believe that they love subtlety and hate melodrama quite so much as they profess.

[2] The Summer, 1940 issue of *The Southern Review,* which is devoted entirely to Hardy.

2. *The Historian of Wessex*

Thomas Hardy was born, June 2, 1840, in Dorsetshire, in the heart of the region he was to immortalize as Wessex,[3] an Old English name as eminently suited to his Saxon genius as that which he himself bore. His father, a building contractor, intended him for the church. Both his father and his grandfather played in the church orchestra and at rural festivals. The orchestra itself was gone by Hardy's time, but he entered as fully as possible into the spirit of the ancient ways. Thus he came to know the people of the countryside intimately, and thus he prepared himself to write *Under the Greenwood Tree.*

The threatened invasion of Napoleon, at the beginning of the century, was still within living memory in the Southern counties, and Hardy heard about it from early childhood. Here is the seed not only of *The Trumpet-Major* (into which he introduced his relative, Captain Thomas Hardy, commander of Lord Nelson's flagship at Trafalgar), but also of the vast conception afterwards developed in the great epic-drama, *The Dynasts.* And the remains of Roman civilization still conspicuous in the country carried him many centuries farther back.

Hardy did not go into the church; instead he became an ecclesiastical architect. Independently he was developing other interests. With his fellow-apprentices he studied Latin and Greek. He attended evening classes at the University of London. He became interested in painting and the theater. He began writing verses under the guidance of the Dorsetshire poet, William Barnes.

Critics have made much of the effect of Hardy's architectural training upon his work. The classical passage is that of Lascelles Abercrombie:

> In the great building, which fancy easily sees Hardy's several books uniting to shape, the pillared nave would be the series of the six principal novels [*Far from the Madding Crowd, The Mayor of Casterbridge,*

[3] "A province bounded on the north by the Thames, on the south by the English Channel, on the east by a line running from Hayling Island to Windsor Forest, and on the West by the Cornish Coast."—General Preface to Anniversary Edition. Cf. also Preface to *Far from the Madding Crowd.*

The Return of the Native, The Woodlanders, Tess of the D'Urbervilles, Jude the Obscure]; unless the last two of them should be seen as transepts, since each of these is large enough to stand somewhat by itself. *Under the Greenwood Tree* might be the porch or antechapel; and certainly *The Dynasts* must be the quire, a place, as sometimes happens, of loftier proportions, more intricate carving and more varied material than the nave through which it is approached. This is the main building; but round about, though not separate, supporting but not intimately concerned in the chief composition of the building, there are, like side-chapels and miscellaneous recesses, the poems, the short stories,[4] and two other novels [*Two on a Tower, The Trumpet-Major*].[5]

That all this is somewhat fanciful Abercrombie was well aware. Hardy himself had little sympathy with those who attempted to connect his early profession with his art. It is clear that his work as an architect affected his writing. But it affected his writing first of all as his music did, by drawing him closer and deeper into the spirit of Wessex.

For it must be remembered, as Joseph Warren Beach once remarked, that Wessex is no mere "physical background" but "an economic order, a social order" as well. Hardy wrote of Wessex because life brought him Wessex; this was the thing he knew best. But he is never a "regionalist." He does not exploit local peculiarities. His interest is not in what is peculiar to Wessex but in what there is in Wessex that illuminates universal values. In his own words, he wished to show that in out-of-the-way places "dramas of a grandeur and unity truly Sophoclean are enacted in the real, by virtue of the concentrated passions and closely-knit interdependence of the lives therein."

Hardy gave twenty-five years to fiction. Before 1870 and after 1895 he concerned himself entirely with poetry. Economic considerations

[4] Collected in *Wessex Tales* (1888); *A Group of Noble Dames* (1891); *Life's Little Ironies* (1894); *A Changed Man and Other Stories* (1913).

[5] *Thomas Hardy, A Critical Study* (Viking Press), p. 77; cf. p. 49, pp. 90-91. Abercrombie also attempts to interpret the relationships between Hardy's characters in terms of algebraic formulas (p. 111). Duffin (*Thomas Hardy*, pp. 99-101) and others prefer to use geometrical figures for this purpose. Carl J. Weber, "Chronology in Hardy's Novels," *PMLA*, LIII (1938), 314-320, would credit Hardy's careful treatment of chronology to his training as an architect. For further discussion of Hardy's chronology, see *PMLA*, LIV (1939), 618-620; *Modern Language Notes*, LIV (1939), 491-501.

inclined him toward the novel after he had become engaged to Emma Gifford;[6] the unfavorable reception of *Jude the Obscure* was the immediate reason why he abandoned fiction when he did. His first novel, *The Poor Man and the Lady,* was rejected by Macmillan and by George Meredith as reader for Chapman and Hall.[7] Meredith told him he needed more plot: he wrote *Desperate Remedies.* John Morley liked the rustic scenes; he wrote *Under the Greenwood Tree.*

During his later years, everybody except George Moore [8] regarded Hardy as the grand old man of English letters. This was partly because his ideas had come to seem less shocking with the passing of time, partly because people were now increasingly disposed to allow a distinguished writer to express his view of life even when they did not agree with him, and partly because the sweetness of Hardy's own spirit had won him so many friends. He received the Order of Merit, the gold medal of the Royal Society of Literature, and many honorary degrees. He died at Max Gate, January 11, 1928.

3. *Three Groups of Novels*

Hardy classified his novels under three heads:

I. NOVELS OF INGENUITY. *Desperate Remedies* (1871); *The Hand of Ethelberta* (1876); *A Laodicean* (1881).

II. ROMANCES AND FANTASIES. *A Pair of Blue Eyes* (1873); *The Trumpet-Major* (1880); *Two on a Tower* (1882); *The Well-Beloved* (1892, 1897).

[6] For the first Mrs. Hardy, who was something of a tartar, see Carl J. Weber's *Hardy of Wessex.* After her death at seventy-two, her husband wrote: "In spite of the differences between us, which it would be affectation to deny, and certain painful delusions she suffered from at times, my life is intensely sad to me now without her."

[7] There is reason to believe that it survives in part in *An Indiscretion in the Life of an Heiress,* published in the *New Quarterly Magazine* in 1878, but quite forgotten for many years, and in part in Hardy's published novels. See Carl J. Weber's edition of the *Indiscretion* (Johns Hopkins University Press, 1935) and W. R. Rutland's discussion in *Thomas Hardy, A Study of His Writings and Their Background,* Chapter IV.

[8] Hatred of Hardy was a mania with Moore. Cf. his *Conversations in Ebury Street* (Boni, 1924) and Middleton Murry's slashing rejoinder, *Wrap Me Up in My Aubusson Carpet* (Greenberg, 1924).

III. Novels of Character and Environment. *Under the Greenwood Tree* (1872); *Far from the Madding Crowd* (1874); *The Return of the Native* (1878); *The Mayor of Casterbridge* (1886); *The Woodlanders* (1887); *Tess of the D'Urbervilles* (1891); *Jude the Obscure* (1895).

The books in the first group call for little comment. *Desperate Remedies* is an intricate country-house melodrama, *The Hand of Ethelberta,* a "somewhat frivolous narrative" of social climbing and matchmaking. Criticism of *A Laodicean* is disarmed by the fact that Hardy dictated it during a severe illness to keep faith with his editor, and afterwards let it stand to "help while away an idle afternoon of the comfortable ones whose lines have fallen to them in pleasant places."

Of the three books, *Desperate Remedies* is probably the most important. Despite all its sensationalism it is the work of a poet, of a reflective mind—note Manston's reflections on death in Chapter 21. Virginia Woolf points out that, as prophetic of Hardy's later treatment of nature, it has the sound of a waterfall booming and echoing through it.

Of the "Romances and Fantasies," *A Pair of Blue Eyes* and *Two on a Tower* are typical of Hardy, while *The Trumpet-Major* and *The Well-Beloved* are not.

The Trumpet-Major is generally called Hardy's only historical novel. Actually, as Professor Weber has shown, Hardy's novels cover almost the entire nineteenth century.[9] But *The Trumpet-Major* is set farther back in time than any of the others, and its spirit is closer to what we ordinarily think of as the historical romance. It is a thoroughly delightful book. Some readers may have to gulp to get down the broadly farcical Festus Derriman, and even the titular hero, who sacrifices himself for his brother, seems a bit too good to be true. But no male reader ever has any trouble with Anne Garland, thoroughly conventional heroine though she is! The subject of *The Well-Beloved,* a Shelleyan fantasy, obviously and avowedly Platonic in its inspiration, whose hero seeks his ideal first in Avice Caro, then in her daughter, and finally in her granddaughter, hardly seems well adapted to prose fiction.

[9] Carl J. Weber, *Hardy of Wessex.* p. 182.

A Pair of Blue Eyes was the first Hardy novel young William Lyon Phelps ever read. Unaware of the bitter irony concealed in that innocent-sounding title, he read on absorbedly, sure that the author would finally bring things out "right." When he came to the end—that bitter, brutal, cynical end, in which both Elfride's lovers, traveling down into the country to "forgive" her, find themselves riding on the same train which carries her corpse for burial, he threw the book across the room, took to his bed and stayed there for a week.[10] *A Pair of Blue Eyes* is a study, first, of the weakness of a girl, then, of the egotism of a man. Knight is like Meredith's quixotic heroes in his tragic demand that his bride must come to him untouched. Elfride herself is Hardy's first study of the vacillating feminine temperament, a work of rich promise rather than real achievement. Like Bathsheba Everdene, Viviette Constantine, Eustacia Vye, and others, Elfride brings to mind some of Ibsen's heroines; the resemblance is strengthened by the stilted dialogue—astonishingly like that in William Archer's translation of Ibsen—which Hardy sometimes employs—and occasionally, as in *Two on a Tower,* by symbolism. This novel is a troubled love story about a young astronomer and his older benefactress. It does not always steer clear of absurdity—there is no sense, for example, to the secret marriage—but the way in which the tortured human drama is set against the passionless serenity of the stars is impressive. Not until *Memoirs of a Midget* was astronomy again to be used so suggestively in English fiction.

4. *The Real Achievement*

We have come now to the third group, and to Hardy's real achievement. It began with *Under the Greenwood Tree,* which, as he himself says, was penned "so lightly, even so flippantly at times." The situation between Fancy Day and her lovers might so very easily have ended in tragedy. But happily it does not. I have spoken of *A Pair of Blue Eyes* as a work of promise. *Under the Greenwood Tree* is not a work of promise. It is the thing itself.

But precisely for that reason, having done it, Hardy must now go

[10] William Lyon Phelps, *Autobiography with Letters* (Oxford University Press, 1939), Ch. 38.

off in another direction, digging more profoundly into the human drama. It was with this that he was experimenting in *A Pair of Blue Eyes*. And it is this that he first achieves completely in *Far from the Madding Crowd*.

When *Far from the Madding Crowd* was serialized in the *Cornhill Magazine* it was widely attributed to George Eliot, though totally unlike her in style, because no other novelist in England was believed good enough to have written it. Professor Beach has remarked that the characters are "conceived in the large grave manner of Scripture pastorals," their very names combining Biblical and rustic associations. In such an environment—and again his title is ironical—Hardy has placed Bathsheba Everdene, the smoldering, unfulfilled woman, so uncharacteristic of her background, so typical of the modern age.

The heroine of *The Return of the Native,* Eustacia Vye, is of the same sisterhood:

> "I do not deserve my lot!" she cried in a frenzy of bitter revolt. "O, the cruelty of putting me into this ill-conceived world! I was capable of much; but I have been injured and blighted and crushed by things beyond my control! O, how hard it is of Heaven to devise such tortures for me, who have done no harm to Heaven at all!"

Her husband, Clym Yeobright, who has known the "civilization" she craves and deliberately rejected it, finds a measure of contentment at last, despite the tragedies that have ravaged his life; and so do Thomasin and Diggory Venn, who are almost a part of the Heath, who have, at least, never rebelled against it.

But the "happy ending" for these two was no part of the original plan; it was added at the insistence of the serial editor. The extent to which Hardy was willing to go in bowdlerizing and mutilating his novels in their serial versions is one of the phenomena of literary history: Tess kills Alec D'Urberville for no particular reason, and Angel Clare is not permitted to carry the dairy girls across the stream in his arms, he must use a wheelbarrow.[11] The change at the end of *The Return of the Native* is the happy exception to all

[11] See Rutland, *Thomas Hardy, A Study of His Writings and Their Background* and Mary Ellen Chase, *Thomas Hardy From Serial to Novel* (University of Minnesota Press, 1927).

this, and Hardy did well to retain it permanently. To have Thomasin and Diggory escape the general doom not only prevents our feeling, as we sometimes do with Hardy, that he has loaded the dice against his puppets, but their fate reinforces the dominant idea of the book, that he who makes terms with the Heath shall live.

Egdon Heath is the real hero of *The Return of the Native.* This dynamic use of scene to determine the lives of the characters—a thing only hitherto suggested, here and there, in English fiction [12]—is technically the most interesting thing in the book.

> The first chapter, "A Face On Which Time Makes But Little Impression" [write Helen and Wilson Follett], raises a curtain on some mighty drama presently to be enacted in shadow. The opening is one of those stupendous effects of mood which can only be compared to such things as the first scene of *Hamlet* or the Prelude to *Tristan und Isolde.*

It is not only in *The Return of the Native* that Hardy uses scene in this manner, though no doubt *The Return of the Native* is the star example. The picture of night among the stars at the beginning of *Far from the Madding Crowd* is very wonderful, and Tess of the D'Urbervilles is never detached from her background. "On these lonely hills and dales her quiescent glide was of a piece with the element she moved in. Her flexuous and stealthy figure became an integral part of the scene." Her surroundings and her activities alike reflect and intensify the deepening emotional overtones of the story, as unerringly and as dramatically as the rising and falling fortunes of Joan of Arc are illuminated in the changing colors of the famous Boutet de Monvel pictures. In a rather different fashion, the horror of *Jude* is strongly accentuated by the deliberate ugliness of its settings.

Sometimes Hardy builds up his scene from its geological foundations, as in the famous cliff passage in *A Pair of Blue Eyes.* He never sentimentalizes nature. It is our "womb" and our "tomb," as Gardner says, our "nurse" and our "destroyer." In *The Woodlanders* the internecine warfare of the forest trees is powerfully imaged.

Between *The Return of the Native* and *Tess of the D'Urbervilles*

[12] As in *Wuthering Heights* and portions of *The Mill on the Floss.* In the drama, there are, of course, the heath scenes in *King Lear.*

—which is the *Native's* only possible rival as Hardy's greatest novel —two other books intervened. These are *The Mayor of Casterbridge* and *The Woodlanders.*

The Mayor of Casterbridge foreshadowed the tendency developed more strongly in the last two novels to concentrate attention on one leading figure, rather than to divide it among a group of characters arranged in relation to each other in terms of an almost formal symmetry, a practice which had tended to prevail up to this time. It has a smashing beginning. Michael Henchard, drunk and careless, sells his wife and children at a fair; eighteen years pass, and he is reintroduced as a prosperous, influential man, the mayor of Casterbridge.

We are at once reminded of *King Lear,* where the climax takes place in the opening scene, and everything that happens to Lear thereafter finds its place in a long falling action. Since Hardy himself is on record as having placed the climax of the book in Chapter 31, he was probably not trying to develop it on the *Lear* pattern;[13] if he was, he can hardly be said to have made out an entirely convincing case. If, on the other hand, he was simply trying to show how the same unfortunate weaknesses in Michael's character that led to his early (and bitterly repented) sin must also lead him into other errors that should destroy him in the end, he may be said to have succeeded. The spectacular beginning seems unrealistic to modern readers, though Hardy himself declares that such occurrences were not unknown in Wessex. The question is, in any case, unimportant. Hardy believed—and we have seen that it was a necessary corollary of his whole conception of life and art that he must believe—that "it is not improbabilities of incident but improbabilities of character that matter." We do not stop to argue about whether or not Lear would divide his kingdom; we accept so much as given and expect the dramatist to work out his situation convincingly from that point.

The Woodlanders combines rustic humor and much out-of-the-way information on woodland customs with a study of marriage.

[13] W. H. Gardner, *Some Thoughts on The Mayor of Casterbridge,* English Association Pamphlet, No. 77 (1930), pp. 27-29, has a detailed comparison between *Lear* and Hardy's novel.

And here, for the first time, Hardy goes in for social, as distinct from cosmic, criticism. When George Melbury finds that his daughter is married to an unfaithful husband a very interesting thing happens, a thing highly symptomatic of what was happening both to English life and the English novel. He begins to question the established morality. "He knew that a woman once given to a man for life took, as a rule, her lot as it came, and made the best of it, without external interference; but for the first time he asked himself why this so generally should be done." But the ending is hardly iconoclastic. Generally in pre-divorce-age fiction, unwanted husbands (or wives) are very kind about dying. In *The Woodlanders* Dr. Fitzpiers refuses to die. Instead (and this is typical Hardyan irony), Grace's lover dies! *The Woodlanders* is a very uneven book. But one character, Marty South, stands on Hardy's highest level, and though Marty advances the action only when she sells her hair to Mrs. Charmond, she is permitted to open and close the book in an atmosphere of high dignity and passion:

> "Now, my own, own love," she whispered, "you are mine, and only mine; for she has forgot 'ee at last, although for her you died! But I—whenever I get up I'll think of 'ee, and whenever I lie down I'll think of 'ee again. Whenever I plant the young larches I'll think that none can plant as you planted; and whenever I split a gad, and whenever I turn the cider wring, I'll say none could do it like you. If ever I forget your name let me forget home and heaven! . . . But no, no, my love, I never can forget 'ee; for you was a good man, and did good things!"

We have left now but *Tess* and *Jude*. If individual characterization is the great thing in fiction, then *Tess* must bear the palm from the *Native,* for there is nothing in the earlier book to match the living, breathing woman we meet here. In general Hardy is not memorable as a creator of individual character. His rustics, in some ways his most wonderful creations, we think of as a community rather than as individuals; of his characters in general it may be said that they have renounced the individual idiosyncrasy in which so much of the glory of English fiction resides, to become instead the embodiments of different aspects of the human soul as it faces the mysteries of life and death. It is interesting to note that ten years before *Jude* Hardy was already speculating on the possibility of "rendering as visible essences, spectres, etc., the abstract thoughts of the analytic school." The last two novels, then, mark a temporary departure from his characteristic method, and *The Dynasts* was the logical consummation of it.

It is not Alec D'Urberville who destroys Tess; life is strong in her; she recovers from that wound. Her destroyer is the "pure" Angel Clare, who because he has lost touch with the good gross earth—(" 'Tis Nature, after all, and what do please God," says Mrs. Durbeyfield, when she learns that her daughter is no longer a virgin)—without growing into the spirit of Christian forgiveness, finds it impossible to forgive Tess when her "past" is revealed to him. Hardy is hitting the double standard and conventional notions of chastity. "Was once lost always lost really true of chastity? . . . The recuperative power which pervaded organic nature was surely not denied to maidenhood alone." A subordinate idea was to criticize the prudery of the time which kept young people ignorant in matters of sex hygiene, thus putting girls like Tess as completely as possible into the power of men like Alec.

Whether Hardy established his "point" is not very important. It is always difficult to reason from particular instances to general laws. Perhaps Hardy begs the question when he gives Tess so beautiful a character that she cannot possibly be typical of "betrayed" girls—or of any other class. It may even be that the sub-title—"A Pure Woman Faithfully Presented"—was a mistake, not at all because the essential purity of the heroine is not established but because it casts a faintly doctrinaire glimmer over the narrative.

Except at the end, where she kills her betrayer, Tess is a modern Griselda. It is interesting to compare her with the great eighteenth-century heroine of seduction-romance, Clarissa Harlowe. Strictly speaking, as we have already noted in these pages, Clarissa is not seduced; she is kidnaped, drugged, and raped. The manuscript of *Tess of the D'Urbervilles* shows that originally Hardy intended to have Tess drugged also. This has now dropped out, but even as the book stands, the girl is hardly more than half-seduced. Alec takes her in her sleep; it was clearly the author's idea to make her as little responsible as he could.

There is melodrama in the book. Perhaps the killing of Alec is melodrama. It was taken from life, and that which is taken from life often seems exaggerated in art, for no artist's imagining can match the monstrous exaggeration which is life itself. Many readers have doubted Alec's appeal for Tess, many more the possibility of her returning to him. Personally I do not for a moment believe in his conversion, nor yet in the possibility of Tess winning him away from it, when she meets him again, by parroting the skeptical arguments of Angel Clare, which she herself only half understands.[14] In the last analysis, Tess is an old-fashioned heroine in the sense that her life is made and marred by sex. The typical heroine of contemporary fiction may be somewhat freer in her sexual relationships, but they mean less to her; and if love never comes she can still manage to live a happy and fairly useful life.

When Jeannette Gilder finished reading *Jude the Obscure* in 1895, she "opened the windows and let in the fresh air, and I turned to my bookshelves and said: 'Thank God for Kipling and Stevenson, Barrie and Mrs. Humphry Ward. Here are four great writers who have never trailed their talents in the dirt.'"

The usual view today is that Miss Gilder was a fool. She was not. She was absurd and hysterical but she had a point. And most of the readers of her time agreed with her.

Jude represents the climax of Hardy's gloom and determinism. Its sexual frankness, its free-thinking, neurotic heroine (one of the earliest examples in English fiction of the unsettling effects of the new "rationalism" on the minds of young people), and its apparently determined pessimism—even aside from the fact that it contains one of the most unbearable scenes in fiction, these things are enough to account for the popular reaction. Says W. R. Rutland:

> Whether or not these things had in them "cathartic qualities," as Hardy afterwards claimed, it is absurd, when he deliberately did all he could to horrify and outrage his readers, to blame the readers for being outraged and horrified. Their horror should rather have been welcomed, as a tribute.

[14] Varley Lang, *Modern Language Notes,* LIII (1938), 369-370, argues Crabbe's influence on Alec's conversion and relapse.

There seems to have been a strange, tense compulsion upon Hardy when he wrote this book; here alone in his novels the demon of the perverse gets into him.

The climax of horror comes, as all the world knows, when Little Father Time, Jude's son by Arabella—who, according to Hardy, represents "the beginning of the coming universal wish not to live" —kills the two children of Jude and Sue and hangs himself, leaving a note "Done because we are too menny." H. C. Duffin calls this scene Hardy's parallel to the gouging out of Gloucester's eyes. It is a tremendous tragic effect which turns instead to sickening horror, and thus fails to come off. Moreover, it is relieved by no Shakespearean ray of hope; there is no servant to give his life to protect Gloucester, no Emilia to defy the Moor. Hardy keeps such comfort for the close of *The Mayor of Casterbridge,* where there is something very like it in the half-witted Abel Whittle's care for the fallen Henchard. Professor Chew has observed justly that Little Father Time "suffers, among his many other miseries, from the responsibility . . . of being an allegory." This is typical of the doctrinaire quality of the book. Powerful as the novel is, some of the criticism of the "university extension chatter" put into the mouths of Jude and Sue is justified.

For the fundamental problem of *Jude the Obscure* is not sexual; the book begins with the vain efforts of a young stone mason to overthrow English snobbery and make his way in the universities. Two women complicate his problem: Arabella Donn, whom he marries—a creature compared to whom the Wife of Bath was an ascetic—and the brittle Sue Bridehead, who lives with him but will not marry him because she does not believe in marriage.[15] From the point of view of conventionally minded people, Hardy's final disposition of Sue was the most unkindest cut of all. After the death of her children she breaks completely, sees her fate as the sign of God's judgment upon her, and repudiates all her former beliefs. But the ways of the Lord are not justified. The pious reader may,

[15] The full explanation of why Sue refused to marry Jude is not given in the novel because Hardy feared public opinion would not tolerate the open discussion of such matters. Cf. F. E. Hardy, *The Later Years of Thomas Hardy,* p. 42.

if he likes, see in the once confident woman's final phase her redemption from sin, but the author makes it perfectly clear that he sees nothing of the kind. Instead of redemption we have a complete mental and spiritual collapse.

5. *The Question of "Pessimism"*

Most readers of Thomas Hardy are firmly convinced that he was a pessimist. To support this position they muster considerable evidence. In *The Return of the Native* he declares that "the new Vale of Tempe may be a gaunt waste in Thule," that "thought is a disease of flesh," and speculates whether physically beautiful women may not soon come to be as great an anachronism as physically beautiful men are today. When Elizabeth-Jane, of *The Mayor of Casterbridge,* finds happiness at last she wonders at it, her youth having taught her that "happiness was but the occasional episode in a general drama of pain." And when Tess of the D'Urbervilles is hanged, we are told that "the President of the Immortals . . . had ended his sport" with her.

Other passages, though less striking, are perhaps even better evidence because less directly required by the narrative. "Somebody" might have come along to help Jude in his perplexity. "But nobody did come, because nobody does." One may well doubt, too, whether a girl like Tess would be so cosmological as to tell her little brothers and sisters that the reason why things are so bad here is that "we live on a blighted star."

Hardy is not above going out of his way to take a fling at "the ingenious machinery contrived by the Gods for reducing human possibilities of amelioration to a minimum." And in one of his poems he perfectly illustrates the popular definition of a pessimist as a man who blows out the gas to see how dark it is when he attributes consciousness and fear of coming death to his dog, Wessex!

Yet Hardy disliked being called a pessimist, and I think he was justified.

Hardy steers away from pessimism at the outset through his respect for humanity. When he was dying he asked to have three poems read to him—Browning's "Rabbi Ben Ezra," "The Listeners," by Walter de la Mare, and the quatrain from *The Rubáiyát of Omar Khayyám* that I have used as an epigraph to head this chapter. His sympathy was all-embracing—"Promethean," John Cowper Powys called it. He abhorred hunting, abhorred the habit of confining pet birds in cages. When W. T. Stead asked him to contribute to an anti-war symposium, he suggested that it might be agreed to take no horses into battle. Whatever the truth about the morality of nature, he was sure that if human beings were to model their conduct on what seem to be the ways of nature, only disaster could result. Darwinian evolution itself, which so many have used to justify a "red in tooth and claw" philosophy, seemed to him, contrariwise, to enlarge "as a *necessity of rightness* the application of what has been called 'The Golden Rule' beyond the area of mere mankind to that of the whole animal kingdom." The Ancient Mariner found salvation through falling in love with the water snakes. But Hardy does not stop with water snakes. In one of the most wonderful passages of *The Return of the Native,* Mrs. Yeobright is made to sympathize with "the maggoty shapes of innumerable obscene creatures" in a shallow pool.

Some men may possibly love maggots without loving their own kind. Not so Hardy. For him a human being was "the focus of a universe." "The universe itself only came into being for Tess on the particular day in the particular year in which she was born." And it must be obvious that a world which can produce a Tess is not all bad, even if as yet it produces her only to destroy her.

All this has been recognized by critics whose own attitude toward life is very different from Hardy's. Roman Catholic priests preparing to become village rectors were once advised first to make a good retreat, and then to undertake a careful study of Hardy's novels. "From Thomas Hardy he [the priest] would learn the essential dignity of country people and what deep and often passionate interest belongs to every individual life." Another Catholic writer, George N. Shuster, goes even further when he says that "the Hardy view of life is a wholly permissible prelude to the redemptive affirmations of the Catholic faith."

But there is a more important reason for not accentuating what is often regarded as Hardy's pessimism. This is the necessity to remember that he was neither a scientist nor a philosopher but an artist. And as Keats perceived, the artist, strictly speaking, has no opinions; he has only perceptions. Hardy was not a didactic writer; none of the novels in which he is most characteristically himself were written to reform anything. He seems to have started didactically in *The Poor Man and the Lady,* but he did not continue along this road. Towards the close of his career as a novelist, didacticism may be seen creeping back upon him—to a certain extent in *Tess,* much more strongly in *Jude.* This is one reason why the latter (the darling of those critics who are primarily responsible for current misapprehensions concerning Hardy) is not quite his kind of book. It is as ridiculous to believe that Hardy gave up fiction merely because *Jude* had been reviewed unfavorably as it is to believe that Keats was "snuffed out by an article." Great writers are not contemptible weaklings, and they know how little criticism is worth. Hardy stopped writing fiction because he had said everything he had to say in fiction and because, for the time being at least, he had rather lost the note. *Jude the Obscure* was not the consummation of his career as a novelist; it was a blind alley.

To pursue the subject beyond this point is, strictly speaking, to pursue irrelevancies. Unfortunately it is necessary to pursue them. For many of the people who pretend to be studying literature in America today are really not interested in literature at all. They are interested in sociology and economics; they are interested in "ideas"; they are interested in propaganda. They simply cannot believe that the mind of a great creative worker does not work exactly like a professor's. So we have detailed considerations of Hardy's dependence upon Schopenhauer, von Hartmann, and other thinkers—most of them resting on the assumption that a poet should be approached as if he were primarily a systematic thinker, a philosopher.[16]

Often such books are right in many of their details. Hardy did read Schopenhauer and von Hartmann, and in his later work he

[16] Cf., among other works, Helen Garwood, *Thomas Hardy, An Illustration of the Philosophy of Schopenhauer* (Winston, 1911); Ernest Brennecke, Jr., *Thomas Hardy's Universe* (Unwin, 1924); Albert Pettigrew Elliott, *Fatalism in the Works of Thomas Hardy* (University of Pennsylvania, 1935).

was somewhat influenced by them. But even if our interest is in Hardy as a "thinker," we ought to be able to do better than that. For long before he turned to the Continentals, and while he was still young and impressionable, Hardy read Darwin, Huxley, Spencer, and Mill. As Rutland has pointed out, he came strongly under the influence of Sir Leslie Stephen, and he was impressed by the controversies that followed the publication of *Essays and Reviews* in 1860. Much more important still, his temperament being what it was, he responded enthusiastically to the magic of Swinburne and Omar Khayyám.

For this is the essential point: the whole idea that Hardy's works are based on a philosophical system, or that a philosophical system can be deduced from them, is utterly erroneous. In so far as he ever formulated his metaphysic at all, he formulated it as an artist.[17]

To be sure of that, one need only listen to Hardy himself. A great writer may not always be able to explain the effects he creates, but he does know what he did not do; if he cannot write a critical study of his own works, he can at least check the studies of others where they go wrong. In Hardy's case, whether he is speaking of fiction or of metaphysics, the emphasis is always the same. Of fiction he declares that "to call the idle trade of story-telling a science, is the hyperbolic flight of an admirable enthusiasm." As to metaphysics, he insists, again and again, that he has no system—"such objectless consistency never has been attempted"—he has "only a confused heap of impressions." When the ubiquitous Joseph McCabe wished to include him in a dictionary of modern "rationalists" he turned him down. He was not a rationalist, he declared; he was an "irrationalist." As a poet he was drawn profoundly toward belief; poetically speaking, he even "believed" many things he could not justify on rational grounds.[18]

[17] The reason why Professor John Livingston Lowes's magnificent essay ("Two Readings of Earth," in *Essays in Appreciation,* Houghton Mifflin, 1936) is so much better than anything else about Hardy's cosmos is that Lowes has kept this fact steadily in mind.

[18] As Professor Lowes says, his earth is "a haunted spot"; his poetry is "pervaded with a sense of the continued presence of the dead," of the past. In the same "Real Conversation" (*Critic,* XXXVIII [1901], 309-318) in which, apparently from memory, he gave the world Hardy's oft-quoted

Even those most concerned to establish Hardy's philosophical pessimism have recognized this. Else why the complaint that "his early belief in Chance breaks out occasionally even after he had accepted Determinism as his guide"? why the suggestion that the "Immanent Will, unconscious but with powers of sight in the far future," was "created" by him "to reconcile his pessimism and hopefulness"? These would be unhappy reflections upon a philosopher. But if Hardy's approach to life is rather the poet's approach, then his withers are unwrung.

For what is the Poet in this particular incarnation? Is he not an almost abnormally sensitive and sympathetic man—a man (for some reason or other) inclined temperamentally toward a dark brooding over the nature of things? And what do we require of him? Is it not required of him simply that he shall embody for us, in forms precious through their exceeding beauty, his impressions of this thing called life as it appears to a man of such temperament from, say, the vantage point of Egdon Heath? Suppose he does shoot indiscriminately—now against "ephemeral remediable wrongs," now against "the very nature of things." Suppose he does depict nature as cruel and unsympathetic at the same time that he advocates the free play of natural impulses. Is not this exactly what such a man might have been expected to do? Suppose that today he sees the Immanent Will as unconscious, indifferent, "that neither good nor evil knows," while tomorrow, under the stress of some fresh disillusionment, it appears to him that only an active cosmic malignancy

declaration that his "practical philosophy" was "distinctly meliorist," William Archer also reports him as having declared that he would have given ten years of his life to be able to see a ghost. In an elaborate study of *Folkways in Thomas Hardy* (University of Pennsylvania Press, 1931), Ruth A. Firor interprets Hardy's interest in psychic matters as follows: "It was evident to him that magic, which is only a rude and undeveloped science, sees the world from a point of view exactly opposite to that of religion; in this respect it is like legitimate science. In both magic and science the element of caprice is eliminated from the workings of natural laws; religion, on the other hand, conceives nature as variable, elastic, and subject to a conscious personal power who may be conciliated." This is less "evident" to me than it is to Dr. Firor; and I do not think it would have been "evident" to Hardy. (Quoted by permission of the University of Pennsylvania Press.)

can cover the facts in the case. Is all this so very unfamiliar to human experience? And need any of it lessen our respect for Hardy as the artist he was, standing over against the metaphysician and logician he never pretended nor desired to be?

Of course none of this means that "ideas" have no place in Thomas Hardy's novels. Without "ideas," without the particular ideas that he apprehended, whether he took them from books or breathed them in from the atmosphere of the world in which he lived, his novels must have been very different. I am even willing to grant that, unlike Joseph Conrad, who, as we shall see later, has sometimes been subjected to the same kind of misinterpretation, and whose books are as nearly one hundred per cent creative as any novels have ever been, Hardy sometimes slips from the creative to the schematic plane. I think he does this too often in *Jude*. But one does not describe the work of a great writer in terms of his failures.

Taking Hardy in the large, one can surely say that his metaphysic is not a matter of logic but a matter of temperament.

> Differing natures [he says] find their tongue in the presence of differing spectacles. Some natures become vocal at tragedy, some are made vocal by comedy, and it seems to me that to whichever of these aspects of life a writer's instinct for expression the more readily responds, to that he should allow it to respond. That before a contrasting side of things he remains undemonstrative need not be assumed to mean that he remains unperceiving.

Of a reasoned philosophical "pessimism" there can, then, in Hardy's case be no question. He lived in an age when science seemed to be cheating the humanity that produced it, when there appeared to be less room in the world for the human soul than there had ever been before, and being an unusually sensitive man he reflected a great deal of the depression of those times. But he reflected it the more strongly because the climate of the age did not agree with him; and even as his pages stand, the soul *is* the important thing always, not "society," not the "system." Sometimes he catches in his mirror what seems merely a reflection of one or another "aspect," one or another "tendency" of human experience; sometimes he creates full bodied individuals. Whatever he does, there is always a dark splendor about him.

CHAPTER XXI

ROMANCE RESURGENT: ROBERT LOUIS STEVENSON *

. . . he reawoke to the poetic facts of life.

Prince Otto

1. *R.L.S. and The Novel*

Stevenson's position in the history of the novel is a very curious one. Though unquestionably "a main-stream *writer,*" he was not, as Galsworthy has observed, "a main-stream novelist,"[1] yet he has had a very large influence on the novel. In a day when naturalistic drabness moved in from all directions to take possession of it, his fiction and his essays alike reaffirmed the immemorial claims of romance. He was indeed the most completely "convinced romanticist" that Britain has ever known; for him the power of romance was the power of salvation.

He was, too, in the narrower sense of the term, the Artist-Novelist; a passionate preoccupation with his medium was the only thing he had in common with the esthetes of the Wilde-Pater school on the one hand, and with his friend, the American, Henry James, on the other. It is interesting that Stevenson's favorite French novelist was Dumas while James's was Balzac; James says of Stevenson that his "ideal of the delightful work of fiction would be the adventures of Monte Cristo related by the author of Richard Feverel."[2] Between them the two writers did much to give English fiction "an air of having a theory, a conviction, a consciousness of itself behind it—of being the expression of an artistic faith, the result of choice and comparison."[3]

* The quotations in this chapter from Stevenson's *A Gossip on Romance, The Lantern Bearers, Treasure Island, Prince Otto,* and *David Balfour* are made with the permission of Charles Scribner's Sons.

[1] "Four More Novelists in Profile," in *Candelabra* (Scribners, 1933).

[2] "Robert Louis Stevenson," in *Partial Portraits* (Macmillan, 1894).

[3] Henry James, "The Art of Fiction," in *Partial Portraits.*

There are those, to be sure, who see both Stevenson's contributions to fiction as the fruit of his weakness, not his strength. For though, in days gone by, Stevenson was often the subject of undiscriminating adulation, it is also true that, during late years, nobody has been more disparaged; if there is a debased interpretation of anything he said or did that Mr. Frank Swinnerton, for example, has not set forth, the reason must be that it is past the wit of man to uncover it. Stevenson wrote romance, we are now asked to believe, because he lacked the courage to deal with modern life in fiction; he would not fight the good fight to which Hardy, George Moore, and George Gissing gave themselves. His interest in form can be explained with equal facility; he had no substance; what can a perpetual invalid possibly know about life? [4]

On Stevenson's attitude toward realism and romance a word will be said later; since I happen to be writing criticism, not psychoanalysis, I need not discuss the objections of the detractors in detail. However Stevenson became the champion of romance, that is what he became. And on that basis he must be evaluated.

2. *Mostly Biographical*

Robert Louis Stevenson was born in Edinburgh, November 13, 1850. He rebelled against his ancestral destiny as a lighthouse engineer. In the early days, indeed, he rebelled against everything. There were only two things he was interested in—one was writing and the other was dissipation.[5] It is true that he found it advisable to

[4] "What lions have these critical fellows shot with a bow and arrow, that they turn up superior noses at Stevenson, who merely consorted with thieves and harlots in the slums of Edinburgh and London, ran through the professions of engineering and law before he was twenty-five, explored the Scotch coast in a sailboat, canoed the Sambre and Oise, slept in a lonely bivouac *à la belle étoile* in the Cévennes, fled to San Francisco by emigrant train, chartered his own schooner, sailed the South Seas for three years, feasted with cannibal chiefs, refused to sleep with their wives, conspired with Kanaka kings, was threatened with deportation, planted a wilderness, governed a small tribe of savages and died in his boots?" Stuart P. Sherman, *Critical Woodcuts* (Scribners, 1926, quoted by permission of the publisher).

[5] There was one fantastic, quixotic, pathetic romance. The girl, Kate Drummond, was a prostitute, who loved Stevenson and would have married him, but parental influence proved too strong, and he dropped her back into the gutter. Did he remember her, I wonder, when he named his best heroine

compromise with his disappointed father to the extent of becoming a barrister, but his heart was never in the law; he was already training himself to write by careful imitation of the authors he admired. His first book, *An Inland Voyage,* the story of a canoeing trip in Belgium and France, appeared in 1878, his second, *Travels with a Donkey,* an account of his journeyings in the mountains of southern France, in 1879.

By this time, Stevenson had met, in France, and fallen in love with, an American woman, Fanny Van de Grift Osbourne, who was living apart from her husband. In 1879 she sent him a message from California, the exact nature of which is unknown, and Stevenson broke with his family to go to her, almost literally starving to death in San Francisco, before, in 1880, he and Mrs. Osbourne, now divorced from her first husband, were married.[6]

Stevenson's first publications following his marriage were two collections of essays originally published in magazines—*Virginibus Puerisque* (1881) and *Familiar Studies of Men and Books* (1882). Though he had been experimenting with fiction for many years, his first published venture in this field was the *New Arabian Nights* (1882), "the result of a very happy idea, that of placing a series of adventures which are purely adventures in the setting of contemporary English life, and relating them in the placidly ingenuous tone of Scheherazade."[7] The first story, "The Suicide Club," opens with brilliant insouciance on the adventures of the Young Man with the Cream Tarts; perhaps no writer could have quite lived up to that beginning.

Catriona Drummond? Was it with her image before him that he wrote of Catriona "but what I remember the most clearly was the way her lips were a trifle open as she turned"? Stevenson did not accept, or consider himself bound by, conventional standards of sexual morality, but when it came to the obligations he did accept, he was punctilious. From his point of view, it could have been no sin to love Kate, but to abandon her—that must have been quite another matter. The story of Stevenson and Kate Drummond is told in John A. Steuart's *Robert Louis Stevenson,* Chapter 5, and is the special subject of the same writer's novel, *The Cap of Youth* (Lippincott, 1927).

[6] *The Amateur Emigrant* (1895) and *Across the Plains* (1892) tell the story of this terrible journey.

[7] Henry James, "Robert Louis Stevenson," in *Partial Portraits.*

Treasure Island, Stevenson's first long fiction, was written ostensibly for the amusement of his stepson, Lloyd Osbourne; here, for the first time in English literature, all the ingenuities of a sophisticated littérateur were lavished upon the subject-matter of the penny dreadful. *Treasure Island* was written around a map, "and it was because I had made two harbours that the *Hispaniola* was sent on her wanderings with Israel Hands." There were literary influences from Irving, Kingsley, and others—"a parrot from Defoe, a skeleton from Poe, a stockade from Marryat." As a serial in a boy's paper the work failed—it was not sufficiently according to formula—but the book, published in 1883, captivated Gladstone and many others. Even so, it was not until the great success of *Strange Case of Dr. Jekyll and Mr. Hyde* in 1886 that the author was at last freed from financial dependence upon his father.

Five other books appeared before that: *The Silverado Squatters* (1883), which was based on Stevenson's honeymoon in the Sierras; *Prince Otto* (1885), a literary godchild of Meredith's *Harry Richmond,* which Stevenson himself judged fairly enough as "not a romance, nor yet a comedy; nor yet a romantic comedy; but a kind of preparation of the elements of all three in a glass jar"; *A Child's Garden of Verses* (1885); and *More New Arabian Nights* (1885), written in collaboration with Mrs. Stevenson.

Jekyll and Hyde was first written as a "shocker" pure and simple; when his wife complained that he had missed his opportunity for a great moral parable, Stevenson angrily destroyed his first draft, then immediately rewrote the tale as we know it today. The subject suited him admirably; both the "sensualist" and the "Shorter Catechist" of Henley's famous description found scope in this half-supernatural, half-scientific yarn, which builds up horror and terror through a fantastic development of the known possibilities of science along the road Bulwer had first marked out so long ago.[8]

[8] The "huge fallacy" which E. F. Benson (*London Mercury,* XII [1925] 374-377) finds invalidating "the whole story" does not seem to me to answer to his description of it, but there is another fallacy to which he does not refer. Why should a second dose of the same drug which had released Hyde from Dr. Jekyll's dual nature have the power to imprison him again? Henry James long ago had "some difficulty in accepting the business of the powders, which seem to me too explicit and explanatory."

The same year that brought *Jekyll and Hyde* also brought *Kidnapped,* an uneven book, which, episodically at least, is magnificent, and with which Stevenson came at last to the theme which all Scottish romancers are foreordained to consider—the Jacobite struggle and its aftermath.

The few remaining years of Stevenson's life were crowded with books. The year 1887 saw three of them—*Underwoods,* a book of verse; *Memories and Portraits,* a collection of essays; and *The Merry Men,* a story particularly impressive in its use of setting, though perhaps not quite unified either in theme or in tone. In 1888 came *The Black Arrow,* a romance of the Wars of the Roses, which took Stevenson's imagination farther away from home than it had yet dared to venture. It was a piece of "tushery" designed to meet the exigencies of serial publication in *Young Folks* better than *Treasure Island* had met them, in which purpose it succeeded. As a work of art it has had but one admirer, John Galsworthy, who, strangely, found in it "a livelier picture of mediaeval times than I remember elsewhere in fiction."

By this time Stevenson, who had sought health in many places—spending one winter at Dr. Trudeau's colony at Saranac in the Adirondacks—had settled in the South Seas, at Samoa. Here he was regarded as a great man by the natives and exercised considerable influence, and here his health seemed to be better. In 1889 he published *The Wrong Box,* an extravaganza kind of novel written with Lloyd Osbourne, and *The Master of Ballantrae,* the most ambitious of his completed stories. *Ballantrae* has the Jacobite background again, but it is a more serious book than *Kidnapped;* it deals with maturer people and deeper problems. *Ballads* and the famous essay on *Father Damien,* the leper priest, came in 1890, *Across the Plains* in 1892. In *The Wrecker* (1892), written with Lloyd Osbourne, and in *Island Nights' Entertainments* (1893), he began to use South Seas material. *David Balfour* (or *Catriona,* as it is called in England), which is a sequel to *Kidnapped,* and a definite advance upon it from the point of view of the novelist's craft, came in 1893. The year of Stevenson's death saw his last book with Lloyd

Osbourne, *The Ebb-Tide*. The long struggle with tuberculosis ended without warning, December 3, 1894, with the rupture of a blood-vessel in the brain.

The Amateur Emigrant and *In the South Seas* were published in 1895 and 1896 respectively. Stevenson left two unfinished novels—*St. Ives* and *Weir of Hermiston*. For the first, which is the story of a Napoleonic prisoner in Scotland—(Sir Walter Scott makes a brief appearance in Chapter X)—neither the author nor anybody else ever seems greatly to have cared; yet nothing can persuade the present writer that it is not a capital romance. It was completed by Sir Arthur Quiller-Couch and published in 1897. But nobody has ever had the nerve to tinker with *Weir of Hermiston,* which, even in its unfinished state, is almost universally regarded as Stevenson's masterpiece. It was published as he left it in 1896.[9]

3. *Character, Plot, and Setting*

I have run through the full list of Stevenson's publications—fiction and non-fiction alike—deliberately. The first fact which emerges is his versatility. He wrote virtually every kind of book that a man can write. "Mr. Stevenson," wrote J. M. Barrie in 1889, "is not to be labelled novelist. He wanders the byways of literature without any fixed address."

Second, one may note his progression. He began with what was closest to him—the adventures he had had, the books that he had read. Probably no other great writer ever made "copy" of so much of his experience; perhaps none other has ever been quite so much preoccupied with himself. But between *An Inland Voyage* and *Weir of Hermiston* he made great progress in his ability to project himself beyond the plane of his immediate, personal concerns.

Third, of course, there is the all-important matter of his romanti-

[9] Frank Swinnerton (*Robert Louis Stevenson, A Critical Study*) mentions and classifies the best of the short stories: (1) stories of the supernatural—"Thrawn Janet," "The Body-Snatcher," "The Bottle Imp," "The Isle of Voices"; (2) psychological stories—"Will o' the Mill," "Markheim," "Olalla"; (3) light comedies—"The Story of a Lie," "John Nicholson," "The Treasure of Franchard," "Providence and the Guitar"; (4) romantic tales of incident—"The Pavilion on the Links," "The Merry Men"; (5) a realistic tale of incident—"The Beach of Falesá."

cism. But of that I wish to postpone consideration for the time being.

Let us look at him first as a novelist. What of his treatment of plot, character, setting?

Structurally he is weak. This weakness does not matter in such works as *Kidnapped* and *Treasure Island*—strictly speaking these are not "novels" but tales of adventure—yet the end of *Kidnapped* is rather a shock; the book does not end, it just stops. *David Balfour* is much better unified. *Weir* can hardly be judged fairly in its fragmentary state. It may be that we value it more highly now than we could if Stevenson had lived to complete it. To fulfill the magnificent promise of the opening chapters, he would have needed to surmount very difficult problems, and they were just such problems as wrecked him in *The Master of Ballantrae*. On the Master himself Chesterton would seem to have spoken the final word; "not only a family demon but also a family ghost," he is splendidly effective on his native heath, but he loses his power when Stevenson starts him off like "the Prince of Wales on an imperial tour."

As narrator, Stevenson uses one special device which must be mentioned. As we have had occasion to notice before in these pages, English novelists since Fielding had, for the most part, committed themselves to the convention of the omniscient author, entering into the minds of all their characters with a fine impartiality. Henry James was to break with this tradition. James preferred always to establish a "point of view," to identify himself with some one of his characters, not the leading character ordinarily, as in the old-fashioned biographical novel, but rather "some more or less detached, some not strictly involved, though thoroughly interested and intelligent, witness or reporter, some person who contributes to the case mainly a certain amount of criticism and interpretation of it." Stevenson does something like this. In *The Master of Ballantrae* the narrator is the old steward, Mackellar. The extravagant story of Dr. Jekyll and Mr. Hyde is told by the dryasdust old lawyer, Utterson, surely the last man to be suspected of credulity! And even in *Treasure Island* Stevenson is closer to Henry James's method than he seems. For it is only nominally that Jim Hawkins can be called the hero of that book; actually he is rather an observer of the action than a director of it. Nor must one fail to observe that when Mackellar comes to what he did not know at first hand he makes long quotations from the memoirs of the Chevalier Burke, and that when it becomes necessary to acquaint the readers of *Treasure Island* with that which fell beyond the range of Jim's experience, Dr. Livesey replaces him temporarily as narrator.

Stevenson's use of the narrator is, however, less successful than that of James. The boy readers of *Treasure Island* are always irritated and puzzled when they are asked to drop Jim's narrative and take up the doctor's, and their instinct in the matter is right; adults have the same difficulty with the Chevalier Burke.

There is all the difference in the world between telling a story, as Wilkie Collins does, in terms of a combination of narratives, which have been artfully arranged so that the whole truth of the affair under consideration is contained in no one of them but emerges instead in terms of the relationship they sustain to each other, and relying principally upon one narrator, yet finding it necessary occasionally to summon help from the outside.

It must be admitted too that Stevenson has created few enduring characters. Barrie thought Alan Breck, of *Kidnapped,* worthy of Scott; not to know Breck and John Silver was like never having been in love! But even Barrie must add the reminder that Scott "created these rich side characters by the score, another before dinner-time."[10]

Stevenson is most severely condemned along this line for his inability to create living women. From this condemnation I, at least, would have to exempt Catriona, "that pearl of maidenhood whom Viola and Perdita would hail as their very sister."[11] Perhaps there are no women like that in the world; I do not know; if not, then the world is poorer. Stevenson himself took no chances; we see Catriona only as she appeared in David's eyes.

With setting he is much more successful. By the time he came along, the English novel was already what Willa Cather calls "over-furnished." Meredith and Hardy solved the problem by making set-

[10] See Barrie's *An Edinburgh Eleven* and the chapter on Stevenson in *Margaret Ogilvy.*

[11] William Archer.

ting itself an actor—sometimes, Hardy especially, by casting it in a determinative role. Stevenson too does this at times. The marvelous description of Seraphina's night wanderings through the forest in *Prince Otto* may perhaps be dismissed as an imitation of Meredith, but there will still be the impressive use of the weather in *The Merry Men,* in "Thrawn Janet," and, in a rather different way, in "Olalla." *The Merry Men* "began with the feeling of one of those islands on the west coast of Scotland, and I gradually developed the story to express the sentiment with which that coast affected me."

He did not always work that way however. Clayton Hamilton observes of Dr. Jekyll's London that it is "nothing but a vacancy of lamplit streets or else a crowded city quenched in fog"; Henry James objected to the lack of background in the Dutch part of *David Balfour.* The point is that while Stevenson was sensitive to setting as few writers have been—("Certain dank gardens cry aloud for a murder; certain old houses demand to be haunted; certain coasts are set apart for shipwreck")—he valued it only for its atmospheric suggestiveness. When he needed it to get the effect he wanted, he used it; otherwise he let it go. But no matter how important it was to him, he always tended to present it impressionistically; instead of trying to describe everything, he concentrated upon some salient feature, thus stimulating the imagination of the reader to reconstruct the scene for himself.

For all Stevenson's charm, there is then a certain thinness in his fiction. It is interesting to note that he never claimed genius. "What genius I had was for *work!*" he told Lloyd Osbourne. "I started out with very moderate abilities; my success has been due to my really remarkable industry—to developing what I had in me to the extreme limit." He passionately loved writing for its own sake; "he went in search of a style," says John Jay Chapman, "like Coelebs in search of a wife." In itself, care in writing is not a thing that may easily be overdone, but it is true that Stevenson began to write before he had anything to say; consequently he is often more concerned with manner than with matter. He strained his muscles sometimes; no doubt this is the reason why it is often a relief to turn from his chiseled elegance to the slovenly, surging power of a Scott.

Frank Swinnerton may be right in ascribing Stevenson's inability to hold the note to his defective health.[12] "These romances are, in fact, the romances of a sick man of tremendous nervous force, but of neither physical nor intellectual nor even imaginative energy." Yet the same thing appears in Mark Twain, whose health was excellent, and who left as many abandoned manuscripts behind him as Stevenson himself, and there was even some of it in Chaucer. Whatever the explanation, the fact is beyond dispute.

4. *The Gospel of Romanticism*

We come now, at last, to the heart of Stevenson and to his real importance, in other words to his romanticism. I have already said that he was a romanticist by conviction. But he was also a romanticist by temperament; those who believe that he would have been Zola if he had not feared the censorship do not understand him very profoundly. Like Dickens, like Browning, he was what James Huneker called a "yes-sayer" to life.

He was a romanticist, for one thing, because he never lost the heart of youth. Whether we agree with his critics that he remained a boy because he was constitutionally incapable of maturity, or whether we take Chesterton's more generous view, that subconsciously he was trying to find his way back to a place where the world of sin could not come between him and the beauty he dreamed, makes no difference. The famous essay on the Victorian toy theaters—"'A Penny Plain and Twopence Colored'"[13]—shows his youthfulness very clearly; "The Lantern Bearers,"[14] in which he takes his point of departure from an incident in the play of children, shows it even more clearly. For the only child who never had anything of the romantic in him was Jude Fawley's son, Little Father Time. And he hanged himself.

"The Lantern Bearers," "A Gossip on Romance,"[15] and "A Hum-

[12] Stevenson himself half-humorously ascribed it to another cause in a letter to Barrie: "Endless cigarettes," he wrote of himself, "except when he coughs or kisses. Always tied to apron strings. Drinks a lot. Swears somewhat. Unstable character."

[13] In *Memories and Portraits.*

[14] In *Across the Plains.*

[15] In *Memories and Portraits.*

ble Remonstrance"[15]—here is the heart of Stevenson's gospel of romanticism. What does it involve?

It involves a love of color and adventure. He likes "scenes." He can perceive no reason why it should be "thought very clever to write a novel with no story at all, or at least with a very dull one," why we should "look somewhat down on incident, and reserve . . . [our] admiration for the clink of teaspoons and the accents of the curate." The fundamental problem in art is to produce illusion, and this need is served better by incident than by character; it is action that "woos us out of ourselves."

> Crusoe recoiling from the footprint, Achilles shouting over against the Trojans, Ulysses bending the great bow, Christian running with his fingers in his ears, these are each culminating moments in the legend, and each has been printed on the mind's eye forever.

Like a good debater, Stevenson sometimes overstates the case for action. Yet he knows that

> In the highest achievements of the art of words, the dramatic and the pictorial, the moral and the romantic interest, rise and fall together by a common and organic law. Situation is animated with passion, passion clothed upon with situation. Neither exists for itself, but each inheres indissolubly with the other.

But this is not the fundamental thing. The fundamental thing—and here Stevenson confronts the naturalists foursquare—is that no objective judgment of human experience is possible, that no life can be judged except by the man who lives it:

> There is one fable that touches very near the quick of life: the fable of the monk who passed into the woods, heard a bird break into song, hearkened for a trill or two, and found himself on his return a stranger at his convent gates; for he had been absent fifty years, and of all his comrades there survived but one to welcome him. It is not only in the woods that this enchanter carols, though perhaps he is native there. He sings in the most doleful places. The miser hears him and chuckles, and the days are moments. With no more apparatus than an ill-smelling lantern I have evoked him on the naked links. All life that is not merely mechanical is spun out of two strands: seeking for that bird and hearing him. And it is just this that makes life so hard to value, and the delight

of each so incommunicable. And just a knowledge of this, and a remembrance of those fortunate hours in which the bird has sung to us, that fills us with such wonder when we turn the pages of the realist. There, to be sure, we find a picture of life in so far as it consists of mud and of old iron, cheap desires and cheap fears, that which we are ashamed to remember and that which we are careless whether we forget; but of the note of that time-devouring nightingale we hear no news.

Literature cannot give us life directly, he says elsewhere; all it can do is to show us how somebody reacts to life. This is a far more "scientific" attitude than that of the naturalists, who assume an unchanging, objective reality, which is the same for all observers. Stevenson hated "realism" because he regarded it as unreal. The realist may report his hero's life truly from the point of view of an hypothetical detached observer, but since no life was ever lived from the point of view of an hypothetical detached observer, all that is quite beside the point.

His life from without may seem but a rude mound of mud; there will be some golden chamber at the heart of it, in which he dwells delighted; and for as dark as his pathway seems to the observer, he will have some kind of a bull's-eye at his belt.

I shall be reminded, no doubt, that Stevenson once wrote a novel about a streetwalker, which was destroyed at the instance of his wife.[16] But there is nothing in Stevenson's gospel of romanticism which should make it unnatural for him to write about a streetwalker. "True romantic art . . . makes a romance of all things. It reaches into the highest abstraction of the ideal; it does not refuse the most pedestrian realism." No doubt Stevenson tried to give us the streetwalker as she must have appeared in her own eyes.

Stevenson's chief contribution to romance, Henry James believed, was psychology. He is never afraid to present the hero David Bal-

[16] George S. Hellman believes that this incident suggested Henry James's story, "The Author of Beltraffio." He may be right, but I mistrust his gift for allegory. Mrs. Stevenson may have been a difficult person, but the evidence is not all in; for the time being I can only return a verdict of "not proven" against the autobiographical interpretation of such stories as "The Waif Woman" and "The Bottle Imp." For a delightful study of the sources of "The Bottle Imp," see Joseph Warren Beach, *Modern Language Notes*, XXV (1910), 12-18; cf. XXVI (1911), 94.

four in unheroic aspects, and St. Ives thinks of a safer way to leave the castle only when he is dangling between heaven and earth in imminent, deadly peril! But Stevenson did more than that for romance. His reasoned, considered defense of the romantic position, on sound psychological grounds, made it once more a possible artistic credo for intelligent men.

That that defense was worth less than, say, Scott's glorious, untheoretical example at the beginning of the century, we may grant freely. But Scotts do not grow on blackberry bushes; there was none available in Stevenson's time. And even if there had been, he would probably have been less successful in meeting the rather finespun, reasoning temper of his time than Stevenson was.

In an age of growing materialism—hostile alike to religion and art—Stevenson vindicated fiction and he vindicated life. "Neo-Christian" he is often called, and the term serves well enough, though actually there was a good deal of neo-Stoicism about it. Intellectually speaking, Stevenson's religious thinking, such as it was, was probably no more important than his early irreligious revolt. His frank subjectivism as a romanticist tends rather to ally him with those who, in an age of crumbling objective verities, would set up their shrine in the world within.

His influence has been enormous, first of all on the Kailyard School in his own Scotland—Barrie, S. R. Crockett, and Ian Maclaren—and probably few of the romancers of these latter days have been entirely unmindful of his example. If romance is dead, says Mr. Swinnerton, Stevenson killed it. But it seems to many of us that he gave it, rather, a new lease on life.

CHAPTER XXII

VICTORIAN SUNSET *

. . . darkling stand
The varying shore o' the world.
Antony and Cleopatra

1. *Mrs. Humphry Ward, Who Popularized Ideas*

Life is always much less systematic than histories of literature; and there are currents and counter-currents in every period. During the latter end of Victoria's reign in England some writers were already giving their allegiance to the ideals of the age that was to come, while others, not necessarily inferior to them, were still finding their creative inspiration in the old patterns. The progressives will be considered in the next chapter; the conservatives we must consider here.

Mrs. Humphry Ward is naturally the first of these. It is the fashion nowadays to see her in a light very similar to that in which Lytton Strachey placed her grandfather, Thomas Arnold. She is the perfect symbol of everything that was "stuffy" in Victorianism. She has been caricatured by H. G. Wells and Arnold Bennett;[1] and even her friend, Henry James, who spent many hours trying to pump some of his wisdom into her, is said to have declared that the dear lady never understood a word he said.

The most remarkable thing about Mrs. Ward is that having first achieved such prestige as surely no other novelist with so little creative power had ever enjoyed before her, she should have been so quickly forgotten. She died as recently as March 24, 1920; though no

* The quotations from Mrs. Humphry Ward's Prefaces to the Westmoreland Edition given in this chapter are cited with the permission of Houghton Mifflin Company.

[1] In *The Sea Lady* and *The Book of Carlotta* respectively.

doubt it would be possible to argue that as an artist she died with Catherine Elsmere in 1911, on the last page of *The Case of Richard Meynell.* Among her later books, *The Coryston Family* (1913), *Eltham House* (1915), and *Lady Connie* (1916) are perhaps the best; from these she descended to the four war novels which stand gathering dust in old bookshops to remind us that she was an important cog in the British propaganda machine to get America into the First World War.

Yet for many years Mrs. Ward was regarded as George Eliot's successor, and her books were approached with comparable reverence. None other than Tolstoy called her the greatest living English novelist. The general public was equally enthusiastic; in America the competition between rival pirate publishers of *Robert Elsmere* waxed so keen that one actually brought out an edition at four cents a copy, only to be outdone at last by the Maine Balsam Fir Company, which gave away a book with every cake of soap! "No book since *Uncle Tom's Cabin,*" wrote William Roscoe Thayer, "has had so sudden and wide a diffusion among all classes of readers; and I believe no other book of equal seriousness ever had so quick a hearing."

Robert Elsmere (1888), *The History of David Grieve* (1892), *Helbeck of Bannisdale* (1898), and *The Case of Richard Meynell* (1911) are Mrs. Ward's distinctively religious novels; here she does what George Eliot always refused to do—she makes religious doubt the subject of fiction. Robert Elsmere, like George Eliot herself, is driven to relinquish orthodoxy through the critical study of Christian evidences; he leaves the Church of England to found a religious-humanitarian center in London, which is motivated by ideals similar to those that inspired Mrs. Ward's own Passmore Edwards Settlement, and at last finds his spiritual equilibrium in a passionate loyalty to a purely human Christ. The most moving part of the book concerns the struggle between the hero and his rigidly orthodox wife, so impervious to his opinions, so unshaken in her love and loyalty. *David Grieve* presents the ideal of a "natural religion" developing spontaneously through conscience and social sensitiveness. *Helbeck of Bannisdale* reverses the *Elsmere* problem on its personal side; this time the man is a passionate Catholic, the girl an unbeliever. And *Richard Meynell* reworks *Elsmere* toward another conclusion. Richard, who marries Elsmere's daughter and inherits his battle, refuses to leave the church; instead he attempts to build a place for Modernists within its fold.

Life had prepared Mrs. Ward very thoroughly for the understanding of such problems. She was born, Mary Augusta Arnold, in Tasmania, June 11, 1851. Her father was the younger Thomas Arnold, whose conversion to Catholicism brought him home from that country, while his daughter was yet a child, to become a professor in the Catholic University of Dublin. Later he left the Catholic Church; still later, he returned to it, this time permanently.

Mary did not go to Dublin; her childhood was spent instead in Wordsworth's Lake Country. When she was sixteen she moved to Oxford, where she was influenced by Mark Pattison and others, and where she specialized in the early Christian history of Spain. Whatever may be said of her as a novelist there can be no question about her scholarship; when she came to deal with the problems that wrecked Elsmere's orthodoxy she knew whereof she spake, for she had been over the ground independently before him. She continued to reside in Oxford until 1881, when her husband, T. Humphry Ward, whom she had married in 1872, went to London as art critic of the *Times*.

This removal brought Mrs. Ward closer to the main stream of English life. In her own austere way she ceased to be a cloistered scholar and became a woman of the world. As a critic she turned from ancient Spaniards to modern Frenchmen. She became interested in politics and enjoyed the friendship of many learned men. In her later years—passionate anti-suffragist though she was—she engineered her son's career in Parliament; the wags called him "the member for Mrs. Humphry Ward." *Marcella* (1894), *Sir George Tressady* (1896), *The Marriage of William Ashe* (1905), and *The Coryston Family* (1913) all involve Parliamentary considerations; as a group they are second in importance only to the religious group.

But whether she writes of politics or of religion, there is still a bookish quality about Mrs. Ward; we know the libraries of her heroes better than we know their hearts. It is not that she fails to understand them. She understands them completely, and she sets them forth so admirably, so justly, and with such admirable detachment, that we sometimes get a touch of smugness or snobbery. But, as Henry James puts it of the people in *Robert Elsmere,* they are "not simply enough seen and planted on their feet."

Five times Mrs. Ward chose to make a novel out of a historic scandal.[2] In no one of these instances does she trust her imagination and dare to present her characters in their native setting. She is too good a scholar for that; she might get something wrong. Instead, she takes them all over into her own time, changes their names, and decks them out in modern dress.[3] She never hesitates to refer openly to history or to literature; the characters she has created always seem more real to her when she can remember that they are like something she has read about. In *The Marriage of William Ashe,* where Cliffe is already Byron, she very nearly breaks the spell altogether by referring several times to his historical prototype.

Much of this Mrs. Ward herself knew as well as any critic. She was, to be sure, rather a pontifical person.

> What is important [writes Katherine Mansfield] is the messages that her characters have to deliver; she sees herself, we fancy, as the person of the great house, receiving these messages and translating them to the eager, inquiring crowd about the gates, and then—returning to the library.[4]

Yet she realized her limitations, and her own analysis of them in the Prefaces to the Westmoreland Edition is fundamentally just. "Had I dragged my heroine through ways of a more commonplace difficulty and miriness," she says of the Marcella of *Sir George Tressady,* "she would have been more appealing, and the scene with Letty stronger." And she repudiates the latter half of *Lady Rose's*

[2] Chateaubriand and Madame de Beaumont in *Eleanor* (1900); Madame du Deffand and Julie de Lespinasse in *Lady Rose's Daughter* (1903); Byron and the Lambs in *The Marriage of William Ashe;* Romney and Lady Hamilton in *Fenwick's Career* (1906); Lord Holland and Lady Webster in *Eltham House.* Elise Delaunay in *The History of David Grieve* is an almost heartless caricature of Marie Bashkirtseff.

[3] For her views on the matter, cf. the significant Preface to *The Marriage of William Ashe* in the Westmoreland Edition.

[4] *Novels and Novelists* (Knopf, 1930, p. 190, quoted by permission of the publisher).

Daughter because she knows she herself lacked the spiritual robustness necessary to achieve the tragic ending the logic of the story demanded.

In general, Mrs. Ward's story-telling impulse was "set in motion by an event, a tale, a character, which causes a stir in the mind like that of a seed germinating, till the leaf and flower of the story are thrown up, one hardly knows how, but with a certain heat and violence, and a happy sense of *discovery";* but among all her books only *The Story of Bessie Costrell* (1895) was, she tells us, written, in anything like its entirety, in what might be called a state of inspiration. For the most part she knew just what she was doing; she wrote "intellectually, following out a logical sequence"; she achieved no effects that she could not explain.

For her immediate popularity, Mrs. Ward's limitations were no doubt quite as valuable as her gifts. A great and original artist in fiction—a Meredith, a Conrad—must create the taste by which he is enjoyed. Mrs. Ward essayed no technical experiments; her technique was as old-fashioned as her morality. She wrote about the subjects which intelligent people in her time wished to consider, and she handled them intelligently, with assured competence and impeccable taste.

It is not quite fair to her to say that "the subjects she treats with complete assurance are those proper to the platform and the lecture-room." Such a statement omits the important fact that she still stands as one of the few writers who have been able to put passion into the novel of ideas. This was what James liked about *Elsmere,* that with all its faults it was still "a history of our moral life and not simply of our physical accidents."

The frightfully insular French portions of *David Grieve* are mere synthetic stuff, but the English scenes here and there suggest *The Old Wives' Tale. Helbeck* has power despite the Gordian knot-cutting of Laura's suicide. And "the tears of things" are in Lady Kitty Ashe's death scene (despite its sentimentality) and in the common tragedy of Bessie Costrell (which is not sentimental at all). In such things we get Mrs. Ward at her best.

2. *Maurice Hewlett,* Who Defies Classification*

Maurice Hewlett was born in Surrey, January 22, 1861, of a family originally French Huguenot but English Puritan at least since St. Bartholomew's time. His father—a poet, a critic, an expert in antiquarian law—named his son, the eldest of a large family, after Frederick Denison Maurice.

> At nine years old [wrote Hewlett in later life], I knew Nelson's ardor and Wellesley's phlegm; I had Napoleon's egotism, Galahad's purity, Lancelot's passion, Tristram's melancholy. I reasoned like Socrates and made Phaedo weep. . . . I was by then Don Juan and Don Quixote, Tom Jones and Mr. Allworthy, Hamlet and his uncle, young Shandy and his. You will gather that I was a reader. I was, and the people of my books stepped out of their pages and inhabited me.

Most of this came, one gathers, from independent reading, rather than from any of the private schools the boy attended, or from the London International College. Hewlett became a barrister and, like his father before him, Keeper of the Land Revenue Records and Enrollments. At one time he lectured on medieval subjects at South Kensington University College. In later life he sank himself deep into the life of Wiltshire, a passionate anti-imperialist with a pronounced tendency toward Quaker and pacifist views, and with all his faith for the future centered in those "so rooted in the soil of this England that they cannot be torn out of it." He died, June 15, 1923.

Hewlett challenged fame and earned a fortune as a writer of medieval and Renaissance romances,[5] but having won his place he stubbornly refused to consolidate it. He had done his *Queen's Quair;* there could be no possible point in doing that over again, especially when the fools who read your books persisted in calling that which you considered serious history, "romance." On the other

* All quotations from Hewlett's writings are by permission of Charles Scribner's Sons.

[5] *The Forest Lovers* (1898); *The Life and Death of Richard Yea-and-Nay* (1900); *The Queen's Quair* (1904). Similar interests and backgrounds appear in the stories and sketches included in *Earthwork Out of Tuscany* (1895); *Little Novels of Italy* (1899); *New Canterbury Tales* (1901). In 1911 Hewlett published two more chivalric books—*Brazenhead the Great* and *The Song of Renny*—but neither is very important.

hand, there might be considerable point in writing about eighteenth-century Italy,[6] or nineteenth-century Spain;[7] about England as Byron knew it,[8] or Gladstone and Disraeli;[9] or even as you knew it today;[10] and then when you got tired of all that, you could go back to the Icelandic sagas and rewrite them.[11]

It did not in the least concern Hewlett that he must be heroic in one book, romantic in a second, and coolly ironic in a third; nor that he must finally drop the tapestried splendor of his Renaissance novels for the stark nakedness of his saga tales. Neither did it concern him that the public refused to buy his later books, for he wrote to please himself, and by that time he had discovered the values of poverty. Even ignoring the fact that Hewlett came to the end of his life more or less ready to consign all his novels to Limbo, and stake his claim to remembrance on his essays and his poetry of English history and the English peasant,[12] what we have here must be something very close to an unmatched phenomenon.

Yet I oversimplify the man. For while his medieval and Renaissance romances form a group against the others, they are by no means alike.

The Forest Lovers was the point of departure. This book—Malory dashed with Pre-Raphaelitism—is worthy of its lovely title. Frederic Harrison describes it as "the rapid improvising of an omnivorous reader of poems, romances, old ballads; Decameronic *Novelle;* Orlandic epics; sagas, folk-songs; Spenser's *Faerie Queene,* and Sidney's *Arcadia.*" It carries the reader into a world of Howard Pyle enchantment.

[6] *The Fool Errant* (1905).

[7] *The Spanish Jade* (1908).

[8] *The Stooping Lady* (1907); *Mrs. Lancelot* (1912); *Bendish* (1913, sequel to *Mrs. Lancelot*).

[9] *Mainwaring* (1920).

[10] Most importantly in the trilogy: *Halfway House* (1908); *Open Country* (1909); *Rest Harrow* (1910).

[11] *A Lover's Tale* (1915); *Frey and His Wife* (1916); *Thorgils of Treadholt* (1917); *Gudrid the Fair* (1918); *The Outlaw* (1919); *The Light Heart* (1920).

[12] Of which *The Song of the Plow* (1916) and *The Village Wife's Lament* (1918) are the most important. Cf. John Freeman, *English Portraits and Essays* (Hodder and Stoughton, 1924); J. B. Priestley, *Figures in Modern Literature* (Dodd, Mead, 1924).

Doubtless the book has its "modern" side; for Hewlett, the many-faceted, was radical as well as reactionary. Though he came to the end of his days cursing the libertinism of the age, he himself had been reproached for his "fleshly" note; and he had crusaded for freer divorce laws when that was still a daring thing to do. There is a "modern," realistic touch in the villainess Maulfry; there is even a mild touch of perversity in the situation of the mother and the daughter, their identity unknown to each other, both in love with Prosper le Gai. Modern psychology casts its shadow over the book also. "The problem," says Hewlett, "is, how love gets into the man." But the remarkable thing about *The Forest Lovers* is not that there should be a "modern" touch in it here and there but the fact that at the end of the nineties a writer should still have been able to find his way back into so alien a world.

It was a literary achievement, of course, a scholar's achievement. This appears even more clearly in *Richard Yea-and-Nay* and *The Queen's Quair*. For in both these books Hewlett essays genuine historical reconstruction; he attempts to cast light on that which history has left shrouded in darkness.

Differing from the Mantuan as much in sort as in degree [he writes of himself], I sing less the arms than the man, less the panoply of some Christian king offended than the heart of one in its urgent private transports; less treaties than the agony of treating, less personages than persons, the actors rather than the scenes.

In *Richard Yea-and-Nay* he is not wholly successful; the narrative is nearly as mannered as the style. But *The Queen's Quair* had the inestimable benefit of starting with one of the richest and most moving and most pitiful stories men know—the history of the Queen of Scotland. Hewlett's Mary is sympathetically presented, though by no means guiltless. "You say she had sought wrongly. I say she had overmastering need to seek. Love she must; and if she loved amiss it was that she loved too well." I do not believe that she is the Mary Stuart of history, though Hewlett did. He uses the methods of the biographer as well as those of the novelist; cites authorities and quotes from imaginary documents; presents his material from many different points of view, yet himself retains control of the narrative; and addresses the reader, whenever he chooses, in his own person.

In later books, Hewlett sometimes presented historical figures under aliases: Lord Bendish is the coxcomb side of Byron, Gervase Poore is Shelley, and the Duke of Devizes is Wellington. But more important than *Mrs. Lancelot* and *Bendish*—the books in which these men figure—are *The Fool Errant, The Stooping Lady,* and the contemporary trilogy.

The Fool Errant marries Hewlett's own idealistic purity to the traditional charms of the picaresque novel. It has been called *The Forest Lovers* in a new setting. Like Isoult le Désirée of that novel, like Jehane Saint-Pol of *Richard Yea-and-Nay,* like Manuela of *The Spanish Jade,* Virginia Strozzi is a woman who can be soiled by no degradation so long as she is faithful to her love. It also suggests in some of its aspects that much vaster panorama of an earlier Italy, *The Cloister and the Hearth.*

The Stooping Lady has another gallant girl, though of a different variety, in the person of Hermia Mary Chambre, a girl of good family, who "stoops" to the gallant young butcher, champion of the rights of man, and who does not scorn to take her place beside him in the pillory.

Like the story she names, Hermia Mary is very Meredithian, and the same might be said of the glorious Sanchia-Josepha, heroine of the modern trilogy—*Open Country, Halfway House,* and *Rest Harrow.* These novels are almost impossible to summarize. They have a philosophical anarchist, George Borrow sort of hero, Jack Senhouse, who refuses either to own property or to live under a roof, and who spends his time making a garden of neglected corners of England, and teaching Sanchia and others that whoever places the yoke of matrimony upon the neck of the woman he loves, degrades her. Sanchia's true mate is Senhouse himself, but neither of them realizes it at the outset, and Sanchia is merely applying the combined wisdom and foolishness of the Senhouse teaching when she gives herself to a scoundrel who is not free to marry, and who, in any event, is not the marrying kind. The result is a comedy of errors which might very easily have turned into a tragedy.

The difficulty of summary here is the danger of creating an impression of absurdity which would not be fair to Hewlett. There are passages in his work to which such an impression would do no injustice. The reactions of some of his characters are truer to Meredith than they are to life; when Hermia Mary, for example, finds herself "handfasted" to an unidentified lover who has been sending her violets, the mildest thing we can say is that Hewlett is using a method which is hardly suitable to prose fiction. But no such judgment can be entered of his work as a whole.

All in all, Hewlett was a puzzling and fascinating writer who challenges more serious critical attention than he has yet received. His independence inspires respect; it also suggests a strong possibility that he never quite found himself. "He was wayward," wrote his friend, Laurence Binyon; "for there was a restlessness in his fibre which is visible enough in his writing."

It is no accident that whatever one reads of his, one is immediately reminded of other writers. "All my life," he himself remarked, "I have used other men's art and wisdom as a springboard." A springboard, not a crutch. His individuality maintained itself triumphantly through several changes of style and manner. He stands outside any given line of development, and rests his claim to remembrance on what he was in himself.

3. *J. M. Barrie, "A Diet All Salt and Sugar"* *

Sir James Matthew Barrie (born, May 9, 1860; died, June 19, 1937) was the last survivor of the men who made great reputations under Victoria. His is a power which, for those capable of feeling it at all, partakes almost of the quality of magic, but it is too closely connected with his curious and enigmatical personality to yield itself readily to analysis. Barrie enthusiasts tend to drool at the very mention of his name; detractors, even more unhappily, snarl and foam.

Barrie was born in Kirriemuir (Thrums), Scotland. His father was a weaver and small employer of weavers, his mother the daughter of a stonemason who had brought up her younger brother from the time she herself was a girl of eight. It is significant that, humble

* All quotations from J. M. Barrie are given by the permission of Charles Scribner's Sons, as is also the quotation from Thomas Moult's *Barrie*.

as the family was, this brother yet succeeded in becoming a clergyman. Barrie himself attended Glasgow Academy and Edinburgh University. His first journalistic appointment was at Nottingham; in 1885 he went to London, where such editors as Frederick Greenwood and W. Robertson Nicoll helped him to establish himself.

Barrie's place in the history of the novel is smaller than his fame might lead one to expect. *Auld Licht Idylls* (1888) is a series of sketches describing life on the author's native heath; in *A Window in Thrums* (1889), still using similar material, he begins to work for continuity. *My Lady Nicotine* (1890) harks back to Goldsmith and the periodical essayists of the eighteenth century. There is more unity in *Better Dead* (1887), but this work is only a *jeu d'esprit,* an imitation of Stevenson's "Suicide Club" which falls far short of its model. *When a Man's Single* (1888) was meant to be a novel, but Robertson Nicoll began to serialize it when only the first two chapters had been completed, and the unifying interest of the hero's progress in love and journalism do not take up much more than half of it. *The Little White Bird* (1902), the purest example of the undiluted Barrie magic in fiction, is notable for the first appearance of Peter Pan. But so loosely were Peter's adventures connected with the story of Captain W—— and his little friend David, that they were easily detached from their context and published with the Arthur Rackham illustrations as *Peter Pan in Kensington Gardens* (1906). *Peter and Wendy* (1911) is simply the play, *Peter Pan,* retold in story form.

Barrie's only piece of prose fiction in later years was *Farewell Miss Julie Logan* (1932). There are suggestions here of the same ideas we now often meet in the fiction of those who have been influenced by J. W. Dunne and his "serial time." ("Maybe it was her echo that was back in the glen, and by some mischance you got into the echo.") But having the great tradition of Scottish diablerie behind him, Barrie does not need the clumsy machinery of a Wells or a Maxwell Anderson. He had mastered all that stuff as far back as *The Little White Bird:*

> We hailed a hansom. "Drive back six years," I said to the cabby, "and stop at the Junior Old Fogies' Club."
>
> He was a stupid fellow, and I had to guide him with my umbrella.

This leaves but three of Barrie's books—*The Little Minister* (1891); *Sentimental Tommy* (1896); *Tommy and Grizel* (1900)—as novels; and even these are unsuccessful when judged by ordinary standards. They fail as novels to succeed gloriously as something else—one is never quite sure what.

The Little Minister seems indeed to have begun as a serious picture of a Scottish weaving community in the early nineteenth century. But when Babbie dances into the woods by moonlight (and into the minister's heart)—"a gleam of color, a gypsy elf poorly clad, her bare feet flashing beneath a short green skirt, a twig of rowan berries stuck carelessly into her black hair"—all this is changed. It was the most impressive entrance any British novelist had devised for a heroine since Beatrix Esmond descended the staircase at Walcote House. But Babbie takes possession of the senses differently from Beatrix; there is something in her glamor which causes us to remember that Barrie was the kind of man who worships actresses.

The Little Minister is a quite unbelievable book. The great flood scene was omitted when Barrie dramatized the novel because it could not be staged, but it is quite as theatrical as anything in the play. Nor can one easily believe that Gavin and Babbie lived happily ever after. Yet there is nothing in the book that a sympathetic reader would change. It "dates," no doubt. It is not the kind of romanticism we go in for nowadays; neither is it Emily Brontë's kind, which is independent of time. But if we remember Chesterton's admonition not to confuse our age with the Day of Judgment we may still realize that *The Little Minister* is a remarkable book for what it triumphs over.

The two *Tommy* books cut deeper. Here Barrie revives the Sterne-Mackenzie tradition. Unlike his predecessors, he lashes sentimentalism even while he indulges it; Meredith himself was no more merciless. But he makes even less attempt to "build" a novel than he did in *The Little Minister.*

Sentimental Tommy started out to be *Tommy and Grizel,* but Tommy's boyhood insisted on getting itself described first, and heaven only knows how long it might all have gone on had not Barrie hanged the philandering hero by a borrowed overcoat at the end of the second novel! Thomas Moult defends this horrible scene, which is too brutal for comedy and too undignified for tragedy, as "the most masterly contrivance in the story"!

> It was apparently intended at first that he should die of consumption—"for Tommy had inherited his mother's cough." . . . But the idea of the boy who wouldn't grow up is sufficiently fixed in the author's mind to persuade him that just as Tommy has lived boyishly so he must die boyishly.

But Barrie himself was much less logical about it. For Tommy was in part a portrait of Robert Louis Stevenson, and Stevenson was indirectly responsible for the unsatisfactory scene. When Barrie told him there was a bad end in prospect, he inquired joyfully, "Am I hangit?"

Yet one must admit that in one way or another Tommy had to die. His history is an elaborate study of the moral dangers which accompany the "artistic temperament." In *Sentimental Tommy* the boy had dramatized the last Jacobite rising. It is his tragedy that becoming a man, he cannot put away childish things; he inhabits the world of reality only at meal times. For this reason he is much less pleasant as a man than he was as a boy; it was kinder even to hang him than to let him go on into middle age.

But that, say the detractors, was Barrie's own tragedy. You get mawkish, sentimental "make-believe," and then you get a slap in the face like this hanging of Tommy, or like the almost sadistic killing of little Davy in *When a Man's Single,* for which no compensation of any kind is offered. A cold wind blows through the later plays also, and such glimpses of reality as we catch in *The Will,* in *Dear Brutus,* in the miraculous *Mary Rose* are anything but reassuring.

Well, perhaps. Grizel's own portrait is not untouched by sentimentalism, yet it has its pathos and even its grandeur. Grizel's heroic conduct at her mother's death is a conception worthy of Shakespeare, but it fails to move us as it should because the book in which we meet it is not quite large enough to frame it adequately. In any case, there is a large element of taste in this matter of feeling. At the present moment—which is one wherein, as Barrie himself has observed, all the authors are trying to see which one can say "Damn!" loudest, while all the women are busy maintaining their equal right with men to grow beards—it is natural to emphasize his shortcomings, but to have no difficulty at all with those of Messrs. Faulkner, Caldwell, and Hemingway.

There is not much point in reproaching a writer for the excellent things he has failed to do; neither can his admirers expect nim to be praised for the qualities he never possessed. It was no accident that the definitive edition of Barrie should be called the "Peter Pan Edition"; he did not want to grow up, and he made no secret of his disinclination.

Barrie attempted no complete picture either of life or of Thrums; he left scenery out of his books, for example, because his mother did not care for it. There is a good deal of pepper and mustard in *Auld Licht Idylls;* they start much less like Mrs. Gaskell than like Galt. But, says Barrie significantly, "As unlooked for as a telegram there came to me the thought that there was something quaint about my native place."

Such a man cannot be Shakespeare; perhaps such a man cannot quite escape frustration. But, unlike Tommy Sandys, Barrie loved greatly, and he accepted responsibilities that would have terrified many of his critics. Perhaps he was a writer who preferred his fancy to his imagination. Perhaps even, as Stevenson suggested, he was a genius with a journalist at his elbow. Whatever the explanation may be, it can hardly be summed up in a phrase, for Barrie was a very complex creature, and he became the master of a highly sophisticated art.

4. *The Phenomenon That Was Kipling*

Rudyard Kipling was "the story teller of India, the self-appointed laureate of Tommy Atkins, the Anglo-Saxon Aesop." [13] In his time he was a phenomenon as inescapable as the Boer War, the skyscraper, and the motorcar. His characters became household words; quite without the Boy Scouts, the *Jungle Books* would have fathered a new mythology. Even non-literary people conversed in scraps from his tales and ballads, assuring each other that the female

[13] Frederic Taber Cooper, *Some English Story Tellers.*

of the species was more deadly than the male, that Judy O'Grady and the Colonel's Lady were sisters under the skin, that East was East and West was West and never the twain should meet; and the formula, "But that is another story," was as widely quoted as "Well, hardly ever" at the height of the *Pinafore* epidemic.

Yet Kipling's contribution to the novel proper was smaller even than Barrie's. Disregarding *The Story of the Gadsbys* (1888), which, as a kind of novelette in dialogue, is a pretty specialized thing, and disregarding that monument to the brutality of English schoolboys, *Stalky and Co.* (1899), which is really a group of short stories, one may say that only four times in his long career did Kipling attempt a continued story. Of these works, one—*The Light That Failed* (1890)—is a failure; one—*The Naulahka* (1892), written in collaboration with Wolcott Balestier—is at best a qualified success; one—*Captains Courageous* (1897)—is only a good book for boys. That leaves *Kim* (1901). And *Kim* is, truly, "another story."

The Light That Failed is supposed to be the story of an artist who goes blind and loses his love—there is an alternative version in which Maisie remains true to him—but this is all mixed up with war in the East and man-talk in London, to say nothing of the children in the Prologue. The Maisie of the Prologue and the Maisie of the story proper have nothing in common except the name.

The Naulahka is even less unified. There is India; there is the life of the medical missionary; there is Western American business and politics; and there is the love story. Tarvin goes to India to get the famous jewel known as the Naulahka for the railroad president's wife, in order to make sure that the road shall come to Topaz. He gets it through trickery and intrigue, but having by this time also won Kate Sheriff, he relinquishes it, for Kate's husband must not be a thief. Kate had rejected him in Colorado because she wanted to be a medical missionary, but she now shrinks in horror from the misery that is India—and the moral of that is that woman's place is in the home. In the last chapter, Tarvin addresses the firmament and volunteers the information that the Naulahka was distinctly a side-issue. So the reader feels, though the book is named for it.

Captains Courageous celebrates the redemption of a miserable little rotter who is swept overboard from an ocean liner and picked up by a Gloucester fishing schooner. The moral is sound, but adult readers complain that Harvey's redemption is stated, not portrayed, and that it seems quite unconvincing. Another fault of the book is that it goes on for some time after what should have been its end—Harvey's restoration to his parents.

Even about *Kim* grave questions have been raised. There is the ethical objection that all Kim's striving must eventuate in his betraying to the British those whom he has always regarded as his people. And, as Edmund Wilson has remarked, this connects closely with the esthetic objection that "the parallel lines never meet," that "the adventures of the Lama and of Kim simply arrive at different consummations." Kipling himself could not see *Kim* as a "real novel"; he thought of it as "nakedly picaresque and plotless—a thing imposed from without." It is true that the book has no more "development" than *Captains Courageous,* yet the latter is slick journalese compared to it. It is also true that Kim's character does not develop greatly, but it is shown vividly in many different lights and illuminated by manifold experiences. *Kim* is a book without ancestors and without descendants. It was not made; it grew; it was; no other writer could possibly have produced it. It is a long story in which a well-defined central character travels through circumstances toward a goal. Novel let it be. But it is the only one of importance.

Yet one cannot quite leave the matter of Kipling's contribution to the novel on this note. For there is a sense in which the whole vast body of his short stories make up a kind of novel. This is not merely because he links his tales by referring from one to another, nor even because we know that favorite characters like the Soldiers Three may appear again and again. The fundamental unity is a more subtle thing than that. "Bit by bit my original notion grew into a vast, vague conspectus—Army and Navy List, if you like—of the whole sweep and meaning of things and efforts and origins throughout the Empire." Obviously I can attempt no comprehensive interpretation of these stories here. But neither can I pass them by in complete silence.

Kipling's literary sources were many. Stevenson influenced him.

Mark Twain influenced him. His local color shows obvious indebtedness to Bret Harte. And along with all this, and often in opposition to it, the Bible influenced him in many ways. But his life experiences influenced him more.

Like Thackeray, Kipling was born in India—at Bombay, December 30, 1865. His father was a talented artist and professor. Burne-Jones was his uncle; Stanley Baldwin and Angela Thirkell are cousins. He was sent home to North Devon and went to school at Westward Ho. But, unlike Thackeray, he returned to India, where at seventeen he found himself sub-editor of a paper. It was from India and from that paper that the wonderful stories of *Plain Tales from the Hills, Under the Deodars, Soldiers Three,* and the other early collections were sent forth. "As one turns over the pages . . ." said Oscar Wilde wearily, "one feels as if one were seated under a palm tree reading life by superb flashes of vulgarity."

Despite its malice, this was good criticism. Kipling was no more innocent than he was perverse. "Once upon a time there was a Man and his Wife and a Tertium Quid"—that was a sufficiently daring beginning for a story in the nineties. Kipling's treatment of the courtesan was more French than English, and more Indian than French; and there was some excuse for horror over his cool, objective description of Oriental vices in such tales as "The Gate of a Hundred Sorrows."

The *Plain Tales* smell of whisky, sweat, blood, and tobacco. They are smart and cocky, with the surface sophistication of the newspaper cub who has seen everything and understood nothing. Her Majesty's privates make something of a point of having small time to cultivate the virtues on which her Majesty prides herself. On the whole it is just as well that many of the people who were shocked by these things in Kipling did not live to read some of his successors. But he helped pave the way for those successors. And there are passages in his horror stories that are still almost unreadable.

To be sure, there have always been those who insisted that he never got very deep into India, never left the camp of the British Army far behind. But except for the specialists his dazzling technique made such questions unimportant. He is a late-Victorian Defoe; he is the trickiest of all great writers. In their own way, his opening sentences are the most wonderful in literature. "It came without warning, at the very hour his hand was outstretched to crumple the Holz and Gunsberg Combine." Or: "Let it be clearly understood that the Russian is a delightful person till he tucks in his shirt." You may not like to be screamed at—but you read on. You may disapprove of the several pages he devoted to the advertisements of the future in "With the Night Mail"—but you admit that Sterne would have used them if he had thought of it. As you read Kipling the atmosphere of the smoking-room enfolds you. He talks desultorily about characters and backgrounds not directly connected with the story. He hints at further, perhaps forbidden, knowledge. "This part is not to be printed."

His vocabulary enriched the English language. Whatever he is writing about, he gets up all the technical terms. Perhaps there is not enough to deceive the expert, but there is often enough to obscure the story and bewilder the hero. And when, as in *Puck of Pook's Hill* (1906), he deals with the past, one feels that, like the hero of "The Finest Story in the World," Kipling must have lived before, must be merely remembering.

Perhaps he did live before, for there are many Kiplings. There is the journalist and imperialist (whom we may scrap if we will). But there will still be the student of occult lore, the primitivist, the maker of myths. Kipling himself, in a well-known poem, recognized that he had two sides to his head, and declared himself willing to lose friends, tobacco, or bread rather than give up either. Possibly he might have been better off if he had given up one of them, for the greater Kipling rarely gets completely out of the lesser Kipling's shade.

Some of the attacks that have been made on his stories about machines—"The Ship That Found Herself" or ".007"—seem to me unfair. I do not think such tales show his materialism. Rather, they show his grasp of the ability that primitive man had to spiritualize his surroundings by attributing consciousness to objects. But though it is true that in *Puck of Pook's Hill* and its successor, *Rewards and Fairies* (1910), Kipling invented a new kind of fairy lore, it is also true that these tales are a glorified review of English history for children with all Rudyard Kipling's Tory prejudices thrown in.

And F. A. Waterhouse has, I fear, a plausible case when he makes the beloved *Jungle Books* themselves the starting-point for an attack on Kipling as both decadent and superficial. He worked on the borderline of converging worlds without entering very deeply into any: with him it is East vs. West; Man vs. Animal; Past vs. Present; Animate vs. Inanimate. And Mowgli is "the ultimate *reductio ad absurdum* of the hero as understood by the romanticists, the 'man of nature.' . . ."

Kipling's admirers are very busy apologizing for his militarism and anti-democracy; the gist of the argument seems to be that it was not war he admired but the heroic virtues, and that war in the nineties was a rather pleasant little thing anyway. It was a bitter joke on Kipling when the swastika he had been using as a trademark for many years was adopted as the symbol of the Nazi Party. It was no joke at all but unmixed agony when, even earlier, the war he had long been urging England to prepare for took the life of his own son when it came.

This was the last of the terrible blows Kipling endured. The first came in childhood when a fanatical aunt to whose care he and his sister had been entrusted in England while their parents were still in India, mistreated him shamefully; when his mother returned and bent over his bed, the child put up his arm to ward off the expected blow. What life was like at Westward Ho we may infer from *Stalky and Co.* On top of these unhappy experiences of childhood came the quarrel with his Vermont wife's brother, which, unimportant as it was in itself, drove him out of America—once more he had failed to adjust himself to his environment—and later still the death of his dearly-beloved daughter.[14] It is no wonder that the man who settled down at last in ungracious retirement at Burwash was in some respects a psychic cripple.

[14] Kipling himself told the story of his childhood in *Something Of Myself,* having previously used it as fiction in "Baa, Baa, Black Sheep." The story of the quarrel with Beatty Balestier is told by Frederic Van de Water, *Rudyard Kipling's Vermont Feud* (Reynal & Hitchcock, 1938). Edmund Wilson's heavily Freudian essay in *The Wound and the Bow* performs the good service of bringing all these matters together, but trips over its own feet by attempting to prove too much. There were a good many imperialists with no Westward Hos or murderous aunts in their background.

Yet many wonderful stories were written at Burwash, and Edward Shanks is just when he complains that they have never been adequately studied. The public read Kipling avidly as long as he lived—he died January 17, 1936, a day or so before King George V—but the critics had long since given him up. Perhaps it was his own fault. But it was their loss.

For whether with Edmund Wilson we see in Kipling's last stories an increasing preoccupation with disease, or whether with Mr. Shanks we see him as "concerned with the immortal problems of pain and death, of ill-doing and punishment, of the other world, and of religion," the fact remains that he had now mastered an immensely supple and subtle art; the old slapdash enthusiasm was far behind him. And however impatient one may be with Kipling for some of the things that he could not see, one must gladly admit that no man ever better deserved to be called incorruptible, that no artist ever developed more inevitably, as Miss Geraldine Farrar once said the artist must develop, "in his own orbit, according to his light."

CHAPTER XXIII

TOWARDS A NEW CENTURY

I am not saying that one went out, as one might into a garden, and there saw that a rose had flowered or a hen had laid an egg. The change was not sudden and definite like that. But a change there was, nevertheless; and since one must be arbitrary, let us date it about the year 1910. The first signs of it are recorded in the books of Samuel Butler, in *The Way of All Flesh* in particular; the plays of Bernard Shaw continue to record it. . . . All human relations have shifted—those between masters and servants, husbands and wives, parents and children. And when human relations change there is at the same time a change in religion, conduct, politics, and literature.

VIRGINIA WOOLF *

1. *George Gissing, a Scholar in Grub Street*

It is ironical that many readers should know George Gissing only by the bookish pages of *The Private Papers of Henry Ryecroft* (1903). But it was far more ironical that a man who wanted to spend all his life in scholarly retirement should have become the special historian of "new Grub Street" and "the Nether World." Gissing's heart was never with the slum-dwellers who people his pages; in a way he did not even sympathize with them; he kept his sympathy for superior persons like himself who were compelled for lack of means to dwell among them. Gissing was a classical scholar, and he used his scholarship as a refuge from life. His posthumous *Veranilda* (1904), that elaborate reconstruction of Roman life in the days of Justinian, was far more characteristic of the man as he knew himself than any of the volumes which now seem to constitute his primary contribution to fiction.

Gissing had no faith in the ability of the proletariat to improve their lives, and the thought that they might some day attempt to control the lives of others only filled him with fear and horror. He knew the times were bad, but there was nothing he could do to

* Quoted from "Mr. Bennett and Mrs. Brown" by permission of Doubleday, Doran and Co.

make them better; as early as 1883 he commits himself to the thesis that the artist's job is simply to study and reproduce in art the "collection of phenomena" which is the world.

It may be asked why such a man felt constrained to occupy himself with the particular phenomena which concern the life of the slums. In Gissing's case there were a number of reasons. From his childhood he admired Hogarth and Dickens passionately, and both Hogarth and Dickens had been much concerned with these things. "Paint a faithful picture of the crowd we have watched," says Tolladay, of *Workers in the Dawn,* "be a successor of Hogarth, and give us the true image of our social dress, as he did of those of his own day."

But Hogarth and Dickens were reinforced—and, in a sense, superseded—by Dostoevsky and the French naturalists. Gissing admired Daudet. He loved Murger's *Vie de Bohème.* He believed that art was "an expression, satisfying and abiding, of the zest of life." He never got much of that into his novels. But he also believed that "art nowadays must be the mouthpiece of misery, for misery is the keynote of modern life." Describing the "preposterous" conditions of his own existence to Mrs. Frederic Harrison in 1884, he found "one consolation, that if I live through it, I shall have materials for a darker and stronger work than any our time has seen." Waymark, of *The Unclassed,* expresses this same idea more elaborately:

> Let me get a little more experience, and I will write a novel such as no one has yet ventured to write, at all events in England. . . . The fact is, the novel of every-day life is getting worn out. We must dig deeper, go to untouched social strata. Dickens felt this, but he had not the courage to face his subjects; his monthly numbers had to lie on the family tea-table. Not virginibus puerisque will be my book, I assure you, but for men and women who like to look beneath the surface and who understand that only as artistic material has human life any significance.

It was unfortunate that Gissing so managed his life that the Nether World was what he himself knew best. He was born in Wakefield, Yorkshire, November 22, 1857, the son of a druggist. His start in life was as hopeful as that of any bright boy in moderate circumstances; he made a brilliant record at Owens College, Manchester; then he wrecked his future by getting mixed up with a streetwalker. Convinced that only economic need had driven the girl to prostitution, Gissing stole for her from his fellow-students, was detected, and went to prison.

After his release he fled to America, where he taught high school in Waltham, Massachusetts, wrote his first fiction for the Chicago *Tribune,* almost starved to death on peanuts in Troy, New York, and seriously considered throwing himself into Niagara Falls. Upon his return to England he sealed his fate by marrying the streetwalker, with whom he lived in misery until the inevitable separation, and whom he continued to support afterwards until she drank herself to death.

His second wife was a shrew, whom he married with little pre-acquaintance to escape from overwhelming loneliness. Towards the end of his life he formed a common law tie with a French girl, who seems to have treated him well enough, though he detested French food and always claimed that her mother, the third member of their *ménage à trois,* was starving him. He died in France, December 28, 1903.

Gissing wrote twenty-three novels; and not all of them deal with the slums. Both the powerful but chaotic *Workers in the Dawn* (1880) and its successor, *The Unclassed* (1884) are slum novels; they concern themselves with the tragedy of Gissing's own first marriage. With *Isabel Clarendon* (1886) he made his first attempt to break away from the slum theme. But Meredith urged him to stick to his own subject: he wrote *Demos* (1886); *Thyrza* (1887); and *The Nether World* (1889). *New Grub Street* (1891) gives us the poor writing hacks who struggle for a living in an uncongenial atmosphere; *Born in Exile* (1892) concerns the personal tragedy of an intelligent rationalist of the lower classes who poisons the springs of his own life when he pretends an eagerness to take orders as a step toward winning the woman he loves and taking the position he feels he must occupy in the eyes of the world.

Born in Exile was the last book quite in the old manner, though it is true that *The Odd Women* (1893), which involves a study of a group of spinsters for whom society can find no adequate place, reflects some of the same interests. But Gissing had already sent out new feelers with *A Life's Morning* (1888) and *The Emancipated*

(1890); he is now turning increasingly toward the middle class and toward personal, not social, problems. *In the Year of Jubilee* (1894) gives a hostile picture of a cheap commercial England; *Eve's Ransom* (1895) is a strange and complicated love story; *The Whirlpool* (1897), which has been much praised, is a portrait of a neurotic woman. A somewhat unexpected phenomenon of Gissing's last period was a group of light humorous novels, some of which show the Meredith influence—*The Paying Guest* (1895); *Sleeping Fires* (1895); *The Town Traveller* (1898), and others.

To his special admirers, Gissing was a great novelist; others complain that, like many transitional writers, he falls between two stools. The old Victorian three-decker was still in vogue during his earlier career; and he conformed to its demands, in spite of the fact that its complicated plot-machinery, its heavy melodramatic devices, and its multitudinous characters balanced over against each other were not really congenial to his aims. Since he wrote one of the very best critical studies we have of Dickens, it is not surprising that the Dickens influence should appear even in so grim a book as *The Nether World*. Jane Snowdon is Dickens's angel-child; Mrs. Peckover and Clem descend from Dickens's criminals; Sam and Bessie Byass are, in their earlier aspects, Dickens clowns. And it is very clear that Mr. Peggotty's finding of Em'ly was in Gissing's mind when he wrote of Hewett's recovery of Clara.

Gissing, then, is old-fashioned in his technique, but he is forward-looking in his materials—unromantic, frank, skeptical in religion and politics alike. A pacifist, he proffered "peace made a religion" as "the religion of the future" and "the world's only hope." He was no Socialist, but he saw the connection between modern industrial capitalism and the war system as clearly as any Socialist ever did. "We may reasonably hope, old man, to see our boys blown into small bits by the explosive that hasn't got its name." And when the First World War came, his son was blown to bits.

Gissing has some limitations, however, which cannot be charged to his period. What George Stearns, his sympathetic pupil at Waltham, Massachusetts, says of his teaching has a curious suggestiveness: "Most teachers are popular or unpopular among their pupils, but Gissing was neither." He himself complained of Zola that he "writes deliberate tragedies; his vilest figures become heroic from the place they fill in a strongly imagined drama." In the Preface to *Isabel Clarendon* he limited himself narrowly:

He who is giving these chapters of her history may not pretend to do much more than exhibit facts and draw at times justifiable inference. He is not a creator of human beings, with eyes to behold the very heart of the machine he has himself pieced together; merely one who takes trouble to trace certain lines of human experience, and, working here on grounds of knowledge, there by and of analogy, here again in the way of colder speculation, spins his tale with what skill he may till the threads are used up.

The really great novelist is everything Gissing here declares that the novelist is not; and he does everything Gissing says the novelist cannot do. Indeed, in so far as Gissing's own novels are successful, he himself was false to this creed.

Yet the creed was there, and the drabness characteristic of his work is not unconnected with it. There were altogether too many things that he would not or could not do. "He could not discuss speculative metaphysics," writes his friend, Morley Roberts, "because they were disturbing, and speculative sociology, for him, was grinding the wind." And Gissing himself laments: "If I could write a book that recognized the spiritual side of man, where I now appeal to one reader, I should then speak to thousands."

He never lacked emotion, but his emotion was somewhat specialized. He was more closely tied to his own experiences than many authors are. "I identified myself with the poor and ignorant," says Waymark; "I did not make their cause my own, but my own cause theirs." Hence Gissing's preoccupation with scholars who have been "born in exile," hence his failure to fill his tragedies full of universal significance, and hence Virginia Woolf's complaint that "we establish a personal rather than an artistic relationship" with him.

All these factors must be considered in judging Gissing's work, but it is important not to overstress them. His awkwardness in handling transitions plus his failure to emphasize climaxes ought to have made him a very dull writer. Yet with all his faults he is not a dull writer. It is impossible not to be interested in his characters; it is impossible not to respect his own integrity and independence.

His novels made little popular success when they were published, yet they have stubbornly refused to lose themselves in the shuffle-dance of time. On the contrary, they seem to be gaining in prestige.

2. *George Moore, the Man of Wax*

"I don't know exactly when Mr. George Moore began to write novels," wrote Maurice Hewlett, "but cannot recall any striking example of the French novel in English before his time, and should be inclined to commence our series of the grubby and illicit with him."

Moore was the best example among all British novelists of the man of letters pure and simple. Though he sometimes prided himself on being "feminine, morbid, perverse," he was not even that really; it is hardly an exaggeration to say that he had no character; indeed he himself declared that he "came into the world apparently with a nature like a smooth sheet of wax, bearing no impress but capable of receiving any."

It was Oscar Wilde who pointed out that Moore conducted his literary education in public. When he began he could not write a decent sentence; he rewrote his books constantly; he yielded to influence after influence, experimented with type after type of fiction; it was not until sixteen years after Oscar had gone to his grave that he achieved, in *The Brook Kerith,* a style which really satisfied him. But while he was creating his books he was also creating something that meant more to him than any book—himself; and it may even be that the succession of studies he made of that self, as it was and as he imagined it to be,[1] will turn out as his most lasting contribution to literature.

Yet susceptible as Moore was to the influence of environment, he began with revolt. He was born at Moore Hall, County Mayo, Ireland, February 24, 1852, the son of an M.P. He revolted against his church as soon as he was old enough to recognize it; his country he can hardly be said to have discovered until 1901, when, disgusted over the Boer War, he moved from London to Dublin, convinced

[1] *Confessions of a Young Man* (1888); *Memoirs of My Dead Life* (1906); *"Hail and Farewell!" Ave* (1911), *Salve* (1912), *Vale* (1914); *Avowals* (1919); *Conversations in Ebury Street* (1924).

that "the Messiah Ireland was waiting for was in me and not in another." Long before that time he had received the imprint of the rather decadent literary and artistic Paris in which, at first desiring not to write but to paint, he had established himself at eighteen, where he had come in contact with Impressionist painters and naturalistic novelists, and where he is said to have lived with a tame python which he nourished on live guinea pigs.

It was under French naturalistic influences—Zola, Gautier, the Goncourts, Flaubert—that Moore wrote his first group of novels: *A Modern Lover* (1883); *A Mummer's Wife* (1885); *A Drama in Muslin* (1886); *A Mere Accident* (1887); *Spring Days* (1888); *Mike Fletcher* (1889); *Vain Fortune* (1890).

The important book of this early group is *A Mummer's Wife,* the clinical record of how Kate Ede ran away from a pious home and a cranky, asthmatic husband in the Potteries region, with a strolling actor, herself achieved some success on the stage, and forthwith proceeded, for no very apparent reason, to drink herself to death. Zola's influence shows clearly in the elaborate occupational background of the book—(from it Arnold Bennett derived the inspiration for the studies of the Potteries upon which his own fame rests)—and Moore actually went about with a traveling opera company to get the feel of theatrical life.

If we can pass over the imperfect motivation at the outset, Kate's progress on her way to hell must be admitted to have been portrayed with terrible fidelity; English fiction had never known such a scene as that in which the unhappy woman vomits all over herself and the red plush upholstery of the cab, and, fortunately, it has not known many like it since. A pious reader may see *A Mummer's Wife* as a sermon against whoring and drunkenness, a superb example of teaching by the horrible example, but Moore himself did not thus conceive it; he was giving us his "slice of life," and the nasty subject appealed to him for its vividness, not for its moral suggestiveness. Yet there is pity in the book, and the author is not so fanatical in his adherence to the objective creed of the naturalists that he refrains from giving the reader his own opinions of what he records.

Esther Waters (1894) is much less extreme; what naturalism there is blends comfortably into the English tradition; the great pontiff Gladstone seriously embarrassed the lending library which had sought to ban the book by publicly placing the seal of his approval upon it; and though it is not a novel of purpose it led directly to the establishment of a home for foundling children. The servant girl as heroine was not new in English fiction. Richardson had used her almost simultaneously with the emergence of the novel, and Hardy was currently investing someone rather like her with cosmic significance. There is nothing cosmic about *Esther Waters,* but there is plenty of humanity, and the theme—"Hers is a heroic adventure if one considers it—a mother's fight for the life of her child against all the forces that civilization arrays against the lowly and the illegitimate"—is infinitely greater and warmer and more appealing than the theme of *A Mummer's Wife*. *Esther Waters* is by all odds Moore's most important book, since even those who see *The Brook Kerith* and *Héloïse and Abélard* as the great masterpieces must admit that they lie outside the main line of development of the English novel.

In *Evelyn Innes* (1898) and *Sister Teresa* (1901), which are really one novel divided into two parts, Moore passes under the influence of J. K. Huysmans and gives himself to an elaborate analysis of mental states. Moore's "official" interpreters parrot his own dislike of this work, and even more independently minded critics are often repelled by what they call the Ouida-like background of the book and the Sunday supplement character of the tempter, Sir Owen Asher. But Asher does not make the book; primarily it is an analysis of the soul of a girl who was drawn powerfully toward worldly sensuality and toward the religious life at the same time. As a great Wagnerian soprano, Sir Owen's mistress conquers Europe, but conscience drives her to forsake her sinful life and enter a nunnery.

Evelyn Innes is one of the best novels of the opera ever written; it shows a real understanding of how a characterization is conceived and projected. In the religious part of the novel, too, Moore is surprisingly sympathetic for so rabid an anti-Catholic; he knows that a woman cannot change her nature by taking vows; he understands the terribly complicated business of sainthood, and gives a moving picture of the struggles of a soul. The picture is inevitably a harrowing one, for while the reader always sympathizes with Evelyn, he is never convinced that she has a vocation; it is her tragedy that she can be happy neither in the world nor out of it. In the 1901 version she remains in the convent; in the complete revision of 1909 she deserts it. Neither version really arrives anywhere.

By the time *Sister Teresa* came out, Moore had already begun his attempt to identify himself with the Gaelic revival in Ireland. The attempt on the whole proved abortive, but both Yeats and Æ. had some influence upon him, and it was in Ireland that he began the development of what Charles Morgan calls his absolute prose, and abandoned "the literary approach to narrative for that of a *raconteur*."

The first fruits of this new effort were the short stories in *The Untilled Field* (1903), then *The Lake* (1905), a strange, disturbing novel about an Irish priest who, gradually becoming conscious that jealousy, not purity, was the motive which impelled him to drive from his parish the pretty schoolmistress who was about to bear a child, swims across the lake, leaving his clothes on the bank to suggest that he has been drowned, and sets out for a new life in America. "There is a lake in every man's heart. And every man must ungird his limbs for the crossing."

For Moore himself the story was more than a bit of symbolism; it was an allegory, "a sun myth." The lyricism of the Irish landscape is appealing, but the interminable letters which Rose sends Father Gogarty while traveling about Europe, presumably as the mistress of another man, letters full of art criticism and Biblical criticism, are an unpleasantly extraneous element.

Eleven years passed between *The Lake* and *The Brook Kerith* (1916). During the interval Moore returned to London and perfected the style in which both *The Brook Kerith* and *Héloïse and Abélard* (1921)—to say nothing of the less important *Ulick and Soracha* (1926) and *Aphrodite in Aulis* (1930)—were written.

Of this style sharply opposed judgments have been entered. Charles Morgan speaks for the faithful when he finds "a new cadence and discipline" in it, "a new reconciliation between the written and the spoken word." More specifically, he praises Moore for interweaving narrative and speech, "as they have never before been interwoven on the printed page," and for having found a way "to preserve at once the impression of natural speech and the continuity of a prose that would have been broken by photographic naturalism." Bernard Shaw, on the other hand, stopped after reading thirty pages, finding "no mortal reason" why Moore should not go on thus for 50,000 pages or even for 50,000,000; and Yeats agreed with the "Dublin critic" who could only think of "ribbons of tooth-paste squeezed out of a tube."

A fair judgment lies, probably, somewhere between the two extremes. Moore's final style is beautiful and it is artificial. It is difficult to read. It creates a soporific effect. There is passion in *Héloïse and Abélard,* but Moore's method makes it very hard to get at. This will appear very quickly if *Héloïse and Abélard* is compared with Helen Waddell's superbly dramatic treatment of the same story in her *Peter Abelard* (1933).

Yet *Héloïse and Abélard* is probably a better book in which to judge Moore's final style than *The Brook Kerith.* For *The Brook Kerith* is a novel about Jesus, and Moore's Jesus is an Essene and an eschatologist who did not die on the cross but merely swooned, and whose life was restored by Joseph of Arimathea; whence, among other things, the post-Resurrection appearances recorded in the New Testament. Worse still, he thinks of himself, after his Resurrection, as having been brought to the cross by his own monstrous blasphemy in making himself God, and at last concludes that even "God is but desire, and whosoever yields to desire falls into sin." In a dramatic encounter with Saint Paul, who has dedicated himself to preaching Jesus Christ and him crucified, the real Jesus, now a fifty-two-year-old shepherd, does his utmost to stop the perpetuation of his transgression in the world, but without avail. It will be a long time before a completely disinterested judgment of such a book can be entered.

It will be a long time also before the passions and prejudices awakened by Moore's fantastic existence shall have quieted sufficiently to make a completely cool-headed estimate of his work as a whole possible. (He died as recently as January 21, 1933.) His service to English naturalism is indisputable, and the stylistic achievement of his final period is indisputable, whether one happens to enjoy such a style or not. But when his press-agents declare that there was no form in the English novel before him, they show an ignorance of his predecessors which is lamentable.

It was no accident that he should have finished not with *Esther Waters* but with *Héloïse and Abélard;* for John Freeman is right when he says that "the mood of imaginative reverie is the peculiar kingdom of our novelist, and the communication, the expression of its human sweetness and sadness, his peculiar office." But that judgment, little as Freeman intended it, must itself place Moore with the minor novelists. I have already maintained the humanity of *Esther Waters*. Yet Freeman declares that the book does not touch "passionate heights and depths." Katherine Mansfield agreed with him, and it was on this ground that she rejected it.[2] How could one expect "passionate heights and depths" of a man who had no character, who never lived? Even in his erotic adventures Moore habitually "abandoned the prey for the shadow," so that a wise lady declared, "Some men kiss and tell; Mr. Moore tells but does not kiss." Such a man must inevitably find material relayed to him at second hand better for his purposes in fiction than anything derived from first-hand contacts; such a man may create beauty, but there will be something lacking in it, and the lack will make itself felt. Character is fate, for the novelist as well as for the butcher, the baker, and the candlestick-maker. George Eliot knew that and proclaimed it. Perhaps this is the reason why Moore did not like George Eliot.

3. *Samuel Butler* * *and His Influence*

No history of the novel can embrace a rounded picture of the literary activities of Samuel Butler. Though he influenced the novel tremendously, he was no novelist. Strictly speaking he produced but one novel, *The Way of All Flesh* (written 1872-1884, published 1903), and it is not a particularly good one. Primarily Butler was a thinker, a philosopher, and a critic of life.

He was born in Nottinghamshire, December 4, 1835. His father

[2] See her *Novels and Novelists* (Knopf, 1930), pp. 242-246.

* The scattered quotations from *The Way of All Flesh* are made by permission of E. P. Dutton and Co.

was a clergyman; his grandfather, Dr. Samuel Butler, had been headmaster of Shrewsbury School and later Bishop of Lincoln. He himself was destined for the church, and, though never ordained, went so far as to engage in parish work in London, before he rebelled and left for New Zealand in 1859 as a sheepfarmer. Five years later he returned with a competence and settled down in Clifford's Inn, where he stayed until he himself went the way of all flesh, June 18, 1902—painting pictures which the galleries refused to hang, and composing music in the manner of his god, Händel; paying his publishers to bring out books which nobody even considered worth attacking; supporting a vile scoundrel named Charles Pauli, and failing to respond to the devotion of a noble, though possibly eccentric, woman, Eliza M. A. Savage, who lived for him in the flesh almost as exclusively as she lives in him posthumously.

All this seems tame and flat compared to what Butler himself wrote of his experience in *The Way of all Flesh,* for as his most illustrious disciple, Bernard Shaw, has said, "Butler is the only man known to history who has immortalized and actually endeared himself by parricide and matricide long drawn out."

If it be asked whether the real Canon Butler and his wife were actually as their son has drawn them in the Reverend Theobald Pontifex and his Christina, the answer must, of course, be in the negative. I do not mean that he fabricated; I simply mean that he sees his parents as subjectively as ever Charlotte Brontë saw the Reverend Mr. Brocklehurst. Butler's own master at Shrewsbury, Dr. Kennedy, appears, in quite the brightest passage of his novel, as the eccentric who told his wife that all he wanted for dinner was a glass of hot water and a small piece of bread and butter, but who, when he sat down to the table actually disposed of "a good plate of oysters, a scallop shell of minced veal nicely browned, some apple tart, and a hunk of bread and cheese," and chased that down with gin and water, "hot and stiff too." Yet when a contemporary sent Butler an admiring pen portrait of Dr. Kennedy, he replied, "your description of him is perfectly just." It is clear, then, that he was not a photographer.

The Way of All Flesh is an attack on the family, the church, and the school. The Reverend Theobald Pontifex is a brute; his wife prepares her servant for confirmation by teaching her the geography of the Holy Land, and in secret daydreams sees herself crowned by a loving Savior while angels gaze upon her with envy and admiration. Unlike Butler, Ernest submits to ordination, but finds himself a hopeless square peg in a round hole until he is lucky enough to bring his house down around his ears by getting himself sentenced to six months imprisonment for having made improper advances to a lady. Upon emergence, he marries an amiable prostitute, whose drunken orgies he incredibly attributes to the psychic distresses incident to pregnancy, and establishes a second-hand clothing shop. Just when the situation has become intolerable, it transpires that Ellen already had a husband when she married Ernest. The latter, now happily inoculated against matrimony, returns to contented bachelorhood. Another windfall, in the shape of a legacy from Aunt Alethea, now enables him to make his final adjustment to life as a happy and unsuccessful author.

Ernest's story is told by Overton, a friend of the Pontifex family. Both Overton and Ernest represent Butler himself at different stages of his development. This device gives Butler almost complete license to comment upon and interpret the significance of his material.

The Way of All Flesh is the study of a family group. Like Gissing in *Demos,* Butler goes back to the third generation to explain his hero. Ernest's father and grandfather are both bad. About his own great-grandfather Butler knew nothing. In John Pontifex, the village carpenter, he hypothesized a source for the elements of strength and decency in Ernest's character. John Pontifex is an unconscious knower; he lives "under grace." His son George is "an irregular, abnormal growth," "a sudden divergence." George's sons, especially Theobald, "suffer from this sudden interruption to the normal evolutionary development." [3] For *The Way of All Flesh* is a dramatization of Butler's evolutionary philosophy, which was also his religion.

Of this philosophy all that can be said here is that, rejecting "natural selection" as the clue to the origin of species, Butler returns to and develops the ideas of the French biologist, Lamarck. Briefly

[3] See Claude T. Bissell, "A Study of The Way of All Flesh," in *Nineteenth Century Studies,* ed. Davis, De Vane, and Bald (Cornell University Press, 1940).

and very roughly, Darwin taught that new species arrive through the development of accidental differences; these changes, which are undirected either by the creature who is changing or by any outside power, establish themselves as they are found to possess survival values. According to the Lamarckian view, on the other hand, the creature may be said to have a share in his own evolution, being aided by "unconscious memory" and exercising a power corresponding to that which in human beings we call the will. To Butler's way of thinking, this hypothesis gave a more "human" universe and was more easily reconcilable with the religious view of life than straight, unadulterated Darwinism. Butler's deity, however, is no transcendent god but the god within life and matter who has been made famous by Bernard Shaw as the Life-Force.[4]

All this is warp and woof of *The Way of All Flesh;* no novel was ever more successful in dramatizing a creed. What the book shows is that

> If a man is to enter the Kingdom of Heaven, he must do so, not only as a little child, but as a little embryo, or rather as a little zoösperm—and not only this, but as one that has come of zoösperms which have entered into the Kingdom of Heaven before him for many generations.[5]

I have already risked the wrath of the Butlerites by declaring that *The Way of All Flesh* is not a very good novel. Admitting that the enormously disproportionate space given to Ernest's ancestors is necessitated by Butler's special views, and admitting that the summary character of the last chapter is due to the fact that Butler never really completed the novel, I still do not see how the book can be regarded as other than the work of a brilliant amateur. The Butlerites may reply that the very absence of any suggestion of the pro-

[4] For Butler's own complete exposition of these ideas, cf. *Life and Habit* (1878); *Evolution Old and New* (1879); *Unconscious Memory* (1880); *Luck, or Cunning* (1887); *God the Known and God the Unknown* (1909).

[5] A number of other important ideas in *The Way of All Flesh* have been conveniently summarized by Bissell: "the identity of memory and heredity, the transmission of acquired characteristics, the essential unity of life and the absence of any complete break between the generations, and the conception of evolutionary growth as a gradual, conservative absorption of improvements that have developed, half by the conscious desire of the organism, half by lucky accident."

fessional novelist makes the charm of the book, and that Butler is to be praised for throwing over musty conventions in fiction as he did in life. But this is not quite the point, for one does not write a great novel by simply throwing over conventions.

One cannot create character by throwing over conventions, for example. Now, Christina is a character. The bawdy old Mrs. Jupp, whose backbone simply curdled at the sight of a cool-livered man, is a character. Theobald is momentarily a character. But Ernest's own history is quite in the line of the educational novels of the eighteenth century. It is a controlled experiment; it smacks of the laboratory; and Overton hovers in the background with the terrible ace of Aunt Alethea's legacy up his sleeve. Ernest's relations with Ellen are quite unbelievable; developments are stated, not shown; and one finds it quite impossible to believe him capable of the emancipation he achieves.

No, the vogue of *The Way of All Flesh* has not been due to enthusiasm for the art of fiction. It has not enriched the art of fiction. On the contrary, it has tended to encourage novelists to make their books a carry-all for whatever ideas they could thrust into them.[6] Thus Butler has been as strong an influence toward formlessness as Henry James was toward form. Between them, the two writers have pretty well divided the fiction of the twentieth century.

Butler's vogue has been due to his wit, his gift for satire, and his aphoristic style, to his ideas, and to the fact that he was felt to have described a man's life honestly, in terms free from moral humbug. He struck note after note that sounded in the ears of his followers with insistent charm. He was an unbeliever. He championed sexual freedom. He anticipated Freud in perceiving the importance of the subconscious, and he skirted the fringe of the stream-of-consciousness novel. He was a Vitalist, roughly in the manner of Bergson; he foresaw the Gestaltist reply to Behaviorism. He even knew there

[6] Among the books generally mentioned as belonging to the school of Butler are *Of Human Bondage,* by W. Somerset Maugham; *Changing Winds,* by St. John Ervine; the Jacob Stahl trilogy, by J. D. Beresford; *Young Earnest,* by Gilbert Cannan; *The Clayhanger Family,* by Arnold Bennett; *The New Machiavelli,* by H. G. Wells; *Sons and Lovers,* by D. H. Lawrence; *Mary Olivier,* by May Sinclair.

was "a horrible screw loose" somewhere in the Newtonian system, though he never got round to figuring out where it was.

A word must be said in closing about Butler's Utopia, *Erewhon* (1872) and its successor, *Erewhon Revisited* (1901). *Erewhon* takes off directly from Butler's own experiences in New Zealand: a sheep-herder, seeking new pastures, finds a passage through the range, and stumbles into the unknown country. At the close he escapes in a balloon, taking the Erewhon girl he wishes to marry with him.

There is a suggestion of Swift or Defoe about the matter-of-factness of the opening chapters; and Swift is imitated again at the close, where persons interested in sending the Gospel to Erewhon are invited to mail their contributions to the Lord Mayor of London. But it was too late in the day for anybody to be taken in by that.

In *Erewhon Revisited* the pious Higgs returns to find that a new religion has been developed around him. The years have been re-numbered for him and sayings attributed to him that he never dreamed of uttering. Already the cult of the Sunchild has identified itself very thoroughly with the existing order, and when Higgs asserts his presence at the dedication exercises of the new temple he nearly loses his life. So, Butler implies, Christians would re-crucify Jesus were he to appear among men once more.

As a piece of narrative the sequel is far ahead of the first book. "The sense and honesty of Chaucer"—such is Aldous Huxley's great tribute—"these he [Butler] had always displayed. In this last book he reveals something of the delicate sensibility and emotional depth of his greater predecessor." [7] As Butler himself says, *Erewhon* has "no central idea" and "hardly any story." But it bites, and it has left its mark. Whether they were meant seriously or not, the chapters on the tyranny of the machine were strangely prescient of the terrible dilemma of the twentieth century, as Karel Čapek described it in *R.U.R.*, as mankind experienced it in the sickening horror of the Second World War. In Erewhon they nurse the criminal and punish the sick man for bad judgment. There is much fooling in

[7] There had been something of the same kind of charm in the portrait of the Nausicaä whom Butler believed to have written the *Odyssey;* cf. *The Authoress of the Odyssey* (1897). It was a strangely mellow tribute from a man ordinarily somewhat unresponsive to the charms of women.

Butler's presentation of these procedures, but there is much sound criminology and common sense also.

It should be clear by now that Butler did not keep all his shafts for the traditionalists. He was by no means a complete determinist. Some things are predetermined, but within our own sphere we can still exercise freedom of the will. Ernest gets a bad start, but life does not down him. In spite of misfortune and disappointment he is happy and useful in the end.

Butler was far from orthodox Christianity, yet he was a very religious man. Even if we do not take his considered statement that he thought of himself as a member of the Broad Church seriously, it still remains true that in his own view he was building a better foundation for the religion of the future. He believed "that if a man loves God he cannot come to much harm." But like the Quakers, he felt that to achieve this security a man must disregard theological dogmas and social conventions completely and listen to the voice of God to within himself.

> Above all things [he pleaded], let no unwary reader do me the injustice of believing in *me*. . . . If he must believe in anything, let him believe in the music of Handel, the painting of Giovanni Bellini, and the XIIIth Chapter of St. Paul's Epistle to the Corinthians.

His disciples have not always obeyed him, but that is the way of disciples, as he himself must well have known.

CHAPTER XXIV

VALUES AND JOSEPH CONRAD *

I have been called a writer of the sea, a descriptive writer, a romantic writer—and also a realist. But as a matter of fact all my concern has been with the "ideal" value of things, events, and people. That and nothing else. The humorous, the pathetic, the passionate, the sentimental aspects came in of themselves. . . .

JOSEPH CONRAD

1. *Conrad's Approach to Fiction*

Jozef Teodor Konrad Nałecz Korzeniowski lived three lives, and they constituted a more spectacular romance than any he was ever able to write. That a Polish boy, born far away from all sight and sound of the sea, should be impelled by some inner compulsion to make himself a British sailor is itself an amazing fact; that after his retirement from the sea that sailor should have become one of the most distinguished of British novelists is a feat without parallel. Yet this was Conrad's experience. He was born into the Polish landed gentry, in the Ukraine, December 3, 1857. His father, translator of Shakespeare, Victor Hugo, and others, was banished by the Russian government in 1862, and his wife and son followed him into exile. The mother died in 1865, the father four years later. The boy studied in the Royal and Imperial Gymnasium of St. Anne and elsewhere, but the sea was ever sounding in his ears. He came to it at Marseilles in 1874; for the next twenty years he followed it. In 1886 he

* The quotations from Conrad's books and from his critics given in this chapter are from *The Nigger of the Narcissus,* by Joseph Conrad, copyright, 1897, 1914; *Lord Jim,* by Joseph Conrad, copyright, 1899, 1920; *Chance,* by Joseph Conrad, copyright, 1913; *The Shadow-Line,* by Joseph Conrad, copyright, 1908, 1921; *A Critical Study of Joseph Conrad,* by Wilson Follett, copyright, 1915; *Joseph Conrad: Life and Letters,* by G. Jean Aubry, copyright, 1926, 1927; *The Last Twelve Years of Joseph Conrad,* by Richard Curle, copyright, 1928; all quotations being used by permission of Doubleday, Doran and Company, Inc.

became a master in the English Merchant Service. He sailed to the West Indies and the Gulf of Mexico; to India, Australia, and the Far East; to the Straits Settlements and the Malay Archipelago. He engaged in gun-running activities in behalf of the Spanish Pretender; and he piloted a boat up the Congo with his head full of Mark Twain on the Mississippi.

The Congo journey cost him his health and ultimately his life, for there he picked up the disease that wracked his body until it killed him thirty years afterwards. There too he saw life naked and was permanently disillusioned. "The sinister voice of the Congo with its murmuring undertone of human fatuity, baseness and greed had swept away all the generous illusions of his youth," wrote his friend, Edward Garnett, "and left him gazing into the heart of an immense darkness."

Like William Morris, Conrad could not remember learning to read; he only knew that he was reading Polish books at five and that French was added soon thereafter. Abridged versions of *Don Quixote* and *Gil Blas* came his way; he read Shakespeare and Victor Hugo in his father's translations. But Dickens, whom he always loved, was his introduction to English literature: "It is extraordinary how well Mrs. Nickleby could chatter disconnectedly in Polish. . . ." Scott enthralled him also, as did Cooper and Marryat, that "enslaver of youth." But the great explorers—Livingstone and his peers—meant as much to him as the novelists; sometimes he thought they meant more.

His mature literary allegiance Conrad gave to the French school—Flaubert, de Maupassant, and that Gallicized Russian, Turgenev. Henry James was the only other writer who influenced him deeply. He liked Daudet, France, Mérimée, and Balzac; he liked Trollope, Howells, and Stephen Crane. Ford Madox Ford credits him with considerable reading in Mrs. Henry Wood, Miss Braddon, and the *Family Herald*. He disliked Melville, Stevenson, and Meredith; and poetry in general meant little to him; Keats and Christina Rossetti are the only poets in whom he ever took much interest. He disliked Tolstoy and above all he disliked Dostoevsky, for him the pre-eminent incarnation of the forces of unreason that he thought of as having their stronghold in Russia.

Conrad was never a facile inventor. "The sustained invention of a really telling lie demands a talent which I do not possess." As John D. Gordan has pointed out, we must go to his own life to find the sources of his books. Sometimes he used his individual experiences; sometimes he depended on observation, sometimes on hearsay, sometimes even on reading. In *Lord Jim* all four sources were tapped.

Of course this does not mean that Conrad was a reporter. Many of his characters were drawn from personages he had only glimpsed. Mr. Gordan's elaborate independent study of the life-models used for *Almayer's Folly* concludes with the observation that the book "was not a record of the life of William Charles Olmeijer but an expansion of the impression made upon the novelist by the man's personality." And Sir Frank Swettenham and Sir Hugh Clifford, authorities on Malaysia, see Conrad's Malays as the result "of a series of flash-light impressions absorbed by a mind of strangely sensitive and imaginative quality, rather than of any deep understanding of the people we both knew so well."

But if none of this means that Conrad was a reporter, it certainly does mean that his personality is an immensely important factor in his books. Mr. R. L. Mégroz is quite accurate when he points out that Conrad "belongs to the Miltonic type of artist, whose vision of reality is always a reflection of his own tragic and aspiring self." [1]

2. *Conrad's Writing Career*

Conrad's first two books—*Almayer's Folly* (1895) and *An Outcast of the Islands* (1896)—are somber studies in degeneration. They are authentic Conrad, but they seem unimportant compared to *The Nigger of the Narcissus* (1897), the book which brought him fame though not fortune, and by which he was content to stand or fall as an artist.

Though the treatment of the sailors in the forecastle derives directly from Flaubert's description of the barbarians in the Gardens of Hamilcar at the beginning of *Salammbô, The Nigger* is still one of the most original books ever written. Essentially it is a study of the influence of a dying black sailor upon the men who sail home

[1] *Joseph Conrad's Mind and Method* (Faber, 1931).

with him from Bombay. Wait is half-invalid, half-charlatan, and there are times when he is Death itself. Though one is never quite convinced that in life he would have met with the patience he meets with here, one must still be impressed by the unforgettable characters with which the book is crowded.

The Nigger has much in common with the three collections of shorter pieces which followed it—*Tales of Unrest* (1898); *Youth* (1902); *Typhoon* (1903).[2] The first of these is unimportant. But the other two volumes are still held by most seasoned Conradians as standing among their author's greatest achievements. "Youth" is the story of an apparently "hoodooed" voyage which the spirit of youth makes glorious; "Typhoon" contains the most wonderful description of a storm at sea in all literature; in "Heart of Darkness" (which is included in the *Youth* volume), the Congo assails not merely our eyes and ears and nostrils but our very souls.

The first period of Conrad's work culminates logically, if not quite chronologically, in *Lord Jim* (1900), that acute study in "the consciousness of lost honor." So far, though Conrad had established himself as a writer, he had done little to prove that he was a novelist. *Lord Jim* began as a short story, but it grew upon his hands, and by the time he finished it he had passed an important milestone. Yet as a novel it is still far from perfect. It breaks definitely in the middle—this is the "plague spot" upon which Garnett put his finger and which Conrad ruefully acknowledged—and the second half is much inferior to the first.[3]

After *Lord Jim,* Conrad marked time by collaborating with Ford Madox Ford (then Ford Madox Hueffer) in *The Inheritors* (1901), *Romance* (1903), and *The Nature of a Crime,* which was not published in book form until 1924. *Romance* is the only one of these

[2] Later collections of short stories were entitled *A Set of Six* (1908); *'Twixt Land and Sea* (1912); *Within the Tides* (1915); *Tales of Hearsay* (1925). It will be convenient also to list here four non-fiction books by Conrad: *The Mirror of the Sea* (1906); *A Personal Record* (1912); *Notes on Life and Letters* (1921); *Last Essays* (1926).

[3] *Lord Jim* was probably influenced by the career of Rajah Brooke; see J. D. Gordan, *Studies in Philology,* XXXV (1938), 613-634, XXXVII (1940), 130-132; see also, for an interesting analysis of certain incidents in the story, Richard Hoffman, "Proportion and Incident in Joseph Conrad and Arnold Bennett," *Sewanee Review,* XXXII (1924), 79-92.

books to which Conrad contributed importantly. But apparently his collaboration with Ford increased his confidence, for he turned next to one of the most ambitious novels in the language, his most neglected and in his own opinion his greatest book, *Nostromo* (1904).

If he was wrong, it must be because there is too much of the book, and because its complicated method of narration makes it extremely difficult to read. Yet much may be forgiven a novelist who creates a whole country, as Conrad did in these pages.[4] In a way, indeed, he may be said to have recreated a world; for Costaguana is our modern world in little, with its greed and its twisted motives, its strange passion for bloodletting, its vain, tortured attempts to serve ideal ends by impure means, thus twisting its means and betraying its ends. In the usual sense of those terms, *Nostromo* is Conrad's most original, his most creative book. And surely it left no doubt concerning his ability to handle a long, highly wrought narrative.

For the time being he seemed to have exhausted his memories; he wrote two novels about anarchists and revolutionaries—*The Secret Agent* (1907) and *Under Western Eyes* (1911). Of the first of these, which was suggested by the 1894 attempt to blow up the Greenwich Observatory, Conrad remarks that it was not a book he needed to write. He might have said the same of *Under Western Eyes.* Yet both books exemplify his humanity, and the latter, while un-Conradian in its method, is very characteristic of him in its point of view.

Razumov, the hero of *Under Western Eyes,* is in some sense comparable to Lord Jim. At the beginning he betrays the young revolutionary who had cast himself upon his confidence; as the game proceeds, he takes every trick. Victor's comrades accept him as one of themselves; Victor's saintly sister is just on the point of loving him. It is then, when he is entirely safe, that he must tell the truth and accept his terrible fate.

With the unbelievably rich and beautiful book he called *Chance* (1914), Conrad seems to be getting his second wind. And here, too, he begins at last to find his public. In a way, this is surprising, for *Chance* is the most complicated as to method of all Conrad's books.

[4] Cf. Richard Curle, "The Background of 'Nostromo,'" in *Caravansary and Conversation* (Stokes, 1937).

But it is a very appealing story; it has a fascinating heroine; and many readers found the characters with which it deals better suited to Conrad's analytic method than the natives of Malay and Borneo. Flora de Barral, daughter of a crooked financier, has suffered a "brutally murdered childhood." Captain Anthony, "The Knight," marries her, and takes her off to sea with her incubus of a father. From this poignant situation, complicated as it is by de Barral's murderous hatred for his benefactor, Conrad extracts the last bit of emotion and—what is more—the last bit of significance it can be made to yield. The resolution comes at last through a "scene" which could be guaranteed to thrill the most hardened habitué of Drury Lane, but the author's psychological probing never ceases.

There is more melodrama perhaps in *Victory* (1915). Here again gallantry plays its part, for Heyst carries Alma off to his desert island to save her from the lecherous scoundrel, Schomberg. Greed follows them, to rob them of imagined wealth, in the likeness of the bored "Mr. Jones" and his shadow Ricardo, and Alma dies at last to win the victory over Heyst's inertia and her own fears. She gives her life as she had already given her body; it is an important element in her characterization that she should not have been "what they call a good girl." Conrad himself had something of Heyst's skepticism; he cannot plant himself foursquare in opposition to his hero, as Meredith might have done. But the Swede's habit of drifting as a defense against life is a method that fails him in the end, and Conrad is as didactic as he ever gets in the dying cry, "Ah, Davidson, woe to the man whose heart has not learned while young to hope, to love—and to put his trust in life!" [5]

In his next two books Conrad went back to autobiography. ***The Shadow-Line*** (1917) is a companion-piece to "Youth." In the earlier story a succession of material disasters cursed the voyage. The situa-

[5] At several points, *Victory* suggests the possible influence of the Elizabethan drama. Heyst and his opponents fence as lengthily as Hamlet and Claudius, and the full exposition given of the ruthlessness of Jones and Ricardo serves the same function as Hamlet's self-exhortations, i.e., it helps to delay the decisive action which there is no psychological reason for holding off. Alma does not tell Heyst of his peril, though in life she would certainly have done so, thus increasing the sensationalism of the close. Finally there is the orgy of slaughter in which the book ends.

tion in *The Shadow-Line* is more awful, for this time the vessel seems to lie under a psychic curse. The book hovers on the edge of the unknown; it could be interpreted either as a study in coincidence and superstition or as a piece of supernaturalism. In a later Preface Conrad violently repudiated the latter view.

The Arrow of Gold (1919) harks back to Conrad's gun-running days. But there is no action in the book; its subject is glamour, the glamour which a woman of the world can cast over a generous and imaginative young man. I do not happen to find Rita attractive, but the objection sometimes heard, that she is unreal, is silly. She was not meant to be real. We never see her as she is. We see her as she enthralled M. George.

In 1920 Conrad at last published *The Rescue,* which had been more than twenty years in the writing, and had given him more trouble than all the rest of his books together. To make up for that, as the saying goes, it gives trouble to many readers also. The hero is again Tom Lingard, whom we heard of first in *Almayer's Folly;* but this time he is engaged in an unfamiliar battle, pitting his powers against an ultra-sophisticated woman who is more than a match for him, and through whom he at last betrays the primitive people whom he really loves and understands. The last page of this book is an example of almost Dantesque restraint in the expression of powerful emotion; it is one of the greatest pages in English fiction.

Conrad died, August 3, 1924, over *Suspense,* an ambitious historical novel in the classic tradition, a story of the period between the Peace of Paris and Waterloo. It was published, as he left it, in 1925. He might perhaps have had time to complete it, had he not put it aside to write a briefer novel which grew out of it. This is *The Rover* (1923), a tale of Napoleonic days on the Escampobar Peninsula. This picturesque novel, through which breathes the aftermath of the days of the Terror, hardly admits of summary, but the old pirate-patriot, Peyrol, is one of Conrad's unforgettable characters.

3. *Conrad's Vision of Life*

This was the work that he did. How, now, was it wrought—by what methods and to what end?

Fundamentally Conrad saw art as "a single-minded attempt to render the highest kind of justice to the visible universe, by bringing to light the truth, manifold and one, underlying its every aspect." To do this, he tried to bring out "in the aspects of matter and in the facts of life what of each is fundamental, what is enduring and essential—their one illuminating and convincing quality—the very truth of their existence." Of course, art can appeal only through the senses. If literature is to succeed, "it must strenuously aspire to the plasticity of sculpture, to the color of painting, and to the magic suggestiveness of music. . . ."

On this basis Conrad is often called an impressionist. He visualized the stories he wished to tell, himself went through the emotional reactions he desired from his readers. He was never quite sure whether it was his habit or his weakness or his gift to do these things. Certainly impressionism could hardly go farther than it goes in the description of Winnie Verloc's murder of her husband in *The Secret Agent* or the description of what young Powell saw through the glass in *Chance*.

But this is not all. If it were, Conrad could hardly be more than the superb descriptive writer which is all those who search out his "purple passages" know him to be.

Conrad had nothing but scorn for overt didacticism in fiction, yet he realized fully that "every subject in the region of intellect and emotion must have a morality of its own if it is treated at all sincerely; and even the most artful writer will give himself (and his morality) away in about every third sentence." His own morality was that of a passionate Puritan; only Walter de la Mare, among his greater contemporaries, can match him on this score. He saw the world as resting squarely on a few ancient fundamentals, the most important of which was fidelity. "My task . . . is, by the power of the written word to make you hear, to make you feel—it is, before all, to make you *see*. That—and no more, and it is everything. If I succeed, you shall find there according to your deserts: encouragement, consolation, fear, charm—all you demand—and, perhaps, also that glimpse of truth for which you have forgotten to ask."

What is that "glimpse of truth"? Nominally, at least, Conrad was a Roman Catholic. Personally I can find little specifically Catholic doctrine in him, though it is only fair to add that Patrick Braybrooke thinks he finds a good deal.[6] It is certainly not true, as has been stated, that Conrad never mentions God. The dead Almayer's soul stands "in the presence of Infinite Wisdom"; the country he inhabited, like our own, "lies under the inscrutable eyes of the Most High." And of *The Nigger of the Narcissus* Conrad wrote to a friend: "I am conceited enough about it,—God knows,—but He also knows the spirit in which I approached the undertaking to present faithfully some of His benighted and suffering creatures: the humble, the obscure, the sinful, the erring upon whom rests His Gaze of Ineffable Pity." When Bancroft summarizes Conrad's "philosophical principles" as suggesting "not only the Kantian notion of the Moral Law, but Hegel's treatment of 'existence and reality,' and, somewhat, Bosanquet's 'World,'" his whole systematic, ideational approach is foreign to Conrad's way of functioning, as foreign as Mr. Mencken's attribution to him of his own moral and spiritual nihilism, or Arthur Symons's curious attempt to read into him the deep diabolism that so fascinated the critic himself. What was said in these pages of Hardy must be repeated with even greater emphasis of Conrad. He believed that "Nothing humanly great . . . has come from reflection." His attitude toward life was a working attitude, and it was determined by his temperament.

Conrad saw the world as a spectacle, "a spectacle for awe, love, adoration, or hate, if you like . . . never for despair." It can be called a world that is friendly to man only in the sense that it has afforded conditions under which it has been possible for human values to develop. It gives no sign of being itself committed to those values; on the contrary, man faces "the immense indifference of things"; only in activity can he find "the sustaining illusion of an independent existence. . . ." But it is still a world in which a Jim, a Razumov, an Alma can win a spiritual victory. It is true that victory cost every one of them his life. But then, that was also true of Christ.

The problem is complicated by the spotty character of humanity

[6] *Dublin Review,* CLXXXIX (1931), 318-325.

itself. Human nature is "not very nice clear through." It is cursed by "poignant miseries" and "passionate credulities," "tragically eager for its own destruction." Man wants to be saint and devil at the same time, and his life is too short for the full utterance of whatever meaning it may be capable of sustaining; perhaps the artist who made him was a little mad.

None of this, in any sense, invalidates the value of values. And for Conrad values are most likely to be found upon the sea. There has been considerable controversy as to whether or not Conrad loved the sea. Certainly there was no sentimental nature-pantheism in his attitude toward it. It has "no compassion, no faith, no law, no memory . . . nothing can touch the bitterness of its heart." And yet . . . and yet . . . "The true peace of God begins at any spot a thousand miles from the nearest land." Perhaps that was it. At sea you can get away from the ugly mess that men have made of the world. The non-essentials disappear; the fundamentals get their chance. Here man meets his ordeal—"the test of manliness, of temperament, of courage and fidelity—and of love."

The peculiar circumstances of Conrad's life-experience must always be taken into consideration as conditioning the subject-matter, if not the fundamental character, of his books. There are some things one cannot imagine Conrad doing under any circumstances. One cannot imagine him writing what is now called a "proletarian" novel, and the disparagement of him on the part of radical critics of the thirties was due largely to this fact. Conrad detested autocracy, but he knew that there was nothing to be hoped for from revolution; for him all governments were bad, and the last refuge of comedy was in the courts. I am not forgetting that he loved England, but he loved her because she had gone farther than any other nation toward learning the sublime truth that the function of government is not to govern. His love was not blind; he opposed the Boer War; there was not much about imperialistic exploitation that he did not know; he had no illusions that even representative government could guarantee liberty against the disturbing force of human passions. Fundamentally, as Sir William Rothenstein has remarked, Conrad was an aristocrat; "he believed that the object of life was the perfection of individual conduct—the education of man's own spirit. For panaceas of human perfection he had neither patience nor respect."

That "perfection of individual conduct" is the theme of all his books, and it is inconceivable that, being what he was, he could ever have chosen another, but it is true that if he had not followed the sea, he might have studied conduct in very different aspects. For one thing, there might have been much less melodrama in his books. Even when he turned away from the sea to write of Europe, as in *The Secret Agent* and *Under Western Eyes,* he found melodramatic themes. Apparently it was inconceivable to him that a novel could be written in any other way, for when he came to give advice to the young Norman Douglas what he said was, "Try to make it a novel of *analysis* on the basis of some strong situation."

In short, Conrad's materials hark back to the epic stage in the development of literature, but he treats them with all the introspective subtlety of a James or a Proust. The early critic who rejected *Almayer's Folly* on the ground that "Borneo is a fine field for the study of monkeys, not of men," was not a very discerning creature, and Conrad's own ringing eloquence is a sufficient answer:

> I am content to sympathize with common mortals, no matter where they live; in houses or in tents, in the streets under a fog, or in the forests behind the dark line of dismal mangroves that fringe the vast solitude of the sea. For, their land—like ours—lies under the inscrutable eyes of the Most High. Their hearts—like ours—must endure the load of the gifts from Heaven: the curse of facts and the blessing of illusions, the bitterness of our wisdom and the deceptive consolation of our folly.

Yet it is still possible to feel that there is a clash at times between Conrad's materials and his method.

In pursuing this study of individual conduct, Conrad again and again uses the theme of the psychic wound. Lord Jim deserted the ship. Dr. Monygham betrayed his friends under torture.[7] Falk ate human flesh.[8] Captain Whalley went on sailing the ship after his eyesight had begun to fail.[9] Flora de Barral was made to think herself unlovable. Arlette was crazed when she saw her parents butch-

[7] *Nostromo.*
[8] "Falk," in *Typhoon and Other Stories.*
[9] "The End of the Tether," in *Youth and Other Stories.*

ered under the Terror.[10] And these persons are no anomalies. "The commonest sort of fortitude prevents us from becoming criminals in a legal sense; it is from weakness unknown, but perhaps suspected, as in some parts of the world you suspect a deadly snake in every bush—from weakness that may lie hidden, watched or unwatched, prayed against or manfully scorned, repressed or maybe ignored more than half a lifetime, not one of us is safe." Even the young captain of *The Shadow-Line,* who is Conrad himself, is haunted by a "strange sense of insecurity." "I always suspected that I might be no good." The best any of us can hope to do is to pick his way through the world, hoping that he may be given the grace to make a decent end.

The most elaborate study of the psychic wound is, of course, in Lord Jim, who blights his career by deserting an apparently doomed ship which yet miraculously comes to shore. Edward Crankshaw says rightly that the book "is not so much a thesis on the theme of honor as a fantasia." It was not cowardice that caused Jim's dereliction; it was "nerves"; it was hypnosis, a paralysis of will; it was something he could not understand himself. The people who come to his trial are drawn by a keen psychological interest; for Conrad—and for us—no trouble that we may take to understand Jim can be too great, for he was one of us; and if that sort can go wrong, what hope is there for anybody? We must believe in Jim before we can believe in anybody else; humanity itself is to be vindicated in him.

Scandal pursues Jim from job to job; he cannot escape from his past; he will not escape from himself. Suicide could solve nothing; he must yield to the destructive element; he must have another chance to find out the truth about himself.

It comes at last in Patusan, where he has made himself a great man, but it comes in amazing guise.

> We are offered [says Wilson Follett], not the old—and how familiar!—story of the man who fails dismally in a crisis and is whipped by his failure into a spectacular atoning success, but the new and far less obvious story of the man who fails twice over, deliberately invoking the undeserved consequences of the second failure and turning them into one splendid triumph. . . . And that there may exist not one of even

[10] *The Rover.*

the external trappings of melodrama, Jim is allowed to die without material justification or forgiveness.

The woman he loves wants Jim to fight those who would take his life, but he replies that there is nothing to fight for because nothing has been lost; nothing can touch him. He ends his life "an obscure conqueror of fame, tearing himself out of the arms of a jealous love at the call of his exalted egoism."

It would have been too much to hope that we might have been spared a Freudian interpretation of all this. It was offered in 1930 by Gustav Morf,[11] and it ran true to formula. Conrad himself was Lord Jim, and Poland was his *Patna.* This is about as convincing as most Freudian analyses, but one need not go with Morf and Freud to see Conrad's solitariness as peculiarly accentuated by the circumstances of his life. That every man spends his life in impenetrable loneliness, and that the peculiar quality of his existence is a thing he can never communicate to anybody else is, of course, a commonplace of human experience, but few have ever felt it so keenly as Conrad did. Yet he believed that "we exist only in so far as we hang together," and he saw crime itself as "a breach of faith with the community of mankind." When *Chance* brought him at last his wider hearing, he rejoiced "because what I always feared most was drifting unconsciously into the position of a writer for a limited coterie; a position which would have been odious to me as throwing a doubt on the soundness of my belief in the solidarity of all mankind in simple ideas and in sincere emotions."

4. *Conrad's Narrative Method*

It has been necessary to raise these considerations before turning to the matter of Conrad's narrative method, for the reason that the latter cannot be understood apart from them. The most distinctive feature of that method is, in the apt words of William Lyon Phelps, that he "does not have us look directly at the object, but rather at a mirror in which the object is reflected." To be sure he does not always do this. In his most difficult book, *Nostromo,* he contented himself almost entirely with direct, objective narrative; in such

[11] *The Polish Heritage of Joseph Conrad* (Richard R. Smith).

works as *The Shadow-Line* and *The Arrow of Gold* he wrote in the first person as an actor in the story. More characteristic of him, however, are such narratives as "Youth," "Heart of Darkness," *Lord Jim,* and *Chance,* all of which are told by "that preposterous master-mariner" (as Henry James called him), Marlow, "a most discreet, understanding man," whose "slightly mocking expression . . . covers up his sympathetic impulses of mirth and pity before the unreasonable complications the idealism of mankind puts into the simple but poignant problem of conduct on this earth." And Conrad often uses Marlow in such fashion as to cause even so determined a devotee of "point of view" as James himself to feel that he seemed determined to find the hardest possible way. In *Chance,* Marlow relates what Fyne, Mrs. Fyne, young Powell, Flora, and others told him to "I," who is never identified and who contributes nothing; sometimes we actually get the narrative at the fifth remove.

As for chronology specifically, the bewildered reader's first feeling must be that Conrad has only one principle: never under any circumstances must the incidents in a story be related in the order in which they occurred! Galsworthy speaks of his folding his story over and over itself, and Conrad himself has a phrase about stopping "in the very fullness of the tick." In *The Secret Agent* the bomb outrage is first reported on p. 70. Then we dig back into its antecedents and do not reach it again until p. 190, while it is not until p. 210 that Winnie is made aware that the man who was blown to pieces was her brother. In *Under Western Eyes,* Part IV follows Part I chronologically. In the account of Powell's adventures in *Chance,* Chapter I is continued on p. 273; and the dog's disloyalty to Flora, which seemed a trifling thing when reported on p. 43, is brought up again on p. 202 and shown to have exercised an almost determinative influence upon the plot.

Conrad's critics have been very busy explaining these apparent eccentricities.[12] He lends both intensity and plausibility to his characters, we are told, by giving them to us as they appear in the eyes of a

[12] Practically all critical studies touch on the matter. See especially two articles in the *Sewanee Review*—Frances Westworth Cutler, "Why Marlow?" XXVI (1918), 28-38; Donald Davidson, "Joseph Conrad's Directed Indirections," XXXIII (1925), 163-177.

keen observer. He may have felt that he was doing his characters "less violence dragging them out into the open, when some third person intervened between himself and them." He was "a subjective visionary committed to the [Flaubertian] ideal of objectivity." Being unable to thrust himself into his story directly, as Thackeray and Trollope do, he used this other method of commenting indirectly; thus he achieved "simultaneous intimacy and detachment," "a fusion of memory and thought," a synthesis of disparate materials. Through Marlow Conrad "detaches the problem from immediacy," achieves "an effect of distance or perspective." The fact that the story is presented from more than one point of view underlines both the complexity and the subjectivity of the events recorded; the novelist creates "a dome of many-colored glass," involving the reader himself in the tale, and causing him to possess it "as a web of events and characters acting and reacting as living things."

All this has considerable cogency, but perhaps none of it quite reaches the heart of the matter. Nor can one be entirely satisfied with Ford Madox Ford's report on Conrad's theory of story-telling. For Conrad was one of the most profoundly intuitive of all writers. He created his characters without knowing what they were going to do; he thrust them into a situation without the remotest idea of how he was going to get them out again. With such a writer, theories and principles, however sincerely held, are mere rationalizations imposed upon the deep urges of his fundamental temperament.

Conrad's close friend, Richard Curle, reports that "he never said all he thought about any one subject at any one time." "There was a curious caution about him, and he would walk round a subject examining it from different angles." Well, that is exactly what he did in his novels! In the last analysis, Conrad told his stories as he did because that was the natural way for him.

There was more to it than that, of course. Nor do I wish to imply that Conrad did not understand the implications of what he was doing. I have already said that he was not a didactic writer. Neither are his tales allegories like Franz Kafka's. But there is many a halfway house between preaching and mere "yarning"; and there are times when Conrad does begin to approach Kafka—in *Victory,* for example, where Mr. Jones and his confederates are intended to typify "evil intelligence, instinctive savagery, arm in arm." Miss M. C. Bradbrook goes further still when she sees Mr. Jones as Death. ("Davy Jones" is the sailor's name for Death.) "I am he who is," says Mr. Jones of himself, reminding Miss Bradbrook of Milton's "Myself am hell" and Shelley's "He who reigns."

In a sense, every novel of quality is an allegory; how else could it possibly have any significance for human life? Conrad's supreme interest was always in values, in the essential significance of his tale. That is why he is out of the local color movement, why it is absurd to speak of him, as he was once described at the beginning of his career, as "the Kipling of the Malay Archipelago." And that is why he is right when he remarks of the story he tells in *The Arrow of Gold* that, though it happens in Marseilles, "it might have happened anywhere." He chooses his method, and he establishes the order of his narrative, with an eye to the effects he has in view. The important thing is not point of view, and the important thing is not chronology. The important thing is significance.

Whether the method is "good" or not must depend, as such things generally do, on its effect on the reader. Here and there, legitimate exceptions may surely be taken. In *The Nigger of the Narcissus* there is some unmotivated shifting between the first person and the third. The chapter of *The Secret Agent* in which Verloc is murdered is written from Verloc's point of view, but naturally Verloc dies in the course of it; at this moment, Conrad shifts abruptly to the vantage-point of his wife, the murderess.

But there are larger matters than these. Not only is it impossible to believe that Marlow could have talked so long as he does in *Lord Jim,* but, as J. M. Robertson has pointed out, the novel is not a spoken "but a consummately written tale"; "Marlow is reciting written Conrad." Robertson also speaks of Decoud's impossible letter in *Nostromo,* which it must have taken at least seven hours to achieve, without intervening rest, at the end of a period of forty hours of intense strain! In *Chance,* I for one cannot believe that Flora would tell Marlow all she does tell him "on the pavement," while Fyne is remonstrating with her protector within. I do not believe that Marlow could have remembered all the dialogue he reports in the first part of *Chance,* nor do I think he could have figured out people's motives as he did with the material he had in nand.

It will not do, however, to object that Conrad's method has a tendency to leave too much enshrouded in mystery. That was precisely where Conrad thought it belonged. Not that he went in for the kind of mystery that enthralls devotees of *The Cat and the Canary;* such child's play must have seemed to him to stand on the intellectual level of the jig-saw puzzle. For him, human character itself is the great mystery. He once told Richard Curle that "Explicitness is fatal to the glamour of all artistic work." He was speaking of the identification of backgrounds, but his words have a wider application. Hence his "atmosphere." Hence the peculiar brooding quality which distinguishes him from a writer like Henry James. Hence his tendency to project a dramatic concept, as Elizabeth Bowen has remarked, "not by means of a development but by means of a soaking."

Aldous Huxley, therefore, though absolutely correct, is strangely irrelevant when he declares that Conrad did not fathom his own creations. Conrad never pretended to understand himself. Marlow does not profess to understand Lord Jim. And Jim himself is never sure what kind of person he is until he has made the final sacrifice.

Edwin Muir, on the other hand, is miles from the truth when he speaks of Conrad's characters in general as "specimens of humanity" who "exist in a laboratory of psychology"; indeed this is an excellent statement of what they are not. We never, never know them as we know a historical character, for example, whom we have analyzed in the light of all the available evidence, with every trait and impulse neatly classified under the appropriate heading. We know them rather in the infinitely warmer but less systematic way that we know the people we live with, of whom we can never be sure what they will do next. What misled Mr. Muir was the fact that Conrad sometimes carries his search for essential meanings so far that we cannot see the tree for the woods. This is particularly likely to be true of his women. Rita has in her something of the women of all time; she is "part of the indestructible," has at her service "the everlasting charm of life." Winnie Verloc is much more concrete, but when she kills her husband, and flees, and slips at last beneath the waters of the channel, breathless as the narrative is, we feel that it is the very spirit of flight and terror that enthralls us; we are gripped by the emotions of a tortured woman rather than by those of this woman in particular.

5. *A Last Word*

Like Phoebe of *As You Like It* Conrad is not for all markets. His art was so profoundly individual in its method—and that individuality was so pronounced—that many, even among cultivated readers, find it very difficult to meet him on his own ground. But there can be little question that he was the greatest novelist of his time. His work was remarkable in itself, and when one considers the conditions under which he wrought one bows the head in the presence of a miracle. No man ever wrote with greater difficulty than Conrad; it is hardly an exaggeration to say that every word he got on paper cost him a drop of his blood. He was cursed too by long periods of sterility, during which his heroic attempts to force himself only made matters worse. In addition to all this, he was—until *Chance* turned the tide for him—desperately poor; and he was rarely free from pain.

Of his metaphysic, if we are to call it that, as of Hardy's, we must say that while it may or may not have been adequate for life, it served him well as an artist. He wrote in a "spirit of piety towards all things human," and a great soul shines through his work. For all the role chance plays in his books, he never believed life to be all chance, nor could any but the most superficial reading of the novel which bears that title so interpret it. The title-page gives the first clue, for it carries this quotation from Sir Thomas Browne: "Those that hold that all things are governed by Fortune had not erred, had they not persisted there." At the end of the novel the "gospel truth" is proclaimed, that "the science of life consists in seizing every chance that presents itself." Conrad himself seized chance by the forelock and expended all his art and all his manhood in making it serve the needs of life.

CHAPTER XXV

NOVELIST OF BEING: ARNOLD BENNETT*

> But at my back I always hear
> Time's winged chariot hurrying near;
> And yonder all before us lie
> Deserts of vast eternity.
>
> ANDREW MARVELL

1. *"Time Goes"*

At the west end of the Midway Pleasance at the University of Chicago stands Lorado Taft's great statue of "The Fountain of Time." A vast cloaked and hooded figure with scythe and hourglass gazes across the water at an immense sculptured procession in which almost every conceivable kind of human being is depicted. On the base of the monument are these words from Austin Dobson:

TIME GOES YOU SAY, AH NO. ALAS TIME STAYS, WE GO

After viewing "The Fountain of Time" the traveler may go downtown to the Fine Arts Building on Michigan Avenue. Over the portal he will read:

ALL PASSES—ART ALONE ENDURES

This sense of time passing was a thing that never left Arnold Bennett. "He had once been young, and he had grown old, and was now dead. That was all. Everything came to that."

All Bennett's best work strikes this note. Mr. Shushions, the aged Sunday School teacher, who years before had befriended Darius Clayhanger, and who is baited by the hoodlums at the festival, is "Time's obscene victim." When Edwin Clayhanger stands by the

* Quotations from Bennett's *The Clayhanger Family* (copyright, 1910, 1938), *The Old Wives' Tale* (copyright, 1909, 1937), *Leonora* (copyright, 1910, 1938), *Buried Alive* (copyright, 1913, 1941), *Anna of the Five Towns* (copyright, 1915), *Whom God Hath Joined* (copyright, 1906, 1934), and *Riceyman Steps* (copyright, 1923), are used by permission of Doubleday, Doran and Company, Inc.

death-bed of Auntie Hamps, he cannot help thinking of what she had been fifty years ago. "She was a young girl—and now she is sentenced." *The Old Wives' Tale* began with its author's similar reaction toward an absurd old woman in a Paris restaurant.

Only, Bennett always remembered "that the change from the young girl to the stout, aging woman is made up of an infinite number of infinitesimal changes, each unperceived by her." Not for him the bold sharp contrasts of a Thackeray. In *Henry Esmond* we see Beatrix in her youth. In *The Virginians* we see her in old age. And she is the same woman, which is a marvelous thing. But we do not actually see the change coming about. This is precisely what we do see in Constance and Sophia Baines of *The Old Wives' Tale.*

Of the four most famous Edwardian novelists, Bennett is the easiest to underestimate. He has none of Conrad's exoticism, none of Wells's intellectual bravura, none of Galsworthy's "fineness." If Wells is the Novelist of Becoming, then Bennett is the Novelist of Being; and he is too much enthralled by the spectacle ever to want to change it. He deals with basic human experiences. His ideas are not "original"; he does not sing; he never sends up skyrockets to call attention to his "effects." None of his virtues are of the flamboyant variety. And he is enough of a classicist always to cause one to think of his novels as novels, not as so many summaries of brilliant parts.

2. *Bennett's Life-Experience and Literary Ideals*

Enoch Arnold Bennett, the son of a solicitor, was born near Hanley, in "The Potteries," May 27, 1867. Pottery-making, iron-smelting, and coal-mining are the industries of this district; its culture is predominantly Wesleyan. Bennett began as a journalist, first in the Five Towns, then in London. He edited a woman's magazine; he acted as publisher's reader, book reviewer, and dramatic critic. Bennett never indeed relinquished journalism. He earned a great deal of money from such "Pocket Philosophies" as *How to Live on 24 Hours a Day, Married Love,* and *Friendship and Happiness;* in the last year of his life he was still one of the most influential reviewers in London.

In 1900 he resigned his editorship of *Woman,* and went to live on a farm in Bedfordshire. By March, 1903, he was settled in Paris. In 1907 he married a Frenchwoman, Marguerite Soulié. He toured the United States in 1911; in 1912 he earned £16,000, which was more than he had earned in all his other years together. During the war he did propaganda work for the government, and found it a great lark. In 1921 he separated from his wife; two years later he formed his intimacy with the actress, Dorothy Cheston, who later became the mother of his only child, Virginia Bennett. He died March 27, 1931.

Bennett is the historian of the "Five Towns,"[1] by which he was profoundly conditioned, and out of which nearly all his best work grew. He hated them and rebelled against them—"I do not think the Five Towns will ever be described. Dante lived too soon."—yet in some moods he was profoundly touched by them and even hurt when others could not see the beauty of their fierce drabness. He never forgot that an artist must himself be under the spell of the life he describes.

Bennett was reared in an unliterary atmosphere. As late as 1896 he calls Jane Austen the only author he knows well; he did not read *David Copperfield* until he was thirty. He admired Blake and Wordsworth, Trollope and Meredith; he found comfort in the mysticism of the English Bible. Among standard English novelists only Samuel Butler and George Moore would seem to have affected him strongly. The Gallic naturalism of Moore, who had already written of the potteries, appealed strongly to Bennett's temperament, while Butler's influence can be seen in the study of family groups in *Clayhanger* and elsewhere. In addition to these writers there was Ouida, whom Bennett read avidly in his youth and from whom he never really recovered. If it had not been for Ouida, we might have escaped *The Book of Carlotta* and even certain passages in *The Pretty Lady* and *Imperial Palace*.

But Bennett was growing up in a time in which all really "ad-

[1] Tunstall, Burslem, Hanley, Stoke-upon-Trent, and Longton, in northern Staffordshire, which appear in the novels as Turnhill, Bursley, Hanbridge, Knype, and Longshaw. He left out the sixth town, Fenton, because he liked the sound of "Five Towns" better than "Six Towns." See the maps and the "Note on the Topography of the Five Towns," in Harvey Darton, *Arnold Bennett,* pp. 44-50.

vanced" young Englishmen were giving their allegiance to Continental writers. He read Zola and Balzac; he also read Leblanc and Gaboriau, who influenced his "thrillers"; more importantly, he read de Maupassant, Flaubert, Gautier, Huysmans, and the Goncourts. He began keeping a journal because the Goncourts had kept a journal; at the very end of his life he draws on the Goncourt journal for *Imperial Palace.*

It may be that at the time he thought their spirit more congenial to him than it actually was, for in his own novels he never achieved either a complete naturalism or a thoroughgoing objectivity. Something deeper in him responded later to the Russian influence, in connection with which Lafourcade speaks of his "vague oriental tenderness for the poor," the "strange passivity" of his heroes, the "nondescript mysticism" of *The Glimpse,* and the "inverted romanticism" so characteristic of his work.

3. *An Attempt at Classification*

Arnold Bennett's fiction may be divided into four groups:

I. MELODRAMAS. *The Grand Babylon Hotel* (1902); *The Gates of Wrath* (1903); *Teresa of Watling Street* (1904); *The Loot of Cities* (1905); *Hugo* (1906); *The Sinews of War* (with Eden Phillpotts) (1906); *The Ghost* (1907); *The City of Pleasure* (1907); *The Statue* (with Eden Phillpotts) (1908).

II. FARCES. *A Great Man* (1904); *Buried Alive* (1908); *Helen with the High Hand* (1910); *The Card* (American edition: *Denry the Audacious*) (1911); *The Regent* (American edition: *The Old Adam*) (1913); *The Lion's Share* (1916); *Mr. Prohack* (1922); *The Strange Vanguard* (American edition: *The Vanguard*) (1928).

III. SERIOUS NOVELS. *A Man from the North* (1898); *Anna of the Five Towns* (1902); *Leonora* (1903); *Sacred and Profane Love* (1905) (Revised edition: *The Book of Carlotta,* 1911); *Whom God Hath Joined* (1906); *The Old Wives' Tale* (1908); *The Glimpse* (1909); *The Clayhanger Family,* a trilogy comprising *Clayhanger* (1910), *Hilda Lessways* (1911), and *These Twain* (1915); *The Price of Love* (1914); *The Pretty Lady* (1918); *The Roll Call* (1918); *Lilian* (1922); *Riceyman Steps* (1923); *Lord Raingo* (1926); *Accident* (1928); *Imperial Palace* (1930); *Venus Rising from the Sea* (American edition: *Stroke of Luck*) (1931); *Dream of Destiny* (unfinished) (1932).

IV. SHORT STORIES. *Tales of the Five Towns* (1905); *The Grim Smile of the Five Towns* (1907); *The Matador of the Five Towns* (1912); *Elsie and the Child* (1924); *The Woman Who Stole Everything* (1927).[2]

4. *"The* Grand Babylon Hotel *Cycle"*

The Melodramas do not call for extended comment. Bennett had the example of Balzac before him in writing them; in addition to the other authors already mentioned, there was some influence from Wilkie Collins and Eugène Sue. *The Grand Babylon Hotel* is by all means the best known of the group: an American millionaire buys the most luxurious hotel in London on a whim, and forthwith finds himself involved in the intrigue of imaginary European kingdoms of the Anthony Hope or George Barr McCutcheon variety. The most unusual of the group is *The Ghost,* in which a peer who had loved an opera-singer wreaks vengeance from beyond the grave upon all who dare to love her after his death.

5. Buried Alive *and Other Farces*

The Farces are worth more. Bennett himself called them "fantasias on modern themes" and "idyllic diversions." But there is nothing either fantastic or idyllic about them. As Harvey Darton remarks, each deals "with a characteristic phenomenon of material civilisation" in a spirit of gay irresponsibility.

Bennett has one really distinguished book in this field—*Buried Alive,* the universally known and loved story of the shy painter, Priam Farll, who allowed his rascally valet, Henry Leek, to be buried in the Abbey under his name, and went on to marry the Mrs. Challice whom the villain had been in the process of courting through a matrimonial agency.

> She was balm to Priam Farll. She might have been equally balm to King David, Uriah the Hittite, Socrates, Rousseau, Lord Byron, Heine, or Charlie Peace. She would have understood them all. They would all have been ready to cushion themselves on her comfortableness. Was she a lady? Pish! she was a woman.

[2] "The Death of Simon Fuge" and the title stories in *The Matador* and *Elsie and the Child* are universally regarded as Bennett's finest short stories. The only really significant item among his many plays is *Milestones,* which he wrote in collaboration with Edward Knoblock (1912).

Complications arise when Leek's deserted wife arrives with her self-righteous sons (both curates and both fools) to claim Farll as her husband, and when, Alice's brewery shares having failed, her husband finds it necessary to go back to painting. Critics rightly discern resemblances to Dickens, Shaw, and Wells in this book. As easily as the author of "The Rime of the Ancient Mariner," Bennett secures "that willing suspension of disbelief . . . which constitutes poetic faith."

I find this same "suspension" in *The Card,* the history of how a clever and not unlovable young smart-aleck of the Five Towns pulls himself up from nowhere by an ingenious use of savings and loan associations, excursion boats, lemonized chocolate, and many other means of persuading fools to part with their money. But I can find none of it in the much-praised *Mr. Prohack,* in which a Treasury official, hard hit by post-war depressions, unexpectedly comes into wealth, and, by a lucky fluke, enormously increases it.

Harvey Darton comes down as heavily on the morality of *The Card* as Macaulay came down on the Restoration drama. It is clear that he resents Bennett's affection for Denry. But how could Bennett help it? He was a "card" himself on one side of him; no doubt this explains why his "fantasias" satisfied something in him which his more important novels did not satisfy. In *The Regent* Denry gets out of the Five Towns into theatrical speculation in London. To become concerned over sharp dealing in such narratives is as beside the mark as it would be to shudder over the killing in a sword and cloak romance.

6. *Serious Fiction: Before* The Old Wives' Tale

Five serious novels preceded the acknowledged masterpieces—*The Old Wives' Tale* and *The Clayhanger Family.* With these we may consider *The Glimpse,* which falls chronologically between the two great books.

Of these six books, the first—*A Man from the North*—is promising. Two—*Sacred and Profane Love* and *The Glimpse*—are bad. The other three are the work of an important writer.

In *A Man from the North,* Bennett's career began with portentous seriousness. Here is the sedulous ape of Flaubert sweating blood over every sentence to achieve an impossible perfection. And here is the self-absorbed young man who wants to be a great writer, writing about a self-absorbed young man who wants to be a great writer. But the young man in the book never does become a great writer. "In obedience to my philosophy I made myself a failure. . . . I decided that . . . [the hero] should go through most of my experiences, but that instead of fame and a thousand a year he should arrive ultimately at disillusion and a desolating suburban domesticity." Otherwise the book would not be French and brave and disillusioned and unashamed, and everybody knows that these are the qualities which an emancipated young writer of the nineties must aim at!

Sacred and Profane Love was intended as the picture of a woman of genius, self-portrayed; it succeeds only in achieving a sickly, semi-hysterical sentimentality. *The Glimpse,* which had its origin in a dream, is not so bad as that, though there is some hysteria here also. The story of a man who has apparently died and come to life again, it presents a picture of life beyond the veil which is much in the manner of second-rate theosophical scribblings.

Anna of the Five Towns was the first of the Potteries novels, and it is the only one in which the background is elaborately described. It is also Bennett's most elaborate study of Wesleyanism, which appears at its best in Mrs. Sutton, and at its worst in the Sunday school superintendent, Titus Price, who kills himself over financial troubles, and in Anna's miserly father, Ephraim Tellwright, whose talents had early been directed toward the business side of evangelism, and who had "reduced the cost per head of souls saved, and so widened the frontiers of the Kingdom of Heaven." In the description of Anna's agony during the great revival we get a fine picture of a sensitive girl whose spiritual experience simply will not conform to the accepted pattern. A large part of the book is taken up with Anna's romance with Henry Mynors, whose religion is entirely sincere as far as it goes but who never forgets that he has to live in this world as well as another.

A deeper note is struck in the record of Anna's relations with Willie Price, Titus's son, toward whom she feels responsibility because she had been, on her father's instigation, the old man's most pressing creditor. Unhappily the last part of the book is hurried and underdeveloped; Willie's death, which recalls Eustacia's in *The Return of the Native,* seems motivated by the same youthful conviction that gloom is more "artistic" than cheerfulness which had already appeared in *A Man from the North.* "The whole story," says L. G. Johnson, "has been subjected to the the imposition of a short story climax." But at least *Anna of the Five Towns* has none of the worship of success with which Bennett has often been reproached. "Blessed are the meek, blessed are the failures, blessed are the stupid, for they, unknown to themselves, have a grace which is denied to the haughty, the successful, and the wise."

The heroine of *Leonora* is as sympathetic as Anna Tellwright, but unlike Anna she is forty years old, which was itself unusual in the fiction of the period. Her detestable husband, John Stanway, accommodatingly kills himself in the course of the narrative, which is a favorite method of shuffling off this mortal coil for such superfluous Bennett characters as cannot manage to develop cancer. Meanwhile the strong man, Twemlow, who might have crushed John by revealing his oldtime dishonesty, has brought love into Leonora's life. She meets it more frankly than a Victorian heroine would have done, but she does not fling her cap over the windmill; it seems to her that she must stay in England to look after her three self-centered daughters. But by this time the stern literary conscience that had decreed failure for the Man from the North and death for Willie Price had begun to make terms with its native optimism and the demands of the market. Twemlow sells out his interests in New York to remain in London, and so dear Leonora can have her cake and eat it too!

Whom God Hath Joined tells the story of two divorce suits. Lawrence Ridware, "admitted" clerk in a solicitor's office, divorces his wife for infidelity in Scotland, after an English judge had thrown the case out on a technicality; but his chief, Charlie Fearns, gets a reprieve when his daughter, the chief witness against him in his wife's divorce suit, faints on the stand. He soon returns to his old ways, and the inflexible girl never sees him again. She goes to work as a nurse, and is engaged to look after an old cousin of Lawrence Ridware's. Though Lawrence himself had always admired her, he refrains from making love to her because he has not the heart to bring all the tortures of sex into her life. This is the most pessimistic passage in all Bennett. *Whom God Hath Joined* lacks unity and precision—it "troubles" its readers as Elijah troubled Israel—yet several good critics put it in the forefront of Bennett's achievement.

7. *The Masterpieces*

Bennett was now ready to write *The Old Wives' Tale*. He was determined to stand or fall by this book; to signalize its importance he wrote it in a beautiful calligraphic hand, without blotting a line. On the morning it was published he exclaimed to his wife: "This day is the most important of my life. . . . I have done my best. . . . I shall never be able to do better. . . . It will decide our future!"

Everybody knows the "story" of *The Old Wives' Tale;* the book concerns two sisters—Constance and Sophia Baines—from their girlhood in a Bursley emporium until they die in their sixties. Constance stays in Bursley, marries the good apprentice, Samuel Povey, and inherits the business. Sophia, more adventurous of spirit, elopes to Paris with a young ne'er-do-weel, and is deserted. Originally Bennett intended that at this point she should go to the bad, but this plan was wisely abandoned. The shock of her desertion puts an end to Sophia's flightiness, and the vein of iron in her Five Towns ancestry and training begins to show through; ultimately she establishes herself as the very successful keeper of a Paris pension. In her old age she returns to Bursley to live—and die—with her sister.

It was significant that Bennett should give such a story the name of a highly romantic Elizabethan play.

The author himself has told us how the book was born from the sight of an eccentric old woman in a Paris restaurant and the desire to create an English counterpart of de Maupassant's *Une Vie*. "One ought to be able to make a heartrending novel out of the history of such a woman as she." Constance was the original heroine. Sophia was added later out of bravado, just to go de Maupassant one better.

There is plenty of "interesting" material in *The Old Wives' Tale:* the shooting of the elephant (which was taken from a newspaper account, quite in the manner of Charles Reade); old Mr. Baines's death, when Sophia leaves him alone for a moment to flirt with her worthless lover; the murder by Daniel Povey of his drunken wife; the execution at Auxerre; the siege of Paris; Sophia's involuntary contacts with the Parisian demi-monde. But Bennett de-sensationalizes all these things. They have their place in the relentless succession of human days, but their place is secondary.

Probably he got the key from an old couple who had lived through the siege of Paris. When he questioned them, he found that they hardly remembered it; thus he came to realize "that ordinary people went on living very ordinary lives . . . during the siege, and that to the vast mass of the population the siege was not the dramatic, spectacular, thrilling, ecstatic affair that is described in history." Sophia, for example, was not at all interested in the political questions involved; what interested her was how she was going to buy food and keep her pension running through these difficult times.

Life is time, after all, and nobody lives through two moments together. So insignificant a thing as Sophia's refusal to take her castor oil may mark "a historic moment in the family life." Detail after detail impresses the passing of time on our minds. One man sits in a chair formerly identified with another; an elaborate signboard goes up before an establishment whose former owner thought it ungenteel to have any sign at all. After Sophia's return to Bursley, Paris fades gradually in our minds as it does in hers; the aging Constance speaks of her old complaint as "my sciatica," but the upstart newcomer is "this rheumatism." And always we are kept busy exploring the tangled jungle of human motives. One reason her good-for-nothing husband came to resent Sophia is that she is taller than himself! One cannot but agree, as one turns the last page, that this is "What Life Is."

Bennett spent nine months in accumulating notes and documents for *Clayhanger;* this was the most elaborate piece of research he ever did for a novel. Printing now replaces draping, the occupational background of *The Old Wives' Tale,* but retrospectively we explore the potteries during the childhood of Edwin's father, Darius, a terrible episode which connects Bennett directly with the humanitarian novel of Dickens and Holcroft. The antagonism between Edwin and his father, who thwarts his desire to be an architect, and keeps him in the printing business at a pittance on which he finds it impossible to marry, shows the influence of *The Way of All Flesh.* Edwin's friends, the Orgreaveses, live very differently, and their home, with its lovely garden, is everything that the Clayhanger home is not. Janet Orgreaves, who loves Edwin in silence and waits for him in vain, grows old as gradually as the old wives, and the life of the Five Towns is linked up with the life of England in frequent references to Bishop Colenso, the Bradlaugh case, Gladstone's Home Rule speech, Victoria's jubilee, and other matters of current interest.

It is through the Orgreaveses that Edwin meets that strange, rude, passionate, disconcerting, vital person, Hilda Lessways, whom he so ardently loves. At the end of *Clayhanger* she has apparently jilted him, and neither he nor the reader knows why. To explain the reason Bennett found it necessary to write *Hilda Lessways,* which first builds up Hilda's background, as *Clayhanger* had developed Edwin's, and then takes us through the same experiences we have already savored once, with the significant difference that this time we look at them not through the man's eyes but through the woman's! "He would not see the real Hilda any more," Bennett had written after his hero had fallen in love, "unless some cataclysm should shatter the glass." So far as the reader is concerned, it is shattered now with a vengeance; and it is startling to see the girl we had hitherto considered so formidable, now diffident, shrinking, tortured, as she seems to herself, as she appears to the author of her being. Such a commentary on the relativity of all human judgments of personality, English fiction had not, I think, hitherto achieved.

Finally, having given us Edwin and Hilda separately, Bennett brings them together in *These Twain,* the greatest study of the ordeal called marriage in all fiction. It is marriage itself that Bennett deals with; there are no complicating elements, like sexual antagonism in the case of Soames and Irene in *The Forsyte Saga.* "This woman will kill me," cries Edwin, "but without her I shouldn't be interested enough to live."

The author again borrows Edwin's eyes, but we see his stupidity and pig-headedness quite as vividly as his wife's utter lack of tact;

and when we are inclined to sympathize more with him than with her, we cannot help remembering what a difference the shift in viewpoint made once before. Having no mystery to clear up, Bennett did not find it necessary to retell the story of *These Twain,* though he did later attach an addendum to his trilogy—*The Roll Call,* which is the record of the adventures of Hilda's son, George Cannon, in love and business up to the time of his enlistment in the First World War.

The solution of his marital problem comes to Edwin at last on the town bridge—the same place where the trilogy opened—and it is "the great discovery of his career." "If Hilda had not been unjust in the assertion of her own individuality, there could be no merit in yielding to her. . . . He himself was unjust. . . . To reconcile oneself to injustice was the master achievement." "I'm not going to be beaten by Hilda!" he vows. "And I'm not going to be beaten by marriage. Dashed if I am! A nice thing if I had to admit that I wasn't clever enough to be a husband!"

8. *The Best of the Later Novels*

We have now brought Bennett's serious fiction up to the First World War. He wrote no "war novel" in the ordinary sense of the term; he came closest in *The Pretty Lady. The Roll Call* and *Mr. Prohack* were influenced by the war. *Lilian,* while not a war book, reflects the loosening of moral fiber which follows in the wake of war. *Lord Raingo,* a careful study of the mentality of Britain's rulers during the crisis, is the story of a rich man who was made a peer and director of propaganda. His wife dies in an automobile accident; his mistress commits suicide; he himself takes more than a hundred solid pages to expire of pneumonia.

The Pretty Lady itself is a book of undeveloped possibilities. For one thing it lacks a center. Sometimes we are with Christine, sometimes with Hoape; in the last paragraph, which is our key to the understanding of the woman's character, the author finds it necessary to speak to us directly. Christine has much the same obsession as Nina in Eugene O'Neill's *Strange Interlude;* and her devotion to the Blessed Virgin is as startling as in the most amoral of the medieval tales. Hoape's final decision to marry the repulsive neurotic,

Concepcion, is quite unconvincing, and the prominence given to Lady Queenie Paulle, whose own recklessness causes her death in a Zeppelin raid, can hardly be justified even on the ground that she is the "high-society" counterpart of the harlot who gives the book its name.

Of the post-war books, *Accident* is an inconsequential tour-de-force, while *Venus Rising from the Sea* hardly does more than reflect the renewed interest in the theater which came to Bennett with Dorothy Cheston. The significant books of the period were *Riceyman Steps* and *Imperial Palace.*

Riceyman Steps is a less ambitious book than *Imperial Palace,* but it is a much better one. The scene is Clerkenwell; the theme is miserliness. In *The Old Wives' Tale,* Bennett doubled his old women; here he doubles his misers—the bookseller, Mr. Earlforward, and Mrs. Arb, the confectioner from over the way, whom he marries. As a miser, Earlforward is "done" as completely as Molière could have done him. He turns in his wife's old wedding ring toward the price of the new one, and when his shop is cleaned by vacuum he wants to know if the cleaners are planning to sell the dirt. Sordidness runs by the side of humor in these pages, for the man dies at last of cancer, and the undernourished woman fails to rally after an operation. But this is not the remarkable thing about *Riceyman Steps.* Bennett has actually made his misers lovable; one returns to the old bookshop again and again. The book also contains Elsie, the servant-girl, who is far and away Bennett's tenderest characterization.

Bennett almost killed himself to produce *Imperial Palace,* which he hoped would equal *The Old Wives' Tale.* There are eighty-five speaking characters; he counted them and recorded the number in a prefatory note. The novel gives a detailed picture of the workings of a great luxury hotel in all its ramifications from restaurant to laundry. Closely interwoven is the personal history of the "panjandrum," Evelyn Orcham, and his adventures with two women—Gracie Savott, a rich girl of genius and insight but fundamental instability, and Violet Powler, whom he makes head housekeeper and finally marries. Evelyn is endeared to us by the same kind of fundamental simplicity which Bennett himself possessed; Violet is an excellent example of his ability to find romance in what most writers would consider rather dull material. Gracie is a more complicated matter. Here is a showy, spectacular characterization of one of the most elaborately studied women in all Bennett; only, unfortunately, one is never quite sure that the woman is real.

With all its faults, *Imperial Palace* still has more value than is generally attributed to it. I can find no foundation for the charge that in it "the artistic and personal decadence of the man sold to materialism is complete."

9. *The Spirit of Arnold Bennett*

What now emerges from this welter of words as Arnold Bennett's contribution to the English novel?

I think we may say that he helped make the English novel part of the European novel, and that he considerably widened its scope.

Take, first, his use of backgrounds. It will be remembered that both Thackeray and Trollope thought that all an author could do was to depict men out of their businesses. Bennett, on the other hand, finds it necessary to give us the whole professional background of his characters, whether it be hotel-keeping in *Imperial Palace,* printing in *Clayhanger,* draping in *The Old Wives' Tale,* or prostitution in *The Pretty Lady*. It must be admitted, however, that he is often less successful than, say, Hardy in making his background a part of the play. Perhaps his immense gusto betrayed him here, his appetite for facts as facts, and consequent inability at times to choose between them and to reject irrelevant items.

He saw human nature as a more complicated thing than many of his predecessors, and he had great skill in recording the changing reactions of human beings toward each other. Like Eugene O'Neill, in *Strange Interlude,* he filled many pages with the record of what his characters thought and felt but did not say.

It is commonly held that he led the novel toward French naturalism, but this view needs some qualification. He neither desired nor attempted complete objectivity, and he rejected as ridiculous the idea that the naturalists "have at last lighted on a final formula which ensures truth to life."

His own attitude, like Lord Raingo's, was one of "sturdy rationalism" but he never denied "that the universe was moved by mysterious forces of which men know nothing. . . ." He believed in the decent reasonableness of the average reader, and maintained that success as a writer could only be based on "some central righteousness." He believed also that "the great principles, spiritual and moral, remain intact," and that "there is something higher in man than the mind." He deplored the lack of nobility in Flaubert and de Maupassant, and he knew that *The Old Wives' Tale* would be a failure unless he could get into it "a lofty nobility," "a Christ-like, all-embracing compassion." His wife was not far wrong when she said that he might have made a very good Christian if only he had not been afraid to let himself go.[3]

The truth of the matter is that fundamentally Arnold Bennett was a romantic writer. He found it impossible to "walk along a common street . . . without being imbued with a deep sense of the majesty and beauty of the whole inexplicable affair. The older I grow the more keenly I delight in the marvel of life." A girl like Annunciata is "the supreme excuse for the universe, a miraculous vase from which the pure fluid of life itself seems to gush forth." Earlforward's Elsie is a common drudge, yet she comes to Joe as a "celestial visitant," "a savior, a powerful protectress, a bright angel."

This tremendous zest for life balks at no phase of human experience—"there is no such thing as ugliness in the world." His characters find it impossible to be unhappy after the most harrowing experiences; instead, they have "a tingling consciousness of being unusually alive"; they are thrilled by the weather, or "the beauty and order and silence of the room," or "the geometrically regular creases in the damask tablecloth." When Lawrence Ridware and his brother Mark lie down to sleep it is no "spectacle of ideal romantic loveliness" that they present; yet it "touches" the author of their being "profoundly." Evelyn Orcham is similarly impressed by "the unconsciousness of undefended sleep" as he prowls the corridors of the Imperial Palace. For all the luxuries at their command, his guests are "as touching as the piteous figures crouching and shivering in the lamp-lit night on the benches of the Thames Embankment."

[3] See Arnold Bennett, *My Religion* (Appleton, 1926) and "My Religious Experience," *Century*, CXI (1926), 539-546.

It was indeed "the common grey things" of life that were most congenial to what Rebecca West calls Bennett's strangely Protestant art. Leonora is not excited particularly when she arrives just in time to prevent Stanway from killing Uncle Meschach with a cold compress. "She thought: 'So that is murder, that little thing, that thing over in a minute!'" And when Stanway later kills himself, both Leonora and the whole family feel "that suicide was mysteriously different from their previous notion of it." What does thrill Leonora is that she should be able to give a simple command to her daughter, that "little morsel of a child which she had borne one night," and which now "had become a daughter of Eve, with a magic to mesmerize errant glances and desires." How strange that she herself, "a wistful, wayward atom in the universe," should be able to lay a command upon another wayward atom!

J. B. Priestley goes so far as to find Bennett's distinctive contribution to fiction in this tendency: he runs romantic obstacle-races and performs romantic conjuring tricks. If he had tried to rewrite *Romeo and Juliet* he would have turned out five acts of gush; it is only when he responds to the things that most people do not find appealing at all that his taste is impeccable. What he calls realism is precisely what Stevenson calls romanticism, and he shares Stevenson's subjectivism to the full; he insists on looking at life from the point of view of the man who lives it. "His life," he writes of Evelyn Orcham, "was of enthralling interest to him. No other kind of life could be as interesting."

Yet he was not Stevenson. And the most curious thing about him is that though the popular impression of his "greyness" can be proved wrong in a hundred details, fundamentally it is just. Like Henry James,[4] one comes to the end of a Bennett novel asking what it all means. Bennett's own more sensitive characters are always asking this question; Evelyn Orcham goes about muttering, "What am I alive for?"; they are all painfully anxious to be reassured of the value of life.

This is often attributed to Bennett's "materialism," but his "materialism" has been greatly exaggerated. He was, as Wells called

[4] In *Notes on Novelists* (Dent, 1914).

him, a "dear, delightful person," who was probably as little contaminated by his luxuries as any man who ever lived. His yacht, his pretty clothes, his expensive hotels, and his place in the world to which all these things belonged, he regarded with the wide-eyed wonder with which the boy regards his "junk," and there was hardly more worldliness about him than there is in the boy. In themselves these things may have been cheap but they were not cheap for him; his imagination transformed them. He was a lavish spender, but unlike many of the breed, he spent even more lavishly on others than on himself; "he was great," says Rebecca West, "he was grand; he was Coquelin's Cyrano de Bergerac, but tenderer, more lovable."

He failed in important particulars, nevertheless, and Wells may possibly have the clue when he writes, "You're always taking surface values that I reject. . . . For some unfathomable reason you don't penetrate." Beside all his tremendous zest, he had the melancholy which oppresses all sensitive men who can find no justification for life outside of life itself. That is why, as we turn his pages, while feeling unceasingly that this is "What Life Is," we also find ourselves saying, "Yes, but life is something more than this."

CHAPTER XXVI

H. G. WELLS, "REALIST OF THE FANTASTIC"

To love without illusions is to be secure against surprise. It is the quintessence of love. I follow in the tradition of Hogarth and Tom Jones and not in the footsteps of Richardson, and I shall count myself wholly damned if I let my friendly advisers induce me to pander to these people for whom reading is nothing better than material for Grandisonian reverie.

You Can't Be Too Careful

1. *Approach to a Phenomenon*

A vigorous contemporaneity seized the English novel with Herbert George Wells. Hardy and George Eliot had been iconoclasts in their way, but both respected tradition and cast many a lingering, longing look behind. In his own words, Wells was "a typical Cockney without either reverence or a sincere conviction of inferiority to any fellow creature." The English novel had never been the genteelest form of literature; such gentility as Scott and others had given it had already cracked badly in Dickens; Wells made it his job to destroy gentility altogether.

He has, of course, been much more than a novelist, though it is only as a novelist that he can be considered here. Criticism has as yet done singularly little with Mr. Wells, though it seems generally agreed that he is not The Writer-He-Once-Was. Like Punch, in the old saying, he never was. There is a quality of "Peter-pantheism" about him which has often left him open to ridicule. First he would have Socialism save us, then history, then education. During the First World War he discovered God, and since he has never been in the habit of doing things by halves, he discovered two gods while he was about it, but never did succeed in getting them to speak to each other. Today he sees the very name of Deity as a word "that ought to be forcibly removed from circulation." He has done as much to make modern men hate war and love peace as any man alive, yet he has supported both the great wars in which England has engaged during his time, so that he finds himself in the rather strange position of opposing war in general but supporting wars in particular.

All this is less troublesome than it would otherwise be when we remember how skeptical Mr. Wells is of the ability of the human mind to seize a knowledge of final reality, how assured of the "quiver of idiosyncrasy in every sequence," how ready to believe that though there is clearly an order in the universe it has no necessary correspondence to the order in our minds.[1] As a matter of fact he has been a consistent Socialist since his student days. His work upon history never affected that. *The Outline of History* is a contribution to the study of human ecology, a study of the effect of developing means of communication upon the size and composition of human societies. As for religion, he evidently feels that a human being needs some standard of reference by which he may maintain a certain consistency of conduct, and he tries to find out what can be done by personifying and externalizing this. And for him to call himself "Atheist," so far as any of *our* gods go, is perhaps part of that "Peter-pantheism" to which I have already referred.

H. G. Wells was born in Bromley, Kent, September 21, 1866. His father was unsuccessful both as a gardener and as a shopkeeper, though he became well known as a professional cricketer and bowler. His mother was an innkeeper's daughter who began life as a lady's maid and became a housekeeper after the final collapse of her husband's business when their youngest son was thirteen. Desperate attempts to make a draper or a chemist of the boy were unsuccessful; in 1881 he secured a pupil-teacher's appointment at Midhurst Grammar School; three years later a scholarship sent him to study biology under Huxley at the Royal College of Science. His career as a teacher of science was cut short by invalidism consequent upon a smashed kidney at football and a ruptured pulmonary blood vessel. His first "strike" as a writer came in 1891 when Frank Har-

[1] Cf. "The Rediscovery of the Unique," *Fortnightly Review,* N.S., L (1891), 106-111; Appendix to *A Modern Utopia* (1905); Book I of *First and Last Things* (1908); General Preface to Atlantic Edition; Chapter II of *The Work, Wealth, and Happiness of Mankind* (1931); *Experiment in Autobiography* (1934), pp. 178-183.

ris accepted his essay, "The Rediscovery of the Unique"; later Henley took him on, and he found inspiration for a series of sketches of every-day life in *When a Man's Single,* by J. M. Barrie.

A fortunate accident in Wells's boyhood was the fact that his father was a lover of books. When the boy broke his leg at the age of nine he discovered the joys of reading. The Up Park Library, where his mother was housekeeper, and the London libraries during his student days widened his horizon notably, and he familiarized himself with many authors. Among these Plato,[2] Lucretius, Voltaire, Blake, Shelley, Tom Paine, Herbert Spencer, and Henry George all exercised an important influence on his thinking—(he scorned Karl Marx and all his works)—while Swift, Sterne,[3] Reade, and Dickens [4] (above all others) influenced his art. Unlike Bennett and Galsworthy, he seems to have found little or nothing in French and Russian literature.

2. *A Wonderful Variety*

Mr. Wells's novels may be arranged, though with considerable overlapping, in the following groups.

[2] Cf. *A Modern Utopia.*

[3] He often uses the kind of tricks that Sterne established in the English novel, very boldly if not very effectively in *All Aboard for Ararat,* where he lists his favorite hates and leaves a blank space in which the reader may fill in additional names. The business of setting sketches for *Tono-Bungay* advertisements into the text of that novel is more like Reade than Sterne; and Reade would have sympathized warmly with Wells's desire to achieve a more graphic representation of one of the incidents in *The Wife of Sir Isaac Harman* than present-day literary conventions will permit (Ch. VIII, §11).

[4] His lower middle-class types and his humor have always been recognized as essentially Dickensian. He is very close to Dickens too in his animism. Mrs. Pybus (*Joan and Peter*) lives in "a small oblong room with a faint projection towards the street, as if it had attempted to develop a bow window and had lacked the strength to do so." There is a more elaborate instance in *Mr. Blettsworthy on Rampole Island:* "Frothy water came into the cabin like a lost dog in search of its master, rushed about, wetted abundantly, and went out again. Everything loose in my cabin leapt hither and thither; a pair of boots departed in the custody of a wave and never returned; I twisted my wrist horribly and bruised a knee. My water bottle got free, lived dangerously and broke and left its splinters chasing madly from side to side in search of hand or foot." Cf. Geoffrey West, *H. G. Wells,* Appendix II, "A Note on Dickensian Parallels."

I. Fantastic and Imaginative Romances. *The Time Machine* (1895); *The Wonderful Visit* (1895); *The Island of Dr. Moreau* (1896); *The Invisible Man* (1897); *The War of the Worlds* (1898); *The Sleeper Awakes* (1899); *The First Men in the Moon* (1901); *The Sea Lady* (1902); *The Food of the Gods* (1904); *In the Days of the Comet* (1906); *The War in the Air* (1908); *The World Set Free* (1914); *Men Like Gods* (1923); *Mr. Blettsworthy on Rampole Island* (1928); *The King Who Was a King* (1929); *The Autocracy of Mr. Parham* (1930); *The Shape of Things to Come* (1933); *The Croquet Player* (1937); *Star-Begotten* (1937); *The Camford Visitation* (1937).

II. Novels of Personality and Personal Idiosyncrasy. *The Wheels of Chance* (1896); *Love and Mr. Lewisham* (1900); *Kipps* (1905); *Tono-Bungay* (1909); *The History of Mr. Polly* (1910); *Bealby* (1915); *The Dream* (1924); *Christina Alberta's Father* (1925); *The Bulpington of Blup* (1933); *Brynhild, or The Show of Things* (1937); *Apropos of Dolores* (1938).

III. Novels of Ideas—Love and Sex. *Ann Veronica* (1909); *Marriage* (1912); *The Passionate Friends* (1913); *The Wife of Sir Isaac Harman* (1914); *The Secret Places of the Heart* (1922).

IV. Novels of Ideas—Politics and Citizenship. *The New Machiavelli* (1911); *The Research Magnificent* (1915); *The World of William Clissold* (1926); *Meanwhile, The Picture of a Lady* (1927).

V. Novels of Ideas—War, Religion, and Education. *Mr. Britling Sees It Through* (1916); *The Soul of a Bishop* (1917); *Joan and Peter* (1918); *The Undying Fire* (1919); *The Brothers* (1938); *The Holy Terror* (1939); *Babes in the Darkling Wood* (1940); *All Aboard for Ararat* (1941); *You Can't Be Too Careful* (1942).

In this table I have failed to classify (since it is quite unclassifiable) one of Mr. Wells's fictions, *Boon* (1915), which the author describes as "an outbreak of naughtiness," and "a bundle of personalities and parodies." It contains among other things an outrageous attack upon and a consummate burlesque of Henry James, some extremely good talk about the war, and two humorous stories of the supernatural.

Mr. Wells's short stories, originally collected under such titles as *The Stolen Bacillus* (1895); *The Plattner Story* (1897); *Tales of Space and Time* (1899); and *Twelve Stories and a Dream* (1903) are now conveniently available in a single volume as *The Short*

Stories of H. G. Wells (1927). Many of these belong with the "Fantastic and Imaginative Romances."

3. *The Romances*

Mr. Wells's romances have an obvious affinity with the work of such writers as Bulwer-Lytton, Jules Verne, and the Stevenson of *Dr. Jekyll and Mr. Hyde.* Suppose time is merely a fourth dimension of space; why might not man learn to travel into the past and into the future? (*The Time Machine.*) Suppose a number of three-dimensional universes are packed side by side in space; might not one be subject to incursions from another? (*The Wonderful Visit; Men Like Gods.*) If it is true that "humanity is but animal rough-hewn to a reasonable shape and in perpetual internal conflict between instinct and injunction," why could not a sufficiently clever vivisector carve beasts into men? (*The Island of Dr. Moreau.*) Suppose a physicist to find the means of making himself invisible (*The Invisible Man*); suppose the discovery of a food substance which should make growth continuous instead of intermittent (*The Food of the Gods*); suppose a comet were to engulf the earth, changing the nitrogen in the atmosphere into "a respirable gas, differing indeed from oxygen, but helping and sustaining its action, a bath of strength and healing for nerve and brain" (*In the Days of the Comet*). If a substance could be found "opaque to all forms of radiant energy," why might not earthlings reach the moon? (*The First Men in the Moon.*) Or, if Mars is inhabited, why is it inconceivable that the Martians may some day invade the earth—malevolently, in military fashion (*The War of the Worlds*), or benevolently, by means of cosmic rays, thus effecting changes in our chromosomes and so developing a new and more constructive humanity? (*Star-Begotten.*)

Wells's principal advantages over his predecessors in this field were that he built upon a substratum of genuine scientific knowledge—instead of contradicting nature, he simply carried present tendencies to their logical, often terrifying conclusions—and that he had the imagination to identify himself with characters who were undergoing experiences that no human beings ever have undergone, and to describe their behavior convincingly. The idea of having the irresistible Martians suddenly succumb to the disease germs of this planet because they had developed no immunity against them was perhaps a brilliant guess, but it could have occurred only to a man who had had training in science. Similarly, men have played with the idea of invisibility since imaginative writing began, but Wells was the first to take the trouble to think through the problem of what being invisible would actually involve.

Yet these books are almost as sociological as scientific. The very first, *The Time Machine,* takes us forward to the year 802,701, by which time humanity has long since divided into Eloi and Morlocks, the former on the surface of the earth, the latter underground. The pleasures of life are reserved for the Eloi; the function of the Morlocks is to work. But they have already begun to revenge themselves on their masters by eating them. To such an impasse the present division of the world's goods between "Haves" and "Have-Nots" must bring us; even on a purely selfish basis, greediness is not going to pay. Similarly, in *The Sleeper Awakes,* Graham finds himself after 200 years the nominal master of the world—a streamlined world, a mechanized Dark Age of fascist tyranny; and perceives at once "how necessarily this state of things had developed from the Victorian city." In *The Wonderful Visit* our whole interest is in social criticism; the angel whom the vicar has mistakenly shot for a bird finds it quite impossible to adjust himself to the kind of world in which we live.

Two of Mr. Wells's fantastic stories—one early and one late—are neither scientific nor sociological. *The Sea Lady,* which has more than a hint of Ibsen, is unique among Wells's books in reverting to the unskeptical method of the fairy tales; the unrationalized heroine symbolizes the lure of the unknown, drawing men out to the sea in search of better dreams, and so far as this world goes, to death. And if *The Sea Lady* suggests Ibsen, *The Croquet Player* suggests de la Mare; here is a terrifying picture of a haunted countryside, which is plainly intended to typify our tottering world of today.

Two books of Mr. Wells's middle period employ the fantastic method in a modified form. Both *The War in the Air* and *The World Set Free* were propaganda books designed to warn mankind what the application of science to warfare must mean to the human race. *The War in the Air* is an apocalyptic vision of destruction; appearing more than six years before one fighting plane had mounted the airways, it must have seemed to its first readers as fantastic as a trip to the moon, but as a matter of fact all the destruction is brought about by mechanical means. *The World Set Free* is somewhat closer in method to the earlier books, or does it only seem so to us since the atomic bomb, unlike the fighting plane, is not yet with us? It destroys most of the world's great cities in 1958, whereupon the common sense of the world's rulers is awakened, and a new order is established.

Among Mr. Wells's later books, two—*Mr. Blettsworthy on Rampole Island* and *The Autocracy of Mr. Parham*—give us only make-believe fantasy, and three belong to the fantasies only in a manner of speaking. Mr. Blettsworthy's island exists only in delirium; Lord Paramount, British fascist dictator of the Second World War, is a Martian who "materializes" into Mr. Parham, a reactionary don, but at the end of the book we find that it was all a dream. Lord Paramount wants war with Russia but what he gets is war with the United States, in the course of which both the British and the American fleets are destroyed in good old *War in the Air* tradition. As for the others, *The King Who Was a King,* which was written in the manner of a film scenario, consecrates *Prisoner of Zenda* materials to the cause of world peace; *The Shape of Things to Come* offers a history of the world for the next 150 years, eventuating in the establishment of the World-State; in *The Camford Visitation,* the Voice which speaks from the air to demand justification of the university's way of life is only a device to give Wells an opportunity for an authoritative denunciation of academic ways.

The First Men in the Moon is Mr. Wells's own favorite among his early novels in the fantastic group, though it lacks the moral power of *The Time Machine* and such masterpieces as "The Star" and "The Country of the Blind" among the short stories. Now that the production of fourth-dimensional novels has become a small industry,[5] the idea of using a machine to travel in time may seem

[5] For a discussion of a considerable number of recent examples, cf. Margaret C. Walters, "Space-Time in Literary Form," *Tomorrow,* I, June, 1942, pp. 25-29. Many of these works have been influenced by the "serial time"

rather clumsy, but the extraordinary suggestiveness of the Eloi and Morlocks will remain. In the *Comet* story, gas seems a curious means of effecting a change in human nature; the confusion between moral and physical greatness in *The Food of the Gods* is open to much more serious objection. Among the later books, *Men Like Gods,* with its splendid naked Samurai, largely engaged in scientific experimentation and creative thinking, has been deservedly admired; and I, at least, would wish to add to the honor roll *Mr. Blettsworthy, The Croquet Player,* and *Star-Begotten.*

To be sure, the merits of the *Blettsworthy* book have little to do with fantasy. There is no fantasy in the hero's youthful adventures at Oxford, his business failure, nor the treachery of his partner and Olive Slaughter; and the story of the sea voyage is in the grand old tradition of Marryat, Smollett, and Defoe. After the island dream is over, Mr. Blettsworthy is nursed back to life by a hitherto worthless girl whom he has saved from suicide; in her a boundless capacity for devotion comes into being, and the two derelicts save each other. All this happens to illustrate the valuable point that no absolute line of demarcation can be drawn between the "fantastic romances" and Mr. Wells's more realistic fictions. *The Wonderful Visit, In the Days of the Comet,* and *The Food of the Gods* all involve pictures of the world we know; Bert Smallways, the perky cockney through whose eyes we see the War in the Air and the Artillery Man who, even in the face of the War of the Worlds remains an incarnation of human hope, are close relatives of Kipps and Mr. Polly.

4. *The Charles Dickens Group*

Mr. Wells's second group of fictions is in the Smollett-Dickens tradition. It opened modestly with *The Wheels of Chance,* a picture

of J. W. Dunne; cf. his *An Experiment with Time* (Macmillan, 1927); *This Serial Universe* (Macmillan, 1938); *The New Immortality* (Harper, 1939); *Nothing Dies* (Faber, 1940). As a young man Dunne was greatly impressed by *The Time Machine* and by Wells's anticipations of flying. The Dunne plane was a tailless V-shaped plane, very stable and very slow. It mounted the ether at Eastchurch in 1908, one of the earliest machines to fly. Dunne's theories have been seriously criticized by Wells for his neglect of angles between the time dimension and the three spatial dimensions.

of the cycling holiday of a draper's assistant who came as close to playing Sir Galahad as a helpless little cockney could in the nineties. Even more delightful is *Love and Mr. Lewisham,* which draws freely on Wells's own experiences as a teacher. Neither Lewisham nor his Ethel are very important, or even very admirable, people, yet few things in modern fiction are more touching than the account of their reconciliation after he has unjustly and absurdly suspected her of being unfaithful to him, nor yet than his abandonment of his somewhat priggish, grandiose, and probably impossible schemes for advancement in science, to accept at last the old, old obligation of caring for his family. I am not sure that the deep humanity which lives in Wells side by side with a certain ruthlessness ever again found such perfect, unadulterated expression.

A much more varied and elaborate book was *Kipps,* in which another draper's apprentice comes unexpectedly into money and struggles desperately to live up to it. It was followed in kind by *The History of Mr. Polly* and *Bealby*. The latter novel, which deals with the picaresque adventures of a rebellious young servant boy who runs off from his "place," is merely engaging slapstick, but *Mr. Polly* is a masterpiece, the most completely delightful of all Wells's books.

Mr. Polly is a middle-aged, unsuccessful, dyspeptic tradesman who conceives the brilliant idea of escaping from his domineering wife by committing suicide and at the same time setting fire to his house, so that, his death seeming accidental, she may be able to collect his life insurance. The fire is a glorious success but the suicide is an ignominious failure, and when Mr. Polly finds the flames spreading to neighboring houses, he is forced to become a hero in spite of himself by rescuing an old lady who doesn't mind scrambling but who is no good at jumping and won't jump. How Mr. Polly was finally delivered from his troubles by happier means, and how he established a new life with the fat landlady at the Potwell Inn, there is neither time nor space to tell here. Mr. Polly has "a capacity for joy and beauty at least as keen and subtle as yours or mine," a passion for literature, and an amazing gift for inventing such phrases as "joy de vive" and "sesquippledan verboojuice." All his woes are the result of that peculiarly English "muddling" which Mr. Wells hates with all his soul, but he is so completely satisfying and comes out so very well that he is mighty poor propaganda! There is a curious amoral quality in the book which illuminates not only the transitional period in which it was written but life's endless indifference to human ideals. A man has no right to find happiness by evading his obligations and leaving his wife in the lurch, but that is what Mr. Polly does, and it turns out the best thing he ever does. Moreover when his conscience drives him back to see Miriam, five years later, he finds her quite as contented as he is, and her only anxiety is a dreadful fear lest perhaps he may have come back to stay!

Profounder implications underlie the novel published the year before *Mr. Polly,* the work universally regarded as Wells's masterpiece, *Tono-Bungay.* George Ponderevo, the hero-narrator, is "a spiritual guttersnipe in love with unimaginable goddesses"; Tono-Bungay, the patent medicine which he and his uncle manufacture, serves as a perfect symbol of the disintegrating society which Wells portrays so comprehensively in this book. The uncle, Edward Ponderevo, is to Wells what Merdle is to Dickens and Melmotte to Anthony Trollope, with this significant difference, that Wells sees him not as a villain but as the inevitable product of an iniquitous social order to which we have all contributed. It is a bitter piece of irony that even when George turns from money-making at last to find salvation in science, he can find nothing better to do than build destroyers; in his final aspect he stands beside Undershaft, the mystical munitions-maker of Shaw's *Major Barbara.*

I place only two novels of the twenties and three of the thirties in this second group. Mr. Wells himself lists *The Dream* as one of his fantastic stories. It is fantastic only in its frame. The whole life of Harry Mortimer Smith, a former incarnation of Sarnac, returns to that Utopian of 2,000 years hence in a dream, and is related by him to his friends. But the story itself is altogether realistic—a lower middle class domestic tragedy of the early twentieth century. The first part is as funny as *Kipps,* the second as touching as *Love and Mr. Lewisham. The Dream* is, indeed, without qualification, a masterpiece, and it has never received anything like the recognition it deserves.

Much the same spirit informs *Christina Alberta's Father*. A fake medium gives Mr. Preemby the idea that he is Sargon, King of Kings, returned to earth to bring order into chaos. But society has only the asylum for such people, and before Mr. Preemby dies he realizes that the world can never be saved until we all become Sargons and take hold of it to cleanse and control it. His daughter sees herself as "ugly, rude, inconsiderate," with "no purity, no devotion." But to Bobby, who loves her, and who kidnaps her father from the asylum, she is "incessantly interesting . . . , straight, swift, and endlessly beautiful." Wells makes both judgments seem reasonable.

Of the three books of the thirties, *The Bulpington of Blup* is the most considerable. It is Wells's *Egoist*—"a very direct caricature study of the irresponsible aesthetic mentality"—and he himself thinks Theodore Bulpington as good as Kipps. Perhaps he is right. But Kipps is lovable, while Theodore is perfectly loathsome—a coward in war, a decadent, fire-eating militarist in peace. Yet he will be a fortunate man who never catches a glimpse of his own features in the mirror held up to him.

Both *Brynhild* and *Apropos of Dolores* are among Wells's lightest books. In the former, Rowland Palace, novelist, engages a young man to build a "façade" for him in the most modern and scientific manner. When our interest is shifted to his rival, Alfred Bunter, we may feel that the story is wandering. But it is not. For Bunter's life is all façade, and when his past catches up with him, he ceases to be a serious rival to Rowland Palace. Only, it is Brynhild (Mrs. Palace) to whom he turns for consolation, and Brynhild manifests a skill in erecting her own façade that puts both her husband and his agent to shame. Brynhild's child, fortunately, is said to resemble her mother.

Apropos of Dolores gives us the portrait of one of the most appalling hellions in fiction—we are hardly shocked when her husband casually murders her—together with some interesting speculations on the differences between two kinds of human beings, those who, like Dolores, are completely unsocial, and those who, like her husband, have some unselfish qualities mixed in. The rest of the book is rather desultory, with some few scenes of hilarious comedy.

Wells came closest to being a "straight" novelist in the early books of his second group. There is no overt propaganda here; neither did he yield to the temptation which afterwards engulfed him—to let the story go hang while he read us lectures on his own ideas. It was under the spell of Charles Dickens that this great anti-Victorian was most creative.

5. *Sex, Love, and Marriage*

Four novels of the middle period were devoted to sexual matters. Of these *Ann Veronica* was the earliest and most sensational. Ann was one of the first English heroines to insist on "living her own life." Charlotte Brontë had already written of the girl who dared to love unbidden, but Ann is interested not only in love but also in sex. She lives "in sin" with Capes and is happy; in fact the experiment works so well that even her father is forced to forgive her. *Ann Veronica* gives a vivid picture of the difficulties which a girl had to face who attempted to live alone in London thirty years ago, but its colors have already faded considerably and its interest is now largely historical.

There is more left of *Marriage,* a powerful dramatization of the conflict between a man's passion for research and his desire to give the best he can to his wife and family. We see that Marjorie's extravagance is destroying the work of Trafford's life, but we understand her too well to condemn; nor when Trafford gives up research temporarily for business are we willing to judge him. In *Marriage,* Wells reworks on a larger scale the problem already implied in *Love and Mr. Lewisham*. And this time neither science nor humanity is to be sacrificed.

The Passionate Friends, which deals with the tragedy of possessiveness in love, is pitched higher than *Marriage,* but is considerably less convincing. For good or ill, the world is now far more ready to accept an Ann Veronica than it was thirty years ago, but nothing that has happened in the interval has made it easier than it was then to see a martyr in a woman who refuses to marry the man she loves simply because his rival can give her more of this world's goods, but who considers it perfectly legitimate to carry on an affair with her lover behind her husband's back.

A much better book is *The Wife of Sir Isaac Harman,* the comedy of this group. The central figure is the wife of a rich man who chafes under the limitations her fashionable existence imposes upon her, and whose escape is fostered by the varied agencies of death, militant suffrage agitation, and the kindness of a rather fatuous writer who loves her but wins no love in return.

Though sex plays an important role in most of the later Wells novels, there is only one that I should call distinctively a sex novel—*The Secret Places of the Heart.* This book attempts a study of a man fundamentally idealistic, unselfish, devoted to the common-weal, who depends on erotic experiences for strength and comfort. This is one of the three novels largely in dialogue which Mr. Wells wrote about this time, and it is much the poorest of the three. The other two—*The Undying Fire* and *The Soul of a Bishop*—will be discussed with the religious group.

6. *Politics and Citizenship*

For me, no one of the four novels which Mr. Wells has devoted essentially to politics and citizenship quite fulfills its purpose. The dominating idea in all is "the statesman's idea, that idea of sound service which is the protagonist of my story."

These words are those of the hero of *The New Machiavelli,* which is almost a handbook of English political life on the eve of the First World War. The present writer finds the political part of the book nearly unreadable, and reserves his admiration for the story of Remington's early life, and again for the moving account of his adventures with his wife Margaret and his mistress Isabel. For Isabel he threw away the world, in much the same manner as Parnell did, and went to Italy, where he writes the autobiography which is the novel. *The Research Magnificent* seems a gigantic prelude to a drama on which the curtain never rises. It is Benham's obsession to live nobly, to live the aristocratic life, to free himself from fear, indulgence, jealousy, and prejudice. He wants to achieve a Sense of the Whole; he wants to build the World-State; but up until his death in the South African strike riots of 1913, he is only preparing and observing. Whatever may be said of *The Research Magnificent* as a novel, however, there can be no question that it is one of its author's most important books; it contains virtually all the ideas he was to spend the rest of his life developing.

The World of William Clissold is Wells's longest novel; like *The New Machiavelli* it takes the form of an autobiography; like *Tono-Bungay* it attempts to summarize an age. "If a man is to be given completely, there must first be the man and his universe, then the man and history, and only after that man and other men and other men and womankind." Clissold was a scientist but he was also a rich industrialist. He was "greedy for property and freedom and influence and for many sorts of experience I had better have avoided," and after the war he was "foolish enough to dabble in politics."

Mr. Wells may be right when he argues that the reason why "few fully adult people read modern novels" is that most novels assume "that people's lives and actions are never determined by political and social conditions, but only by personal reactions." Yet I cannot feel that the numerous dissertations which this book contains are ever quite transmuted into the stuff of fiction, or that the book ever lives in them as it lives in its account of the hero's relations with women—Clara, his wife, who betrays him; the notorious Sirrie Evans, whom he stands by in her scandal and cares for until her death; and Clementina, the prostitute whom he picks up out of pure benevolence in the streets of Paris and gives a new lease on life. These are all vivid figures, and Minnie, Dickon Clissold's wife—cold, exquisite, of "a cynicism fine as carved ivory"—is more vivid than any of them. Success or failure, this "Novel at a New Angle" was a very interesting experiment, and it deserved more attention than it received.

After *Clissold, Meanwhile* seemed inconsequential. The first part, which takes place on the Italian estate of a wealthy English mine-owner, is in the Peacock tradition. The General Strike of 1926 calls Rylands back to England, and the second half of the book is composed mainly of the letters to his wife wherein he describes how he discovered his duty toward the building of a better world. It is interesting to compare Wells's treatment of the strike with Galsworthy's in *Swan Song*.

7. *War, Religion, and Education*

The three apparently unrelated themes—war, religion, and education—are curiously intertwined in Mr. Wells's work. It was in his novel of the First World War, *Mr. Britling Sees It Through,* that Mr. Wells announced his discovery of God, his own finite god, the Captain of those who fight for a better world;[6] it was the war too which convinced him that there is a race on "between education and catastrophe."

Mr. Britling and *The Outline of History* (1920), itself a part of Mr. Wells's great educational enterprise in the non-fiction field,[7] have been his sensational best-sellers, especially in America, where the former served as an authentic report on the spiritual life of England during the early months of the war. The book is journalism, of course, yet it is absorbing reading even today; Mr. Wells may not have seen too clearly, but he felt nobly. *Joan and Peter,* that long, fascinating, sprawling, chaotic book, started out to be "The Story of an Education," but it was swamped by the war and the effects of the war on the manners and morals of young people. One agrees with the author that something had to be omitted, but one may still wonder why he chose to omit the very thing that the book was about.

The Second World War and its approaches have already produced several works of fiction. *The Brothers* is committed to the thesis that "The Left and Right in any age are just the two faces of the Common Fool." Leaders on both sides want the same thing—a world of discipline and order—but they are handicapped by the myopia of their followers. "What is really happening is the birth of a new world, out of mankind, almost in spite of mankind." This

[6] The discovery had been foreshadowed in *The Research Magnificent.* It was formally expounded in *God the Invisible King* (1917) and formally withdrawn in the Prefaces to the Atlantic Edition and in *Experiment in Autobiography.* During recent years there has been an important movement in theology in the direction of thinking of God as finite. See F. H. Ross, *Personalism and the Problem of Evil* (Yale University Press, 1940).

[7] *The Science of Life* (1931) and *The Work, Wealth, and Happiness of Mankind* (1931) were intended to supplement *The Outline of History,* the whole constituting a summary of indispensable knowledge for modern men.

thesis is presented in terms of fiction, and the brief narrative is concentrated and highly dramatic. *The Holy Terror* tells how a nasty Englishman named Rud Whitlow became world dictator, how he established peace and order because it is going to take a man with a large capacity for destruction to do that job, and how, when he came to be a menace to his own work, he was put out of the way by his associates. One reader at least finds it difficult to believe that Rud's efforts could achieve Mr. Wells's aims. *Babes in the Darkling Wood* deals directly with the Second World War, which breaks out in the course of the narrative, and gets as far as the invasion of the Lowlands. The "babes" are Stella and Gemini, unbelievers, experimentalists in morals, with the whole state of the world "hammering down on . . . [their] poor little brains." Into their mouths and that of Stella's Uncle Robert, a psychotherapeutist, Wells puts some ninety per cent of the book. In general the dissertations are better assimilated than in *Clissold,* always excepting the long, tiresome, and already old-fashioned discussion of the peculiar psychological approach known as Behaviorism. The present writer finds a coarse, brutal quality in the *Babes* which makes it one of the least attractive of Wells's books.

Two earlier novels which, like the *Babes,* are written largely in dialogue—*The Soul of a Bishop* and *The Undying Fire*—develop the religious ideas set forth by Mr. Britling. The *Bishop* invites comparison with Trollope and Walpole; despite much contrary opinion, I must persist in regarding it as a rather good book. I would agree, of course, that it is vastly inferior to *The Undying Fire.* This is a careful rewriting in modern idiom of one of the greatest works in all literature, the Book of Job. The parallels are uncannily close yet they are never forced. I doubt that a commensurable triumph exists in literature.

Much was hoped from Mr. Wells's latest experiment in dialogue form, *All Aboard for Ararat,* but expectations were not realized. The book starts with God's suggestion to Noah Lammock (who, like Mr. Britling and Mr. Wells, is a novelist) that he prepare a new Ark to save mankind from the flood of war. But the fantastic note is lost as the book advances; the story becomes heavily metaphysical, collapses structurally, and loses itself in talk.

In 1942 Mr. Wells published *You Can't Be Too Careful.* This book is rather difficult to classify. It is a war book; it is a study of personal idiosyncrasy; it is a novel of ideas. Edward Albert Tewler is brother to Kipps and Mr. Polly, but Mr. Wells has not told his story because he is either interested or amused by his eccentricities. Mr. Wells in fact finds Edward Albert both pitiful and detestable. "He is what our civilization has made of him." There can be no hope for the world until Tewlerism is utterly destroyed.

8. *By Way of Summary*

Mr. Wells's theory of fiction is largely negative. He disclaims great care in writing (though the appearance of his manuscripts clearly belies him), calls himself journalist rather than artist, and has no expectation or desire of permanence. Indeed he thinks art in general much inferior to science.

Of course that is not the whole story. As Geoffrey West has clearly pointed out, there is a conflict in Wells between reason and intuition—"In the ultimate I know, though I cannot prove my knowledge in any way whatever, that everything is right and all things mine"—but "he has chosen the intellectual attitude, and therefore has to reject all that he cannot rationalise." Naturally such a man would find scientific fairy tales very congenial to him.

He wanted to write about the whole of human life, and to him life was raw material for change. He was not satisfied to look at it; he wanted to do something about it.[8] As a serious man and a reformer, he could not "pander to the vulgar appetite for stark stories"; he had to get ideas into his books, as Shaw was getting them into his much less flexible plays. Neither could he accept the estheticism of a Ford Madox Ford or a Henry James; a fine Jacobean unity could only be had at the price of leaving a great many valuable things out.

Such a writer experiments with many methods, yet has no "method." The story will get itself told somehow (since he has a

[8] See his essay on "The Contemporary Novel," in *An Englishman Looks at the World* (1914); his introduction to Frank Swinnerton's *Nocturne* (1917); his Prefaces to the Atlantic Edition; his Preface to *Babes in the Darkling Wood.*

natural gift for story-telling); and if in the course of the narrative he chooses to indulge a natural levity which lies deep in him despite all his fundamental seriousness, no one can have the right to complain. If he wishes to set down an adventurous episode in the midst of a realistic book, as when he sends George Ponderevo off to Africa to search for a wholly imaginary "quap," or ships Marjorie and Trafford to the Labrador, where they first have Jack London adventures, and then sit down to deliver lectures at each other and talk the book to death, that is his business; for it is his novel that he is writing, and Samuel Butler has taught him that he can do whatever he likes with it.

He has a tendency toward the autobiographical novel of the Victorians—since that is a very loose form—though the materials he thrusts into it are not very Victorian in tone. Sometimes his arrangement is topical rather than strictly chronological; in *William Clissold* the hero's relations with Sirrie Evans are mentioned as having affected his intercourse with his brother's wife before we have met Sirrie or learned her history. This weaving back and forth adds notably to the impression of reality.

Of late Mr. Wells has been much in love with the novel in dialogue; it is interesting that most of the models he cites—the Socratic dialogue, the Book of Job, the work of Peacock and W. H. Mallock, the plays of Bernard Shaw—should lie outside the novel field. But unlike the stream-of-consciousness writers he will not trust his readers to interpret his dialogue for themselves. He remembers always that art is communication; the lack of a common experiencial background makes the interpreter's service indispensable.

His minor characters, his comic characters, and such heroes as Kipps and Mr. Polly have a Dickens-like vitality, but in the novels of ideas most of his personages live only to illuminate a thesis. The typical Wells hero is a scientist or man of affairs whose mind is set on disinterested ends but who is liable to be seduced into the ways of private profit by the urgencies of his animal nature. His wife, likely as not, will fail to satisfy him because she prefers clothing to nakedness, after which he will turn to find his true mate outside of marriage. These type characters are not always clearly differentiated. We are not prepared for the swift moral collapse of Amanda in *The*

Research Magnificent; at the outset she seems to have as much stuff in her as Marjorie in *Marriage;* it is largely an arbitrary decision of the author's that Marjorie should climb to the heights while Amanda must crash.

I do not come to embalm Mr. Wells; fortunately there is no need for that as yet. I am not called upon to evaluate his views on sex and on religion; his work as a publicist does not concern me. As a novelist, his principal fault has been a lack of respect for his medium, which has served, I think, neither the novel itself nor the ideas to which he has sacrificed it. Mr. Wells has influenced the thinking of his generation both when he has addressed it in his own person and when he has succeeded in fusing his ideas with the stuff of fiction, but when he has only pretended to write novels he has been productive mainly of annoyance.

Yet beyond question he has widened the scope of fiction, and others will build on the foundation he has laid. No intelligent man can read him through without often being impatient with him, but no open-minded man can read him through without often being enlightened and uplifted. His own considered self-judgment is just: "There is . . . something said in these volumes that was not said before, and something shaped that was not shaped before."

CHAPTER XXVII

PITY, IRONY, AND JOHN GALSWORTHY *

It is befitting to you that you take a stand against your own class. Every man can pass judgment on, and censure, only his own class.

GOETHE

1. *March to Mastery*

When John Galsworthy killed his most famous character, at least one London paper headlined the event

DEATH OF SOAMES FORSYTE

as if a man of flesh and blood had passed. At the writer's own death in 1933 he was generally regarded as the most distinguished of British novelists. It had not always been so. Paging through the publishers' advertisements in old *Harpers* and *Atlantics,* one can still find a new novel "by John Galsworthy"—*Fraternity* or maybe *The Patrician*—modestly listed in small type among the "also rans," while the bold face at the top of the page proudly proclaims another piece of trash by some already forgotten writer. This was the period when a distinguished British ecclesiastic, visiting the University of Chicago, picked up a book from the desk of the president's secretary, and mumbled, "Galsworthy? Galsworthy? And is he, then, one of your rising young American writers?" As late as 1916, in the first critical study of Galsworthy's books ever to be graced with the dignity of boards, Sheila Kaye-Smith permitted herself one of the worst prophecies on record: "Galsworthy will never be widely read. . . ."

Galsworthy had almost deliberately made haste slowly. He was born in Surrey, August 14, 1867; his father, a prosperous attorney, descended from Devonshire yeoman stock, his mother from a line of

* The quotations from Galsworthy's books are made by permission of Charles Scribner's Sons.

provincial squires, gentlemen farmers, and men of commerce. He was not a remarkable student either at Harrow or at Oxford, where his literary passions were *Ruff's Guide* and the novels of Whyte-Melville; and he finally became a barrister not because he loved the law but because it was considered a genteel profession for a dandified young sportsman with no particular ambition in life. Foreign travel may have helped destroy his insular outlook, but the really determinative influence was that of his cousin, Ada Galsworthy. "Why don't you write?" she had asked him in 1894, when she was still the wife of his cousin Arthur. "You're just the person." Through the difficult years up to their marriage in 1905, Galsworthy played Young Jolyon to her Irene;[1] thus he attained his spiritual maturity. An elegant young trifler died; a serious artist was born. It is not too much to say that John Galsworthy experienced a non-religious conversion.

The first-fruits were two volumes of short stories—*From the Four Winds* (1897) and *A Man of Devon* (1901)—and two novels—*Jocelyn* (1898) and *Villa Rubein* (1900). These books are interesting as prefiguring the work that an important writer was to do rather than as positive achievements. No doubt the same might be said of *The Island Pharisees* (1904), but if this book is only a prologue it is a remarkable one; every motif later employed in Galsworthy's work is already sounded in it.

Complete maturity came suddenly in 1906 with *The Man of Property,* at about the same time that *The Silver Box* marked its author's arrival as a dramatist. But not until the complete *Forsyte Saga* appeared in 1922 did Galsworthy become a world figure. He refused knighthood in 1918 but accepted the Order of Merit in 1929 and the Nobel Prize in 1932. His death occurred January 31, 1933.

2. *The Forsytes*

Though *The Forsyte Saga* was the title he first had in mind for *The Man of Property,* Galsworthy did not then see that novel as one of a series. In the terrible last chapter, Irene, utterly defeated by the death of her lover, returns to her husband's house; and as

[1] The story is told in H. V. Marrot's *Life and Letters,* I, 6, to which the essay in Ford Madox Ford's *Portraits from Life* is an important addendum.

late as 1911 Galsworthy was still telling questioners that he did not know what they did afterwards. In "Indian Summer of a Forsyte," written in 1917, Irene is described as having left Soames again that same night, but it was not until one Sunday in the summer of 1918 that the idea of the complete *Saga* came into Galsworthy's mind.

The Forsytes are rich London bourgeoisie, "the very people," as Wilbur Cross has remarked, "who entered largely into the novels of Dickens and Thackeray." Dickens hated them; Thackeray was impressed principally by their snobbery. There is considerable sensitiveness in the Jolyon branch of the family, but there is less in Soames's line, for though Soames is a noted connoisseur, he is never able to forget the monetary value of his pictures. We are told that "In my father's house are many mansions" is one of Aunt Juley's favorite texts; it comforts her "with its suggestion of house property." The tragedy of it is that a Forsyte cannot stop with regarding houses as property. Everything is property. Wives are property. Soames regards Irene as property, and the climax of their history is a legalized rape—a "supreme act of property"—which poisons the lives of the Forsytes through two generations.

The Man of Property, which opens with a gathering of the clan on June 15, 1886, and which ends in 1888, is the most "packed" of all the Forsyte novels, and the most discursive as to method. All ten of the old Forsytes are still alive at the beginning of this book—(Soames himself, James's son, "the man of property," belongs to the younger generation)—and after the author gets through the tedious "charactery" of his opening chapters, he is very successful in welding diverse materials together. The material is presented from many different points of view, but never from that of Irene or her lover, Bosinney. Irene is a "concretion of disturbing Beauty impinging on a possessive world"; we see her only as she is reflected in the minds of others; Bosinney we can hardly be said to see at all. In the first draft Galsworthy actually had Bosinney commit suicide after Soames's crime on Irene, and it took all Edward Garnett's persuasive powers to convince him that this would not do. The accidental death of the published text is a skillful evasion.

In Chancery (1920) opens in 1899 and ends with the famous description of Queen Victoria's funeral. After an abortive attempt to rewin Irene, which only succeeds in driving her into the arms of Young Jolyon, Soames finally frees himself of the past, and marries the French girl, Annette, in the hope that she may bear him a son. *In Chancery* is lighter and far less complicated than *The Man of Property,* and though it has its own merits, many readers think of it as preparing the way for the moving love-affair between Fleur, daughter of Soames and Annette, and Jon, Irene's son by Young Jolyon.

Skipping the First World War, *To Let* (1921) opens May 12, 1920. Galsworthy's epigraph deliberately challenges the comparison with *Romeo and Juliet:*

> From out [*sic*] the fatal loins of these two foes
> A pair of star-crossed lovers take their life.

Ignorant of the bitter past, the children meet and love. When the revelation comes, Fleur would go on, but Jon draws back. Juliet does not kill herself with Romeo's dagger, for the day of old heroic passions has gone by; instead she marries Michael Mont, who is much too good for her. But one may bleed to death internally without a dagger.

The Man of Property left us speculating about the future of Soames and Irene. In the same way, *To Let* leaves us wondering about Fleur and Jon and Michael. So Galsworthy gave us his second Forsyte trilogy, *A Modern Comedy.*

In the first novel of this series, *The White Monkey* (1924), the first test of Fleur's marriage comes when Wilfrid Desert, a typical representative of the "lost generation," conceives a passion for her. Fleur is reckless enough to give Michael a pretty bad time temporarily, but in the end she sends Wilfrid on his way. In *The Silver Spoon* (1926) modern "morality" goes on trial in a society scandal which involves Fleur and Marjorie Ferrars. If this seems a flimsy theme for a serious novel, we must remember that the drifting aimlessness of post-war lives is precisely what Galsworthy is writing about. *Swan Song* (1928) rises to a much higher emotional level with its tragic revival of Fleur's passion for Jon and the fatal consequences of that affair for Soames.

Critics generally feel that the *Comedy* does not reach the level of the *Saga,* and they have been very busy trying to figure out why. Galsworthy's sympathies are not with the period covered, they tell us. Or, it is impossible to achieve "completeness . . . in the portrayal of a generation whose destiny . . . [is] still obscure." Sometimes it is even suggested that Galsworthy has now become the professional novelist, "carried forward more by the momentum already acquired than by any powerful creative impulse; each book follows immediately on the year in which the action is placed, as if the author were somewhat hastily and perfunctorily keeping his chronicle up to date."

Certainly there can be no question as to the contemporaneousness of the *Comedy*. Practically every fad and foible of the twenties enters somewhere—jazz, cubism, dadaism, futurism, osteopathy, birth-control, mental healing, psychoanalysis, Couéism, and what-have-you. *Swan Song* opens on a hostile picture of the General Strike of 1926; in *The Silver Spoon* Michael identifies himself with "Foggartism," a scheme for the economic salvation of England which includes, among other things, the emigration of large numbers of English children. The business background of *The White Monkey* is dark and murky, and the lower-class story of Bicket and Victorine is not closely enough connected with the main plot to be judged other than an extraneous element.

But if the *Comedy* has not quite the force of the *Saga,* it has gained in humanity. This is due largely to the fact that Soames is much more attractive as an old man than he was in middle age—to that and to Fleur.[2] Fleur is the Beatrix Esmond of post-war fiction. She has Beatrix's limitations of character, Beatrix's clear-sighted realization of her own shortcomings, and Beatrix's incapacity to do anything about them. She has too—and here she is unlike Beatrix—an endearing childlikeness, which crops out, despite her sophistication, in every crisis, and which disarms the reader as completely as it disarms her husband. Doubtless our kindliness toward her, despite all her faults, is largely a tribute to the skill and fine humanity with

[2] See H. C. Duffin's fine article, "The Rehabilitation of Soames Forsyte," *Cornhill Magazine,* LXVIII (1930), 397-406; Edward Wagenknecht, "The Selfish Heroine—Thackeray and Galsworthy," *College English,* IV (1943), 293-298.

which Galsworthy has portrayed her. By the time we get through the *Comedy,* we have suffered with her through her terribly young heartbreak over Jon; we have stood by her side through the agonies of motherhood; we have trembled for her soul when she flings her cap over the windmill; and we have tasted the salt tears of her bitter remorse when her father is killed. There are not many women in English fiction whom we know so well.

Her brief reappearances in *End of the Chapter* are not wholly satisfactory. In *Maid in Waiting* she has nothing to do save motor Dinny and her friends around the country! But Galsworthy leaves us in no doubt that she has kept the promise she made her dying father when she said, "Yes, Dad; I will be good!" Only her own soul knows what it has cost her. Something vivid, something lovable has gone from the willful girl we used to know. To achieve such self-mastery a woman must either become a saint or else she must partly kill herself.

I have got over now into another trilogy, *End of the Chapter,* which is a kind of addendum to the story of the Forsytes, its heroine, Dinny Charwell, being a connection of Fleur's on her husband's side. These books may be dismissed quickly; here if anywhere Galsworthy transgressed his own advice to Ralph Mottram never to write anything unless he must. The first, *Maid in Waiting* (1931), is the worst; it scatters; its pictures of contemporary society lack vividness and pass too rapidly before our eyes; the staccato dialogue is all on the surface. In *Flowering Wilderness* (1932), Wilfrid Desert returns to England much less a rotter than one might have expected after *The White Monkey,* but his genuine romance with Dinny is wrecked by the fact that public opinion will not condone his having abjured Christianity at the point of an Arab's pistol. *Over the River* (American title: *One More River*) (1933) has value merely as one more illustration of Galsworthy's ability to write breathless courtroom scenes.[3]

[3] I have disturbed chronology somewhat for the sake of keeping the Forsyte material together. The student should remember that the first Forsyte, Swithin, made his initial appearance in "Salvation of a Forsyte," as far back as *A Man of Devon.* There is a whole volume of short stories, *On Forsyte 'Change* (1930). There are short stories which serve as links in both the *Saga* and the *Comedy*—"Indian Summer of a Forsyte" and "Awakening" in the

3. The Others

The non-Forsyte novels divide themselves into two groups: four novels of social criticism and three novels of passion. The first group comprises *The Country House* (1907); *Fraternity* (1909); *The Patrician* (1911); and *The Freelands* (1915). The second group consists of *The Dark Flower* (1913); *Beyond* (1917); and *Saint's Progress* (1919).

Galsworthy himself was inclined to regard *The Country House* as the best of his non-Forsyte books. Among the wealthy landed gentry, "Pendycitis" replaces Forsyteism; "Pendycitis" is indeed as close to Forsyteism as a class can come which cherishes tradition and refuses to place a strictly commercial valuation upon the experience of living. As so often in Galsworthy, *The Country House* uses social scandal to test a society. George Pendyce is in love with Mrs. Bellew, who resembles Irene as an extraneous element in her lover's world, but who differs from her in being a thoroughly bad woman. His father would disinherit George on principle, but Mrs. Pendyce stands by him—and even risks a break with her husband to do so—not because she thinks him right, but because she loves him, and love is higher than law. In the end, George recovers, and Mrs. Pendyce returns to her husband. Nothing has "happened," but a way of life has been critically examined.

Fraternity, a study in frustration, is Galsworthy's most hopeless book, and technically it is probably the most perfect. Nearly every one of the upper middle-class intelligentsia who occupy the foreground has his "shadow" among the submerged; but despite the best intentions in the world the gulf between the classes cannot be bridged. If you try, the most elementary facts of life defeat you; Hilary's marriage-vow does not keep him from running off with the Little Model, but "the scent of stale violet powder . . . warmed by her humanity," when she throws her arms round his neck and kisses him on the mouth, can and does. So the girl drops into the underworld presumably, and the man's last chance to escape utter

first, "A Silent Wooing" and "Passers-By" in the second. Finally, there are references to the Forsytes in *Villa Rubein* and in "Danaë," which is the first draft of *The Country House* (cf. *Forsytes, Pendyces, and Others,* 1935).

sterility has passed him by. Fraternity exists only in the interminable pages of old Mr. Stone's crazy book, which he goes on writing and writing in that hopeless household where no human being ever meets another on common ground.

In *The Patrician,* which goes over into the world of the aristocracy, the conflict is between Lord Miltoun's love for Audrey Lees Noel, whose clergyman-husband refuses to divorce her, and his career. The man cannot take his love in secret, for he will not be a hypocrite. At one time he decides to relinquish his career, but Lord Dennis convinces him that this would be unfair to Mrs. Noel. In the end she solves her lover's problem by going away.

Miltoun's young sister, Barbara, the most splendid of all Galsworthy's girls, is wiser. Barbara loves Courtier, a radical democrat, and she would have taken him, too, if circumstances had not defeated her. In the end she makes a sensible, suitable, and eminently fitting marriage with a fine young man whom she does not love.

The Freelands is Galsworthy's most unappreciated novel and one of his best. This, as Leon Schalit has remarked, is a rural *Fraternity;* the problem of the poor is now presented in a country setting. The Preface expounds the moral, which is "that England will never be sound and safe till the land is again what it once was, the very backbone and blood of our race." There is surprising variety in the Freeland clan, and much fine characterization.

It seems strange that Galsworthy, who handled passion so movingly in the Fleur-Jon romance and in the greatest of his shorter pieces, "The Apple Tree," should have failed when he tried to make passion the theme of a whole novel. Perhaps *Beyond* is not really a novel of passion. Gyp gives her worthless first husband, Fiorsen, an embodiment of the "artistic temperament" at its worst, "everything except her heart"; the reader finds it nearly as difficult as her father does to explain why she married him. *Beyond* is a "woman's novel"; it reminds me of Margaret Ayer Barnes, though it is far below the best of that author's work. In *Saint's Progress,* which is the story of a clergyman's daughter and her "war baby," Galsworthy fails for a different reason. He had often used social scandal to test society; here he seems to be using it for its own sake, and this proves much less interesting. He is handicapped also by his failure to understand mystical experience; because the author is quite unable to describe Edward Pierson's religious life, it must seem to the reader that he has none. Indeed *Saint's Progress* has little value save as a social document depicting life in England during the First World War, and as an expression of Galsworthy's own humane and civilized refusal to surrender to a savage wartime mood.

Galsworthy would not have objected to anything I have said about these two books; he set little store by either of them. On the other hand, he regarded *The Dark Flower* highly, and this is a view which I cannot share.[4] This book presents three detached episodes in the love life of Mark Lennan. As a young man, he spurns the middle-aged professor's wife who has conceived a passion for him; in his maturity, he finds the grand passion, only to have it snatched from him by death; growing old, he is pursued by a young girl, whom he rejects at last out of consideration for his wife. Mark's passion is considerably more real than he is, which is likely the inevitable result of omitting everything in his life that does not bear upon the erotic experience. Galsworthy's tendency to shift his point of view continually does not help this story either; very likely we might find Part I more palatable if we saw Anna only through Mark's eyes.

4. *Literary Ideals and Practice*

Galsworthy regarded Tolstoy's *War and Peace* as the greatest modern novel, but he claimed to have learned less from Tolstoy than he learned from Turgenev and de Maupassant. There has been much discussion as to just how these literary idols affected him. Sheila Kaye-Smith derives his pity from Russia, his irony from France. But, she adds, his Russian pity is "shorn of its mysticism," his French irony of its gaiety. Frank Swinnerton, who calls him the first English novelist "to turn for what may be called technical inspiration to Russia," points out that while French realism is objective, Russian realism "was always tinged with philosophy (that is to say, with ethics and metaphysics) and with politics." Ford Madox

[4] It is only fair to record that some critics do. Cf. Thomas Mann, "An Impression of John Galsworthy," *Virginia Quarterly Review,* VI (1930), 114-116.

Ford thought that Turgenev was responsible for transforming Galsworthy from the Trollope he might otherwise have been to the novelist of pity he became.

Personally I do not take any of this too seriously. As for Ford, the dates plainly contradict his assumption that *Villa Rubein,* which he liked, was free of Turgenev's influence, and that this entered first in *The Island Pharisees* and *The Man of Property,* which he did not like. In general, I believe that Galsworthy wrote sympathetically because he was Galsworthy. He did not learn pity out of anybody's book. And if he needed an example there were plentv before him in nineteenth-century England.

Except in the play, *Justice* (1910), which did produce changes in English prison administration, Galsworthy did not actually work for reform in the good old fashion of Charles Dickens and Charles Reade.[5] Again and again he insists that he is not trying to reform anything; he is simply expressing his view of life, describing the world as it appears to him in the light of his particular temperament. He thought of art as "the one form of human energy in the whole world, which really works for union, and destroys the barriers between man and man." To his way of thinking, the artist could only see life as in a state of flux; for him no questions were closed questions; he could have no desire to impose his temperament upon another.

Galsworthy might possibly have been more strongly tempted to use his art for propaganda purposes had he possessed a more hopeful nature. Wells and Shaw are great crusaders because they are great believers in human perfectibility. To be sure, everything is wrong now, but everything might so easily be made right if only we would listen to them! Galsworthy had no such faith. For him the roots of human maladjustments lay deep in the stuff of human nature itself. Palliation might be possible, but there could never be a cure.

Naturally none of this obviates the necessity for pity, and it was along this line that Galsworthy was sometimes reproached for his

[5] For Dickens, Galsworthy always had a passion, but it is difficult to trace any specific influence on his work. For a list of other writers of fiction who meant much to him, see the first page of his introduction to *Bleak House,* as reprinted in *Forsytes, Pendyces, and Others.*

"sentimentality." "The sight of a butterfly," remarks Philip Guedalla, "makes him think of wheels." I am not surprised to learn through Mr. H. V. Marrot that Galsworthy greatly admired the work of Robert Nathan, for some of his references to animals are curiously like Nathan's. But on the whole I think Galsworthy's "sentimentality" very nicely balanced by his love of irony, by the under-expression to which he and his characters alike (nearly all modern cultivated Englishmen) are so notoriously given, and by his preference for what he himself calls "the negative method." He did not admire Jane Austen, but he might have said with her that "pictures of perfection" made him "sick and wicked." What he did say was that angelic conceptions are for poetry, not prose. A novelist must not "look up" to his characters.

As for the influence of de Maupassant and Turgenev on Galsworthy's form specifically, this is made difficult to determine by the fact that in the novel, as distinguished from the medium-length story of the *Five Tales,* he never considered form of any particular importance. Yet he is "arty" (for want of a better word) as few of his English predecessors before Meredith had been. He lacks the companionable quality of Dickens and Thackeray; not for him is the novel a long conversation between author and reader. No, he holds himself in reserve; he carves his statue with far more regard than they showed for purity and clarity of line; he is fastidious; he must load every rift with ore. This aristocratic reserve was, no doubt, largely a matter of temperament, but was it not this fastidiousness in his temperament that caused him to turn to continental models, and must it not have been immensely encouraged by them? So it comes about that Galsworthy is emphatically one of the novelists that need to be savored. His pages are full of delicate perceptions and lovely but quite unpretentious turns of expression, and this is a large part of the charm he has for his devotees.[6]

The profoundest of Galsworthy's critics, André Chevrillon, has

[6] Yet on occasion he is capable both of bad writing and of bad taste. "Wrapped in an old Guards' blanket, they carried the almost inanimate dog to the divan" (*Flowering Wilderness*). Sir James Foskisson "nodded almost imperceptibly three times, precisely as if he had seen the Holy Ghost" (*The Silver Spoon*).

paid warm tribute to his use of indirect speech. He has also tried to justify Galsworthy's frequent shifts in point of view:

> The idea that governs his art is that the inner life of a man is seen only in flashes, that we never get a direct view of it—therefore that no direct description of it can be true—and further, that a character is part of an ever-moving group, where no single figure appears for a moment in the foreground without being eclipsed by others—therefore that it should not be kept too long before the footlights, and studied separately.

But this tendency is not universally praised. Professor Joseph Warren Beach, for example, goes so far as to connect Galsworthy's "paleness" with "his inability to regard any person, place, or object steadily for any length of time." It would be difficult to deny that this "paleness" does exist at times in all save his very finest work. He himself recognized variations even within the same book; he knew that he had failed with Bosinney, for example. It is interesting that he did not always succeed with the characters he liked best. In *The Patrician* he admires Mrs. Noel and dislikes Miltoun, but Miltoun is the one he makes real.

5. *Criticism of Life*

As a critic of life, Galsworthy is sometimes judged nihilistic. He believed that life is a mess and that we should be kind; and this, say the authoritarians, is not enough. Religiously speaking, he rejected all the distinctive Christian doctrines; to him a creed was only the expression of a temperament, and he attributed the decline of the church in modern times to its vain attempt to cling to an outgrown conception of religious authority.

Yet he had a vague metaphysic of his own, and here and there we find traces of a Meredith-like nature-mysticism. Now and again, his characters discuss their religious problems. In *The Freelands,* Cuthcott finds belief in God inevitable, "some kind of instinct toward perfection," "some kind of honor forbidding one to let go and give up." A conversation between Young Jolyon and Jolly in *In Chancery* comes closer to orthodox Christianity than Galsworthy gets anywhere else. Young Jolyon proclaims his faith in "the Unknowable Creative Principle" and also in "the Sum of altruism in man":

it remains for Jolly to point out that these two ideas have been joined in Christ.

As Galsworthy himself draws nearer the Mystery, his interest in religion seems to be increasing, though his orthodoxy clearly is not. In *Maid in Waiting,* God is defined as "perpetual motion in perpetual quiet," but not as a God of mercy in the ordinary sense, or as "of much immediate use to mortals." Hilary, the good parson, who admits that he would be unfrocked if his real beliefs were known, reads to a dying child not from the Bible but from *Alice in Wonderland!*

Galsworthy has commented on the difference between himself and Dickens in this matter of faith, and it troubled him, for he wished to preserve the Christian ethic, and he was intelligent enough to know that this is difficult to do without Christian sanctions. In *Maid in Waiting* there is a long didactic passage from Hubert's diary, arguing against the view that with religious values gone, "There's nothing for it but to enjoy ourselves as best we can." Hubert argues that "You can't . . . disbelieve in consideration for others without making an idiot of yourself and spoiling your own chances of a good time." Galsworthy had no faith in sacrifice as a virtue in and for itself, but even Fleur must learn in the end that sacrifice is a necessary prerequisite to conquest. This is the subject of Michael's meditation during the terrible hours when Fleur writhes in childbirth: "To have a creed that nothing mattered—and then run into it like this! Something born at such a cost, must matter, should matter. One must see to that!"

It was not hard for Michael to learn that, for Michael was, as it were, a "natural" Christian. It is harder for Soames and for Fleur. Wisdom comes to him through his love for his daughter, the first selfless, unpropertied love he has ever known. He learns the truth perhaps more completely than she ever does, but he learns it later in life than it comes to her. And in the end he dies for her, as the only way he can pass his knowledge on. Very nearly the last words Fleur speaks in *Over the River* make the point inescapable:

> Of course I know what you've been through [she tells Dinny], but the past buries its dead. It is so, I've been through it, too. It's the present

and the future that matter, and we're the present, and our children are the future.

So, in the last analysis, the comparison between Fleur and Beatrix Esmond becomes a contrast. Beatrix's last years are a degradation redeemed only by her vitality; Fleur, like Gwendolen Harleth, though quite unemotionally, in her hard little post-war way, is saved, "as by fire."

But all this comes about through man, not God, for it is only in human life that justice can be found, and so humanism comes to seem increasingly the only possible faith for a modern man. Perhaps "being in love with life" is enough; it is Soames's great criticism of Fleur's contemporaries that they have no interest in being alive. And it is Galsworthy himself who tells us that "life for those who still have vital instinct in them is good enough in itself even if it lead to nothing, and we have only ourselves to blame if we, alone among animals, so live that we lose the love of life for itself."

This passionate humanism is the key to his inmost spirit; he disliked metaphysics as he disliked institutionalism because he was not ready to sacrifice his direct experience of human reality to either. On the same ground he hated "systems" of morality, hated "watertight compartments" and glib assumptions of superiority; he was always against the rule and for the exception.

This leads him at times to dispose somewhat cavalierly of the great conflict between freedom and authority, between mercy and justice which lies at the root of so much great art; if there is any true sentimentality in Galsworthy, here is where it is to be encountered. There is nothing gross about John Galsworthy, but theoretically he goes the whole way in his demand for freedom. If a departure from established codes can justify itself pragmatically no other questions need be asked. It is interesting that this disillusioned intellectualist should be at one with the medieval romancers in his feeling that love is irresistible. He was one of the first to state frankly in English fiction that a man cannot live celibate without suffering psychic injury, and sexual antagonism—a theme never treated as such by Victorian novelists—is the very mainspring of the vast *Saga*. His best heroines are never vulgar in their attitude toward sex, but they do not feel that celibacy in itself is very important; from the men who love them, they demand devotion first of all. Galsworthy has been accused of evasion because he calls Irene, Beauty, instead of frankly calling her Sex; the criticism quite misses the point that for him Sex is Beauty, and there can be no Beauty without it. In Sex is the fundamental manifestation of the creative impulse in human nature, the thing which stands opposed to the lust to possess and to destroy.

6. *Vale*

All this cuts sharply across many sacred beliefs and even more sacred prejudices; the reader's response must be determined by many things. Nor has the time come yet to pass the final esthetic judgement upon John Galsworthy, to assign him his "place" in the development of the novel. At the present time, few critics would claim for him either the massive solidity of Hardy or the puckish vitality of Meredith. Yet perhaps no other novelist builds a book more artfully, joining various elements, pulling threads together, looking backwards and forwards, yet never forcing the note, never over-analyzing and wearying the reader. And perhaps none other makes us feel that we are more steadily in the presence of a fastidious intelligence.

Fastidiousness, to be sure, has its own dangers in art, and it would be too much to say that Galsworthy has escaped them all. There are artificialities even in the Forsyte chronicles; the transmission and transmutation of Soames's hapless passion for Irene into Fleur's passion for Irene's son, and the magnificently theatrical death of Soames (Greek proverb-wise) through her he has loved most—all these things are impressive, but they can hardly be said to have been achieved with complete spontaneity.

Similar reservations must be made with regard to his penchant for characterization by types and his use of symbolism. The charge that his characters are types has often been made insensitively, and he did well to resent it; modern men, he points out, "are part of the warp and woof of a complicated society"; they cannot "exactly be depicted isolated by the sea, or standing out against the sky." Yet it is a far cry from this admission to the allegory of the scene in

The Country House in which Horace Pendyce, Hussel Barter, Edmund Paramor, and Gregory Vigil discuss George's affairs from the point of view of the Church, the State, the Law, and philanthropy.

At its best, Galsworthy's symbolism is wonderfully effective. Hilary's dog in *Fraternity,* who can only find his perfect mate in a manufactured article—"The latest—sterilised cloth—see white label underneath: 4s. 3d"—is a perfect commentary on Hilary's sterility and that of his class. Nor could there be a better image of the post-war futilitarians than the picture of the White Monkey who has sucked the orange dry and still feels dissatisfied as he looks about helplessly for—what? On the other hand, the symbolical hornet in *The Patrician* is treated almost as cruelly by Galsworthy as by Lady Casterley; and when the Forsytes themselves go in for symbolism, and find Bosinney's whole personality in his very unsuitable soft, gray hat, which Aunt Hester tries to shoo off the chair in the dark hall, "taking it for a strange, disreputable cat," it is time to realize that even in symbolism one may have too much of a good thing.

No doubt it was unfortunate for Galsworthy's immediate reputation that his last three novels should have fallen so far below the level of his best work. Here he seemed to have abandoned the thing for which he had always been honored most—his fulfillment of Goethe's adjuration to pass judgment upon his own class. The "Service-classes" are the acknowledged heroes of these novels, and the books are not quite free of smugness. In *Flowering Wilderness,* society is not on trial; society is trying a man. Wilfrid had no religious faith. None of his critics have any religious faith. Yet they feel he ought to have permitted the Arab fanatic to blow him to bits rather than make his recantation because, forsooth, he showed the white feather, he let England down!

Ernest Sutherland Bates may have the correct explanation of this when he sees Galsworthy reverting to a narrower, more nationalistic standpoint with the bitter post-war conviction that England will never again hold her old place in the sun.[7] Or he may be running true to form in championing the under-dog; in *The Silver Box* the

[7] "John Galsworthy," *English Journal,* XXII (1933), 437-446.

poor man found it impossible to get justice in the courts, but now judges are trying so hard to be fair that they lean over backwards, and the upperclassman must hesitate to bring a suit, no matter how just his cause! Whatever the final explanation, the matter will not, at long last, prove very important, for every novelist has a right to ask that he be judged by his best work. That granted him, Galsworthy's place may not be with the greatest, but it must always, I think, be a high and honorable one.

CHAPTER XXVIII

D. H. LAWRENCE, PILGRIM OF THE RAINBOW *

One has to be so terribly religious, to be an artist.

D. H. LAWRENCE

1. *The Man and His Books*

Yesterday's rebel is the conservative of today. In a whimsical meditation on the changing climate of the literary world, John Galsworthy once reminded himself that D. H. Lawrence and his school were no more shocking to him than he himself had been to old-fashioned people in the days of his youth.

The highest compliment we can pay to Lawrence is to say that his life was a pilgrimage toward a goal which has not even yet been satisfactorily defined. One may discount the hysterical rhapsodies of the female adorers who swarmed about him—and squabbled over his remains; sufficient testimony remains to make it clear that he was one of the most extraordinary men that have appeared in our time.

"Different and superior in kind"—such is Aldous Huxley's astonishing tribute. David Garnett was unimpressed by his philosophy, "but his *values,* his instinctive code of ethics, always seemed to me incontrovertible." "I have not met anybody who knew Lawrence who did not love him," says Frank Swinnerton. And even Middleton Murry, who saw him at last as Antichrist, bears willing testimony to his great sensitiveness, his ability to immerse himself in experience, his astonishing capacity for tenderness, and insists that though finally he chose hate rather than love, became the prophet

* In this chapter the quotations from *The Plumed Serpent* are used by permission of Alfred A. Knopf, Inc.; the quotations from *The Rainbow* (Copyright, 1915) and from *Studies in Classic American Literature* (Copyright, 1923, 1930) by permission of The Viking Press, Inc.

of death, not life, he must not be judged except by one of comparable temptations and endowments.

Lawrence's people are "naked," "vulnerable." And there is nothing about nakedness that touches him more than its vulnerability. As a little girl, Ursula Brangwen fell one day as she was running toward her father with outstretched arms, and when he raised her from the ground her mouth was bleeding. "He could never bear to think of it, he always wanted to cry, even when he was an old man and she had become a stranger to him."

David Herbert Lawrence was born in Eastwood, Nottinghamshire, September 11, 1885, the son of a drunken coal-miner and his "superior" wife. He was educated at the Nottingham Day Training College, and became a teacher, a great passer of examinations and winner of scholarships. His literary career began about 1909 under the aegis of Ford Madox Ford in *The English Review*.[1]

His first novel, *The White Peacock* (1911), struck the lyrical note characteristic of much of his best work; his second, *The Trespasser* (1912), was more melodramatic. With *Sons and Lovers* (1913) he definitely "arrived."

The first part of *Sons and Lovers*—the description of the boy's life in the miner's household and his wonderful yet terrible relationship with his mother—has been universally recognized as one of the great pieces of English autobiographical fiction. The history of Paul's relations with the two women, Miriam and Clara, is much inferior, not only, as Galsworthy objected, because "that kind of revelling in the shades of sex emotions seems to me anemic,"[2] but more because, as we now know, there is a fundamental falsity in it. The moving reminiscences of E.T.,[3] Lawrence's real-life Miriam, have now made it clear that not only did he use his novel to give himself imaginatively the sexual gratification he could not find in life, but he re-

[1] Lawrence was an extraordinarily prolific writer; the Manly and Rickert bibliography lists nearly sixty titles under the headings: Novels, Poems, Plays, Short Stories and Tales, Essays and Studies, and Travel. Only the novels concern us directly here.

[2] Cf. Galsworthy's letter to Edward Garnett in Marrot's *Life and Letters*, p. 724, a passage in which the old fiction and the new are made to stand in sharp juxtaposition. Lawrence has an hysterical attack on Galsworthy in *Phoenix* (1936).

[3] *D. H. Lawrence, A Personal Record* (Knight, 1935).

fused to face the truth of his difficulty when he insisted on placing the blame for his failure upon the girl rather than on his mother, where it belonged. Before the book appeared, however, Lawrence had turned away from "Miriam" altogether, to solve his own sexual problem (in so far as he ever did solve it), with another woman. In 1912 he eloped with Frieda, Mrs. Ernest Weekley, nee von Richthofen, daughter of the German ex-governor of Lorraine. Two years later they were married.

Sons and Lovers is a realistic book, strongly suggestive of Samuel Butler and Arnold Bennett. *The Rainbow* (1915) starts in much the same manner, but there is far more poetry in it and far more limpid beauty. The first 125 pages or so of *The Rainbow* belong with the most precious things in English fiction; perhaps the tenderness and painful awareness that were the real D. H. Lawrence never found such perfect expression again. Before the book is finished, however, the sexual side of his subject has rather begun to run away with the author; moreover, he stops writing a novel and begins sketching a rather weird allegory. Yet from the worst of *The Rainbow* to the best of its purported sequel, *Women in Love* (1921), the descent is abysmal. *Women in Love* is a bad-smelling variant of the Peacock country house novel; it has the odor of death about it. In fairness to Lawrence it must be said that he pictured society as he saw it, and that it was his conviction that his readers must tread in the footsteps of Birkin and Ursula if they were to find salvation. Personally I find the solution neither clear nor convincing; neither can I follow Miss Dorothy Hoare in her attempt to differentiate between the three pairs of lovers:

> The Hermione-Birkin situation collapses because of Hermione's insistence on the "power to will": the Gerald-Gudrun situation collapses because of their entire reliance on direct and intense feeling: the Birkin-Ursula situation is valid because, loving each other, they realize that each personality is entirely separate.

I must agree rather with Murry that all the lovers merely "writhe continually, like the damned, in a frenzy of sexual awareness of one another."

Women in Love came out of a bad time in Lawrence's life; its publication was delayed several years by the suppression of *The*

Rainbow, a circumstance which nearly wrecked its author's career. His alleged obscenity, his failure to sympathize with the war, and the fact that his wife was a German made him the target for a good deal of petty persecution, which culminated when he was removed from Cornwall so that he could not signal to German submarines in the Channel! He tried to make his peace with the reading public in *The Lost Girl* (1920), a comparatively innocent but, unfortunately, rather inferior book, with a mining background, an emporium background, a theatrical background, a medical background, and an Italian background! In the Italian scenes Lawrence's feeling for nature appears at its best.

By this time Lawrence had left England on a pilgrimage which took him through Italy, Ceylon, Australia, Mexico, and the American Southwest, in search of "some older, half-forgotten way of consciousness." *Aaron's Rod* (1922), which has been much overpraised by Murry and other critics, begins the important discussion of the theme of male comradeship and leadership which is continued in the Australian novels, *Kangaroo* (1923) and *The Boy in the Bush* (with M. L. Skinner, 1924). This motif culminates in that appalling Mexican novel, *The Plumed Serpent* (1926), in which Lawrence turns his back on everything that man has achieved since he began his long climb out of the dust.

After *The Plumed Serpent,* Lawrence had but one more important novel to write; it is the *Lady Chatterley's Lover* (1928), in which, as all the world knows, he returned to the sex theme. *The Virgin and the Gypsy* (1930) is a minor novel in similar mood, while the earlier *St. Mawr* (1925), which, like *The Plumed Serpent,* came out of the American sojourn, embodies the Life Force in a vicious stallion, and quite unconsciously provides a *reductio ad absurdum* of all Lawrence's theories of blood and mindlessness.

D. H. Lawrence died of tuberculosis, March 2, 1930, at Vence, in the south of France.

2. *"I, Who Loathe Sexuality . . ."*

To the man in the street Lawrence is still the great "sex" novelist. "I, who loathe sexuality so deeply, am considered a lurid sexuality specialist." Yet he detested promiscuity; he was even fussy in matters of small propriety; Casanova shocked him; he thought Joyce indecent and Freud a blasphemer; he spat upon Ben Hecht's *Fantazius Mallare.* If there were nothing worse in Lawrence than the sexual passages which have caused such a turmoil, a very strong case might be made out for him. He was a passionate Puritan, forever in search of the Rainbow which should over-arch the whole of man's life and fuse all his powers into unity. "I always labor at the same thing," he declared, "to make the sex relation valid and precious, instead of shameful." This was true even in *Lady Chatterley's Lover.* Now it may very well be that what Lawrence was trying to do in that book cannot be done. But however offensive his method may have been, his aim was clean as fire. "I want," he said, "to make an *adjustment in consciousness* to the basic physical realities."

His sexual ideal was high and lofty. He was sure that there can be no satisfying union on the physical plane alone. "There is such a thing as sin, and that's the center of it." Marriage is the inescapable basis for a new order of society. "Once a man establishes a full dynamic communication at the deeper and the higher centers, with a woman, this can never be broken. . . . Very often not even death can break it." If you can't find such a relationship, it is better not to have any:

> Leave sex alone.
> Sex is a state of grace
> and you'll have to wait.

For if you make sex itself your goal you drive on toward anarchy and despair; man's living purpose collapses. Sex is a door. Beyond lies an ultimate, impersonal relationship, free of all emotional complications. Beyond lies the splendid service of God.

If Lawrence had stopped there he might have become one of the great moral liberators of his age. But alas! he could not stop there. His haunted preoccupation with the necessity of making "an *adjustment in consciousness* to the basic physical realities" is in itself a confession that he found that adjustment lacking in himself, for Lawrence believed in "art for my sake"; for him, his books had a cathartic value. "One sheds one's sicknesses in books—repeats and presents again one's emotions to be master of them." And it is clear that Lawrence's sexual life was not normal. *Sons and Lovers* alone would suffice to show that he suffered from what the Freudians call the Oedipus complex; we have also the testimony of E.T. that he told her he loved his mother "like a lover. That's why I could never love you." She adds: "I could not help feeling that the whole question of sex had for him the fascination of horror. . . ." That he was also impotent, as Murry maintains, is more questionable, though the assumption would explain some things in his books that are otherwise difficult to understand. Even his sane characters rarely find satisfaction in sexual intercourse; enmity lies close to love, and love always contains "a developing germ of hate." Like the tortoise in the poem, man is "divided into passionate duality," "doomed in the long crucifixion of desire, to seek his consummation beyond himself." Man needs woman terribly, and because he is ashamed of his dependence he hates her. There are many illustrations of all this in *The Rainbow;* in *Women in Love* the limits of sanity are passed. Hermione finds the "consummation of voluptuous ecstasy" in trying to smash Birkin's skull, and so far from feeling resentment, the latter reconciles himself to life by going out to love the vegetation.

It will be clear that Lawrence describes this impasse from the man's point of view; he resents man's subjection to woman, not woman's subjection to man. Indeed it is the modern woman's rebellion against man which lies at the heart of the disease that is killing civilization. Unless man is supreme, the relation he sustains to the woman is a filial relation; in other words it is incest. In *The Plumed Serpent* Kate blindly submits all she has to a Mexican Indian who deliberately denies her even sexual satisfaction, to say nothing of recognizing her spiritual heritage as a European woman. E.T. tells us that when Lawrence was young he saw Sarah Bernhardt in *Camille.* "I feel frightened," he cried. "I realize that I, too, might become enslaved to a woman." It must have been a unique reaction to that play. And the inability it shows to appreciate the woman's point of view is terrifying. Unique too is his view of *The Scarlet Letter* as an allegory of the destruction of man by woman, and of *Moby Dick* as an image of "crucifixion into sex," and of Cooper's Chingachgook and Natty Bumpo as presenting a "stark, stripped human relationship of two men, deeper than the deeps of sex."

The suggestions of personal suffering in all this, especially when we remember that we are dealing with an exponent of "art for my sake," are terrible. No wonder there were times when Lawrence "wanted sex to revert to the level of the other appetites, to be regarded as a functional process, not as a fullfillment." No wonder he sought death, lapse, immolation in it. No wonder he was tempted to turn away from passion to a cold, calculated sensuality, seeking a consciousness deeper than the phallic consciousness. No wonder he tried in vain to exorcise the haunting figure of Jesus.[4]

All this was intimately associated with Lawrence's philosophy—my "pseudo-philosophy" he called it. He never defined it clearly or convincingly. Definition is one of the things he is revolting against, and it is part of his philosophy that philosophy is no good. You must know with your blood, not your mind; you must surrender yourself to forces that are greater than you are.

> Not I, not I, but the wind that blows through me,
> A fine wind is blowing the new direction of Time
> If only I let it bear me, carry me, if only it carry me.

So the people who were forever exhorting him to forget about sex were asking the impossible. For sex is the one means readily available of taking us out of ourselves and uniting us with the primal, elemental things that lie below the conscious mental level.

There alone can you find salvation. That is the great conviction that underlies all of Lawrence's tiresome talk about plexuses and ganglions, his deep-seated conviction that "the vast bulk of consciousness is noncerebral." He early became convinced that the state of contemporary civilization was desperate, that "the living intuitive faculty was dead as nails," and that man had cut himself off from the living cosmos, which is God. Unless that contact can be restored society must perish. Obviously the mind cannot restore it; the mind is the very thing that has destroyed it. But man is not all mind. "My

[4] In one of his most wonderful stories, *The Man Who Died* (1931), which had originally been published in Paris in 1929 as *The Escaped Cock*, Lawrence takes a leaf from George Moore and Samuel Butler, brings Jesus back to a natural life after his crucifixion, converts him to the Lawrencian gospel of individualism, and reconciles him once more to life in sexual intercourse with a priestess of Isis. As an interpretation of Jesus the thing is fantastic, but as art it stands in the forefront of Lawrence's achievement.

great religion is a belief in the blood, the flesh, as being wiser than the intellect. We can go wrong in our minds. But what the blood feels, and believes, and says, is always true." So you must "let your will lapse back into your unconscious self."

This is not materialism. The machine is materialism; to it the true physical stands forever opposed. Husbands, fathers, mine-owners, and vicars (to borrow Professor Tindall's effective summary) are the great servants of the machine; to escape their dominance you must turn to grooms, game-keepers, gypsies, crooners, and even horses. Horses, cows, cats, fish, and snakes all serve as symbols, for while the "polarity" that a man needs to achieve with another man or woman is an eightfold thing, this is only a part of the completer polarity for which he is striving, "a mineral, animal, vegetable, many-fold polarity" that takes in all of life.

Once you have achieved that, you are ready to build the new community, to destroy "the old Moloch of greediness and love of property and love of power," in order to seek "joy and understanding rather than getting and having." You cannot get that merely by "going native." But there have been peoples on this earth who knew more about it than we know today—perhaps the Etruscans, the Hindus, the Aztecs, the American Indians. It is unfortunate that the men of Atlantis, who knew more about it than any of these, should have left no descendants.

Perhaps the study of Hindu philosophy and Aztec remains does not seem much like the "mindlessness" for which Lawrence was striving. In our day and age nobody can be quite so artificial as the primitivist. Professor Tindall has made an effective study of Lawrence's sources, and they range from Schopenhauer and Nietzsche to Madame Blavatsky and the Theosophists. But Professor Tindall is the very one who brings out most clearly the fact that Lawrence did not use his books like a scholar but like a poet. He was always true to himself, to some aspect of himself at least, though unhappily he never buckled down to the difficult task of fusing the varied aspects and elements of his personality into a unified whole. When Aldous Huxley presented scientific evidence for his consideration he brushed it aside. "But I don't care about evidence. Evidence doesn't mean anything to me. I don't feel it *here*."

3. *Lawrence and the Novel*

Lawrence's art needs less analysis than his ideas. He was no more an artist in the usual sense of the term than he was a novelist. He did not care to be. To him art was simply an attempt to convey a complete truth, the writer's feeling about a particular state; and a work of art lost its value when it lost its pure, direct spontaneity. His style, in prose and verse alike, is both miraculous and slovenly; at his best he achieved effects without parallel, because he had gifts which God had never given to a human being before him; but he never worked for an effect, and when inspiration failed him he could write as badly as a third-rate journeyman.

For the plots of his novels he cared nothing. When his setting happened to interest him he did wonders with it; otherwise he did not even trouble to give the reader a clear picture. He had no interest in most of the activities in which human beings engage, and most of his characters are not individuals but mere incarnations of impulses. In *Lady Chatterley's Lover* the scene is set as for a chemical experiment in the laboratory or the demonstration of a proposition in mathematics upon the blackboard. Ursula and Gudrun are forever melting into one another; the mature Anna Brangwen is not the same person we knew in her girlhood and her young married life. When she dances before her mirror in naked pregnancy, it is beside the point to argue that no woman would do such a thing under the circumstances; Anna is not a woman to Lawrence; she is the joy of fecundity, of female fulfillment. Similarly, the death of Gerald in the snow-covered Alps typifies the fate which threatens to overtake a whole generation of cold, futile, sterile men.

One may be willing to grant Lawrence his method here and still remain far from convinced that it is a method which makes for the writing of successful fiction. "*Fiction* is about persons; and I am not interested in persons." He disregarded deliberately the old stable ego of character; if you object that his personages behave inconsistently, he will retort that that is the way human beings behave. Which may be quite true and still wholly beside the point so far as the art of the novel is concerned.

Yet he had special gifts of his own, and it was not his only contribution to the novel that in him the fight for freedom which perhaps began with Hardy has at last been won. It is true that *Lady Chatterley's Lover* is still suppressed, but it hardly needs to be; certainly the contemporary novelist has all the freedom he can conveniently use. Lawrence's ability to describe and communicate sensation was unprecedented; what Glenn Hughes has to say of his poems is almost equally true of his novels:

> Keats may have looked through his window at a sparrow pecking among the gravel and felt himself pecking among the gravel too; but Lawrence sucks blood with the mosquito, darts with a fish, swoops with a bat, wriggles over the desert floor with a snake, shuffles through the tropics with an elephant, hops with a kangaroo, and makes love with goats and tortoises.[5]

His people are like no others in fiction, and he describes their subconscious flow toward and away from each other, the "exchange of feeling . . . apart from their consciousness" as it had never been described before. Their emotional life is as abnormally ardent as the intellectual life of Henry James's personages is abnormally keen. In both writers a stimulus so slight that most novelists would pass it over altogether may produce overwhelming results: both, therefore, enlarge the scope and the sensitivity of fiction.

But art was not the thing that interested Lawrence primarily, and it is not as an artist that he will finally be judged. It will be a long time before that final judgment can be entered. He understood the disease of modern civilization—and on that score alone he did not even live in the same world with the Pharisees who threw stones at him. That he found the remedy is more doubtful. He knew that "man is responsible to God alone," and that the clue to the universe can only be found in "the individual soul within the individual being." But the Quakers have known that for three hundred years without ever falling under the condemnation that visits Lawrence. A gospel which eventuates in a *Plumed Serpent* must still be viewed with extreme suspicion.

It is true, as Ramon maintains in that terrible book, that from

[5] *Imagism and the Imagists* (Stanford University Press, 1931).

time to time man loses his connection with the unchanging God. "And then he can never recover it again, unless some new Savior comes to give him his new connection." But that does not at all mean that Ramon is right when he goes on to contend "that the world had gone as far as it could go in the good, gentle, and loving direction, and anything further in that line meant perversity." Bluntly, *The Plumed Serpent* is the story of the establishment of a Fascist dictatorship in Mexico, and the idea at the heart of the establishment is the assumption that Jesus and Mary are now ready to withdraw from a land with which they have made no vital connection so that the Aztec gods, Quetzalcoatl and Huitzilopochtli, may take possession of it once again—blood sacrifice and all. To these demon-gods a European woman surrenders herself through her marriage to the Indian reincarnation of the Aztec god of war! "Man is a column of blood, with a voice in it. And when the voice is still, and he is only a column of blood, he is better." To get excited about *Lady Chatterley's Lover* because it reduces to cold type a few words which every schoolboy knows, while such a book is passed by as innocuous—this surely is to betray a sexual obsession and lack of fundamental judgment appalling enough to justify the worst of Lawrence's own tirades!

It is true that Horace Gregory and others have opposed Murry's argument that hate had the last word with Lawrence. After *The Plumed Serpent,* they remind us, came *Lady Chatterley's Lover,* a novel informed by a vast tenderness. If so, Sir Clifford and Bertha Coutts are clearly outside the bounds of that tenderness, and it is the essence of the Christian view which Lawrence rejected that nothing can be left outside. If *Lady Chatterley's Lover* does reach a solution, the answer is on the level of a mere mindless sensuality. To solve the problem of civilization this is not enough.

CHAPTER XXIX

STREAM-OF-CONSCIOUSNESS *

"It was Knockespotch," Mr. Scogan continued, "the great Knockespotch, who delivered us from the dreary tyranny of the realistic novel. My life, Knockespotch said, is not so long that I can afford to spend precious hours writing or reading descriptions of middle-class interiors. He said again, 'I am tired of seeing the human mind bogged in a social plenum; I prefer to paint it in a vacuum, freely and sportively bombinating.' "

"I say," said Gombauld, "Knockespotch was a little obscure sometimes, wasn't he?"

"He was," Mr. Scogan replied, "and with intention. It made him seem even profounder than he actually was."

Aldous Huxley: *Crome Yellow*

1. *On the Stream: Dorothy M. Richardson*

In a suggestive essay on "The Break-Up of the Novel,"[1] Mr. J. Middleton Murry has commented on the nearly simultaneous appearance of "three significant books, calling themselves novels. . . ."

In France Marcel Proust published *Du Côté de Chez Swann* . . . ; in America the Irishman James Joyce published *A Portrait of the Artist as a Young Man;* in England Dorothy Richardson published *Pointed Roofs.* These books had points of outward resemblance. Each was in itself incomplete, a foretaste of sequels to come. Each was autobiographical and, within the necessary limits of individuality, autobiographical in the same new and peculiar fashion. They were attempts to record immediately the growth of a consciousness. Immediately; without any effort at mediation by means of an interposed plot or story. All three authors were trying to present the content of their consciousness as it was before it had been re-shaped in obedience to the demands of

* In this chapter the quotation from Huxley's *Crome Yellow* is used by permission of Harper and Brothers; the quotations from Dorothy Richardson's *Pointed Roofs, Backwater,* and *The Tunnel* by permission of Alfred A. Knopf, Inc.; the quotations from John Cowper Powys's *Dorothy M. Richardson* by permission of Joiner and Steele, Ltd., London.

[1] *Yale Review,* XII (1923), 288-304.

practical life; they were exploring the strange limbo where experiences once conscious fade into unconsciousness.

With Proust this book is not directly concerned. But it is concerned with Miss Richardson, with Joyce, and with Virginia Woolf.

Of these writers, Miss Richardson is the one who shows the stream-of-consciousness method in its simplest form. She is perhaps the most "original" of the three. She is the only one still living. And certainly she has always been the least "popular."

Joyce and Virginia Woolf are not "popular," of course, in the sense in which an Edna Ferber or a Kathleen Norris can be "popular." But Joyce certainly became a legend—and a tremendous influence—and Virginia Woolf was the leading pythoness of post-war British fiction. Compared to either, Dorothy Richardson remains obscure.

She was born in Berkshire, when, she does not say. Her formal education ended at seventeen. She has been a teacher and a clerk, has made translations and written criticism. In private life she is Mrs. Alan Odle, wife of the artist.

Though Dorothy Richardson is one of the worst self-advertisers on record, her comparative obscurity has not been due to any lack of effort on the part of her admirers. Though she has not blown her own horn, it has been blown for her by as devoted a body of distinguished contemporaries as ever undertook a hopeless cause. For years, the American publisher, Alfred A. Knopf, published each of the successive "chapters" of *Pilgrimage* with a laudatory introduction by a well-known writer, and when they still stubbornly refused to sell, he made a virtue of necessity by giving them to us in numbered copies! After nine volumes had thus appeared, Mr. Knopf gave up the fight for the time being, and it was not until Dent brought out the complete four-volume *Pilgrimage* in England in 1938 that Mr. Knopf imported some sheets, and Dorothy Richardson again found herself in print in America.[2] And once more the sales were unimpressive.

[2] *Pilgrimage* comprises *Pointed Roofs* (1915); *Backwater* (1916); *Honeycomb* (1917); *The Tunnel* (1919); *Interim* (1919); *Deadlock* (1921); *Revolving Lights* (1923); *The Trap* (1925); *Oberland* (1927); *Dawn's Left Hand* (1931); *Clear Horizon* (1935); *Dimple Hill* (1938).

Stream-of-consciousness did not spring into being full-armed from Miss Richardson's forehead. This book has already noted stream-of-consciousness implications in Samuel Richardson, Sterne, Dickens, and other writers.[3] More important than any of these was Henry James. The somewhat sarcastic Preface to *Pilgrimage* is inclined to make light of James, but in *The Trap* Miss Richardson is more generous. "There *was* something holy about it," so Miriam muses of *The Ambassadors*. "Something to make, like Conrad, the heavens rejoice."

Perhaps the best introduction to Dorothy Richardson is the little book about her by John Cowper Powys.[4] To Mr. Powys, Miss Richardson's single heroine, Miriam Henderson, is not only the most completely portrayed woman in literature; she was immensely worth portraying. She continues "the great egoist life-quest of Montaigne, Goethe, Wordsworth, Pater, and Proust." If one would find her superior "in intellectual interest," one must "turn to such world-famous figures as Hamlet and Faust." And she fills a need which Faust and Hamlet cannot meet, for she alone draws *"from the abyss of the feminine subconscious."* In her, literature gives us for the first time "the peculiar feminine reaction to life, not only in humour and sentiment, but in what might be called cosmic apprehension, or planetary aestheticism."

Miss Richardson's method is to identify herself with Miriam absolutely, and to permit nothing to find its way to the printed page that does not pass through Miriam's mind; we see the world, and we see other persons, only as they impinge upon her consciousness.

[3] In his *James Joyce,* p. 91 ff., Harry Levin cites stream-of-consciousness passages from Fanny Burney, Fenimore Cooper, Dickens, and Melville. Joyce acknowledged the influence upon himself of Edouard Dujardin, *Les lauriers sont coupés* (1887), who defined the term "internal monologue" as follows: "The internal monologue, in its nature on the order of poetry, is that unheard and unspoken speech by which a character expresses his inmost thoughts (those lying nearest the unconscious) without regard to logical organization—that is, in their original state—by means of direct sentences reduced to the syntactic minimum, and in such a way as to give the impression of reproducing the thoughts just as they come into the mind."

[4] *Dorothy M. Richardson* (London, Joiner and Steele, 1931). Harvey Eagleson's article, "Pedestal for a Statue," *Sewanee Review,* XLII (1934), 42-53, is a useful guide to reading, with helpful notes on all the first ten titles, but the final verdict is against Miss Richardson.

Sometimes the vividness which results is essentially cinematic, as in the omnibus ride of *The Tunnel:*

The lane of little shops flowed away, their huddled detail crushing together, wide shop windows glittered steadily by and narrowed away. When the bus stopped at Gower Street, the tower of St. Pancras church came into sight soaring majestically up, screened by trees.

Or here, in the delightful description of the *Haarwaschen* in the German school of *Pointed Roofs:*

Miriam's outraged head hung over the steaming basin—her hair spread round it like a tent frilling out over the table.

For a moment she thought that the nausea which had seized her as she surrendered would, the next instant, make flight imperative. Then her amazed ears caught the sharp bumping of an eggshell against the rim of the basin, followed by a further brisk crackling just above her. She shuddered from head to foot as the egg descended with a cold slither upon her incredulous skull. Tears came to her eyes as she gave beneath the onslaught of two hugely enveloping, vigorously drubbing hands—'sh—ham—poo' gasped her mind.

But such passages as this, in which Miriam lies in her bed in Germany and conjures up "a vision of the back of the books in the book-case in the dining-room at home" are beyond the cinema. Unfortunately the section is too long to quote in its entirety.

Iliad and *Odyssey* . . . people going over the sea in boats and someone doing embroidery . . . that little picture of Hector and Andromache in the corner of a page . . . he in armour . . . she, in a trailing dress, holding up her baby. Both, silly. . . . She wished she had read more carefully. She could not remember anything in Lecky or Darwin that would tell her what to do . . . *Hudibras* . . . *The Atomic Theory* . . . *Ballads and Poems,* D. G. Rossetti . . . Kinglake's *Crimea* . . . Palgrave's *Arabia* . . . Crimea . . . *The Crimea* . . . Florence Nightingale; a picture somewhere; a refined face, with cap and strings. . . . She must have smiled. . . . Motley's *Rise of* . . . *Rise of* . . . Motley's *Rise of the Dutch Republic* and the *Chronicles of the Schönberg-Cotta Family.* She held to the memory of these two books. Something was coming from them to her. She handled the shiny brown gold-tooled back of Motley's *Rise* and felt the hard graining of the red-bound *Chronicles.* . . . There were green trees outside in the moonlight . . . in Luther's Germany . . . trees and fields and German towns and then Holland.

Luther . . . pinning up that notice on a church door. . . . (Why is Luther like a dyspeptic blackbird? Because the Diet of Worms did not agree with him.) . . . and then leaving the notice on the church door and going home to tea . . . coffee . . . some evening meal . . . Käthe . . . Käthe . . . happy Käthe. . . . They pinned up that notice on a Roman Catholic church . . . and all the priests looked at them . . . and behind the priests were torture and dark places. . . .

Darwin had come since then. There were people . . . distinguished minds, who thought Darwin was true.

No God. No Creation. The struggle for existence. Fighting. . . . Fighting. . . . Fighting. . . . Everybody groping and fighting. . . . Fräulein. . . . Some said it was true . . . some not. They could not both be right. It was probably true . . . only old-fashioned people thought it was not. It was true. Just that—monkeys fighting. But who began it? Who made Fräulein? Tough leathery monkey. . . .

Miss Richardson has found the ideal method to serve the ends she has in view in such passages. And there are hundreds of them in *Pilgrimage.*

Other needs of fiction are less ideally served. There are the needs of the story, for instance. *Pilgrimage* has no plot. Miriam teaches school, first in Germany, then in London. She becomes a governess in a fashionable household. She acts as secretary and assistant to a group of dentists. She falls in love with a Russian Jew but decides not to marry him; later she becomes the mistress of a writer, the husband of an old school friend. She goes to Switzerland for two weeks and finds a spiritual freedom. She is ordered to rest and lives in a farmhouse with a Quaker family at Dimple Hill.

Time and place relationships are indicated only casually. *Lohengrin* is a "new piece" in *Pointed Roofs;* Oscar Wilde is being tried in *Honeycomb;* Conrad's *Typhoon* is a current book in *Revolving Lights,* Bennett's *Clayhanger* in *Dawn's Left Hand.* As late as *Clear Horizon,* motor-cars and planes are just beginning to be used.

Of the hundreds of people who cross Miriam's horizon we are told nothing except what she naturally tells herself in the course of her contacts with them. If we do not understand, that is our loss. Important events affecting Miriam's life occur between novels; several matters about her family never are made clear to us. This does not mean that Miss Richardson is out to mystify us; she is not really thinking about "us" at all. She is like the actress for whom the perfect audience is the audience which allows her to forget its presence.

Perhaps this is one reason why Miss Richardson's audience often elects not to be present. One might, for example, have expected Katherine Mansfield to admire Dorothy Richardson. She did not. "Miss Richardson," she said, "has a passion for registering every single thing that happens in the clear shadowless country of her mind." To Katherine Mansfield, Dorothy Richardson seemed to be playing tricks with her mind, holding it out, as it were, for Life to hurl objects into it. She seemed, too, always to be living at a breathless pace, never taking time to creep away into the "caves of contemplation." Finally, Katherine Mansfield complains of Dorothy Richardson, that she has no discrimination: ". . . she leaves us feeling . . . that everything being of equal importance to her, it is impossible that everything should not be of equal unimportance."[5]

Miss Richardson's style changes somewhat as her work advances. She gets more "literary," less spontaneous, and she meets Katherine Mansfield's criticism, to a certain extent, by including more reflective passages. The later books are more difficult also; the sympathetic R. A. Scott-James thinks we can understand the last novel only "by knowing something of what . . . [Miriam's] spirit has been through, what these various intimate recollections are which color all her thinking, all her sensibility, and make her speech what it is." But *Dimple Hill* does not "arrive" any more than, say, *Oberland;* and only authorial fiat could have decreed that the "pilgrimage" must end here rather than three books back or twenty books ahead.

"Pilgrimage" may seem a strange word for it; in making pilgrimages it has always been customary to define a goal. But that, cries John Cowper Powys, is only the masculine point of view, and it is Dorothy Richardson's peculiar glory that she does not accept it! "Women represent the eternal growth of life itself. And of life, as we know, there is necessarily no end." Miriam, he thinks, has "a

[5] *Novels and Novelists* (Knopf, 1930), pp. 15-16, 145-146. If I were writing a history of English *fiction* instead of a history of the English novel, Katherine Mansfield herself would inevitably have her distinguished place in this chapter. Since she wrote only short stories, she must regretfully be excluded See my article about her in *The English Journal,* XVII (1928), 272-284.

very deep and original system of life based upon a mystical quietude; an intensity of entranced contemplation." (It is not for nothing that Miss Richardson has written a book about the Quakers.) Miriam's is, however, a "non-moral, anti-social, lonely zest for the pure Life-Sensation, stripped of all surplusage. . . ." The kind of salvation she achieves is "only to be attained by a certain peculiar awareness of an apparently purposeless life-flow." Miriam is looking for "the Beatific Vision," but she seeks it "as it manifests itself in diffused glory, throughout the whole inflowing and outflowing tide of phenomena."

This may all be true. There are times when one is sure that it is true. "What is much more astonishing than things behaving after their manner," Miriam observes, "is that there should be anything anywhere to behave. Why *does* this pass unnoticed?" And one recalls Wordsworth's desire to make his readers conscious of the beauty and the emotion in quiet lives, after which the mind jumps to a bored Oscar Wilde reflecting beside Niagara Falls that it would have been much more wonderful if the water had been running the other way. Miss Richardson is an excellent antidote to the writers who are only impressed by water running the other way. In this connection, the passage in *Backwater* in which Miriam, mounting the stairs, becomes aware of the "curious buoyancy rising within her," has been quoted again and again:

> For a second, life seemed to cease in her and the staircase to be swept from under her feet. . . . 'I'm alive.' . . . It was as if something had struck her, struck right through her impalpable body, sweeping it away, leaving her there shouting silently without it. I'm alive. . . . I'm alive.

Moreover, Miss Richardson's skill is not limited to the recording of such exceptional moments. She has succeeded in getting down into cold type nuances of human experience with which we are all familiar but which have scarcely been recorded before. "People go about saying, 'Ibsen's *Brand*' as if it were the *answer to something,* and Ibsen knows no more than any one else. . . ." And, to take one very trivial example, one wonders whether any other novelist has ever been so successful in recapturing the pleasure a woman feels in so simple an act as tying up a neat package.[6]

[6] *The Tunnel,* Ch. 3.

One may gladly admit all this, however, and still have numerous questions to dispose of. One never doubts that Miriam's life is absorbingly interesting to herself. (Most people's lives are interesting to themselves.) But that does not necessarily mean that it can interest the reader through 2,000 pages. If Mr. Powys is right in his feeling that here, and here alone in literature, we have the feminine point of view, it is easily possible to retort that if that is true, then the anti-feminists, who have always claimed that women are incapable of conceiving and executing a great work of art, are going to turn out to have been right after all! Is not a pilgrimage whose goal is never defined too close to life to be very satisfactory as art? To create a great work of art on an heroic scale, does not one need to be able to do something more than make an incomparably vivid record of the moments as they pass? Does not one need, perhaps, the design, the sense of consummation and completeness—masculine, or even melodramatic, if you like—which Miss Richardson disdains? What do we learn about women from *Pilgrimage* that we did not already know from the Journal of Marie Bashkirtseff? What does it mean as fiction, which is an art?

Enthusiasts for the stream-of-consciousness method maintain that it is superior to all other methods because here alone you get everything in. That, of course, is nonsense. You do not get everything in, and if you did get everything in, you would not have a work of art, you would have a universe. The difference between art and life is precisely that art is selection, interpretation, while life is all-inclusive. And there is a sense in which a method which pretends to attempt the impossible is more artificial than a method like Fielding's or Trollope's or Conrad's—to take three very different examples—which frankly accepts the limitations imposed upon it by the conditions of its being.

2. *Below the Stream: James Joyce* *

James Joyce's experiments with the stream-of-consciousness were far more elaborate than Miss Richardson's. But it should be realized

* The quotations in this section from Joyce's *A Portrait of the Artist as a Young Man* are by permission of The Viking Press, Inc.

at the outset that my discussion of Joyce necessarily must be very inadequate. Joyce is said to have told Max Eastman that what he asked of his readers was that they should spend their whole lives studying his works. This pleasure I must unhappily deny myself.

Joyce believed that the personality of the artist expresses itself in his work first as "a cry or a cadence or a mood," passes on thence to "a fluid and lambent narrative," and finally "refines itself out of existence, impersonalizes itself, so to speak." His own "cry" sounds in the poems first collected in 1907 under the title, *Chamber Music*. He achieved "fluent and lambent narrative" in the wonderful stories called *Dubliners* (1914), a collection which no reader who loves Chekhov or Katherine Mansfield should miss. The process of withdrawal begins in *A Portrait of the Artist as a Young Man* (1916); it is continued in *Ulysses* (1922). In the *Portrait* the stream-of-consciousness on which we float is the author's own, but in *Ulysses* Joyce can lose himself altogether in persons so utterly unlike himself as Leopold and Marion Bloom. And he flings us into their world without priest or bible to chart our way.

James Joyce was born in Dublin, February 2, 1882. He received a Jesuit education at Clongowes Wood College, Belvedere College, and University College, Dublin. Having resisted all attempts to make a priest of him, he flirted with the idea of a medical career and a singing career but followed neither. He did work, for bread, at various times, as a bank clerk, as the manager of a motion picture theater, and as a teacher of languages. From 1904 to 1914 he lived mainly in Trieste. During the First World War he made his home in Zurich; after the war he came to Paris. When France fell to Hitler he returned to Zurich, and here he died, after an intestinal operation—he had survived I know not how many operations on his eyes—on January 13, 1941.

An indispensable prerequisite to the reading of *Ulysses* is *A Portrait of the Artist as a Young Man,* for here is the history of Stephen Dedalus, the Telemachus of Joyce's Odyssey, from the time when "there was a moocow coming down along the road and this moocow that was down along the road met a nicens little boy named baby tuckoo" until, having rejected his family, his country, and his church, Stephen goes "to encounter for the millionth time the reality of experience and to forge in the smithy of my soul the uncreated conscience of my race." Whether the *Portrait* has quite the unity and "development" which a great novel needs may still be something of a question, but there can be no question as to its power. Ireland lives in the description of the Christmas dinner ruined by bitter squabbling over the respective merits of Parnell and the Church. The sins and remorse of adolescent erotism could hardly have been presented more vividly, while the sermons on hell must still strike terror to the heart of anyone raised under the old orthodoxy, whatever his present opinions may be. And no doubt it would be foolish to allow our enjoyment to be seriously marred by the touch of the fin de siècle about the epiphany scene, in which the pure fleshly beauty of the bathing girl—

> Her bosom was as a bird's, soft and slight, slight and soft as the breast of some dark-plumaged dove. But her long fair hair was girlish: and girlish, and touched with the wonder of mortal beauty, her face—

the gleaming wet bodies of the naked boys, and the sound of his own, strange name, "Stephanos Dedalos"—

> Now, at the name of the fabulous artificer, he seemed to hear the noise of dim waves and to see the winged form flying above the waves and slowly climbing the air—

all unite to bring Stephen to his consecration to art:

> Yes! Yes! Yes! He would create proudly out of the freedom and power of his soul, as the great artificer whose name he bore, a living thing, new and soaring and beautiful, impalpable, imperishable.

In the presence of so splendid a spiritual experience, it seems ungracious to point out that Joyce has confused the business of being an artist with his own private rebellion against his environment. Rebellion is not *necessary* to creativeness; neither, to be sure, is conformity; both are, in a sense, beside the point. Great artists have lived and died within the bounds of the Catholic Church (and even in the service of Dark Rosaleen). But when a man makes rebellion itself his artistic credo, it should surprise nobody (especially when that man has had a strictly logical Jesuit training), that he must arrive at last, as Joyce apparently did in *Finnegans Wake* (1939), at the enfranchisement of writing from meaning altogether and the worship of words as things.

Ulysses devotes 768 very large pages (in the American edition) to describing the lives of Stephen Dedalus, Leopold Bloom, and his wife, Marion Tweedy Bloom, between eight o'clock on the morning of June 16, 1904, and two A.M. the following day. In the first section (51 pages) our attention is centered upon Stephen; thereafter it is generally focused on Bloom. Twice in the course of the day the paths of the two men cross, but they do not actually meet until night, when Bloom follows the drunken Stephen to a brothel, where he guards him tenderly, and from which he takes him to the Bloom home, which, however, the young man shortly leaves. The last section (45 pages) consists of the (unpunctuated) stream of Mrs. Bloom's consciousness before she drops off to sleep.

Nothing of great importance happens. Bloom attends a funeral, visits a newspaper office, flirts with a girl on the beach, innocently gets into a brawl. Stephen does hardly that much. Mrs. Bloom, we learn indirectly, commits adultery in the course of the afternoon, but she has done that so often that it can hardly be taken as specially marking the day for her.

The theme of *Ulysses* has been variously defined. It is Telemachus's search for a father and Ulysses's search for a son. It is a study of remorse—"agenbite of inwit," Joyce calls it, out of an obscure medieval theological treatise; and if you do not know what that means, he will be the last to tell you! Other suggestions have been made also, all apparently on good authority. The aim of the book is clearer. In Edmund Wilson's words, Joyce is trying "to render as exhaustively, as precisely, and as directly as it is possible in words to do, what our participation in life is like. . . ."

The devices Joyce employs to set forth his picture of life are multitudinous; the book which seems to the uninitiated the most chaotic ever written is actually the most elaborately organized fiction in all literature. It is not enough that every episode should find its parallel in the *Odyssey*. As Valéry Larbaud, the French critic, through whom the "key" to Ulysses was first given to the world, has put it,

Each episode treats of a science, or a particular art, contains a particular symbol, represents an organ of the human body, has a particular color (as in the Catholic liturgy), has an individual technique, and, in time, corresponds to one hour of the day.

Put all the organs together and you have the complete human body; combine all the arts and sciences and you have the sum of human knowledge.

The ingenuity of the Odyssean parallels is amazing. Joyce has, to be sure, shifted order and emphasis; he has not hesitated to give Bloom a daughter in place of Ulysses's son, and a cat instead of a dog. But let us take one or two examples of correspondence.

Buck Mulligan lords it over Stephen as Antinous lorded it over Telemachus. Stephen pays the rent for the Martello tower, where the two are living, but Mulligan keeps the key. Like Telemachus, Stephen uses the arms of "silence, exile, and cunning." Mr. Deasy, under whom Stephen teaches, is Nestor, and because Nestor was a tamer of horses, his walls must be covered with pictures of horses, and there must be much talk of horses in the episode in which he figures. Moreover, when he speaks of Kitty O'Shea, who ruined Parnell, she must be likened to Helen of Troy, for there are many minor parallels in every episode besides the major ones. Because Circe drugged the companions of Ulysses, Bloom must fear that Stephen has been "doped" in the brothel scene. Even Gerty MacDowell's care for her "undies" goes back to Nausicaä's passion for clean clothes, an historical trait of the Phaeacians, as Joyce knows. And there are Homeric precedents for Joyce's penchant for variety of style.

Joyce, indeed, has not derived his knowledge of the Greeks from the *Odyssey* alone. Tradition affirmed a connection between the Greeks and the early Irish, and the Milesians were supposed to have made a long stay in Spain on their way north; whence, no doubt, the Spanish strain in Mrs. Bloom. The Hebrew strain in both the Blooms was suggested by Joyce's acceptance of Victor Bérard's theory of the Phoenician (hence, Semitic) origin of the *Odyssey.*

Many critics see the parallelism between *Ulysses* and the *Odyssey* as merely a satiric commentary on modern life, in the vein of Masefield's "Cargoes." The Sirens become Dublin barmaids, and in our world the lovely Nausicaä becomes the crippled Gerty MacDowell, who can only stimulate her futile Ulysses to a boyish auto-eroticism. The blind Polyphemus hurls a mountain-top; the "blind-drunk" Citizen hurls a biscuit-tin. And when it comes to Marion Bloom as the chaste Penelope . . . !

Joyce was fully aware of the humor of all this. But, on the whole, the satirical interpretation of *Ulysses* is shallow. "It may first be noted," says Stuart Gilbert, "that Homer's account of the absolute fidelity of Penelope was not endorsed by later classical writers." Joyce is not merely perpetrating a gigantic hoax; he is trying—whether successfully or not is entirely another question—to present the whole of human experience. There is a great deal of occultism in *Ulysses*. From occult tradition comes the idea that our parents are not our spiritual progenitors; hence Stephen's search for a father, though his father is still alive. And from the occult point of view there is a sense in which the infinitely great equals the infinitely little. Metempsychosis ("met-him-pike-hoses" is Marion Bloom's word for it) and the omphalos haunt the book, and there was some influence also from the idea of the eternal return as conceived and set forth non-mystically by the Italian philosopher, Vico.

One reason why many people favor the satirical interpretation is that they feel a decided dissatisfaction when Joyce offers them Leopold Bloom in the Ulysses-role. And there is enough in Bloom that is weak, whining, frustrate, bungling, masochistic, clumsy, and downright unclean to afford much apparent justification for this feeling. But let us see.

Bloom is the ordinary man. He stands between Stephen, who is the creative imagination, and Marion, who is the flesh. As opposed to Marion's sensualism, Stephen is "spiritual," but still, as in the *Portrait,* he cries "Non serviam!" and so, like Lucifer before him, he is also the pride of life. According to Frank Budgen, Joyce believed that character is best indicated in the commonest acts of life. "How a man ties his shoelaces or how he eats his egg will give a better clue to his differentiation than how he goes forth to war."

Now Ulysses was Joyce's boyhood hero. Compared to Achilles, Ulysses was an ordinary man. But as Homer describes him, he is more nearly the complete man than Achilles, more nearly the complete man than Hamlet or Faust. For Ulysses is son, lover, husband, father, war-dodger, warrior, ruler—"a good man."

Despite all his childish (largely mental) philandering, Bloom's love for his grossly unfaithful wife has its touching side. Equally touching is his idealistic (and certainly most unsophisticated) reaction, after his physical response to Gerty MacDowell's wiles—

What a brute he had been! At it again? A fair unsullied soul had called to him and, wretch that he was, how had he answered? An utter cad he had been. He of all men!

Bloom is humble, non-violent; the brutal callousness of the medical students shocks him; he champions love as the active principle in human life. At first blush, Foster Damon seems to blaspheme when he says that as Stephen is Lucifer, Bloom is the Christ. But there is authority for that interpretation in the text, and the real blasphemy is in us who have dared to forget that there is an Eternal Incarnation, that God is forever trying to impregnate the common stuff, the Bloom-stuff of human life.

It should not be supposed that a thorough familiarity with stream-of-consciousness technique will alone suffice to equip the reader of *Ulysses;* in other words, it should not be supposed that the graduate, with honors, of the Dorothy Richardson Academy is necessarily ready to go on to the James Joyce University. For Joyce does not confine himself to stream-of-consciousness; his method is all methods.

Thus the very form of Joyce's book is an elusive and eclectic *Summa* of its age [says Harry Levin]: the *montage* of the cinema, impressionism in painting, *leit-motif* in music, the free association of psycho-analysis, and vitalism in philosophy. Take of these elements all that is fusible, and perhaps more, and you have the style of *Ulysses.*

There are 260,430 words in the book, Mr. Levin tells us further, and 29,899 different words, of which over half are used only once. Joyce gives us the minds of his characters; he gives us also, if there be such a thing, the mind of his scenes. It takes Stuart Gilbert four pages of microscopic type to *name* and *illustrate* the rhetorical devices employed in the chapter on Bloom's visit to the newspaper office; hundreds of musical effects are *reproduced verbally* in the

Sirens chapter; Gerty MacDowell's cheap little flirtation is perfectly described in terms borrowed from an Ethel M. Dell novel; and embryonic development is suggested in the episode in the maternity ward in a series of brilliant parodies of outstanding English writers from medieval times to the present.

On Joyce's much-mooted indecency, opinions have ranged all the way from Herbert Read's declaration that *Ulysses* is "the most wholesome purgative that has been offered to mankind for more than a century. That it should be banned and burned by the public hangman is a mad example of the way mankind refuses salvation" to Shane Leslie's declaration that it is "only an Odyssey of the sewer." Like many men who have been reproached for the violence and immorality of their writings, Joyce was blameless and of uncommon gentleness in his private life, a good husband and a good father.[7] The morality of his work is another question, and it should not be assumed that only conventionally minded people have condemned it. Shaw disclaimed all interest in Joyce's "infantile clinical incontinencies"; D. H. Lawrence denounced his book as "a clumsy *olla putrida*." Richard Aldington accused him of having libeled humanity; E. M. Forster saw him simplifying human character "in the interests of hell." And even H. G. Wells, whose review [8] did so much for the *Portrait* in America, lamented Joyce's "cloacal obsession." The present writer is willing to grant that indecency must have its place in a book which attempts a comprehensive picture of life, but it still seems to him that in Joyce this side is over-developed in comparison with more constructive (and more interesting) aspects. Dante passed through the inferno, but he did not pitch his tent there.

I do not find it necessary to speak in this place of Joyce's last book, *Finnegans Wake*, which concerns the unconscious of sleep, and which is written in a dream language of Joyce's own invention. I am informed that the episode of "The Ondt and the Gracehoper"

[7] See Padraic Colum, "A Portrait of James Joyce," *New Republic*, LXVI (1931), 346-348; Elliot Paul, "Farthest North," *Bookman* [New York], LXXV (1932), 156-163; and Maria Jolas's letter to *The Commonweal*, XXXV (1942), 392-393.

[8] *New Republic*, X (1917), 158-160.

is woven of "a mosaic of seventeen or more tongues," and I am willing to accept so much on faith.[9] For all the difficulties of *Ulysses,* the book still rests on what David Daiches calls a "realistic narrative basis." Since this is lacking in *Finnegans Wake,* the latter can hardly claim to be considered a novel; and so far there have been few signs that it will influence the novel.

Herbert J. Muller writes in his *Modern Fiction:*

> Joyce's gifts for observation and insight into character, for parody and satire, for shimmering poetry and robust comedy, for hewing out a colossus, and carving a cherry stone—separately they may be surpassed, but in combination they are unique. There can be no doubt, I believe, that he is the most amazing genius of this age, and one of the greatest of all ages.

This is not exuberance; it is simple justice. In Joyce's own words: "Thou art, I vow, the remarkablest progenitor barring none in this chaffering allincluding most faragineous chronicle"!

One may say all this, however, without admiring James Joyce's mind, and without emulating the rootless young iconoclasts of the twenties whose militant anti-puritanism obliged them to find in *Ulysses* the bible of a great new age.

Of course, Joyce himself was never a pagan; he was a renegade Catholic. Aquinas furnished the framework of his thinking, and he was always powerfully under the sway of the great ceremonial of the Mass. Only a man who had once believed in Christian symbolism could have achieved the horrible blasphemy of the *Walpurgisnacht* brothel scene. "I imagine," says Stephen, in the *Portrait,* "that there is a malevolent reality behind those things I say I fear."

The technical faults of *Ulysses* and its spiritual faults are therefore one. *Finnegans Wake* ends in the middle of the sentence whose

[9] Those who are interested may be referred to Harry Levin's discussion of *Finnegans Wake* in his *James Joyce,* to John Peale Bishop's article in *The Southern Review,* V (1940), 439-452, and to Edmund Wilson's essay in *The Wound and the Bow* (Houghton Mifflin, 1941). A more elaborate study than any of these will be found in Samuel Beckett and others, *An Exagmination of James Joyce* (New Directions, 1939). This was originally published in Paris in 1929 as *Our Exagmination Round his Factification for Incamination of Work in Progress.*

conclusion opens the book; it is interesting that Carl Jung should find in *Ulysses* itself a circular movement; it has neither beginning nor end, he declares; you may read it backwards or forwards. In other words, it fails in movement. Neither Bloom nor Stephen is capable of action, for action involves the assertion of the will, and it is by the will that souls are lost or saved. They drift together and drift apart again; the "mastodon of contemporary literature" is an encyclopaedic picture of futilitarianism.

Mr. Daiches sees Joyce observing his environment in *Dubliners,* rejecting it in the *Portrait,* recreating it from a distance in *Ulysses.* Unlike some of his contemporaries, he goes on—and, he might have added, unlike Shakespeare—Joyce never made the journey back to reacceptance, reintegration on a new plane, reconciliation. What he did was to move on into a private world, to become increasingly what Max Eastman once described in another connection as the poet talking to himself. Joyce felt, as many modern writers have felt—as Virginia Woolf felt so strongly—the lack of a common experiencial background, a sense of the Great Community which reader and writer share. And his method of solving the problem was to make himself a god, to create his own frame of reference, which should be sufficient unto itself, so that the "meaning" of *Ulysses* must be sought in its completeness as art, and not in anything it may have to say about the life that lies outside its pages. (In that sense, Joyce's champions are right when they say that the question of indecency is totally irrelevant as applied to *Ulysses,* but by the same token everything else that concerns human life is equally irrelevant!) And that, I take it, is what accounts for our feeling of dissatisfaction at last in the face of his tremendous, his superhuman achievement. No saint in the calendar ever surpassed this perfect artist of unquestionable integrity on the score of perfect patience and devotion. No martyr ever paid more for the Kingdom of Heaven than he paid for his book. Yet for all its greatness it stands strangely alone, a masterpiece withdrawn from humanity, with the suggestion of something monstrous about it.

3. *The Stream and the World: Virginia Woolf* *

Virginia Woolf inherited the Liberal tradition of the great Victorian intellectuals; study widened her own horizon till it swept at last from Plato and Sophocles to the most advanced contemporary experimentalists. She was born in 1882, daughter of Sir Leslie Stephen, distinguished editor of the *Cornhill Magazine* and the *Dictionary of National Biography*. Family connections bound her to the Thackerays, the Darwins, and the Symondses.

She began her writing career as a reviewer for the London *Times Literary Supplement*. After her marriage, in 1912, to Leonard Woolf, husband and wife founded the Hogarth Press. Through the Press and other channels, they established close relations with E. M. Forster, V. Sackville-West, the Sitwells, John Maynard Keynes, Lytton Strachey, and other distinguished writers.

Virginia Woolf was a lovely personality—elusive, a bit strange, yet simple, unpretentious, and of manifold witchery and charm. Her life ended in tragedy. Her health had always been bad, and she hated war with every fiber of her being.[10] When it came again in 1939 she faced it courageously but the strain proved too great. Feeling herself trembling on the verge of madness, and determined not to be a burden to her husband, she took her walking-stick on the morning of March 28, 1941, strolled across the Downs, and slipped beneath the waters of a Sussex stream.

She was the only first-flight novelist to die by suicide in English literary history. Yet her death was less a suicide than a mercy-killing, self-administered. As James Southall Wilson has remarked, she did not choose between life and death but merely between death and insanity.

Virginia Woolf's first two novels—*The Voyage Out* (1915) and *Night and Day* (1919) are more or less conventional in form. *Night and Day* is social comedy, reflecting, perhaps, her interest in Jane

* The quotations from Virginia Woolf's essay "Mr. Bennett and Mrs. Brown" are from *The Hogarth Essays* by Leonard and Virginia Woolf with permission of Doubleday, Doran and Co. All other quotations from Virginia Woolf are by permission of Harcourt, Brace and Co.

[10] Cf. especially her *Three Guineas* (1938).

Austen. *The Voyage Out* is more characteristic of her mind than of her method. The voyage of Rachel Vinrace is both actual and symbolic. She sails across the ocean to South America; she sails into the expanding world of her own being; she sails out of this life altogether.

Virginia Woolf's stream-of-consciousness novels are four in number: *Jacob's Room* (1922);[11] *Mrs. Dalloway* (1925); *To the Lighthouse* (1927); and *The Waves* (1931). *Orlando* (1928) and *Flush* (1933), each subtitled "A Biography," are *jeux d'esprit;* and the last two books—*The Years* (1937) and the posthumous *Between the Acts* (1941)—are only mildly experimental in technique.

By whom her method may have been influenced has so far been somewhat indeterminately discussed. She may be presumed to have read Dorothy Richardson. She read *Ulysses*—"a memorable catastrophe—immense in daring, terrific in disaster"—in 1919, when it was serialized in part in *The Little Review*. Apparently she did not read Proust until 1922. And I believe she claimed not to have read Bergson at all, despite the fact that she herself constantly suggests him to some readers, and though her sister-in-law published a book about him.

Each of Virginia Woolf's stream-of-consciousness novels is a fresh experiment, a new creative effort. She did not live in a static world; she could not, therefore, establish an absolute style.

Jacob's "room" is the world he lived in; we get the boy himself in a series of carefully arranged snap-shots preserving all the apparent chance and disarray of life itself. He goes to Cambridge; he visits the Scilly Islands; he lives alone in London, where he gets mixed up with an alluring little prostitute; he studies in the British Museum; he follows art to Athens; he is killed in the First World War. But the reader sees him only as his "room" reflects him, that is as he is observed by those who came in contact with him, as he established, or failed to establish, himself with them. The action is external mainly; *Jacob's Room* is a picture book.

In Clarissa Dalloway's story, on the other hand, there is little ex-

[11] She had prepared for *Jacob's Room* by writing the sketches now collected in the volume called, in this country, *Monday or Tuesday* (1921).

ternal action. *Jacob's Room* covers twenty years; *Mrs. Dalloway* passes in twelve hours. The heroine is

> caught, immobilised, as it were, for one moment in time, with her life revolving round her, so that we see her with her thoughts darting back into the past and forward into the future, and catch a glimpse of the infinite . . . number of revolving lives which touch the circle of hers at one or many points and in their turn touch and are touched by others, a world-wide pattern of interlaced and separately revolving circles.[12]

The striking of Big Ben follows Mrs. Dalloway through the day as she goes about London preparing for her party, but Mrs. Dalloway does not live one day at a time any more than the rest of us do. For everything that ever happened to her has made her what she is and determined what she does this day, and everything in English history—and in the history of the planet for that matter—has created the background against which she moves.

The structure of *To the Lighthouse,* on the other hand, is as loose as that of *Mrs. Dalloway* is tight. In Part I we see Mrs. Ramsay with her family at their summer house in the Hebrides, planning an excursion to the lighthouse. Bad weather intervenes, and the excursion is never made. In Part III Mrs. Ramsay is dead, and the little boy who had been so bitterly disappointed in Part I now goes to the lighthouse as a young man—after he has lost all desire to go. These two parts are connected by the section, "Time Passes," in which the decay of the old house is described. There are no human characters in "Time Passes" save the charwomen, and they hardly count. The real characters are wind and dust and time. To the present writer, "Time Passes" is one of the most beautiful pieces of writing in English literature.

Finally, in *The Waves* the whole structure of the novel as we usually understand it is scrapped. The book consists of a series of soliloquies uttered by six friends at various stages of development from childhood to age or death. What happens to them, and between them, must be inferred from what they say. The passing of time is marked, however, by a series of prose-poems about the sea, which are printed in italics at the beginning of each division of the

[12] Storm Jameson, *The Georgian Novel and Mr. Robinson.*

book. No attempt has been made to provide a distinctive speech for the six different characters; the language throughout is the author's, not theirs. For, as will appear more clearly later on, Virginia Woolf was less interested in individual characterization than in interpreting the *essential* nature of universal experience.

The revolutionary aspect of Virginia Woolf's novels often comes as a surprise to those who approach them after having read any of the essays [13] in which such a fine appreciation of traditional values is expressed. But there is no real contradiction here. Virginia Woolf was never the iconoclast. She had no sympathy with "the smashing and the crashing . . . the prevailing sound of the Georgian age"; she never shared the Georgian (or Lawrencian) tendency to abandon reason in favor of instinct and emotion, nor did she ever forget the importance of convention as "a means of communication [not, as it so often was with Joyce, 'an obstacle and an impediment'] between writer and reader." She did not love the world of crumbling values in which her lot was cast; she looked back enviously to the days of faith. "To believe that your impressions hold good for others is to be released from the cramp and confinement of personality. It is to be free, as Scott was free, to explore with a vigor which still holds us spell-bound the whole world of adventure and romance." For good or for ill, the great Victorian agnostic's daughter could not find such certainty for herself, though she never ceased to cherish the hope that some time the great days of Sir Walter might come again. Until that time we must content ourselves with "the spasmodic, the obscure, the fragmentary, the failure." At least that was better than to fall back on the arid materialism of her fellow-Georgians, all so much more preoccupied with the environment of their characters than with their souls.

Spasmodic, too, are her glimpses of reality. "In the midst of chaos there was shape; the eternal passing and flowing was struck into stability." But that is faith. We *know* nothing; we do not even know ourselves or each other. The "great revelation" never comes. "Instead there were little daily miracles, illuminatings, matches struck

[13] Such as those collected in *The Common Reader* (1925), *The Second Common Reader* (1932), and *The Death of the Moth and Other Essays* (1942).

unexpectedly in the dark." If you could put all these moments of illumination together, "write them out in some sentence," you could get at "the truth of things." But you cannot. "Touched by human penitence and all its toil, divine goodness" will now and again part the curtain. But divine goodness knows that we do not deserve to dwell in the presence of unbroken vision; "twitching the cord," he "draws the curtain" again before we are satisfied.

If you believe that, you can hardly be expected to compose a novel according to pattern. Life is not patterned. You cannot ever get it into "orderly and military progress," and if you pretend you can, it is "a convention, a lie."

> There is always deep below it, even when we arrive punctually at the appointed time with our white waistcoats and polite formalities, a rushing stream of broken dreams, nursery rhymes, street cries, half-finished sentences and sights—elm trees, willow trees, gardeners sweeping, women writing—that rise and sink, even as we hand a lady down to dinner. . . .

To get into that world you must "record the atoms as they fall" and patiently "trace the pattern . . . which each sight and incident scores upon consciousness." Like Joyce, and unlike Dorothy Richardson, Virginia Woolf does not confine herself to any one consciousness but moves freely from mind to mind. Unlike Joyce, she does not plunge us into an uncharted, alien consciousness. Using a variety of subtle devices, she reserves her right to comment upon her material.

Virginia Woolf was often reproached for her failure to create memorable characters. She was less interested in Mrs. Brown than in "Mrs. Brownness," less concerned about individuals than about "the meaning which, for no reason at all," sometimes descended upon them, "making them representative," not, say, Mr. and Mrs. Ramsay, but "the symbols of marriage, husband and wife." Even when you speak of a beautiful woman, "you mean only something flying fast which for a second uses the eyes, lips or cheeks of Fanny Elmer, for example, to glow through." And Mrs. Ramsay herself is described in her highest manifestation as "the spirit we live by—life itself."

"Nobody sees any one [or anything] as he is. . . ." The material, unlovely lighthouse that James Ramsay sees finally is not the symbol of infinite allurement he yearned towards as a child. And is it the only lighthouse there is? "No, the other was also the Lighthouse. For nothing was simply one thing. The other Lighthouse was true too."

This attitude toward character appears in all Mrs. Woolf's novels. Part of Jacob's "room" is made up of people who meant nothing to him, some of whom never crossed the screen of his consciousness at all. "It is no use trying to sum people up." Clarissa Dalloway feels a much closer connection with the shell-shocked Septimus Smith than would seem to be justified by the mere fact that his suicide is reported at her party by the distinguished physician whose heartlessness and lack of comprehension was its immediate cause. But in the introduction written for the Modern Library reprint of 1928 Mrs. Woolf explained that Septimus was Clarissa's "double." Originally she was intended to kill herself, or to die, at the close of her party; later Septimus was brought in to do it for her.[14]

"We are members one of another," says the rather fatuous clergyman of *Between the Acts*. "Each is part of the whole." For the best expressions of this feeling we must go to *The Waves*. "I am not one person," cries Bernard; "I am many people; I do not know who I am—Jimmy, Susan, Neville, Rhoda, or Louis: or how to distinguish my life from theirs." Approaching Neville, he finds himself all mixed up with him. And when Percival dies, Bernard feels, "You have gone across the court, further and further drawing finer and finer the thread between us. But you exist somewhere. Something of you remains. A judge. That is, if I discover a new vein in myself I shall submit it to you privately."[15]

[14] "The societified lady and the obscure maniac are in a sense the same person. His foot has slipped through the gay surface on which she still stands —that is all the difference between them." So E. M. Forster, in "The Novels of Virginia Woolf," *Yale Review,* XV (1926), 505-514. It is an interesting commentary on the difficulties of reading Mrs. Woolf that the first time this close friend and gifted novelist read *Mrs. Dalloway* he thought the heroine had killed herself. On a second reading he thought not; when he wrote his essay he was not sure but had decided the question was not important!

[15] It is no burlesque of Virginia Woolf's method, though it is a manifestation of her subtle and delicious humor, that she should find Flush and Elizabeth Barrett resembling and complementing each other, and surely the ob-

And it is not only to our friends that we are bound. We are bound also to the "long, long history that began in Egypt, in the time of the Pharaohs, when women carried red pitchers to the Nile,"[16] to "the old brute, too, the savage, the hairy man who dabbles his fingers in ropes of entrails; and gobbles and belches; whose speech is guttural, visceral. . . ." Louis feels his roots going down "to the depths of the world, through earth dry with brick, and damp earth, through veins of lead and silver." He takes "the trees, the clouds, to be witnesses of my complete integration." Virginia Woolf is very close here to the American novelist, Mary Johnston, whose mystical experience was, however, much wider and profounder, and who achieved the certainty that eluded Mrs. Woolf. It is still true, however, that the unity for which she is striving is, as Joseph Warren Beach has called it,

> a metaphysical unity, the unity which the old scholastic philosophers saw binding creature to creature and all created things to God. It is also a psychological unity, such as the most modern Viennese psychologists see binding infancy to age, and making the whole individual human life a "recherche du temps perdu."

T. S. Eliot, in his treatment of tradition, has something very close to this. The idea of the present moment as the recapitulation of the past haunts the imagination of the modern writer.

So much, then, for Virginia Woolf's unorthodox treatment of character. Her treatment of time is equally unorthodox. The problem of time (and death) is the theme of nearly all her fictions, but the most startling illustrations occur in the history of Orlando, who lives through three centuries at a speed peculiar to himself, who is a child in Queen Elizabeth's time, who arrives at the age of thirty as a contemporary of Alexander Pope, and who is still in the prime

servation is no less striking and original because she found abundant authority for it in the Browning sources.

[16] But even while this realization is fully upon him, Louis feels he must take care lest he shall fail fully to realize the present moment completely; if this happens, "human history is defrauded of a moment's vision." This eagerness perhaps explains Virginia Woolf's absorption in the moment, her concern to "record the atoms as they fall," a passion which might otherwise seem out of harmony with her metaphysical inclinations.

of life as the clock strikes midnight on October 11, 1928. Ruth Gruber points out that the book is "a poetization of Einstein's hypothesis. . . . Orlando is a physical possibility in a time-space continuum."

I must make it clear that in referring to *Orlando* as a *jeu d'esprit,* as I did a while back, I intend no disrespect toward it. It is incomparably Virginia Woolf's most brilliant, though not her most endearing, book, and it has qualities which do not appear elsewhere in her work. If there is anything more vivid in English fiction than the description of Queen Elizabeth's hand—the reconstruction, indeed, of her whole personality from the sight of her hand—which Orlando achieves as he sinks upon his knees to offer her a bowl of rosewater, or more electrifying than the description of the Great Frost with the Thames frozen over, I should much like to encounter it. Not all the keys to *Orlando* have been turned over to us. But it is clear that the book is both a history of the Sackvilles and a history of English literature.[17]

The most startling thing in *Orlando* is, of course, the fact that something less than half way through the book, the hero goes to bed a man and wakes up a woman. Winifred Holtby and others have speculated at some length as to why Virginia Woolf used this feature. Perhaps the best reason of all is that in no other way could she so brilliantly, and so wickedly, have manifested her contempt for the conventions of the realistic novel. But there are other reasons also. In some way or other, Orlando is Virginia Woolf's friend, Miss V. Sackville-West, the novelist. Orlando lives at Knole House, the ancestral home of the Sackvilles; Miss Sackville-West's poem, *The Land,* is quoted in the book and attributed to Orlando; Miss Sackville-West's portraits and those of her ancestors are used as illustrations. V. Sackville-West is a writer and a woman, and Vir-

[17] In its second aspect, it includes many brilliant parodies of famous styles, which should be compared and contrasted with those in *Ulysses*. "But let other pens treat of sex and sexuality; we quit such odious subjects as soon as we can." One critic innocently quotes this passage from Chapter III as evidence of Virginia Woolf's squeamishness! It is, of course, quoted, with studied inaccuracy, from Jane Austen. This is an excellent illustration of the perils with which Woolfian criticism is beset.

ginia Woolf was interested in the writer as woman.[18] But in the early days the writers of England were not women but men.

The change of sex also made it easier for Virginia Woolf, who believed that there are many potential selves in every human being, to make Orlando a study in multiple personality, and it gave the character him/herself additional data in his/her quest for the meaning of life, upon which, like all Virginia Woolf's characters, he/she was passionately embarked. But more important than all this is the fact that Mrs. Woolf believed with Coleridge and Sir Thomas Browne in the androgynous mind. This is particularly important for a writer, for only the androgynous mind is fully fertilized and can use all its faculties in creation.

Personally I am less enthusiastic about the last two novels. The posthumous *Between the Acts* seems to me to lack definition, possibly because Virginia Woolf did not live to revise it completely. Evidently it was her idea in some way to portray the history of England in the pageant, but the performance itself is horribly dull, and I think the point is not made clear. I feel a certain vagueness also in *The Years,* which presents multitudinous members of a typical English family in manifold experiences from 1880 to the present day. But I think my comparative coldness here is probably my fault. For Virginia Woolf at this stage in her development, it was perhaps not necessary that a book should have a "theme" or a "point." It was enough if it had life. In the course of *The Years,* Lady Kitty takes a journey, which Mrs. Woolf describes. She is the only novelist I know who could have done that. Anybody else would have concerned herself with what happened on the journey. The journey itself would have been treated as merely a means to an end. On Lady Kitty's journey nothing happens. It does not lead to anything except Lady Kitty's destination.

And this, I think, brings us very close to the heart of Virginia Woolf. She loved life. She did not pretend to understand it, but she loved it. She believed in the vital surge which springs up again and again in the face of defeat. "The sun had risen, and the sky above the houses wore an air of extraordinary beauty, simplicity and

[18] Cf. *A Room of One's Own* (1929).

peace.' Such are the last words of *The Years,* and they are typical. Look at the gallant close of *The Waves,* which is unfortunately too long to quote. Look at the frustrate Giles and Isa at the end of *Between the Acts.* "Before they slept, they must fight; after they had fought, they would embrace. From that embrace another life might be born." Lust defies despair. And the face of the world defies it. "For, Heaven knows why, just as we have lost faith in human intercourse some random collocation of barns and trees or a haystack and a waggon presents us with so perfect a symbol of what is unattainable that we begin the search again."

Virginia Woolf knew that, and she knew more than that. She knew that the meaning of our world lies in the human soul, that there are people on this planet who radiate harmony. Her fiction celebrates such people. Mrs. Ramsay furnishes a standard of reference in life and in death. "That woman sitting there writing under a rock resolved everything into simplicity; made these angers, irritations fall off like old rags. . . ." The scientist Bankes sees her reading a fairy tale to her little boy and she has upon him "precisely the same effect as the solution of a scientific problem, so that he rested in contemplation of it, and felt, as he felt when he had proved something absolute about the digestive system of plants, that barbarity was tamed, the reign of chaos subdued." Mrs. Ramsay herself, though in perfect humility, understands something of her own significance, knows that death itself can make no difference. "They would, she thought, going on again, however long they lived, come back to this night; this moon; this wind; this house; and to her too."

This may be an inadequate symbol, an inadequate answer to the riddle of life. But let us remember that it is fundamentally the same symbol that the men of the Middle Ages used. The Mother of God did for them what Mrs. Ramsay does for those who come in contact with her; the Mother of God through whom alone, as Henry Adams believed, order had been imposed upon a chaotic world.

It is too early to assign Virginia Woolf her permanent place in the history of the novel. Stream-of-consciousness as such will not progress, I think, beyond the point to which she and Joyce carried it; even the distinguished Elizabeth Bowen [19] shows no signs of introducing fresh technical innovations. As a type, the Stream-of-Consciousness Novel may well disappear altogether, while the experiments which its practitioners made remain, like the free verse experimentation in another field, to widen and enrich more orthodox patterns. Virginia Woolf herself did not escape the deficiencies of her superb virtues. In a very real sense, *The Waves,* though less extreme than Joyce's work, was, in the current phrase, a novel "to end all novels"; it is significant that Virginia Woolf herself could go on producing fiction only by ignoring this book and returning to more conventional patterns. And while one must not, in the matter of the creation of character, for example, condemn her for failing to accomplish something she never attempted, one must also admit, I think, that it is at least very doubtful whether the novel can long survive having substituted "Mrs. Brownness" for Mrs. Brown.

Literature, of course, will survive. And the human spirit will survive because it is of God and therefore indestructible. And in Virginia Woolf's case probably the only thing we can say in the last analysis is that it is the beauty of her own spirit that draws us to her.

[19] See, especially, *The House in Paris* (Knopf, 1936) and *The Death of the Heart* (Knopf, 1939).

CHAPTER XXX

NEWS OF TISHNAR: WALTER DE LA MARE *

Tishnar is a very ancient word in Munza, and means that which cannot be thought about in words, or told, or expressed. So all the wonderful, secret, and quiet world beyond the Mulgars' lives is Tishnar—wind and stars, too, the sea and the endless unknown.

The Three Mulla-Mulgars

1. *"Not Matter-of-Fact—But Matter-of-Truth"*

From time to time we have had occasion in these pages to speak of books and writers somewhat outside the main tradition of the English novel, writers more interested in the soul than in society, books brooded over by the consciousness of another world. There are those who refuse to rely exclusively upon the testimony of the senses for the simple reason that the senses "can tell us only what they are capable of being sensible *of*." For themselves they know "that what we see and hear is only the smallest fraction of what is." Even when the phenomena they describe are frightfully "real," "it doesn't follow . . . that they didn't mean something else too."

These quotations are all from stories by Walter de la Mare, the greatest writer of this group.

Mr. de la Mare was born at Charlton, Kent, April 25, 1873, of Scottish and French Huguenot ancestry. On his mother's side he is related to Robert Browning. Among the few facts concerning his early life that have been made available one has a deep significance. His formal education at Saint Paul's Cathedral Choir School ended when he was fourteen, and from 1890 to 1908 he worked in the statistical department of the Anglo-American Oil Company.

I am not much impressed by the Freudian view that because he spent his working hours at an uncongenial task, Mr. de la Mare's

* All quotations from de la Mare's work are given by permission of Alfred A. Knopf, Inc.

creative energies *must* necessarily have expended themselves in the poetry of dream. What does interest me is his stamina. "I think one can find an interest in any task that has *got* to be done"—such was his quiet answer to a question from Mr. R. L. Mégroz about these years. Tennyson was ready to relinquish even love, if necessary, in order that he might continue to devote all his energies to poetry. "We must bear or we must die," he wrote Emily Sellwood, breaking off, as he then believed, their three-year-old engagement. De la Mare knew from the beginning that he wanted to write, yet he married and gave hostages to fortune in the shape of four children; in other words, he knew that if a man is to be a great artist he must be a human being first.

I dwell on this matter because it seems to me very important for the understanding of Mr. de la Mare's work. He is the poet of supernatural wonder and terror, but his dominant note is a heart-warming, quite unsentimental humanity. "Dusk, as a matter of fact," says one of the narrators of *Ding Dong Bell,* "is my mind's natural illumination." But there is more light in the de la Mare dusk than in other men's noonday. Among those who have ventured with him along the difficult frontiers of consciousness, I wonder is there any other whom we dare to think of as quite so completely sane?

Mr. de la Mare's poetry as such falls outside the range of this book, but one should remember that his work, in prose and verse alike, though diversified in form, is wonderfully single in its inspiration. There are four extended works of fiction: *Henry Brocken* (1904); *The Three Mulla-Mulgars* (later renamed *The Three Royal Monkeys*) and *The Return* (both 1910); *Memoirs of a Midget* (1921). *Ding Dong Bell* (1924), a collection of enchanting epitaphs in a slight prose fiction setting, defies classification. The short stories have been collected, so far, in six volumes: *The Riddle* (1923); *Broomsticks* (1925); *The Connoisseur* (1926); *On the Edge* (1930); *The Lord Fish* (1933); *The Wind Blows Over* (1936).

The key to de la Mare's art is the distinction he himself makes (in his lecture on *Rupert Brooke and the Intellectual Imagination*) [1] between two kinds of poets—"those who in their idiosyncrasies re-

[1] Harcourt, Brace (1919). Reprinted in *Pleasures and Speculations* (Faber, 1940).

semble children and bring to ripeness the faculties peculiar to childhood; and those who resemble lads." He put Brooke in the second class. He himself belongs emphatically in the first. "Children . . . live in a world peculiarly their own." "They are not bound in by their groping senses. Facts to them are the liveliest of chameleons. Between their dream and their reality looms no impassable abyss." When a writer carries this spirit into mature years we classify his work as intuitive, inductive, visionary. The source and origin of his inspiration is in the world within, and that world, "old as Eden and remote as the stars, lies like the fabric of a vision, bathed in an unearthly atmosphere."

That all this applies to de la Mare's fiction as well as to his poetry there is, as I have already suggested, the character of the work itself to testify; but if we prefer we may have his own testimony. He believes that "a fine work of fiction must reflect truly the firsthand knowledge and experience of the life of its writer." But "it is neither a copy of life in general nor of the author's particular life." It is "not matter-of-fact—but matter-of-truth." Realism, "in the accepted sense," is only "a kind of scientific reporting." . . . "An imaginative experience is not only as real but far realer than an unimaginative one." For it is "in our individual imagination" that "the essential truth for each one of us" lies.

2. *The Four Long Stories*

Of the four works which are my principal concern here, the first, *Henry Brocken,* is both the palest and the most "poetic." It opens with the picture of a little boy who has been left in charge of an elderly relative (a favorite situation of de la Mare's) starting out one morning on Rosinante—but by this time he seems already a man—to encounter the "wild and faithful" and "strange and lovely" people he has loved in books.[2] De la Mare did not succeed in capturing the manner of the various authors whose characters are encountered, and the patterned beauty of his writing was less suited to fiction than was the rich, cerebrated prose he developed later.

[2] An article by de la Mare on "Books and Reading," *Living Age,* CCC (1919), 744-747, connects with the Gulliver episode in *Henry Brocken,* and shows clearly that the traveler's temperament is de la Mare's own.

Yet, with all its immaturity, *Henry Brocken* is a book which only young genius could have written. The Criseyde episode, though a little vague, is very beautiful; even at thirty, de la Mare's comments on the subtlest creation of "the shrewdest and tenderest of [his] countrymen" went as deep as anything the Chaucerians have done. The passionate Puritanism of the Bunyan episode is pure de la Mare; and when the Yahoo loses his life to save Brocken in the stampede, Swift's bitterest creation is turned to the uses of faith and hope.

The passive quality of *Henry Brocken* disappears altogether in that glorious adventure story, *The Three Mulla-Mulgars*. Ostensibly written for the amusement of the de la Mare children, it is really an epic of courage, a song of loyalty and love; its mood is that of the noble sonnet on "Virtue":

> Yet, yet: O breast how cold! O hope how far!
> Grant my son's ashes lie where these men's are!

The three mulla-mulgars are monkeys, royal monkeys, born in exile, who are called upon to undertake the unspeakably perilous journey to the Kingdom of Assasimmon in the glorious vale of Tishnar. De la Mare is closer to Blake here than anywhere else in his work; he has created his own mythology. The book plunges us into forest depths, terrifies us with immense heights, and dazzles our eyes in the snow fields. It is neither an allegory nor a sermon, but it is a serious picture of human life in the guise of a wonder-tale. In the Andy Battle episode love bridges even the seemingly impassable gulf between man and beast.

In *The Return* we give our attention to the darker side of occult lore. It is interesting to remember that it was designed as a pot-boiler, in exactly the manner in which Henry James had described Ray Limbert as having created his masterpiece; [3] instead, it won the Polignac Prize! Of this book Forrest Reid has remarked that "it is the story of a spiritual upheaval such as might be produced by any violent emotional crisis, religious or otherwise." And it is true that a materialistically inclined writer might very well have taken his point of departure from some medically recognized maladjustment,

[3] "The Next Time" (*Embarrassments*).

while de la Mare preferred instead to have the convalescent Arthur Lawford possessed by the spirit of a long-dead French roué, Nicholas Sabathier, beside whose grave he had slumbered for a moment in a neglected cemetery. Once the element of "given" has been accepted, however, the situation is developed with psychological exactitude. Like a magic talisman, Lawford's strange experience tests his life in its every aspect. His wife it condemns utterly; in a crisis, that shallow selfish woman has nothing to give. Alice, the daughter, is a very different story; so is the good clergyman, Mr. Bethany, who does not understand the situation but refuses to relinquish faith in his friend. More important than either of these is Grisel. Her loyalty and understanding at last make it possible for Lawford to solve the problem she herself has greatly accentuated, for he loves her increasingly as Sheila draws away from him, and he wonders whether, now that he is no longer Lawford but Lawford-*plus*-Sabathier, he is still morally bound to his wife. Grisel herself cannot be ensnared by casuistry. "Life is a little while. . . . I know in my heart that to face the worst is your only hope of peace." The real question that has been put up to Lawford is whether the power that has achieved a physical entry into his body shall be permitted to assume control of his spirit also. With this the ever present temptation to suicide is closely connected, for Sabathier took his own life. "What peace did *he* find who couldn't perhaps, like you, face the last good-bye?" It is victory for Lawford in the end—"it seemed . . . as if . . . some obscure detestable presence as slowly, as doggedly had drawn worsted aside"—and one hopes it is rest at last for Sabathier.

Few novels of our time have awakened such enthusiasm as *Memoirs of a Midget*. Storm Jameson hailed it when it was published as "the most notable achievement in prose fiction of our generation";[4] Wilson Follett went farther still when he called *Nostromo* "its only peer in the language."[5] It is much the longest and most closely wrought of Mr. de la Mare's novels, and while it is not obscure, it was written, and it should be read, imaginatively and intensely. But it is not a puzzle-book or a case-history. It is a picture of human life. The reader immerses himself in Miss M.'s experience

[4] *English Review,* XXXIV (1922), 424-430.
[5] *Literary Review,* II (1922), 331.

with the same complete absorption encouraged by the great Victorian novels which the setting of the book suggests. And with such a protagonist, this is a great deal to say.

The fundamental idea is clearly the conflict between society and the individual;[6] to accentuate the problem by making the heroine a midget was a very daring thing. There may have been some influence at this point from Wilkie Collins, whom de la Mare greatly admires, and who is suggested again by the use of documents.

A Miss M. of normal stature must still have participated in a very bitter conflict; her passionate devotion to truth, her unswerving determination to maintain her integrity, to work out the significance of her own experience, no matter where it leads or what it costs her—none of these things could have made for an easy life. To Mr. Crimble, the young clergyman who kills himself because of his unrequited love for Fanny Bowater, she cries, "I have had my desperate moments too—more alone in the world than you can ever be! And I swear before God that I will never, never be *not* myself." Miss M., too, loves the heartless Fanny and, in her own way, is spurned by her. Fanny's dislike of poetry, her inability to see anything of value in *Wuthering Heights,* show us that her cruelty is caused, partly at least, by her lack of imagination. It is not the mere mention of *Wuthering Heights* that makes the reader feel that the Brontë influence upon *Memoirs of a Midget* was at least as important as that of Wilkie Collins. Miss M. herself, with her intensity and her independence, would make a very good Brontë heroine.

Though the first part of the narrative is studded with passages in which Miss M. is shown in relation to hairbrushes, watches, cats, books, etc., figures are never given. It is the mental and spiritual differences which result from her diminutive stature that really interest de la Mare; what might have been a mere trick is here filled full of creative significance, and we enter upon a tract of human experience hitherto unexplored. The data the midget accumulates

[6] Rebecca West, *New Statesman,* XVII (1921), 496, would say the conflict between society and the artist. There are suggestions of this in the way Mrs. Monnerie "shows off" Miss M., also in the circus episode. But all in all the interpretation is too narrow. The artist, of course, is a pronounced type of individualist.

are rather different from ours. Her descriptions of the minuter aspects of nature and of such of the smaller animals as "humanity has left unslaughtered" are of breath-taking beauty. But she does not stop with beauty.

> Again and again, as I have pored over the scenes of my memory, I have asked myself: What can life be about? What does it mean? What was my true course? Where my compass? How many times, too, have I vainly speculated what *inward* difference being a human creature of my dimensions really makes.

But to take Miss M. thus far was only half de la Mare's task. Having separated her from humanity, he must at once unite her with it again; otherwise she is a freak and his book merely a tour de force. It must not be supposed that she is always right and society always wrong. For all his love of another world, de la Mare has never sacrificed this one to it; he loves solitude but he knows its dangers, its limitations; he knows, too, the social values. Mrs. Monnerie, the lion-hunter, is wrong; Fanny is wrong. But Sir Walter Pollocke is right, and the "somewhat Dickensian" housekeeper, Mrs. Bowater, has all the sanity of common, uncorrupted humanity. Miss M. coarsens a little when she conquers the world or surrenders to it—there is a little of both—by exhibiting herself in a circus, but this is less shameful than her simpering under Mrs. Monnerie's patronage. And she is completely at fault in her treatment of her dwarf-lover, Mr. Anon; indeed, she treats Mr. Anon almost as badly as Fanny had treated her. She learns better in the end; indeed, she goes so far as to realize "that it will be impossible to free myself, to escape from this world, unless in peace and amity I can take every shred of it, every friend and every enemy, all that these eyes have seen, these senses discovered with me." But it costs Mr. Anon his life to teach her.

By this time she has carried the lesson of the stars into human relationships. From the beginning she had loved them passionately; only in this rapt contemplation had she and her friends of ordinary size stood on a common level. So—the implication would seem to be though it is never stated—so in the light of eternal things all the differences and distinctions which make personality, make life-experience as we know it today, will be swept away. There is no supernaturalism in *Memoirs of a Midget,* but Miss M. would not be a de la Mare heroine if she never looked over the edge; and it was more than a love of mystification which impelled her creator to remove her from the book—and our ken—with the laconic message, "I have been called away." So she typifies universal experience in the end, and so we get the marvelous suggestion that she goes on and on. . . .

3. *On a Smaller Scale*

Many readers of the *Midget* have wondered why de la Mare should not have seen fit to follow it with other novels in later years. Some ask still another question. Why should a man whose creative gifts have the quality of magic in them choose to devote so much of his time to non-creative work? Why, when he might be giving us wonderful stories of his own, should he choose instead to be rewriting *Animal Stories* (1940), *Stories from the Bible* (1929), and traditional folk tales (*Told Again,* 1927)? And why does he compile anthologies? Why such an elaborately annotated lecture as *Desert Islands and Robinson Crusoe* (1930)? Why an encyclopedic compilation of child lore like *Early One Morning in the Spring* (1935)?

At the outset one feels that such questions must come from those who have never read the books named. *Told Again* and *Stories from the Bible* are creative work; in *Come Hither!* (1923)—incomparably the finest selection of poems for children that has ever been published—and in *Behold, This Dreamer!* (1939), whose field is "Reverie, Night, Sleep, Dream, Love-Dreams, Nightmare, Death, the Unconscious, the Imagination, Divination, the Artist, and Kindred Subjects," anthology-making itself becomes a work of genius. As for *Early One Morning,* it seems to me worth all the scientific treatises on child-rearing ever written if for no other reason than because its pages are studded with the secrets which reveal themselves to love alone.

Of course the proletarian critics, with customary ineptitude, find de la Mare guilty of "escapism." They are answered very effectively by the *London Times* reviewer of *The Connoisseur:* "How can you be said to be fleeing the real, or the actual, when you are merely opening your eyes to what the simplest fragment of it, in your view, involves?" Surely the critic who remarked that de la Mare alone among contemporary English poets had failed to show the influence of the First World War must have read *Motley* and its successors to little purpose! Even the precious economic problem plays its part—and it is very nearly a determinative part—in Miss M.'s history. Miss M. never "funks"; neither does her creator. I think it significant also that in spite of all his love for children de la Mare is never sentimental about them. The small hero of "An Ideal Craftsman" (*On the Edge*) is positively sinister, and no "realist" could have given a less sentimental description than de la Mare has written of the "reactions" of Nicholas in "The Almond Tree" (*The Riddle*) when he finds his father a suicide in the snow.

There is no evasion even in the de la Mare Otherworld. Immanâla, "who preys across these shadows," plays a large role in the mythology of the *Mulla-Mulgars*. Where in literature are the powers of evil more terrifying than in that dread tale of spiritual vampirism, "Seaton's Aunt" (*The Riddle*), where more inexplicable than in "All Hallows" (*The Connoisseur*)? It was on this ground that G. K. Chesterton, with his customary perspicacity, distinguished de la Mare's wonderland from that of Barrie and other writers who "make believe." They confine themselves to "the things that we want to exist." Not so de la Mare. For his fairy tales "are not those of the Sceptic but of the Mystic."

The refusal to look society in the eye can be no explanation, then, for de la Mare's increasing preoccupation with short fiction during recent years. Nor need any technical shortcomings be invoked. The architectonics of fiction have never disturbed him, and few writers since Dickens[7] have had his ability to invent distinctive turns of speech.[8] It may well be, however, that, while de la Mare's power to

[7] J. B. Priestley finds in de la Mare "the other half of the Dickens world, the poetical, mysterious, aristocratic half that Dickens, with his eyes fixed on the democratic, humorous, melodramatic elements, never gave us."

[8] I do not mean that de la Mare always does this. Sometimes, as at the eloquent close of "At First Sight" (*On the Edge*), he prefers to transmute the living speech of men into something resembling the dialogue of Henry James, whose influence upon him has been very strong. "He strains his in-

work is continuous, his inspiration is intermittent; he himself tells us that his "inward eye . . . can see its object in detail with the utmost clearness; but it cannot . . . except for a moment or two remain fixed and watch it." Moreover, while de la Mare does not shy from social problems, they do not particularly concern him as an artist; he is concerned, as I have already said, with the soul, particularly as it explores the frontiers of consciousness. In some of his most wonderful achievements, indeed—in "The Creatures" and "The Vats" (*The Riddle*), for example, and, in a quite different manner, in "Maria-Fly" (*Broomsticks*)—he has no story to tell, he has only a mood to develop.

His shorter pieces classify themselves conveniently in several groups. First of all, there are stories of "real" life, like "The Almond Tree," "Miss Duveen" (*The Riddle*), "The Lost Track"—the only American story—(*The Connoisseur*), "Willows" (*On the Edge*), and "'A Froward Child'" (*The Wind Blows Over*). There is no supernatural element in these stories, but they are all brooded over by a sense of the mystery of human life and destiny; it is impossible to read them without feeling that they come from a mind with strong mystical tendencies.

Sometimes de la Mare's stories of this type are sinister, horrible, like "The Three Friends" (*The Riddle*), "Missing" (*The Connoisseur*), or "An Ideal Craftsman" (*On the Edge*). But the method is still indirect. Forrest Reid calls "Missing" "the most appalling murder story ever written," but the word murder is never mentioned in it.

In some stories, though this world is our principal concern, we find ourselves subject to incursions from another. Such are "Miss Jemima," "Broomsticks," "Lucy," and "Alice's Godmother" (all in *Broomsticks*).

A special subdivision under this group might contain stories of

sights through a double mesh of consciousness," writes Clifton Fadiman of de la Mare, "and suffuses the original outlines of his men and women in a shifting haze of retrospection." It is interesting to compare "Out of the Deeps" (*The Riddle*) with *The Turn of the Screw,* as Forrest Reid suggests, or "Seaton's Aunt" with *The Sacred Fount* (cf. *Spectator,* CXXX [1923], 930), or "The Picnic" with "Theodolinde" (*Master Eustace*). De la Mare's memorial essay on James (*Living Age,* CCLXXXIX [1916], 122-125), is important.

ghosts and haunting, like "Out of the Deep" (*The Riddle*), "The Green Room" (*The Connoisseur*), "A Revenant" (*The Wind Blows Over*)—which is, however, a piece of literary and biographical criticism cast into narrative form rather than a ghost story per se—and "Strangers and Pilgrims," an enchanting series of epitaphs in a setting of prose fiction, which appeared originally in *The Wind Blows Over* but has now been taken up into *Ding Dong Bell.*

There is a considerable group of out-and-out fairy tales: "The Dutch Cheese," "The Lovely Myfanwy," "The Three Sleeping Boys of Warwickshire" (all in *Broomsticks*), and the stories in the volume called *The Lord Fish.*

Finally, there are a number of parables and apologues, all of which definitely seem to "mean" something, one is not always sure what: "The Riddle," "The Tree," "The Creatures," "The Vats" (all in *The Riddle*).

The tales are full of sensitive children, recluses, sinister old women, and spinsters quite divinely mad. Sometimes the psychic element lays violent hold upon a suburban, middle-class, matter-of-fact world. Sometimes we are taken out to an imaginary locality which hangs upon the naked shingles of the world as fantastic dream-states attach themselves to consciousness. The fact that in many of his stories de la Mare goes back to a Victorian setting should puzzle nobody. Having, as we have seen, the child-type of imagination, he would naturally feel most at home in a world which was still present, actually, or in living memory, during his formative years.

4. *Significances*

In speaking of de la Mare's mysticism, I have (I am aware) begged an important question. Some of his admirers see him suffering in later years from a spiritual nostalgia; the gates of the Kingdom of Dream are gradually closing themselves against him. Storm Jameson does not go nearly so far as some critics along this line, but even she compares de la Mare disadvantageously with Blake:

> For Blake, who wrote of humble things with an exquisite tenderness, was never shaken in his conceit of himself; he lived in this world as an audacious heir. Mr. de la Mare's humility is rooted with his self-mockery;

it trammels his fantasy, and he is conscious of his mortal weakness all the more sharply that he sees it—sometimes—through the ironic regard of the elf his brother.

Probably every romanticist living in this day and age must, to a certain extent, find his fantasy trammeled; however uncompromising he may be in his romanticism, he can hardly avoid being a little self-conscious about it. It is true that de la Mare has some of the frank subjectivism of Stevenson; it is also true that he does not attempt to give us more than a glimpse of the Ultimate Vision. As he sees it, the "poet's faith" should express itself implicitly throughout his work. We have no right to ask of him that he "shall answer each of our riddles in turn; 'tidy things up.' He shares our doubts and problems; exults in them, and at the same time proves that life in spite of all its duplicity and deceits and horrors, is full of strangenesses, wonder, mystery, grace and power: is 'good.'" I find no nihilism in de la Mare, though I find much of the discouragement which touches all sensitive men in these troubled times. "Illuminated by the imagination, our life—whatever its defeats and despairs—is a never-ending, unforeseen strangeness and adventure and mystery. This is the fountain of our faith and of our hope." The implicit testimony is even clearer. You get it again and again. You get it in the novels, with their imperious, merciless call for courage. You get it in the profoundest, the most puzzling, and probably the most beautiful of his short stories, "The Connoisseur." You get it in that amazing tale, "The Wharf" (*The Connoisseur*), where a pile of manure in the barnyard is made to serve bewilderingly as a completely adequate symbol of salvation!

All this is pretty closely connected with de la Mare's celebrated obscurity, no greater obscurity surely than that to which a relative of Robert Browning is legitimately entitled! Raymond Mortimer has remarked that, like Hoffmann's, his stories often end in anticlimax. "And this is no doubt very intentional. 'That,' he suggests, 'is the way things are.'"[9] Obscurity has its own values in this way of writing. The mysterious Old Man in "The Pardoner's Tale" is

[9] *New Statesman,* XXI (1923), 201.

much more impressive in his mystery than he could be if Chaucer had taken a hint from his interpreters to identify him with Death, Old Age, the Wandering Jew, or something else. So, too, it does not seem to me that I really wish to work out a detailed allegorical interpretation for that exquisite fairy tale turned parable, "The Riddle," which seems to me already among the imperishable things. On the other hand, I should like to know more about "The Connoisseur" which apparently nobody has ever understood in its entirety. But we tread on dangerous ground here, and perhaps we only reveal our own stupidity. At any rate the matter is highly subjective.

5. *"Heere Taketh the Makere of This Book His Leve"*

We have seen the history of the novel in many convolutions since Queen Elizabeth's day, and have brought it now not to the end but to the present. Doubtless I have made many mistakes. The worst of all I propose to avoid by remembering the wise caution of George Eliot that of all the forms of human error prophecy is the most gratuitous.

Walter de la Mare may seem a strange writer with which to close the record, for Walter de la Mare is "hardly a novelist." But is not that very much the point? Fiction has grown steadily more oblique, more indirect since Dickens's time. Many of its most interesting developments have been brought about by those who were "hardly novelists"; many of its most interesting publications have been "hardly novels."

I am not for a moment asserting that in Mr. de la Mare, or in the stream-of-consciousness writers, or anywhere else, we have what Zona Gale once referred to as "the allotrope of the novel." I am not even asserting (remembering, once more, George Eliot) that here is "the novel of the future." I hope it will be a long time yet before our Storm Jamesons and our Sheila Kaye-Smiths turn away from the study of man in society; I hope it will be even longer before the Scheherazade-like talents of a John Buchan or a Marjorie Bowen shall cease to make it possible for us to forget all about man in society. Nevertheless I am persuaded that in so far as the writing of English fiction is a serious art, it will continue to depend in the future, as it has always depended in the past, upon the peculiar talents of extraordinarily gifted writers, many of whom have established, and will establish, no school, for the quite sufficient reason that they are unique and inimitable. And so here is a prophecy in spite of all, and George Eliot's caution was at last in vain.

APPENDIX

SOME NINETEENTH AND TWENTIETH CENTURY NOVELISTS NOT CONSIDERED IN THE TEXT

"Here's richness!"

Nicholas Nickleby

The possible usefulness of this book to students of English fiction will be increased, I hope, by the following series of notes on a number of writers whom considerations of space and proportion have excluded from the body of the book.

Once I hoped that the names of all important writers of their periods might be found written here. This ideal has proved impracticable even in the nineteenth century, and in the twentieth I have frankly abandoned it. It has seemed to me quite unnecessary that I should seek to rival Fred B. Millett's guide to *Contemporary British Literature* (HB, 1939); I have, therefore, listed only those outstanding writers who could not, without absurdity, be omitted from any book which deals with the English novel. To these I have added, however, a number of names not included in Millett (and in other widely used books on the contemporary novel), in some cases, no doubt, because of too recent emergence, in others for some reason which I do not pretend to understand.

Because I cannot expect anybody to agree with all my omissions and inclusions, I apologize in advance to the reader who will not find his favorite authors listed, and to the authors themselves. Could I have written as much as I should like to write about the contemporary novel, the length of my book must have been doubled.

The symbol sometimes used following an author's name indicates the publisher or publishers who issue or have issued his works. For abbreviations employed, here and elsewhere, see p. 578.

AINSWORTH, William Harrison (EL) (1805-1882), editor, man of fashion, friend of Dickens, and author of forty-two novels, was one of the great historic purveyors of romantic melodrama. His first important book, *Rookwood* (1834), was an attempt to revivify the Gothic novel by transfusions from Hoffman, Tieck, Victor Hugo, Dumas, and other continental writers. In such novels of place as *The Tower of London* (1840), *Old Saint Paul's* (1841), and *Windsor Castle* (1843), he dealt with some of the most romantic figures in English history—Lady Jane Grey, Anne Boleyn, etc.—but he attempted no minute characterization of them, for he was trying "to contrive such a series of incidents as should naturally introduce every relic of the whole pile . . . so that no part of it should remain un-illustrated." Yet Ainsworth was an antiquarian, if not a scholar, and *The Lancashire Witches* (1849) was based on careful study. Ainsworth pioneered in the use of slang and cant terms in dialogue, though his "noble" characters talk Wardour Street. He was much interested in the more sensational aspects of crime; Jonathan Wild is the villain of *Jack Sheppard* (1840). Many of his books were illustrated by Cruikshank. The fullest study is S. M. Ellis, *WHA and His Friends* (Lane, 1911). See Malcolm Elwin, *Victorian Wallflowers* (C, 1934).

Banim, John (1798-1842) and Michael (1796-1874), were the first important novelists of the Irish peasantry. John, who died young, after enough physical and mental suffering to kill a dozen ordinary men, took the lead in *O'Hara Tales* (1825-1826), which avowedly attempts to do for Ireland what the Waverley Novels had achieved for Scotland. Scott is imitated again in John's *The Boyne Water* (1826). Michael's most important historical novel, *The Croppy* (1828), concerns the Rebellion of 1798. The Banims are nationalist and Catholic; there is much violence and melodrama in their books and some supernaturalism. P. J. Murray published a *Life of JB* in 1857. See H. S. Krans, *Irish Life in Irish Fiction* (ColUP, 1903).

Besant, Sir Walter (1836-1901), wrote *Ready-Money Mortiboy* (1872), *The Golden Butterfly* (1876), and ten other novels (largely of a sensational character) with James Rice (1843-1882), and more than twenty-five of his own after Rice's death. Some of these are historical novels of the eighteenth century—*Dorothy Forster* (1884), *For Faith and Freedom* (1889), *The Orange Girl* (1899), etc.—but the books by which he is best remembered are *All Sorts and Conditions of Men* (1882) and *Children of Gibeon* (1886), which picture life in London's East End; the former led directly to the establishment of the People's Palace. Besant was first chairman of the Society of Authors, and wrote an immense number of nonfiction books on the topography of London and other themes. His *Autobiography* appeared in 1902. See Lewis Melville, *Victorian Novelists* (Co, 1906).

Black, William (1841-1898), was a professional journalist of Glasgow and London who wrote some thirty romances distinguished for their conventionally but charmingly romantic heroines and their picturesque scenery. Black develops the contrast between his dour countrymen and their more volatile contemporaries, either by bringing an alien into Scotland, as the French girl, Coquette, in *A Daughter of Heth* (1871), or by taking a Scottish protagonist to London. Among his best-known books are *A Princess of Thule* (1874), *Madcap Violet* (1876), *Macleod of Dare* (1878), and *Judith Shakespeare* (1884). There is a biography by Sir T. Wemyss Reid (Cassell, 1902). See "WB Reaches His Centenary," *LTLS,* Nov. 8, 1941, p. 557.

Blackmore, R[ichard] D[oddridge] (1825-1900), wrote novels to recoup the losses he sustained on fruit-gardening, which was his primary interest. It was his misfortune as a writer that he could never again come within hailing-distance of the success of the glorious romance which generations have now loved as *Lorna Doone* (1869); "It's a pity the book was ever written, a pity it cannot be destroyed." Among his other titles are *The Maid of Sker* (1872), *Alice Lorraine* (1875), and *Springhaven* (1887), a tale of the days when England waited for Napoleon. Blackmore used history for background, but his real subject is love. His plots depend on such time-honored romantic devices as abduction, forged letters, and disputed inheritance, and his black villains are sharply contrasted to his virile, fighting heroes and the fragile, lovely girls they protect and adore. Blackmore's rhythmic, imaginative descriptions of Devon are saved from lushness by his deep and genuine feeling and his intimate knowledge of the ways of peasants and fisher-folk. The fullest study of his work is Quincy G. Burris, *RDB: His Life and Novels, ISLL,* XV, No. 4 (1930). See M. Elwin, *Victorian Wallflowers.*

Borrow, George (1803-1881), linguist, compiler, traveler, authority on gypsies, and agent of the British Bible Society, was one of the great English eccentrics. His name is usually included in histories of the novel, though he was not a novelist, for his famous autobiography, *Lavengro* (1851) (EL), and its sequel, *The Romany Rye* (1857), use the old picaresque methods, and are developed imaginatively rather than literally. Equally famous is *The Bible in Spain* (1843) (EL). W. I. Knapp wrote the basic *Life, Writings, and Correspondence* (Murray, 1899); a considerable literature has developed since.

Bowen, Marjorie, pseud. Gabrielle Margaret Vere Campbell Long, b. 1888, wrote her first novel, *The Viper of Milan* (1906), while still in her teens, and has now published more than 130 books, mostly historical fiction and biography. Among her best-known titles are *The Glen o' Weeping* (1907); *Black Magic* (1909); *Defender of the Faith* (1911); *Dickon* (1929), which rehabilitates Richard III; *The English Paragon* (1930), the story of the Black Prince; *Dark Rosaleen* (1932), which treats of the Irish Rebellion of 1798; a trilogy on Renaissance themes, comprising *The Golden Roof* (1928), *The Triumphant Beast* (1934), and *Trumpets at Rome* (1937); and a trilogy on the spiritual life of England in the seventeenth century, comprising *God and the Wedding Dress* (1938), *Mr. Tyler's Saints* (1939), and *The Circle in the Water* (1939). Of late years she has published many books under the pseudonyms of George R. Preedy (*General Crack*, 1928; *The Rocklitz,* 1930; *Painted Angel,* 1938, etc.) and Joseph Shearing (*The Golden Violet,* 1936; *Blanche Fury,* 1939; *The Crime of Laura Sarelle,* 1941, etc.). As Shearing, she anticipated Rachel Field's *All This and Heaven Too* by telling the story of the Praslin murder in *Forget-Me-Not* (*The Strange Case of Lucile Cléry*) (1932). Though Mrs. Long's reputation has suffered somewhat from the literary snobbery which insists that we ought to be less grateful to a writer who has given us a hundred good books than we should be if he had given us only ten, Hugh Walpole calls her the greatest historical novelist England has had in a generation. She is a brilliant writer with an uncanny gift for atmosphere, especially of a sinister or supernatural variety. Her autobiography, *The Debate Continues,* by Margaret Campbell (He, 1939), tells the poignant story of a hard, noble, and spiritually triumphant life.

Braddon, Mary Elizabeth (Mrs. John Maxwell) (1837-1915), owned Bulwer as her master but is generally thought of as belonging to the school of Wilkie Collins sensationalism. Among her more than eighty books, the great success was *Lady Audley's Secret* (1862), which stands in literary history with Mrs. Henry Wood's *East Lynne*. Writing on her centenary in *LTLS* (Oct. 2, 1937, p. 711), Michael Sadleir gives her credit for having created a detailed picture of Victorian life with a subtone of malice. She did not take the pomposities of her time (or of life itself) too seriously, he thinks, and, though personally a devout woman, she would have gone farther in her rebellion had she dared.

Broughton, Rhoda (1840-1920), composed her own epitaph when she pointed out that she had begun her career as Zola and was to finish it as Charlotte M. Yonge. "It's not I that have changed, it's my fellow countrymen." Her early novels (*Not Wisely But Too Well,* 1867; *Cometh Up As a Flower,* 1867; *Red As a Rose Is She,* 1870) were published anonymously, and it is said that her father forbade her to read them. *Belinda* (1883) has been called her best novel; in her last work, *A Fool in Her Folly* (1920), she reworked early materials in the light of her maturer experience. Trollope, who did not like her attitude, praised her in his *Autobiography,* for taking the trouble "to make her personages stand upright on the ground" and for causing them to speak "as men and women do speak." She had energy and, when not too busy with rebellion, much humor. Her historical importance is that, though much less an extremist than Ouida, she helped break the mold of Victorian decorum in fiction. Rhoda Broughton is considered briefly in Walter de la Mare's essay, "Some Women Novelists," in his *Pleasures and Speculations* (FF, 1940) and in Forrest Reid's "Minor Fiction in the Eighteen-Eighties," in his *Retrospective Adventures* (FF, 1941).

Buchan, John (HM) (1875-1940), led a full, distinguished life as author, publisher, sportsman, and public servant, and died as Lord Tweedsmuir, Governor-General of Canada. His widest popularity came with the long series of adventure stories about Richard Hannay and his friends, of which three (*The Thirty-Nine Steps,* 1915; *Greenmantle,* 1916; and *Mr. Standfast,* 1919) have now been collected as *Adventures of Richard Hannay* (1939), and three more (*Huntingtower,* 1922; *The Three Hostages,* 1924; *John McNab,* 1925) as *Adventurers All* (1942). His more substantial work as historical novelist in the Scott tradition will be found in such books as *Midwinter* (1925); *Witch Wood* (1927); *The Blanket of the Dark* (1931); and *The Free Fishers* (1934). Buchan had the ancient gift of tale-telling, "which holdeth children from play and old men from the chimney corner," a well-stored, deeply reflective mind, and a keen spiritual sensitiveness; the combination produced the best fiction of its kind that has been written in our time. In his autobiography, *Pilgrim's Way* (1940), pp. 193-199, he himself classified and evaluated his books. For an interesting description of the Hannay cycle, cf. Howard Swiggett's introduction to the last novel, *Mountain Meadow* (1941).

Caine, Hall (Cassell, CW) (1853-1931), and Marie Corelli, pseud. Mary Mackay (Me) (1864-1924), are as typical of the taste of their time in "thrillers" as Miss Braddon and Mrs. Henry Wood were typical of the Victorian period. Caine began as companion of Rossetti during the last year of his life (*Recollections of Rossetti,* 1882) and London correspondent of a Liverpool paper, and made himself the laureate of the Isle of Man, where primitive conditions among the folk lent themselves to the wild sensationalism, which, coupled with scandal and religiosity, constituted his stock-in-trade. A shrewd self-advertiser, he presented his stories on the stage (and, later, screen) as well as between covers, and died, having been knighted for his propaganda work in the First World War, the richest novelist in English history. His books include *The Deemster* (1887), *The Manxman* (1894), *The Christian* (1897), *The Eternal City* (1901), and *The Woman Thou Gavest Me* (1913). Like him, Marie Corelli took herself with prodigious seriousness, but she was not a regionalist. Her "line" was the sensational exploitation of pseudo-scientific, pseudo-occult wisdom. Among her most successful books were *Thelma* (1887), *Wormwood* (1890), *Barabbas* (1893), *The*

Sorrows of Satan (1895), and *The Master Christian* (1900). Her admirers are said to have included Queen Victoria, Edward VII, Gladstone, Tennyson, Ellen Terry, and Oscar Wilde; and she was translated by Rostand. George Bullock gave her an intelligent modern biography (Co, 1940), and see Mark Twain's amusing comments on her egregious vanity in *Mark Twain in Eruption* (H, 1940). Caine published an autobiography, *My Story* (AC, 1909). Malcolm Elwin treats both writers briefly and hostilely in *Old Gods Falling* (M, 1939); Michael Sadleir's sketch of Marie Corelli in the *Dictionary of National Biography, 1922-1930* is more temperate and larger-minded.

Corelli, Marie. See Caine, Hall.

Crockett, S[amuel] R[utherford] (1860-1914), and Ian Maclaren, pseud. John Watson (1850-1907), both Scottish clergymen, stand with the early Barrie as members of the "Kailyard School," which devoted itself to a loving, and sometimes rather pious, exploitation of the quainter aspects of Scottish life and character. The famous books are Crockett's *The Stickit Minister* (1893) and Maclaren's *Beside the Bonnie Briar Bush* (1894) and *A Doctor of the Old School* (1896). Crockett left the kailyard to write a very long line of historical romances. George Douglas, i.e., George Douglas Brown (1869-1902) protested against what seemed to him the sentimentality of these writers in a novel preoccupied with all the worst aspects of Scottish character, *The House with the Green Shutters* (1901). See M. M. Harper, *Crockett and Grey Galloway* (H&S, 1907); W. R. Nicoll, *Ian Maclaren* (H&S, 1908); C. and A. M. Lennox, *George Douglas Brown* (H&S, 1903).

De Morgan, William (Ht) (1839-1917), maker of fine pottery, turned novelist at sixty-seven, with *Joseph Vance* (1906). In this and its successors, of which the best are *Alice-for-Short* (1907), *Somehow Good* (1908), and *When Ghost Meets Ghost* (1914), De Morgan is generally considered as an imitator of Dickens—"my idol in childhood, boyhood, youthhood, manhood, and so on, to a decade of senility—even until now"—but Will T. Hale has shown ("W DM and the Greater Early Victorians," *Indiana University Studies,* VIII, No. 50, 1921) that this is a narrow view. Turning to fiction in old age, De Morgan naturally derives from the writers who were at the height of their vogue in his youth, but he does not confine himself to any one writer, nor is he ever a slavish imitator. With him may be mentioned the distinguished explorer and colonial administrator, Sir Harry H. Johnston (1858-1927), who took the characters of *Dombey and Son* and *Our Mutual Friend* into another generation in *The Gay-Dombeys* (1919) and *The Veneerings* (1922), and who also continued Shaw's play, *Mrs. Warren's Profession,* in *Mrs. Warren's Daughter* (1920).

Douglas, George. See Crockett, S. R.

Douglas, Norman, b. 1868, takes an amoral position which makes him something of a phenomenon among English writers. As a novelist—he is also scientist and essayist—his reputation rests almost entirely on *South Wind* (1917) (Modern Library), whose setting is the Capri of which Mr. Douglas has written so much nonfiction, and which is a brilliant, kindly, and perverse novel in the Peacock tradition. Mr. Douglas has published an autobiography, *Looking Back* (HB, 1933); see Elizabeth D. Wheatley, *SR,* XL (1932), 55-67.

Doyle, Sir Arthur Conan (L, Murray) (1859-1930), physician, historian of the Boer War, authority on spiritualism, found it as impossible to escape from the master-detective, Sherlock Holmes (one of the few pieces of contemporary folklore) as Haggard from Allan Quartermaine or Hope from Ruritania. Between *A Study in Scarlet* (1887) and *The Case-Book of Sherlock Holmes* (1927), the great detective figures in eight novels and collections of tales; Doyle killed him off in *Memoirs of Sherlock Holmes* (1892) but was compelled to resurrect him in *The Return of Sherlock Holmes* (1905). *Micah Clarke* (1888), a story of Monmouth's rebellion, and *The White Company* (1891), a story of the fourteenth century, are standard historical novels. *The Lost World,* one of the first stories about dinosaurs, created a sensation in 1912. There is a memoir by J. Lamond (Murray, 1931); see M. Elwin, *Old Gods Falling.*

Du Maurier, George (H) (1834-1896), who gave most of his time to his famous satirical drawings of society life for *Punch* and other media, wrote three novels—*Peter Ibbetson* (1892), *Trilby* (1894), and *The Martian* (1897). The third has not held its place, but the first two have enjoyed extraordinary success, both between covers and on the stage; more recently (1931) Deems Taylor made *Peter Ibbetson* into an opera. Du Maurier's books owe their vogue to his pleasant, Murger-like pictures of artist-life in the Latin Quarter—the author was half French—and to their pleasant, diluted occultism. Trilby can sing only when under the hypnotic influence of the evil Jew, Svengali; the love-life of Mimsey Seraskier and Peter Ibbetson exists only in the dreams they have learned to "dream true"; Barty Josselin is guided from the spirit world by an inhabitant of Mars who later incarnates as his daughter. Daphne du Maurier, author of *Rebecca* (1938), etc., is George du Maurier's grand-daughter; see her *The Du Mauriers* (DD, 1937).

Eddison, E[ric] R[ücker] (D), b. 1888, and employed in public service until 1938, has possibly gone farther into "pure" romance than any other fictionist of our time. There are echoes of world mythology in Eddison's work, as there are echoes of many literatures in his elaborately mannered prose, but instead of identifying himself with any old tradition he is creating a new one. He insists that his books must be read as stories, and not as parables, but since they are drenched in metaphysical wisdom, "escapism" is not the dominant motive. In *The Worm Ouroboros* (1922), he laid his scene in Mercury, but apparently this did not strike him as sufficiently "created." He descended to earth to tell the saga-tale of *Styrbiorn the Strong* (1926), and then took off for his private Valhalla, Zimiamvia, the scene of *Mistress of Mistresses* (1935) and (in part) of *A Fish Dinner in Memison* (1941). Eddison's books cannot be described, for there is nothing with which to compare them, but one wonders whether it is anything more than the fancy of a capricious public which has made James Joyce the major mystery of the modern novel while Eddison remains virtually unknown. See James Stephens's introductions to *The Worm Ouroboros* and *A Fish Dinner in Memison.*

Egan, Pierce (1772-1849), sports writer, made his contribution to fiction with *Tom and Jerry* (*Life in London; or the Day and Night Scenes of Jerry Hawthorn, Esq., and his Elegant Friend, Corinthian Tom, accompanied by Bob Logic, the Oxonian, in their Rambles and Sprees through the Metropolis,* 1821-1828), which was as well-known to the men of the Regency as Buster Brown and the Keystone Comedies have been to us. It is a long, anecdotal account (with pictures by Cruikshank) of the exploits of a pair of gay young men about town. *Tom and Jerry* inherited a tradition which runs back to the fabliaux and beyond, and it shows what kind of world *The Pickwick Papers* emerged from. In a sequel of 1828, Egan devised moral or tragic ends for his rascals!

Ferrier, Susan (1782-1854), author of *Marriage* (1818) (EL), *The Inheritance* (1824), and *Destiny* (1831), is the worthy Scottish counterpart of the novelists described in Chapter X of this book. Miss Ferrier had a keen eye for absurdities, a quick mind, and a pungent style; she did as much as can be done in the "tea table" novel without the supreme gifts of a Jane Austen. There is a *Memoir and Correspondence,* ed. by J. A. Doyle (Murray, 1898).

Ford, Ford Madox, originally Ford Madox Hueffer (Duckworth) (1873-1939), whose father was a German physician and whose grandfather was the painter, Ford Madox Brown, was brought up in a Pre-Raphaelite atmosphere, and derived his view of the novel from Henry James. As editor of *The English Review* and *The Transatlantic Review,* Ford discovered many writers and exercised much influence on contemporary literature. Yet, thanks to his aloofness from many later "movements," and possibly to his personal idiosyncrasies, he has received less attention as a novelist than his talents would seem to warrant. In his earlier days,

Ford wrote many romances, including the trilogy about Henry VIII and Catherine Howard (*The Fifth Queen,* 1906; *Privy Seal,* 1907; *The Fifth Queen Crowned,* 1908), and the three books with Conrad. More important are the searching psychological novel, *The Good Soldier* (1915) and the tetralogy inspired by the First World War—*Some Do Not* (1924); *No More Parades* (1925); *A Man Could Stand Up* (1926); and *The Last Post* (1928). Ford's autobiographical works include *Thus to Revisit* (1921); *Return to Yesterday* (1931); and *It Was the Nightingale* (1933). See Granville Hicks, *B*(NY), LXXII (1930), 364-370.

Forster, E[dward] M[organ] (HB), b. 1879, a Cambridge man, is the voice of English Liberalism—anti-imperialist, anti-capitalist, anti-regimentarian, pro-mystical, anti-ecclesiastical. Forster's humanistic ideal shows in his love for Greece and Italy. Greek mythology plays its part in his supernatural tales (*The Celestial Omnibus,* 1911, etc.); two novels (*Where Angels Fear to Tread,* 1905, and *A Room with a View,* 1908) concern Italy. *The Longest Journey* (1907) reflects the author's contacts with Cambridge. But his reputation rests finally on *Howard's End* (1910), an elaborate picture of pre-war society, and on that perspicacious and prophetic picture of Anglo-Indian relations, *A Passage to India* (1924). Forster's faith is all in the individual; as Rose Macaulay points out in *The Writings of EMF* (HB, 1938), his villains always prefer things to people, and for all his skeptical urbanity, his primary preoccupation is with the old struggle between good and evil. See Lionel Trilling, *Kenyon Review,* IV (1942), 160-173.

Galt, John (1779-1839), wrote many novels, though novel-writing was but one of the many activities in which he engaged during his adventurous life. The best known are *The Ayrshire Legatees* (1821) (EL), an imitation of *Humphry Clinker; Annals of the Parish* (1821) (EL), in which a Scottish Dr. Primrose, the historian of his township, is also called upon to view such world events as the American, the French, and the Industrial Revolutions, as they impinge upon the life of his people; *The Provost* (1822), the self-told story of a self-made man, which Coleridge considered a masterly study of the "Irony of Self-delusion"; and *The Entail* (1823) (WC), which follows a Scottish family through three generations. Galt, who was a writer of considerable power, has been most recently evaluated by Frank Hallam Lyell, *A Study of the Novels of John Galt* (PUP, 1942).

Gore, Catherine, née Moody (1799-1861), was burlesqued in Thackeray's *Novels by Eminent Hands* as the author of "Dukes and Déjeuners," "Hearts and Diamonds," "Marchionesses and Milliners," etc. In such books as *Romances of Real Life* (1829), *Women as They Are* (1830), and *The Fair of Mayfair* (1832), Mrs. Gore had perhaps left herself open to his attack. But not all her work is fashionable or "silver fork." She began with historical fiction, including a *Richelieu* (1826). *Mothers and Daughters* (1831) and *Mrs. Armytage* (1836) are in the Jane Austen tradition. In *Cecil, Adventures of a Coxcomb* (1841) and *Cecil a Peer* (1841), she takes in a wider, and much less feminine, swathe on the Continent. Mrs. Gore's general attitude is mildly worldly and cynical, but satire, sympathy, and didacticism were all within her range. See M. W. Rosa, *The Silver Fork School* (ColUP, 1936).

GOUDGE, Elizabeth (CM), b. 1900, is the most gifted English woman writer of recent emergence. A clergyman's daughter, Norman-French on her mother's side, Miss Goudge has lived all her life in church and university centers. Among her best-known books are *Island Magic* (1936); *Towers in the Mist* (1938), which deals with Queen Elizabeth's Oxford; *The Middle Window* (1939), which deals with second sight in a Scottish setting; *The Bird in the Tree* (1940); and *The Castle on the Hill* (1942), which includes a distinguished treatment of the problem of the conscientious objector, an amazing book to come out of England in the third year of war. Miss Goudge is especially fine in her portrayal of children. Her growing popularity rebukes those who complain that the modern novel is indifferent to spiritual values, and at the same time helps reassure all who feel that the naturalistic mold must be shattered if the novel is to live.

GRANT, James (1822-1887), soldier and military authority, a relative of Scott, produced some sixty works of fiction, beginning with *The Romance of War, or The Highlanders in Spain* (1846-1847). Though generally preoccupied with military matters, he achieves variety by placing his scenes all over the world, and roving far enough back in time to produce, among others, the inevitable historical novels about Mary Queen of Scots (*Bothwell,* 1854) and Montrose (*Memoirs of James, Marquis of Montrose,* 1858). *First Love and Last Love* (1868) deals with the Indian Mutiny, *Lady Wedderburn's Wish* (1870) with the Crimean War. See S. M. Ellis, *Mainly Victorian* (Hu, 1925).

GRIFFIN, Gerald (1803-1840), like the Banims, wrote of the Irish peasantry. Both his historical novels—*The Invasion* (1832) and *The Duke of Monmouth* (1836)—are unimportant; but *The Collegians* (1829) (Talbot Press) is often called the best of all Irish novels. The plot, which is based on fact, deals with the murder of a peasant girl by her socially superior husband, and is not without its sensationalism, but the book includes a comprehensive picture of Irish society. Dion Boucicault dramatized it as *The Colleen Bawn,* which, in turn, was made into an opera by Sir Julius Benedict, *The Lily of Killarney*. Griffin's *Tales of the Munster Festivals* (1827-1832) use materials similar to those of the

Banims in *O'Hara Tales*. He died a Christian Brother. Daniel Griffin published a *Life* (Simpkin, 1843). See H. S. Krans, *Irish Life in Irish Fiction*.

HAGGARD, Sir Henry Rider (L) (1856-1925), used his first-hand knowledge of Africa in *King Solomon's Mines* (1885), which was written in emulation of *Treasure Island;* his second great triumph was *She* (1887), the story of an immortal sorceress, again in an African setting. From the bondage of these successes he finally gave up trying to deliver himself; *Ayesha* (1905) is a sequel to *She,* and the further adventures of Allan Quartermaine fill many books. During his earlier years, however, Haggard attempted many other things. *Jess* (1887), *Colonel Quarich, V. C.* (1888), and *Beatrice* (1890) deal with modern life and society; *Cleopatra* (1889) and *Montezuma's Daughter* (1893) are serious historical novels. *Eric Brighteyes* (1891) is in the manner of the Icelandic sagas, and *Nada the Lily* (1892) applies a similar literary method to the Zulu materials its author knew so well. *The World's Desire* (1890), a half-allegorical tale written with Andrew Lang, concerns the rather esoteric theme of the Egyptian Helen. Haggard was essentially a storyteller, with little interest in style. Like many servants of Empire, he had his blind spots, but he was far from being an uninformed or insensitive man. A son of the old squirearchy, and a devout Christian with a touch of fatalism in his make-up, he gave up hunting because he believed the souls of animals immortal. A transparent honesty and simplicity informs his autobiography, *The Days of My Life* (L, 1926). See M. Elwin, *Old Gods Falling*.

HOBBES, John Oliver (St) (1867-1906), was the pseudonym of a writer born (in Boston) as Pearl Mary Teresa Richards. She married Reginald W. Craigie in 1887 and divorced him in 1895. A "society novelist," influenced by Disraeli, Meredith, and Henry James, Mrs. Craigie was profoundly committed, 'neath all superficies, to the conception of life as a quest; for her personally this quest ended in the Roman Catholic Church. She first attracted attention with such books as *The Sinner's Comedy* (1892), *A Study in Temptations* (1893), and *The Gods, Some Mortals, and Lord Wickenham* (1895), but her most ambitious and characteristic effort was the Catholic and historical novel, *The School for Saints* (1897) with its sequel, *Robert Orange* (1900). See *The Life of JOH, Told in Her Correspondence with Her Friends,* etc. (Du, 1911); Isabel C. Clarke, *Six Portraits* (Hu, 1935).

HOOK, Theodore (1788-1841), was a playwright, public entertainer, famous practical joker, society reporter, scandal-sheet editor, and (in his earlier phase at least) egregious snob. *Sayings and Doings* (1824-1828), ten stories in nine volumes, are short dramatic pieces, each exemplifying a proverb. *Maxwell* (1830) and *The Parson's Daughter* (1833) are novels of middle-class life, with many coincidences and improbabilities, and a moral; *Gilbert Gurney* (1836), *Jack Brag* (1837), and *Peregrine Bunce* (1842) are picaresque farces. Hook had no style, no skill in plot construction, and no gift for the selection of detail, but he is of considerable importance as a link between Smollett and Dickens and a pioneer of nineteenth-century realism; he gives a fuller picture of London life than any of his contemporaries. There is a fine study by Myron F. Brightfield, *TH and His Novels* (HUP, 1928). See also Agnes Repplier's delightful *In Pursuit of Laughter* (HM, 1936).

Hope, Anthony, i.e., Sir Anthony Hope Hawkins (1863-1933), had two great popular triumphs: *The Dolly Dialogues* (1894), amusing pictures of smart society, and *The Prisoner of Zenda* (1894), with its sequel, *Rupert of Hentzau* (1898), tales of Ruritania, an imaginary European kingdom, honeycombed with intrigue, which is the British fictional equivalent of the American, George Barr McCutcheon's, Graustark. Yet Hope had begun his career by being rebuked in the press for the political cynicism of *A Man of Mark* (1890) and for daring to write of the priest who falls in love in *Father Stafford* (1891). Nor was there any end of variety in his later experiments. He wrote of Cecil Rhodes in *The God in the Car* (1894), of Disraeli in *Quisanté* (1900), of Catherine the Great in *Sophy of Kravonia* (1906). He even tried audaciously to rework Ruritanian materials toward more serious ends in *The King's Mirror* (1899). But the public clung stubbornly to its preference for *Zenda,* and it is as the author of *Zenda* that Hope will be remembered. There is a biography by Sir Charles Mallet, *AH and his Books* (Hu, 1935). See F. T. Cooper, *Some English Story Tellers* (Ht, 1912) and M. Elwin, *Old Gods Falling.*

Hope, Thomas. See Morier, J. J.

Hudson, W[illiam] H[enry] (K) (1841-1922), was born in Buenos Aires of American parents; he came to England in 1869 but was not naturalized until 1900. Primarily Hudson was not a fictionist but a poet-naturalist; the hyphenization is necessitated not by any lack of precise and exact knowledge on his part but rather by the fact that in him close observation was reinforced by so deep a conviction of the fundamental oneness of all life that even the city-bound reader experiences no shock when Rima, the heroine of the forests in *Green Mansions* (1904), is compared to birds, insects, and even reptiles. This book, which did not fully come into its own until Alfred Knopf brought out an American edition in 1916, with a Preface by John Galsworthy, owes its vogue partly to its lovely title and style, but more to the fact that it takes us out of the civilization Hudson loathed into the half primitivistic, mystical realm where he had his being. It is one of the few novels which have really voiced the deeper longings of the spirit of man during our time. Hudson used more conventional South American materials in *The Purple Land* (1885) and the five stories known as *El Ombú* (*Tales of the Pampas*) (1902). *A Little Boy Lost* (1905), like *Green Mansions,* hovers between allegory and realism; *A Crystal Age* (1887) is Hudson's Utopia. There is a book-length study by Morley Roberts (Nash & Grayson, 1924). See R. H. Charles's essay, "The Writings of WHH," *E&S,* XX (1935).

HUGHES, Thomas. See LAWRENCE, G. A.

HUXLEY, Aldous (H), b. 1894, is the son of Leonard Huxley, grandson of Thomas Henry Huxley, grand-nephew of Matthew Arnold, nephew of Mrs. Humphry Ward. He is the most brilliant and possibly the most learned of modern British authors. In his earlier aspects, Huxley was *l'enfant terrible,* the spokesman of the "lost generation." *Crome Yellow* (1921), which imitates Peacock, *Antic Hay* (1923), *Those Barren Leaves* (1925), and *Point Counterpoint* (1928) are largely devoted to the anatomy of ultra-sophisticates in a world from which all values have disappeared. But discerning critics found heartbreak in these books as well as gusto; *Point Counterpoint* preserves the record of its author's attempt to find a way of life through D. H. Lawrence, and later speculations are foreshadowed at the close of *Those Barren Leaves.* Huxley's next two books showed interesting developments. *Brave New World* (1932) expressed the humanist's horror of a coming mechanical Utopia, while *Eyeless in Gaza* (1936) propounded both mysticism and pacifism. The next year, the extended essay, *Ends and Means,* made all this more specific, for here Huxley cried *peccavi,* and dedicated himself to a spiritual view of life. Though his philosophy has not yet been completely formulated, he has already taken up a position of leadership among those who are not content either to accept established creeds or to satisfy themselves with mere negation, as he once did. The influence of Huxley's new way of thinking upon his fiction is not yet important, however, for the only novel he has written since *Ends and Means* is *After Many a Summer* (1939), an amusing picture of some of the more spectacular aspects of life in Southern California; while this book contains considerable discussion of Huxley's later ideas, it is not essentially different in kind from his earlier fictions. Indeed, Mr. Huxley is not interested in the "problem" of fiction, nor is he basically a novelist; he uses the novel for the expression of his ideas, which he has also set forth in poems, essays, books of travel, etc. There is a long study by Alexander Henderson (CW, 1935); Herbert Muller has a good brief analysis, in *Modern Fiction* (FW, 1937).

JAMES, G[eorge] P[ayne] R[ainsford] (1799-1860), was, like Ainsworth, a follower of Scott. His immense productivity, his habit of repeating himself, and his florid, formal style always let him in for a good deal of ridicule (cf. Thackeray, in *Novels by Eminent Hands*), but he was admired by many distinguished writers—he had some influence on Hardy—and enjoyed enormous sales. Among his best-known titles are *Richelieu* (1829) (EL), *Darnley* (1830), *Philip Augustus* (1831), *Mary of Burgundy* (1833). *The Brigand* (1841) and *The Smuggler* (1845) are more picaresque than historical, and *Forest Days* (1843) is a romance of Robin Hood. The fullest study is *The Solitary Horseman* (Cayme Press, 1927), by S. M. Ellis, who reports that the "two cavaliers" or "solitary horseman" which served in the popular mind as a kind of trade-mark for James's books actually appear in only seventeen out of a total of fifty-seven romances.

JAMESON, (Margaret) Storm (Mrs. Guy Chapman) (K,M), was born in Yorkshire in 1897. Her first real success was *The Pitiful Wife* (1923), which is said to have had autobiographical significance. Her reputation was established by the trilogy, *The Triumph of Time* (*The Lovely Ship,* 1927; *The Voyage Home,* 1930; *A Richer Dust,* 1931), which draws on first-hand knowledge of the Yorkshire shipbuilding trade. In *The Captain's Wife* (1939), whose heroine is the daughter of Mary Hervey of the trilogy, some of the same material is presented from another point of view, in a manner which recalls Arnold Bennett's *The Clayhanger Family.* Mary Hervey's granddaughter is the heroine of *The Mirror in Darkness* (*Company Parade,* 1934; *Love in Winter,* 1935; *None Go Back,* 1936), which started out to be a comprehensive picture of English life between two wars, but which has now apparently been abandoned. The ordeal of this generation is presented in Miss Jameson's pages as poignantly as anywhere in contemporary fiction; she brooded over the war for years before it came; *In the Second Year* (1936) is a British *It Can't Happen Here;* in *Here Comes a Candle* (1938) we see a rotten society awaiting its doom. Storm Jameson's problem is complicated by the fact that she thinks of herself as having "fallen out of the hands of the Absolute"; in her world there is no infinite in which parallel lines may meet. When she published her autobiography, *No Time Like the Present* (1933)—which see for her own views on her novels and on fiction generally—she proclaimed herself an absolute pacifist, but she abandoned this position when the storm broke. One of her best books is *The Moon Is Making* (1937), in which she achieved a perfect fusion between the Jane Eyre-like romanticism of *The Pitiful Wife* and the significance of her later, more conscientious, but less exciting, books.

JOHNSTON, Sir Harry H. See DE MORGAN, William.

KAYE-SMITH, Sheila (Mrs. Theodore Penrose Fry) (H), b. c. 1887, whose special field is Sussex, is England's most distinguished living woman novelist. As a child, she "composed forty-two novels in her head"; she wrote out thirteen more during her last two years at school. She used some of the materials of her juvenilia in her first two published novels, *The Tramping Methodist* (1908) and *Starbrace* (1909). For eleven years, she never earned more than £60 from a novel; the first book to attract much attention was *Sussex Gorse* (1916). *Joanna Godden* (1921), the story of a woman-farmer, is her most famous book; *The End of the House of Alard* (1923) has been her best-seller; she herself thinks *Green Apple Harvest* (1920) a better book than either. In her early days, Miss Kaye-Smith wrote intuitively; when she could no longer do this, she felt that her work began to fail; it was not until *Rose Deeprose* (1936) that she could believe herself to be achieving a blend of "thought and instinct, conscious and unconscious." Her development as a writer has run hand in hand with her religious development; in her autobiography, *Three Ways Home* (1937), she has traced both with such fairness and clarity as almost to obviate the necessity of further analysis. In 1929 she and her husband, an erstwhile Anglican priest, became Roman Catholics. Though she does not believe in using fiction for propaganda purposes, she calls *Superstition Corner* (1934), a story of religious persecution under Elizabeth (cf. *Late Harvest* [M, 1940], by the American novelist, Olive B. White), her first Catholic novel. Other notable titles include *Little England* (*The Four Roads*) (1918), *Tamarisk Town* (1919), *Shepherds in Sackcloth* (1930), *Susan Spray* (1931), *Gallybird* (1934), *The Valiant Woman* (1938).

KINGSLEY, Henry (1830-1876), younger brother of Charles Kingsley, was one of the casualties of English literature; dissipation and misfortune combined to wreck his career. *Geoffrey Hamlyn* (1859) (EL) and *The Hillyars and the Burtons* (1865) were described as "the Charter of Australia" by a one-time Prime Minister of that country. *Ravenshoe* (1861) (EL, WC) and *Austin Elliott* (1863) (WC) are English tales with Continental excursions, including one to the Crimea in *Ravenshoe*. Historical novels include *Mademoiselle Mathilde* (1868), a tale of the French Revolution, and *Old Margaret* (1871), a story of Antwerp in the days of the Van Eycks. Kingsley fails in structure, and his "wholesomeness" and "nobility" are sometimes very trying; but he had a flair for thrilling narrative, a fine feeling for nature, a good style, and an exceptional gift for creating attractive characters. For his delightful children, see especially *The Lost Child* (1871), extracted from *Geoffrey Hamlyn*, and the fantasy, *The Boy in Grey* (1871). See S. M. Ellis, *HK, 1830-1876, Towards a Vindication* (Richards, 1931); Michael Sadleir, "HK: A Portrait," *Edinburgh Review*, CCXL (1924), 330-348.

Lawrence, George Alfred (1827-1876), showed how Charles Kingsley's "Muscular Christianity" can degenerate in the hands of a coarse, unspiritual, though very "thoroughbred," man. Lawrence's mother was the daughter of an earl; he himself became a barrister. When the Civil War broke out in America, he came over to enlist in the Confederate Army, but the vulgar, unromantic Yankees clapped him in jail, and would not let him out again until he promised to go back to England and stay there! Like Thomas Hughes (1822-1896), Lawrence was a Rugby product; he may even have been the original of one of the smaller boys in a book still much read by young people and others who admire the English public school ideal, *Tom Brown's Schooldays* (1857). Lawrence's key book is *Guy Livingstone, or Thorough* (1857), cruelly caricatured in Bret Harte's *Sensation Novels Condensed* as "Guy Heavystone, or Entire." This hero's pedigree runs back to Samson; his descendants include such recent pests as *The Sheik* of E. M. Hull and the Superman heroes of the degenerate modern comic strip. Lawrence was a favorite novelist of military men, and it was no accident that he admired the Prussians. He also wrote *Sword and Gown* (1859), *Barren Honor* (1862), *Maurice Dering* (1864), etc. *Brakespeare* (1868) deals with the Hundred Years War. See S. M. Ellis, *Wilkie Collins, Le Fanu, and Others* (Co, 1931).

Le Fanu, Joseph Sheridan (1814-1873), proprietor of the *Dublin University Magazine* and other periodicals, was the great Irish mid-Victorian master of terror. His stories of the supernatural, some of which are still reprinted in virtually every new collection of twilight tales, were based on an immense knowledge of occult matters; he was far less professional in his attitude toward such things than Wilkie Collins; toward the end of his life, indeed, he seems to have been somewhat thrown off his balance by them. *The House by the Church-Yard* (1863), *Wylder's Hand* (1864), and *Uncle Silas* (1864) (WC) are all so good that his devotees cannot agree which one was his masterpiece. Other titles include *Guy Deverell* (1865), *Haunted Lives* (1868), *The Wyvern Mystery* (1869), and the short stories, *In a Glass Darkly* (1872). Much earlier than any of these are the historical novels, *The Cock and Anchor* (1845) and *The Fortunes of Colonel Torlogh O'Brien* (1847). Le Fanu still awaits the full study his merits demand; see S. M. Ellis, *Wilkie Collins, Le Fanu, and Others*.

Lover, Samuel (1797-1868), was a professional humorist and entertainer. Like Lever, though with less force and talent, and unlike Carleton, Griffin, and the Banims, he exploited the stage Irishman. The best known of his three novels is *Handy Andy* (1842) (EL), a record of the diverting adventures of "a fellow who had the most singularly ingenious knack of doing everything the wrong way," but *Rory O'More* (1837), one of the many Irish novels of the Rebellion of 1798, is a far more solid piece of work. W. B. Bernard published a *Life* (H. S. King, 1874). See Lewis Melville, *Victorian Novelists.*

MACHEN, Arthur (De, Secker), b. 1863, son of a Welsh clergyman, presents one of the most remarkable examples of sustained devotion to creative work in literary history. In forty-two years of unremitting toil he produced eighteen books which earned him a total of £635. Industriously "boomed" in the twenties, he came into a brief period of something approaching popularity—Secker brought out the limited Caerlon Edition in 1923—but this seems now largely to have disappeared. Machen is a devotee of the mystic contemplation which induces ecstasy; he seeks to bridge "the world of sense and the world of spirit"; and to him no book is great unless it embodies "the eternal quest of the unknown." Though an ardent Churchman, he is much preoccupied with diabolism; cf. especially *The House of Souls* (1906), where he reveals a gift for breathless narrative to match Le Fanu's. This is lacking in the book generally regarded as his masterpiece, *The Hill of Dreams* (1907), the story of a Welsh boy, not unlike Machen himself, whom not even his hard-won citizenship in the world beyond phenomena could save from making shipwreck of his life. In 1914 the short story, "The Bowmen," became the source of the legend of the Angels of Mons. Other works by Machen in the fiction field include *The Three Impostors* (1895), *The Great Return* (1915), *The Terror* (1917), *The Shining Pyramid* (1923). Machen has written his autobiography in *Far Off Things* (1922) and *Things Near and Far* (1923); in *Hieroglyphics* (1902), he described his values in literature. There is no adequate study, but see Vincent Starrett, *Buried Caesars* (Washington Book Company, 1923); R. Ellis Roberts, *SR,* XXXII (1924), 353-356; and Robert Hillyer's reviews in *NY Times Book Review,* Nov. 5, 1922, p. 6, and March 4, 1923, pp. 5, 21.

MACDONALD, George (1824-1905), Scottish mystic, a clergyman who rebelled against Calvinism, is best loved today for his fairy-tales, *At the Back of the North Wind* (1871) and *The Princess and the Goblin* (1872). But there is more of the real MacDonald in the less conventional *Phantastes* (1858) (EL), which so comforted Marjorie Bowen during a difficult period of her life, and *Lilith* (1895). The same religious mysticism apparent in these books informs MacDonald's novels, for he was a follower of Novalis. Perhaps the most important novel is *Robert Falconer* (1868), whose hero fights the same fight against constricting and insensitive creedalism which MacDonald himself had waged. *Sir Gibbie* (1879) (EL) is the Fool in Christ. See also *David*

Elginbrod (1863), *The Portent* (1864), *Alec Forbes of Howglen* (1865), and *Annals of a Quiet Neighborhood* (1867). There is a biography by Greville MacDonald, *GMD and His Wife* (Allen & Unwin, 1924), and an excellent essay by K. N. Colville, *Fame's Twilight* (Philip Allan, 1923).

MACLAREN, Ian. See CROCKETT, S. R.

MALLOCK, W[illiam] H[urrell] (1849-1923), wrote nine novels dedicated to the same defense of religion against scientific materialism, and of society against the Socialist Radicalism which is the ally of materialism, that is found in his essays and studies. The first two fictions are the best known. *The New Republic* (1877), which is a book of talk, constructed on the same plan as Peacock's country-house novels, presents many famous Victorian writers under thin disguises. *The New Paul and Virginia* (1878) is in the manner of Voltaire's *Candide*. With much flamboyance, Mallock was still an intelligent defender of established values in a changing age. He had some influence on H. G. Wells. See Amy B. Adams, *The Novels of WHM, University of Maine Studies,* Second Series, No. 30, 1934.

MANNING, Anne (1807-1879), a scholarly woman, the author of many novels, is best known today for *The Maiden and Married Life of Mary Powell* (1849), *Deborah's Diary* (1859), and *The Household of Sir Thomas More* (1851) (all EL). These are the imaginary journals, respectively, of Milton's first wife, of his daughter, and of More's daughter, Margaret Roper. They are beautiful works of art—brief, un-Victorian, appealing in content, and highly successful in form. *Cherry and Violet, A Tale of the Plague* (1853) is likewise a beautiful book. See Charlotte M. Yonge, in *Women Novelists of Queen Victoria's Reign* (Hurst & Blackett, 1897).

MARTINEAU, Harriet (1802-1876), propagandist and political economist, wrote fiction to inculcate the principles of the Manchester School. *Deerbrook* (1839) and *The Hour and the Man* (1841), which is the story of Toussaint L'Ouverture, are novels; but the tales collected under such formidable titles as *Illustrations of Political Economy* (1832-1834) and *Poor Laws and Paupers Illustrated* (1833) are more characteristic. The continued popularity of such stories as "Feats on the Fiord" (from *The Playfellow,* 1841) suggests a comparison with Maria Edgeworth. See the biography by Theodora Bosanquet (Etchells & Macdonald, 1927).

MAUGHAM, W[illiam] Somerset (DD), b. 1874, is perhaps the outstanding contemporary British novelist in the naturalistic tradition. He is prolific both in fiction and in drama, but his serious reputation rests essentially upon *Of Human Bondage* (1915), which is generally considered the best of the frank, unsentimental autobiographical novels which followed *The Way of All Flesh*. Among the most important of his other fictions are *Liza of Lambeth* (1897), a slum story, which suggests comparisons with Gissing and with such writers as Arthur Morrison (*Tales of Mean Streets,* 1894), William Pett Ridge, Edwin Pugh, and Israel Zangwill (*Children of the Ghetto,* 1892); *The Moon and Sixpence* (1919), whose hero is an Englished Gauguin; *The Painted Veil* (1925), which has a Chinese setting, and which inspired the cruel bon-mot—"Too much paint and too little veil"; and *The Narrow Corner* (1932), a tragedy in a Malay setting. *The Circle* (1921) and *The Letter* (1925) were great stage successes; greater still was *Rain,* the play made by John Colton and Clemence Randolph, from a South Seas story in *The Trembling of a Leaf* (1921). Maugham has much culture, competence, and urbanity; but he has no poetry, no philosophy, and little imagination; and like all materialists he finds no significance in life. Richard Cordell has published a careful analysis of his work (N, 1937), and Maugham himself has achieved a disarmingly honest self-evaluation in *The Summing-Up* (1938). See Theodore Spencer, *College English,* II (1940), 1-10.

Merriman, Henry Seton, pseud. Hugh Stowell Scott (1862-1903), whose carefully wrought books show the influence of French literary ideals, attempted a more psychological type of historical romance than his contemporaries, Haggard and Hope. Among his best-known titles are *With Edged Tools* (1894), *The Sowers* (1896), *In Kedar's Tents* (1897). See M. Elwin, *Old Gods Falling.*

Morgan, Lady (Sydney Owenson) (1776-1859), was an actor's daughter, who became a great figure in the salons of Dublin, London, and Paris, and long used fiction to exploit both Ireland's charm and Ireland's wrongs. *The Wild Irish Girl* (1806), her first considerable success, owed its vogue as much to its fervent patriotism and its use of the then fresh materials of old-time Irish glories as to its almost hysterical romanticism. *The O'Briens and O'Flahertys* (1827) is probably the best of Lady Morgan's nationalistic books. See the biography by Lionel Stevenson, *The Wild Irish Girl* (Chapman and Hall, 1936); H. S. Krans, *Irish Life in Irish Fiction.*

Morier, James Justinian (1780-1849), a British diplomat born in Smyrna, wrote a vast Persian farce-comedy on the *Gil Blas* pattern, called *The Adventures of Hajji Baba of Ispahan* (1824). It had several close contemporaries of similar character, notably Thomas Hope's *Anastasius* (1819), which has a villain-hero, much given to remorseful, Byronic self-analysis, and Edward John Trelawny's brutal, and probably autobiographical, *Adventures of a Younger Son* (1831). But Morier's work is more entertaining than that of the others, and it has outlived them all. It may also be compared with a much later work, *Saïd the Fisherman* (1903), the most important novel of the Orientalist, Marmaduke Pickthall (1875-1936). Morier wrote other novels, in one of which he brought his Persian hero to England. See Scott's introduction to the EL edition of *Hajji Baba.*

Mulock, Dinah Maria, Miss Mulock, afterwards Mrs. Craik (1826-1887), a prolific writer of fiction, is now remembered only as the author of *John Halifax, Gentleman* (1856) (EL) and the children's classics, *The Adventures of a Brownie* (1872) and *The Little Lame Prince* (1875). *Halifax* is a "success" story with a strong evangelical cast; few English novels have been more passionately loved, though one must admit that many of its admirers are people who do not care much for fiction in general. Miss Mulock never feared to "speak out": *A Life for a Life* (1859) opposes capital punishment, and *Hannah* (1872) urges lifting the ban on marriage with a deceased wife's sister. See Louisa Parr's memoir, *The Author of John Halifax, Gentleman* (Hurst, 1898) and her briefer study in *Women Novelists of Queen Victoria's Reign.*

O'Faoláin, Sean, b. 1900, is an Irish nationalist, who, being impatient with the limitations of the naturalistic novel, writes of recent Irish history in a manner very different from Liam O'Flaherty (*The Informer,* 1925, etc.). O'Faoláin made his reputation with *A Nest of Simple Folk* (1933); in it and its successors—*Bird Alone* (1936) and *Come Back to Erin* (1940)—he at once reflects revolutionary movements, and enters deeply into the experiences of his people, in nearly all the events of their lives. See his "Plea for a New Type of Novel," *VQR,* X (1934), 189-199, and cf. J. Donald Adams's enthusiastic review of *A Nest of Simple Folk, NY Times Book Review,* Jan. 7, 1934, p. 1.

O'Flaherty, Liam. See O'Faoláin, Sean.

Oliphant, Margaret O. W., born Wilson, known as Mrs. Oliphant (1828-1897), was a saint with all the humanity of the sinners, a strong woman perpetually surrounded by weaklings, who literally wrote her fingers to the bone to provide for her dependents; her life was such a succession of sorrows that even today her *Autobiography* (1899) is a heart-breaking document. Mrs. Oliphant began with stories of her native Scotland—*Passages in the Life of Mistress Margaret Maitland* (1849), *Katie Stewart* (1853), etc. *The Chronicles of Carlingford,* in which she challenges comparison with Trollope's Barchester series, probably constitutes her principal claim to fame; these are *Salem Chapel* (1863) (EL), *The Rector and the Doctor's Family* (1863), *The Perpetual Curate* (1864), *Miss Marjoribanks* (1866), and *Phoebe Junior* (1876).

But her powerful stories of the supernatural, written not for bread but for love, lay very close to her own heart. In *A Beleagured City* (1880), she relates, with Defoe-like verisimilitude, how the dead of Semur compelled the living "to yield their places, which they had not filled aright, to those who knew the meaning of life, being dead"; *A Little Pilgrim in the Unseen* (1882) attempts a tender and audacious picture of heaven; its complement, *The Land of Darkness* (1888), no less audaciously, portrays hell. Mrs. Oliphant's historical and biographical studies are generally considered hack-work, but books like *The Makers of Florence, The Makers of Venice,* and the biographies of Saint Francis of Assisi and Joan of Arc have stubbornly refused to die. There are good papers about Mrs. Oliphant in Isabel C. Clarke's *Six Portraits* and in Stephen Gwynn's *Saints and Scholars* (Butterworth, 1929). Henry James's obituary notice is reprinted in his *Notes on Novelists* (De, 1914).

Ouida, pseud. Marie Louise Ramé, later, by her own fiat, de la Ramée (CW) (1839-1908), was the author whose books the Victorians hid under sofa-pillows. Though her father was French she was reared in a stifling atmosphere of respectability; she lived her later life in Italy, where she died in abject poverty. Ouida was a notorious eccentric, the "lady novelist" of the comic valentine. She began as a protegée of Ainsworth; her first famous novel was *Strathmore* (1865), which was soon followed by the still popular *Under Two Flags* (1867), and later by *Friendship* (1878), *Moths* (1880), *Othmar* (1885), and many others. For all Ouida's fantasticality, her novels fought hypocrisy and championed truth; in a roundabout way she prepared the way for the realists. Her latest biographer, Yvonne ffrench, *Ouida, A Study in Ostentation* (AC, 1938), sees *Pascarel* (1873) as the pioneer study of modern Italy in fiction, with an important influence on d'Annunzio and Norman Douglas; it was followed in kind by *Signa* (1875), *Ariadne* (1877), *A Village Commune* (1881), and *In Maremma* (1882), all of which show keen interest in social conditions. *A Dog of Flanders* (1872) is still a sentimental classic; *Two Little Wooden Shoes* (1874) inspired Mascagni's opera, *Lodoletta.* Some critics, including Quiller-Couch, see Ouida as one of the glories of Victorian literature, but the majority, though no longer much more impressed by her alleged wickedness than by that of Elinor Glyn (*Three Weeks,* 1907), who, in some respects inherited her tradition, are still repelled by her unhealthy exuberance, and by the coarse, undisciplined quality of what they admit was a genuine imagination. Ouida was pacifist and humanitarian; her essays—*Views and Opinions* (1895) and *Critical Opinions* (1900)—show much clear thinking and seeing. See Carl Van Vechten's appreciative essay in *Excavations* (K, 1926), and Malcolm Elwin's unsympathetic account in *Victorian Wallflowers.*

Pater, Walter (1839-1894), anticipated the esthetes of the nineties as early as 1873 when he set forth his conception of life as a fine art at the close of his book on *The Renaissance*. "To burn always with this hard, gem-like flame . . . is success in life." In Pater's single completed novel, *Marius the Epicurean* (1885), one of the great spiritual autobiographies in the form of fiction, the hero, a sensitive young man of Marcus Aurelius's time, keeps always in mind "the purpose of preparing himself towards some possible further revelation some day," and at last gives his life for his friend. This is very different from the coarse-grained sensationalism of *The Picture of Dorian Gray* (1891), by the literary leader of the fin de siècle esthetes, Oscar Wilde (1856-1900). *Dorian Gray* was written under the influence of Huysmans and Balzac, and borrows from Wilde's great uncle, C. R. Maturin, the magic portrait which reflects every change in the original as he wastes his life.

Phillpotts, Eden (M), b. 1862, made his first outstanding success in *Lying Prophets* (1897), in which "the woman pays" against a background of religious fanaticism in picturesque Cornwall. But the larger number of his more notable novels—*Children of the Mist* (1898), *The River* (1902), *The Secret Woman* (1905), *The Whirlwind* (1907), *The Mother* (1908), etc.—are loosely-woven chronicles of Dartmoor, in which close observation of the folk is apparent, beside a very free use of the traditional machinery inherited from earlier novelists; these books have sometimes caused Phillpotts to be thought of as the Hardy of Devon. Among his more than 150 titles, the reader will also find many mystery stories, of which the trilogy comprising *Bred in the Bone* (1932), *Witch's Caldroun* (1933), and *A Shadow Passes* (1933) is the most important; a series of fairy stories on classical or medieval themes—*Evander* (1919), *The Lavender Dragon* (1923), *Arachne* (1927), etc.; the "Human Boy" stories—*The Complete Human Boy* (1930); and many other types. See F. T. Cooper, *Some English Story-Tellers* and Helen and Wilson Follett, *Some Modern Novelists* (Ht, 1918).

Pickthall, Marmaduke. See Morier, J. J.

Preedy, George R. See Bowen, Marjorie.

Reid, Forrest, b. 1876, is one of the outstanding individualists among contemporary British novelists, and, in America at least, one of the most unjustly neglected. Mr. Reid is an Irishman who has kept free of Irish "movements" to devote his energies to the expression of his personal vision of reality. He writes of nature, of animals, of friendship, and, above all, of sensitive, not quite "normal," boys; his interest, he confesses, always tends to flag at the point where the boy begins to turn man. As is the case with his close friend, Walter de la Mare, there is something of the supernatural in his books, but this is "only because that was inseparable from my conception of reality." Reid looks at nature essentially from the animist's point of view; he believes that human beings can love only the good, but he takes Greeks rather than Christians as his guides back to the "friendly and benevolent" world he is sure he must once have known, and to which he desires to return. His literary masters have been Pater, d'Annunzio, James, and France. *The Garden God* (1906), which shocked and alienated James, was an attempt to create a whole novel in the mood of Pater's "The Child in the House"; in *The Bracknels* (1911), on the other hand, the story of an Irish family is developed around the idyll of the moon-worshiping boy who kills himself at last because the revelation of the world's evil is too much for him to bear. This was Mr. Reid's first important book; it "came" to him "out of a mysterious region of 'other' reality." Much later, *Uncle Stephen* (1931), which suggests J. W. Dunne's "Serial Time," came similarly, as did also *The Retreat* (1936); both, in fact, had their origin in dreams. *Peter Waring* (1937), which is as close to the conventional autobiographical novel as Reid can come, reworks the earlier *Following Darkness* (1912). Other titles include *At the Door of the Gate* (1915), *The Spring Song* (1916), *Pirates of the Spring* (1920), *Pender Among the Residents* (1922), and *Brian Westby* (1934). A number of Mr. Reid's short stories have been reprinted in *Retrospective Adventures* (1941). He has published two volumes of autobiography—*Apostate* (1926) and *Private Road* (1940). The latter includes an excellent analysis of his work. Cf. also E. M. Forster, *Abinger Harvest* (HB, 1936).

RICE, James. See BESANT, Sir Walter.

RICHARDSON, Henry Handel (i.e., Henrietta) (Norton), b. ? , is the author of *The Fortunes of Richard Mahony,* a trilogy comprising *Australia Felix* (1917), *The Way Home* (1925), and *Ultima Thule* (1929). She wrote it because earlier novels of Australia had all been stories of adventure, devoted to the exploits of those who succeeded in the new country; she wanted, instead, to tell the story of a man who failed. Miss Richardson's technique is old-fashioned, her manner uncompromising; her allegiance is to an honest, straightforward realism. Though her work was published under every conceivable disadvantage it has made its way until it is now generally regarded as the most distinguished of Australian novels. Its success has redirected attention to an earlier book of Miss Richardson's, *Maurice Guest* (1908), also a tragedy, which recreated the Leipsig musical milieu of which the author was a part as a young girl. See her "Some Notes on My Books," *VQR,* XVI (1940), 334-347.

Rutherford, Mark, pseud. William Hale White (OUP) (1831-1913), who has affinities with Gissing and with *Robert Elsmere,* is the outstanding novelist of the spiritual struggle of sensitive men in a world of unimaginative provincial Nonconformity. These struggles he presents as inevitable but useless; Mark Rutherford (*The Autobiography of Mark Rutherford,* 1881, and *Mark Rutherford's Deliverance,* 1885), the hero whose experience is closest to White's own, finds his solution, if it can be called that, in terms borrowed from Job and Ecclesiastes: the ways of God are past finding out, but man can enjoy life if he will gratefully accept the blessings which have been prepared for him and not concern himself with matters which are too high for him. *The Revolution in Tanner's Lane* (1887) includes a picture of the depression which followed Waterloo. *Catherine Furze* (1893) and *Clara Hopgood* (1896) deal with emotional problems. White has a gift for characterization if not for structure, and his books are necessary to the understanding of one phase of the intellectual struggle through which the modern world was born. See A. E. Taylor, *E&S,* V, 1914.

Sabatini, Rafael (HM), was born in Italy in 1875, the son of John McCormack's famous singing teacher. He was importantly influenced by the American novelist, Mary Johnston. Though Sabatini began as early as 1904 with *The Tavern Knight,* it was not until the sensational American success of his novel of the French Revolution, *Scaramouche* (1921), that Sabatini came into his own. Among the best of his many novels are *The Sea Hawk* (1915); *Captain Blood* (1922); *The King's Minion* (1930), which deals with the Overbury scandal—(cf. *My Tattered Loving* [1937], by George R. Preedy); *The Lost King* (1937)—(Louis XVII of France); and *Columbus* (1941). Sabatini's Latin blood shows in his special fondness for the intriguer-hero. He carried the banner of the sword-and-cloak romance triumphantly straight through the futilitarian era. A careful and intelligent workman, with a hearty scorn of many contemporary vagaries, Sabatini has set forth the creed on which his novels are based in his "Historical Fiction" in Dale Warren's *What Is a Book?* (HM, 1935).

Schreiner, Olive (1855-1920), author of *The Story of an African Farm* (1883), was essentially a crusader. She crusaded against war and British exploitation of the Boers in *Trooper Peter Halket* (1897); against the God of her German missionary-father and her mother's Hebrew ancestors; above all, against the unfair discriminations suffered by women. Yet, says Forrest Reid, "The Woman's Rights novel, the Religious Doubts novel, the Sex novel—seeds of all these were wafted from her farm in Africa." Olive Schreiner refused to follow up her great success; she had larger fish to fry. *Dreams* (1891) and *Dream Life and Real Life*

(1893) are tales with a strong allegorical cast; the fearfully rebellious *Undine* (1928) is a piece of juvenilia. Olive Schreiner's husband, S. G. Crownright-Schreiner wrote her *Life* (Unwin, 1924). See Margaret Lawrence's essay in *The School of Femininity* (St, 1936).

SHEARING, Joseph. See BOWEN, Marjorie.

SHORTHOUSE, Joseph Henry (1834-1903), is famous as the author of *John Ingelsant* (1880) (M), which if not, indeed, "the one great religious novel of the English language" (More), is something better yet—one of the most beautiful novels in all literature. Shorthouse was a literary amateur, a Birmingham manufacturer of chemicals, who took both his devotion to Plato and his inherited Quaker faith in the Inner Light with him when he entered the Anglican Church. The scene of *John Ingelsant* is the seventeenth century, and Hobbes, Crashaw, Nicholas Ferrar, and others are among its characters. But it is not really an historical novel, for the author's real preoccupation (standing in the wake of Tractarianism but not identifying himself with any party) was the spiritual problem of his own time. Shorthouse's other novels—*The Little Schoolmaster Mark* (1883-4), *Sir Percival* (1886), *The Countess Eve* (1888), and *Blanche, Lady Falaise* (1891)—have now fallen into desuetude, but they are all filled with the mystic beauty which was the natural result of their author's conviction that "all history is nothing but the relation of . . . the struggle of the divine principle to enter into human life." Shorthouse's *Life and Letters* appeared posthumously, edited by his wife (M, 1905). The most elaborate study is Meijer Polak's *The Historical, Philosophical, and Religious Aspects of "John Ingelsant"* (Purmerend, Holland: J. Muusses, 1933), which makes much too much of his borrowings. See also Joseph E. Baker, *The Novel and the Oxford Movement* (PUP, 1932), and Paul Elmer More's paper in *Shelburne Essays,* III.

SINCLAIR, May (M), b. ? , published her first novel in 1897, her twenty-fourth just a generation afterwards. She is interested in the family-group and in the relationship of the individual to it, and she is an adept in ferreting out the hidden depths of monstrous selfishness in "good" parents and in "nice" people generally; thus the wronged wife of *The Helpmate* (1907) is told bluntly that while her husband has kept all his marriage vows except one, she herself has broken all except one. Miss Sinclair declares war on the Victorian virtue of self-sacrifice; Harriet Frean (*The Life and Death of Harriet Frean,* 1922), accomplished nothing except to make everybody thoroughly miserable when, because she had been brought up to behave beautifully, she refused to marry her friend's fiancé. Miss Sinclair's work shows many influences. Her attitude toward the family suggests Butler and Shaw; Freud seems both reflected and anticipated. *The Three Sisters* (1914) reminds us that she had recently been engaged in studying the Brontës; *The Belfry* (1916), which used her own war experiences, also testifies to her interest in H. G. Wells; the famous *Mary Olivier* (1919) adapts the method of Dorothy Richardson; both *Mr. Waddington of Wyck* (1921) and *A Cure of Souls* (1924) recall Meredith's *Egoist*. Though both hard-headed and much preoccupied with sex, Miss Sinclair is not sordid; she has written two books on philosophical idealism. Her first great success was *The Divine Fire* (1904), which is at once a picture of literary life in London and a study in soul-making. Jean de Bosschere has an enthusiastic appreciation, "Charity in the Work of MS," *YR*, XIV (1924), 82-94; see also the chapters in Cooper, *Some English Story Tellers*, and in Burrell and Brewster, *Modern Fiction* (ColUP, 1934).

Stephens, James (M), b. 1882, who is said by those who know him to resemble a leprechaun, is distinguished as poet and story-teller alike. In *Irish Fairy Tales* (1920), *Deirdre* (1923), and *In the Land of Youth* (1924), he retells ancient Celtic stories, but in *The Charwoman's Daughter* (*Mary, Mary*) (1912) and *The Demi-Gods* (1914), he straddles the borderland of two worlds and keeps one foot in either. This may be said also, if anything can be said that is not misleading about an absolutely indescribable book, of *The Crock of Gold* (1912), an insouciant fairy-tale and a learned treatise, a book in which many moods and many kinds of material are blended with fine recklessness and complete harmony.

Strong, L[eonard] A[lfred] G[eorge] (K,M,L), b. 1896, is half-Irish, half-English. He has written of Dublin and its environs (*The Garden*, 1931; *Sea Wall*, 1933; *The Bay*, 1941); once he set his scene in a boy's school near Oxford (*The Last Enemy*, 1936). But it is more characteristic of him to take his readers to distant places: to Dartmoor, in *Dewer Rides* (1929); to the Scottish Highlands, in *The Jealous Ghost* (1930) and *The Brothers* (1932); to a peninsula off the west coast of Scotland, in that glorious romance, *The Seven Arms* (1935); to an island west of Ireland in *The Open Sky* (1939). When one compares Strong with Hardy and Conrad, one is not saying that he is so great as they. He leaves many loose ends lying about; he sometimes fails to define his theme; his characters do not always match his atmosphere. (He once confessed that he sees his novels first in terms of landscape.) But he is like Hardy and Conrad in his attitude, in his penchant for fresh, sometimes exotic, materials, and in the strange quality of excitement inseparable from his work; whatever else men may be in Strong's novels, they are never mannikins in store clothes. Among his special interests are boys; folklore, superstitions, and the supernatural; and illness, which he knows intimately at first hand. *Corporal Tune* (1934), his most "inward" book, is the odyssey of a man's soul on its way to death. Strong has written three volumes of short stories, fiction for children, poems, essays, and biographies of Tom Moore and John McCormack. See R. L. Mégroz, *Five Novelist-Poets of To-day* (Joiner & Steele, 1933).

TRELAWNY, E. J. See MORIER, J. J.

WALPOLE, Hugh (DD) (1884-1941), was probably the most successful romantic novelist of his time. Among his nearly forty novels, we may distinguish: (1) *The Herries Chronicle* (*Rogue Herries,* 1930; *Judith Paris,* 1931; *The Fortress,* 1932; *Vanessa,* 1933), to which he later added an Elizabethan prelude, *The Bright Pavilions* (1940), which introduces Mary Queen of Scots; the tetralogy proper tells the story of an English family of the Lake District from 1745 to the present day, as a part of the history of England; (2) the Cathedral, or Provincial, Novels (*The Cathedral,* 1922; *The Old Ladies,* 1924; *Harmer John,* 1926; *The Inquisitor,* 1935), which are Trollope plus symbolism; (3) a series of terror-tales, which includes *Portrait of a Man with Red Hair* (1925); *Above the Dark Tumult* (1931); *A Prayer for My Son* (1936); *The Sea Tower* (1939); and *The Killer and the Slain* (1942); (4) two books which came out of Walpole's Red Cross service in Russia during the First World War—*The Dark Forest* (1916) and *The Secret City* (1919); (5) a number of books about boys and children, including *The Golden Scarecrow* (1915), *Jeremy* (1919), *Jeremy and Hamlet* (1923), and *Jeremy at Crale* (1927). Other well-known titles are *Fortitude* (1913); *The Duchess of Wrexe* (1914); *The Captives* (1920); *Wintersmoon* (1928); and *Hans Frost* (1929). Walpole had the fecundity, though perhaps not the intensity—and certainly not the style—of the great novelist. Much of his work must be rejected by those who insist on applying to the novel the strict criteria of serious art; viewing the matter from a more humanistic standpoint, one finds it difficult to reject him without also rejecting much that is of great value in the life of his people and in the tradition of the English novel. Marguerite Steen's *HW, A Study* (DD, 1933) is not accomplished criticism but it serves as a useful survey of his books; his own *Roman Fountain* (1940) has autobiographical passages.

WARD, Robert Plumer (1765-1846), a distinguished politician and jurist, used the novel to work out moral equations. *Tremaine* (1825) presents a rich young man suffering from ennui who finds his bearings through lengthy discussions, theological and otherwise, with a wise clergyman; *De Vere* (1827) is one of the early political novels. Ward had some influence on both Bulwer and Disraeli. See M. W. Rosa, *The Silver Fork School.*

Warner, Rex (K), b. 1905, is the leading English disciple of the Czecho-Jewish novelist, Franz Kafka (1883-1924), author of *The Castle* (see Max Lerner, *SRL*, XXIV, June 7, 1941, pp. 3-4, 16-17); his principal native association (he is also a poet) has been with Auden, Lewis, and Spender. "I should like to see the characters of the novel invested with the kind of poetic quality that makes them, in their own way, more, not less, impressive than the characters of everyday life. I should like to see the epic and allegorical qualities in the place of the photographic methods which now seem to be popular." This ideal Mr. Warner has tried to attain in *The Wild Goose Chase* (1937), which begins with the ancient fairy tale situation of the three brothers who set out on a quest. The development is complicated somewhat by the author's sympathy with Communism. A second novel, *The Professor* (1939), is less daring in its departures. With Rex Warner it is interesting to compare the French novelist, Robert Francis, part of whose work has been translated as *The Wolf at the Door* (HM, 1935).

Warren, Samuel (1807-1877), used his medical training for *Passages from the Diary of a Late Physician* (1832-1838) (R) and his experiences as a distinguished lawyer for *Ten Thousand a Year* (1841) (Sweet & Maxwell), the story of a draper's assistant, Tittlebat Titmouse, who comes into an estate through the machinations of a pair of Dodson and Foggs, misbehaves scandalously, is finally proved illegitimate, and lands in the asylum. This book has had a longer life than its merits would seem to warrant. Warren claimed to be describing real life as a guide to righteous conduct, but his development is coarse and sensational, and in the medical book he is somewhat sadistic.

Webb, Mary, née Gladys Mary Meredith (Du) (1883-1927), a gnome-like little woman with a goiter, died in poverty—she eked out her income by selling flowers in Shrewsbury market—then, puffed by Stanley Baldwin, Barrie, John Buchan, and others, came posthumously to a considerable vogue. *Precious Bane* (1924) is her most famous novel, though many prefer *Gone to Earth* (1917); the others are *The Golden Arrow* (1916), *The House in Dormer Forest* (1920), *Seven for a Secret* (1922), and *Armour Wherein He Trusted* (1929). To her admirers Mary Webb is the Hardy of Shropshire, but Hardy is by no means the only writer she echoes. Her nature mysticism has much charm, she has a variety of fascinating folk-material, and her attitude toward life is passionate and earnest. But her mastery of the technique of fiction leaves much to be desired, and there is a deliberate artfulness—and even, at times, an archness—about her presentation which repels some readers. Thomas Moult, *MW, Her Life and Work* (Ca, 1932) is the authoritative interpretation; A. Edward Newton's slight essay in *End Papers* (LB, 1933) has some valuable material.

WEYMAN, Stanley J. (1855-1928), is known for his revival of the Dumas school of romance in *A Gentleman of France* (1893) and *Under the Red Robe* (1894), but he wrote of many periods and always showed intimate knowledge of the life he portrayed. His own favorite book was *Chippinge* (1906), which concerns England at the time of the Reform Bill. See M. Elwin, *Old Gods Falling.*

WHYTE-MELVILLE, George James (1821-1878), succeeded Surtees as the novelist of the hunt but was always more "regular" in his attitude toward it. Besides his hunting novels—*Captain Digby Grand* (1853), *Market Harborough* (1861), etc.—he wrote such historical romances as *Holmby House* (1860), *The Queen's Maries* (1862), and *Katerfelto* (1875), which is said to be as popular in the Exmoor country as *Lorna Doone.* Bulwer's influence is seen in *The Gladiators* (1863) (EL) and *Sarchedon* (1871), which go as far afield, respectively, as Rome and Palestine in the days of Vitellius and Titus, and Egypt and Assyria under Semiramis. *The Interpreter* (1858) came out of the author's service in the Crimean War. The devotion of the Forsytes, and of Galsworthy himself in his unregenerate days, testifies to Whyte-Melville's long popularity with old-fashioned English gentlemen, whose life is nostalgically evoked in Sir John Fortescue's essay on him in *The Eighteen-Sixties,* ed. John Drinkwater (CUP, 1932). See also the essays by Lewis Melville, in *Victorian Novelists,* and by S. M. Ellis, in *Mainly Victorian.*

WILDE, Oscar. See PATER, Walter.

WOOD, Mrs. Henry, née Ellen Price (M, Collins) (1814-1887), proprietor of *The Argosy,* was one of Wilkie Collins's most successful followers in the field of domestic sensation fiction. A pretty invalid, she began by contributing her tales gratis to Ainsworth's magazines, for the mere love of story-telling, and did not turn to the systematic exploitation of her talent until after her husband had suffered financial disaster. Her first novel, *Danesbury House* (1860) was written as propaganda for the Scottish Temperance League. Though *The Channings* (1862) is still in EL, the only book by which Mrs. Wood is now widely known to the general public is *East Lynne* (1861), a work which has created prosperity for publishers, actors, and theater-managers through more than two generations. Among the best of her many other novels are *Mrs. Halliburton's Troubles* (1862), *Verner's Pride* (1863), *The Shadow of Ashlydyat* (1863), *Lord Oakburn's Daughters* (1864), *Roland Yorke* (1869), and *Dene Hollow* (1871). Lovers of sensation fiction could always read Mrs. Wood in serene confidence that their sense of propriety would never be outraged. Charles W. Wood published a fulsome *Memorials of Mrs. HW* (Bentley, 1894). See M. Elwin, *Victorian Wallflowers.*

YONGE, Charlotte M. (1823-1901), spiritual and literary godchild of John Keble, author of *The Christian Year,* was the great Church of England novelist in Victorian times. But the feeling that *The Heir of Redclyffe* (1853) (EL) was one of the best novels ever written was not confined to Anglican churchmen; the book was adored with equal fervor by leading Pre-Raphaelites and by the soldiers in the Crimea. Miss Yonge published more than 150 books, her novels being mainly stories of English domestic life or historical romances. In the latter field, her most famous book is probably *The Dove in the Eagle's Nest* (1866) (EL), which has a German background; *The Caged Lion* (1870) concerns James I of Scotland—cf. Evan John, *Crippled Splendour* (1938); *Unknown to History* (1882) introduces Mary Queen of Scots. Other well-known books by Miss Yonge include *Heartsease* (1854); *The Daisy Chain* (1856), whose plain heroine made almost as great an appeal as the hero of *Redclyffe; The Trial* (1864), a sequel to *The Daisy Chain; Dynevor Terrace* (1857); and *The Clever Woman of the Family* (1865). Christabel Coleridge (M, 1903) has the authorized biography. There is a recent brief study by Sarah Bailey, *Cornhill,* CL (1934), 188-198. Charlotte Yonge also plays her part in E. M. Delafield's *Ladies and Gentlemen in Victorian Fiction* (H, 1937), which includes many extracts from her books.

SELECTED BIBLIOGRAPHY WITH ANNOTATIONS

A man will often turn over a whole library to make one book.

DR. JOHNSON.

This section pretends to no bibliographical erudition. It has but one aim—to aid the reader who wishes to know more about any of the authors treated in this book than I have been able to tell him. Books and articles in foreign languages have been included only when of outstanding importance.

British books are generally cited in American editions, when such have been issued. It should be remembered, however, that a book may be in print in one country and out of print in the other.

Important sources of this bibliography are *The Cambridge Bibliography of English Literature,* ed. F. W. Bateson, 4 vols. (Macmillan, 1941); *The United States Catalogue* and *Cumulative Book Index; The Reference Catalogue of Current Literature; Essay and General Literature Index* with Supplements; the *Readers' Guide to Periodical Literature,* the *Supplement* to the *Readers' Guide,* and the *International Index to Periodicals;* the *Annual Bibliographies* of the Modern Humanities Research Association, and the Annual Bibliographies in *PMLA;* Edith Batho and Bonamy Dobrée, *The Victorians and After* (McBride, 1938); Edwin Muir, *The Present Age from 1914* (McBride, 1940); Fred B. Millett, *Contemporary British Literature* (Harcourt, 1939). See also E. A. Baker and James Packman, *A Guide to the Best Fiction,* revised ed. (Macmillan, 1932); Elbert Lenrow, *Reader's Guide to Prose Fiction* (Appleton-Century, 1940).

To save space the following rules will be followed:

1. Works to which adequate reference has already been made in footnotes to the text are excluded from the following list.

2. When a book is cited more than once, bibliographical information is given only the first time.

3. When the title of a book or article is merely the name of the author with whom it deals, the title is generally omitted; when the author's name is part of a longer title, initials are employed.

4. The abbreviations listed hereinunder are used.

AC	D. Appleton & Co., Century Co., D. Appleton-Century Co.
AM	*Atlantic Monthly*
B(L)	*Bookman* (London)
B(NY)	*Bookman* (New York)
Bl	Basil Blackwell
Bla	*Blackwood's Magazine*
BM	Bobbs-Merrill Co.
C	Jonathan Cape
Ce	*Century Magazine*
CM	Coward-McCann
Co	Constable & Co.
ColUP	Columbia University Press
CoM	*Cornhill Magazine*
CorUP	Cornell University Press
CR	*Contemporary Review*
CUP	Cambridge University Press
CW	Chatto & Windus
DD	Doubleday, Doran & Co. and their predecessors, Doubleday, Page & Co.
De	J. M. Dent & Sons
DM	Dodd, Mead & Co.
Do	Geo. H. Doran Co.
Du	E. P. Dutton & Co.
EAP	*English Association Pamphlets*
EL	Everyman's Library (Du)
ELH	*English Literary History*
ER	*Edinburgh Review*
E&S	*Essays and Studies by Members of the English Association*
FF	Faber & Faber and their predecessors, Faber & Gwyer
Fort	*Fortnightly Review*
FP	Fortune Press
FR	Farrar & Rinehart
FW	Funk & Wagnalls Co.
G	Ginn & Company
H	Harper & Brothers
HaM	*Harper's Magazine*
HB	Harcourt, Brace & Co.
He	William Heinemann
HM	Houghton Mifflin Co.
HS	*Harvard Studies and Notes in Philology and Literature*
Ht	Henry Holt & Co.
Hu	Hutchinson & Co.
HUP	Harvard University Press
H&S	Hodder & Stoughton
ISLL	*Illinois Studies in Language and Literature*
JEGP	*Journal of English and Germanic Philology*
JHP	Johns Hopkins University Press
K	Alfred A. Knopf
L	Longmans, Green & Co.
LA	*Living Age*
LB	Little, Brown & Co.
LM	*London Mercury*
LTLS	*London Times Literary Supplement*
M	The Macmillan Co.
Me	Methuen Publishers
MLN	*Modern Language Notes*
MLR	*Modern Language Review*
MP	*Modern Philology*
N	Thomas Nelson & Sons
NAR	*North American Review*
NQ	*Notes & Queries*
OUP	Oxford University Press
P	G. P. Putnam's Sons
PMLA	*Publications of the Modern Language Association of America*
PQ	*Philological Quarterly*
PUP	Princeton University Press
QR	*Quarterly Review*
R	G. Routledge & Sons, Ltd.
RES	*Review of English Studies*
S	Charles Scribner's Sons
SAQ	*South Atlantic Quarterly*
Sc	Walter Scott
SCS	*Smith College Studies in Modern Languages*
SHP	Shakespeare Head Press
SM	*Scribner's Magazine*
SP	*Studies in Philology*
SPr	Scholartis Press
SR	*Sewanee Review*
SRL	*Saturday Review of Literature*
St	Frederick A. Stokes Co.
UCP	University of Chicago Press
UNCP	University of North Carolina Press
UTSE	*University of Texas Studies in English*
VP	Viking Press
VQR	*Virginia Quarterly Review*
WC	World's Classics (OUP)
XIX C	*Nineteenth Century and After*
YR	*Yale Review*
YSE	*Yale Studies in English*
YUP	Yale University Press

General References

European Backgrounds of English Fiction. J. C. Dunlop, *History of Prose Fiction,* rev. H. Wilson (Bell, 1906); F. M. Warren, *History of the Novel Previous to the Seventeenth Century* (Ht, 1895).

General History of the English Novel. The most elaborate *History of the English Novel* is by Ernest A. Baker, 10 vols. (Witherby, 1924-1939). The most widely used single-volume histories are Wilbur L. Cross, *The Development of the English Novel* (M, 1899) and R. M. Lovett and H. S. Hughes, *The History of the Novel in England* (HM, 1932). See also Walter Raleigh, *The English Novel* (S, 1894), which stops with Scott; George Saintsbury, *The English Novel* (Du, 1913); Cornelius Weygandt, *A Century of the English Novel* (AC, 1925); Pelham Edgar, *The Art of the Novel* (M, 1933). Sir Walter Scott's *Lives of the Novelists* (EL edition, 1910) treats most of the important eighteenth-century novelists. Derek Verschoyle's *The English Novelists* (HB, 1936) is a symposium constituting "A Survey of the Novel by Twenty Contemporary Novelists."

Four books by Amy Cruse constitute a delightful approach to English literature (including fiction) from the point of view of the readers' interests: *The Shaping of English Literature* (Crowell, 1927), *The Englishman and His Books in the Early Nineteenth Century* (Crowell, 1930), *The Victorians and Their Reading* (HM, 1935), *After the Victorians* (Allen & Unwin, 1938). Lord Ernle's *The Light Reading of Our Ancestors* (Brentano's, 1927) offers delightful comment on the older English novels. *Pamela's Daughters,* by R. P. Utter and G. B. Needham (M, 1936), a study of the heroines of English fiction, is one of the most entertaining books ever written about English literature. R. N. Whiteford, *Motives in English Fiction* (P, 1918), though sometimes uncritical, is remarkable from the point of view of tracing themes and attitudes. Annette B. Hopkins and Helen S. Hughes, *The English Novel Before the Nineteenth Century* (G, 1915) is an anthology of selections from standard novels.

Technique of Fiction. In America the two best-known manuals are Bliss Perry, *A Study of Prose Fiction,* rev. ed. (HM, 1920) and Clayton Hamilton, *The Art of Fiction,* rev. ed. (DD, 1939). Cf. also Wilson Follett, *The Modern Novel* (K, 1918); Percy Lubbock, *The Craft of Fiction* (S, 1921); E. M. Forster, *Aspects of the Novel* (HB, 1927); Van Meter Ames, *Aesthetics of the Novel* (UCP, 1928); Carl H. Grabo, *Technique of the Novel* (S, 1928); Edwin Muir, *The Structure of the Novel* (Hogarth Press, 1928); John Carruthers, *Scheherazade, or The Future of the English Novel* (Du, 1928).

For early theories of fiction in England, cf. A. J. Tieje, "The Critical Heritage of Fiction in 1579," *Englische Studien,* XLVII (1913), 415-448, "The Expressed Aim of the Long Prose Fiction from 1579 to 1740," *JEGP,* XI (1912), 402-432, *The Theory of Characterization in Prose Fiction Prior to 1740, University of Minnesota Studies in Language and Literature,* No. 5, 1916, and "A Peculiar Phase of the Theory of Realism in Pre-Richardsonian Fiction," *PMLA,* XXVIII (1913), 213-252; Joseph B. Heidler, *The History from 1700 to 1800 of English Prose Fiction, ISLL,* Vol. XIII, No. 2, 1928; W. F. Gallaway, Jr., "The Conservative Attitude Toward Fiction, 1770-1830," *PMLA,* LV (1940), 1041-1059.

The Victorian Novel. *The Great Victorians,* ed. H. J. and Hugh Massingham (DD, 1932), includes studies of a number of Victorian novelists. Lord David Cecil, *Early Victorian Novelists* (BM, 1935) deals brilliantly with Dickens, Thackeray, the Brontës, Mrs. Gaskell, Trollope, and George Eliot; several of these are also considered by Sir Arthur Quiller-Couch, *Charles Dickens and Other Victorians* (CUP, 1925) and by Frederic Harrison, *Studies in Early Victorian Literature* (Arnold, 1895). S. M. Ellis, *Mainly Victorian* (Hu, 1925), like Lewis Melville, *Victorian Novelists* (Co, 1906) is an extensive miscellany; Malcolm Elwin, *Victorian Wallflowers* (C, 1934) concerns the minor writers. The women writers are studied in *Women Novelists of Queen Victoria's Reign,* a compilation (Hurst & Blackett, 1897), H. H. Bonnell, *Charlotte Brontë, George Eliot, Jane Austen* (L, 1902), Marjory A. Bald, *Women Writers of the Nineteenth Century* (CUP, 1923), Muriel Masefield, *Women Writers from Fanny Burney to George Eliot* (Ivor Nicholson & Watson, 1934). Important ideas concerning the backgrounds of the Victorian novel are presented in Louis Cazamian, *Le roman social en Angleterre, 1830-1850* (Paris, Les Belles-Lettres, 1903); Madeleine L. Cazamian, *Le roman et les idées en Angleterre, L'influence de la science, 1860-1890* (OUP, 1923); John W. Cunliffe, *Leaders of the Victorian Revolution* (AC, 1934); Leo J. Henkin, *Darwinism in the English Novel, 1860-1910* (Brooklyn, The Author, 1940).

The Contemporary Novel. The following books deal with various phases of the recent and contemporary novel: F. T. Cooper, *Some English Story Tellers* (Ht, 1912); Firmin Roz, *Le roman anglais contemporain* (Paris, Hachette, 1912) (Meredith, Hardy, Mrs. Ward, Kipling, Wells); Stuart Sherman, *On Contemporary Literature* (Ht, 1917) (Meredith, Moore, Butler, Bennett, Wells); John Freeman, *The Moderns* (Crowell, 1917) (Conrad, Wells, de la Mare); Helen Thomas Follett and Wilson Follett, *Some Modern Novelists* (Ht, 1918) (Meredith, Hardy, Gissing, De Morgan, Phillpotts, Conrad, Bennett, Galsworthy); Harold Williams, *Modern English Writers* (K, 1919); Douglas Goldring, *Reputations* (Seltzer, 1920) (Gissing, Bennett, Wells, Lawrence, etc.); St. John Ervine, *Some Impressions of My Elders* (Allen & Unwin, 1923) (Moore, Bennett, Wells, Galsworthy); Gerald Gould, *The English Novel of Today* (John Castle, 1924); Abel Chevalley, *The Modern English Novel* (K, 25); Elizabeth A. Drew, *The Modern Novel* (HB, 1926); Edwin Muir, *Transition* (VP, 1926) (Joyce, Lawrence, Woolf, Stephen Hudson, Huxley); Walter L. Myers, *The Later Realism* (UCP, 1927); Bonamy Dobrée, *The Lamp and the Lute* (OUP, 1929) (Hardy, Kipling, Lawrence, Forster); Storm Jameson, *The Georgian Novel and Mr. Robinson* (He, 1929); W. L. Cross, *Four Contemporary Novelists* (M, 1930) (Wells, Bennett, Conrad, Galsworthy); Joseph Warren Beach, *The Twentieth Century Novel* (AC, 1932); J. W. Cunliffe, *English Literature in the Twentieth Century* (M, 1933); *The Post-Victorians,* with an Introduction by W. R. Inge (Ivor Nicholson & Watson, 1933); Dorothy Brewster and Angus Burrell, *Modern Fiction* (ColUP, 1934); Frank Swinnerton, *The Georgian Scene* (FR, 1934); André Maurois, *Prophets and Poets* (H, 1935) (Kipling, Conrad, Wells, Lawrence, Huxley, Katherine Mansfield); H. J. Muller, *Modern Fiction* (FW, 1937); H. V. Routh, *Towards the Twentieth Century* (M, 1937); Ford Madox Ford, *Portraits from Life* (HM, 1937) (W. H. Hudson, Conrad, Lawrence, Hardy, Wells, Galsworthy); Dorothy M. Hoare, *Some Studies in the Modern Novel* (CW, 1938) (Moore, Conrad, Hardy, Forster, Lawrence, Joyce, Mansfield, Woolf); Malcolm Elwin, *Old Gods Falling* (M, 1939); G. U. Ellis, *Twilight on Parnassus* (Michael Joseph, 1939); Granville Hicks, *Figures of Transition* (M, 1939) (Hardy, Moore, Butler, Stevenson); David Daiches, *The Novel and the Modern World* (UCP, 1939) (Galsworthy, Conrad, Mansfield, Joyce, Woolf, Huxley); William C. Frierson, *The English Novel in Transition, 1885-1940* (University of Oklahoma Press, 1942).

MISCELLANIES. The following books contain valuable criticism of novelists not confined to any one period. Each title is followed by a list of the writers treated. George Saintsbury, *Corrected Impressions* (He, 1895) (Dickens, Thackeray, Charlotte Brontë, George Eliot, Trollope); Leslie Stephen, *Studies of a Biographer,* Second Series, Vols. 3-4 (P, 1902) (Vol. 3—Godwin; Vol. 4—Trollope, Stevenson); Paul Elmer More, *Shelburne Essays,* Series 1-11 (HM, 1904-1921) (Series 2—Meredith, Kipling; Series 3—Sterne, Scott, Shorthouse; Series 4—Walpole, Burney; Series 5—Dickens, Gaskell, Gissing; Series 6—Bunyan; Series 8—Beckford; Series 9—Disraeli; Series 10—Mrs. Behn, Swift; Series 11—Mrs. Ward, Butler); Andrew Lang, *Essays in Little* (S, 1907); Leslie Stephen, *Hours in a Library,* 4 vols. (P, 1907) (Vol. 1—Defoe, Richardson, Scott; Vol. 2—Walpole, Disraeli; Vol. 3—Fielding, Kingsley, Charlotte Brontë; Vol. 4—Sterne, George Eliot); Virginia Woolf, *The Common Reader*

(HB, 1925) (Defoe, Edgeworth, Austen, the Brontës, George Eliot, Conrad, "Modern Fiction"); M. P. Willcocks, *Between the Old World and the New* (St, 1926) (Dickens, Thackeray, Trollope, the Brontës, George Eliot, Meredith, Hardy, Butler); Augustus Ralli, *Critiques* (L, 1927) (Austen, the Brontës, Borrow, Hardy); Leonard Woolf, *Essays on Literature, History, and Politics* (HB, 1927) (Stevenson, Moore, Butler, Conrad); Paul Elmer More, *New Shelburne Essays,* Series 1-3 (PUP, 1928-1936) (Series 1—Trollope, Butler; Series 3—Joyce); Edmund Blunden, *Votive Tablets* (H, 1932) (Bunyan, Defoe, Goldsmith, Mackenzie); Virginia Woolf, *The Second Common Reader* (HB, 1932) (Sidney, Defoe, Swift, Sterne, Mary Wollstonecraft, Burney, Meredith, Hardy, Gissing); George Saintsbury, *Prefaces and Essays* (M, 1933) (Swift, Fielding, Smollett, Sterne, Austen, Peacock); Herbert Read, *Collected Essays in Literary Criticism* (FF, 1938) (Swift, Smollett, Sterne, the Brontës); Isabel C. Clarke, *Six Portraits* (Hu, 1935) (Austen, George Eliot, Mrs. Oliphant, John Oliver Hobbes, Katherine Mansfield).

Chapter I: Fiction in Shakespeare's Time

General. Useful collections of Elizabethan fiction will be found in *Shorter Novels, Elizabethan and Jacobean* (EL, Du, 1929), Turner and Turner, *Malory to Mrs. Behn* (N, 1930), Edward J. O'Brien, *Elizabethan Tales* (HM, 1937). Detailed studies of the fiction of the Elizabethan period will be found in J. J. Jusserand, *The English Novel in the Time of Shakespeare* (Unwin, 1890) and Volume II of Baker's *History*. The standard work on the Greek romances is S. L. Woolf, *The Greek Romances in Elizabethan Prose Fiction* (ColUP, 1912); cf. Gamaliel Bradford's essay, "The Novel Two Thousand Years Ago," in *A Naturalist of Souls* (DM, 1917). For rogue stories, cf. F. W. Chandler, *The Literature of Roguery,* 2 vols. (HM, 1907). Louis B. Wright, *Middle-Class Culture in Elizabethan England* (UNCP, 1935) includes some interesting comment on fiction.

Gascoigne and Grange. P. W. Long, "From Troilus to Euphues," *Kittredge Anniversary Studies* (G, 1913); Leicester Bradner, "The First English Novel, A Study of George Gascoigne's *Adventures of Master F.J.,*" *PMLA,* XLV (1930), 543-552; F. T. Bowers, "Notes on Gascoigne's *A Hundreth Sundrie Flowers* and *The Posies,*" *HS,* XVI (1934), 13-35; Hyder E. Rollins, "John Grange's *The Golden Aphroditis,*" same, pp. 177-198. The Gascoigne story, in its revised form, may be read in J. W. Cunliffe's edition of *The Posies* (CUP, 1907).

Lyly. The most elaborate edition of *Euphues* is by M. W. Croll and Harry Clemons (Routledge, 1916). An excellent introduction to the study of Lyly is an article by S. L. Woolf, "The Humanist as Man of Letters: JL," *SR,* XXXI (1923), 8-35. Cf. also J. Dover Wilson (Macmillan and Bowes, 1905). A more elaborate study (in French) is that of A. Feuillerat (CUP, 1910). For Lyly's style, cf. C. G. Child, "JL and Euphuism," *Münchener Beiträge zur romanischen und englischen Philologie,* VII (1894), which includes a history of earlier studies.

SIDNEY. All versions of the *Arcadia* are included in A. Feuillerat's edition of Sidney (CUP, 1912-1926). A recent biography of Sidney is A. H. Bill, *Astrophel* (FR, 1931). Two important studies of Sidney's art are M. S. Goldman, *Sir PS and the Arcadia, ISLL,* XVII, Nos. 1-2, 1934, and K. O. Myrick, *Sir PS as a Literary Craftsman* (HUP, 1935). Both these works include elaborate bibliographies. See, also, Kenneth T. Rowe, "Elizabethan Morality and the Folio Revisions of Sidney's *Arcadia, MP,* XXXVII (1939-1940), 151-172.

NASHE. *The Unfortunate Traveler* may be read in the EL *Shorter Novels.* Cf. F. T. Bowers, "Thomas Nashe and the Picaresque Novel," *Studies in Honor of John Calvin Metcalf* (University of Virginia, 1941).

DELONEY. The standard edition is that of F. O. Mann (OUP, 1912). The most elaborate study is in French—Abel Chevalley (Paris, Gallimard, 1926). For an enthusiastic appreciation, cf. Llewellyn Powys, *VQR,* IX (1933), 578-594.

GREENE. *Pandosto* and *Menaphon* may be read in Greene's *Works* (Huth Library, 1881-1886). Cf. also S. L. Woolf, "RG and the Italian Renaissance," *Englische Studien,* XXXVII (1907), 321-374; J. C. Jordan (CUP, 1915); and Gwyn Jones's absorbing novel, *Garland of Bays* (M, 1938).

LODGE. *Rosalynde* has been edited by E. C. Baldwin (G, 1910). For Lodge, cf. N. B. Paradise, *TL, The History of an Elizabethan* (YUP, 1931); E. A. Tenney, (CorUP, 1935).

Chapter II: The Seventeenth Century

GENERAL. Charlotte E. Morgan, *The Rise of the Novel of Manners* (ColUP, 1911); Franklin P. Rolfe, "On the Bibliography of Seventeenth Century Prose Fiction," *PMLA,* XLIX (1934), 1071-1086; C. E. Miller, "The Influence of the French Heroico-Historical Romance on Seventeenth Century English Prose Fiction," *University of Virginia Abstracts of Dissertations,* 1940, pp. 13-17.

MRS. BEHN. To the material listed on p. 20, add Wylie Sypher, "A Note on the Realism of Mrs. Behn's *Oroonoko,*" *Modern Language Quarterly,* III (1942), 401-405.

John Bunyan. Editions of Bunyan are legion. A volume ed. Edmund Venables (OUP, 1900) contains both parts of *The Pilgrim's Progress* and *Grace Abounding.* There is a CUP edition of *Mr. Badman* and *The Holy War,* 1905. The standard biography is John Brown, *JB, His Life, Times, and Work,* rev. ed. F. M. Harrison (London, Hulbert, 1928). The most valuable of recent books is W. Y. Tindall, *JB, Mechanick Preacher* (ColUP, 1934), where see excellent bibliography. Cf. also Jack Lindsay, *JB, Maker of Myths* (Me, 1937).

Harold Golder has a very important (and highly entertaining) series of articles about Bunyan: "JB's Hypocrisy," *NAR,* CCXXIII (1926), 323-332; "The Chivalric Background of *Pilgrim's Progress," Harvard University Summaries of Theses* (HUP, 1928); "B's Valley of the Shadow," *MP,* XXVII (1929-1930), 55-72; "B and Spenser," *PMLA,* XLV (1930), 216-237; "B's Giant Despair," *JEGP,* XXX (1931), 361-378.

Famous essays about Bunyan by Macaulay and Carlyle may be found in their Collected Works. Other studies worth consulting include J. B. Baillie, "The Mind of JB," *Hibbert Journal,* XXVII (1928-1929), 385-405; Daniel Gibson, Jr., "On the Genesis of *Pilgrim's Progress,"* MP, XXXII (1934-1935), 365-382; Sir Charles Firth, *Essays Historical and Literary* (OUP, 1937); J. W. Mackail, *Studies in Humanism* (L, 1938); C. E. Dugdale, "B's Court Scenes," *UTSE* (1941), 64-78.

Chapter III: Defoe and His Contemporaries

Defoe and Swift. John F. Ross, *S and D, A Study in Relationship* (University of California Press, 1941).

Defoe. A recent, handsome edition of Defoe's *Novels and Selected Writings* is that of SHP, 14 vols. (HM, 1927). The best biography is James Sutherland's (Lippincott, 1938). A more elaborate study is Paul Dottin, *DD et ses Romans,* 3 vols. (OUP, 1924). The biographical volume was translated by Louise Ragan as *The Life and Strange and Surprising Adventures of DD* (Macaulay, 1929), where see further bibliography. A. W. Secord, *Studies in the Narrative Method of Defoe, ISLL,* IX (1924) is the best study of Defoe's art, and the same writer's introduction to his edition of *A Journal of the Plague Year and Other Pieces* (Odyssey Press, 1935) is an excellent starting-place for the study of Defoe. G. D. H. Cole has a good brief account in Bonamy Dobrée (ed.), *From Anne to Victoria* (S, 1937); cf. also Louis Kronenberger, *Kings and Desperate Men* (K, 1942). W. P. Trent's fine chapter in *The Cambridge History of English Literature,* Vol. IX, and his *DD, How to Know Him* (BM, 1916) have long been valued by students. The fullest study of Defoe's Puritanism is Rudolf G. Stamm, *Der aufgeklärte Puritanismus DDs*

(Leipzig & Zurich, M. Niehaus, 1936); Stamm has a briefer consideration of the same subject in English in "DD: An Artist in the Puritan Tradition," *PQ,* XV (1936), 225-246. Cf. J. R. Moore, "D's Religious Sect," *RES,* XVII (1941), 461-467; James Moffatt, "The Religion of Robinson Crusoe," *CR,* CXV (1919), 664-669. Quite in a class by itself is Walter de la Mare's enchanting book, *Desert Islands and Robinson Crusoe* (FF, 1930). For additional studies, cf. R. P. Utter, *Pearls and Pepper* (YUP, 1924); Virginia Harlan, "D's Narrative Style," *JEGP,* XXX (1931), 55-73; H. W. Häusermann, "Aspects of Life and Thought in Robinson Crusoe," *RES,* XI (1935), 299 ff.; G. D. H. Cole, *Persons and Places* (M, 1938); J. R. Moore, *Defoe in the Pillory and Other Studies, Indiana University Publications, Humanities Series,* No. 1 (1939); C. N. Greenough, *Collected Studies* (HUP, 1940); J. R. Moore, "Defoe and Scott," *PMLA,* LVI (1941), 710-735, a paper rich in appreciation of both writers.

THE WOMEN WRITERS. Joyce M. Horner, *The English Women Novelists and Their Connection with the Feminist Movement, 1688-1797, SCS,* XI, Nos. 1, 2, 3 (1929-1930). For Mrs. Manley, cf. two articles by P. B. Anderson, "Mistress Delariviere Manley's Biography," *MP,* XXXIII (1936), 261-278, and "Delariviere Manley's Prose Fiction," *PQ,* XIII (1934), 168-188. Mrs. Haywood has been honored with an elaborate monograph by G. F. Whicher, *The Life and Romances of Mrs. Eliza Haywood* (ColUP, 1915).

SWIFT. The standard book on Swift is now Ricardo Quintana, *The Mind and Art of JS* (OUP, 1936). Cf. also Émile Pons, *S: Les années de jeunesse et le 'Conte de tonneau'* (Les Belles-Lettres, 1925); Carl Van Doren, *Swift* (VP, 1930). Scott's essay in his edition of Swift's Works has often been reprinted, as has Thackeray's in *The English Humorists.*

For the attack on the old view of Swift as cynic and misanthrope and the development of the modern view, cf. Charles Whibley (CUP, 1917) and "Gulliver's Travels," *Bla,* CCXX (1926), 549-560; Ernest Bernbaum, in his ed. of *Gulliver's Travels* (HB, 1920); T. O. Wedel, "On the Philosophical Background of Gulliver's Travels," *SP,* XXIII (1926), 434-450; W. L. Phelps, "A Note on Gulliver," *YR,* XVII (1927), 92-98; Ricardo Quintana, "Recent Discussion of Swift," *College English* II (1940-1941), 11-18; M. D. Clubb, "The Criticism of Gulliver's 'Voyage to the Houhynhmns,' 1726-1914," in *Stanford Studies in Language and Literature* (Stanford University, 1941); F. M. Darnall, "Old Wine in New Bottles," *SAQ,* XLI (1942), 53-63.

The definitive study of "The Political Significance of 'Gulliver's Travels'" is that of Sir Charles Firth, originally in the *Proceedings of the British Academy,* 1919-1920, now reprinted in his *Essays Historical and*

Literary. What Firth did for Swift's politics, Marjorie Nicholson and Nora M. Mohler have done for his science in "The Scientific Background of Swift's Voyage to Laputa," *Annals of Science,* II (1937), 299 334, 405-430. Cf. J. R. Moore, "The Geography of 'Gulliver's Travels,'" *JEGP,* XL (1941), 214-228. Other studies of *Gulliver* are W. A. Eddy, *Gulliver's Travels, A Critical Study* (PUP, 1923), which is the most elaborate work in its field; H. M. Dargan, "The Nature of Allegory as Used by Swift," *SP,* XIII (1916), 159-179; J. B. Moore, "The Role of Gulliver," *MP,* XXV (1928), 469-480; J. R. Moore, "A New Source for Gulliver's Travels," *SP,* XXXVIII (1941), 66-80. Harold Williams edited the text of the first edition of *Gulliver* elaborately for the First Edition Club (1926).

John Hayward's essay on Swift in *From Anne to Victoria* grapples with the fundamental problem of Swift's personality, adequately for its space. See also W. B. C. Watkins, *Perilous Balance* (PUP, 1939); G. Wilson Knight, *The Burning Oracle* (OUP, 1939). Edith Sitwell's novel, *I Live Under a Black Sun* (DD, 1938) puts the life of Swift into a modern setting.

Chapter IV: Psychological Realism Begins: Samuel Richardson

Richardson. Twentieth-century editions include the He edition (1902) and the SHP edition (HM, 1930), each 19 vols. *Pamela* and *Clarissa* are both available in EL. *Familiar Letters* has been reprinted with introduction by B. W. Downs (DM, 1928).

The ultimate source for biography is Mrs. Barbauld's edition of Richardson's *Correspondence,* 6 vols. (1804). The best modern study is Alan D. McKillop, *SR, Printer and Novelist* (UNCP, 1936), where see further bibliography. Cf. also W. M. Sale, Jr., *SR, A Bibliographical Record of His Literary Career with Historical Notes* (YUP, 1936).

Special attention may be called to the following brief studies: F. S. Boas, "R's Novels and Their Influence," *E&S,* II (1911), reprinted in his *From Richardson to Pinero* (ColUP, 1937); H. G. Ward, "R's Character of Lovelace," *MLR,* VII (1912), 494-498; H. S. Hughes, "Characterization in Clarissa Harlowe," *JEGP,* XIII (1914), 110-123; W. L. Phelps, *Essays on Books* (M, 1914); Stephen Gwynn, *QR,* CCLIX (1932), 315-330; E. K. Broadus, "Mr. R Arrives," *LM,* XXVIII (1933), 425-435; Charlotte Lefever, "R's Paradoxical Success," *PMLA,* XLVIII (1933), 856-860; K. G. Hornbeak, "R's Familiar Letters and the Domestic Conduct Books," *SCS,* XIX, Jan. 1938, pp. 1-30; William White, "R: Idealist or Realist?" *MLR,* XXXIV (1939), 240-241. J. W. Krutch's study in *Five Masters* (Cape & Smith, 1930) must be used with caution.

The Epistolary Novel in General. H. S. Hughes, "English Epistolary Fiction Before Pamela," *Manly Anniversary Studies* (UCP, 1923); G. F.

Singer, *The Epistolary Novel* (U. of Pennsylvania Press, 1933); F. G. Black, "The Technique of Letter Fiction in English from 1740 to 1800," *HS*, XV (1933), 291-312; K. G. Hornbeck, *The Complete Letter-Writer in English, 1568-1800, SCS*, XV (1934), Nos. 3-4: F. G. Black, *The Epistolary Novel in the Late Eighteenth Century* (U. of Oregon, 1940).

Chapter V: Fielding and the Prose Epic

The SHP edition of Fielding, 10 vols., was published by HM in 1926. *Jonathan Wild* has been specially annotated by Wilson Follett (K, 1926) and *Joseph Andrews* by J. Paul de Castro (Scholartis Press, 1929).

W. L. Cross, *The History of HF*, 3 vols. (YUP, 1918) is a monumental work, which supersedes all previous studies. Frederic T. Blanchard, *F the Novelist* (YUP, 1926) is an elaborate history of Fielding's reputation. There are two recent books on his theory of the novel: Ethel M. Thornbury, *HF's Theory of the Comic Prose Epic, University of Wisconsin Studies in Language and Literature*, No. 30 (1931), and F. O. Bissell, Jr., *F's Theory of the Novel* (CorUP, 1933); cf. R. C. Beatty, "Criticism in F's Narratives and His Estimate of Critics," *PMLA*, XLIX (1934), 1087-1100. W. R. Irwin, *The Making of Jonathan Wild* (ColUP, 1941) is an important study. Two recent general critical studies are Aurelien Digeon, *The Novels of F* (Du, 1925) and H. K. Banerji, *HF, His Life and Works* (Bl, 1929). See also A. R. Humphreys, "F's Irony: Its Methods and Effects," *RES*, XVIII (1942), 183-196.

Chapter VI: Smollett and the Novel of Humors

The SHP edition of Smollett, 11 vols., was published by HM in 1925-1926.

There is no really adequate study of Smollett. The best known of the older books are by David Hannay (S, 1887) and Oliphant Smeaton (Edinburgh, Oliphant, 1897). Lewis Melville, *The Life and Letters of TS* (HM, 1927) is a collection of materials rather than a biography.

Important ground is broken in Edward S. Noyes's edition of Smollett's *Letters* (HUP, 1926). To this, these highly specialized studies should be added: Howard S. Buck, *A Study in S, Chiefly "Peregrine Pickle"* (YUP, 1925); Arnold Whitridge, *TS, A Study of His Miscellaneous Works* (Brooklyn, The Author, 1925); Louis L. Martz, *The Later Career of TS* (YUP, 1942); Claude E. Jones, *Smollett Studies, U. of California Publications in English*, IX, No. 2 (1942); James R. Foster, "Smollett's Pamphleteering Foe, Shebbeare," *PMLA*, LVII (1942), 1053-1100. See also essays by Andrew Lang, *Adventures Among Books* (L, 1905), Frederic Harrison, *De Senectute* (AC, 1923), and Alice Parker, "TS and the Law," *SP*, XXXIX (1942), 545-558.

Chapter VII: The Triumph of Sensibility: Laurence Sterne

W. L. Cross edited Sterne's *Works,* 12 vols., including Percy Fitz-Gerald's *Life* for J. F. Taylor & Co., N. Y., 1904. A more recent edition is that of the SHP, 7 vols. (HM, 1926-1927). Herbert Read edited *A Sentimental Journey* for the Scholartis Press, 1929. But the best introduction to the study of Sterne is James A. Work's edition of *Tristram Shandy* (Odyssey Press, 1940), where see biography, criticism, and bibliography.

W. L. Cross, *The Life and Times of LS,* rev. ed. (YUP, 1929) is the standard biography. Cf. also L. P. Curtis's edition of Sterne's *Letters* (OUP, 1935) and the same writer's *The Politicks of LS* (OUP, 1929). Arie de Froe, *LS and His Novels Studied in the Light of Modern Psychology* (Groningen, Noordhof, 1925) is behavioristic and Freudian.

Important brief studies include Edwin Muir, *B* (NY), LXXIII (1931), 1-5; W. B. C. Watkins, *Perilous Balance;* Rufus Putney, "The Evolution of *A Sentimental Journey,*" *PQ,* XIX (1940), 359-369.

Chapter VIII: Sentimentalists and Revolutionaries

General. The best general survey of the period covered by this chapter is J. M. S. Tompkins, *The Popular Novel in England, 1770-1800* (Co, 1932). See also the following works on the subjects indicated by their titles: C.B.A. Proper, *Social Elements in English Prose Fiction between 1770 and 1832* (Amsterdam, H. J. Paris, 1929); Allene Gregory, *The French Revolution and the English Novel* (P, 1915); Lois Whitney, *Primitivism and the Idea of Progress in English Popular Literature of the Eighteenth Century* (JHP, 1934); Walter F. Wright, *Sensibility in English Prose Fiction, 1760-1814, A Reinterpretation, ISLL,* XXII, Nos. 3-4 (1937); Edith Birkhead, "Sentiment and Sensibility in the Eighteenth Century Novel," *E&S,* XI (1925).

Goldsmith. The best edition of *The Vicar of Wakefield* is edited by Oswald Doughty (SPr, 1928). A recent biography is that by Stephen Gwynn (Ht, 1935).

Mackenzie. *The Man of Feeling* has been edited by Hamish Miles (SPr, 1928). The best study is H. W. Thompson, *A Scottish Man of Feeling* (OUP, 1931).

Brooke. *The Fool of Quality* was edited by E. A. Baker (Du, 1906). Cf. Helen M. Scurr, Thesis (U. of Minnesota, 1927); Eric Gellert, "The Fool of Quality," *LM,* XXX (1934), 420-428.

Day. G. W. Gignilliat, *The Author of Sandford and Merton* (ColUP, 1932); Sir S. H. Scott, *The Exemplary Mr. D* (FF, 1935).

Mrs. Inchbald. S. R. Littlewood, *EI and Her Circle* (O'Connor, 1921); William McKee, *EI, Novelist* (Washington, The Catholic University of America, 1935); G. Louis Joughin, "An I Bibliography," *UTSE,* July 8, 1934, pp. 59-74.

Holcroft. *The Life of TH,* Written by Himself, ed. Elbridge Colby, 2 vols. (Co, 1925); E. Colby, "TH, Radical," *Mid-West Quarterly,* V (1917), 44-60, and "TH, Man of Letters," *SAQ,* XXII (1923), 53-70; Virgil R. Stallbaumer, "TH: A Satirist in the Stream of Sentimentalism," *ELH,* III (1936), 31-62.

Godwin. The best biography is Ford K. Brown, *The Life of WG* (Du, 1926). The best critical study is in two articles by B. Sprague Allen: "WG as a Sentimentalist," *PMLA,* XXXIII (1918), 1-29, and "The Reaction against WG," *MP,* XVI (1918), 57-75. Cf. also "WG, Apostle of Universal Benevolence," *LTLS,* April 4, 1936, p. 285.

Bage. Carl H. Grabo, "RB, A Forgotten Novelist," *Mid-West Quarterly,* V (1917), 201-226.

Chapter IX: The Renascence of Wonder

General. The three most detailed studies of the Gothic Novel are Edith Birkhead, *The Tale of Terror* (Co, 1921); Eino Railo, *The Haunted Castle* (R, 1927); Montague Summers, *The Gothic Quest* (FP, 1938). See also Summers's extensive list, *A Gothic Bibliography* (FP, 1941). Railo must be used with caution, as must Mario Praz, *The Romantic Agony* (OUP, 1933), a study of the abnormal aspects of romanticism. For the non-literary aspects of Gothicism, cf. Kenneth Clark, *The Gothic Revival* (S, 1929).

Walpole. The two most important editions of *The Castle of Otranto* are those of M. Summers (HM, 1924) and Oswald Doughty (SPr, 1929). Recent biographies include those by Dorothy M. Stuart (M, 1927) and R. W. Ketton-Cremer (L, 1940). See also K. K. Mehrotra, *HW and the English Novel* (Bl, 1934).

Mrs. Radcliffe. *The Mysteries of Udolpho* may be had in EL (1931) and *A Romance of the Forest* in *Three Eighteenth Century Romances* (S, 1931). The two most elaborate studies of Mrs. Radcliffe are Clara F. McIntyre, *AR in Relation to Her Time, YSE,* LXII (YUP, 1920); Alida A. S. Wieten, *Mrs. R, Her Relation Towards Romanticism* (Amsterdam, H. J. Paris, 1926). See also Andrew Lang, *Adventures Among Books* (L, 1905), and M. Summers, *Essays in Petto* (FP, 1928).

Maturin. *Melmoth the Wanderer* was reprinted by Bentley, London, in 1892. Cf. Niilo Idman, *CRM, His Life and Works* (Co, 1923); William Scholten, *CRM, The Terror Novelist* (Amsterdam, H. J. Paris, 1933).

The Oriental Tale. Martha Pike Conant, *The Oriental Tale in England in the Eighteenth Century* (ColUP, 1908).

Beckford. *Vathek* is easily available. *The Episodes of Vathek* was published in "The Abbey Classics" (Small, Maynard, 1912). Beckford has been the subject of two recent extensive studies: J. W. Oliver, *The Life of WB* (OUP, 1932) and Guy Chapman (S, 1937). See also Sacheverell Sitwell, *B and Beckfordism* (Duckworth, 1930).

Chapter X: The Romance of the Tea-Table

Fanny Burney. The most scholarly edition of *Evelina* is that edited by F. D. Mackinnon (OUP, 1930). *Evelina* is available also in EL and *Cecilia* in the Bohn Library. There is an edition of the *Diary and Letters,* ed. Muriel Masefield (Du, 1931). The most important biographical and critical studies are Austin Dobson (M, 1903); Will T. Hale, *Madame D'Arblay's Place in the Development of the English Novel, Indiana University Studies,* No. 28, 1916; Edith Morley, *EAP,* No. 60 (1925); R. B. Johnson, *FB and the Burneys* (St, 1926); Muriel Masefield, *The Story of FB* (CUP, 1927); A. A. Overman, *An Investigation into the Character of FB* (Amsterdam, H. J. Paris, 1933); Christopher Lloyd (L, 1936); A. B. Tourtellot, *Be Loved No More* (HM, 1938). Gamaliel Bradford's *Portraits of Women* (HM, 1916) contains papers on both Miss Burney and Miss Austen.

Maria Edgeworth. Du published a 12 vol. edition of Maria Edgeworth's novels in 1893. *Castle Rackrent* and *The Absentee* are now available in a single volume in EL. The fundamental biographical study is F. A. Edgeworth, *A Memoir of ME, with a Selection from Her Letters,* 3 vols. (Privately printed, 1867); see also Harriet J. & Edgeworth Butler, *The Black Book of Edgeworthstown and Other Edgeworth Memoirs, 1585-1817* (FF, 1927). F. V. Barry's *ME: Chosen Letters* (HM, 1931) is delightful reading, and the introduction makes better biography than some of the longer accounts, which include Grace Oliver, *A Study of ME* (Boston, A. Williams & Co., 1882); Helen Zimmern, *ME* (W. H. Allen, 1883); A. J. C. Hare, *The Life and Letters of ME,* 2 vols. (HM, 1894); Emily Lawless, *ME* (M, 1904). Two recent theses, each published only in part, are valuable critical studies: Theodore Goodman, *ME, Novelist of Reason* (New York University, 1936); Robert G. Mood, *ME's Apprenticeship* (U. of Illinois, 1938). Cf. also Lady Ritchie, *A*

Book of Sybils (H, 1883); Milton Millhauser, "ME as a Social Novelist," *NQ*, CLXXV (1938), 204-205.

JANE AUSTEN. R. W. Chapman's edition of Jane Austen, 2 vols., in the 1934 edition (OUP) is one of the few thoroughly scholarly editions we have of any English novelist. Unfortunately it is not complete. The *Miscellanea* volume of the Maximilien Vox edition (Du, 1934) comprises *Sanditon, The Watsons,* and *Lady Susan,* together with "Plan of a Novel" and "Cancelled Chapter of 'Persuasion.'" See also *Love and Freindship* (CW, 1922) and *Volume the First,* ed. R. W. Chapman (OUP, 1933).

Chapman has also edited *JA's Letters to Her Sister Cassandra and Others,* 2 vols. (OUP, 1932) and J. E. Austen-Leigh's *Memoir of JA,* originally published 1870-1871 (OUP, 1926), the basis of all later biographies. The "official" biography at present is that of W. and R. A. Austen-Leigh, *JA, Her Life and Letters* (Smith, Elder, 1913). To this may be added M. A. Austen-Leigh, *Personal Aspects of JA* (Du, 1920).

Geoffrey Keynes has edited *JA: A Bibliography* (Nonesuch Press, 1929). G. L. Apperson's *JA Dictionary* (Palmer, 1932) is disappointing.

There are many biographical and critical studies including Goldwin Smith, *Life of JA* (S, 1890); W. H. Pollock, *JA, Her Contemporaries and Herself* (L, 1899); Geraldine Mitton, *JA and Her Times* (P, 1905), which is invaluable for backgrounds; F. W. Cornish, *JA* (M, 1913); O. W. Firkins, *JA* (Ht, 1920); Léonie Villard, *JA, A French Appreciation* (Du, 1924); C. Linklater Thomson, *JA, A Survey* (Marshall, 1929); R. B. Johnson, *JA, Her Life, Her Work, Her Family, and Her Critics* (Du, 1930), a very useful book which brings a considerable variety of material together; John Bailey, *Introductions to JA* (OUP, 1931); David Rhydderch, *JA, Her Life and Art* (C, 1932); Guy Rawlence, *JA* (M, 1934); Lord David Cecil, *JA* (M, 1935), a brilliant evaluation; Beatrice Kean Seymour, *JA, Study for a Portrait* (Michael Joseph, 1937), a lively, but somewhat desultory book, by a good novelist; Mona Wilson, *JA and Some Contemporaries* (Cresset Press, 1938); Mary Lascelles, *JA and Her Art* (OUP, 1939), the fullest critical study of Jane Austen. See also Lady Ritchie, *A Book of Sybils* (H, 1883); Alice Meynell, *Second Person Singular* (OUP, 1922).

Chapter XI: The Heights: Sir Walter Scott

The Border Edition of the *Waverley Novels,* 48 vols. (Nimmo, 1892-1894) is still valuable for Andrew Lang's notes. An edition of Scott's *Miscellaneous Prose Works* was published by Houlston, 1843-1846.

The best edition of the authorized biography, *The Life of Sir WS,* by

John Gibson Lockhart, is the Large Paper Edition (HM, 1901). The Riverside Popular Edition, 5 vols. (HM, 1926) is much less expensive, and there is an abridgement in EL. Sir H. J. C. Grierson, *Sir WS, Bart.* (ColUP, 1938) was designed as a supplement to Lockhart.

The Journal of Sir WS, 1825-1832 was published in 1890. There is a recent edition by N, 1932.

The standard collection of *Letters* is the Centenary Edition, ed. Grierson, 12 vols. (Co, 1932-1937). Cf. also Wilfrid Partington (ed), *The Private Letter-Books of Sir WS* (St, 1930) and *Sir W's Post-Bag* (Murray, 1932).

The standard bibliography is Greville Worthington, *A Bibliography of the Waverley Novels* (Co, 1931). There is a useful book of *Waverley Synopses,* ed. J. Walker McSpadden (Crowell, 1909). An admirable book of selections from Scott is *The Waverley Pageant,* ed. Hugh Walpole (H, 1932). Four numbers of *The Sir WS Quarterly* were published 1927-1928.

The best introduction to the study of Scott is John Buchan (CM, 1932). Other centenary literature of value includes Lord David Cecil (Co); H. J. C. Grierson, *Sir WS* and *Sir WS Today* (both, Co); *S Centenary Articles* (OUP).

James T. Hillhouse, *The Waverley Novels and Their Critics* (U. of Minnesota Press, 1936) is a fine history of Scott's reputation. The best study of his non-creative work is Margaret Ball, *Sir WS as a Critic of Literature* (ColUP, 1907). Cf. A. M. Williams, "S as a Man of Letters," *Englische Studien,* XXXVII (1907), 100-124.

Among many biographical and critical studies, I may mention the following: R. H. Hutton (M, 1878); C. D. Yonge, *The Life of Sir WS* (Sc, 1888); George Saintsbury (S, 1897); Andrew Lang (H&S, 1906); C. A. Young, *The Waverley Novels, An Appreciation* (James Maclehose & Sons, 1907); Stephen Gwynn, *The Life of Sir WS* (LB, 1930). Donald Carswell's *Scott and His Circle* (DD, 1930), the work of the *advocatus diaboli* of Scott criticism, is worth reading for the attempt it makes to straighten out the tangle of Scott's business affairs.

There are famous essays on Scott by Carlyle, Emerson, Ruskin ("Fiction Fair and Foul"), and Walter Bagehot. Of many recent articles, I have space to mention only the following: John Erskine, *The Delight of Great Books* (BM, 1928); Sir Arthur Quiller-Couch, *Studies in Literature,* Third Series (P, 1930); Agnes Muir Mackenzie, "The Survival of S," *LM,* XXV (1932), 270-278; Dorothy M. Stuart, "Sir WS, Some Centenary Reflections," *EAP,* No. 59 (1934); Paul Landis, "The Waverley Novels, or a Hundred Years After," *PMLA,* LII (1937), 461-473.

Chapter XII: From Scott to Dickens

GENERAL. M. W. Rosa, *The Silver Fork School* (ColUP, 1936) concerns the fashionable novelists of the period. Lionel Stevenson deals with Bulwer and Disraeli in "Stepfathers of Victorianism," *VQR,* VI (1930), 251-267, and with Lever, Marryat, and G. P. R. James in "The Novelist as Fortune Hunter," *VQR,* XIII (1937), 376-390.

BULWER. The New Knebworth Edition, 29 vols. (1895-1898) is standard; some volumes are still carried by R. In America, L. C. Page has published an Illustrated Cabinet Edition, 24 vols. The authorized biography is *The Life of EB, First Lord Lytton,* by his grandson, The Earl of Lytton, 2 vols. (M, 1913). It is a pity that Michael Sadleir's *Bulwer, A Panorama,* which promised to be one of the great biographies of our time, should never have progressed beyond the first volume, *Edward and Rosina, 1803-1836* (LB, 1931). See also T. H. S. Escott, *EB, First Baron L of Knebworth* (R, 1910). E. G. Bell, *Introductions to the Prose Romances, Plays and Comedies of EB, Lord L* (Chicago, Walter M. Hill, 1914) is an incompetent approach to a Bulwer dictionary. Two recent studies of scholarly value are E. B. Burgum, *The Literary Career of EB, Lord L,* Ph.D. thesis, U. of Illinois (1924), and Harold H. Watts, "L's Theories of Prose Fiction," *PMLA,* L (1935), 274-289. There are two essays by W. F. Lord, "Lord L's Novels," *XIX C,* L (1901), 449-458, and "The Wand of Prospero," *XIX C,* XCV (1924), 59-68, and another by Edmund Gosse, *Some Diversions of a Man of Letters* (S, 1919).

DISRAELI. The Bradenham Edition, 12 vols., was published by K (1926-1927). The authorized biography is *The Life of BD,* by W. F. Monypenny and George E. Buckle, rev. ed., 2 vols. (Murray, 1929). Two recent entertaining books are by André Maurois (AC, 1928) and Elswyth Thane, *Young Mr. D* (HB, 1936). But the only elaborate discussion of Disraeli's novels is in M. E. Speare, *The Political Novel* (OUP, 1924). All the important articles published prior to 1924 are mentioned in Speare's notes. To these may be added Frank Swinnerton, "Disraeli as a Novelist," *YR,* XVII (1927-1928), 283-300; Rowland Grey, "D in Fancy Street," *CoM,* N.S. LXVI (1929), 102-110, and Stanley B. James, "The Tragedy of D," *Catholic World,* CLII (1940-1941), 414-419.

THE IRISH NOVELISTS. H. S. Krans, *Irish Life in Irish Fiction* (ColUP, 1903); Stephen J. Brown, *Ireland in Fiction, A Guide to Irish Novels, Tales, Romances, and Folklore* (Dublin, Talbot Press, 1916); Stephen Gwynn, *Irish Literature and Drama in the English Language, A Short History* (N, 1936).

Lever. No collected edition of Lever's novels is now in print. Downey published one, 37 vols. (1897-1899), and an American edition was formerly issued by LB. *Harry Lorrequer* is available in EL. For Lever's biography, cf. W. J. Fitzpatrick, *The Life of CL* (H, 1879); Edmund Downey, *CL, His Life in His Letters* (S, 1906), and especially Lionel Stevenson, *Dr. Quicksilver* (Chapman & Hall, 1939). See also "CJL," *Bla,* CXII (1872), 327-360; Lewis Melville, *LA,* CCL (1906), 649-658; J. M. Spaight, "CL Re-read," *Bla,* CCXXVII (1930), 679-693.

Carleton. Many editions of Carleton are listed in Brown, *Ireland in Fiction,* but the only book now in print is *Stories of Irish Life* (Talbot Press, 1936). The authorized biography is David J. O'Donoghue, *The Life of WC* (Downey, 1896), which includes Carleton's unfinished Autobiography. The only recent book is Rose Shaw, *Carleton's Country* (Talbot Press, 1930). For criticism, cf. L. McManus, *Academy and Literature,* LXV (1903), 719-720; G. Barnett Smith, "A Brilliant Irish Novelist," *Fort,* LXVII (1897), 104-116.

Surtees. The best edition is the ten-volume set, with the original illustrations hand-colored, issued by S (1929-1930). It was supplemented in 1931 with uniformly-made editions of *Jorrocks's Jaunts and Jollities* and *The Analysis of the Hunting Field.* For biographical material, cf. E. D. Cuming, *RSS (Creator of 'Jorrocks'), 1803-1864* (S, 1924), which prints Surtees's hitherto unpublished papers; Frederick Watson, *The Life of RSS* (Hersant, 1933). Watson has also published *RSS, A Critical Study* (Harrap, 1933). Anthony Steel, *Jorrocks's England* (Du, 1932) is concerned largely with backgrounds. Hugh S. Gladstone's *Shooting with Surtees* (Stokes, 1928), though primarily a compilation, contains some bibliography and an approach toward a Surtees dictionary. Cf. also F. J. Harvey Darton, *From Surtees to Sassoon* (Kennerley, 1931). There are two Surtees papers in Una Pope-Hennessy, *Durham Company* (CW, 1941). Briefer studies include: Moira O'Neill, "Some Novels by S," *Bla,* CXCIII (1913), 535-542, and "The Author of 'Jorrocks,'" *Bla,* CCXC (1924), 857-868; Frank J. Wilstach, "S and Charles Dickens," *N. Y. Times Book Review and Magazine,* July 23, 1922, pp. 13, 26; E. D. Cuming, "'Handley Cross' Behind the Scenes," *Bla,* CCXVI (1924), 462-471; W. C. Rivers, "The Place of RSS," *LM,* X (1924), 605-613; "RSS," *LTLS,* Mar. 27, 1930, pp. 257-258; W. L. Renwick, "Jorrocks: A Conversation," *E&S,* XVII (1932); A. Edward Newton, *End Papers* (LB, 1934); Quentin Bell, *New Statesman & Nation,* XIX (1940), 335.

Marryat. De's edition of Marryat's novels, 26 vols., ed. R. B. Johnson, was published 1929-1930. L. C. Page publish the Illustrated Cabinet Edition in 24 vols. The authorized biography is Florence Marryat, *Life and Letters of Captain M* (AC, 1872); see also David Hannay, *Life of*

FM (Sc, 1889) and Christopher Lloyd, *Captain M and the Old Navy* (L, 1939). The following essays are all worth reading: "Captain M," by the Earl of Iddlesleigh, *LA,* CCXLIII (1904), 212-220; Michael Sadleir, "Captain M, A Portrait," *LM,* X (1924), 495-510; Maurice McGrath, "A Century of M," *XIX C,* CVI (1929), 545-555; "The Captain's Death Bed," *LTLS,* Sept. 26, 1935, pp. 585-586; F. S. Boas, "Captain M," *Queen's Quarterly,* XLIV (1937), 230-241.

Peacock. The Halliford Edition of Peacock's *Works,* ed. H. F. B. Brett-Smith and C. E. Jones, 10 vols. (Co, 1924-1934) is magnificently definitive. There is a five-volume edition of the *Novels,* with prefaces by George Saintsbury, in M's "Pocket Classics," 1927. *The Misfortunes of Elphin* and *Crotchet Castle* are published in WC; *Headlong Hall* and *Nightmare Abbey* appear both in WC and EL. The first extensive biography was Carl Van Doren's *Life of TLP* (Du, 1911); for what had been accomplished before this date, cf. Van Doren, pp. 267-270. A more recent biography has been included in Volume I of the Halliford Edition. There are two other long studies in English: A. Martin Freeman, *TLP, A Critical Study* (Secker, 1911) and J. B. Priestley (M, 1927). There is one long study in French—Jean-Jacques Mayoux, *Un Epicurean Anglais: TLP* (Paris, Nizet et Bastard, 1933)—and one in Italian—Benvenuto Cellini, *TLP* (Rome, Cremonese, 1937). The following essays are of interest: Richard Garnett, *Essays of an Ex-Librarian* (He, 1901); Herbert Paul, "The Novels of P," *LA,* CCXXXVIII (1903), 158-169; H. W. Boynton, *AM,* XCVIII (1906), 765-774; Clive Bell, *Pot-Boilers* (New York, The Sunwise Turn, 1919); Osbert Burdett, *LM,* VIII (1923), 21-32; R. W. Chapman, *SRL,* I (1925), 685-686; Herbert Wright, "The Association of TLP with Wales," *E&S,* XII (1926).

Chapter XIII: White Magic: Charles Dickens

The handsomest and most complete edition is the limited *Nonesuch Dickens,* 23 vols. (Nonesuch Press, 1937-1938), the last three volumes of which comprise the most comprehensive collection of Letters that has yet been printed. The Heritage Press is now engaged in publishing a handsome edition of Dickens's novels, each work being illustrated by a different artist.

J. W. T. Ley edited John Forster's authorized *Life of CD* (Cecil Palmer, 1928); his annotations sum up all the additional biographical information available in 1928. There is considerable new material in Ralph Straus, *CD, A Biography from New Sources* (Cosmopolitan, 1928). The most elaborate study of Dickens's personality is Edward Wagenknecht, *The Man CD* (HM, 1929), where see further bibliography. The best *Dickens Dictionary* is by G. A. Pierce and W. A. Wheeler

(HM, 1878). Humphry House, *The D World* (OUP, 1941) is a picture of Dickens's environment. The Dickens Fellowship has been publishing the magazine, *The Dickensian,* since 1905.

The most famous critical studies are by George Gissing (DM, 1898), by G. K. Chesterton (DM, 1906), and George Santayana's brilliant essay in *Soliloquies in England* (S, 1922). To these may be added W. A. Ward (M, 1882); E. P. Whipple, 2 vols. (HM, 1912); Wilhelm Dibelius (Leipzig, Teubner, 1916), in German, the most elaborate study ever published; J. B. Van Amerongen, *The Actor in D* (AC, 1927), an exhilarating study; Stefan Zweig, *Three Masters* (VP, 1930); Osbert Sitwell (CW, 1932) André Maurois (H, 1934).

From the thousands of articles that have been published any selection must be more or less arbitrary. In addition to the titles mentioned elsewhere, I should like to list here, first of all, Swinburne's essay, now included in his Collected Works; then S. M. Crothers, *Humanly Speaking* (HM, 1912); W. L. Phelps, *Essays on Books;* Alice Meynell, *Hearts of Controversy* (S, 1917); Pearl S. Buck, "My Debt to D," *English Review,* LXII (1936), 408-412; Earle R. Davis, "D and the Evolution of Caricature," *PMLA,* LV (1940), 231-240; Alfred Noyes, *Pageant of Letters* (Sheed and Ward, 1940).

Chapter XIV: The Disciples of Dickens

General. Walter C. Phillips, *Dickens, Reade, and Collins, Sensation Novelists* (ColUP, 1919).

Collins. Wilkie Collins's novels are published by CW. *The Woman in White* and *The Moonstone* appear as a single volume in the Modern Library Giants series. There is no extended biographical or critical study (though Dorothy Sayers is said to have one in preparation); the most extensive account now available is in S. M. Ellis, *WC, Le Fanu, and Others* (Co, 1931). "Reminiscences of a Story-Teller," *Universal Review,* I (1888), 182-192, is the only article Collins ever published about himself. Some of his letters appear in Mary Anderson, *A Few Memories* (H, 1896); R. C. Lehmann, *Memories of Half a Century* (Smith, Elder, 1908); Frank Archer, *An Actor's Notebooks* (Stanley Paul, 1912). Cf. also H. Chartres, *London Society,* LVI (1889), 515-523; [N. Beard], "Some Recollections of Yesterday," *Temple Bar,* CII (1894), 315-339; W. Reeve, "Recollections of WC," *Chambers's Journal,* LXXXIII (1906), 458-461. The most distinguished pieces of criticism are Swinburne's essay in his Collected Works; Walter de la Mare, "The Early Novels of WC," in *The Eighteen-Sixties,* ed. John Drinkwater (CUP, 1932); T. S. Eliot, "WC and Dickens," in *Selected Essays, 1917-1932* (HB, 1932). Cf. also Harry Quilter, "A Living Story Teller," *CR,* LIII

(1888), 572-593; Andrew Lang, "Mr. WC's Novels," *CR,* LVII (1890), 20-28; Arthur Compton-Rickett, *B*(L), XLII (1912), 107-114; Malcolm Elwin, *Victorian Wallflowers.*

Reade. Charles Reade's novels are published by CW and L. C. Page. The best edition of *The Cloister and the Hearth* is ed. C. B. Wheeler (OUP, 1915). The original brief serial form of this novel, *A Good Fight,* has been reprinted with introduction by Andrew Lang (OUP, 1910). Malcolm Elwin's biography (C, 1931) is much better than either the authorized biography by Charles L. Reade and Compton Reade (H, 1887) or John Coleman's *CR as I Knew Him* (Du, 1903), but the definitive book is now Léonie Rives, *CR: sa vie, ses romans* (Toulouse, Lion et Fils, Imprimerie toulousaine, 1940). There are valuable biographical data in Annie Fields, "An Acquaintance with CR," *Ce,* N.S. VII (1884), 67-79, and in E. H. House, "Anecdotes of CR," *AM,* LX (1887), 525-539. The critical studies which count are Turner (see p. 249) and a series of articles by Emerson Grant Sutcliffe: "CR's Notebooks," *SP,* XXVII (1930), 64-109; "The Stage in R's Novels," *SP,* XXVII (1930), 654-688; "Foemina Vera in CR's Novels," *PMLA,* XLVI (1931), 1260-1279; "Plotting in R's Novels," *PMLA,* XLVII (1932), 834-863; "Psychological Presentation in R's Novels," *SP,* XXXVIII (1941), 521-542. See also Swinburne's essay; W. L. Courtney, "CR's Novels," *Fort,* XLII (1884), 460-471; Sir Arthur Quiller-Couch, *Studies in Literature,* First series (P, 1918); E. W. Hornung, "CR," *LM,* IV (1921), 150-163.

Mrs. Gaskell. The Knutsford Edition, 8 vols. (P, 1906) was edited by A. W. Ward. Clement K. Shorter edited the volumes in WC, some of which are now out of print. There is no authorized life; the only considerable collection of letters is the *Letters of Mrs. G and Charles Eliot Norton, 1855-1865,* ed. Jane Whitehill (OUP, 1932). The following books are all worth consulting. Sanders makes a good beginning; both Sanders and Whitfield contain good bibliographies. Mrs. Ellis H. Chadwick, *Mrs. G, Haunts, Homes, and Stories* (St, 1911); J. J. Van Dullemen, *Mrs. G, Novelist and Biographer* (Amsterdam, H. J. Paris, 1924); Gerald DeWitt Sanders, *EG,* Cornell Studies in English, XIV (YUP, 1929); A. Stanton Whitfield, *Mrs. G, Her Life and Work* (R, 1929); George A. Payne, *Mrs. G, A Brief Biography* (Manchester, Sherratt and Hughes, 1929); Elizabeth Haldane, *Mrs. G and Her Friends* (AC, 1931). Brief studies include: W. Minto, "Mrs. G's Novels," *Fort,* XXX (1878), 353-369; Lewis Melville, "The Centenary of Mrs. G," *XIX C,* LXVIII (1910), 467-482; K. L. Montgomery, *Fort,* XCIV (1910), 450-463; A. K. Tuell, *Cont,* C (1911), 681-692; Margaret B. Samson, "Mrs. G's Place as a Novelist," *Queen's Quarterly,* XXVII (1919-1920), 93-

100; Annette B. Hopkins, "Mrs. G in France, 1849-1890," *PMLA,* LIII (1938), 545-573.

KINGSLEY. Charles Kingsley's novels are readily available in Macmillan editions and others. Mrs. Kingsley's *CK, His Letters and Memories of His Life* (S, 1877) is a typical Victorian memoir; the standard modern book is Margaret F. Thorp, *CK, 1819-1875* (PUP, 1937). Stanley E. Baldwin's *CK* (CorUP, 1934), a useful book with a good bibliography, is spoiled somewhat by the author's tendency to take Kingsley at his wife's valuation. See also W. F. Lord, "The K Novels," *XIX C,* LV (1904), 996-1004; Stanley T. Williams, "Yeast: A Victorian Heresy," *NAR,* CCXII (1920), 697-704; Mary W. Hanavalt, "CK and Science," *SP,* XXXIV (1937), 589-611; W. M. Conacher, *Queen's Quarterly,* XLV (1938), 503-511.

Chapter XV: Counter-Blast: W. M. Thackeray

The Biographical Edition of Thackeray, published first by Smith, Elder, later by Murray, contains introductions by his daughter, Lady Ritchie. There is a valuable edition of *Henry Esmond,* ed. T. C. and W. Snow (OUP, 1915) and of *Vanity Fair,* ed. Paul Elmer More (Odyssey Press, 1935). The best bibliography is *A T Library,* ed. Henry Sayre van Duzer (New York, privately printed, 1919). There is a *T Dictionary* by Mudge and Sears (Du, 1910).

There is no authorized biography. The latest biography, and probably the best, is Malcolm Elwin, *T, A Personality* (C, 1932), which contains an annotated list of sources for Thackeray's biography. Lady Ritchie has written informally in *Chapters from Some Unwritten Memoirs* (H, 1894) and *Thackeray and His Daughter* (H, 1924). Lewis Melville has two useful books: *The Life of WMT,* 2 vols. (Stone, 1899), republished as *WMT* (DD, 1928), and *Some Aspects of T* (LB, 1911).

The fullest studies of Thackeray's art are in Charles B. Hale's unpublished Ph.D. thesis, *The Art of T* (Cornell, 1924), and in John W. Dodds, *T, A Critical Portrait* (OUP, 1941). There are two full, scholarly studies of Thackeray's early work: Miriam M. H. Thrall, *Rebellious Fraser's* (ColUP, 1934) and H. S. Gulliver, *T's Literary Apprenticeship* (Valdosta, Georgia, privately printed, 1924); cf. Gulliver's very full bibliography.

Other biographical and critical studies include: John Brown, *T, His Literary Career* (Osgood, 1877); Anthony Trollope (M, 1879); Herman Merivale and Frank T. Marzials, *Life of WMT* (Sc, 1891); A. A. Jack, *T, A Study* (M, 1895); Charles Whibley (DM, 1903); Sidney Dark (Cassell, 1912); Raymond Las Vergnas, *WMT, l'homme, le penseur, le romancier* (Paris, Champion, 1932), a full and important study; H. N. Wethered, *On the Art of T* (L, 1938). Among briefer studies, consult: W. C. Brownell, *Victorian Prose Masters* (S, 1901); E. G. Sutcliffe, "T's Romanticism," *SAQ*, XXI (1922), 313-321; Chauncey W. Wells, "T and the Victorian Compromise," *Essays in Criticism, University of California Publications in English*, I (1929), 177-199; W. A. Hirst, "The Chronology in T's Novels," *CoM*, N.S. LXVII (1929), 553-563; Violet A. Simpson, "T's Last Heroine," *CoM*, N.S. LXVII (1930), 577-590; S. M. Smith, "In Defence of T," *XIX C*, CXIV (1933), 103-113, a reply to Michael Sadleir's attack on Thackeray in his *Bulwer, A Panorama;* Ernest Boll, "The Author of *Elizabeth Brownrigge:* A Review of T's Techniques," *SP*, XXXIX (1942), 79-101.

Chapter XVI: The Novelist as Novelist: Anthony Trollope

There is no complete edition of Trollope's novels. The SHP edition started to be just that but stopped with the first group, The Barsetshire Novels and the *Autobiography*, 14 vols. (HM, 1929). DM have published three sets: The Barsetshire Novels, The Parliamentary Novels, and The Manor House Novels, which comprise *Orley Farm, The Belton Estate, Is He Popenjoy?, John Caldigate,* and *The Vicar of Bullhampton.* Titles of individual novels available in EL and WC are indicated on pp. 289-290. The *Autobiography* may also be had in WC. Recent editions of special Trollope items comprise: *The Noble Jilt* (a play) (Co, 1923); *London Tradesmen* (S, 1927); *Hunting Sketches* (Mitchell, 1929); *Four Lectures* (Co, 1938); *The Tireless Traveller,* ed. B. A. Booth (University of California, 1941).

The first full-length study of Trollope's work was T. H. S. Escott, *AT, His Work, Associates, and Literary Originals* (Lane, 1913). But Michael Sadleir's *AT, A Commentary* (HM, 1927) is now the standard authority; cf. also his introduction to the SHP set, to the WC *Autobiography,* and to *The Noble Jilt.* Other books on Trollope are Hugh Walpole (M, 1928) and John H. Wildman, *AT's England* (Brown University, 1940). Spencer Van Bokkelen Nichols's essay, *The Significance of AT* (Douglas MacMurtie, 1925) is of no great importance in itself, but the book contains a beautiful map of Barsetshire by George F. Muendel.

The standard bibliography is M. Sadleir, *T, A Bibliography* (Co, 1928). Mary Leslie Irwin's *AT, A Bibliography* (H. W. Wilson, 1926) lists considerable criticism. R. W. Chapman has attempted to apply the canons of textual criticism to Trollope; see *RES,* XVII (1941), 322-331, and *MP,* XXXIX (1942), 287-294, with the references contained in both articles.

The following short papers are all well worth reading: Julian Hawthorne, in *Confessions and Criticisms* (HM, 1887); Henry James, in *Partial Portraits* (M, 1888); W. F. Lord, "The Novels of AT," *XIX C,* XLIX (1901), 805-816; James Bryce, in *Studies in Contemporary Biography* (M, 1903); F. G. Bettany, "In Praise of AT's Novels," *Fort,* LXXXIII (1905), 1000-1011; Gamaliel Bradford, in *A Naturalist of Souls;* A. Edward Newton, in *The Amenities of Book-Collecting* (LB, 1918), a paper which contributed outstandingly to the Trollope renascence in America; George Saintsbury, "T Revisited," *E&S,* VI (1920); Wilfrid L. Randell, "AT and His Work," *Fort,* CXIV (1920), 459-467; R. A. Knox, "A Ramble in Barsetshire," *LM,* V (1922), 378-385; M. E. Speare, in *The Political Novel;* M. Sadleir, "AT Love Story and Mary Thorne," *XIX C,* XCVI (1924), 355-366; Hilaire Belloc, *LM,* XXVII (1932), 150-157; Charles R. Brown, in *They Were Giants* (M, 1934); Ashley Sampson, "T in the Twentieth Century," *LM,* XXXV (1936-1937), 371-377.

Chapter XVII: Fire over Yorkshire: The Brontës

The SHP Brontë (HM, 1932 ff.), edited by T. J. Wise and J. A. Symington, is now the definitive edition. It comprises Novels (11 vols.), Miscellaneous Writings (2 vols.), Poems (2 vols.), Bibliography (1 vol.), and a four-volume biography, *The Bs, Their Lives, Friendships, and Correspondence,* which attempts to assemble all essential biographical material. At this writing (1942) all except the Bibliography volume have appeared.

Mrs. Gaskell's *Life of CB* (1857) was the foundation biography. It is now available in EL, ed. May Sinclair. Later publications include Sir T. Wemyss Reid, *CB, A Monograph* (M, 1877); Augustine Birrell, *Life of CB* (S, 1887); Clement K. Shorter, *The Bs and Their Circle* (with W. R. Nicoll) (DM, 1896), *CB and Her Sisters* (S, 1905), *The Bs: Life and Letters,* 2 vols. (S, 1908), a series of publications which contributed much to the understanding of the Brontës; A. M. Mackay, *The Bs: Fact and Fiction* (DM, 1897); May Sinclair, *The Three Bs,* rev. ed. (Hu, 1914), a deeply sympathetic and perceptive study; Ernest Dimnet, *The B Sisters* (C, 1927), a fine brief account; K. A. R. Sugden, *A Short History of the Bs* (OUP, 1929); Rosamond Langbridge, *CB, A Psychological Study* (DD, 1929), which, like most "psychological" works, should be used cautiously; Emilie and Georges Romieu, *Three Virgins of Haworth* (Du, 1930), a fascinating but inaccurate book; E. M. Delafield (ed.), *The Bs: Their Lives Recorded by Their Contemporaries* (Hogarth Press, 1935); E. F. Benson, *CB* (L, 1932), the latest full biography, which is unfortunately rather unsympathetic; W. B. White,

The Miracle of Haworth (Du, 1937); Edith Kinsley, *Pattern for Genius* (Du, 1939). Naturally these works vary greatly in merit, and all should now be checked against Fanny E. Ratchford, *The B's Web of Childhood* (ColUP, 1941), which, as indicated in the text, has now revolutionized Brontë criticism.

The Transactions and Publications of the B Society have contained much valuable material. Cf. also their *CB, 1816-1916* (Du, 1918).

A. Mary F. Robinson, *EB* (LB, 1883) was the first book devoted to Emily Brontë alone. Charles Simpson, *EB* (S, 1929) is the only good recent book; both *All Alone, The Life and Private History of EJB,* by Romer Wilson (CW, 1928) and *The Life and Eager Death of EB,* by Virginia Moore (Rich & Cowan, 1936) illustrate some of the worst vagaries of contemporary biographical writing. On Emily Brontë, see also J. C. Smith, *E&S,* V (1914); Prince D. S. Mirsky, *LM,* VII (1923), 266-272; Arthur Symons, *Dramatis Personae* (BM, 1923); Augustus Ralli, *NAR,* CCXXI (1925), 495-507; Ralph Aiken, "Wild-Heart: An Appreciation of EJB," *SAQ,* XXXIV (1935), 202-210; Martin Turnell, "Wuthering Heights," *Dublin Review,* CCVI (1940), 134-149.

The only independent study of Anne Brontë is Will T. Hale, *AB: Her Life and Writings, Indiana University Studies,* Vol. XVI, No. 83 (1929).

In addition to the foregoing, the following items may be noted: A. C. Swinburne, "EB" and "A Note on CB" in his *Works;* H. H. Bonnell, *CB, George Eliot, and Jane Austen;* Alice Meynell, *Hearts of Controversy;* Janet Spens, "CB," *E&S,* XIV (1929); Julien Green, "CB and Her Sisters," *VQR,* V (1929), 42-58; G. F. Bradby, *The Bs and Other Essays* (OUP, 1932); Elizabeth Haldane, "The Bs and Their Biographers," *XIX C,* CXII (1932), 752-764.

E. Thornton Cook, *They Lived* (S, 1935) and Dorothy H. Cornish, *These Were the Bs* (M, 1940) are both novels about the Brontës. The following are all plays: Clemence Dane, *Wild Decembers* (DD, 1933); R. Ferguson, *CB* (Benn, 1933); Dan Totheroh, *Moor Born* (French, 1934); J. Davison, *The Bs of Haworth Parsonage* (Muller, 1934); A. Sangster, *The Bs,* New ed. (Co, 1938); Elizabeth Goudge, *The Bs of Haworth,* in *Three Plays* (Duckworth, 1939).

Chapter XVIII: The "New" Novel: George Eliot

The Warwickshire Edition of George Eliot's Writings, 25 vols. (HM, 1908) includes the authorized *Life, Letters, and Journals* by J. W. Cross. Roland Stuart, *Letters of GE to Elma Stuart, 1872-1880* (Simpkin, Marshall, 1909) and Arthur Paterson, *GE's Family Life and Letters* (HM, 1928) supplement Cross's collection with more personal letters. There is a

GE Dictionary by I. G. Mudge and M. E. Sears (H. W. Wilson, 1924). The best modern biography is Blanche Colton Williams (M, 1936).

Most of the books in the following list include both biography and criticism. I have marked the more important items with an asterisk. * Oscar Browning, *Life of GE* (Sc, 1890); Clara L. Thomson (Small, Maynard, 1901); * Leslie Stephen (M, 1902); * Mathilde Blind (LB, 1904); William Mottram, *The True Story of GE* (McClurg, 1906), which contains an elaborate study of the autobiographical background of *Adam Bede* and a great deal of information about Elizabeth Evans; * Charles Gardner, *The Inner Life of GE* (Pitman, 1912); * Mary H. Deakin, *The Early Life of GE* (Manchester University Press, 1913); * Elizabeth S. Haldane, *GE and Her Times* (AC, 1927); J. Lewis May (BM, 1930); E. & G. Romieu, *The Life of GE* (Du, 1932), a fictionized biography, much inferior to the work by the same authors on the Brontës; P. Bourl'honne, *GE, Essai de biographie intellectuelle et morale* (Paris, Champion, 1934). Charles S. Olcott, *GE, Scenes and People in her Novels* (Crowell, 1910) is a richly illustrated study of backgrounds. J. E. Buckrose, *Silhouette of Mary Ann* (BM, 1931) is a novel.

Critical essays on George Eliot are so numerous that it seems hopeless even to attempt a selection. I venture, nevertheless, to add the following list, some items in which have become famous: Edward Dowden, *Studies in Literature, 1789-1877* (Kegan, Paul, 1878); F. W. H. Myers, *Ce,* N.S. I (1881), 57-64; Sidney Lanier, *The English Novel* (S, 1883); George W. Cooke, *GE, A Critical Study of Her Life, Writings, and Philosophy* (HM, 1883); John C. Brown, *The Ethics of GE's Works,* Fourth edition (Blackwood, 1884); Lord Acton, "GE's 'Life,'" *XIX C,* XVII (1885), 464-485; R. H. Hutton, *Essays on Some of the Modern Guides of English Thought in Matters of Faith* (M, 1887); Henry James, *Partial Portraits;* Frederic Harrison, "GE's Place in Literature," *Forum,* XX (1895), 66-78, and "Reminiscences of GE," *HaM,* CIII (1901), 577-584; W. C. Brownell, *Victorian Prose Masters;* H. H. Bonnell, *Charlotte Brontë, GE, and Jane Austen;* Edward A. Parry, "The Humor of GE," *Fort,* CXII (1919), 883-895; H. C. Minchin, "GE: Some Characteristics," *Fort,* CXII (1919), 896-903; W. L. Cross, "GE in Retrospect," *YR,* N.S. IX (1920), 256-270; Josiah Royce, *Fugitive Essays* (HUP, 1920); R. M. Wenley, "Marian Evans and 'GE,'" *Washington University Studies,* IX (1921), 3-34; Edmund Gosse, *Aspects and Impressions* (S, 1922); Charles Gardner, "GE's Quarries," *AM,* CXXXVI (1925), 659-665; B. C. Williams, "GE: Social Pressure on the Individual," *SR,* XLVI (1938), 235-241; W. F. Wright, "GE as Industrial Reformer," *PMLA,* LVI (1941), 1107-1115.

Chapter XIX: The Poetic Comedy of George Meredith

The Memorial Edition of Meredith, 29 vols. (S, 1909-1912) includes fiction, poetry, and letters. There are bibliographies by A. J. K. Esdaile, *Bibliography of the Writing in Prose and Verse of GM* (Spencer, London, 1907) and *A Chronological List of GM's Publications* (Co, 1914) and two by M. B. Forman, *A Bibliography of the Writings in Prose and Verse of GM* and *Meredithiana* (Bibliographical Society, 1922 and 1924).

J. B. Priestley's little book (M, 1926) is a good introduction to the study of Meredith. James Moffatt, *GM, a Primer to the Novels* (H&S, 1909) is an excellent handbook and guide to reading.

R. E. Sencourt attempts a full biography in *The Life of GM* (S, 1929). Cf. also S. M. Ellis, *GM: His Life and Friends in Relation to His Work* (DM, 1920); Mary Sturge Gretton, *The Writings and Life of GM* (HUP, 1926).

The following studies of Meredith all appear between independent covers: Hannah Lynch (Me, 1891); Richard Le Gallienne (Lane, 1900); W. Jerrold, *GM, An Essay Towards Appreciation* (Greening, 1902); G. M. Trevelyan, *The Poetry and Philosophy of GM* (S, 1906); E. J. Bailey, *The Novels of GM* (S, 1907); M. S. Gretton, *GM, Novelist, Poet, Reformer* (S, 1907); Richard Henry Parnell Curle, *Aspects of GM* (Du, 1908); M. B. Forman (ed.), *GM, Some Early Appreciations* (S, 1909); Joseph Warren Beach, *The Comic Spirit in GM* (L, 1911); Constantin Photiadès, *GM, His Life, Genius, and Teaching* (S, 1913); H. Bedford, *The Heroines of GM* (H&S, 1914); J. H. E. Crees (Bl, 1918); Lady A. M. Butcher, *Memories of GM* (S, 1919); J. M. Barrie, *GM, A Tribute* (Co, 1922); W. Chislett, *GM, A Study and an Appraisal* (Badger, 1925); Robert Peel, *The Creed of a Victorian Pagan* (HUP, 1931). J. A. Hammerton's *GM, His Life and Art in Anecdote and Criticism* (Kennerley, 1909) presents a useful summary and digest of material up to the date of its publication.

Among briefer studies of Meredith, I will mention the following: W. C. Brownell, *Victorian Prose Masters;* Oliver Elton, *Modern Studies* (L, 1907); Archibald Henderson, *Interpreters of Life* (Kennerley, 1911); Alice Meynell, *Second Person Singular* (OUP, 1922); Osbert Burdett, *Critical Essays* (FF, 1925); Frederick P. Mayer, "GM, An Obscure Comedian," *VQR,* I (1925), 409-422; Ramon Fernandez, *Messages* (HB, 1927); Thomas Hardy, "GM, A Reminiscence," *XIX C,* CIII (1928), 145-148; John Erskine, *The Delight of Great Books;* A. K. Tuell, *A Victorian at Bay* (Marshall Jones, 1932); J. L. Lowes, *Essays in Appreciation* (HM, 1936); E. Arthur Robinson, "M's Literary Theory and Science: Realism Versus the Comic Spirit," *PMLA,* LIII (1938), 857-868.

Chapter XX: Hardy and the Cosmic Drama

Standard editions of Thomas Hardy include the Wessex Edition, 23 vols. (M, 1912-1914) and the Mellstock Edition, 37 vols. (M, 1919-1920). Carl J. Weber edited *Tess of the D'Urbervilles* (H, 1935) and *Far from the Madding Crowd* (OUP, 1937). An important, though unauthorized, collection of critical essays by Hardy is *Life and Art,* ed. Ernest Brennecke, Jr. (Greenberg, 1925).

Carl J. Weber has built up an immense Hardy library at Colby College, which has now become a great center for the study of Hardy. Most of Weber's pre-1940 publications are omitted from this list as all are now listed in his *First Hundred Years of TH, 1840-1940* (Colby College Library, 1942), which attempts a complete listing of everything written about Hardy to 1940. There is *A TH Dictionary,* by F. Outwin Saxelby (Du, 1911).

Hardy's authorized biography is in two books by his second wife, Florence Emily Hardy, *The Early Life of TH* and *The Later Years of TH* (M, 1928, 1930). Weber's *Hardy of Wessex* (ColUP, 1940) is a splendid critical biography. Cf. also E. Brennecke, Jr., *The Life of TH* (Greenberg, 1925).

The following books are all critical studies. I have placed an asterisk before the most important titles. Annie Macdonell (H&S, 1894); F. A. Hedgcock, *TH: Penseur et Artiste* (Paris, Librairie Hachette, 1911); *Lascelles Abercrombie, *TH, A Critical Study* (Secker, 1912; VP, 1927); Lina Wright Berle, *George Eliot and TH* (Kennerley, 1917); A. Stanton Whitfield, *TH, The Artist, The Man, and The Disciple of Destiny* (Richards, 1921); *Joseph Warren Beach, *The Technique of TH* (UCP, 1922); *Lionel Johnson, *The Art of TH,* New edition (DM, 1923); R. Williams, *The Wessex Novels* (De, 1924); H. B. Grimsditch, *Character and Environment in the Novels of TH* (Witherby, 1925); Arthur Symons, *A Study of TH* (Sawyer, 1927); *Samuel C. Chew, *TH, Poet and Novelist* (K, 1928); Pierre d'Exideuil, *The Human Pair in the Work of TH* (Toulmin, 1930); H. M. Tomlinson (Crosby Gaige, 1929); Arthur S. McDowall (FF, 1931); D. H. Lawrence, "Study of TH," *Phoenix* (VP, 1936); *H. C. Duffin, *TH, A Study of the Wessex Novels, The Poems, and The Dynasts,* Third Edition (Manchester University Press, 1937); Alfred Colling, *Le Romancier de la Fatalité: TH* (Emile-Paul, 1938); *W. R. Rutland, *TH, A Study of His Writings and Their Background* (Bl, 1938); H. W. Nevinson (Allen & Unwin, 1941); *Edmund Blunden (M, 1942).

The following brief studies may also be noted: J. M. Barrie, "TH, The Historian of Wessex," *CR,* LVI (1889), 57-66; W. L. Phelps, *Essays on Modern Novelists* (M, 1910); Harold Williams, "The Wessex Novels of

TH," *NAR,* CXCIX (1914), 120-134; John Gould Fletcher, "The Spirit of TH," *YR,* XIII (1923-1924), 322-333; R. P. Utter, *Pearls and Pepper;* Robert Shafer, *Christianity and Naturalism* (YUP, 1926); J. H. Fowler, *The Novels of TH, EAP,* No. 71 (1928); John Freeman, *English Portraits and Reviews* (H&S, 1924); W. L. Phelps, "TH's Fifteen Novels," *Forum,* LXXIX (1928), 436-447; J. C. Squire, *LM,* XVII (1928), 337-341; S. M. Ellis, "TH: Some Personal Recollections," *Fort,* CXXIX (1928), 393-406; G. B. Berry, *XIX C,* CXXVIII (1940), 377-389; Carl J. Weber, "Chronology in H's Novels," *PMLA,* LIII (1938), 314-320—cf. John P. Emery, LIV (1939), 618-619, and Weber's reply, p. 620; also A. A. Murphree and C. F. Strauch, "The Chronology of *The Return of the Native,*" *MLN,* LIV (1939), 491-497; Phyllis Bentley, "TH as a Regional Novelist," *Fort,* CLIII (1940), 647-652; Carl J. Weber, "Ainsworth and TH," *RES,* XVII (1941), 193-200; and "H's Grim Note in *The Return of the Native,*" *Bibliographical Society of America Papers,* XXXVI, No. 1, 37-45 (1942).

Chapter XXI: Romance Resurgent: Robert Louis Stevenson

Standard editions of Stevenson include the Thistle, 26 vols. (1902), Vailima, 26 vols. (1922-1923), South Seas, 32 vols. (1925), and Tusitala, 35 vols. (He, 1923-1924). The later editions include new material. All books listed in this note are published by S unless otherwise indicated.

There is *A Bibliography of the Works of RLS,* by W. F. Prideaux, revised by Flora L. Livingston (Miner Co., St. Louis, 1917). George E. Brown's *A Book of R.L.S.* (1919) is the closest approach that has been made to a dictionary.

The authorized biography is *The Life of RLS* by Graham Balfour (1901). Sidney Colvin edited Stevenson's *Letters* (1899), *Vailima Letters* (1895), and *New Letters* (1912); these are often included in editions of Stevenson. A modern biography is Rosaline O. Masson, *The Life of RLS* (St, 1923). John A. Steuart, *RLS, Man and Writer,* 2 vols. (LB, 1926) and George S. Hellman, *The True S, A Study in Clarification* (LB, 1925) are both iconoclastic, which is to say that they bring out into the full light of day a number of matters concerning which earlier writers were more discreet. Jean Marie Carré, *The Frail Warrior, A Life of RLS* (CM, 1930) is a French book, based on Steuart and Hellman; Malcolm Elwin takes the same point of view in two long chapters on Stevenson in *Old Gods Falling.*

The following list contains, I hope, all the most important items among the many books that have been published about Stevenson: Margaret M. Black (Oliphant, 1898); L. Cope Cornford (Blackwood, 1899); H. B. Baildon, *RLS, A Life Study in Criticism* (CW, 1901);

Isobel Strong and Lloyd Osbourne, *Memories of Vailima* (1902); Leslie Stephen (P, 1902); Arthur Johnstone, *Recollections of RLS in the Pacific* (CW, 1905); W. R. Nicoll & G. K. Chesterton (1906); Walter Raleigh (1908), which was originally given as a lecture in 1895, one of the very earliest critical studies of Stevenson; J. H. Moors, *With S in Samoa* (Small, Maynard, 1910); J. A. Hammerton, *Stevensoniana,* revised ed. (Edinburgh, John Grant, 1910), a vast collection of material from printed sources; Katherine D. Osbourne, *RLS in California* (McClurg, 1911); Isobel Strong (1911); E. B. Simpson, *The RLS Originals* (1913); Francis Watt, *R. L. S.* (M, 1913); E. B. Simpson, *RLS's Edinburgh Days* (H&S, 1898); Clayton Hamilton, *On the Trail of Stevenson* (DD, 1915), which was the first book to take up the attitude afterwards expressed by Steuart and Hellman; Amy Cruse (St, 1915); Stephen Chalmers, *The Penny Piper of Saranac* (HM, 1916), *Enchanted Cigarettes* (HM, 1917); Lord Guthrie, *RLS: Some Personal Recollections* (Edinburgh, Green, 1920); R. O. Masson, *I Can Remember RLS* (St, 1923), a collection of living reminiscences; Frank Swinnerton, *RLS, A Critical Study,* revised ed. (Do, 1923), which stands with E. F. Benson's article, noted below, as the most intelligent expression of the views of the anti-Stevensonians; Lloyd Osbourne, *An Intimate Portrait of R.L.S.* (1924); A. St. John Adcock, *RLS, His Work and His Personality* (H&S, 1924); G. K. Chesterton (DM, 1928), a stimulating study; Sidney Dark (H&S, 1931); Doris L. Dalglish, *Presbyterian Pirate, A Portrait of S* (OUP, 1937), an eccentric and affected book; Isobel Field, *This Life I've Loved* (L, 1937), the enthusiastic autobiography of Stevenson's stepdaughter, formerly known as Isobel Strong; Janet Adam Smith (Duckworth, 1937); Richard A. Bermann, *Home from the Sea, RLS in Samoa* (BM, 1939), "an imaginative recreation of S's last two years"; Anne R. Issler, *S at Silverado* (Caxton Printers, 1939).

Reference may also be made to the following brief studies: John Jay Chapman, *Emerson and Other Essays* (1898); W. L. Phelps, *Essays on Modern Novelists;* John Freeman, *English Portraits and Reviews;* E. F. Benson, "The Myth of RLS," *LM,* XII (1925), 268-283, 372-384; Louise M. Rosenblatt, "The Writer's Dilemma: A Case History and a Critique," *International Journal of Ethics,* XLVI (1935-1936), 195-211; Janet Adam Smith, "Henry James and RLS," *LM,* XXXIV (1936), 412-420.

Chapter XXII: Victorian Sunset

Mrs. Ward. The Westmoreland Edition, 16 vols. (HM, 1909 ff.) stops with *The Case of Richard Meynell.* For biography, cf. Mrs. Humphry Ward, *A Writer's Recollections,* 2 vols. (H, 1918) and Janet Penrose Trevelyan, *The Life of Mrs. HW* (Co, 1923). There are two brief critical studies in book form, neither of which is very good: J. Stuart Walters, *Mrs. HW, Her Work and Influence* (Kegan, Paul, 1912) and Stephen Gwynn, *Mrs. HW* (Ht, 1917). M. E. Speare, *The Political Novel* considers *Marcella* and *Sir George Tressady*. The best critical study is in an article by O. W. Firkins, *Weekly Review,* III (1920), 368-370. Cf. also H. W. Mabie, "The Work of Mrs. HW," *NAR,* CLXXVI (1903), 481-489; W. L. Phelps, *Essays on Modern Novelists;* Alfred Fawkes, "The Ideas of Mrs. HW," *LA,* CCLXXV (1912), 3-15; Charles S. Olcott, *The Lure of the Camera* (HM, 1914); Arnold Bennett, *Books and Persons* (CW, 1917); R. M. Lovett, "Mary in Wonderland," *Dial,* LXVI (1919), 463-465; Rowland Grey, "The Heroines of Mrs. HW," *Fort,* CXIII (1920), 886-896; Muriel Harris, *NAR,* CCXI (1920), 818-825; Edmund Gosse, *Silhouettes* (S, 1925).

HEWLETT. Maurice Hewlett's earlier books were published in America first by M, later by S; the later books were divided between many publishers. Biographical information will be found in *The Letters of MH,* ed. Laurence Binyon (Small, Maynard, 1926). The only detailed and authoritative critical study is Arthur Bruce Sutherland, *MH: Historical Romancer* (The Author, Department of English, Pennsylvania State College, 1938), where cf. excellent bibliography. Milton Bronner's book (Luce, 1910) is much less ambitious. See also Frederic Harrison, *Fort,* LXXV (1901), 61-71; Edith Lyttleton, *National Review,* XXXVII (1901), 444-452; Barrington O'Reardon, *SR,* XXI (1913), 99-107; J. C. Squire, "MH, Man of Many Talents," *LA,* CCCXVIII (1923), 362-365; Stephen Gwynn, *Edinburgh Review,* CCXXXIX (1924), 61-72; John Freeman, *English Portraits and Reviews;* W. H. Graham, *Fort,* CXXIV (1925), 47-63; Richard Church, "MH Reconsidered," *Fort,* CXLI (1934), 96-102.

BARRIE. The Peter Pan Edition, 18 vols. (1929-1941), is definitive, but the earlier and cheaper Thistle Edition contains all the fiction except *Farewell Miss Julie Logan. The Greenwood Hat,* 1938, was as close as Barrie came to autobiography, though there is much about him in the book he wrote about his mother, *Margaret Ogilvy* (1896). The authorized biography is Denis Mackail, *Barrie, The Story of J.M.B.* (1941). Cf. also Thomas Moult (1928); F. J. Harvey Darton (Ht, 1929); J. A. Hammerton, *B, The Story of a Genius* (DM, 1929); James A. Roy, *JMB, An Appreciation* (1938); W. A. Darlington (Blackie, 1938). The two best articles are Dixon Scott's in *Men of Letters* (H&S, 1916) and J. B. Priestley's, *English Journal,* XVIII (1929), 106-119. Cf. also W. M. Parker, *Modern Scottish Writers* (Hodge, 1917); Louis Wilkinson, "Sir JB, Confectioner and Parlour-Magician," *Dial,* LXXV (1923), 167-169; Henry Bett, *London Quarterly Review,* CLXII (1937), 477-488. For bibliography cf. Herbert Garland, *A Bibliography of the Writings of Sir JMB, Bart., O.M.* (The Bookman's Journal, 1928); H. D. Cutler, *Sir JMB, A Bibliography* (Greenberg, 1931). All books not otherwise assigned in this note are published by S.

Kipling. The Burwash Edition, 28 vols. (DD, 1941), is complete and definitive. (DD publish all books in this note not otherwise accredited.) Earlier editions include the Outward Bound (S, 1897-1937), the Seven Seas (1913-1926) and the Sussex (M, 1937-1938). *Something of Myself* (1937) was a kind of autobiography. The most recent bibliography is Flora V. Livingston, *Bibliography of the Works of RK* (Edgar H. Wells, 1927); cf. her supplement in *Colophon,* Part VII (1931). W. Arthur Young has a *Dictionary of the Characters and Scenes in the Stories and Poems of RK, 1886-1891* (Du, 1911). *A K Primer,* by F. L. Knowles (Brown & Co., 1899) has small value as criticism but is useful for many descriptive notes. Probably the two best critical studies are Richard Le Gallienne, *RK, A Criticism* (Lane, 1900), which is definitely anti-Kipling, and Edward Shanks, *RK, A Study in Literature and Political Ideas* (1940), which is a defense. Other book-length studies are Cecil Charles, *RK, The Man and His Work* (Hewetson, 1911); Cyril Falls, *RK, A Critical Study* (Secker, 1915); John L. Palmer (Ht, 1915); W. M. Hart, *K The Story-Writer* (U. of California Press, 1918); Patrick Braybrooke, *K and His Soldiers* (Daniel, 1926); Robert T. Hopkins, *RK, The Story of a Genius* (Palmer, 1930). Among shorter pieces, cf. G. K. Chesterton, *Heretics* (DM, 1905); W. L. Phelps, *Essays on Modern Novelists;* A. R. Sarath-Roy, "RK Seen Through Hindu Eyes," *NAR,* CXCIX (1914), 271-281; Dixon Scott, *Men of Letters;* F. A. Waterhouse, "The Literary Fortunes of K," *YR,* X (1921), 817-831; Philip Guedalla, *A Gallery* (P, 1924); R. Ellis Roberts, *LA,* CCCXXXIV (1928), 1217-1224; Maurice Hutton, *Many Minds* (Ht, 1927); Archibald Henderson, *Contemporary Immortals* (AC, 1930); Angela Thirkell, *Three Houses* (OUP, 1931); Katharine F. Gerould, *Modes and Morals* (S, 1933); Edith Mirrielees, "Time and Mr. K," *VQR,* XI (1935), 37-46; Hugh Kingsmill, *English Review,* LXII (1936), 150-156, cf. discussion, pp. 373-376, 507-508; Rebecca West, *LA,* CCCL (1936), 38-43; Hilton Brown, "RK, A Reassessment," *XIX C,* CXXVIII (1940), 39-50.

Chapter XXIII: Towards a New Century

Gissing. A number of novels by Gissing are published in America by Du. *New Grub Street* and *The Private Papers of Henry Ryecroft* are in The Modern Library, *Veranilda* in WC. *Workers in the Dawn,* 2 vols., ed. Robert Shafer, is published by the Odyssey Press (1935), and Shafer's introduction is the best place to begin the study of Gissing; cf. also his article, "The Vitality of GG," *American Review,* V (1935), 459-487. In 1929, C published a volume of *Selections, Autobiographical and Imaginative, from the Works of GG,* ed. A. C. Gissing, introduction by Virginia Woolf.

There is a substantial collection of *Letters of GG to Members of His Family,* ed. Algernon and Ellen Gissing (HM, 1927). Morley Roberts, who knew Gissing well, unfortunately chose to write his biography in the form of a novel, *The Private Life of Henry Maitland,* revised ed. (Geo. H. Doran, 1912); for key, cf. Shafer's *Workers in the Dawn,* p. li. For further comments by Roberts on Gissing, cf. *Queen's Quarterly,* XXXVII (1930), 617-632, "Letters of GG," *VQR,* VII (1931), 409-426, and his introductions to the Gissing novels published by Du. Other friends and relatives who have written of Gissing include H. G. Wells, "The Novels of Mr. GG," *Contemporary Review,* LXXII (1897), 192-201, "GG, An Impression," *Monthly Review,* XVI, August, 1904, pp. 160-170, and *Experiment in Autobiography* (M, 1934)—(cf. Shafer, *Workers in the Dawn,* pp. xxxi-xxxiv); Frederic Harrison, Introduction to *Veranilda* (Co, 1904); Thomas Seccombe, Introduction to *The House of Dreams* (Co, 1906); Austin Harrison, *LA,* CCLI (1906), 216-225; Anon., "Some Recollections of GG," *Gentleman's Magazine,* N.S. LXXVI (1906), 11-18; Edward Clodd, *Memories* (Chapman & Hall, 1916); George A. Stearns, "GG in America," *B*(NY), LXIII (1926), 683-686; Ellen Gissing, "GG, A Character Sketch," *XIX C,* CII (1927), 417-424; A. C. Gissing, "GG, Some Aspects of His Life and Work," *National Review,* XCIII (1929), 932-941.

The fullest studies of Gissing's work are May Yates, *GG, An Appreciation* (Manchester University Press, 1922) and Frank Swinnerton, *GG, A Critical Study,* revised ed. (DD, 1923). Swinnerton has been critically examined by A. Rotter, *Frank Swinnerton und GG* (Prague, Rudolf M. Rohrer, 1931) and by Ruth C. McKay, *GG and His Critic, Frank Swinnerton,* Thesis, Ph.D., University of Pennsylvania (1933). Leslie Lisle Lewis did a Cornell thesis (1933), and Samuel Vogt Gapp produced another, *GG, Classicist,* for the University of Pennsylvania (1936). A number of other theses in German are listed by Shafer. Briefer studies include: James H. Findlater, "The Spokesman of Despair," *LA,* CCXLIII (1904), 733-741; Arthur Waugh, *LA,* CCXL (1904), 714-723; Stanley Alden, "GG, Humanist," *NAR,* CCXVI (1922), 364-377. The London *Bookman* had a Gissing number in Vol. XVII—1915.

MOORE. The Works of George Moore have been collected in the Carra Edition, 21 vols. (Boni & Liveright, 1922-1924) and the Ebury Edition, 20 vols. (He, 1936-1938). Joseph Hone, *The Life of GM* (M, 1936) is the "official" biography. There is a volume of *Conversations with GM* by Geraint Goodwin (K, 1929). Cf. also Susan L. Mitchell (DM, 1916);

John Freeman, *A Portrait of GM in a Study of His Work* (AC, 1922); Humbert Wolfe (Shaylor, 1931); Charles Morgan, *Epitaph on GM* (M, 1935). Briefer studies include: G. K. Chesterton, *Heretics* (Lane, 1905); Forrest Reid, "The Novels of GM," *Westminster Review,* CLXXII (1909), 200-208; James Huneker, *Overtones, The Pathos of Distance, Unicorns* (S, 1904, 1913, 1917); Duncan Phillips, *YR,* VI (1916-1917), 342-357; Joseph Hergesheimer, *Literary Review,* IV (1923), 361-362; Humbert Wolfe, *Dialogues and Monologues* (K, 1929); Hellmut Bock, "GM: The Brook Kerith, Eine kritische Studie," *Die Neueren Sprachen,* XXXIX (1931), 340-355; Osbert Burdett, *LM,* XXVII (1932-1933), 415-426; Thomas J. Lynch, *Commonweal,* XVII (1933), 629-631; Mercury Patten, *New Statesman & Nation,* V (1933), 103; R. Ellis Roberts, *XIX Century,* CXIII (1933), 369-383.

Butler. The Shrewsbury Edition of Samuel Butler, ed. Henry Festing Jones and A. T. Bartholomew, 20 vols. (Du, 1923-1926), is definitive. In 1936, OUP published an edition of *The Way of All Flesh* with an introduction by Bernard Shaw. For bibliography, cf. A. J. Hoppé, *A Bibliography of the Writings of SB* (Bowker, 1925). The authorized biography is H. F. Jones, *SB, A Memoir,* 2 vols. (M, 1919), to which may be added *Letters Between SB and Miss E. M. A. Savage* (C, 1935). But the student will find his best introduction to the study of Butler in Clara G. Stillman's admirable biographical and critical study, *SB, A Mid-Victorian Modern* (VP, 1932). Mrs. Stillman may be somewhat too enthusiastic about her subject, but this is better than to err in the opposite direction, as does the devil's advocate of Butler criticism, Malcolm Muggeridge, *The Earnest Atheist* (P, 1937). In addition to the foregoing there are the following books about Butler: Gilbert Cannan (Secker, 1915); John F. Harris (DM, 1916); C. E. M. Joad (Small, Maynard, 1924); Mrs. R. S. Garnett, *SB and His Family Relations* (Dutton, 1926). To the works of continental origin listed in Mrs. Stillman's working bibliography one should add at least J. B. Fort, 2 vols. (Bordeaux, Bière, 1934). From the multitudinous briefer discussions I have chosen the following either because they concern themselves particularly with Butler's fiction or because they present an interesting point of view: Howard Maynadier, "A Brick at a New Literary Idol," *SR,* XXVII (1919), 303-319; J. Middleton Murry, *Aspects of Literature* (Collins, 1920); Maurice Hewlett, *In a Green Shade* (Bell, 1920); Joseph B. Harrison, "SB Revisited," *Pacific Review,* II (1921-1922), 257-272; Edmund Gosse, *Aspects and Impressions* (S, 1922); Horace J. Bridges, *As I Was Saying* (Marshall Jones, 1923); Stuart Sherman, *Points of View* (S, 1927); R. M. Lovett, *Preface to Fiction* (Rockwell, 1931); Robert Shafer, *Christianity and Naturalism* (YUP, 1932); Edmund Wilson, *The Triple Thinkers* (HB, 1938); Nevin Dilworth, "The

Second Passing of SB," *SAQ,* XL (1941), 37-45; Lee E. Holt, "SB and His Victorian Critics," *ELH,* VIII (1941), 146-159, and "SB's Rise to Fame," *PMLA,* LVII (1942), 867-878. See also the Samuel Butler number of *Life and Letters,* October, 1931.

Chapter XXIV: Values and Joseph Conrad

DD are Conrad's authorized publishers in America. This house has published the limited Sun Dial Edition and the popular-priced Concord and Complete Editions. All books in this note not otherwise accredited bear the imprint of this house.

The authorized biography is G. Jean Aubry, *JC Life and Letters,* 2 vols., 1927. More letters will be found in *JC's Letters to His Wife* (London, privately printed, 1927); Edward Garnett, *Letters from JC, 1895-1924* (BM, 1928); Richard Curle, *Conrad to a Friend* (1928); John A. Gee and Paul J. Sturm, *Letters of JC to Marguerite Poradowska* (YUP, 1940); Carl Bohnenberger and Norman Mitchell Hill, "The Letters of JC to Stephen and Cora Crane," *B*(NY), LXIX (1929), 225-235, 367-374. Richard Curle edited "C's Diary [in the Congo, 1890]," *YR,* XV (1926), 254-266; cf. Otto Lütken, "JC in the Congo," *LM,* XXII (1930), 40-43, 261-263, 350-351.

The foundation for bibliographical work has been laid in T. J. Wise, *A Bibliography of the Writings of JC, 1895-1920* (London, privately printed, 1921). Cf. also *A C Library, A Collection of Printed Books, Manuscripts, and Autograph Letters, by JC, Collected by T. J. Wise* (Same, 1928); *A C Memorial Library. The Collection of George T. Keating* (1929); J. T. Babb, "A Check List of Additions to a C Memorial Library," *Yale University Library Gazette,* XII (1938), 30-40.

The following books deal with C's life and personality: Ford Madox Ford, *JC, A Personal Reminiscence* (LB, 1924) and *Return to Yesterday* (Lippincott, 1931); Jessie Conrad, *JC as I Knew Him* (1926) and *JC and His Circle* (Du, 1935), which should be checked by reference to E. Garnett's review, *LM,* XXXII (1935), 385-387; Richard Curle, *The Last Twelve Years of JC* (1928); J. H. Retinger, *C and His Contemporaries* (FF, 1941). Less detailed remembrances will be found in Ernest Rhys, "An Interview with JC," *B*(NY), LVI (1922-1923), 402-408; R. B. Cunninghame Graham, *Inveni Portum* (Rowfant Club, 1924); Cecil Roberts, "JC, A Reminiscence," *B*(NY), LXI (1925), 536-542; Walter Tittle, "The C Who Sat for Me," *Outlook,* CXL (1925), 333-335, 361-362; Ernest Dawson, "Some Recollections of JC," *Fort,* CXXX (1928), 203-212; Robin Douglas, "My Boyhood with C," *CoM,* N.S. LXVI (1929), 20-28; Sir Henry Newbolt, *My World as in My Time* (FF, 1932); William Rothenstein, *Men and Memories, Recollections,*

1900-1922 (CM, 1932); Elbridge L. Adams, "JC the Man," *Outlook*, CXXXIII (1933), 708-712; John Galsworthy, *Candelabra* (S, 1933); Richard Curle, "JC: Ten Years After," *VQR*, X (1934), 420-435; H. G. Wells, *Experiment in Autobiography* (M, 1934).

The most scholarly book yet written about Conrad is John D. Gordan, *JC, The Making of a Novelist* (HUP, 1940); this is a study of the sources and development of *Almayer's Folly, The Nigger,* and *Lord Jim*. It is curious that in spite of the tremendous amount of critical writing that has appeared, there should as yet be no comprehensive critical study. The most elaborate book in English is Richard Curle, *JC, A Study* (1914), which necessarily stops with *Chance*. The most brilliant is Edward Crankshaw, *JC, Some Aspects of the Art of the Novel* (Lane, 1936). There are three introductory studies: Hugh Walpole (Ht, 1929); F. W. Cushwa, *Introduction to C* (1933); M. C. Bradbrook (M, 1941). Cf. also Wilson Follett (1915); Ruth M. Stauffer, *JC, His Romantic Realism* (Four Seas Co., 1922); Ernest Bendz, *JC, An Appreciation* (Gothenburg, N. J. Gumpert, 1923); Arthur Symons, *Notes on JC with Some Unpublished Letters* (London, Myers & Co., 1925)—cf. *Forum*, LIII (1915), 579-592; V. Walpole, *C's Method, Some Formal Aspects* (Beperk, Nasionale Pers, 1928); Liam O'Flaherty, *JC, an Appreciation* (E. Lahr, 1930); Arthur J. Price, *An Appreciation of JC* (Newport, Joyce & Son, 1931); R. L. Mégroz, *JC's Mind and Method* (FF, 1931).

From the vast assortment of critical articles about Conrad, I can only offer a selection from those I personally found most stimulating: Mary Austin, "A Sermon in One Man," *Harper's Weekly*, LVIII, May 16, 1914, p. 20; James Huneker, *Ivory, Apes, and Peacocks* (S, 1915); H. L. Mencken, *A Book of Prefaces* (K, 1917); J. M. Robertson, "The Novels of JC," *NAR*, CCVIII (1918), 439-453; Edward Moore, "A Note on Mr. C," *New Statesman*, XIII (1919), 590-592; F. Melian Stawell, *E&S*, VI (1920); William McFee, *Harbors of Memory* (1921) and *Swallowing the Anchor* (1925); R. M. Lovett, "The Realm of C," *Asia*, XXIII (1923), 325-327; Edward Shanks, *LM*, IX (1923-1924), 502-511; Cornelius Weygandt, "The Art of JC," *Schelling Anniversary Papers* (AC, 1923); C. K. Allan, *CR*, CXXV (1924), 54-61; George W. Whiting, "C's Revision of Lord Jim," *Eng. Jour.*, XXIII (1934), 824-832, "C's Revision of Six of His Short Stories," *PMLA*, XLVIII (1933), 552-557, and "Conrad's Revision of 'The Lighthouse' in *Nostromo*," LII (1937), 1183-1190; H. T. Burt, *Hibbert Journal*, XXIII (1924-1925), 141-157; Edwin Muir, *Latitudes* (Huebsch, 1924); Leonard Woolf, *Nation and Athenaeum*, XXXV (1924), 595; H. J. Bridges, *The God of Fundamentalism* (Covici, 1925); J. B. Priestley, *English Journal*, XIV (1925), 13-21; P. A. Hutchison, "JC, Alchemist of the Sea," *Essays in Memory of Barrett Wendell* (HUP, 1926); Ramon Fernandez, *Messages;*

E. E. Kellett, *Reconsiderations* (M, 1928); A. R. Thompson, "The Humanism of JC," *SR,* XXXVII (1929), 204-220; Granville Hicks, "C After Five Years," *New Republic,* LXI (1930), 192-194; Irwin Anthony, "The Illusion of JC," *B*(NY), LXXIV (1931-1932), 648-653; R. G. Lillard, "Irony in Hardy and C," *PMLA,* L (1935), 316-322; Florence Clemens, "C's Favorite Bedside Book," *SAQ,* XXXVIII (1939), 305-315, and "C's Malaysia," *College English,* II (1940-1941), 338-346; James V. Fletcher, "Ethical Symbolism in C," *College English,* II (1940-1941), 19-26; M. D. Zabel, "C: The Secret Sharer," *New Republic,* CIV (1941), 567-574.

Chapter XXV: Novelist of Being: Arnold Bennett

Nearly all Bennett's books were published in the United States by Do and DD. Most of these are now out of print but English editions are still available.

For his personality, cf. *The Journal of AB* (VP, 1933) and Richard Bennett, *The Letters of AB to His Nephew* (He, 1936). Among Bennett's own non-fiction writings the following contain interesting sidelights on his personality and literary theories: *Fame and Fiction* (1901); *The Truth About an Author* (1903); *How to Become an Author* (1903); *The Author's Craft* (1914); *Books and Persons, 1908-1911* (1917); *Things That Have Interested Me* (1921, 1923, 1925).

Mrs. Arnold Bennett has published two books: *AB* (Adelphi Co., 1925) and *My AB* (Du, 1931). Dorothy Cheston Bennett has written *AB, A Portrait Done at Home* (C, 1935). The following friends and acquaintances have all recorded their memories: Walter Tittle, "Portraits in Pencil and Pen," *Ce,* CVIII (1924), 497-500; William Gerhardi, "Reminiscences of AB," *Saturday Review,* CLI (1931), 709-710; R. Ellis Roberts, *XIX C,* CIX (1931), 611-624; Rebecca West, *AB Himself* (John Day, 1931); Violet Hunt, "AB in Paris," *B*(NY), LXXV (1932), 345-348; Pauline Smith, *A.B., A Minor Marginal Note* (C, 1933); W. S. Maugham, "Living in the Grand Hotel," *SRL,* IX (1933), 601-602; H. G. Wells, *Experiment in Autobiography;* George H. Doran, *Chronicles of Barabbas* (HB, 1935); Frank Swinnerton, *Swinnerton, An Autobiography* (DD, 1936).

The most penetrating and comprehensive critical study is Georges Lafourcade (Frederick Muller, 1939). J. B. Simons, *AB and His Novels* (Bl, 1936) is quite as comprehensive but much less penetrating. Geoffrey West, *The Problem of AB* (Joiner & Steele, 1932) is as penetrating but much less comprehensive. Other studies between covers are F. J. Harvey Darton (Ht, 1913) and L. G. Johnson (C. W. Daniel, 1924).

The following appear as magazine articles or as chapters in books: F. G. Bettany, "AB, An Appreciation," *LA,* CCLXIX (1911), 131-136; W. D. Howells, "Editor's Easy Chair," *HaM,* CXXII (1911), 633-636; R. A. Scott-James, *Personality in Literature* (Secker, 1913); Dorothea Price Hughes, "The Novels of Mr. AB and Wesleyan Methodism," *CR,* CX (1916), 602-610; H. L. Mencken, *Prejudices, First Series* (K, 1919); Sidney Hayes Cox, "Romance in AB," *SR,* XXVIII (1920), 358-366; Clara F. McIntyre, "AB and Old Age," *Personalist,* IV (1923), 31-38; Brian W. Downs, *NAR,* CCXIX (1924), 71-81; J. B. Priestley, *Figures in Modern Literature* (DM, 1924); George B. Dutton, "AB, Showman," *SR,* XXXIII (1925), 64-72; Virginia Woolf, *Mr. Bennett and Mrs. Brown* (Hogarth Press, 1925); Lucy L. Hazard, "AB, Optimist," *Overland Monthly,* LXXXIII (1925), 13-17, 43; Rebecca West, *The Strange Necessity* (DD, 1928); M. St. Clare Byrne, "AB and His Critics," *National Review,* XCVI (1931), 702-706; Orlo Williams, "The Old Wives' Tale," *National Review,* XCIX (1932), 387-397; Desmond McCarthy, "Notes on AB," *LA,* CCCXLIV (1933), 526-533; Elizabeth D. Wheatley, "AB's Trifles: His Novels for the Gay Middle-Aged," *SR,* XLII (1934), 180-189.

Chapter XXVI: H. G. Wells, "Realist of the Fantastic"

The Atlantic Edition of *The Works of H. G. Wells,* 28 vols., was published by S (1924-1927). It stops with *The Dream.*

The most valuable commentaries are the author's own *Experiment in Autobiography* (M, 1934) and two authorized works by Geoffrey H. Wells (Geoffrey West), *The Works of HGW, 1887-1925, A Bibliography, Dictionary, and Subject-Index* (Wilson, 1926), and *HGW* (Norton, 1930).

To these may be added: J. D. Beresford (Ht, 1915); Van Wyck Brooks, *The World of HGW* (Kennerley, 1915); Edouard Guyot (Paris, Payot, 1920); Sidney Dark, *An Outline of W* (P, 1922); R. Thurston Hopkins, *HGW, Personality, Character, Topography* (Palmer, 1922); John S. Price, *The World in the Wellsian Era* (Cardiff, Stacy Hall, 1923); Ivor Brown (Ht, 1924); Patrick Braybrooke, *Some Aspects of HGW* (Daniel, 1928). The controversies growing out of *God the Invisible King* and *The Outline of History* produced a number of books which need not be listed here. F. H. Doughty's *HGW, Educationist* (Do, 1927) is also a specialized study.

Personal impressions of Wells will be found in Sir Harry H. Johnston, *The Story of My Life* (BM, 1923); St. John G. Ervine, *Some Impressions of My Elders;* Mary Austin, *Earth Horizon* (HM, 1932); Frank Swinnerton, *Swinnerton, An Autobiography.*

There is no extensive or adequate critical study of Wells's novels. Geoffrey West's *HGW* started out to be just that but turned instead to biography. Brief studies will be found in: G. K. Chesterton, *Heretics* (DM, 1905); Thomas Seccombe, *LA,* CCLXXXII (1914), 392-405; W. Handley Jones, "The Message of Mr. HGW," *LA,* CCLXXXVI (1915), 281-290; John Haynes Holmes, "HGW, Novelist and Prophet," *B*(NY), XLIII (1916), 507-514; E. E. Slosson, *Six Major Prophets* (LB, 1917); Wilfrid Lay, "HGW and His Mental Hinterland," *B*(NY), XLV (1917), 461-468; H. L. Mencken, *Prejudices, First Series;* Edward Shanks, "The Work of Mr. HGW," *LM,* V (1921-1922), 506-518; Brother Leo, "A Poet Frustrate: HGW," *Catholic World,* CXVIII (1923-1924), 297-305; A. Wyatt Tilby, *ER,* CCXXXVII (1923), 113-132; James M. Gillis, *False Prophets* (M, 1925); J. B. Priestley, *English Journal,* XIV (1925), 89-97; Stuart Sherman, *Contemporary Woodcuts* (S, 1926); Maxwell Struthers Burt, *The Other Side* (S, 1928); Harold Laski, *LA,* CCCXXXIX (1930-1931), 287-289.

Chapter XXVII: Pity, Irony, and John Galsworthy

The Manaton Edition of Galsworthy's *Works,* 30 vols. (1922 ff.), is complete and definitive; the Devon Edition, 22 vols. (1926-1927), covers *Novels, Tales, and Plays* but does not take in any fiction later than *A Modern Comedy.* All books not otherwise accredited in this note are published in America by S.

H. V. Marrot, *The Life and Letters of JG* (1936) is the authorized biography. The same writer has published *A Bibliography of the Works of JG* (1928). Further letters appear in Edward Garnett, *Letters from JG, 1900-1932* (1934) and in *Autobiographical Letters: A Correspondence with Frank Harris* (English Bookshop, New York, 1933). There are volumes of reminiscences by Galsworthy's wife, Ada Galsworthy, *Over the Hills and Far Away* (1938), and by his sister, M. E. Reynolds, *Memories of JG* (St, 1937).

The following critical studies are available: Sheila Kaye-Smith (Ht, 1916); André Chevrillon, *Three Studies in English Literature* (He, 1923); Leon M. Schalit, *JG, A Survey* (1929), which includes a detailed criticism of all works through *A Modern Comedy;* Natalie Croman, *JG, A Study in Continuity and Contrast* (HUP, 1933); Edouard Guyot, *JG, Le Romancier* (Paris, H. Didier, 1933); Hermon Ould (Chapman & Hall, 1934). Brief critical studies are numerous but not particularly distinguished. Among those worth consulting are May Bateman, *Catholic World,* CXIV (1921-1922), 732-747; Dorothy Martin, "Mr. G as Artist and Reformer," *YR,* XIV (1924), 126-139; J. B. Priestley, *English Journal,* XIV (1925), 347-355; A. Watt Tilby, "The Epic of Property," *ER,* CCXLI (1925), 271-285; Wilbur Cross, "The Forsytes," *YR,* XIX (1930), 527-550; H. P. Austin, *Dublin Review,* CLXXXIX (1931), 95-106; Homer E. Woodbridge, *Literary Review,* III (1923), 617-618; R. Colenutt, "The World of Mr. G's Fiction," *CoM,* CXLIX (1934), 55-64.

Chapter XXVIII: D. H. Lawrence, Pilgrim of the Rainbow

Lawrence's books are divided in America between K and VP. The standard bibliography is Edward D. McDonald, *A Bibliography of the Writings of DHL* (Philadelphia, The Centaur Book Shop, 1925). A *Supplement* was published in 1931. A useful check-list of books about L, with lively, highly personalized comments, is L. C. Powell, "DHL and His Critics," *Colophon,* New Graphic Series, No. 4 (1939).

A veritable library has been written about Lawrence, and not everything can be recorded here. The most important source of information for his life is *The Letters of DHL* (VP, 1932), Aldous Huxley's sympathetic introduction to which is an excellent taking-off place for serious study. To this may be added Horace Gregory, *Pilgrim of the Apocalypse* (VP, 1933). The most elaborate and challenging biographical study is J. Middleton Murry, *Son of Woman* (C, 1931). The only scholarly piece of research so far is W. Y. Tindall, *DHL and Susan His Cow* (ColUP, 1939).

The following friends and relatives have published their reminiscences of Lawrence: George H. Nevill, "The Early Days of DHL," *LM,* XXIII (1930-1931), 477-480; William Gerhardi, "Literary Vignettes, II," *Sat. Rev.,* CLI (1931), 893-894; Rebecca West, *Ending in Earnest* (DD, 1931); Ada Lawrence and G. Stuart Gelder, *The Early Life of DHL* (Secker, 1932); Mabel Dodge Luhan, *Lorenzo in Taos* (K, 1932); Catherine Carswell, *The Savage Pilgrimage* (HB, 1932), with which should be compared J. M. Murry's reply, *Reminiscences of DHL* (Ht, 1933); Dorothy Brett, *L and Brett, A Friendship* (Lippincott, 1933); Norman Douglas, "Chapters from an Autobiography," *B*(NY), LXXVI (1933), 105-109; David Garnett, Introduction to *Love Among the Haystacks* (VP, 1933); Earl and Achsah Brewster, *DHL: Reminiscences and Correspondence* (Secker, 1934); Frieda Lawrence (Mrs. D. H.), *"Not I, But the Wind . . ."* (VP, 1934); Knud Merrild, *A Poet and Two Painters* (VP, 1939); Richard Aldington, "DHL Six Years After," *SRL,* XX, June 24, 1939, pp. 3-4, 14. Hugh Kingsmill tried to bring scattered biographical data together in *The Life of DHL* (Dodge, 1938). Edward Shanks comments sarcastically on Lawrencian personalia in "Friends of DHL," *LM,* XXIX (1933-1934), 142-150.

The following books and articles are critical studies. I have marked those definitely hostile to Lawrence with an asterisk. Alfred Booth Kuttner, " 'Sons and Lovers,' A Freudian Appreciation," *Psychoanalytic Review,* III (1916), 295-317; * Joseph Collins, *The Doctor Looks at Literature* (Do, 1923); Edward Shanks, "Mr. DHL, Some Characteristics," *LM,* VIII (1923), 64-75; * W. P. Witcutt, "The Cult of DHL," *American Review,* III (1923), 161-166; * Stuart Sherman, *Critical Woodcuts;* Richard Aldington, *DHL, An Indiscretion* (University of Washington Book Store, 1927); Roger Chance, "Love and Mr. L," *Fort,* CXXXII (1929), 500-511; * Wyndham Lewis, *Paleface* (CW, 1929); F. R. Leavis (Cambridge, Minority Press, 1930); Melisandra, "DHL, Mystic of Sex," *Canadian Forum,* XI (1930), 15-17; Stephen Potter, *DHL, A First Study* (C, 1930); R. Ellis Roberts, *New Statesman,* XXXIV (1930), 701-702; Hugh R. Williamson, "DHL, The Last of the Puritans," *B*(L), LXXIX (1930), 177-178; Ruth F. Moore, "Spades and DHL," *B*(NY), LXXII (1930-1931), 118-125; Dayton Kohler, *SR,* XXXIX (1931), 25-38; * A. R. Thompson, "DHL, Apostle of the Dark God," *B*(NY), LXXIII (1931), 492-499; Frederick Carter, *DHL and the Body Mystical* (London, Denis Archer, 1932); Olive Moore, *Further Reflections on the Death of a Porcupine* (Blue Moon Press, 1932); * A. W. Harrison, "The Philosophy of DHL," *Hibbert Journal,* XXXII (1933-1934), 554-563; R. L. Mégroz, *Five Novelist-Poets of Today* (Joiner & Steele, 1933); * T. S. Eliot, *After Strange Gods* (HB, 1934); Dilys Powell, *Descent from Parnassus* (M, 1934); Henry Alexander, "L and Huxley," *Queen's Quarterly,* XLII (1935), 96-108; Stephen Spender, *The Destructive Element* (HM, 1935); John Hawley Roberts, "L and Huxley," *VQR,* XIII (1937), 546-557; M. Wildi, "The Birth of Expressionism in the Work of DHL," *English Studies,* XIX (1937), 241-259; T. M. Pearce, "The Unpublished 'Lady Chatterley's Lover,' " *New Mexico Quarterly,* VIII (1938), 171-179; Sigrid Undset, *Men, Women and Places* (K, 1939); Eliseo Vivas, "L's Problems," *Kenyon Review,* III (1940), 83-94.

Chapter XXIX: Stream-of-Consciousness

Dorothy Richardson. It may be useful to add the following reviews to the basic material, all of which is mentioned in the text: Babette Deutsch, "Imagism in Fiction," *Nation,* CVI (1918), 656; Anon., "Pilgrimage," *Nation,* CIX (1919), 720-721; Constance Rourke, *NR,* XX, Nov. 26, 1919, Pt. 2, pp. 14-15; Philip Littell, "Books and Things," *NR,* XXVI (1921), 267; Una Hunt, "Deadlock," *NR,* XXIX (1922), 313-314; Joseph Collins, *The Doctor Looks at Literature* (Do, 1923); Earl A. Aldrich, "The Vista of the Stream," *SRL,* IV (1928), 841; R. A. Scott-James, "Quintessential Feminism," *LM,* XXXIII (1935), 201-203; Paul Rosenfeld, "The Inner Life," *SRL,* XIX, Dec. 10, 1938, p. 6.

JOYCE. Joyce's books are published in America by Random House (Modern Library). The authorized biography is by Herbert Gorman (FR, 1939). To attempt to read Joyce's later writings without guidance is madness; to do this successfully, a reader would need Joyce's own Jesuit training, an intimate knowledge of early twentieth-century Dublin, and a familiarity with all the books Joyce ever read. The best general introduction is Harry Levin (New Directions, 1941). As to *Ulysses* specifically, it is well to begin with a good simple introductory essay, like Angus Burrell's in Burrell and Brewster, *Modern Fiction,* or Herbert J. Muller's in his *Modern Fiction,* or Edmund Wilson's in *Axel's Castle* (S, 1931). From this one must go on to Stuart Gilbert's 379-page exposition, *JJ's Ulysses, A Critical Study* (K, 1930). This is absolutely indispensable; Paul Jordan Smith's *A Key to the Ulysses of JJ* (Covici, 1927) is too brief, and was prepared before essential information was available. Cf. also Charles Duff, *JJ and the Plain Reader* (Desmond Harmsworth, 1932); L. Golding (Butterworth, 1933); Frank Budgen, *JJ and the Making of Ulysses* (Smith and Haas, 1934), an authorized interpretation combining commentary with personal reminiscences of Joyce. Valéry Larbaud, *Nouvelle Revue Française* (1922), was the pioneer discussion. Other very important articles are Bernhard Fehr, "JJ's 'Ulysses,'" *Englische Studien,* LX (1925-1926), 180-205, and S. Foster Damon, "The Odyssey in Dublin," *Hound and Horn,* III (1929).

Cf. also Richard Aldington, "The Influence of Mr. JJ," *English Review,* XXXII (1921), 333-341; Shane Leslie, "Ulysses," *QR,* CCXXXVIII (1922), 219-234; Arnold Bennett, *Things That Have Interested Me,* Second Series (Do, 1923); Joseph Collins, *The Doctor Looks at Literature;* Robert Cantwell, "The Influence of JJ," *NR,* LXXVII (1933-1934), 200-201; A. J. A. Waldock, *JJ and Others* (Williams & Norgate, 1937); Joseph Prescott, "JJ, A Study in Words," *PMLA,* LIV (1939), 304-315; Edwin B. Burgum, "*Ulysses* and the Impasse of Individualism," *VQR,* XVII (1941), 561-573; Theodore Spencer, "Stephen Hero: The Unpublished Manuscript of JJ's Portrait of the Artist as a Young Man," *Southern Review,* VII (1941), 174-186.

VIRGINIA WOOLF. Nearly all of V. W.'s books are published in America by HB. The most important of her critical writings for the understanding of her fiction are *Mr. Bennett and Mrs. Brown* (1924), the essays, "Modern Fiction" and "How It Strikes a Contemporary," in *The Common Reader,* and *A Room of One's Own.* There are three monographs in English: Winifred Holtby (Wishart, 1932); Ruth Gruber (Leipzig, Tauchnitz, 1935); David Daiches (New Directions, 1942), where cf. further bibliography. Cf. also E. M. Forster's brief study (HB, 1942). The following brief studies and reviews are all worth consulting: Clive Bell, *Dial,* LXXVII (1924), 451-465; Dudley Carew, *LA,* CCCXXX

(1926), 47-54; Edwin Muir, *Transition* (VP, 1926); Robert Herrick, "The Works of Mrs. Woolf," *SRL,* VIII (1931), 346; Mary E. Kelsey, "VW and the She-Condition," *SR,* XXXIX (1931), 425-444; Peter Burra, *XIX C,* CXV (1934), 112-125; John Hawley Roberts, "Toward VW," *VQR,* X (1934), 587-602, and "The End of the English Novel?" *VQR,* XIII (1937), 437-439; Joseph Warren Beach, *English Journal,* College Edition, XXVI (1937), 603-612; Lodowick Hartley, "Of Time and Mrs. W," *SR,* XLVII (1939), 235-241; B. G. Brooks, *XIX C,* CXXX (1941), 334-340; David Garnett, *New Statesman & Nation,* N.S. XXI (1941), 386; R. Ellis Roberts, "VW: 1882-1941," *SRL,* XXIII, Apr. 12, 1941, pp. 12, 19; Rose Macaulay, *Spectator,* CLXVI (1941), 394; N. Elizabeth Monroe, *The Novel and Society* (UNCP, 1941); James Southall Wilson, "Time and VW," *VQR,* XVIII (1942), 267-276; Warren Beck, "For VW," *American Prefaces,* VII (1942), 316-327; W. H. Mellers, "VW: The Last Phase," *Kenyon Review,* IV (1942), 381-387.

Chapter XXX: News of Tishnar: Walter de la Mare

All Walter de la Mare's fiction except *The Wind Blows Over* (M) has been published in this country by K. The most important critical studies are by R. L. Mégroz (Do, 1924) and Forrest Reid (Ht, 1929). There is an important addition to the Mégroz study in his later book, *Five Novelist-Poets of Today* (Joiner & Steele, 1933).

Among the best brief critical studies are Alice Lothian, *NAR,* CCXVI (1922), 663-672; Llewellyn Jones, "WdlM, Poet of Tishnar," *B*(NY), LVII (1923), 528-532; John Freeman, *English Portraits and Essays* (H&S, 1924); J. B. Priestley, *Figures in Modern Literature* (DM, 1924); R. H. Coats, "The World of WdlM," *Fort,* CXXVIII (1927), 483-491; G. K. Chesterton, *Fort,* CXXXVIII (1932), 47-53; R. Church, *Eight for Immortality* (De, 1941).

For interesting personal glimpses of Mr. de la Mare, cf. *B*(NY), LVI (1922-1923), 50-52; *Ce,* N.S. CVI (1923), 61-62; *B*(NY), LX (1924-1925), 677-678; *LA,* CCCXXVIII (1926), 694-695, and the autobiographies of Sir Henry Newbolt, *My World as in My Time* (FF, 1932) and of William Rothenstein, *Men and Memories, Recollections, 1900-1922* (CM, 1932).

SUPPLEMENTARY BIBLIOGRAPHY

The bibliography which begins on p. 577 of this book was prepared in the fall of 1942. This Supplementary Bibliography goes to the publishers in September, 1953. The attempt has been to list all relevant material published up to this date, but this has not been achieved in all cases. The indexing of material necessarily postdates its publication; moreover, learned journals are often published later than their date-lines would indicate. Some of the material which has not been smoked out at the time this bibliography is sent to the printer will no doubt be added in galley-proof, but it would be too much to hope that nothing will be overlooked.

The following abbreviations should be added to those listed on p. 578:

ACC	Appleton-Century-Crofts
AL	*American Literature*
AQ	*American Quarterly*
AS	*American Scholar*
AU	Allen & Unwin
BPLQ	*Boston Public Library Quarterly*
CE	*College English*
Col	*Colophon*
D	Doubleday & Co.
DA	*Dissertation Abstracts*
DalR	*Dalhousie Review*
EC	*Essays in Criticism*
FR	*Fortnightly Review*
FSY	Farrar, Straus and Young, Inc.
HH	Hastings House
HLQ	*Huntington Library Quarterly*
JHI	*Journal of the History of Ideas*
KCP	King's Crown Press
KR	*Kenyon Review*
Li	J. B. Lippincott Co.
LL	*Life and Letters*
NSN	*New Statesman and Nation*
NYTBR	*New York Times Book Review*
PC	Pellegrini & Cudahy (now absorbed by FSY)
PR	*Partisan Review*
QQ	*Queen's Quarterly*
RH	Random House
Sl	William Sloane Associates
Sp	*Spectator*
SS	Simon & Schuster
SW	Sheed & Ward
Tr	*Trollopian*
UKCR	*University of Kansas City Review*
UOP	University of Oklahoma Press
UTQ	*University of Toronto Quarterly*
WHR	*Western Humanities Review*
XIX CF	*Nineteenth Century Fiction*

The Saturday Review of Literature changed its name to *The Saturday Review* during our period. To avoid confusion, the abbreviation *SRL* has been retained throughout.

General References

S. Diana Neill, *A Short History of the English Novel* (M, 1952) stresses social and intellectual backgrounds. Elizabeth Bowen contributed a brief account of "English Novelists" to W. J. Turner, ed., *Romance of English Literature* (HH, 1944). General, overall consideration of the history of the English novel is also included in A. C. Baugh, ed., *A Literary History of England* (ACC, 1948) and in Hardin Craig, ed., *A History of English Literature* (OUP, 1950). See, also, Arnold Kettle, *An Introduction to the English Novel,* Vol. I (L, 1952), Vol. II (L, 1953).

Selected novelists are studied in a number of works: Bruce McCullough, *Representative English Novelists from Defoe to Conrad* (H, 1946); V. F. Pritchett, *The Living Novel* (Reynal & Hitchcock, 1947), and *Books in General* (HB, 1953); Irène Simon, *Formes du Roman Anglais de Dickens à Joyce* (Université de Liége, 1949); E. K. Brown, *Rhythm in the Novel* (U. Toronto Pr., 1950); John Cournos and Sybil Norton, *Famous British Novelists* (DM, 1952); Dorothy Van Ghent, *The English Novel* (Rinehart, 1953).

Benedict Kiely's *Modern Irish Fiction: A Critique* (Dublin: Golden Eagle Books, 1951) begins with Carleton.

XVII-XVIII CENTURIES. B. G. McCarthy considers *Women Writers: Their Contribution to the English Novel, 1621-1744* (Cork U. Pr., 1944); see also her *The Later Women Novelists* (same, 1947). There are books by John T. Taylor on *Early Opposition to the English Novel: The Popular Reaction from 1760 to 1830* (King's Crown Pr., 1943); by James R. Foster on *The History of the Pre-Romantic Novel in England* (Mod. Lang. Assn., 1949); and by Gilbert Highet on *The Classical Tradition: Greek and Roman Influences on Western Literature* (OUP, 1949). A number of XVII-XVIII C prefaces have been collected in Benjamin Boyce, *Prefaces to Fiction* (Augustan Reprint Soc. Publ. No. 32, 1952). Studies of XVIII C novelists are included in *The Age of Johnson: Essays Presented to Chauncey B. Tinker* (YUP, 1949).

XIX CENTURY. For bibliography, see Michael Sadleir, *XIX C Fiction: A Bibliographical Record,* 2 vv. (U. Cal. Pr., 1951). In *Bulletin of Bibliography,* Vol. XVII (1943), Leo J. Henkin began a long series of bibliographical articles on "Problems and Digressions in the Victorian Novel."

Consideration of the novel is involved in: John L. Cooke and Lionel Stevenson, *English Literature of the Victorian Period* (ACC, 1949); Joseph E. Baker, ed., *The Reinterpretation of Victorian Literature* (PUP, 1950); Jerome H. Buckley, *The Victorian Temper* (HUP, 1951); and in John Holloway, *The Victorian Sage* (M, 1953), which involves three novelists—Disraeli, George Eliot, and Hardy. Special themes are treated by Phyllis Bentley, *The English Regional Novel* (AU, 1941); by Susanne Howe, *Novels of Empire* (ColUP, 1949); and by Andrew L. Drummond, *The Churches in English Fiction* (Leicester, Edgar Backus, 1950). F. E. Bailey's *Six Great Victorian Novelists* (MacDonald, 1947) has little or no value; but Lucy P. Stebbins, *A Victorian Album: Some Lady Novelists of the Period* (ColUP, 1947) has some material of interest. In general, more "popular" novelists are treated in F. Alan Walbank's anthology, *Queens of the Circulating Library* (Evans, 1950). Many XIX C novelists play a part in Charles Morgan's *The House of Macmillan, 1843-1943* (M, 1944). The same author's *Reflections in a Mirror* (M, 1945) includes papers on Austen, Thackeray, Trollope, E. Brontë, and Hardy. Alexander Woollcott speaks of E. Brontë and Barrie in *Long Long Ago* (VP, 1943), and G. M. Young of Thackeray and Hardy in *Last Essays* (Hart-Davis, 1950).

The ff. articles deal with special topics: David D. Johnson, "'Without Benefit of Clergy' in Victorian Fiction," *W. Va. U. Bull., Philological Studies,* IV (1943), 15-21, and "The Artist in the English Novel," *ibid.,* pp. 77-80; J. Gordon Eaker, "Emergent Modernism in Late Victorian Fiction," *SAQ,* XLIV (1945), 286-293; L. Stevenson, "The Second Birth of the English Novel," *UTQ,* XIV (1945), 366-374; Mark Schorer, "Fiction and the 'Matrix of Analogy,'" *KR,* XI (1949), 539-560; L. Stevenson, "The Intellectual Novel in the XIX C," *Personalist,* XXXI (1950), 42-56, 157-166; J. A. Bramley, "Religion and the Novelists," *CR,* CLXXX (1951), 348-353; Robert G. Davis, "The Sense of the Real in English Fiction," *Comp. Lit.,* III (1951), 200-217; Marion Troughton, "Elections in English Fiction," *CR,* CLXXX (1951), 280-294; H. R. Collins, "His Image in Ebony: The African in British Fiction during the Age of Imperialism," *DA,* XII (1952), 60-61; E. H. Conn, "The Impact of *Madame Bovary* on the English Novel (1857-1915)," *DA,* XII (1952), 616; A. S. Kerr, "Victorian Parents and Children: Family Conflict in the Novels of Lytton, Trollope, Meredith, and Butler," *DA,* XII (1952), 65; Jacqueline Krump, "The Clergyman in the Victorian Novel," *Sum. of Doct. Diss., Northwestern U.,* XIX (1952), 25-30.

XX Century. The ff. books deal with XX C fiction, not exclusively British in every case: Edwin B. Burgum, *The Novel and the World's Dilemma* (OUP, 1947); E. K. Brown, *Rhythm in the Novel* (U. Toronto Pr., 1950); Alexander Comfort, *The Novel in Our Time* (AS, 1950). See also these titles, which are not entirely concerned with the novel: H. V. Routh, *English Literature and Ideas in the XX C* (Me, 1946); W. Y. Tindall, *Forces in Modern British Literature, 1885-1946* (K, 1947); B. Ifor Evans, *English Literature Between the Wars* (Me,

1948); J. Isaacs, *An Assessment of XX C Literature* (Secker & Warburg, 1951); R. A. Scott-James, *Fifty Years of English Literature, 1900-1951* (L, 1951). R. W. Church, *British Authors, A XX C Gallery* (L, 1948) includes many novelists. Eric Bentley, ed., *The Importance of Scrutiny* (George W. Stewart, 1948) has essays on Kipling, Lawrence, Forster, Joyce, Woolf. Horace Gregory, *The Shield of Achilles* (HB, 1944) has essays on Moore, Lawrence, Woolf. James M. Gray, *On Second Thought* (U. Minn. Pr., 1946) has essays on Bennett, Wells, Galsworthy, etc. Orville Prescott comments on many British and American writers in *In My Opinion* (BM, 1952).

The ff. articles deal with special aspects of XX C fiction, as indicated: Van Meter Ames, "The Novel: Between Art and Science," *KR,* V (1942), 34-48; N. J. Endicott, "The Novel in England Between the Wars," *UTQ,* XII (1942), 18-31; Mark Schorer, "The Chronicle of Doubt," *VQR,* XVIII (1942), 200-215; Bertha Linn, "The Fiction of the Future," *YR,* XXXIV (1944), 241-253; N. Elizabeth Monroe, "Freedom of the Novelist," *Thought,* XIX (1944), 455-464; Allen Tate, "Techniques of Fiction," *SR,* LII (1944), 210-225; Jacques Barzun, "Our Non-Fiction Novelists," *AM,* CLXXXVIII (1946), 129-136; Thomas J. Beary, "Religion and the Modern Novel," *Cath. World,* CLXVI (1947), 203-211; Desmond Pacey, "The Future of the Novel," *QQ,* LIV (1947), 74-83; Augustus H. Able, III, "A Short View of Contemporary Fiction," *Delaware Notes,* 21st series (1948), 19-35; Ernest Boll, "A Rationale for the Criticism of the Realistic Novels," *MLQ,* IX (1948), 208-215; Dayton Kohler, "Time in the Modern Novel," *CE,* X (1948), 15-24; V. S. Pritchett, "The Future of English Fiction," *PR,* XV (1948), 1063-1071; Jean Stafford, "The Psychological Novel," *KR,* X (1948), 214-227; L. Trilling, "Manners, Morals, and the Novel," *ibid.,* pp. 11-27; Herschel Brickell, "The Present State of Fiction," *VQR,* XXV (1949), 92-98; L. E. Bowling, "What Is the Stream-of-Consciousness Technique?" *PMLA,* LXV (1950), 333-345; Wallace Stegner, "Fiction: A Lens on Life," *SRL,* XXXIII, Apr. 22, 1950, pp. 9-10+; Douglas Grant, "The Novel and its Critical Terms," *EC,* I (1951), 421-429; John Lydenberg, "Mobilizing Our Novelists," *AQ,* IV (1952), 35-48; Horace Gregory, "Mutations of Belief in the Contemporary Novel," in F. E. Johnson, ed., *American Education and Religion* (H, 1952); Ian Watt, "Realism and the Novel," *EC,* II (1952), 376-396.

Miscellanies. The ff. books contain essays on the writers indicated: J. W. Aldridge, ed., *Critiques and Essays on Modern Fiction* (Ronald Pr., 1952) (Austen, Brontës, George Eliot, Lawrence, Woolf); Hilaire Belloc, *The Silence of the Sea* (SW, 1940) (Bunyan, Austen, Scott);

John Peale Bishop, *Collected Essays* (S, 1948) (Defoe, Lawrence, Joyce, de la Mare); Elizabeth Bowen, *Collected Impressions* (K, 1950) (many XIX-XX C novelists); Huntington Cairns, ed., *Invitation to Learning* (RH, 1941) (Bunyan, Defoe); Lord David Cecil, *Poets and Story-Tellers* (M, 1949) (Burney, Austen, Woolf); Harold H. Child, *Essays and Reflections,* ed. S. C. Roberts (CUP, 1948) (Trollope, Stevenson, de la Mare, etc.); Cyril Connolly, *The Condemned Playground* (M, 1946) (Sterne, Joyce); C. N. Greenough, *Collected Studies* (Harvard Coöperative Society, 1940) (Defoe, Galsworthy); Graham Greene, *The Lost Childhood* (VP, 1952) (Fielding, Sterne, Dickens, Kipling, Butler, Conrad, Dorothy Richardson, de la Mare, Buchan, etc.); Gilbert Highet, *People, Places, and Books* (OUP, 1953) (Dickens, Lawrence); Laura H. Hinkley, *Ladies of Literature* (HH, 1948) (Burney, Austen, the Brontës, George Eliot); F. R. Leavis, *The Great Tradition* (George W. Stewart, 1949) (Dickens, George Eliot, Conrad); W. S. Maugham, *Great Novelists and Their Novels* (Winston, 1949) (Fielding, Austen, Dickens, E. Brontë); Desmond MacCarthy, *Portraits* (OUP, 1953) (Trollope, Hardy, Kipling, Galsworthy, Bennett, Wells, Joyce); R. L. Mégroz, *Thirty-One Bedside Essays* (Tower Bridge Publications, 1951) (Scott, Conrad, Wells, de la Mare, etc.); Alice Meynell, *Prose and Poetry* (Cape, 1947) (Dickens, the Brontës); Edwin Muir, *Essays on Literature and Society* (Hogarth Pr., 1949) (Sterne, Scott, Hardy); W. L. F. Murdoch, *Collected Essays* (Angus & Robertson, 1938) (Austen, Dickens, Thackeray, Trollope, Hardy, Conrad); W. V. O'Connor, ed., *Forms of Modern Fiction* (U. Minn. Pr., 1948) (The Brontës, Lawrence, Joyce, Woolf, etc.); Katherine Anne Porter, *The Days Before* (HB, 1952) (Hardy, Lawrence); Peter Quennell, *Singular Preference: Portraits and Essays* (VP, 1953) (Defoe, Dickens, Borrow, Kipling, Wells); J. J. Reilly, *Of Books and Men* (Messner, 1942) (More, Hardy, Conrad, Galsworthy); A. L. Rowse, *The English Spirit* (M, 1943) (More, Swift, etc.) and *The English Past* (M, 1951) (Swift, Hardy, Lawrence, John Buchan); George Saintsbury, *A Last Vintage,* ed. J. W. Oliver, etc. (Me, 1950) (Swift, Smollett, Sterne, Scott, Marryat, Thackeray, etc.) and *A Saintsbury Miscellany* (OUP, 1947) (Goldsmith, Disraeli, Stevenson, etc.); Vincent Starrett, *Bookman's Holiday* (RH, 1942) (Stevenson, Doyle, etc.) and *Books and Bipeds* (Argus, 1947) (many novelists); Francis Thompson, *Literary Criticisms,* ed. T. L. Connolly (Du, 1948) (Bunyan, Meredith, Hewlett); Rex Warner, *The Cult of Power* (Li, 1947) (Bunyan, Swift, Dickens); Edmund Wilson, *Classics and Commercials* (FSY, 1950) (Austen, Peacock, Thackeray, Joyce), and *Shores of Light* (FSY, 1952) (Beckford, Butler, Lawrence); Virginia Woolf, *The Moment and Other Essays* (HB, 1948) (Sterne, Scott, Dickens, Lawrence, etc.) and *The Captain's Deathbed and Other Essays* (HB,

1950) (Goldsmith, Marryat, Hardy, Conrad, etc.); Walter de la Mare, *Private View* (FF, 1953) (Defoe, Thackeray, Hardy, Butler, Ouida).

Chapter I: Fiction in Shakespeare's Time

GENERAL. Mary Patchell has studied *The Palmerin Romances in Elizabethan Prose Fiction* (ColUP, 1947); George Parks contributed "Before *Euphues*" to *Joseph Quincy Adams: Memorial Studies* (Folger Shakespeare Library, 1948).

ST. THOMAS MORE. H. W. Donner has written an *Introduction to Utopia* (Sidgwick, 1946); Russell Ames has studied *Citizen TM and his Utopia* (PUP, 1949), and J. H. Hexter has written *M's Utopia: The Biography of an Idea* (PUP, 1951). See, further, Helen C. White, *Social Criticism in Popular Religious Literature of the XVI C* (M, 1944) and Arthur E. Morgan, *Nowhere Was Somewhere: How History Makes Utopias and How Utopias Make History* (UNCP, 1946); also the ff. articles: R. P. Adams, "Designs by M and Erasmus for a New Social Order," *SP,* XLII (1945), 131-145, and "Social Responsibilities of Science in *Utopia, New Atlantis,* and Elsewhere," *JHI,* X (1949), 374-398; R. Hamilton, "M's *Utopia:* Its Bearing on Present Conditions," *Hibbert J.,* XLIV (1946), 242-247; E. L. Surtz, "Epicurus in *Utopia,*" *ELH,* XVI (1949), 89-103, "TM and Communism," *PMLA,* LXIV (1949), 374-398, and "Defense of Pleasure in M's *Utopia,*" *SP,* XLVI (1949), 99-112; George Sanderlin, "The Meaning of TM's *Utopia,*" *CE,* XII (1950), 74-77; J. K. Sowards, "Some Factors in the Reëvaluation of TM's *Utopia,*" *Northwest Mo. State Coll. Studies,* XVI (1951), 29-60; E. L. Surtz, "Interpretations of *Utopia,*" *Catholic Hist. R.,* XXXVIII (1952), 156-174.

GASCOIGNE AND GRANGE. Charles T. Prouty has published *GG, Elizabethan Courtier, Soldier, and Poet* (ColUP, 1942). He has also edited GG's *A Hundreth Sundrie Flowers,* with introduction and notes, *U. Mo. Studies,* Vol. XVII, No. 2 (1942), and has contributed an article, "Elizabethan Fiction: Whetstone's *The Discourse of Giletta* and Grange's *The Golden Aphroditis*" to *Studies in Honor of A. H. R. Fairchild* (U. of Mo., 1946). See, also, Samuel Tannenbaum, *GG, A Concise Bibliography* (N.Y., The Author, 1942), and two anonymous articles in *LTLS,* Sept. 19, 1942, pp. 462+ and 463: "Elizabethan Poet: GG as Pioneer; Problems of his Life and Writings" and "A Pioneer Novel."

SIDNEY. There is a new, extended French study: Michael Poirier, *Sir PS: Le chevalier poète élizabéthain* (Bibliotheque Universitaire de Lille, 1948). There have also been a number of studies of various aspects of the *Arcadia:* A. G. D. Wiles, "Parallel Analyses of the Two Versions of S's *Arcadia,*" *SP,* XXXIX (1942), 167-206; C. M. Dowlin, "S and Other Men's Thought," *RES,* XX (1944), 257-271; F. L. Townsend, "S and Ariosto," *PMLA,* LXI (1946), 97-108; Kenneth T. Rowe, "Romantic Love and Pastoral Authority in S's *Arcadia,*" *U. Mich. Contributions in Modern Philology,* No. 4 (1947); P. A. Duhamel, "S's *Arcadia* and Elizabethan Rhetoric," *SP,* XLV (1948), 119-133; S. Scribner, *Figures of Word Repetition in the First Book of Sir PS's* Arcadia (Catholic U. of America, 1948); I. Ribner, "Machiavelli and S: The *Arcadia* of 1590," *SP,* XLVII (1950), 152-172; D. E. Ewing, "S's Defence of the Earl of Leicester and the Revised *Arcadia,*" *JEGP,* LI (1952), 25-41.

Nashe. See F. T. Bowers, "TN and the Picaresque Novel," in *Humanistic Studies in Honor of J. C. Metcalf, U. Va. Studies,* Vol. I (1941); A. K. Croston, "The Use of Imagery in N's *The Unfortunate Traveler,*" *RES,* XXIV (1948), 90-101; Agnes M. C. Latham, "Satire on Literary Themes and Modes in N's *Unfortunate Traveller,*" *E&S,* N.S. I (1948).

Greene. See John S. Weld, "Some Problems of Euphuistic Narrative: RG and Henry Wotton," *SP,* XLV (1948), 165-171.

Chapter II: The Seventeenth Century

General. Benjamin Boyce has edited *The Adventures of Lindamira, A Lady of Quality* (U. Minn. Pr. 1949). A. O. Aldridge has considered "Polygamy in Early Fiction: Henry Neville and Denis Veiras," *PMLA,* LXV (1950), 464-472.

Mrs. Behn. There has been an edition of Mrs. B's *Selected Writings,* ed. Robert Phelps (Grove Pr., 1950). George Woodcock has written *The Incomparable Aphra* (Boardman, 1948), a much longer biography than V. Sackville-West's, and Emily Hahn has published a novel about Mrs. B: *Purple Passage* (D, 1950). See, also, D. L. Hobman, "Restoration Petticoat," *LL,* LI (1946), 137-145; R. M. Hill, "AB's Use of Setting," *MLQ,* VII (1946), 189-203.

Bunyan. Book-length studies, both of value, are M. P. Willcocks, *B Calling* (AU, 1943) and Vera Brittain, *Valiant Pilgrim* (M, 1950). H. A. Talon's *JB, The Man and His Work* (HUP, 1951) gives a French view of B. Briefer studies, mostly, of *The Pilgrim's Progress,* include: R. Sharrock, "B and the English Emblem-Writers," *RES,* XXI (1945), 105-116, and "Spiritual Autobiography in *The Pilgrim's Progress,*" *RES,* XXIV (1948), 102-120; M. Hussey, "B's Mr. Ignorance," *MLR,* XLIV (1949), 483-489; R. E. Fitch, "A Tale of Two Pilgrims: A Comparison of B's *Pilgrim's Progress* and Voltaire's *Candide,*" *Hibbert J.,* XLVIII

(1950), 388-393; Perry Miller, in the symposium, *Classics of Religious Devotion* (Beacon Pr., 1950).

Chapter III: Defoe and His Contemporaries

DEFOE AND SWIFT. Jan Kott, *Szola klasków* (Warsaw, Czytelnik, 1946).

DEFOE. See William Freeman, *The Incredible D* (Jenkins, 1950); F. Watson, *DD* (L, 1952); and these articles: William T. Morgan, "The Versatility of DD," *More Books,* XXI (1946), 327-346; John R. Moore, "D's Workshop," *More Books,* XXIII (1948), 323-330; Ian Watt, "The Naming of Characters in D, Richardson, Fielding," *RES,* XXV (1949), 322-338—cf. *RES,* N.S.I (1950), 252; Mark Schorer, "A Study in D: Moral Vision and Structural Form," *Thought,* XXV (1950), 275-287; Alan Swallow, "D and the Art of Fiction," *WHR,* IV (1950), 129-136; A. M. Wilkinson, "Meditations of DD," *MLR,* XLVI (1951), 349-354; J. Bishop, "Knowledge, Action, and Interpretation in D's Novels," *JHI,* XIII (1952), 3-16; C. I. Patterson, "Charles Lamb's Insight into the Nature of the Novel [and interest in D]," *PMLA,* LXVII (1952), 375-382; W. M. Peterson, "Gide and D," *NQ,* CXCVII (1952), 202-203; Ian Watt, "D and Richardson on Homer: A Study of the Relation of Novel and Epic in the Early XVIII C," *RES,* N.S. III (1952), 325-340; Benjamin Boyce, "The Question of Emotion in D," *SP,* L (1953), 45-58; A. E. Rodway, "*Moll Flanders* and *Manon Lescaut,*" *EC,* III (1953), 303-320; J. R. Moore, "D and the South Sea Company," *BPLQ,* V (1953), 175-188.

The ff. deal specifically with *Robinson Crusoe:* Charles E. Burch, "*The Tempest* and *RC,*" RES, XXI (1945), 52-56; Irving Howe, "*RC:* Epic of the Middle Class," *Tomorrow,* VIII, June 1949, pp. 51-54; E. B. Benjamin, "Symbolic Elements in *RC,*" *PQ,* XXX (1951), 206-211; Edwin Honig, "*Crusoe, Rasselas,* and the Suit of Clothes," *UKCR,* XVIII (1951), 136-142; E. D. Seeber, "Oroonoko and Crusoe's Man Friday," *MLQ,* XII (1951), 286-291; Ian Watt, "*RC* as a Myth," *EC,* I (1951), 95-119; Harry F. Robins, "How Smart was RC?" *PMLA,* LXVII (1952), 782-789.

Willa Cather's introduction to *Roxana* was reprinted in *WC on Writing* (K, 1949).

MRS. MANLEY has been studied by Gwendolyn B. Needham, "Mrs. M, Tory Defender," *HLQ,* XII (1949), 253-288, and "Mrs. M, An XVIII C Wife of Bath," *HLQ,* XIV (1951), 259-284.

SWIFT. Carl Van Doren edited a valuable volume of selections in *The Portable S* (VP, 1948). There have been book-length studies by R. C.

Churchill, *He Served Human Liberty* (AU, 1946); Herbert Davis, *The Satire of JS* (M, 1947); B. Acworth (Eyre & Spottiswoode, 1947); Evelyn Hardy, *The Conjured Spirit: S, A Study in the Relationship of S, Stella, and Vanessa* (Hogarth Pr., 1949); J. M. Bullit, *JS and the Anatomy of Satire* (HUP, 1953). Monty Jacobs, *JS* (Berlin, Wedding-Verlag, 1948) is in German. R. W. Jackson's *S and his Circle* (Talbot Pr., 1945) is a book of essays on various Swiftian themes.

See, further, these articles: L. A. Landa, "S, the Mysteries, and Deism," *UTSE* (1944), pp. 239-256, "JS and Charity," *JEGP,* XLIV (1945), 337-350, and another paper in *Eng. Inst. Essays, 1946* (ColUP, 1947); Lois M. Scott-Thomas, "The Vocabulary of JS," *DalR,* XXV (1946), 442-447; R. Quintana, "Situational Satire: A Commentary on the Method of S," *UTQ,* XVII (1948), 130-136; D. S. Savage, *Western R.,* XV (1950), 25-36; Ernest Tuveson, "S and the World-Makers," *JHI,* XI (1950), 54-74; Clarence L. Kulischeck, "Hudibrastic Echoes in S," *NQ,* CXCVI (1951), 339; Ellen D. Leyburn, "S's View of the Dutch," *PMLA,* LXVI (1951), 734-745; H. Davis, "Some Free Thoughts of a Tory Dean," *VQR,* XXVIII (1952), 258-272; I. Ehrenpreis, "S on Liberty," *JHI,* XIII (1952), 131-146; J. R. Moore, "S as Historian," *SP,* XLIX (1952), 583-604; R. C. Olson, "The Scientific Milieu of JS," *U. of Colo. Studies,* General Series, XXIX: i (1952), 206-209.

There has been an extraordinary amount of material published about *Gulliver's Travels.* Sir Harold Williams has studied *The Text of "Gulliver's Travels"* (CUP, 1952). Arthur E. Case has published *Four Essays on GT* (PUP, 1945). See, also, these articles: Philip Gove, "Gildon's *Fortunate Shipwreck* as Background for *GT,*" *RES,* XVIII (1942), 470-478; Joe Horrell, "What Gulliver Knew," *SR,* LI (1943), 476-504; M. F. Ashley-Montagu, "Tyson's Ourang-Outang, sive homo sylvestris and S's *GT,*" *PMLA,* LIX (1944), 84-89; Norman Ault, "Pope and Gulliver," *Nat.R.,* CXXII (1944), 510-516; Frederick Bracher, "The Maps in *GT,*" *HLQ,* VIII (1944), 59-74; S. H. Gould, "Gulliver and the Moons of Mars," *JHI,* VI (1945), 91-101; Margaret R. Grennan, "Lilliput and Leprecan: Gulliver and the Irish Tradition," *ELH,* XII (1945), 188-202; Samuel Kliger, "The Unity of *GT,*" *MLQ,* VI (1945), 401-415; Z. S. Fink, "Political Theory in *GT,*" *ELH,* XIV (1947), 151-161; Aline Mackenzie, "Another Note on *GT,*" *NQ,* CXCIII (1948), 533-538; Philip Sauers, "Wisdom Is a Nut; or, The Idols of JS," in *If By Your Art, Testament to Percival Hunt* (U. Pitt. Pr., 1948); F. Bracher, "The Name 'Lemuel Gulliver,'" *HLQ,* XII (1949), 409-413; Edward Stone, "S and the Horses: Misanthropy or Comedy?" *MLQ,* X (1949), 367-376; N. Joost, "Gulliver and *The Freethinker,*" *MLN,* LXV (1950), 197-199—cf. E. W. Rosenheim, Jr., *PQ,* XXXI (1952),

208-211; Ellen D. Leyburn, "Certain Problems of Allegorical Satire in *GT*," *HLQ*, XIII (1950), 161-189; J. R. Moore, "The Yahoos of the African Travelers," *NQ*, CXCV (1950), 182-185; George Orwell, in *Shooting an Elephant and Other Essays* (HB, 1950); Eric Partridge, in *Here, There, and Everywhere* (M, 1950); R. S. Hunting, "Gulliver Among the Brobdingnagians," *NQ*, CXCVI (1951), 413; H. D. Kelling, "Some Significant Names in *GT*," *SP*, XLVIII (1951), 761-778; K. M. Williams, "Gulliver's Voyage to the Houhynhmns," *ELH*, XVIII (1951), 275-286; E. E. Calkins, "How Small Is Lilliput?" *AM*, CXC, July 1952, pp. 77-78; I. Ehrenpreis, "S and Satire," *CE*, XIII (1952), 309-312; R. C. Elliott, "Gulliver as a Literary Artist," *ELH*, XIX (1952), 49-63; H. D. Kelling, "*Gulliver's Travels:* A Comedy of Humours," *UTQ*, XXI (1952), 362-375.

Chapter IV: Psychological Realism Begins: Samuel Richardson

Important bibliographical data appear in William M. Sale, Jr., *SR, Master Printer* (Cornell U. Pr., 1950). See, also, Francesco Cordasco, *SR: A List of Critical Studies Published from 1896 to 1946* (Long Island U. Pr., 1948).

Charles F. Millett has edited *The Letters of Doctor George Cheyne to SR* (1733-1743), *U. of Missouri Studies*, Vol. XVIII, No. 1 (1943). There is a letter by SR in Alison Bishop, "R Discusses his *Clarissa* and *Grandison*," *BPLQ*, IV (1952), 217-221.

Alan D. McKillop, whose book on SR is noted in the main bibliographical entry, has edited *Critical Remarks on* Sir Charles Grandison, Clarissa, *and* Pamela, *Augustan Reprint Society Publications*, No. 21, Series IV, No. 3 (Los Angeles, W. A. Clark Memorial Library of U. of Cal., 1950). He has also published the ff. articles: "SR's Advice to an Apprentice," *JEGP*, XLII (1943), 40-54; "The Mock-Marriage Device in *Pamela*," *PQ*, XXVI (1947), 285-288; "A Letter from SR to Alexis Claude Clairaut," *MLN*, LXIII (1948), 109-113; "Wedding Bells for Pamela," *PQ*, XXVIII (1949), 323-325; "Epistolary Technique in R's Novels," *Rice Inst. Pamphlet*, XXXVIII (1951), 36-54.

Other articles include: A. E. Carter, *UTQ*, XVII (1948), 390-397; G. A. Bonnard, "SR and Guillaume-Antoine de Luc," *MLR*, XLVI (1951), 440-441; D. Van Ghent, "Clarissa and Emma as Phèdre," *PR*, XVII (1950), 822-827; T. C. Duncan Eaves, "Graphic Illustrations of the Novels of SR, 1740-1810," *HLQ*, XIV (1951), 349-383; Robert E. Moore, "Dr. Johnson on Fielding and R," *PMLA*, LXVI (1951), 162-181; S. O. Lesser, "A Note on *Pamela*," *CE*, XIV (1952), 13-17. See, also, Ian Watt, "Defoe and R on Homer," listed under Defoe.

Chapter V: Fielding and the Prose Epic

Bibliographical data appear in F. Cordasco, *HF: A List of Critical Studies Published from 1895 to 1946* (Long Island U. Pr., 1946).

Frederick H. Dudden, *HF: His Life, Work, and Times,* 2 vols. (OUP, 1952) is the most ambitious study of F since Wilbur Cross. Two other biographical studies which belong to our period are Elizabeth Jenkins (AS, 1948) and M. P. Willcocks, *A True-Born Englishman* (M, 1948). E. L. McAdam, Jr., has published a Fielding letter, *YR,* XXXVIII (1948), 300-310. T. M. Cleland has illustrated magnificently both *Jonathan Wild* (Limited Editions Club, 1943) and *Tom Jones* (LEC and Heritage Pr., 1952). He had already done Sterne's *Tristram Shandy* (LEC, 1935).

Consult the ff. articles: R. M. Hill, "Setting in the Novels of HF," *Bull. of The Citadel,* VII (1943), 26-52; W. H. Rogers, "F's Early Aesthetic and Technique," *SP,* XL (1943), 529-551; C. R. Greene, "A Note on the Authorship of *Shamela," MLN,* LIX (1944), 571; Leo Hughes, "The Influence of F's Milieu upon his Humor," *UTSE,* 1944, pp. 268-297; W. R. Irwin, "Satire and Comedy in the Works of HF," *ELH,* XIII (1946), 166-188; C. B. Woods, "F and the Authorship of *Shamela," PQ,* XXV (1946), 248-272; A. L. Cooke, "HF and the Writers of Heroic Romance," *PMLA,* LXII (1947), 984-994; E. C. Mack, "Pamela's Stepdaughters: The Heroines of Smollett and F," *CE,* VIII (1947), 293-301; R. M. Wallace, "F's Knowledge of History and Biography," *SP,* XLIV (1947), 89-107; J. C. Stephens, Jr., "The Verge of the Court and Arrest for Debt in F's *Amelia," MLN,* LXIII (1948), 104-109; R. S. Crane, "The Plot of *Tom Jones," Journ. Gen. Ed.,* IV (1950), 112-130; Robert Halsband, "F, The Hogarth of Fiction," *SRL,* XXXIII, Sept. 30, 1950, pp. 20-21; M. E. Willy, in *Life Was Their Cry* (Evans, 1950); R. E. Moore, "Dr. Johnson on F and Richardson," *PMLA,* LXVI (1951), 162-181; A. B. Shepperson, "F on Liberty and Democracy," *U. Va. Studies,* IV (1951), 265-275; H. O. Brogan, "Fiction and Philosophy in the Education of Tom Jones, Tristram Shandy, and Richard Feverel," *CE,* XIV (1952), 144-149; R. S. Crane, in his *Critics and Criticism, Ancient and Modern* (UCP, 1952).

Chapter VI: Smollett and the Novel of Humors

Bibliographical data appear in F. Cordasco, *S Criticism, 1770-1924: A Bibliography Enumerative and Annotative* and *S Criticism, 1925-1945* (Long Island U. Pr., 1948, 1947). See, also, F. B. Newman, "A Consideration of the Bibliographical Problems Connected with the First Edition of *Humphrey Clinker*," *Papers Bibl. Soc. of Am.*, XLIV (1950), 340-371.

For Letters, see Cordasco, *Letters of TGS: A Supplement to the Noyes Collection, with a Bibliography of Editions of the Collected Works* (Imp. Avelina Ortega, 1950). For other biographical and miscellaneous data by Cordasco, see *NQ*, CXCIII (1948), 141-142, 142-143, 383-384, 428-429, 533, 563; CXCIV (1949), 557-558.

Three books about S have appeared: Lewis M. Kahrl, *TS, Traveler-Novelist* (UCP, 1945); Fred W. Boege, *S's Reputation as a Novelist* (PUP, 1947); Lewis M. Knapp, *TS, Doctor of Men and Manners* (PUP, 1949). All are important; Knapp's is the fullest general study of S we have.

See, further, these articles: Rufus Putney, "The Plan of *Peregrine Pickle*," *PMLA*, LX (1945), 1051-1065; R. B. Heilman, "Falstaff and S's Micklewhimmen," *RES*, XXII (1946), 226-228; F. Cordasco, "S and Patronius," *MLQ*, IX (1948), 415-417; Judd Kline, "Three Doctors and S's Lady of Quality," *PQ*, XXVII (1948), 219-228; F. Cordasco, "S's German Medical Degree," *MLN*, LXV (1950), 117-119—cf. LXVII (1952), 69-71, 360; Carmine R. Linsalata, "S's Indebtedness to Jarvis' Translation of *Don Quijote*," *Symposium*, IV (1950), 84-106; James R. Foster, "*Peregrine Pickle* and the *Memoirs of Count Grammont*," *MLN*, LXVI (1951), 469-471; C. L. Almirall, "S's 'Gothic': An Illustration," *MLN*, LXVIII (1953), 408-409.

Chapter VII: The Triumph of Sensibility: Laurence Sterne

Bibliographical data appear in F. Cordasco, *LS: A List of Critical Studies Published from 1896 to 1946* (Long Island U. Pr., 1948). For Letters, see Earl R. Wasserman, "Unedited Letters by S, Hume, and Rousseau," *MLN*, LXVI (1951), 73-79.

There are three book-length studies: Lodowick Hartley, *This Is Lorence* (UNCP, 1943); Thomas Yoseloff, *A Fellow of Infinite Jest* (Prentice-Hall, 1945); Ernest N. Dilworth, *The Unsentimental Journey of LS* (KCP, 1948).

See, further, Walter L. Myers, "O, the Hobby Horse," *VQR*, XIX (1943), 268-277; G. L. Barnett, "Gay, S, and *Tristram Shandy*," *NQ*, CLXXXV (1943), 346-347; H. K. Russell, "*TS* and the Technique of the Novel," SP, XLII (1945), 581-593; R. D. S. Putney, "Alas, Poor Eliza!" *MLR*, XLI (1946), 411-413, and "S's Eliza," *LTLS*, Mar. 9, 1946, p. 115; Peter Quennell, in *The Profane Virtues* (VP, 1946); L. Hartley, "Tristram and the Angels," *CE*, IX (1947), 62-69; Wilfred Watson, "The Fifth Commandment: Some Allusions to Sir Robert Filmer's Writings in *TS*," *MLN*, LXII (1947), 234-240; Kenneth Mc-

Lean, "Imagination and Sympathy: S and Adam Smith," *JHI*, X (1949), 399-410; Louis D. Rubin, Jr., "Joyce and S: A Study in Affinity," *Hopkins R.*, III (1950), 1-15; Wayne Booth, "Did S Complete *TS*?" *MP*, XLVIII (1951), 172-183; Richard C. Boys, "*TS* and the Conventional Novel," *Papers of the Michigan Academy of Science, Arts, and Letters*, XXVII (1951), 423-436; Donald Cornu, "Shandy in America," *NQ*, CXCVI (1951), 273-274; Gwin J. Kolb, "A Note on *TS*: Some New Sources," *NQ*, CXCVI (1951), 226-227; W. Booth, "The Self-Conscious Narrator in Comic Fiction before *TS*," *PMLA*, LXVII (1952), 163-185; Ernest Dilworth, "S: Some Devices," *NQ*, CXCVII (1952), 165-166. See, also, Brogan, "Fiction and Philosophy," etc. under Fielding.

Chapter VIII: Sentimentalists and Revolutionaries

GOLDSMITH. William Freeman, *OG* (Phil. Libr., 1952); C. P. Barbier, "G en France au XVIIIe siècle: les Essays et le *Vicar of Wakefield*," *R. Litt. Comp.*, XXV (1951), 385-402; W. H. Graham, *CR*, CLXXXI (1952), 304-308.

BROOKE. F. L. Barber, "John Wesley Edits a Novel," *London Q. R.*, CLXXI (1946), 150-154.

MRS. INCHBALD. Lucy Poate Stebbins, in *London Ladies* (ColUP, 1952).

HOLCROFT. V. R. Stallbaumer, "TH as a Novelist," *ELH*, XV (1948), 194-218.

GODWIN. There have been two new books about G: George Woodcock, *WG, A Biographical Study* (Porcupine Pr., 1946) and David Fleischer, *WG* (AU, 1951). Neither pays much attention to his fiction.

Chapter IX: The Renascence of Wonder

GENERAL. See Robert K. Black, *The Sadleir-Black Gothic Collection* (Bibl. Soc. U. of Va., 1949); also these articles: Robert D. Mayo, "The Gothic Short Story in the Magazines," *MLR*, XXXVII (1942), 448-454, and "How Long Was Gothic Fiction in Vogue?" *MLN*, LVIII (1943), 58-64; Samuel Kliger, "The 'Goths' in England: An Introduction to the Gothic Vogue in XVIII C Aesthetic Discussion," *MP*, XLIII (1945), 107-117; Arthur L. Cooke, "Some Sidelights on the Theory of Gothic Romance," *MLQ*, XII (1951), 429-436; F. Cordasco, "A Poetic Stricture on the Gothic Romance Craze, 1810," *NQ*, CXCVI (1951), 258.

WALPOLE. W. S. Lewis, "HW Reread," *AM*, CLXXVI (1945), 48-51.

REEVE. John K. Reeves, "The Mother of *Fatherless Fanny*," *ELH*, IX (1942), 224-233.

MRS. RADCLIFFE. See Aline Grant, *AR, A Biography* (AS, 1951) and two articles: W. Sypher, "Social Ambiguity in a Gothic Novel," *PR,* XII (1945), 50-60; R. D. Havens, "AR's Nature Descriptions," *MLN,* LXVI (1951), 251-255.

LEWIS. A variorum edition of *The Monk,* with commentary by Louis F. Peck and John Berryman, has been published by the Grove Press, 1951. See, also, W. B. Todd, "The Early Editions and Issues of *The Monk,* with a Bibliography," *Papers Bibl. Soc. Va.,* II (1949), 3-24; L. F. Peck, *"The Monk* and *Le Diable Amoureux," MLN,* LXVIII (1953), 406-408.

THE ORIENTAL TALE. On BECKFORD, see Karl F. Thompson, "Henley's Share in B's *Vathek," PQ,* XXXI (1952), 75-80. On JOHNSON, see R. P. Metzdorf, "The Second Sequel to *Rasselas," New Rambler,* No. 16 (1950), pp. 3-6; Gwin J. Kolb, "The Structure of *Rasselas," PMLA,* LXVI (1951), 698-717; Mary Lascelles, *"Rasselas* Reconsidered," *E&S,* N.S. IV (1951).

MRS. SHELLEY. Mrs. Shelley's *Letters,* 2 vv., and her *Journal* have been published, both ed. Frederick L. Jones (UOP, 1944, 1947). Elizabeth Nitchie has published a study, *MS: Author of Frankenstein* (Rutgers UPr, 1953). See, further, Milton Millhauser, "The Noble Savage in MS's *Frankenstein," NQ,* CXC (1946), 248-250; Ernest Lovell, Jr., "Byron and the Byronic Hero in the Novels of MS," *UTSE,* XXX (1951), 158-183.

MATURIN. P. Riboul, "Villiers de l'Isle-Adam et le *Melmoth* de M," *R. Litt. Comp.,* XXV (1951), 479-481.

Chapter X: The Romance of the Tea-Table

FANNY BURNEY. There are new biographies by Averyl Edwards (Staples Pr., 1948) and by Emily Hahn, *A Degree of Prudery* (D, 1950). See, also, Joyce Hemlow, "FB and the Courtesy Books," *PMLA,* LXV (1950), 732-761; T. C. Duncan-Eaves, "Edward Burney's Illustrations to *Evelina," PMLA,* LXII (1947), 995-999; Eugene White, "FB, Novelist: A Study in Technique," *DA,* XII (1952), 73.

MARIA EDGEWORTH. Harold E. Butler has published ME's *Tour in Connemara, and the Martins of Ballinahinch* (Co, 1950), and there are two new biographies: Isabel C. Clarke, *ME: Her Family and Friends* (Hu, 1950), a full-length study, and P. N. Newby, *ME* (AS, 1950), which is a brief one. See, also, Mary Maxse, *Nat. R.,* CXVIII (1942), 483-488, and Katharine West, *Sp,* CLXXXII (1949), 672.

Jane Austen. The JA canon has been enriched by the publication of more juvenilia, *Volume the Third,* ed. R. W. Chapman (OUP, 1951). The ff. books about JA have appeared: Sheila Kaye-Smith and G. B. Stern, *Speaking of JA* and *More About JA* (H, 1944, 1949)—discursive commentary and appreciation by two well-known novelists; Richard Aldington, *JA* (Pasadena, Castle Pr., 1948); R. A. Austen-Leigh, *JA and Southampton* (Ballantyne, 1949); R. W. Chapman, *JA: Facts and Problems* (OUP, 1949)—lectures on varied aspects of JA's life and art by the foremost authority on the subject; Elizabeth Jenkins, *JA* (PC, 1949)—a detailed critical study; Margaret Kennedy, *JA* (Sw, 1952); Marvin Mudrick, *JA, Irony as Defense and Discovery* (PUP, 1952)—an exceptionally close reading of the text of the novels; Andrew H. Wright, *JA's Novels* (OUP, 1953). Jean Gould, *Jane* (HM, 1947) and May Lamberton Becker, *Presenting Miss JA* (DM, 1952) are intended primarily for younger readers.

See, further, these articles: Q. D. Leavis, "A Critical Theory of JA's Writings," *Scrutiny,* X (1941-1942), 61-87, 114-152, 272-294, XII (1944), 104-119; Leonard Woolf, "The Economic Determinism of JA," *NSN,* XXIV (1942), 39-41; Louis F. Doyle, "JA, How Could You?" *Cath. W.,* CLX (1944), 144-150; G. C. Haddow, *DalR,* XXIV (1945), 379-392; Elsie Greenwood, "*Lovers' Vows* at Mansfield Park," *Nat. R.,* CXXVII (1946), 72-76; S. Kliger, "JA's *Pride and Prejudice* in the XVIII C Mode," *UTQ,* XVI (1947), 357-370; D. Daiches, "JA, Karl Marx, and the Aristocratic Dance," *AS,* XVII (1948), 289-296; E. N. Hayes, "*Emma:* A Dissenting Opinion," *XIX CF,* IV (1949), 1-20—cf. William Frost's reply, pp. 325-328; Alan Dent, "Jane—& a Fig for Jena," *SRL,* XXXIII, Oct. 14, 1950, p. 21+; C. B. Hogan, "JA and her Early Public," *RES,* N.S. I (1950), 39-54; A. D. McKillop, "Allusions to Prose Fiction in JA's *Volume the Third,*" *NQ,* CXCVI (1951), 428-429; Edd W. Parks, "JA's Art of Rudeness," *UTQ,* XX (1951), 381-387, "Exegesis in JA's Novels," *SAQ,* LI (1952), 103-119, and "JA's Lure of the Next Chapter," *XIX CF,* VII (1952), 56-60; S. M. Scott, "Pride, Prejudice, and Property," *Mich. Alum. Q. R.,* LVII (1951), 172-199; Noel J. King, "JA in France," *XIX CF,* VIII (1953), 1-26.

Chapter XI: The Heights: Sir Walter Scott

There is *A Bibliography of Sir WS, A Classified and Annotated List of Books and Articles Relating to His Life and Works, 1797-1940,* by J. C. Corson (Oliver and Boyd, 1943). Dame Una Pope-Hennessy has written a brief biography (AS, 1949). G. H. Needler has produced a study of *Goethe and S* (OUP, 1951). Lectures by Sir Herbert Grierson, Edwin Muir, G. M. Young, and S. C. Roberts have been collected in

Sir WS Lectures, 1940-1948 (Edinburgh U. Pr., 1950). E. H. Cady and H. H. Clark have reprinted three pieces on S in *Whittier on Writers and Writing* (Syracuse U. Pr., 1950).

H. W. Häusermann has printed a S letter in *RES,* XXV (1949), 248-249, and G. Struve has reported the discovery of some S letters in Russia, *John Rylands Lib. Bull.,* XXVIII (1944), 477-484. In "Historical Novels," *Trans. Royal Soc. Lit., Essays by Divers Hands,* XXIII (1947), 53-71, G. P. Gooch has considered the influence of S on British and American fiction. Two articles by R. K. Gordon deal with S and Shakespeare: "Sh's *Henry IV* and the Waverley Novels," *MLR,* XXXVII (1942), 304-316, and "S and Sh's Tragedies," *Trans. Royal Soc. of Canada,* Series 3, XXXIX, Section 2 (1945), pp. 111-117.

The ff. concern varied themes as indicated: W. M. Dixon, in *Apology for the Arts* (L, 1944); J. R. Moore, "S's *Antiquary* and Defoe's *History of Apparitions,*" *MLN,* LIX (1944), 550-551; C. O. Parsons, "The Deaths of Glossin and Hatteraick in *Guy Mannering,*" *PQ,* XXIV (1945), 169-174; R. D. Mayo, "The Chronology of the Waverley Novels; Evidence of the MSS," *PMLA,* LXIII (1948), 935-949; D. Daiches, "S's Achievement as a Novelist," *XIX CF,* VI (1951), 81-95, 153-173; G. P. Gooch, in *Maria Theresa and Other Studies* (L, 1951); R. K. Gordon, "S's Prose," *Trans. Royal Can. Soc.,* Series III 45, sec. 2, pp. 13-18 (1951); S. S. Gordon, "*Waverley* and the 'Unified Design,'" *ELH,* XVIII (1951), 107-122; W. B. Todd, "Twin Titles in S's *Woodstock,*" *Papers Bib. Soc. of Am.,* XLV (1951), 256; Russell Kirk, "S and Bentham," *FR,* N.S. CLXXII (1952), 397-403; Paul Roberts, "Sir WS's Contributions to the English Vocabulary," *PMLA,* LXVIII (1953), 189-210.

To these should be added a series of articles by C. O. Parsons, mostly concerned with S's interest in and use of the supernatural: "S's Fellow Demonologists," *MLQ,* IV (1943), 473-493; "WS in Pandemonium," *MLR,* XXXVIII (1943), 244-249; "Sir John Sinclair's Raspe in S's Dousterswivel," *NQ,* CLXXXIV (1943), 62-66; "The Bodach Ghas in *Waverley,*" *NQ,* CLXXXIV (1943), 95-97; "Minor Spirits and Superstitions in the Waverley Novels," *NQ,* CLXXXIV (1943), 358-363, and CLXXXV (1943), 4-7; "The Interest of S's Public in the Supernatural," *NQ,* CLXXXV (1943), 92-100; "The Dalrymple Legend in *The Bride of Lammermoor,*" *RES,* XIX (1943), 51-58; "The Original of the Black Dwarf," *SP,* XL (1943), 567-575.

Chapter XII: From Scott to Dickens

Bulwer. The Earl of Lytton has published a brief biography, *Bulwer-Lytton* (AS, 1949). For letters, see *More Books,* XXII (1947), 123-136,

175-182. There are articles by Keith Hollingsworth, "Who Suggested the Plan for B's *Paul Clifford?" MLN,* LXIII (1948), 489-491—cf. LXIII (1951), 288; C. H. Shattuck, "E. L. Bulwer and Victorian Censorship," *Q.Jour.Speech,* XXXIV (1948), 65-72; F. Cordasco, "Notes on B-L's Classical Scholarship," *NQ,* CXCVI (1951), 191-192. See, also, William Howard Taft III, "Lytton as a Literary Critic," *DA,* XII (1952), 312-313.

DISRAELI. Biographical studies are Hesketh Pearson, *Dizzy* (H. 1951); R. G. Stapledon, *D and the New Age* (Transatlantic, 1944); Cecil Roth, *BD, Earl of Beaconsfield* (Phil. Libr., 1952). D is included in Richard Aldington, *Four English Portraits* (Evans, 1948) and in Percy Colson, *Their Ruling Passions* (Hu, 1949). Muriel Masefield's *Peacocks and Primroses* (Geoffrey Bles, 1953) is a detailed commentary on the novels. H. H. Hoeltje's article, *PQ,* XXXI (1952), 17-26, deals with his letters to Robert Carter. C. L. Cline has written a number of articles about D: "The Failure of D's Contarini Fleming," *NQ,* CLXXXIII (1942), 69; "D at High Wycombe," *UTSE,* 1942, pp. 124-144; "Unfinished Diary," etc., *UTSE,* 1943, pp. 94-114; "D and Thackeray," *RES,* XIX (1943), 404-408; "Coningsby and Three Victorian Novelists," *NQ,* CLXXXVI (1944), 41-42. See, also, Eric Forbes-Boyd, "D the Novelist," in *E&S,* N.S. III (1950); Robert Hamilton, "D and the Two Nations," *QR,* CCLXXXVIII (1950), 102-115; Russell Kirk, "The Social Imagination of D," *QQ,* LIX (1952), 471-485.

LEVER. F. Genn, *NSN,* XXIV (1942), 159; J. Hennig, "CL and Rodolphe Toepffer," *MLR,* XLIII (1948), 88-92.

CARLETON has acquired a new biography, *Poor Scholar,* by Benedict Kiely (SW, 1948). See, also, Robert Bratton, *LTLS,* Apr. 20, 1946, p. 187.

SURTEES. See Leonard Cooper, *RSS* (Barker, 1952). Cyril Ray has edited a volume of selections: *RSS: Scenes and Characters* (Falcon Pr., 1948). See, further, Una Pope-Hennessy, *Durham Company* (CW, 1941) and G. G. French, *John Jorrocks and Other Characters* (Hu, 1947), as well as these articles: John Shand, *AM,* CLXXV, Jan. 1945, pp. 91-96; W. L. Burn, "S and Trollope," *Bla,* CCLXI (1947), 301-307; Robert L. Collison, "RSS: Satirist and Sociologist," *XIX CF,* VII (1952), 202-207.

MARRYAT. There is a new book-length study—Oliver Warner, *Captain Marryat, A Rediscovery* (M, 1953). See also Sir H. W. Richmond, "The Naval Officer in Fiction," *E&S,* XXX (1944).

PEACOCK. H. Steuert, *Dublin R.,* CCXVI (1945), 67-74; J. B. Price, *CR,* CLXXXI (1952), 365-369.

Chapter XIII: White Magic: Charles Dickens

Bibliographical data will be found in William Miller, *The D Student and Collector, A List of Writings Relating to CD and His Works,* 1846-1945 (HUP, 1946), with a *Supplement,* privately printed in Brighton, England (1947)—cf. P. Calhourn and H. J. Heaney, *Papers Bibl. Soc. Am.,* XLI (1947), 293-320. Another article of bibliographical interest is J. Butt, "*David Copperfield:* From MS to Print," *RES,* N.S. I (1950), 247-251.

Two anthologies worth noting are Trumbull Huntington, ed., *The D Reader* (Howell, Soskin, 1948) and Edward Wagenknecht, ed., *An Introduction to D* (Scott, Foresman, 1952), which contains *Great Expectations, The Chimes,* and "George Silverman's Explanation" complete, and numerous other selections, arranged to show D's development as a novelist, with introductions and annotations.

The Heart of CD, ed. by Edgar Johnson (LB, 1952) presents a substantial selection from D's letters to Miss Angela Burdett-Coutts. Letters by and to D will also be found in F. P. Rolfe, *Dickensian,* XXXVIII (1942), 113-123, 161-166, 189-195, and *XIX CF,* IV (1949), 243-244; R. D. Altick, *Pa. Mag. Hist. and Biog.,* LXXIII (1949), 326-337; W. E. Buckler, *Papers Bibl. Soc. of Am.,* XLV (1951), 160-166; C. W. Miller, *U. of Va. Studies,* IV (1951), 67-71; K. J. Fielding, *RES,* N.S. II (1951), 154-157 and III (1952), 141-154; *English,* IX (1952), 17-19, and *XIX CF,* VII (1952), 103-110. See, also, *HLQ,* XIV (1951), 385-413.

The most elaborate Dickens book published during our period is Edgar Johnson, *CD: His Tragedy and Triumph,* 2 vv. (SS, 1953). This is the only biography constructed on a scale comparable to Forster's, and it includes a great deal of material that Forster did not have. Other substantial biographies are Una Pope-Hennessy, *CD* (Howell Soskin, 1946); Hesketh Pearson, *CD, His Character, Comedy, and Career* (H, 1949); and Jack Lindsay, *CD, A Biographical and Critical Study* (Phil. Libr., 1950). Pope-Hennessy was the first biography to be able to make use of the Nonesuch *Letters.* Except for their naïve treatment of the Ternan scandal (see p. 218, ftn. 2 in this volume), both Pope-Hennessy and Pearson are, in general, acceptable books. Lindsay, on the other hand, is fantastically and unbelievably bad; see Gerald Grubb's review, *XIX CF,* V (1950), 317-324.

In "D and the Scandalmongers," *CE,* XI (1950), 373-382, Edward Wagenknecht summarized and evaluated the evidence then available in the Dickens-Ternan controversy (see p. 218 of this volume, ftn. 3). See, further, Wagenknecht's *Introduction to D,* p. 425, ftn. 4. Richard B. Hudson replied to Wagenknecht's *CE* article in *CE,* XIII (1951),

111-113, and Ada B. Nisbet replied indirectly in *D and Ellen Ternan* (U. of Cal. Pr., 1952). Wagenknecht replies to both Hudson and Nisbet in *The Dickensian,* Winter Number, 1953/1954.

Julian Symons' brief biographical and critical study, *CD* (As, 1951) has little or no value. McEwen Lawson, *Challenge to Oppression* (London, Student Christian Movement, 1948) is a biography stressing the reform angle and addressed to younger readers, as is also Eleanor Graham's *The Story of CD* (Br. Bk. Service, 1952). The year 1946 brought two books from France: Leon Lemmonier, *Life of CD* (Albert Michel) and Alain, *En lisant D* (Gallimard, 1946).

More specialized books are R. J. Cruikshank, *CD and Early Victorian England* (Pitman, 1949), which provides delightful reading on backgrounds; Richard M. Baker, *The Drood Murder Case* (U. of Cal. Pr., 1951); I. I. Rantavaara, *D in the Light of English Criticism* (Helsinki U., 1944); Elias Bredsdorff, *Hans Christian Andersen on CD* (Copenhagen: Rosenkilde og Baggers Forlog, 1952); F. Dubrez Fawcett, *D the Dramatist* (W. H. Allen, 1952), which includes an account of D novels on stage, screen, etc. See, also, George Orwell, *D, Dali, and Others* (Reynal & Hitchcock, 1946), which is stimulating criticism, and Richard Aldington, *Four English Portraits* (Evans, 1948).

Gerald Grubb's contributions to Dickensian biography and criticism during the period under consideration have been very important. See: "D's Pattern of Weekly Serialization," *ELH,* IX (1942), 141-156; "A Hogarth Influence on D," *Dickensian,* XXXIX (1943), 144-145; "The Editorial Policies of CD," *PMLA,* LVIII (1943), 1110-1124; "D's Editorial Methods," *SP,* XL (1943), 79-100; "D's Influence as an Editor," *SP,* XLII (1945), 811-823; "D and the *Daily News:* The Origin of the Idea," *Booker Memorial Studies* (UNCP, 1950); "The Personal and Literary Relationships of D and Poe," *XIX CF,* V (1950), 1-22, 101-120, 209-221; "D and the *Daily News:* Preliminaries to Publication," *XIX CF,* VI (1951), 174-194; "D's Western Tour and the Cairo Legend," *SP,* XLVIII (1951), 87-97; "D and the *Daily News:* The Early Issues," *XIX CF,* VI (1952), 234-246; "D and the *Daily News:* Resignation," *XIX CF,* VII (1952), 19-38; "Personal and Business Relations of CD and Thomas Coke Evans," *Dickensian,* XLVIII (1952), 106-113, 168-173; "D's Marchioness Identified," *MLN,* LXVII (1953), 162-164. For further discussion of some of the matters considered by Professor Grubb, see W. E. Buckler, "D the Paymaster," *PMLA,* LXVI (1951), 1177-1180; Ada Nisbet, "New Light on the D-Poe Relationship," *XIX CF,* V (1951), 295-302.

Three articles have been devoted to the subject of D's relationships, personal and literary, with Washington Irving: Ernest Boll, *MLQ,* V (1944), 453-467; W. C. D. Pacey, *AL,* XVI (1945), 332-339; C. Wegelin,

MLQ, VII (1946), 453-467. Other articles of biographical interest are Wilfrid Partington, *AM,* CLXXX, Aug. 1947, pp. 56-63; C. H. Vivian, *XIX CF,* IV (1950), 328-330; G. Artour, "Landor and D," *LTLS,* Dec. 28, 1951, p. 837; J. C. Maxwell, "Mrs. Christian's Reminiscences of D," *RES,* N.S. II (1951), 59-63; A. A. Adrian, *PMLA,* LXVII (1952), 341-349.

The ff. articles are of varied, largely critical, interest: L. Stevenson, "D's Dark Novels, 1851-1857," *SR,* LI (1943), 398-409; J. D. Gordan, "The Secret of D's Memoranda," in *Bookmen's Holiday: Notes and Studies Gathered in Tribute to H. M. Lydenberg* (N. Y. Pub. Lib., 1943); E. M. S. Simpson, "Jonson and D: A Study in the Comic Genius of London," *E&S,* XXIX (1943); E. Boll, "The Plotting of *Our Mutual Friend,*" *MP,* XLII (1944), 96-122; G. H. Clarke, "D Now," *QQ,* LII (1945), 280-287; L. Cranfield, *NSN,* XXIX (1945), 95-96, and XXX (1945), 301-302; Carolyn W. Houtchens and Lawrence H. Houtchens, "Contributions of Early American Journals to the Study of CD," *MLQ,* VI (1945), 211-217; R. B. Heilman, "The New World in CD's Writings," *Tr,* No. 3 (1946), pp. 25-43, No. 4 (1947), pp. 11-26; A. B. Hopkins, "D and Mrs. Gaskell," *HLQ,* IX (1946), 357-385; Harold Nicolson, *Sp,* CLXXVI (1946), 87; E. P. Vandiver, Jr., "D's Knowledge of Shakespeare," *Sh. Assn. Bull.,* XXI (1946), 124-128; Mildred G. Christian, "Carlyle's Influence upon the Social Theory of D," *Tr,* No. 4 (1947), pp. 27-35, II (1947), 11-26; Robert Hamilton, "D in his Characters," *XIX C,* CXLII (1947), 40-49; Louise Pound, "The American Dialect of CD," *Am. Speech,* XXII (1947), 124-130; L. Stevenson, "Who Was Mr. Turveydrop?" *Dickensian,* XLIV (1947), 39-41; J. Wenger, "Character-Types in Scott, Balzac, D, Zola," *PMLA,* LXII (1947), 213-232; E. K. Brown, *"David Copperfield," YR,* XXXVII (1948), 650-666; W. L. Burn, "The Neo-Barnacles," *XIX C,* CXLIII (1948), 98-103; Donal O'Sullivan, "CD and Thomas Moore," *Studies,* XXXVII (1948), 169-178, 342; A. J. A. Waldock, "The Status of *Hard Times,*" *Southerly,* IX (1948), 33-39; Warrington Winters, "D and the Psychology of Dreams," *PMLA,* LXIII (1948), 984-1006; A. A. Adrian, *"Nicholas Nickleby* and Educational Reform," *XIX CF,* IV (1949), 237-241; Clifton Fadiman, "Pickwick Lives Forever," *AM,* CLXXXIV, Dec. 1949, pp. 23-29; Robert Morse, *"Our Mutual Friend," PR,* XVI (1949), 277-289; A. A. Adrian, *"David Copperfield:* A Century of Critical and Popular Acclaim," *MLQ,* XI (1950), 325-331; H. Rouse Blair, "CD and Henry James: Two Approaches to the Art of Fiction," *XIX CF,* V (1950), 151-157; Fred W. Boege, "Point of View in D," *PMLA,* LXV (1950), 90-105; G. K. Chesterton, in *The Common Man* (SW, 1950); Edgar Johnson, "D, Fagin, and Mr. Riah: The Intention of the Novelist," *Commentary,* IX (1950), 47-50; A. Nisbet, "The Mystery of Martin

Chuzzlewit," in *Essays Critical and Historical Dedicated to Lily B. Campbell* (U. of Cal. Pr., 1950); Dorothy Van Ghent, "The D World: A View from Todgers'," *SR,* LVIII (1950), 419-438; John T. Winterich, "D: Young Man River," *SRL,* XXXIII, Nov. 11, 1950, p. 30+; Herbert Autcliffe, "D and Music," *FR,* N.S. CLXIX (1951), 336-341; John Butt and Kathleen Tillotson, "D at Work on *Dombey and Son,*" in *E&S,* N.S. IV (1951); George H. Ford, "D's Notebook and *Edwin Drood,*" *XIX CF,* VI (1951), 275-280; Lauriat Lane, Jr., "D and Scott: An Unusual Borrowing," *XIX CF,* VI (1951), 223-224—cf. VII (1952), 223-244, VIII (1953), 78—and *"Oliver Twist:* A Revision," *LTLS,* July 20, 1951, p. 460; Donal O'Sullivan, "CD: His Biographers and his Times," *Studies,* XXXIX (1951), 141-153; Eleanor Rooke, "Fathers and Sons in D," *E&S,* N.S. IV (1951); A. A. Adrian, "D on American Slavery: A Carlylean Slant," *PMLA,* LXXVII (1952), 315-329; W. O. Aydelotte, "The England of Marx and Mill as Reflected in Fiction," in R. L. Schuyler and H. Ausubel, eds., *The Making of English History* (Dryden Pr., 1952); W. E. Buckler, *"Once a Week* under Samuel Lucas," *PMLA,* LXVII (1952), 924-951; L. F. Mannheim, *"The Personal History of David Copperfield:* A Study in Psychoanalytic Criticism," *Amer. Imago,* IX (1952), 21-43; K. J. Fielding, "CD and the Department of Practical Art," *MLR,* XLVIII (1953), 270-277; Priscilla Gibson, "D's Uses of Animism," *XIX CF,* VII (1953), 283-291; Lionel Trilling, *"Little Dorrit," KR,* XV (1953), 577-590.

The periodical *The Dickensian* is still published quarterly by the Dickens Fellowship; to this publication a general reference is indicated; very few of the articles contained in it have been listed separately here.

Chapter XIV: The Disciples of Dickens

Collins and Reade. Bibliographical data appear in F. Cordasco, *WC and CR: A Bibliography of Critical Notes and Studies* (Long Island U. Pr., 1949).

Collins. WC has at last acquired a biography: Kenneth Robinson, *WC,* A Biography (M, 1952). See, further, Robert P. Ashley, Jr., *WC* (Roy, 1952), and Earle R. Davis, "Charles Dickens and WC," *Bull., Municipal U. of Wichita,* XX, No. 5 (1945). Mr. Ashley has also published a number of articles: "WC's First Short Story," *More Books,* XXIII (1948) 105-106; "WC and a Vermont Murder Trial," *NEQ,* XXI (1948), 368-373; "WC Reconsidered," *XIX CF,* IV (1950), 265-273; "WC and the Detective Story," *XIX CF,* VI (1951), 47-60. See, also, G. F. McCleary, "A Victorian Classic [*The Moonstone*]," *FR,* CLX (1946), 137-141; Douglas B. Maceachen, "WC and British Law,"

XIX CF, V (1950), 121-139; B. A. Booth, "WC and the Art of Fiction," *XIX CF,* VI (1951), 131-145; T. W. Hill, "The Enigma of WC," *Dickensian,* XLVIII (1952), 54-57 and "The Late WC," pp. 114-116.

READE. Emerson G. Sutcliffe has continued his valuable studies of CR's art: "Fact, Realism, and Morality in R's Fiction," *SP,* XLI (1944), 582-598; "Unique and Repeated Situations and Themes in R's Fiction," *PMLA,* LX (1945), 221-230; "CR in his Heroes," *Tr,* No. 2 (1946), pp. 3-15. Wayne Burns has also been prolific: "Pre-Raphaelitism in CR's Early Fiction," *PMLA,* LX (1945), 1149-1164; "More R Notebooks," *SP,* XLII (1945), 824-842; "CR and the Collinses," *MLN,* LXII (1947), 397-399; *"The Cloister and the Hearth:* A Classic Reconsidered," *Tr,* II (1947), 71-81; "The Sheffield Flood: A Critical Study of CR's Fiction," *PMLA,* LXIII (1948), 686-695. Sutcliffe and Burns collaborated in *"Uncle Tom* and CR," *AL,* XVII (1946), 334-337. See, further, Lewis F. Haines, "R, Mill, and Zola: A Study of the Character and Intention of CR's Realistic Method," *SP,* XL (1943), 463-480; H. Bett, "Thomas Coryat and CR," *London Q.R.,* CLXX (1945), 117-121; Carl D. Woodring, "CR's Debt to William Howitt," *XIX CF,* V (1950), 39-46; Royal A. Gettmann, "The Serialization of R's *A Good Fight,"* *XIX CF,* VI (1951), 21-32; R. H. Bowers, "The Canceled 'Song of Solomon' Passage in R's *Hard Cash,"* *XIX CF,* VI (1952), 225-233; J. B. Price, "CR and Charles Kingsley," *CR,* CLXXXIII (1953), 161-166.

MRS. GASKELL. Annette B. Hopkins, *EG: Her Life and Work* (Lehmann, 1952) is the crowning work of the leading authority on Mrs. G. See also her *"Mary Barton:* A Victorian Best-Seller," *Tr,* III (1948), 1-18, and "A Uniquely-Illustrated *Cranford,"* *XIX CF,* IV (1950), 299-314. A briefer biographical and critical study is Yvonne ffrench, *Mrs. G* (AS, 1949). More specialized is A. Rubenius, *The Woman Question in Mrs. G.'s Life and Works* (HUP, 1950). For letters, see *More Books,* XXIII (1948), 229-230. Consult, further, Gilbert Thomas, in *Builders and Makers* (Epworth Pr., 1945); Mrs. D. L. Hobman, "The Art of Life: A Woman's Problem," *Hibbert J.,* XLIV (1946), 258-262; Rosamond Lehmann, "A Neglected Victorian Classic [*Wives and Daughters*]," *Penguin New Writing,* No. 32 (1948), pp. 89-101, and "Three Giants: Charlotte Brontë, Mrs. Gaskell, George Eliot," *NYTBR,* Dec. 21, 1952, p. 5; D. S. Bland, *"Mary Barton* and Historical Accuracy," *RES,* N.S. I (1950), 58-60; H. P. Collins, "The Naked Sensibility: EG," *EC,* III (1953), 60-72.

KINGSLEY. Una Pope-Hennessy, *Canon CK* (M, 1949); Guy Kendall, *CK and his Ideas* (Hu, 1947); Anon., "K as Children's Writer," *LTLS,* Children's Book Section, June 15, 1951, pp. i-ii. Robert B. Martin,

Princeton U. Libr. Chron., XIII (1952), 168, announces acquisition K materials. See, also, under Reade, Price.

Chapter XV: Counter-Blast: W. M. Thackeray

Of prime importance during the period covered by this bibliographical note has been the publication, after many years of refusal by the Thackeray family, of *The Letters and Private Papers of WMT,* ed. Gordon N. Ray, 4 vv. (HUP, 1945-1946). The material itself and Professor Ray's editing of it have occasioned some discussion; see P. F. Baum, *SAQ,* XLVI (1947), 390-406; Michael Sadleir, *Tr,* II (1947), 107-115; Ernest Bernbaum, *JEGP,* XLVII (1948), 246-253; see, also, Ray, *LTLS,* Nov. 15, 1947, p. 591. Ray's book, *The Buried Life, A Study of the Relation between T's Fiction and his Personal History* (HUP, 1952) is based on his Lowell lectures of 1950. See, further, his "T and *Punch:* Forty-four Newly Identified Contributions," *LTLS,* Jan. 1, 1949, p. 16; "*Vanity Fair:* One Version of the Novelist's Responsibility," in *Essays by Divers Hands, Transactions of the Royal Society of Literature,* XXV (1950), 87-101; and the items listed under Ray in *MP,* XLV (1948), 267. For another addition to the WMT canon, see W. O. Pacey, *PMLA,* LX (1945), 606-611. There are biographical data in Jane T. Prynne and Alicia Bayne, "Memorials of the T Family," *NQ,* CXXXVIII (1945), 119-127. See, also, *T's Daughter,* compiled by Hester Thackeray Fuller and Violet Hammersley (Euphorion Books, 1951).

There have been a number of other books, mainly interpretive. Lionel Stevenson, *The Showman of Vanity Fair* (S, 1947) was the last important biography to be written before the Ray collection became available. See, further, Lambert Ennis, *T, The Sentimental Cynic* (Northwestern U. Pr., 1950) and J. Y. T. Greig, *T, A Reconsideration* (OUP, 1950). J. D. Gordan, *WMT* (N. Y. Pub. Lib., 1947), though the catalogue of an exhibition, contains much information of value. T has also, somewhat surprisingly, become the hero of two biographies for young readers: Laura Benét, *T of the Great Heart and Humorous Pen* (DM, 1947) and Jean Gould, *Young Thack* (HM, 1949).

See, further, the ff. articles: Grace D. Huey, "*Henry Esmond* and the XX C," *EJ,* XXXII (1943), 456-459; John R. Moore, "Scott and *Henry Esmond,*" *NQ,* CLXXXVI (1944), 288-289; W. H. Graham, "T's *The Virginians,*" *FR,* CLXVII (1945), 45-48; H. O. Brogan, "Rachel Esmond and the Dilemma of the Victorian Ideal of Womanhood," *ELH,* XIII (1946), 223-232; H. H. Scudder, "T and Sir Martin Archer Smee," *PMLA,* LXI (1946), 203-210; Eva B. Touster, "The Literary Relationship of T and Fielding," *JEGP,* XLVI (1947), 383-394; Clara Lederer, "*Vanity Fair* After One Hundred Years," *Tr,* III (1948), 159-161; L.

Winegarner, "T's Contributions to the *British and Foreign Review,*" *JEGP,* XLVII (1948), 237-245; Russell A. Fraser, "Sentimentality in T's *The Newcomes,*" *XIX CF,* IV (1949), 187-196; R. Maitre, "Balzac, T, et Charles de Bernard," *R. Litt. Comp.,* XXIV (1950), 279-283; B. G. MacCarthy, "T in Ireland," *Studies,* XL (1951), 55-68; John E. Tilford, Jr., "The 'Unsavoury Plot' of *Henry Esmond,*" *XIX CF,* VI (1951), 121-130 and "The Love Theme of *Henry Esmond,*" *PMLA,* LXVII (1952), 684-701; E. P. Vandiver, Jr., "T and Shakespeare," *Bull. Furman U.,* XXXIV (1951), 30-45; R. C. Tobias, "American Criticism of T, *XIX CF,* VIII (1953), 53-65.

Chapter XVI: The Novelist as Novelist: Anthony Trollope

More of T's novels have been restored to print since pp. 289-290 of this volume were first printed; see, especially, current OUP catalogues. The same house has also begun the publication of "The Oxford T," ed. Michael Sadleir and Frederick Page, with illustrations, introductions, etc. Another handsome edition, "The Borzoi T," has been begun by K. In 1951, D published a well-printed edition of *The Eustace Diamonds,* illustrated by Kenneth Riley; the text, unfortunately, is not complete. Williams and Norgate have republished *Sir Harry Hotspur* (1948). The Folio Society has brought out two handsome collections of short stories: *The Parson's Daughter* (1949) and *Mary Gresley* (1951), both ed. by John Hampden and illustrated by Joan Hassall. *Christmas Day at Kirby Cottage* was reprinted by Greetings Books in 1947; it has also been included in *A Fireside Book of Yuletide Tales,* ed. Edward Wagenknecht (BM, 1948). See, also, *Hunting Sketches,* illustrated, and with an introduction, by Lionel Edwards (John Day, 1953), and T's play, *Did He Steal It?,* with introduction by Robert H. Taylor (PUP, 1952)—cf. discussion in *Princeton U. Libr. Chron.,* XIV (1952), 41. The German publisher, Georg Westermann, brought out two stories, *Journey to Panama* and *Malachi's Cove* in a single volume in 1951. There have also been two volumes of selections: *The T Reader,* ed. Esther C. Dunn and Marion E. Dodd (OUP, 1947) and *The Bedside Barsetshire,* ed. L. O. Tingay, and charmingly illustrated by Gwen Raverat (K, 1951).

The Letters of AT (OUP, 1951) are now available. These have been edited by Bradford A. Booth, who has also brought out new editions of T's *Autobiography* (U. of Cal. Pr., 1947), and, in collaboration with Donald Smalley, of *North America* (K, 1951). See, further, *A Letter from AT Describing a Visit to California in 1875* (Colt Pr., 1946).

The most important general biographical work of the period is Lucy Poate Stebbins and Richard Poate Stebbins, *The T's, The Chronicle of a Writing Family* (ColUP, 1945). A revised edition of Michael Sadleir's standard *AT, A Commentary* was published by FSY in 1945. Beatrice C. Brown, *AT* (AS, 1950) is a brief biographical and critical study; more specialized is Marcie Muir, *AT in Australia* (Adelaide, Wakefield, 1949). There is *A Guide to T,* by Winifred Gregory Gerould and James T. Gerould (PUP, 1948). The Grolier Club published (1950) *Two Addresses Delivered to Members of the GC:* "T's America," by Willard Thorp, and "The Lawyers of AT," by Henry S. Drinker.

The ff. are predominantly critical articles: C. Hollis, "The Meaning of AT," in Douglas Woodruff, ed., *For Hilaire Belloc* (SW, 1942); Clement Greenberg, *PR,* XI (1944), 234-238; Frank P. Jones, "AT and the Classics," *Classical Weekly,* XXXVII (1944), 227-231; W. B. Brash, "The Triumph of AT," *London Q.R.,* CLXX (1945), 293-299; W. M. Parker, "AT and Maga," *Bla,* CCLVII (1945), 57-64; C. J. Vincent, "T: A Victorian Augustan," *QQ,* LII (1945), 415-428; Ernest Boll, "The Infusions of Dickens in T," *Tr,* No. 3 (1946), pp. 11-24; Gladys Green, "T on Sidney's *Arcadia* and Lytton's *The Wanderer," Tr,* No. 3 (1946), pp. 45-54; John H. Wildman, "AT Today, *CE,* VII (1946), 397-399, and "About T, in a Postwar Mood," *Tr,* No. 2 (1946), pp. 17-22; D. M. Alexander, "T's Cosmopolitanism," *Tr,* II (1947), 3-10; B. A. Booth, "T, Reade, and 'Shilly-Shally,' " *Tr,* No. 4 (1947), 45-54, and II (1947), 43-51; Norris D. Hoyt, *"Can You Forgive Her?* A Commentary," *Tr,* II (1947), 57-70; Raymond Mortimer, *NSN,* XXXIII (1947), 83-89; B. A. Booth, "T and *Little Dorrit," Tr,* II (1948), 237-240; W. L. Burn, "AT's Politics," *XIX C,* CXLIII (1948), 161-171; R. W. Chapman, "Personal Names in T's Political Novels," in *Essays Mainly on the XIX C, Presented to Sir Humphry Milford* (OUP, 1948); T. A. Sherman, "The Financial Motive in the Barchester Novels," *CE,* IX (1948), 413-418; Chauncey B. Tinker, *Essays in Retrospect* (YUP, 1948); E. L. Skinner, "Mr. T's Young Ladies," *XIX CF,* IV (1949), 197-207; L. Stevenson, "T as a Recorder of Verbal Usage," *Tr,* III (1948), 119-125; J. F. Wildman, "T Illustrates the Distinction," *XIX CF,* IV (1949), 101-110; M. W. Bloomfield, "T's Use of Canadian History in *Phineas Finn," XIX CF,* V (1950), 67-74; B. A. Booth, "T on the Novel," in *Essays Critical and Historical Dedicated to Lily B. Campbell. . . .* (U. of Cal. Pr., 1950); Virginia W. Pringle, "Barsetshire Under Fire," *XIX CF,* IV (1950), 330-333; David Stryker, "The Sign of T's *American Senator," XIX CF,* V (1950), 141-149; G. M. Tracy, "L'oeuvre de T; ou Le paradis perdu," *Mercure de France,* CCCVIII (1950), 434-445; W. Coyle, "T and the Bi-Columned Shakespeare," *XIX CF,* VI (1951), 33-46, and "An Error in T's Last Novel," *ibid.,* 122; R. A. Fraser, "AT's Younger Characters," *XIX CF,* VI (1951), 96-106; Charles Morgan, in *Liberties of the Mind* (M, 1951); F. E. Robins, "Chronology and History in T's Barset and Parliamentary Novels,"

XIX CF, V (1951), 303-316; L. O. Tingay, "The Reception of T's First Novel," *XIX CF,* VI (1951), 195-200; B. A. Booth, "T and the Royal Literary Fund," *XIX CF,* VII (1952), 208-216; Asa Briggs, "T, Bagehot, and the English Constitution," *Camb. J.,* V (1952), 327-338; William Coyle, "The Friendship of AT and Richard Henry Dana, Jr.," *New England Quarterly,* XXV (1952), 255-262; C. F. Robinson, "T's Jury Trials," *XIX CF,* VI (1952), 247-268; Robert M. Adams, "*Orley Farm* and Real Fiction," *XIX CF,* VII (1953), 27-41; Edd W. Parks, "T and the Defence of Exegesis," *XIX CF,* VII (1953), 265-271; M. W. Hess, "AT's One Hundred Years," *America,* LXXXIX (1953), 624-626.

In Trollope's honor, Professor Bradford A. Booth founded *The Trollopian* in 1945. The title of this journal was afterwards changed to *Nineteenth Century Fiction.* The earlier numbers of this journal contain a number of Trollope items—especially letters, items of biographical or bibliographical interest, etc.—which are not separately listed here. However, see, especially, Muriel R. Trollope, "What I Was Told," *Tr,* II (1948), 223-235. Other items of the character here indicated appear elsewhere; *Sp,* CLXXVII (1946), 613, 644, 676; *Papers Bibl. Soc. Am.,* XLI (1947), 123-139; *New Eng. Q.,* XXV (1952), 255-262.

Chapter XVII: Fire Over Yorkshire: The Brontës

An addition to the B canon has been made by Fannie E. Ratchford, ed., *Five Essays Written in French by EJB,* tr. Lorine W. Nagel (U. of Texas Pr., 1948).

A number of new books about the B's have been published: Laura L. Hinkley, *Charlotte and Emily* (HH, 1945); Phyllis Bentley, *The B's* (AS, 1948)—see, also, her pamphlet, *The B Sisters* (L, 1950); Ernest Raymond, *In the Steps of the B's* (Rich & Cowan, 1948); Lawrence and E. M. Hanson, *The Four B's* (OUP, 1949); W. S. B. Braithwaite, *The Bewitched Parsonage* (CM, 1950); Kathleen Wallace, *Immortal Wheat* (P, 1951), which is somewhat fictionized; and Margaret Lane, *The B Story* (LB, 1953), which brings Mrs. Gaskell's biography up to date. G. Elsie Harrison has written *The Clue to the B's* (Me, 1948); she finds it in Methodism. There are also two French books: Lucienne Escombe, *EB et ses dèmons* (Paris, F. Serlot, 1941) and Jacques Debri-Bridel, *Le secret d'EB* (Paris, Ferenczi, 1950). These are reviewed by F. J. Carmody, *XIX CF,* V (1950), 239-242.

The ff. are mainly critical articles: M. H. Dodds, "Heathcliff's Country," *MLR,* XXXIX (1944), 116-129, which is further discussion of the juvenilia; W. S. H. Jones, *London Q.R.,* CLXX (1945), 347-350; Margaret Willy, "EB: Poet and Mystic," *English,* VI (1946), 117-122; Richard Chase, "The B's; or, Myth Domesticated," in W. V. O'Connor, ed.,

Forms of Modern Fiction (U. of Minn. Pr., 1948); Margiad Evans, "Byron and EB," *LL,* LVII (1948), 193-216; D. Capetanakis, in *Shores of Darkness* (Devin-Adair, 1949); Margaret Lane, "Mr. Nicholls," *CoM,* No. 983 (1950), 351-375; Leslie A. Marchand, "An Addition to the Census of B MSS," *XIX CF,* IV (1950), 81-84; B. G. MacCarthy, "EB," *Studies,* XXXIX (1951), 15-30; J. H. Dugas, "The Literary Reputation of the B's, 1846-1951," *DA,* XII (1952), 61-62; F. Ratchford, "Family of Scribblers," *SRL,* XXXVI, June 20, 1953, p. 21. See, also, under Gaskell, Lehmann.

On *Wuthering Heights,* see G. D. Klingopulos, *Scrutiny,* XIV (1947), 269-286; Melvin R. Watson, *XIX CF,* IV (1949), 87-100. On *Jane Eyre,* see *LTLS,* Aug. 23, 1947, p. 427; M. H. Scargill, *UTQ,* XIX (1950), 120-125; W. E. Buckler, *XIX CF,* VII (1952), 51-55; Dorothy Van Ghent, *ibid.,* pp. 189-197.

The *Transactions of the B Society* are not analyzed in this note. In 1947 a volume of selections was published: *The B's Then and Now* (Haworth: Parsonage Museum). *The Trollopian,* Vol. II, No. 3 (Dec. 1947) was a B Centenary number, with contributions by Ratchford, Bentley, Willis, etc.

Chapter XVIII: The "New" Novel: George Eliot

YUP has now begun the publication of GE's *Letters.* Volume I appeared in 1952.

Three important biographical-critical studies have appeared: Joan Bennett, *GE: Her Mind and Art* (M, 1948); Gerald Bullett, *GE: Her Life and Books* (YUP, 1948); Lawrence and Elisabeth Hanson, *Marian Evans and GE: A Biography* (OUP, 1952). GE is important, also, in F. R. Leavis, *The Great Tradition* (George W. Stewart, 1948). Anna T. Kitchel's *Quarry for* Middlemarch (U. of Cal. Pr., 1950) prints, with introduction and notes, the notebook used by GE while writing *Middlemarch.* There is a GE letter in *More Books,* XXIII (1948), 269-270.

Critical articles and studies include: N. Annan, *NSN,* XXVI (1943), 355; Cecile de Banke, "Week-End with *Middlemarch,*" *QQ,* LII (1945), 346-351; M. H. Dodds, "GE and Charles Dickens," *NQ,* CXC (1946), 143-145, which compares *Felix Holt* and *Bleak House;* Frank G. Halstead, "Medical Digressions in *Middlemarch* and E's State of Health," *Bull. Hist. of Medicine,* XX (1946), 413-425; C. O. Parsons, "Background Material Illustrative of *Silas Marner,*" *NQ,* CXCI (1946), 266-270; V. R., "GE and the Classics," *NQ,* CXCII (1947), 544-546, 564-565, CXCIII (1948), 148-149, 272-274; Morris Greenhut, "George Henry Lewes as a Critic of the Novel," *SP,* XLV (1948), 491-511; Graham Hough, *Horizon,* XVII (1948), 50-62; Walter Naumann, "The Architecture of GE's Novels," *MLQ,* IX (1948), 37-50; B. Willey, in *XIX C Studies* (ColUP, 1949), which is important for GE's literary background; G. S. Haight, "Cross's Biography of GE," *Yale Lib. Gazette,* XXV (1950), 1-9; C. T. Bissell, "Social Analysis in the Novels by GE," *ELH,* XVIII (1951), 221-239; S. Liptzin, *"Daniel Deronda . . . ," Jewish Bk. Annual,* X (1951), 1-4; Floyd W. Casey, "GE's Practice as a Novelist in Relation to her Critical Theory," *Summaries of Doctoral Diss., U. of Wis.,* XII (1952), 441-443. See also, under Gaskell, Lehmann.

Chapter XIX: The Poetic Comedy of George Meredith

Three important, extensive studies have appeared: Siegfried Sassoon, *M* (VP, 1948); Lionel Stevenson, *The Ordeal of GM* (S, 1953); Walter F. Wright, *Art and Substance in GM* (U. of Neb. Pr., 1953). Sir Osbert Sitwell's *Novels of GM, and Some Notes on the English Novel* (OUP, 1947) is his Presidential Address for the English Association. Viscountess Milner has recorded her memories in "Talks with GM," *Nat. R.,* CXXXI (1948), 449-458. For letters, see Evelyn Grantham, *More Books,* XX (1945), 335-357.

There is an excellent working bibliography of M in Stevenson, *op. cit.*

See, further, the ff. articles: H. C. Lancaster, in *Adventures of a Literary Historian* (Johns Hopkins U. Pr., 1942), which deals with *Harry Richmond;* Robert D. Mayo, "Sir Willoughby's Pattern," *NQ,* CLXXXIII (1942), 362-363; Sir John Pollock, *CR,* CLXI (1942), 285-288; W. H. Graham, "A Lord of Creation: Sir Willoughby Patterne, The Complete Egoist," *Nat. R.,* CXXII (1944), 342-345; H. W. Hewett-Thayer, "Ferdinand Lassalle in the Novels of Spielhagen and M," *Germanic R.,* XIX (1944), 186-196; C. L. Cline, *"Diana of the Crossways* and the Wonderful Old Quarto," *NQ,* CLXXXVIII (1945), 187-189; Lord Dunsany, *XIX C,* CXXXIX (1946), 32-35; Gladys W. Ekeberg, *"The Ordeal of Richard Feverel:* A Tragedy," *CE,* VII (1946), 387-393; Anon., "M Revisited," *LTLS,* Jan. 10, 1948, p. 23; R. B. Hudson, "The Meaning of Egoism in GM's *The Egoist," Tr,* III (1948), 163-176, and "M's Early Life," *LTLS,* Dec. 4, 1948, p. 681; R. A. Gettmann, "M as Publisher's Reader," *JEGP,* XLVIII (1949), 44-56, and "Serialization and *Evan Harrington," PMLA,* LXIV (1949), 963-975; J. G. Eaker, "M's Human Comedy," *XIX CF,* V (1951), 253-272; J. T. Fain, "M and the Cuckoo Song," *MLN,* LXVI (1951), 324-326; W. R. Mueller, "Theological Dualism and the 'System' in *Richard Feverel," ELH,* XVIII (1951), 138-154; Dorothy D. Bailey, "American Literary Criticism of GM, 1860-1917," *Summaries of Doctoral Diss., U. of Wis.,* XII (1952), 439-441; W. E. Buckler, "The Artistic Unity of *Richard Feverel:* Chapter XXXIII," *XIX CF,* VII (1952), 119-123; James Stone,

"M and Goethe," *UTQ,* XXI (1952), 157-166; Charles J. Hill, "GM's Plain Story," [*Rhoda Fleming*], *XIX CF,* VII (1952), 90-102, and "The Portrait of the Author in *Beauchamp's Career,*" *JEGP,* LII (1953), 332-339; Adrian Harley, "The Limits of M's Comedy," *XIX CF,* VII (1953), 272-282; L. Stevenson, "M and the Interviewers," *MP,* LI (1953), 50-63; Bernard A. Brunner, "M's Symbolism: *Lord Ormont and His Aminta,*" *XIX CF,* VIII (1953), 124-133.

Chapter XX: Hardy and the Cosmic Drama

For bibliographical data, see Carl J. Weber, *The First Hundred Years of TH, 1840-1940: A Centenary Bibliography of Hardiana* (Colby Coll. Libr., 1942); *TH in Maine* (Colby Coll. Pr., 1942); *Hardy Music at Colby: A Check-List* (Colby Coll. Libr., 1945).

H's story for boys, *Our Exploits at West Poley,* was published by OUP in 1942.

Critical studies of H, mainly as fictionist, are Lord David Cecil, *H the Novelist* (BM, 1946); Orhan Burian, *An Introduction to H's Novels, Les Annales de l'Université d'Ankara,* No. III (1948-1949), 4451-4522; Albert J. Guerard, *TH, The Novels and the Stories* (HUP, 1949); Desmond Hawkins, *TH* (AS, 1952). Harvey C. Webster, *On a Darkling Plain* (UCP, 1947) stresses philosophical perspectives. See, also, R. A. Scott-James's pamphlet, *TH* (London, Longmans, for the British Council and the National Book League, 1952). Special topics are treated in Weber's *Hardy in America: A Study of TH and his American Readers* (Colby Coll. Pr., 1946) and *Hardy and the Lady from Madison Square* [Rebekah Owen] (Colby Coll. Pr., 1952)—cf. Robert Slack, *LTLS,* May 30, 1952, p. 361; Clive Holland, *TH's* Wessex Scene (Dorchester, England: Longmans, Ltd., 1948); Marguerite Roberts, *Tess in the Theatre* (U. of Toronto Pr., 1950); May O'Rourke, *The Young TH* (Dorchester, Dorset Pr., 1951). There are references to H in Siegfried Sassoon, *Siegfried's Journey, 1916-1920* (VP, 1946), and in Eden Phillpotts, *From the Angle of 88* (Hu, 1951). There is a French study by Louise de Ridder-Barzin, *Le Pessimisme de TH* (Presses Universitaires de France, 1948) and one by a Japanese scholar, M. Osawa, *Studies of TH's Literature* (Tokyo, Kenkyusha, 1949). Some letters are printed in *Jour. Rutgers U. Libr.,* XIII (1949), 1-6.

See, also, the ff. articles: Cyril Clemens, "My Chat with TH," *DalR,* XXIII (1943), 87-94; F. R. Leavis, "H and Criticism," *Scrutiny,* XI (1943), 230-237; J. O. Bailey, "H's 'Imbedded Fossil,'" *SR,* XLII (1945), 663-674, and "H's 'Mephistophelian Visitants,'" *PMLA,* LXI (1946), 1146-1184; C. J. Weber, "Tragedy and the Good Life," *DalR,* XXV (1945), 225-233, "*Jude* from Obscurity via Notoriety to Fame," *Colby*

Libr. Q., I (1946), 209-215, "The Tragedy in Little Hintock: New Light on TH's Novel, *The Woodlanders*," in *Booker Memorial Studies* (UNCP, 1950), and "Hardy: A Wessex Seesaw," *SRL,* XXXIV, Jan. 6, 1951, pp. 24-25; R. W. Stallman, "H's Hour-Glass Novel [*The Return of the Native*]," *SR,* LV (1947), 283-296; H. C. Darby, "The Regional Geography of H's Wessex," *Geog. R.,* XXXVIII (1948), 426-443; J. I. M. Stewart, "The Integrity of H," *E&S* (1948); J. C. Blankenagel, "A Note on H's *Tess of the D'Urbervilles* and Goethe's *Faust*," *German Q.,* XXII (1949), 202-203; Mary C. Richards, "TH's Ironic Vision," *Tr,* III (1949), 265-279, and *XIX CF,* IV (1949), 21-35; G. W. Sherman, "The Wheel and the Beast: The Influence of London on TH," *XIX CF,* IV (1949), 209-219, and "Hooper Tolbort's Influence upon TH," *NQ,* CXCVI (1951), 280-281; Clarice Short, "TH and the Military Man," *XIX CF,* IV (1949), 129-135; H. O. Brogan, "'Visible Existences,' in *The Mayor of Casterbridge*," *ELH,* XVII (1950), 307-323; Havelock Ellis, in *From Marlowe to Shaw* (Williams, 1951); J. R. Moore, "Two Notes on TH," *XIX CF,* V (1950), 159-163—on *The Mayor of Casterbridge;* J. E. Harrison, "H's Tragic Synthesis," *Durham U. Jour.,* XLIII (1950-1951), 20-26; F. A. Hedgcock, "Reminiscences of TH," *Nat. & Eng. R.,* CXXXVII (1951), 220-228, 289-291; Clive Holland, "My Walks and Talks in Wessex with TH," *John o' London's Weekly,* LX (1951), 170-171; W. Newton, "Chance as Employed by H and the Naturalists," *PQ,* XXX (1951), 154-175 and "H and the Naturalists: Their Use of Physiology," *MP,* XLIX (1951), 28-41; John T. Sheppard, in *Music at Belmont* (HM, 1951); L. A. G. Strong, "Dorset H," *EC,* I (1951), 42-50; Gilbert Thomas, "The Dark Horse: TH," *DalR,* XXX (1951), 403-411; Cleanth Brooks, "A Note on TH," *Hopkins R.,* V (1952), 68-73; D. A. Dike, "A Modern Oedipus: *The Mayor of Casterbridge*," *EC,* II (1952), 169-179; C. I. Glicksberg, "H's Scientific Pessimism," *W. Humanities R.,* VI (1952), 273-283; G. W. Sherman, "TH and the Agricultural Laborer," *XIX CF,* VII (1952), 111-118.

Many articles on Hardy, by Carl J. Weber and others, have appeared in the *Colby Library Quarterly;* very few of these can be listed here. In addition to the material by Weber listed above, see *Papers Bibl. Soc. Am.,* XL (1946), 1-21. Other articles on specialized themes by Richard L. Purdy are in *LTLS,* Oct. 3, 1942, p. 487; Jan. 2, 1943, p. 7; Mar. 6, 1943, p. 120; June 26, 1943, p. 307; Nov. 20, 1943, p. 559; *Yale U. Libr. Gazette,* XVII (1943), 51-52.

Chapter XXI: Romance Resurgent: Robert Louis Stevenson

A very large number of books about RLS have been published during the period covered by this note. Those marked with a * contain new materials of a biographical character: H. J. Cowell, *RLS* (Epworth Pr., 1945); * Anne B. Fisher, *No More a Stranger* (Stanford U. Pr., 1946); David Daiches, *RLS* (ND, 1947)—cf. his pamphlet, *RLS and the Art of Fiction* (The Author, 1951); Lettice Cooper, *RLS* (AS, 1948); * Anne R. Isller, *Happier for His Presence: San Francisco and RLS* and * *Our Mountain Hermitage: Silverado and RLS* (Stanford, 1949, 1950); Malcolm Elwin, *The Strange Case of RLS* (Macdonald, 1950); Laura L. Hinkley, *The S's: Louis and Fanny* (HH, 1950); * Sister Mary Martha McGaw, *S in Hawaii* (U. of Hawaii Pr., 1950); Moray McLaren, *S and Edinburgh: A Centenary Study* (Chapman & Hall, 1950); * J. C. Furnas, *Voyage to Windward: The Life of RLS* (Sl, 1951); J. W. Ellison, *Tusitala of the South Seas* (HH, 1953). Many letters appear in Janet A. Smith, ed., *Henry James and RLS: A Record of Friendship* (S, 1948); for others, see Roger L. Green, "S in Search of a Madonna," *E&S,* N.S. III (1950). G. B. Stern's novel, *No Son of Mine* (M, 1948) contains an oblique critical study of RLS.

Of bibliographical interest are Rober B. Martin, *Princeton U. Lib. Chron.,* XIII (1952), 167-168; Marjorie G. Wynne, *Yale U. Lib. Gazette,* XXVI (1952), 117-136.

See, further, these articles: J. R. Moore, "S's *Catriona,*" *NQ,* CLXXXIII (1942), 36-38, "Defoe, S, and the Pirates," *ELH,* X (1943), 35-60, and "S's Sources for *The Merry Men,*" *PQ,* XXIII (1944), 135-140; Tom B. Haber, "RLS and Israel Hands," *EJ,* XXXII (1943), 399; J. Ashe, "S After Fifty Years," *Cath. World,* CLX (1944), 241-245; C. O. Parsons, "S's Use of Witchcraft in 'Thrawn Janet,'" *SP,* XLVI (1946), 551-571; Mildred Wilsey, "*Kidnapped* in MSS," *AS,* XVII (1948), 213-220, and *E&S,* N.S. III (1950); J. R. Baird, "Noble Polynesian," *Pac. Spect.,* IV (1950), 463-465; R. L. Green, "The RLS Centenary," *CR,* CLXXVIII (1950), 289-292; C. Keith, "S Today," *QQ,* LVII (1950), 452-458; John Mason Brown, "RLS and *Dr. Jekyll,*" *SRL,* XXXIV, Dec. 1, 1951, pp. 30-33, and Dec. 8, 1951, pp. 28-30; D. Daiches, "Which RLS?" *XIX CF,* VI (1951), 61-70; J. C. Furnas, "Full Circle: S and His Critics," *AM,* CLXXXVIII, Oct. 1951, pp. 67-71; G. A. Hayes-McCoy, "RLS and the Irish Question," *Studies,* XXXIX (1951), 130-140, and "The Centenary of RLS," *ibid.,* pp. 395-406; Mark Kanzer, "The Self-Analytic Literature of RLS," in George B. Wilbur and Warner Muensterberger, eds., *Psychoanalysis and Culture* (International Universities Press, 1951); Sir James Ferguson, "The Appin Murder Case," *Scottish Hist. R.,* XXXI (1952), 116-130—which deals with the case that supplied background for *Kidnapped* and *David Balfour;* D. C. and L. P. Peattie, "The Treasure of RLS," *Reader's Digest,* LXI, Oct. 1952, pp. 83-87; J. C. Furnas, "RLS in Samoa," *Vogue,* CXXII, Aug. 15, 1953, p. 102+.

Controversy has developed with regard to RLS's alleged affair with Kate Drummond, referred to in ftn. 5, pp. 374-375 of this book; see *LTLS,* Jan. 26, 1951, p. 53; Feb. 9, p. 85; Feb. 16, p. 101; Mar. 2, p. 133; Mar. 9, p. 149.

Chapter XXII: Victorian Sunset

MRS. WARD. Clara Lederer, "MAW and the Victorian Ideal," *XIX CF,* VI (1951), 201-208; Anon., *LTLS,* June 15, 1951, p. 372; J. Trevelyan, "Mrs. HW and *Robert Elsmere,*" *Sp,* CLXXXVI (1951), 745.

BARRIE. Barrie's *Letters,* ed. Viola Meynell has been published by S (1947). See, also, George Blake, *B and the Kailyard School* (Roy, 1952) and John Buchan, in *Comments and Characters* (N, 1940).

KIPLING. *RK's Letters from San Francisco* (Colt Pr., 1949) comprises correspondence and articles written for the *Civil and Military Gazette* of Lahore and the Allahabad *Pioneer.* There have been a number of books about RK: Lucile R. Carpenter, *RK, A Friendly Profile* (Argus Books, 1942); Coulson Kernahan, *Nothing Quite Like K Had Ever Happened Before* (Epworth Pr., 1944); Hilton Brown, *RK* (H, 1945)—an extensive critical study; Rupert Croft-Cooke, *RK* (AS, 1948); Howard C. Rice, *RK in New England,* rev. ed. (Brattleboro, Vt., The Book Cellar, 1951). Bonamy Dobrée, *RK* (L, 1951) is a pamphlet. Nella Braddy's *RK, Son of Empire* (Messner, 1941) is a biography for young readers. See, further, these articles: H. M. McLuhan, "K and Forster," *SR,* LII (1944), 332-343; George Orwell, in *Dickens, Dali, and Others* (Reynal & Hitchcock, 1946); R. L. Green, "RK in London: 1889-1891," *English,* VI (1946), 54-58; DeLancey Ferguson and J. E. Scott, "RK: Two Footnotes," *New Col.,* I (1948), 335-348, 407; J. M. S. Tompkins, "K's Later Tales: The Theme of Healing," *MLR,* XLV (1950), 18-32; Esther Kaufman, "K and the Technique of Action," *XIX CF,* VI (1951), 107-120; Donald L. Hill, "K in Vermont," *XIX CF,* VII (1952), 153-170; Geoffrey Wagner, "Some Current K Scholarship," *Kipling Journal,* XIX (1952), 8-9; H. L. Varley, "Imperialism and RK," *JHI,* XIV (1953), 124-135. A. W. Yeats, "The K Collection at the U. of Texas," *Libr. Chron. of the U. of Texas,* IV (1952), 118-122 is of bibliographical interest.

Chapter XXIII: Towards a New Century

GISSING. Myfanwy Evans has published *GG, 1857-1903* (Barker, 1951). Bibliographical data appear in *Yale U. Libr. Gazette,* XVI (1942), 47-50; XXVII (1952), 52. Jacqueline Steiner has printed some of GG's letters to his sister in *More Books,* XXII (1947), 323-336, 376-386. See, also, these articles: Norman L. Daley, "Some Reflections on the Scholarship of GG," *Classical J.,* XXXVIII (1942), 21-30; W. Plomer, *NSN,* XXXI (1946), 140; Anon., *LTLS,* Feb. 14, 1947, p. 92; Russell Kirk, "Who Knows GG?" *WHR,* IV (1950), 213-222; Jacob Korg, "GG's Outcast Intellectuals," *AS,* XIX (1950), 194-202; James J. Wolff, "G's Revision of *The Unclassed,*" *XIX CF,* VIII (1953), 42-52; J. D. Thomas, "The Public Purpose of GG," *XIX CF,* VIII (1953), 118-123.

Moore. S. Nejdefors-Frisk has produced a book-length study of *GM's Naturalistic Prose* (HUP, 1952). See also: R. A. Gettmann, "GM's Revisions of *The Lake, The Wild Goose,* and *Esther Waters,*" *PMLA,* LIX (1944), 540-555; F. Cordasco, "GM and Edouard Dujardin," *MLN,* LXII (1947), 244-251; W. C. Frierson, "GM Compromised with the Victorians," *Tr,* No. 4 (1947), pp. 37-44; R. J. Niess, "GM and Paul Alexis: The Death of La Pellegrin," *Romanic R.,* XXXVIII (1947), 34-42; Kathleen Fitzpatrick, "A Plea for *Evelyn Innes,*" *Southerly,* IX (1948), 198-203; Barret H. Clark, *Intimate Portraits* (Dramatists Play Service, 1951); Ruth E. Temple, *The Critic's Alchemy: A Study of the Introduction of French Symbolism into England* (Twayne, 1953).

Butler. Of bibliographical interest are *Catalogue of the Collection of SB (of Erewhon) in the Chapin Library, Williams College* (Southworth-Anthoensen Pr., 1945), which contains much interesting information about B, and L. E. Holt, "SB's Revisions of *Erewhon,*" *Papers Bibl. Soc. Am.,* XXXVIII (1944), 22-38. There have been three book-length studies: G. D. H. Cole (AS, 1948); P. N. Furbank (M, 1948); Philip Henderson, *SB, The Incarnate Bachelor* (Cohen and West, 1953). Cole has also edited a volume of selections, *The Essential SB* (D, 1950); Geoffrey Keynes and Brian Hall have edited *SB's Notebooks* (C, 1951). See, further, L. E. Holt, "SB's Rise to Fame," *PMLA,* LVII (1942), 867-878; E. M. Forster, *NSN,* XXVIII (1943), 43—cf. Holt, *PMLA,* LXI (1946), 804-819; Betty Miller, "Miss Savage and Miss Bartram," *XIX C,* CXLIV (1948), 285-292; R. M. Myers, "SB: Handelian," *Musical Q.,* XXXIV (1948), 177-198; T. Y. Booth, "Criticism of Machinery and Mechanism by Four Victorian Writers," *Abstracts of Dissertations, Stanford U.,* XXVI (1950-1951), 131-132; E. M. Forster, *Two Cheers for Democracy* (HB, 1951).

Chapter XXIV: Values and Joseph Conrad

Scholarship has been very active with JC during our period. See: J. H. Retinger, *C and his Contemporaries* (Roy, 1943); Albert J.

Guerard, *JC* (ND, 1947); Walter F. Wright, *Romance and Tragedy in JC* (U. Neb. Pr., 1949); Oliver Warren, *JC* (L, 1951); Douglas Hewitt, *C, A Reassessment* (Bowes & Bowes, 1952). There are also two French books by M-R. Mélisson-Dubreil, *Le Vocabulaire Maritime de JC* and *La Personnalité de JC* (Paris, Maurice Lavergne, both 1943). There are letters in Fred B. Johnson, "Notes on C's Finance," *Ind. Q. for Bookmen, III* (1947), 27-30. Of bibliographical interest are J. A. Gee, "The Final Typescript of Book III in C's *Nostromo*," *Yale U. Libr. Gazette,* XVI (1942), 80; F. B. Johnson, "Conrad, Joseph. *Suspense*," *Papers Bibl. Soc. Am.,* XI (1946), 237-238.

The following are mainly critical articles: James Norman Hall, "My Conrad," *AM,* CLIX (1942), 583-587; Leonard F. Dean, "Tragic Pattern in C's *The Heart of Darkness*," *CE,* VI (1944), 100-104; F. H. Lowther, "C After Twenty Years," *London Q. R.,* CLXIX (1944), 145-152; W. F. Wright, "JC's Critical Views," *Research Studies, State Coll. Wash.,* XII (1944), 155-175, "C's *The Rescue* from Serial to Book," *ibid.,* XIII (1945), 203-224, and "How C Tells a Story," *Prairie Schooner,* XXI (1947), 290-295; E. K. Brown, "James and C," *YR,* XXXV (1945), 265-285; H. T. Webster, "JC: A Reinterpretation of Five Novels," *CE,* VII (1945), 125-134, and "C's Changes in Narrative Conception in the MSS of *Typhoon and Other Stories* and *Victory*," *PMLA,* LXIV (1949), 953-962; M. D. Zabel, "JC: Chance and Recognition," *SR,* LIII (1945), 1-22; Lionel Cranfield, *NSN,* XXXI (1946), 28; R. L. Morris, "The Classical Reference in C's Fiction," *CE,* VII (1946), 312-318; E. Crankshaw, "JC and Today," *Nat. R.,* CXXVIII (1947), 224-230; G. Jean-Aubry, "Le jeunesse de C," *Revue de Paris,* LIV (1947), 92-107; Louis J. Halle, Jr., "JC: An Enigma Decided," *SRL,* XXIX, May 22, 1948, pp. 7-8+; Robert F. Haugh, "JC and Revolution," *CE,* X (1949), 273-277; D. Hewitt's, "JC's Hero: 'Fidelity' or 'The Choice of Nightmares,'" *Camb. J.,* II (1949), 684-691; C. Morley, "A New Estimate of a Great Novelist," *NYTBR,* Aug. 14, 1949, p. 1+; R. W. Stallman, "C and The Secret Sharer," *Accent,* IX (1949), 131-143; V. Young, "JC: Outline for Reconsideration," *Hudson R.,* II (1949), 5-19; Wallace Stegner, "Variations on a Theme by C," *Camb. J.,* III (1950), 727-740; L. H. Turner, "The Genius of JC," *U. of Cal. Abstracts of Diss.,* 1950, pp. 59-61; D. C. Weber, "C's *Lord Jim*," Colby Libr. Q., Series II (1950), pp. 266-268; Katherine H. Gatch, "C's Axel," *SP,* XLVIII (1951), 98-106; R. F. Haugh, "Structure in *Lord Jim*," *CE,* XIII (1951), 137-141; J. E. Miller, Jr., "*The Nigger of the Narcissus:* A Reexamination," *PMLA,* LXVI (1951), 911-918; R. P. Warren, "*Nostromo*," *SR,* LIX (1951), 363-391; Arthur H. Wilson, "The Complete Narrative of JC," *Susquehanna U. Studies,* IV (1951), 229-262; A. Grove Day, "Pattern in *Lord*

Jim," *CE,* XIII (1952), 396-397; F. Downing, "The Meaning of Victory in JC," *Commonweal,* LV (1952), 613-614; R. F. Haugh, "Death and Consequences: JC's Attitude Toward Fate," *UKCR,* XVIII (1952), 191-197; John Lehmann, *Open Night* (HB, 1952); V. Young, "Trial by Water: JC's *The Nigger of the Narcissus,*" *Accent,* XII (1952), 67-81, and "Lingard's Folly," *KR,* XV (1953), 522-539; G. H. Bantock, "The Two Moralities of JC," *EC,* III (1953), 125-142; Irving Howe, "JC: Order and Anarchy: The Political Novels," *KR,* XV (1953), 505-521.

Chapter XXV: Novelist of Being: Arnold Bennett

Reginald Pound's *AB* (HB, 1953) has now provided a full biography of AB. See also Walter Allen, *AB* (AS, 1949). Frank Swinnerton has defended B against his critics in a pamphlet, *AB* (L, 1950). See, also, Jim Tully, *Dozen to One* (Murray and McGee, 1943); W. S. H. Jones, "The Card from the Five Towns," *London Q. R.,* CLXXIII (1948), 124-132; W. M. Conacher, "AB and the French Realists," *QQ,* LVI (1949), 409-417; W. Somerset Maugham, *The Vagrant Mood* (D, 1953); John Van Druten, "My Debt to AB," *SRL,* XXXVI, July 18, 1953, pp. 7-8.

Chapter XXVI: H. G. Wells, "Realist of the Fantastic"

H. G. Wells died on August 13, 1946, and some of the evaluations hereinunder were called forth by the event. There have been three book-length studies: Norman Nicholson, *HGW* (AS, 1950); Antonina Vallentin, *HGW, Prophet of Our Day* (John Day, 1950); Vincent Brome, *HGW* (L, 1951). There is an interview with HGW in Robert van Gelder's *Writers and Writing* (S, 1946). *SRL,* XXIX, Aug. 31, 1946, contained articles on HGW by Elmer Davis, Clifton Fadiman, Waldemar Kaempffert, and H. S. Canby. See, also, the ff. articles: W. J. Sykes, "Is W Also Among the Prophets?" *QQ,* XLIX (1942), 284-293; E. K. Brown, "Two Formulas for Fiction: Henry James and HGW," *CE,* VII (1946), 7-17; Sir Richard Gregory, "HGW: A Survey and a Tribute," *Nature,* CLVIII (1946), 399-402; George Orwell, *Dickens, Dali, and Others* (Reynal & Hitchcock, 1946); W. S. H. Jones, "The World of HGW," *London Q. R.,* CLXXII (1947), 26-34; Gerald Heard, "HGW: The End of a Faith," *SRL,* XXXI, Mar. 13, 1948, p. 9+; S. Spencer, "HGW, Materialist and Mystic," *Hibbert J.,* XLVI (1948), 385-361; Richard H. Costa, "HGW: Literary Journalist," *Jour. Q.,* XXVIII (1951), 63-68; Robert P. Weeks, "HGW as a Sociological Novelist," *DA,* XII (1952), 314. See, also, Maugham, under Bennett.

Chapter XXVII: Pity, Irony, and John Galsworthy

See the ff. articles: Richard M. Kain, "G, the Last Victorian Liberal," *Madison Q.*, IV (1944), 84-94; Frederick P. Grove, "Morality in *The Forsyte Saga*," *UTQ*, XV (1945), 54-64; J. Gordan Eaker, "G and the Modern Mind," *PQ*, XXXIX (1950), 31-48; James C. Freeman, "Whyte-Melville and G's 'Bright Beings,'" *XIX CF*, V (1950), 85-100; Barrett H. Clark, *Intimate Portraits* (Dramatists Play Service, 1951).

Chapter XXVIII: D. H. Lawrence: Pilgrim of the Rainbow

Bibliographical data appear in E. W. Tedlock, Jr., *The Frieda Lawrence Collection of DHL Manuscripts* (U. of N. Mexico Pr., 1948). See, also, William White, *DHL: A Check-List. Writings About DHL, 1931-1950* (Wayne U. Pr., 1950).

The DHL canon has been enlarged by the publication of *The First Lady Chatterley* (Dial Pr., 1944) and *A Prelude*, with intr. by P. B. Wadsworth (Merle Press, 1949). Harry T. Moore has edited *DHL's Letters to Bertrand Russell* (Gotham Bookmart, 1948); see, also, *More Books*, XXIII (1948), 23-24. Diana Trilling has edited *The Portable DHL* (VP, 1947), and W. Y. Tindall has edited *The Later DHL: The Best Novels, Stories, Essays, 1925-1940* (K, 1952).

Harry T. Moore's *The Life and Work of DHL* (Twayne, 1951) is the fullest biographical and critical study of L that has yet been written. See, also, the ff. books: Richard Aldington, *DHL: Portrait of a Genius But—* (Duell, Sloan and Pearce, 1950); Anthony West, *DHL* (AS, 1950); Witter Bynner, *Journey with Genius* (John Day, 1951); William Tiverton, *DHL and Human Existence* (Rockliff, 1951)—a Jesuit study; Dallas Kenmore, *Firebird: A Study of DHL* (Phil. Libr., 1952); E. G. Fay, *Lorenzo in Search of the Sun* (Bookman Associates, 1953). A revised edition of *The Savage Pilgrimage*, by Catherine Carswell, was published by Secker in 1951.

See, also, the ff. mainly critical articles: F. J. Hoffman, in *Freudianism and the Literary Mind* (LSUP, 1945) and "From Surrealism to the Apocalypse: A Development in XX C Irrationalism," *ELH*, XV (1948), 147-165; Frieda Lawrence, "A Prophet: DHL," *Southwest R.*, XXXI (1946), 257-259; Henry Miller, "The Apocalyptic L," *ibid.*, pp. 254-256; Dion Byngham, in Denys Baker, ed., *Modern British Writing* (Vanguard, 1947); Charles I. Glicksberg, "DHL, The Prophet of Surrealism," *XIX C*, CXLIII (1948), 229-237, and "DHL and Science," *Scientific Mo.*, LXXXIII (1951), 99-104; C. Jeffries, "Metaphor in *Sons and Lovers*," *Personalist*, XXIX (1948), 287-292; W. S. H. Jones,

"DHL and the Revolt Against Reason," *London Q. R.,* CLXXIII (1948), 25-31; E. L. Nichols, "The 'Simile of the Sparrow' in *The Rainbow* of DHL," *MLN,* LXIV (1949), 171-174; H. Steinhauer, "Eros and Psyche: A Nietzschean Motif in Anglo-American Literature," *MLN,* LXIV (1949), 217-228; F. R. Leavis, *"St. Mawr," Scrutiny,* XVII (1950), 38-53, *"Women in Love," Scrutiny,* XVII (1950-1951), 203-220, 318-330, XVIII (1951-1952), 18-31, "Mr. Eliot and L," *ibid.,* pp. 66-73, *"The Rainbow," ibid.,* pp. 197-210, 273-287, XIX (1952), 15-30; Leavis and R. D. Wagner, *ibid.,* pp. 136-143; H. T. Moore, "New Light on DHL," *Sp,* CLXXXV (1950), 341; J. Vallette, *Mercure de France,* CCCIX (1950), 742-744; Thomas Greene, "L and the Quixotic Hero," *SR,* LIX (1951), 559-573; C. N. Stavrow, "William Blake and DHL: A Comparative Study of their Thought," *DA,* XII (1952), 430-431; Bertrand Russell, "Portraits from Memory," *HaM,* CCVI, Feb. 1953, pp. 93-95—cf. discussion, CCVI, April 1953, p. 22.

Chapter XXIX: Stream-of-Consciousness

Dorothy Richardson. New fiction by DR has been published in *LL,* XLIX (1946), 20-44, 99-114, LI (1946), 79-88, and a critical article on "Novels" in *LL,* LVI (1948), 188-192.

Joyce. For bibliography, see Alan Parker, *JJ: A Bibliography of His Writings, Critical Material, and Miscellanea* (Faxon, 1948); William White, "JJ: Addenda to Alan Parker's Bibliography," *Papers Bibl. Soc. Am.,* XLIII (1950), 401-411; John J. Slocum and Herbert Cahoon, *Bibl. of JJ, 1882-1941* (YUP, 1953).

Selections from JJ appear in *The Portable JJ,* ed. Harry Levin (VP, 1947).

There is biographical material in Leon Edel, *JJ: The Last Journey* (Gotham Bookmart, 1947); Stanislaus Joyce, *Recollections of JJ* (JJ Society of N. Y., 1950); Lucie Noel, *JJ and Paul L. Léon, The Story of a Friendship* (Gotham Bookmart, 1950). Eugene Jolas, ed., *A JJ Yearbook* (Paris, Transition, 1949) contains reminiscences, etc. Patricia Hutchins, *JJ's Dublin* (London, Grey Walls Pr., 1951) is a record in text and picture of the city of which J wrote.

R. M. Kain has reprinted "Two Book Reviews by JJ," *PMLA,* LXVII (1952), 291-294.

The ff. are critical studies: W. Y. Tindall, *JJ: His Way of Interpreting the Modern World* (S, 1950); L. A. G. Strong, *The Sacred River* (PC, 1951); D. S. Savage, *The Withered Branch* (P & C, 1952). Seon Givens, ed., *JJ: Two Decades of Criticism* (Vanguard Pr., 1948) is an anthology of critical studies which have not been listed separately here. Several articles about J have been reprinted in *The Little Review Anthology,* ed. Margaret Anderson (Hermitage House, 1953). See, also, Oliver St. John Gogarty's pamphlet, *James Augustine Joyce* (Dallas, Times-Herald, 1949). Books in foreign languages are Louis Gillet, *Stele pour JJ* (Paris, Editions du Sagittaire, 1946) and J. den Haan, *J, Mythe van Erin* (Amsterdam, De Bezige Bij, 1948).

The ff. books and articles deal with the works indicated:

PORTRAIT OF THE ARTIST AS A YOUNG MAN. *Stephen Hero: A Part of the First Draft of A Portrait . . . ,* ed. Theodore Spencer (ND, 1944)—cf. Francis Hackett, *On Judging Books* (John Day, 1947). See, also, Donald R. Pearce, "'My Dead King!'" *MLN,* LXVI (1951), 249-251; C. G. Anderson, "The Sacrificial Butter," *Accent,* XII (1952), 3-13.

ULYSSES. Richard M. Kain, *Fabulous Voyager: JJ's* Ulysses (UCP, 1947: C. G. Jung, *Ulysses: A Monologue* (Analytical Psychology Club of New York, 1949). There is also a *Word Index to JJ's* Ulysses, by Miles L. Hanlet, et. al. (U. Wis. Pr., 1951). See, further, these articles: Joseph Prescott, "Homer's *Odyssey* and J's *Ulysses,*" *MLQ,* III (1942), 427-444; R. P. Blackmur, "The Jew in Search of a Son," *VQR,* XXIV (1948), 96-116; H. E. Rogers, "Irish Myth and the Plot of *Ulysses,*" *ELH,* XV (1948), 306-327; Sylvia Beach, "*Ulysses* à Paris: l'histoire de la publication du volume; avec une lettre inédité de G. B. Shaw," *Mercure de France,* CCCIX (1950), 12-29; Edward Duncan, "Unsubstantial Father: A Study of the *Hamlet* Symbolism in J's *Ulysses,*" *UTQ,* XIX (1950), 126-140; Calvin R. Edwards, "The *Hamlet* Motif in J's *Ulysses,*" *Western R.,* XV (1950), 5-13; A. M. Klein, "The Black Panther," *Accent,* X (1950), 139-155; M. Godwin, "Three Wrong Turns in *Ulysses,*" *W. Humanities R.,* XV (1951), 221-225; Vernon Hall, Jr., "J's Use of Da Ponte and Mozart's *Don Giovanni,*" *PMLA,* LXVI (1951), 78-84; A. Mounier, "J's *Ulysses* and the French Public," in *The Kenyon Critics,* ed. J. C. Ransome (World, 1951); Joseph Prescott, "Leopold Bloom's Memory concerning Cormac's Death," *NQ,* CXCVI (1951), 434; W. Y. Tindall, "Dante and Mrs. Bloom," *Accent,* XI (1951), 85-92; M. Godwin, "Rushlight for the Labyrinth," *Pac. Spect.,* VI (1952), 84-96; W. P. Jones, "The Common Reader and JJ's *Ulysses,*" *AS,* XXI (1952), 161-171; Hugh Kenner, "J's *Ulysses:* Homer and Hamlet," *EC,* II (1952), 85-104; D. Knight, "The Reading of *Ulysses,*" *ELH,* XIX (1952), 64-80; J. Prescott, "Notes on J's *Ulysses,*" *MLQ,* XIII (1952), 149-162, "Mosenthal's *Deborah* and J's *Ulysses,*" *MLN,* LXVII (1952), 334-336, and "A Song in J's *Ulysses,*" *NQ,* CXCVII (1952), 15-16; Sol Stern, "The Aesthetics of JJ's *Ulysses,*" *UKCR,* XVIII (1952), 241-254; Marvin Magalaner, "Leopold Bloom before *Ulysses,*" *MLN,* LXVIII (1953), 110-111.

FINNEGAN'S WAKE. J. Campbell and H. M. Robinson have published a *Skeleton Key to FW* (HB, 1944). See, also, Ernest Bernbaum, "The Crucial Question Regarding *FW*," *CE,* VII (1945), 151-164; M. Magalaner, "The Myth of Man: J's *FW*," *UKCR,* XVI (1950), 265-277; F. J. Thompson, "A Portrait of the Artist Asleep," *Western R.,* XIV (1950), 245-253; Nathan Halper, "JJ and the Russian General," *PR,* XVIII (1951), 424-431; William Peery, "Shake His Beard at Finnegans Wake," *UTSE,* XXX (1951), 243-257; M. J. C. Hodgart, "Shakespeare and *FW*," *Camb. J.,* VI (1953), 735-752.

See, further, the ff. mainly critical general articles: J. T. Farrell, "J and the Tradition of the European Novel," *NYTBR,* Jan. 21, 1945, p. 4+; Vivienne K. MacLeod, "The Influence of Ibsen on JJ," *PMLA,* LX (1945), 879-898, and LXII (1947), 573-580; R. J. Sender, *Books Abroad,* XIX (1945), 222-227; H. Levin, *AM,* CLXXVIII, Dec. 1946, pp. 125-129; L. A. G. Strong, "JJ and Vocal Music," *E&S,* XXXI (1946); G. McGregor, "Artistic Theory in JJ," *LL,* LIV (1947), 18-27; H. Kenner, "Baker Street to Eccles Street: The Odyssey of a Myth," *Hudson R.,* I (1948), 481-499; M. Magalaner, "JJ and the Myth of Man," *Ariz. Q.,* IV (1948), 300-309; Marion Witt, "A Note on J and Yeats," *MLN,* LXIII (1948), 552-553; R. Fleming, "*Quidditas* in the Tragi-Comedy of JJ," *UKCR,* XV (1949), 288-296; O. St. J. Gogarty, "JJ as a Friend of Music," *Tomorrow,* IX, Dec. 1949, pp. 42-45; Arthur Heine, "Shakespeare in JJ," *Sh. Assn. Bull.,* XXIV (1949), 56-70; Robert G. Kelly, "JJ: A Partial Explanation," *PMLA,* LXIV (1949), 26-39; H. M. Block, "The Critical Theory of JJ," *J. Aesthetics and Art Criticism,* VIII (1950), 172-184; Mary M. Colum, "A Little Knowledge of J," *SRL,* XXXIII, Apr. 29, 1950, pp. 10-12; Richard Elman, "J and Yeats," *KR,* XII (1950), 618-639; Stuart Gilbert, "Souvenirs de Voyage," *Mercure de France,* CCCIX (1950), 45-58; Oliver Gogarty, "JJ as a Tenor," in *Intimations* (Abelard Pr., 1950); P. Hutchins, "JJ on View," *LL,* LXIV (1950), 123-130; M. Jolas, "J en 1939-1940," *Mercure de France,* CCCIX (1950), 45-58; Sean O'Faoláin, in *Summer in Italy* (Devin-Adair, 1950); A. Tate, "Three Commentaries: Poe, James, and J," *SR,* LVIII (1950), 1-15; J. R. Baker, "JJ: Esthetic Freedom and Dramatic Art," *WHR,* V (1951), 29-42; L. Fitzell, "The Sword and the Dragon," *SAQ,* L (1951), 214-216; H. Kenner, "J and Ibsen's Naturalism," *SR,* LIX (1951), 75-96; Herbert M. McLuhan, "J, Aquinas, and the Poetic Process," *Renascence,* IV (1951), 3-11, and "A Survey of J Criticism," *ibid.,* pp. 12-18; B. L. Burman, "The Cult of Unintelligibility," *SRL,* XXXV, Nov. 1, 1952, pp. 9-10; R. Fleming, "Dramatic Involution: Tate, Husserl, and J," *SR,* LX (1952), 445-464; S. Hynes, "Catholicism and JJ," *Commonweal,* LV (1952), 487-489—cf. LVI (1952), 143-145; M. Magalaner, "James Mangan and J's Dedalus Family," *PQ,* XXXI (1952), 363-371; William Peery, "The Hamlet of Stephen Dedalus," *U. of Texas*

Studies in English, 1952, pp. 109-119; J. J. Sweeney, "The World Was His Oyster," *Hudson R.,* V (1952), 404-408; Ellsworth Mason, "J's Categories," *SR,* LXI (1953), 427-432; Arland Ussher, *Three Great Irishmen* (Devin-Adair, 1953).

WOOLF. Two more volumes of VW's essays have been published: *The Moment and Other Essays* and *The Captain's Death Bed and Other Essays* (HB, 1948, 1950).

The following books about VW have been published: Joan Bennett, *VW: Her Art as a Novelist* (CUP, 1945); Deborah Newton, *VW* (Melbourne U. Pr., 1946); R. L. Chambers, *The Novels of VW* (Oliver & Boyd, 1947); Bernard Blackstone, *VW, A Commentary* (HB, 1949). Ines Verga's *VW's Novels and Their Analogy to Music* is an English Pamphlet, No. 11 (Buenos Aires, 1945). See, also, D. S. Savage, *The Withered Branch* (P & C, 1952). Floris Delattre's *Le Roman Psychologique de VW* (Paris, J. Vrin, 1932) ought to have been listed in my first edition. A more recent foreign book is Erik Wiget, *VW und die Konzeption der Zeit in ihren Werken* (Zurich, Juris-Verlag, 1949).

See, also the ff. articles: S. H. Derbyshire, "An Analysis of Mrs. W's *To the Lighthouse,*" *CE,* III (1942), 353-360; Solomon Fishman, "VW on the Novel," *SR,* LI (1943), 321-340; Nathalia Wright, "*Mrs. Dalloway:* A Study in Composition," *CE,* V (1944), 351-358; M. Brace, "Worshiping Solid Objects: The Pagan World of VW," in *Accent Anthology,* ed. K. Quinn and C. Shattuck (HB, 1946); J. H. Roberts, "Vision and Design in VW," *PMLA,* LXI (1946), 835-847; Desmond Pacey, "VW as a Literary Critic," *UTQ,* XVII (1948), 234-244; W. Y. Tindall, "Many-Levelled Fiction . . . ," *CE,* X (1948), 65-71; John Graham, "Time in the Novels of VW," *UTQ,* XVIII (1949), 205-225; Philip Rahv, in *Image and Idea* (ND, 1949); Stephen Spender, "The Life of Literature," *PR,* XVI (1949), 188-192; F. L. Overcarsh, "The Lighthouse, Face to Face," *Accent,* X (1950), 107-123; E. M. Forster, in *Two Cheers for Democracy* (HB, 1951); Aileen D. Lorberg, "VW, Benevolent Satirist," *Personalist,* XXXIII (1952), 148-158.

Chapter XXX: News of Tishnar: Walter de la Mare

Walter de la Mare has published a number of books during the period covered by this note, but most of them do not concern prose fiction. Edward Wagenknecht collected twenty-four of his best stories in *The Collected Tales of W dlM,* with a critical introduction (K, 1950).

The most extensive study of W dlM published during this period concerns only his poetry: Henry Charles Duffin, *W dlM: A Study of his Poetry* (Sidgwick & Jackson, 1949). John Atkins, *W dlM, An Ex-*

ploration (C. and J. Temple, 1947) is a brief essay of no particular significance. But the symposium, *Tribute to W dlM on his Seventy-Fifth Birthday* (FF, 1948), to which many distinguished British writers contributed, contains much valuable material, including studies of dlM's fiction by Lord David Cecil and Graham Greene. See, also, the many references to dlM in Peter Penzoldt, *The English Short Story of the Supernatural* (Peter Nevill, 1952). There is an excellent unpublished Ph.D. thesis by William L. Sullivan on *The Use of the Supernatural in the Prose Fiction of W dlM,* Boston University, 1952.

Finally, see the ff. essays: "Mr. dlM's World: The Reality and the Dream," *LTLS,* June 6, 1942, pp. 282, 286; E. Schneider, "DlM's Märchen," in L. G. Locke, ed., *Readings for a Liberal Education* (Rinehart, 1948); Martin Johnson, *Art and Scientific Thought,* with Foreword by W dlM (ColUP, 1949); Christopher Morley, in *The Ironing Board* (D, 1949); Edward Wagenknecht, "W dlM's 'The Riddle,' A Note on the Teaching of Literature with Allegorical Tendencies," *CE,* XI (1949), 72-80; G. K. Chesterton, in *The Common Man* (SW, 1950); Margery Bianco, in A. C. Moore and B. E. M. Miller, eds., *Writing and Criticism* (Horn Book, 1951); Pamela Bianco, *Horn Book,* XXIX (1953), 173.

INDEX OF NAMES

Excluding characters of fiction and, generally, critics and biographers cited in footnotes and bibliographical references. The principal reference for authors whose work is considered in this book is in italics.

INDEX OF TITLES

This index is largely, though not exclusively, confined to titles of works of fiction. It includes only a selection from the works mentioned in the Appendix.